Encyclopedia of Archaeology
History and Discoveries

Encyclopedia of Archaeology

History and Discoveries

Volume II, E–M

Edited by Tim Murray

A B C 🌐 C L I O
Santa Barbara, California • Denver, Colorado • Oxford, England

Library of Congress Catalog Card Number

Encyclopedia of archaeology : History and discoveries / edited by Tim Murray.
    p. cm.
Includes bibliographical references.
    ISBN 1-57607-198-7 (hardcover : alk. paper) — ISBN 1-57607-577-X (e-book)
    1. Archaeology—History—Encyclopedias. 2. Archaeologists—Biography—Encyclopedias.
3. Antiquities—Encyclopedias. 4. Historic sites—Encyclopedias. 5. Excavations (Archaeology)—
Encyclopedias. I. Murray, Tim, 1955–
    CC100.E54 2001
    930.1—dc21   20011002617

07 06 05 04 03 02 01   10 9 8 7 6 5 4 3 2 1

ABC-CLIO, Inc.
130 Cremona Drive, P.O. Box 1911
Santa Barbara, California 93116–1911

This book is printed on acid-free paper ∞.
Manufactured in the United States of America

Advisory Board

Contents

History and Discoveries

Encyclopedia of Archaeology

History and Discoveries

E

Easter Island

Occupied by people from POLYNESIA at the extreme edge of their range in the early centuries A.D., Easter Island was named by a Dutch navigator by the name of Roggeveen during a visit to the island over Easter in 1722. It seems likely that this was one of the few contacts with the outside world that was made over the entire period of occupation of the island. Detailed archaeological research on Easter Island was begun by the Norwegian explorer Thor Heyerdahl in 1955, although the large statues (*moai*), the platforms (*Ahu*), the quarries, and the Rongorongo script had attracted attention earlier. An air of mystery (and some sadness) pervades Easter Island studies, but archaeologists now have a clear understanding of the means by which the famous statues were created and erected, the source of the island's original inhabitants, and the (devastating) environmental history of the island.

Tim Murray

References
Bahn, Paul, and John Flenley. 1992. *Easter Island, Earth Island.* New York: Thames and Hudson.

Ecuador

Pottery in the New World appeared first in the equatorial and subequatorial tropics. It developed next in the subtropics and, finally, in the temperate zones a few centuries before European contact. Archaeological teaching and research developed inversely. The subject was first taught north of the Tropic of Cancer in the United States, then south of the tropic of Capricorn in ARGENTINA and CHILE and, finally, in Ecuador. References to the pre-Columbian past began with reports by the early Spanish chroniclers who accompanied Francisco Pizarro on his voyages from PANAMA to PERU. This period of Ecuadorean archaeology, which was mainly ethnohistorical, lasted until the last two decades of the nineteenth century—roughly the same as that in any other area of the New World, corresponding to the speculative period defined by GORDON WILLEY and Phillip Phillips for U.S. archaeology.

In the late nineteenth century, Msgr. Federico González Suárez, the archbishop of Quito and a historian, wrote, as an appendix to his *History of Ecuador,* a volume entitled *Archaeological Atlas.* A professor of history at Quito University, he was the first of a generation of historians interested in the aboriginal history of his country. Others, including Carlos Manuel Larrea and Jacinto Jijón y Caamaño, also left their imprint on the archaeology of Ecuador. They conducted research in the Andean intermontane valleys and on the coast of Manabí and Esmeraldas Provinces. However, no serious effort was made to develop professional archaeologists in Ecuador until the 1980s.

During the nineteenth century European naturalists and geographers who visited the New World—such as William Bollaert (from 1860 to 1880), Anatole Bamps (from 1878 to 1888), and Alfons Steuble (from 1875 to 1888)—made the first collections of archaeological artifacts in Ecuador. (The latter's collections were studied by a young MAX UHLE in Dresden from 1889 to 1890 and in 1892.) In the 1890s Marshall Saville from the George Heye Foundation carried out extensive excavations along the Ecuadorean

An example of the famous Easter Island statues (Spectrum Colour Library)

coast, and George Dorsey collected some Inca artifacts from La Plata Island, 36 kilometers southwest of Manta in Manabí Province, for the Field Columbian Museum during the Fourth Centennial Columbian Exhibition in Chicago. Jijón y Caamaño was later instrumental in bringing the German archaeologist Max Uhle to Ecuador, and he financed Uhle's research for nearly two decades (from 1920 to 1939). Beginning in the 1940s coastal archaeological research started to dominate Ecuadorean culture history. This trend needs to be explained for an understanding of the development of archaeological research in the hub of the northern Andean area.

Although small in size, Ecuador presents a great variety of environments and landforms. The upthrust of the Andes divided it into two lowland regions. The coast, west of the Andes, is separated into a Tertiary uplifted plain, bordered by the Pacific Ocean and ancient volcanic mountains. Between these mountains and the Andes, two large riverine basins began to fill with alluvium around 10,000 B.P., providing a western counterpart to the Amazonian jungle. A mantle of recent alluvium covers the Ecuadorian Upper Amazon, and in some areas it overlays ancient alluvial deposits, laid down before the Andean upthrust. The Ecuadorean Andes are divided into two intermontane valleys by the Cordillera Real. Its western valley reaches altitudes higher that 2,000 meters; the eastern valley averages 900 meters in altitude. The western valley is subdivided into smaller valleys that drain both eastward into the Upper Amazon and westward into the coastal lain and the Pacific Ocean.

Beginning in the Holocene the landscape of Ecuador marked by the Andean and coastal uplifts of the Tertiary period underwent great changes. Rapid deposits of recent alluvium modified the landscape of the Guayas and Amazonian basins. Deposits of lava and volcanic tuft caused by the intense volcanic activity in the northern Ecuadorean Andes also changed the early-Holocene landscape. And during the end of the Pleistocene and the beginning of the Holocene, severe climatic and sea-level shifts dramatically altered the landscape as well. Tropical savannahs changed into forests, and the coastline retreated as it gave way to the rising seas. The great mammals of the Pleistocene, which had lived in the area for nearly a million years, disappeared. These changes occurred 2,000 to 3,000 years after the arrival of the Paleo-Indians.

Active floodplain covers great spaces of the Ecuadorean lowlands, and alluvium is added to the Upper Amazon and to the Guayas basin each year. Meandering rivers churn up the alluvium, redepositing it and its cultural contents in newly created point-bar formations, complicating the stratified deposits in new landforms. The accumulated deposits cover the evidence for early occupation of these bottomlands. An example is the Valdivia II site at Colimes de Balzar (with two C-14 assays of 4770 + 210 B.P. or 3200 B.C. [corrected]). This site, buried under 8.20 meters of alluvium strata, shows interspacing by volcanic-ash deposits and habitation floors from several occupational periods. Late-Pleistocene remnants, dating between 18,000 and 10,000 B.C., should be much deeper.

In the northern Ecuadorean highlands, under a soft volcanic tuft about 3 meters deep, Pleistocene faunal remains can be found. A good example is the Paramo del Angel, north of the Chota Valley in Carchi Province, where the remains of several mastodons have been discovered at the bottom of erosion gullies. In the eastern lowlands, Pedro T. Porras found some chipped stone artifacts at Yasuní, apparently belonging to that period, but he did not report faunal associations of any kind. This lack of conclusive evidence is probably the result of unsystematic investigations in preceramic archaeology.

Some 10,000 years of archaeological evidence is buried in this stage. Grave robbers, antiquarians, and some archaeologists have unearthed shards that testify to a complex social-history process based on the exploitation of a landscape rich in ecological niches that supported some of the most diverse floras and faunas in the world.

The Evolution of Archaeology in Ecuador
In trying to systematize the progression of archaeological research in Ecuador, one may be tempted to use Willey and Phillips's CLASSIFICA-

TION for New World archaeology, and in general it does fit. Most archaeological research in Ecuador has been conducted by Americans during several periods, representing the tendencies used as period indicators by Willey and Phillips. In a 1982 article entitled "100 Years of Ecuadorian Archaeology," Donald Collier divided Ecuadorean archaeological research into four periods: the pioneer period, 1878–1899; the developmental period, 1900–1934; the transitional period, 1935–1952; and the florescent period, 1953–1980. Collier's article is chronological in intent and in some ways quantitative-qualitative, and it is useful for showing the increase in archaeological research in Ecuador up to 1980. It does not, however, consider the trends in archaeological research that have dominated Ecuadorean archaeology, and because it was published in the early 1980s, it missed the the recent period in which archaeology in Ecuador attained some degree of maturity.

Archaeology in Ecuador

Archaeological research in Ecuador can be best classified in the following manner. Following is my own thematic version of its development.

The First 350 Years

The initial reports of archaeological monuments in Ecuador appeared in the chronicles of the Spanish priest and soldiers accompanying Pizarro, in the chronicles of the sixteenth century, and in the *Visitas* of the seventeenth century. (Detailed descriptions by naturalists and geographers, who put together the first archaeological collections, came later.) The precursors of Ecuadorean archaeology had appeared. Concomitant with this, the looting of tombs for gold and archaeological materials began with the Spanish conquistadores, settlers, and colonial officials. The first Ecuadorean archaeological and ethnographical materials began to appear in European museums in the 1850s.

1880–1920: The Classificatory Period

This period is best defined by the classification in a museum in Dresden—by young linguist Max Uhle—of the archaeological materials collected by Alfons Steuble and Willhelm Reiss in Ecuador in the 1880s. During this time some local historians (such as Monsignor González Suárez) and foreign residents (such as the linguist Otto von Buchwald) also began to classify their archaeological finds in Ecuador. The collections made by George Dorsey and Marshall Saville in coastal Ecuador for the Field Columbian Museum and for the Museum of the American Indian (George Heye Foundation) were classified and published in the first decade of the twentieth century. About the same time, Paul Rivet and R. Vernau began their Ecuadorean research for the French Academy, and Uhle, who was already acquainted with the Ecuadorean materials collected by Steuble and Reiss in the previous period, arrived in Ecuador from Peru at the invitation of Jacinto Jijón y Caamaño. The two men began a fruitful, twenty-five-year research association that contributed to the development of the first systematic chronology for Ecuadorean archaeology, and together with Carlos Manuel Larrea they carried Ecuadorean archaeology into the culture-historical period.

As Ecuadorean archaeology progressed, grave looters in the southern Ecuadorean Andes began unearthing veritable treasure hoards, which were, for the most part, melted down to be sold as gold from the mines in the area. Saville managed to save a small part of one of the Sigsig/Gualaceo treasures, acquiring it for the Museum of the American Indian from Don Nicol's Ribadeneyra of Guayaquil.

1920–1950: The Culture-Historical Period

Following the momentum of Max Uhle and Jacinto Jijón's archaeological investigations, others individuals, such as G. H. S. Bushnell, Raoul D'Harcourt, and Paul Bergsøe, began conducting research in coastal Ecuador. Two young history and geography teachers, Carlos Zevallos Menéndez and Francisco Huerta Rendón, followed suit, taking their senior students on archaeological field trips. At the beginning of World War II, Bushnell left Ecuador to fight for England, and U.S. anthropologists from the Andean Institute went to Ecuador to do archaeological work and help with the anti-Nazi war effort. Donald Collier and John V. Murra excavated in Cerro Narrío in Cañar Province, and Wendell Bennett conducted research around Cuenca and southern Azuay Province. As World War II came to a close, Hans Dietrich Disselhoff, a former German administrator in occupied Denmark, carried out archaeological research in Manantial de Guangala.

Meanwhile, gold-rich sites continued to be looted, and archaeological gold was melted and formed into ingots. Looters began to keep some of the ceramic and other artifacts, which they sold to a new breed of collectors—those who became interested in local culture-history. A Swiss businessman, Max Konantz, began his collection by buying from looters in the Cuenca area. Local landowners and farmers also started to collect archaeological artifacts.

1950–1965: The Historical Classificatory Period—The Advent of C-14

Bushnell published his coastal chronology in *The Archaeology of the Santa Elena Peninsula in South West Ecuador* (1951), and Collier and Murra published theirs for the cultures of the southern Ecuadorean Andes. However, because stratified materials were not always superimposed, Bushnell, like Jijón y Caamaño before him, inverted part of his sequence. However, Willard Libby's discovery of C-14 DATING was soon conceived as the panacea that would cure all ailments in archaeological chronologies. Establishing a workable chronology was problematic prior to the application of radiometric (C-14) dating. Both Bushnell's coastal chronology and Collier and Murra's chronology of the Southern Ecuadorian Andes experienced difficulties.

With the advent of C-14 the emphasis on excavating archaeological deposits by their "natural stratigraphy" declined, and simpler means of excavation—artificial stratigraphy, for instance, by metric levels—became widespread, providing more secure archaeological sequences. A Guayaquil businessman turned archaeologist, Emilio Estrada, began to build a new chronology for the Ecuadorean coast. Estrada was later joined by Clifford Evans and Betty J. Meggers from the Smithsonian Institution, and together they built the basic chronology for Ecuador. It still stands today, with some addenda and modifications made by others. The single most important modification has been Betsy Hill's 1972–1974 refinement of the Valdivia from four to eight phases, and the more recent eleven-phase refinement by Marcos and Obelic in 1998. During this period the most significant contribution to the knowledge of the archaeology of the Ecuadorian coast derived from the excavations at San Pablo by Carlos Zevallos and Olaf Holm. Although they published only a preliminary report, their excellent excavation permitted a more comprehensive view of Valdivia society. Zevallos later published an article that correctly postulated the agricultural base for the development of Valdivia society.

Meggers and Evans introduced type frequency seriation into Ecuador. This was a laboratory-analysis method developed by JAMES A. FORD for his excavations in the lower Mississippi, which went hand in hand with the excavation of arbitrary levels. The publication of information on Zevallos and Holm's excavations at San Pablo may well have convinced many archaeologists of the limitations of metric stratigraphy and type frequency seriation (*see* Classification; Dating).

Estrada convinced other aficionados to take part in the archaeological research in coastal Ecuador. Richard Zeller, prompted by Estrada, began a long love affair with Guangala sites in the Jabita River basin, north of the Santa Elena Peninsula. Olaf Holm, cooperating at first with Zevallos at San Pablo, moved to Joa in southern Manabí Province to study evidences of copper metallurgy, and in the eastern lowlands Estrada, Meggers, and Evans began supporting Fr. Pedro I. Porras's archaeological research.

During this period archaeologists in Ecuador, following Konantz, began to supplement their excavations with collections, acquiring fortuitous finds from farmers as well as artifacts from merchants who bought from looters, known as *guaqueros*. Zevallos built the gold museum for the Casa de la Cultura de Guayaquil by such acquisitions; the ceramic and other artifacts came from archaeological excavations he and his associates conducted. Estrada supplemented the collection of the Victor Emilio Estrada Museum, buying both whole pots and other artifacts from guaqueros from Manabí. Although this method allowed researchers to supplement museum exhibitions with looted material validated by the archaeological data, it also set a trend that, with time, was exacerbated and became disproportionate, ultimately increasing the looting of archaeological sites.

1965–1974: Questioning Type Frequency Seriation
With the appearance in 1965 of the SMITHSONIAN INSTITUTION's publication *The Formative Period of Ecuador: Valdivia and Machalilla Phases,* by Meggers, Evans, and Estrada, some archaeologists (Donald Collier, Jon Müller, Donald Lathrap, and Henning Bischof, among others) began to question the Jomôn origin for Valdivia, as well as the excavation method used and especially type frequency seriation.

Edward P. Lanning and his students from Columbia University began a research project in the Santa Elena Peninsula, contributing to the refinement of all cultural phases proposed by Estrada and in Meggers's *Ecuador.* Lanning's efforts were also directed at rescuing the excellent data published by Bushnell (1951). Zevallos cooperated with Lanning, and after that point he and his students began to use the stylistic seriation developed by John Rowe in his studies in the Ica Valley in Peru.

Toward the end of this period a florescent epoch for Ecuadorean archaeology commenced. José Alcina Franch and his students at the Universidad Complutense de Madrid began a series of research campaigns in Ecuador that would continue into the next period. Alcina made many contributions to the archaeology of Esmeraldas Province and the Inca site of Ingapirca in Cañar. At Cochasquí, north of Quito, a team from the University of Bonn, under the direction of Udo Oberem, restudied the site that had been excavated by Uhle in the 1920s. Karen Stothert, under the direction of Edward Lanning, began her research at the Vegas preceramic site, and Jorge G. Marcos located the Valdivia site of Real Alto and was pursuing his doctorate at the University of Illinois.

Guillermo Pérez Chiriboga—then president of the Central Bank of Ecuador—decided to create a gold museum at the bank when he realized that much of the gold bullion it bought had been archaeological gold. In some of the ingots he was able to see vestiges of the artifacts that had been melted down to form the bars. In creating the gold museum he intended to save archaeological gold from destruction, and he soon decided to broaden the scope of the museum to include all archaeological artifacts. Going beyond the initial concept, the Central Bank created the Museum for the Archaeology of Ecuador.

The museum fund was built on the acquisition of the Konantz Collection and a few other, smaller private collections. As it grew, its directors began to procure exceptional archaeological pieces from some guaqueros, and in time the negative effect of increased looting became apparent.

1974–1978: The Beginning of Explanatory Archaeology in Ecuador
In August 1974 an interdisciplinary team of archaeologists and other specialists from the University of Illinois—led by Donald W. Lathrap and his student Jorge Marcos—arrived in the Santa Elena Peninsula to begin research at Real Alto, the site that Marcos had discovered. This investigation marked the beginning of explanatory archaeology in Ecuador. Up to that time archaeologists had been content to describe their finds or to construct hypotheses based on routes and ways of diffusion. They also postulated possible social organization based only on their site finds and on prejudices about the level of society reached by the ancestors of the present native population in the area. Another form of prejudice was evident in regard to the environment. A heavily deforested area during the second half of the twentieth century was considered by many archaeologists as a model for the ancient environs of the Santa Elena Peninsula. At Real Alto environmental reconstruction, area excavation, biological and forensic studies of skeletal material, geologic studies of the Tablazo formation, quantification and use patterns in milling stones, and ceramic modal and functional analysis represented a shift in the right direction. The excavation of the Cotocollao site in Quito by Peterson and Villalba, which

began a few months later, followed, in a smaller way, this new trend.

Formally trained Ecuadorean archaeologists working in European and U.S. universities returned to Ecuador at the end of this period. Their impact would soon be felt in the progress of archaeology in their homeland. Examples of the research they started include the project known as Sacred Isles of Ecuador, during which the existence of long-distance maritime trade networks centered on the coast of Ecuador was discovered, and the excavation of the obsidian mine at Mullumica by Ernesto Salazar.

As archaeology progressed, pothunting and looting accelerated due to the increase in international demand and the market pressure created by the acquisition of looted archaeological art by local museums and collectors. The consequent loss of artifacts and sites through disturbance placed the heritage of Ecuador under great pressure.

1980: Formal Training in Anthropological Archaeology Begins

In 1980 the first formal program to graduate professional archaeologists opened at the Escuela Superior Politecnica del Litoral (ESPOL) in Guayaquil. Although the creation of the Institute of National Heritage (Instituto de Patrimonio Cultural) in 1979 had formalized archaeological research, achieving a national consensus on the importance of archaeology for Ecuador is still a pending assignment.

Historically, most Ecuadoreans, including some university and government officials, did not consider archaeology a scientific effort. It was regarded as an activity worthy of dilettantes, the rich, and a few dreamers. The professional archaeologist was seen as strange sort whose career was considered a hobby by most people of means and a job by the poor farmers who became looters as a means of offsetting the chronic scarcity of agricultural jobs.

Such conceptions are now changing. For a long time, however, there was strife between museum directors and museum research personnel. The former felt that archaeologists pulled only potsherds out of the ground, not the beautiful pieces brought to them by grave robbers. The latter wanted museum funds to be used for archaeological investigations, not the acquisition of archaeological art.

1981–1992: Hoarding Archaeological Art versus Archaeological Research

During the 1980s and early 1990s professional archaeologists, on the one hand, and museum directors and collectors, on the other, waged a war that was partially won by the archaeologists, for the national museums in Ecuador halted all forms of acquisition. However, the huge acquisition budgets were not redirected to research, and research funds continued to be meager. The difficulty lay in the fact that archaeology was and still is considered by the cultural elite to be a business for antiquarians and art merchants, rather than a career worthy of historians or anthropologists. Private and archaeological museum collections, including those of the national museums, have been acquired by purchasing from looters rather than through museum-financed archaeological research. Museum directors and collectors justify their actions by saying that they are keeping the archaeological pieces from leaving the country. However, a study made by archaeologists and economists for the Central Bank of Ecuador showed that the internal demand for archaeological art actually finances the looting that yields the small amount of excellent art that is exported clandestinely.

Archaeological research nevertheless grew over this period, thanks to international funding and to some national research funds provided by groups such as Foncultura, or the Social and Cultural Fund of the National Petroleum Company. Studies of the impact of development on archaeological sites were also started, with much of this research carried out by Ecuadorean graduates in archaeology.

1992–2000: Growing Pains—Toward Adulthood and Reproduction

During the last decade of the twentieth century, there was an increase in the number of Ecuadorean archaeologists working in their field, in spite of the economic crisis that affected most cultural and social programs in

Ecuador. This trend was enhanced by an increase in archaeological impact studies, most of which were conducted by Ecuadorean graduates in anthropology and archaeology. However, although the demand for archaeologists increased, a perverse tendency developed in universities where careers were judged by cost-benefit parameters and archaeology or anthropology was not deemed as attractive to the university council as management or business studies.

A number of medium-sized projects to study Ecuadorian biodiversity and native development are now opening up new opportunities for archaeological research, and as a result there has been an increase in the demand for graduates in archaeology. This situation is a welcome preview of better days ahead at the outset of the third millennium.

Jorge G. Marcos

References

Bushnell, Geoffrey H. S. 1951. *The Archaeology of the Santa Elena Peninsula in South West Ecuador.* Cambridge: Cambridge University Press.

Collier, Donald. 1982. "One Hundred Years of Ecuadorian Archeology." In *1o Simposio de Correlaciones Antropológicas Andino-Mesoamericano,* 5–33. Ed. Jorge G. Marcos and Presley Norton. Salinas, Ecuador, 25–31 July 1971. Guayaquil: ESPOL.

Collier, Donald, and John V. Murra. 1943. *Survey and Excavations in Southern Ecuador.* Anthropological Series, vol. 35. Chicago: Field Museum of Natural History.

Estrada, Emilio. 1958. *Las culturas pre-clásicas, formativas o arcaicas del Ecuador.* Guayaquil: Museo Victor Emilio Estrada.

———. 1962. *Arqueología de Manabí Central.* Guayaquil: Museo Victor Emilio Estrada.

Evans, Clifford, and Betty J. Meggers. 1966. "Mesoamerica and Ecuador." In *Archaeological Frontiers and External Connections,* 243–264. Ed. Gordon F. Ekholm and Gordon R. Willey. *Handbook of Middle American Indians,* vol. 4. Gen ed. Robert Wauchope. Austin: University of Texas Press.

Jijón y Caamaño, Jacinto. 1952 [1945]. *Antropología Prehispánica del Ecuador.* Quito: La Prensa Católica.

———. 1997. *Antropología Prehispánica del Ecuador.* 2d ed. Quito: Embajada de España, Agencia de Cooperación Española– Museo Jacinto Jijón y Caamaño.

Lathrap, Donald W. 1966. "Relationships between Mesoamerica and the Andean Areas." In *Archaeological Frontiers and External Connections,* 265–276. Ed. Gordon F. Ekholm and Gordon R. Willey. *Handbook of Middle American Indians,* vol. 4. Robert Wauchope, gen. ed. Austin: University of Texas Press.

———. 1973. "The Antiquity of Long Distance Trade Relationships in the Moist Tropics of Pre-Columbian South America." *World Archaeology* 5, no. 2: 170–186.

———. 1982. "Complex Iconographic Features Shared by Olmec and Chavin and Some Speculations on Their Possible Significance." In *1 Simposio de Correlaciones Antropológicas Andino-Mesoamericanas,* 301–327. Ed. Jorge G. Marcos and Presley Norton. Salinas, Ecuador, 25–31 July 1971. Guayaquil: ESPOL.

Lathrap, Donald W., John Collier, and Helen Chandra. 1975. *Ancient Ecuador.* Chicago: Field Museum of Natural History.

Lathrap, Donald W., Jorge G. Marcos, and James A. Zeidler. 1977. "Real Alto: An Ancient Ceremonial Center." *Archaeology* 30, no. 1: 2–13.

Marcos, Jorge G. 1978. "The Ceremonial Precinct at Real Alto: Organization of Time and Space in Valdivia Society." Ph.D. diss., University of Illinois at Urbana-Champaign. Ann Arbor, Michigan: *University Microfilms International* 7913541.

Meggers, Betty J. 1966. *Ecuador.* New York: Frederick Praeger.

Meggers, Betty J., Clifford Evans, and Emilio Estrada. 1965. "The Early Formative Period of Coastal Ecuador: The Valdivia and Machalilla Phases." *Smithsonian Institution Contributions to Anthropology* 1.

Rowe, John H. 1954. "Max Uhle, 1856–1944. A Memoir of the Father of Peruvian Archaeology." In *University of California Publications in American Archaeology and Ethnology* 46, no. 1: 1–134. Berkeley; Los Angeles: University of California Press.

Egypt: Dynastic
Introduction

The archaeology of Pharaonic Egypt spans three millennia (ca. 3100–332 B.C.) and encompasses a diverse body of artifacts, architecture, texts, and organic remains. Museums throughout the world contain millions of Egyptian antiquities, and an even greater number of remains are still in situ, ranging from the temples, tombs, and cities of the Nile Valley and delta to rock inscriptions carved on remote crags in the Libyan Desert, the Eastern (Arabian) Desert, and the Sinai Peninsula. Three principal factors have facilitated the survival of an unusual wealth of detail concerning pharaonic Egypt: a penchant for grandiose and elaborate funerary arrangements, arid conditions suitable for preservation, and the use of writing on a wide variety of media.

The history of the rediscovery of ancient Egypt is in many respects the same as that of any other civilization in that centuries of ignorance and plundering were gradually replaced by the more enlightened approaches of late-nineteenth-century and twentieth-century scholars. Within this broad trend, however, various specific aspects of Egyptology, such as epigraphy, excavation, philology, and anthropology, have progressed at very different rates.

For most of its history, Egyptian archaeology has tended to be extremely conservative, both in overall conceptual terms and with regard to methods of postexcavation analysis and interpretation of archaeological data. Even in the early 1970s there were still relatively few indications that archaeologists working in Egypt and the Near East were embarking on any radical changes in their methods of analysis and interpretation, particularly when compared with the many advances that were being made in prehistory and historical archaeology elsewhere in the world. While LEWIS BINFORD was laying the foundations of his "middle range theory" (Binford 1972) and Michael Schiffer was formulating the laws of "behavioral archaeology" (Schiffer 1976), most Egyptologists were still preoccupied with the business of pure data gathering and history writing.

In Bruce Trigger's *A History of Archaeological Thought* (1989), there are a mere handful of references to Egyptian archaeology: only the invention by SIR WILLIAM MATTHEW FLINDERS PETRIE of an early form of seriation known as "sequence dating" merits a full page or so of discussion. Although this lack of references may well be a fair assessment of the Egyptologists' contribution to archaeological thought, the excavation of Egyptian sites has, over the last 150 years, provided a steady stream of valuable data. This rapidly expanding database has not only provided new insights into the material culture of the pharaonic period, but it has also made a significant contribution to the creation of a chronological framework for the Mediterranean region. The central role played by Egyptology in the formulation of ancient chronology has lent greater significance to recent attempts to pinpoint flaws in the chronology of the Pharaonic period (James, Thorpe, Kokkinos, Morkot, and Frankish 1991; Rohl 1995), but the established chronology is now a dense matrix of archaeological and textual details that have proved difficult to sort out.

Virtually all nineteenth-century excavations in Egypt were designed to provide art treasures for European and American museums and private collections, since the expeditions' financial support invariably derived from those sources. Even in the late nineteenth century, when scholarly societies, such as the EGYPT EXPLORATION SOCIETY and the Institut Français d'Archéologie Orientale, began to fund excavations with specific research aims in mind, there were still sponsors who required a steady stream of antiquities. It is also evident from excavation records and publications that new archaeological data were regarded primarily as a means of supplementing and illustrating the ample textual record of Egyptian history rather than as the basis for predominantly archaeological reconstructions of the past.

It is symptomatic of the largely historical motivation of pre–World War II archaeologists in Egypt that John Pendlebury, the young director of the British excavations at EL AMARNA, the most important urban site in Egypt, described his enthusiasm for the site in the following way: "One cannot tell in what part of the city some important historical document may come to light. A mere slum house may contain an inscription that will revolutionize history" (Pendlebury 1935, xxviii). The implications of this remark are compounded by the fact that Pendlebury was regarded as an unusually archaeological Egyptologist compared to many of his colleagues in the 1930s (see Powell 1973, 61, where Pendlebury is said to be part of "a new generation of archaeologists openly disapproving of what they regarded as the amateurish policies of the past").

Napoleon, Champollion, and the Problem of Integrating Textual and Archaeological Data

Just as it is difficult to ascertain the date at which European antiquarianism was superseded by archaeology (see Daniel 1967; Piggott 1989), it is difficult to be precise about the point at which the simple enthusiasm for Egyptian antiquities was transformed into something resembling the modern discipline of Egyptology. Most histories of Egyptian archaeology, however, see the Napoleonic expedition at the beginning of the nineteenth century as the first systematic attempt to record and describe the standing remains of Pharaonic Egypt. The importance of the *Description de l'Égypte,* the multivolume publication that resulted from the expedition, lay not only in its high standards of draftsmanship and accuracy but also in the fact that it constituted a continuous and internally consistent appraisal by a single group of scholars, thus providing the first real assessment of ancient Egypt in its totality.

However, the beginning of Egyptology as a complete historical discipline, comprising the study of both texts and archaeology, was made possible by the more deskbound endeavors of the French linguist JEAN-FRANÇOIS CHAMPOLLION. His decipherment of Egyptian hieroglyphs in 1822, closely followed by Thomas Young's decipherment of the demotic script in the late 1820s, transformed Egyptology almost overnight from prehistory into history. The translation of a whole range of documents, containing such information as the names of gods and kings as well as the details of religious rituals and economic transactions, soon enabled the field of Egyptology to take its place alongside the study of the classical civilizations. Champollion's discovery, however, had also set in motion an inexorable process of academic divergence between linguists and excavators, between historians and anthropologists.

From the moment that hieroglyphs, both hieratic and demotic, began to be translated, Egyptology was characterized by a constant struggle to reconcile the kinds of general socioeconomic evidence preserved in the archaeological record with the more specific historical information contained in ancient texts. Although the newly discovered knowledge of the texts had the potential to revive the very thoughts and emotions of the ancient Egyptians, it also introduced the temptation to assume that the answers to questions about Egyptian civilization could be found in the written word rather than in the archaeologist's trench. The purely archaeological view of Egyptian culture, as preserved in the form of buried walls, artifacts, and organic remains, would henceforth have to be seen in the context of a richly detailed corpus of texts written on stone and papyrus. The absence of written records in prehistoric archaeology may be frustrating, but it has undoubtedly allowed prehistoric archaeologists greater freedom to evolve new theories and hypotheses that are based purely on the surviving material culture. In Egyptian archaeology, as in other historical disciplines, the written word, with all its potential for subjectivity and persuasion, has a paradoxical tendency to obscure, and sometimes eclipse, the archaeological evidence (see Kemp 1984).

It is interesting, from the point of view of the dichotomy between texts and archaeology, to compare the history of Egyptian archaeology with that of Mayan studies, given that Mayanists appear to have experienced the reverse situation: their discipline was predominantly anthropological and archaeological until Mayan glyphs began to be deciphered in the 1980s, producing a sudden flood of texts that have significantly altered the perception of the Mayan culture. In some respects, the suspicion with which Mayan archaeologists initially regarded the historical information provided by their philological colleagues (see Coe 1992, 270–274; Schele and Miller 1986) is a mirror image of the reaction of many traditional text-based Egyptologists to the increasingly science-based and anthropological analyses of Pharaonic Egypt produced by archaeologists in recent years. Both Mayanists and

Egyptologists are struggling to come to terms with the basic fact that writing tends to be the product of elite members of society whereas the bulk of archaeological data derives from the illiterate majority of the population. The solution lies in the successful integration of both types of evidence to produce a view of society as a whole.

A related problem in modern Egyptian archaeology is the increasing dislocation between the processes of change in the material culture and the traditional chronological system of dynasties, kingdoms, and "intermediate periods," which may now be approaching the end of its usefulness. The dynastic conventions have become firmly embedded in the literature, but many modern scholars would now question the historic validity of a distinction between Sixth or Seventh Dynasty or between "third intermediate period" and "late period." Excavations since the 1960s have gradually produced a rival and more archaeologically relevant chronological system based simply on changes in material culture and supported by a framework of stratigraphic analysis and radiometric dates (see, for instance, O'Connor 1974; Trigger, Kemp, O'-Connor, and Lloyd 1985). Future chronologies of the pharaonic period will need to integrate political change with the socioeconomic and art-historical fluctuations observable in the archaeological record.

Wilkinson, Lepsius, and Mariette: Exploration and Conservation

The Napoleonic expedition was complemented both by the Franco-Tuscan expedition of 1828–1829 (led by Ippolito Rosellini and Champollion) and by the more piecemeal work of a growing number of European travelers in the late eighteenth and early nineteenth centuries. The British Egyptologist Sir John Gardner Wilkinson, for instance, spent twelve years in Egypt and NUBIA between 1821 and 1833. The publication of *The Manners and Customs of the Ancient Egyptians* in 1837 was to earn him his knighthood, but much of his work, including maps, plans, and drawings of sites that have now been lost or destroyed, remains unpublished. His contemporaries, including English travelers

James Burton, Robert Hay, and Edward Lane, also left behind numerous sketches, notebooks, and unpublished manuscripts that have only recently begun to be researched.

The Prussian expedition of the 1840s, led by KARL RICHARD LEPSIUS, was the next major step forward in terms of the accumulation of a basic archaeological database for Egypt (Lepsius 1849–1859). In many ways, the Napoleonic and Prussian expeditions set the pattern for Egyptology until well into the twentieth century, essentially initiating a quest for more and more information to be cataloged and assimilated into the frameworks of history and art history. From the point of view of data, Egyptian archaeology has always been something of a victim of its own success. The archaeological remains are so rich, diverse, and well-preserved that most Egyptologists have tended to be immersed in the processes of description and categorization, often at the expense of analysis and interpretation. In addition, much of the earlier work was biased by the fact that nineteenth-century archaeologists in Egypt were almost entirely concerned with the study of temples and tombs since those remains were considered most likely to yield the kinds of artistic and textual materials that most Egyptologists then regarded as the backbone of the discipline.

What is remarkable about the European expeditions to Egypt in the first half of the nineteenth century is the rapid pace with which new information was acquired, digested, and assimilated into the overall picture of the pharaonic period. In 1838, the French architect Hector Horeau published a "panorama" of Egypt that included an illustration showing the principal monuments of Egypt. The painting took the form of an imaginary view of the meandering course of the Nile River, with Alexandria and the Mediterranean coast in the foreground and the Temple of Isis on the island of Philae in the far distance. This pictorial view of Egypt, which incorporated the basic essentials of Egyptian architecture from the pyramids at Giza to the temples of eastern and western Thebes, is a good illustration of the speed with which the bare bones of Egyptology were assembled. As early as the 1830s, Gardner Wilkinson was able to present a wide-ranging and detailed view of ancient Egypt in his book on its manners and customs. Certainly there were inaccuracies, misconceptions, and omissions in the publications of the early nineteenth century, but in many respects the fundamentals were already known and the last one and a half centuries have arguably been more concerned with filling in the details than breaking new ground.

Although the greatest individual achievement in the history of Egyptology was undoubtedly the deciphering of hieroglyphs by Champollion, the birth of Egyptian archaeology owes a great deal to the work of another French Egyptologist, AUGUSTE MARIETTE. Born and educated in Boulogne-sur-Mer in northern France, Mariette was inspired to take up Egyptology when he examined the papers bequeathed to his family by his cousin Nestor L'Hote, who had served as a draftsman on Champollion's Franco-Tuscan expedition. In 1850, Mariette was sent to Egypt to obtain papyri for the collection of the Louvre, where he had been employed to inventory the Egyptian inscriptions. Once in Egypt, however, he embarked on a career in excavation, beginning with a remarkable discovery of the Serapeum (the burial place of the sacred Apis bulls) at SAQQARA.

As a result of his prolific archaeological work at many different sites (including Giza, ABYDOS, Thebes, and Elephantine), Mariette was appointed in 1858 to the office of first director of the Egyptian Antiquities Service (now known as the Supreme Council of Antiquities). In this post he was able to reduce the amount of plundering of Egyptian antiquities as well as to create the nucleus of a national archaeological collection (housed initially in a disused warehouse at Bulaq, the port of Cairo, and most recently at the Egyptian Museum in the center of Cairo). During the next twenty years he excavated at some thirty-five different sites and gradually expanded the national museum.

However, despite the efforts of Mariette and his successor Gaston Maspero, the plundering of ancient sites remained a common problem. Such important finds as the Deir el-Bahari cache of royal mummies and the El Amarna archive of cuneiform tablets were initially plundered by local people and only came to scholarly attention when items became available on the art market. Maspero's official discovery of the Deir el-Bahari cache in 1881 involved something of a detective story in which he traced a hieratic papyrus of the Twenty-first Dynasty pharaoh Pinudjem back to the Abd el-Rassul family in the Theban village of Gurna, the family that had first uncovered the mummies ten years earlier.

Flinders Petrie, George Reisner, and the Introduction of Scientific Archaeology

Between the period of organized plundering undertaken by such men as GIOVANNI BELZONI and Drovetti in the early nineteenth century and the excavations of French scholars Emile Amelineau and J. L. De Morgan in the 1890s, there was surprisingly little development in the techniques employed by Egyptian archaeologists. As John Wortham puts it in his history of British Egyptology: "Although archaeologists no longer used dynamite to excavate sites, their techniques remained unrefined" (Wortham 1971, 106).

The concept of "clearance," as opposed to scientific excavation, was arguably one of the most insidious and retrogressive aspects of nineteenth-century archaeology in Egypt. The very word appeared to substantiate the fallacy that the sand simply had to be removed in order to reveal the significant monuments hidden below, thus helping to discourage the proper consideration of stratigraphic excavation and the appreciation of all components of a site such as sand, shards, mud bricks, and towering stone gateways as being equally important and integral elements of the archaeological record. The use of the term *clearance* also encouraged the feeling that the antiquities of Egypt simply needed to be exposed and displayed rather than being analyzed, interpreted, or reconstructed. From the 1880s onward, however, the emergence of more scientific approaches gradually discredited the practice, although it was many years before clearance techniques could be said to have been eradicated.

Two individuals, W. M. Flinders Petrie and GEORGE REISNER, were primarily responsible for the modernization of archaeology in Egypt in the late nineteenth and early twentieth centuries. Although their backgrounds and career paths were quite different in many respects, they shared two important characteristics. Both were able to devote themselves wholeheartedly to Egyptian archaeology primarily because of the considerable financial support they received from female benefactors (in Petrie's case, the British novelist Amelia Edwards, and in Reisner's case, the American philanthropist Phoebe Apperson), and both adopted single-minded and mold-breaking approaches to the survey and excavation of Egyptian sites.

At a time when methods of archaeological fieldwork were still in their infancy, the innovative methods of Petrie and Reisner set new standards for the discipline as a whole. For perhaps the only period in its history, Egyptian archaeology was at the forefront of the development of methodology, setting the pattern for excavations in Europe and America.

One of Petrie's earliest archaeological publications was a metrological analysis ranging from the Giza pyramids in Egypt to Stonehenge in England (Petrie 1877). Although this was a somewhat multidisciplinary work compared with most of his later publications, its meticulous attention to detailed measurement and objective recording methods foreshadowed the rest of his career. By the time Petrie began to work in Egypt in the early 1880s, the motivation of many expeditions had switched from treasure hunting to the authentication of episodes in the Bible. Indeed, the Society for the Promotion of Excavation in the Delta of the Nile (an alternative name for the nascent Egypt Exploration Fund, or EEF) was dedicated to the search for "the documents of a lost period of Biblical history" in the delta region. Petrie was therefore appointed to excavate Tanis, Naukratis, Nabesha, and Defenna, all of which were situated in Lower Egypt.

In complete contrast to the conservative EDOUARD NAVILLE (the other excavator employed by the EEF in the 1880s), Petrie immediately began to create a new style of fieldwork, paying close attention to every detail of the archaeological deposits rather than simply concentrating on the large monumental features of sites. Whereas his predecessors tended to clear large tracts of archaeological material relatively indiscriminately, Petrie dug selectively, excavating trenches in strategically selected parts of each site and thus building up an overall picture of the remains without destroying the entire site in the process. At El Amarna, for instance, he obtained a good overview of a complex urban site in a single season by excavating a range of different types of structures in various parts of the city.

The efficacy of Petrie's methods was particularly evident in his excavations of the early dynastic royal cemetery at Abydos, which had already been despoiled by the French Egyptologist Emile Amelineau for several years. Petrie's meticulous approach enabled him to build up a much clearer picture of the nature and sequence of the tombs, through both new excavation and the dissection of Amelineau's spoil heaps, which contained numerous important small objects such as seal impressions and tiny fragments of ivory labels. Ironically, the same site was reexcavated by the DEUTSCHES ARCHÄOLOGISCHES INSTITUT (German Archaeological Institute) during the 1980s and 1990s, and Petrie's own spoil heaps yielded fresh evidence about this crucial period in Egyptian history.

Petrie's long and fruitful career involved the survey and excavation of at least fifty Egyptian, Palestinian, and British sites, and the publication of numerous site reports, catalogues, and corpora of artifacts, but perhaps the most defining aspect of his work was his invention of the system of "sequence dating." In 1890, he showed in his excavation of the complex stratigraphy of Tell el Hesy in Palestine that careful artifactual synchronisms could be made between the various strata and Egyptian historical phases. About ten years later, he applied the same basic process to the assemblages at predynastic cemetery sites, where the development of the site was horizontal rather than stratigraphic, which made the whole period difficult to date. His use of sequence dates, consisting initially of the matching up of many different slips of paper bearing the details of individual funerary assemblages, allowed him to assign relative dates to each grave within the predynastic cemetery at

Wall relief showing royal barge at the temple of Rameses III at Medinet Habu (Ann Ronan Picture Library)

Diospolis Parva. He was therefore able to create a relative chronology for the predynastic period, which was later to be broadly confirmed both by stratigraphic excavation and by radiocarbon DATING.

Although George Reisner did not begin to excavate in Egypt until about twenty years after the arrival of Petrie, he nevertheless had a comparable impact on the field. Like Petrie, Reisner paid an enormous attention to detail, but he was also the first archaeologist in Egypt to recognize the need to provide such detailed records of his surveys or excavations that any future researcher would be able to reconstruct both the site and the process by which it was originally examined. At the predynastic cemetery of Naga ed-Der, for instance, the records of his excavations of 1901 have proved an invaluable resource to modern anthropologists and prehistorians (see Podzorski 1990). According to a description of Reisner's methods of work, every object found was visually recorded at the time, and as objects were removed from the ground, they were again photographed, sometimes from several angles, and every single object or frag-

ment, potsherd, bead, scrap of every kind as well as important objects was entered in a register with an identifying number, a careful verbal description, usually a measured drawing, measurements, date, place of finding, and a note of photographs taken. The principal drawback of Reisner's painstaking approach was the inherent slowness of preparing the reports for publication, which meant that much of his work was still unpublished at his death.

It was Reisner who introduced the systematic use of section drawing into Egyptian archaeology, some forty years after such stratigraphic analysis had been pioneered by Giuseppe Fiorelli at POMPEII. All previous excavators in Egypt had simply used plans to describe the various stages of excavation at a site, and although Petrie had drawn profiles of the stratigraphy at the Palestinian site of Tell el Hesy in 1890, Reisner was the first to record the stratigraphy of ancient Egyptian sites. He was also one of the earliest archaeologists to take genuinely multidisciplinary teams to Egypt. At Naga ed-Der he was accompanied by the anatomist SIR GRAFTON ELLIOT SMITH, whose detailed observations on the material from cemetery N7000 have provided modern researchers with an extremely reliable anthropological database.

Although the achievements of Petrie and Reisner are comparatively well documented, there was another phase in the development of Egyptian archaeology that has received less attention. In the period between the two world wars, several field-workers in Egypt began to undertake projects that would now be described as experimental and ethno-archaeological. Reginald Engelbach, for instance, undertook a number of experiments in the study of stone procurement and processing (Engelbach 1923) while Winifred Blackman, the wife of the British Egyptologist A. M. Blackman, published a study of Egyptian peasants (Blackman 1927) that was distinctly innovative in its approach to the links between modern and ancient Egyptian culture. These methodological advances, however, were to be thoroughly eclipsed by the discovery of new spectacular treasures by archaeologists HOWARD CARTER at Thebes and Pierre Montet at Tanis.

In 1922, Carter's discovery of the tomb of Pharaoh TUTANKHAMUN, almost exactly a century after Champollion's decipherment of hieroglyphs, opened the floodgates in terms of public appreciation and exploitation of ancient Egypt. Archaeology as a whole attracts a level of popular interest not usually associated with other, more deskbound disciplines such as physics or mathematics, and the study of ancient Egypt has a particularly strong grip on the popular imagination. Even before the discovery of the tomb of Tutankhamun, nineteenth-century poets and novelists, such as Percy Bysshe Shelley and Sir Rider Haggard, were presenting a romanticized view of Pharaonic Egypt that drew heavily on new information provided by adventurers and archaeologists.

There are no doubt many theses that might be written on the impact of Carter's discovery on the popular culture of Europe and America, but from a purely Egyptological point of view, it might be argued that it was something of a mixed blessing. Although both Petrie and Reisner had made other sensational discoveries at certain points in their careers, their principal achievement had been to establish Egyptology as a rigorous scientific discipline concerned with the pursuit of knowledge rather than objets d'art. Yet in one fell swoop, the discovery of Tutankhamun's tomb restored the popular view of Egypt as a treasure hunters' paradise in which sheer persistence might eventually be richly rewarded (after the initial euphoric days, Carter was to spend much of his life cataloging the funerary equipment he had discovered in the tomb). Egyptologists have since been dogged by a public willing them to find something even more exciting than an intact royal tomb, and they have often found that their scientific agenda is at odds with the popular desire for buried treasure. The other side of the coin, however, is the continued existence of a wide audience for Egyptological research, which helps to maintain a subject that might otherwise be a vulnerable minority discipline.

Settlement Prehistory and the "Nubian Campaign": New Directions in Egyptian Archaeology

Most of the work accomplished by archaeologists in Egypt between the mid-nineteenth century and World War II was characterized by two distinct trends. First, the early work in particular was marked by a resolutely art-historic, object-oriented approach to the excavated data. Second, fieldwork was dominated by a preference for the study of religious and funerary architecture rather than the artifacts and architecture of daily life. Both of these tendencies effectively inhibited the intellectual development of Egyptian archaeology until the 1960s when two major influences—the study of the prehistory of the Nile Valley and the increased excavation of pharaonic towns—finally began to exert an influence on the subject as a whole.

Certain town sites had already been investigated by the travelers, antiquarians, and pioneering archaeologists of the early nineteenth century such as Sir John Gardner Wilkinson and Robert Hay. In 1826, for example, Wilkinson made a detailed survey of the Greco-Roman port of Berenice on the Red Sea, which had been discovered a few years earlier by Giovanni Belzoni. Both Wilkinson and Erbkam (Lepsius's

The mortuary Temple of Queen Hatshepsut just over the cliff from the famous Valley of the Kings in Egypt (The Purcell Team / Corbis)

cartographer) produced survey plans of the city at El Amarna that showed the basic structure of the site and several of the major ceremonial buildings in the center of the city. However, the first fully scientific study of an ancient Egyptian town, combining both survey and excavation, was Petrie's excavation of the site of El Amarna in 1891–1892.

In 1950 only a handful of sites could be cited as examples of Egyptian urban life: Kahun, Gurob, and El Amarna (Petrie 1890, 1891), Deir el-Medina (Bruyere 1939), and several fortified towns in NUBIA such as Sesebi and Amara West. These sites were all to some extent unrepresentative of Egyptian urbanization, and only the city at El Amarna was sufficiently well documented to provide any reliable archaeological basis for the analysis of Egyptian urban life. Well-preserved towns of any period were once considered to be rare in Egypt (Fairman 1949; O'Connor 1972, 683), and J. A. Wilson (1960, 24) went so far as to suggest that Egypt was "a civilization without cities." On the few occasions when nineteenth-century and early-twen-

tieth-century archaeologists excavated town sites (rather than simply scouring them for papyri or ostraca), which usually meant that the mud-brick walls of houses were exposed but little or no excavation took place in courtyards, streets, or other potentially significant "open" areas. Since the 1950s, however, there has been a steady increase in the available data from pharaonic urban sites. In an analysis of changing patterns in Egyptological publication, David O'Connor (1990, 241–242) points out that the percentage of published archaeological fieldwork devoted to settlements rose from 13.4 percent in 1924 to 23.2 percent in 1981. The situation, however, appears to have changed even more dramatically in the 1990s, with the 1989–1990 list of Egyptological publications showing no less than 44.4 percent of fieldwork dealing with settlement remains and a correspondingly steep decline in the excavation of nonmonumental cemeteries (see Table 1).

This growth in settlement archaeology has led to the publication of data from numerous surviving fragments of towns and villages exca-

Table 1. Proportions of Published Archaeological Fieldwork (1924–1990)

| Publication | Monumental | | Non-monumental | | Survey |
	Funerary	Religious	Cemetery	Settlement	
1924	34.1	20.7	30.5	13.4	1.0
1981	36.2	13.0	8.7	23.2	15.9
1982	34.6	17.9	11.5	17.9	17.9
1989–1990	27.8	16.7	5.6	44.4	5.6

Source: All details except those for 1989–1990 are taken from D. O'Connor, "Egyptology and Archaeology: An African Perspective," in *A History of African Archaeology,* ed. P. Robertshaw (London: J. Currey, 1990). The data for 1924, 1981, 1982, and 1989–1900 are derived from Pratt (1925), Zonhoven (1985), Leclant (1983), and Hovestreydt and Zonhoven (1992), respectively.

vated in a variety of locations throughout Egypt and Nubia. The houses and living conditions of the Egyptians are still underrepresented, compared with their tombs and temples, but considerably more evidence from urban sites is now available in the form of a relatively unsynthesized collection of examples.

The UNESCO-backed Nubian Salvage Campaign of the 1960s injected a new vigor and urgency into the archaeology of Egypt, but it was the use of innovative techniques by prehistorians—cannibalizing other subjects such as geography, geology, and anthropology—that provided a new toolkit for the study of settlements, whether of the Paleolithic, Pharaonic, or Roman period. The long-neglected study of preliterate Egypt provided the ideal testing ground for techniques of purely archaeological analysis and interpretation in such projects as the excavation and survey of Epipaleolithic remains at Elkab (Vermeersch 1970) and the study of areas of predynastic settlement at Hierakonpolis (Fairservis 1972; Hoffman 1979, 155–164). This type of new fieldwork laid the foundation for more general interpretative works, such as Karl Butzer's groundbreaking study of man-land relationships in the Nile Valley (Butzer 1976).

Michael Hoffman (1979, xvii–xviii) has outlined the differences between traditional Egyptologists and prehistorians: "Although we share with historians a fundamental interest in reconstructing man's past, prehistorians have to depend much more on the often unimpressive scraps of material evidence discarded by our ancestors in their camps, towns, cemeteries and garbage heaps." Seen in this light, prehistorians and settlement archaeologists in Egypt have a

great deal in common. However, there is one major difference between prehistoric and settlement-oriented archaeology in Egypt. Whereas the prehistoric sites of the Nile Valley lie in an intellectual vacuum, the settlement archaeologist's analysis of material culture can be supplemented (and occasionally contrasted) with the very different types of textual information provided by contemporary inscriptions, papyri, and ostraca. The challenge of historical archaeology in Egypt is to synthesize the broad patterns of material culture with the existing historical, textually based framework of events, dates, and personalities (see, for example, Kemp 1984; Shaw 1992).

When less information was available about Egyptian towns, there was a frequent tendency to make generalized comparisons across many hundreds of years and between different functional types of settlement in diverse geographical locations so that, for instance, a Middle Kingdom pyramid town such as Kahun might be compared in detail with a late New Kingdom "harim-town" such as Gurob. Undoubtedly there is evidence to suggest a certain degree of continuity in Egyptian urban planning from the Old Kingdom to the late period, but the routine and indiscriminate comparison of towns and villages separated by several centuries tended to result in a blurred picture in which the particular cultural, chronological, and geographical contexts of settlements were neglected. Such was the dearth of evidence in the 1940s that H. W. Fairman proposed an analogy between social patterning in Old Kingdom cemeteries and that of towns of the same date in an attempt to provide some means of reconstructing Old Kingdom town planning (Fairman 1949, 36).

Now, however, the long-term excavations at sites such as Elephantine in Upper Egypt and Tell el-Dab'a in the eastern delta have provided a more reliable view of the gradual processes of urbanization by revealing successive strata of settlements spanning many centuries. The published evidence from Elephantine (Kaiser et al. 1988), for instance, charts the growth of the site from an Old Kingdom settlement of some 16,000 square meters to a congested late-period city covering more than 70,000 square meters. The excavations at Tell el-Dab'a (Bietak 1975, 1992) have revealed a detailed local socioeconomic history in which the Egyptian inhabitants of the first intermediate period (ca. 2134–2040 B.C.) were gradually supplanted by Asiatics during the second intermediate period (ca. 1640–1532 B.C.). The results of the scientific investigations at Elephantine, Tell el-Dab'a, and other sites have not only vastly increased the knowledge of Egyptian domestic economy but have also begun to show how Egyptian settlements changed over the course of time. The Egyptian urban database has therefore expanded sufficiently to allow the different chronological phases of urbanization in Egypt to begin to be discerned and studied separately (see Kemp 1977, 1989) so that the idiosyncrasies of individual sites and particular periods of urban growth can be clearly distinguished from overall trends.

The Growth of Science in Egyptology

Eric Peet's inaugural lecture as reader in Egyptology at Oxford University in 1934 concerned the "present state of Egyptological studies." Already acutely conscious of the impact of science on Egyptology, he suggested that "many of the questions, especially those of the origins of materials and the technical processes of the arts and crafts, which have puzzled us for years, will eventually reach definite solution through the resources of chemistry and the other sciences" (Peet 1934). He was no doubt mindful of the fact that only eight years earlier the Cairo-based British chemist Alfred Lucas had published the first edition of *Ancient Egyptian Materials and Industries,* a brilliant summary of the surviving evidence for Egyptian materials and crafts that effectively served as the essential manual for

Egyptological science until the 1990s. Lucas had access to much of the material in the Cairo museum, which enabled him to publish data, chemical analyses, and bibliographical references for a great deal of the most important material excavated since the mid-nineteenth century, including the objects from the tomb of Tutankhamun.

Lucas may have been the first scientist to survey the whole range of available data from Egypt, but there were many earlier scholars who pioneered various procedures. The field of bio-anthropology, focusing principally on the study of human and animal remains, has been one of the most active areas of scientific research in Egyptology from the early nineteenth century until the present day (see David 1979, 1986; Davies and Walker 1993). The surgeon Thomas Joseph Pettigrew took part in the unwrapping and dissection of numerous mummies from 1820 onward, and in 1834 he published his *History of Egyptian Mummies* that was to serve as the most reliable volume on the subject until the X-raying work of Grafton Elliot Smith at the beginning of the twentieth century (Elliot Smith 1912). In 1896, the German researcher W. Konig was the first to make radiographs of Egyptian mummies, and two years later, Petrie published radiographs of mummies from his excavations at Deshasheh (Petrie 1898). These photographs are thought to be the earliest instance of the archaeological use of X-rays in Britain, and they were perhaps made by J. N. Collie, who was making pioneering medical X-rays at University College London in the same year. Most of the subsequent work on Egyptian mummies has concentrated on examinations of this type, but some of the most recent research has concentrated on molecular biology and the extraction of DNA (e.g., Goudsmit, Decker, Smit, Kuiken, Geelen, and Perizonius 1993; Nissenbaum 1992).

A growth area in the 1980s and 1990s was the study of human diet in Pharaonic Egypt, based principally on the analysis of surviving fragments of food from both domestic and funerary contexts. Projects of this type have included studies of Egyptian bread and beer making, wine production, and meat processing. A related area of research into Egyptian food technology is the analysis of organic residues in amphorae and other vessels, which is beginning to make a significant contribution to the understanding of trading patterns between Egypt, the Levant, and the Aegean.

Thanks primarily to WILLARD LIBBY's use of Egyptian antiquities as some of his earliest "guinea pigs" in the development of radiocarbon dating, Egyptian archaeologists have been able to take advantage of radiometric methods of dating since the 1950s. In the immediate aftermath of the emergence of dendrochronological curves for the calibration of radiocarbon dates, in the mid-1980s, Egyptology was again one of the yardsticks against which the method was tested (Hassan and Robinson 1987; Shaw 1985). There is broad agreement between the calibrated dates and the conventional pharaonic chronology, but there has never been a concerted attempt to date a wide range of materials from a number of different phases of Pharaonic Egypt (and there are still a small number of disconcerting anomalies, e.g., see Haas, Devine, Wenke, Lehner, and Wolfi 1987). The existing sets of Egyptian radiocarbon dates are too piecemeal (and in many cases too old or too unreliable) to form the basis of an independent radiometric chronological framework for comparison with the conventionally calculated dates.

Another important area of scientific progress in recent years has been the use of geophysical methods of prospecting pharaonic sites, including the use of such techniques as resistivity survey, proton-magnetometer survey, sonic profiling, ground-penetrating radar, and thermal imaging. In the Great Pyramid at Giza, for instance, in 1986–1987 the combined use of microgravimetry (a technique for measuring the relative densities of stone blocks) and the transmission of electromagnetic microwaves revealed the possible presence of hidden chambers behind the stone walls of the so-called king's and queen's burial chambers. On a less sensational level, resistivity surveys at Saqqara, Memphis, and El Amarna, during the 1980s and 1990s have proved particularly suited to Egyptian sites. Resistivity traverses have supplemented conventional survey techniques, which has allowed archaeologists both to select areas showing the greatest potential for excavation and to map major features, such as wells or enclosure walls, without actually having to remove the material under which they are buried (see, for instance, Leclant and Clerc 1988; Mathieson and Tavares 1993).

The processual, multidisciplinary strategies of fieldwork that are now largely taken for granted in Egyptology (and even in some fieldwork at funerary and religious sites, as in the application of Schiffer's "behavioral archaeology" to the excavation of a Theban tomb [see Polz 1987]) have their roots in the archaeology of Egyptian settlements and prehistoric sites. Many sites (e.g., Abydos, Memphis, El Amarna, Elephantine, and Tell el-Dab'a) have been the subject of long-term multidisciplinary research since the late 1970s, thus providing opportunities for the application of numerous innovative scientific approaches to the archaeological remains of the Pharaonic period, including the use of experimental and ethnoarchaeological work (e.g., Guksch 1988; Nicholson 1992).

Theoretical and Practical Problems in Egyptian Archaeology

The sheer consciousness of large amounts of still-unpublished or unexamined data seems to have discouraged archaeologists working in Egypt from experimentation with innovative techniques and fresh theoretical perspectives. Indeed, H. S. Smith sees the apparent theoretical and analytical stagnation of Egyptian archaeology as an inevitable result of the accumulation of vast amounts of relatively unsynthesized data. He argues that the relative lack of explicit method or theory in Egyptology might be an inherent problem for historical archaeologists generally: "Because of the complexity of most of the societies with which they deal, the vast scale of the records and remains known to exist, and the countervailing inadequacy of these to provide a complete cultural picture at any one moment or a complete development through time, historians and historical archaeologists tend to be less analytical in approach, more catholic and less explicit in their assumptions" (Smith 1972, xi).

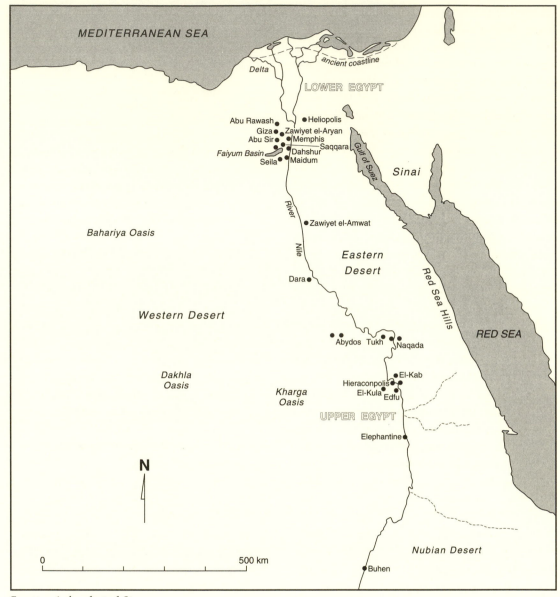

Egyptian Archaeological Sites

Since 1980 however, Egyptian archaeologists have undoubtedly begun to seek what Smith describes as "new types of information," and there has been a massive growth of interest in the investigation of data from prehistoric and urban sites. There have also been a few small signs of movement, or at least a recognition of the need for movement, toward more problem-oriented fieldwork (e.g., Assmann, Burkard, and Davies 1987; van den Brink 1988), with some research projects beginning to be specifically designed to answer long-standing cultural or historical questions as op-

posed to the tendency simply to explore new sites in an indiscriminate fashion.

One of the foremost problems of Egyptology is the recurrent bias toward data from Upper (i.e., southern) Egypt. Despite the work undertaken at delta sites both in the late nineteenth century and the late twentieth century (see van den Brink 1988, 1992), the prevailing view of Egyptian society and history is heavily biased toward Upper Egypt and dominated in particular by the rich remains of the Theban region. This situation stems partly from the survival of more impressive standing architectural remains in

Upper Egypt, but it also stems from the relatively poor conditions of preservation in the delta, where high population, submergence of archaeological deposits below the groundwater level, and the agricultural use of tell sites for fertilizer have all tended to reduce the attraction (and indeed the visibility) of archaeological sites in Lower Egypt. Although the initiation of a number of new projects at delta sites in the 1980s and 1990s has begun to redress this balance, it will be many years before the weight of evidence can be said to be spread equally across southern and northern Egypt.

As a result of the application of scientific methods of survey and analysis (and the simultaneous assimilation of ideas from linguistics, literary criticism, and art history), the field of Egyptology has inexorably expanded into a sprawling multidisciplinary monster with tentacles extending from bio-anthropology and geophysics to philology and sociology. Although this diversification sometimes threatens the integrity of the subject as a whole, it is also increasingly its strength in that the many different academic disciplines utilizing Egyptological data each provide fresh sources of stimulation and new directions for future research.

Ian Shaw

References

Assmann, J., G. Burkard, and W. V. Davies. 1987. *Problems and Priorities in Egyptian Archaeology.* London: Kegan Paul International.

Bietak, M. 1975. *Tell el-Dab'a II.* Vienna: Osterreichische Akademie der Wissenschaften.

————. 1992. *Tell el-Dab'a V.* Vienna: Osterreichische Akademie der Wissenschaften.

Binford, L. R. 1972. *An Archaeological Perspective.* New York: Seminar Press.

Blackman, W. S. 1927. *The Fellahin of Upper Egypt.* London: Harrap.

Bruyere, B. 1939. *Rapport sur les fouilles de Deir el-Medineh (1934–5) III.* Cairo: IFAO.

Butzer, K. W. 1976. *Early Hydraulic Civilization in Egypt: A Study in Cultural Ecology.* Chicago: University of Chicago Press.

Coe, M. D. 1992. *Breaking the Maya Code.* London: Thames and Hudson.

Daniel, G. 1967. *The Origins and Growth of Archaeology.* Harmondsworth, UK: Penguin.

David, A. R. 1986. *Science in Egyptology: The Pro-ceedings of the 1979 and 1984 Symposia.* Manchester, UK: Manchester University Press.

David, A. R., ed. 1979. *The Manchester Museum Mummy Project: Multidisciplinary Research on Ancient Egyptian Mummified Remains.* Manchester, UK: Manchester Museum.

Davies, W. V., and R. Walker. 1993. *Biological Anthropology and the Study of Ancient Egypt.* London: British Museum Press.

Description de l'Egypte. 1809–1822. 9 vols. Paris.

Elliot Smith, G. 1912. *The Royal Mummies: Catalogue General des Antiquites Egyptiennes du Musee du Caire. No 61051–61100.* Cairo: Service des Antiquites de l'Egypte.

Engelbach, R. 1923. *The Problem of the Obelisks: From a Study of the Unfinished Obelisk of Aswan.* London: Fisher Unwin.

Fairman, H. W. 1949. "Town Planning in Pharaonic Egypt." *Town Planning Review* 20: 32–51.

Fairservis, W. A. 1972. "Preliminary Report on the First Two Seasons at Hierakonpolis." *Journal of the American Research Center in Egypt* 9: 7–27, 67–99.

Goudsmit, J., J. Decker, L. Smit, C. Kuiken, J. Geelen, and R. Perizonius. 1993. "Analysis of Retrovirus Sequences in ca. 5300 Years Old Egyptian Mummy DNA Obtained via PCR Amplification and Molecular Cloning." In W. V. Davies and R. Walker, *Biological Anthropology and the Study of Ancient Egypt,* 91–97. London: British Museum Press.

Guksch, C. E. 1988. "Ethnoarchaeology in Egyptology: A View from Anthropology." In *Akten des vierten internationalen Agyptologenkongress: Munchen 1985,* 1:41–51. Ed. S. Schoske. Munich: Helmut Buske.

Haas, H., J. Devine, R. Wenke, M. Lehner, and W. Wolfi. 1987. "Radiocarbon Chronology and the Historical Calendar in Egypt." In *Chronologies in the Near East.* Ed. D. Aurenche, J. Evin, and F. Hours. Oxford: British Archaeological Reports.

Hassan, F., and S. Robinson. 1987. "High-precision Radiocarbon Chronometry of Ancient Egypt and Comparisons with Nubia, Palestine and Mesopotamia." *Antiquity* 61, Shaw no. 231: 119–134.

Hoffman, M. A. 1979. *Egypt before the Pharaohs.* New York: Knopf.

Hovestreydt, W., and L. M. J. Zonhoven. 1992. *Preliminary Egyptologiical Bibliography.* No. 11. Leiden: International Association of Egyptologists.

James, P., I. J. Thorpe, N. Kokkinos, R. Morkot,

and J. Frankish. 1991. *Centuries of Darkness.* London: Jonathan Cape.

Kaiser, W., et al. 1988. "Stadt und Tempel von Elephantine: 15/16, Grabungsbericht." *Mitteilungen des Deutschen Archaologischen Instituts Abteiluna Kairo* 44: 135–182.

Kemp, B. J. 1977. "The Early Development of Towns in Egypt." *Antiquity* 51: 185–200.

———. 1984. "In the Shadow of Texts: Archaeology in Egypt." *Archaeological Review from Cambridge* 3, no. 2: 19–28.

———. 1989. *Ancient Egypt: Anatomy of a Civilization.* London: Routledge.

Leclant, J. 1983. "Fouilles et travaux en Égypte et au Soudan, 1981–1982." *Orientalia* 52: 261–542.

Leclant, J., and G. Clerc. 1988. "Fouilles et travaux en Égypte et au Soudan, 1986–1987." *Orientalia* 57: 329.

Lepsius, K. R. 1849–1859. *Denkmaler aus Agypten und Athiopien.* 12 vols. Berlin: Nicolai. Reprint, Geneva: Centre de Documentation du Monde Oriental, 1973.

Mathieson, I. J., and A. Tavares. 1993. "Preliminary Report of the National Museums of Scotland Saqqara Survey Project, 1990–91." *Journal of Egyptian Archaeology* 79: 17–31.

Nicholson, P. T. 1992. "The Relationship between Excavation, Ethnoarchaeology, and Experiment in Egyptology." In *Atti . . . sesto congresso internazionale di egittologie,* 1:473–480. Turin, Italy.

Nissenbaum, A. 1992. "Molecular Archaeology: Organic Geochemistry of Egyptian Mummies." *Journal of Archaeological Science* 19: 1–6.

O'Connor, D. 1972. "The Geography of Settlement in Ancient Egypt." In *Man, Settlement, and Urbanism,* 681–698. Ed. P. J. Ucko, R. Tringham, and G. W. Dimbleby. London: Duckworth.

———. 1974. "Political Systems and Archaeological Data in Egypt: 2600–1780 B.C." *World Archaeology* 6: 15–38.

———. 1990. "Egyptology and Archaeology: An African Perspective." In *A History of African Archaeology,* 236–251. Ed. P. Robertshaw. Portsmouth and London: Heinemann and James Currey.

Peet, T. E. 1934. *The Present State of Egyptological Studies.* Oxford: Oxford University Press.

Pendlebury, J. D. S. 1935. *Tell el-Amarna.* London: Lovat, Dickson and Thompson.

Petrie, W. M. F. 1877. *Inductive Metrology.* London: Hargrove Saunders.

———. 1890. *Kahun, Gurob, and Hawara.* London: Egypt Exploration Fund.

———. 1891. *Illahun. Kahun, and Gurob.* London: Egypt Exploration Fund.

———. 1898. *Deshasheh.* 1897. London: Egypt Exploration Fund.

Piggott, S. 1989. *Ancient Britons and the Antiquarian Imagination.* London: Thames and Hudson.

Podzorski, P. V. 1990. *Their Bones Shall Not Perish: An Examination of Predynastic Human Skeletal Remains from Naga-ed-Der in Egypt.* New Malden: SIA.

Polz, D. 1987. "Excavation and Recording of a Theban Tomb: Some Remarks on Recording Methods." In *Problems and Priorities in Egyptian Archaeology,* 119–140. Ed. G. Burkard and W. V. Davies. London: Kegan Paul International.

Powell, D. 1973. *Villa Ariadne.* London: Hodder and Stoughton.

Pratt, I. 1925. *Ancient Egypt: Sources of Information in the New York Public Library.* New York: New York Public Library.

Rohl, D. 1995. *A Test of Time: The Bible from Myth to History.* London: Century.

Schele, L., and M. E. Miller. 1986. *The Blood of Kings: Dynasty and Ritual in Maya Art.* Fort Worth: Kimbell Art Museum.

Schiffer, M. B. 1976. *Behavioral Archaeology.* New York: Academic Press.

Shaw, I. 1985. "Egyptian Chronology and the Irish Oak Calibration." *Journal of Near Eastern Studies* 44: 295–317.

———. 1992. "Ideal Homes in Ancient Egypt: The Archaeology of Social Aspiration." *Cambridge Archaeological Journal* 2, no. 2: 147–166.

Smith, H. S. 1972. "Preface." In *Man, Settlement, and Urbanism,* xi–xii. Ed. G. Burkard and W. V. Davies. London: Duckworth.

Trigger, B. G. 1989. *A History of Archaeological Thought.* Cambridge: Cambridge University Press.

Trigger, B. G., B. J. Kemp, D. O'Connor, and A. B. Lloyd. 1985. *Ancient Egypt: A Social History.* Cambridge: Cambridge University Press.

van den Brink, E. C. M. 1988. *The Archaeology of the Nile Delta: Problems and Priorities.* Amsterdam: Netherlands Foundation for Archaeological Research in Egypt.

———. 1992. *The Nile Delta in Transition: 4th–3rd Millennium B.C.* Jerusalem.

Vermeersch, P. 1970. "L'Elkabien: Une nouvelle industrie epipaléolithique Elkab en Haute

Égypte: Sa stratigraphie, sa typologie."
Chronique de l'Egypte 45: 45–68.

Wilkinson, J. G. 1837. *The Manners and Customs of the Ancient Egyptians.* 3 vols. London: Murray. Rev. ed., 1873.

Wilson, J. A. 1960. "Egypt through the New Kingdom: Civilization without Cities." In *City Invincible.* Ed. C. Kraeling and R. M. Adams. Chicago: Chicago University Press.

Wortham, J. D. 1971. *British Egyptological Bibliography: 1549–1906.* Newton Abbot, UK: David and Charles.

Zonhoven, L. M. J. 1985. *Annual Egyptological Bibliography 1981.* Warminster, PA: Aris and Phillips.

Egypt: Predynastic

The term *Predynastic* denotes Egypt before the historically recorded sequence of kings and dynasties that starts ca. 3050 B.C. (*see* EGYPT: DYNASTIC). Although there is no official beginning to the Predynastic, in Egyptian archaeology the term usually refers to the period that follows the appearance, ca. 5000 B.C., of a Neolithic food-producing economy in the Egyptian Nile Valley proper (as distinct from the Sahara at large). Evidence for reliance on food production using domesticated plants and animals (principally sheep, goat, pigs, cattle, wheat, and barley) occurs late in the Nile Valley relative to the fertile crescent of the Near East, possibly suggesting that hunting/gathering remained viable for a longer time span in the rich environment of the Nile floodplain. Once adopted, however, food production is linked with a long-term process of population growth, sedentism, and increasing social complexity in Predynastic cultures in the Nile Valley. The study of Predynastic Egypt has primarily been focused on the development of a series of different cultures in both northern and southern Egypt during the course of the two millennia from ca. 5000 to ca. 3000 B.C. The Predynastic period culminated in a process of political and territorial conquest during the second half of the Fourth Millennium B.C. (ca. 3400–3050) that included the expansion of the southern Egyptian cultural tradition over the rest of the country. The emergence of a politically powerful elite, governmental institutions, royal artistic and architectural styles, and the hieroglyphic writing system can be traced during the terminal stages of the Predynastic period, setting the stage for Egypt's transition to the Dynastic period.

The study of Predynastic Egypt differs in certain ways from that of Dynastic Egypt. The lack of writing until the very end of the Predynastic means that archaeology of the Predynastic does not have at its disposal the written evidence that begins to be increasingly important with the transition to the Dynastic period. This difference is, however, not as pronounced as might appear to be the case since during many periods of Egypt's Dynastic history, the volume of written documents and inscriptions is a small and very selective corpus of material. The archaeology of Predynastic Egypt has been, in recent decades, one of the most rapidly changing areas of work in Egypt, with new insights and discoveries continuing to reshape understanding of the early origins of Egyptian civilization.

Although the concept of the Predynastic period fits well with modern ideas of the distinction between prehistory and history, it is important to recognize that the idea of the Predynastic has been rooted to a large degree in the Egyptians' own ideas of their earliest past. One of the central religious and political ideas of ancient Egypt was the concept of the *Sema-Tawy,* or "Unification-of-the-Two-Lands." The Egyptians organized their history into a sequence of royal dynasties (a version of this that was recorded by Manctho, a priest of the Ptolemaic period, being the basis for the Dynastic history we use today). The beginning of these dynasties was the unification (*Sema-Tawy*) of Upper (southern) and Lower (northern) Egypt by a king Menes, ca. 3100 B.C. Menes was the first pharaoh of the First Dynasty and according to Egyptian tradition founded the capital city of Memphis near the southern apex of the Nile delta so he could live there and rule over this newly unified kingdom.

For many years it was believed that the tradition of the *Sema-Tawy* was a historical reality and scholars frequently followed ancient Egyptian tradition by defining the Predynastic period as Egypt before the unification by Menes. Evidence suggesting that the Egyptian hieroglyphic writing system emerged full-blown at this same time tended to reinforce the clear division between Egypt's literate and sophisticated Dynastic culture and the preliterate, prehistoric past that preceded it. Much of the efforts of recent archaeological work on the Predynastic period has been to understand the process of state formation that culminated in the transition to the Pharaonic Egyptian state. One of the major insights of the work of recent decades has been evidence for the long-term development during the later Predynastic period of features such as hieroglyphic writing, royal iconography, administrative institutions, and increasingly organized trade links both within Egypt as well as between Egypt and foreign lands (including Syro-Palestine areas, MESOPOTAMIA, and NUBIA). The evidence suggests a complicated process of cultural and political unification spanning centuries and not occurring virtually overnight as suggested by the tradition of the *Sema-Tawy*.

Predynastic Egypt was not culturally homogeneous; archaeological work has defined a series of different cultural traditions characterized by different artifacts, tool types, burial practices, and architecture. Broadly speaking, the Predynastic period of Egypt is divided between two cultural spheres: the Nile delta and southern Egypt. Regional variation is, however, a marked feature of both culture areas. Predynastic settlement sites in the northern part of the country include the sites of Merimda Beni-Salama (ca. 4200–3400 B.C.) on the southwest edge of the Nile delta; el-Omari (ca. 3600–3200 B.C.) south of Cairo; and a group of settlements on the edge of the Fayum (Fayum B culture, ca. 4500–4000 B.C.) that display the transition from a fishing/gathering to mixed farming/fishing lifestyle. These sites show regional cultural variations. The main type-sites that have defined the northern cultural tradition are Maadi (just south of modern Cairo) and Buto (near modern Alexandria). The late Neolithic cultural tradition of Lower Egypt has in recent years become generally known as the Buto-Maadi culture and shows many connections with the contemporary culture of Chalcolithic/Early Bronze I of southern Palestine.

A quite different Predynastic cultural tradition occurs in Upper (southern) Egypt. Unlike the wide Nile delta of Lower Egypt, the valley south of the delta is characterized by an undulating low desert terrain that flanks either side of the floodplain of the Nile River. Predynastic Egyptians, like their later Dynastic descendants, used the arid low desert for burying the dead. Cemetery archaeology has been the foundation of work on the southern Predynastic cultures since the end of the nineteenth century. Several major settlement sites (including Nagada, Hierakonpolis, and Mahasna) have been excavated and settlement archaeology in southern Egypt promises to continue to add crucial information on the Predynastic cultural development in southern Egypt.

An early Predynastic culture in Upper Egypt is the Badarian (named after the site of el-Badari) dating ca. 4500–4000 B.C. The Badarian culture displays the earliest reliance on domesticated plants and animals in the Nile Valley. The Badarian most likely represents a regional variant, or facies, of a wider southern cultural sphere that includes the succeeding Nagada culture (dating ca. 4000–3050 B.C.). The Nagada culture is named after the type-site of Nagada in southern Egypt where a series of large cemeteries provided the basis for defining the evolution over time of the Nagada tradition. The early geographical range of the Nagada culture extended approximately from the region of Hierakonpolis (south of modern Luxor) to just north of ABYDOS. However, in its later phases (ca. 3600–3050 B.C.) the Nagada culture expanded dramatically both southward and northward, where it ultimately replaced the Buto-Maadi material culture by the end of the Predynastic period. Understanding how and why this expansion of the Nagada culture occurred is a central topic of current research on Predynastic Egypt.

The first serious work on the archaeology of the Predynastic cultures of southern Egypt was undertaken by WILLIAM FLINDERS PETRIE at the end of the nineteenth century. Petrie applied a technique that he termed *sequence dating* (known today as seriation) to organize a chronological sequence of Predynastic tombs from southern Egypt. This technique was based on an ordering of tombs containing similar groups of artifacts. Based on the principle that pottery and other objects change in style and popularity over time, sequence dating permitted a chronological order to be placed on the (at that time undatable) Predynastic cultural remains. Petrie arbitrarily assigned sequence "dates" to this relative ordering of Predynastic artifacts. Petrie anchored the late end of his Predynastic sequence by recognizing a shift toward mass-produced, less decorated pottery in the late Predynastic period. Following Petrie's Predynastic sequence dating, terms to describe different phases of southern Egyptian Predynastic material culture were coined based on "type-sites" that typified the cultural remains of a given phase of the Predynastic. The terms *Amratian* (adapted from site of el-Amra), *Gerzean* (based on site of Gerza); and *Semainean* (based on site of el-Semaina) came into use.

Although these terms are still employed today, archaeologists working on the Predynastic material use a more detailed chronological sequence that was developed by Werner Kaiser based on detailed analysis of the extensive Predynastic cemetery located at Nagada in southern Egypt. Kaiser defined the Nagada I (dating ca. 4000–3600 B.C.), Nagada II (ca. 3600–3250 B.C.) and Nagada III (ca. 3250–3050 B.C.) periods, with chronological subphases. Physical dating techniques, principally radiocarbon DATING, have served to anchor this Predynastic cultural sequence in absolute years before the present. The Nagada culture has a distinctive assemblage of artifacts. Pottery includes red-ochre polished wares, often with a black topped rim and upper body created by inverting the vessels in the embers during the firing process. Pottery with painted figural and geometric decoration is important in the cemeteries of the Nagada culture. Mud-stone palettes are a standard part of the Nagada culture repertoire. These palettes, usually trapezoidal, or occasionally zoomorphic, in form, were used as tools for grinding cosmetics. Small stone maceheads, at first disc-shaped and then pear-shaped, are a typical weapon type included in burials through the Nagada I and Nagada II. Ivory combs and pins, shell bracelets and a range of figurines are frequent in Nagada culture burials.

One of the major issues in the study of Predynastic Egypt has been the evidence for the development of social stratification. The division of society into distinct social levels with differential access to wealth, resources, and power is one of the hallmarks of complex society throughout the world. The well-preserved Predynastic cemeteries of southern Egypt have provided the principal evidence on this process of social stratification. Unequal control of power and resources is detectable through the appearance of burials that are wealthier, larger, and/or more elaborate than those of contemporaries. For the Badarian culture stratification appears to be minimal, although incipient stratification has been argued based on some differentiation in tomb wealth. Social stratification becomes a more visible feature of Predynastic cemeteries during the later Nagada I period (Amratian culture). This trend toward a more hierarchically organized society reaches a crescendo during the Nagada II (Gerzean culture) and Nagada III period.

The transition from the Nagada II to Nagada III periods (dating ca. 3250 B.C.) is noted for the appearance of a series of tombs at certain sites in southern Egypt that are indicative of the emergence of a super-elite, i.e., individuals occupying positions of wealth and authority far beyond contemporary members of their community. Three sites in southern Egypt—Nagada, Hierakonpolis, and Abydos—have provided indications of this development. At Hierakonpolis, the excavation in 1899 of the so-called Painted-Tomb (Tomb 100) revealed a decorated tomb with wall scenes indicating activities of a chief or proto-king. The decoration in the Painted Tomb at Hierakonpolis includes depictions of a figure wielding a mace and smiting enemies, a type of pose for the king that becomes a standard element of royal iconography at the very end of the Predynastic period. The Nagada Painted Tomb appears to be associated with a powerful chief or proto-king. A similar development is attested in Cemetery T at Nagada.

The best-documented site that displays the evolution of social complexity in the late Predynastic period is the early cemetery of Abydos (known as Umm el-Gaab). Work by E. Amélineau followed by Petrie at Abydos at the turn of

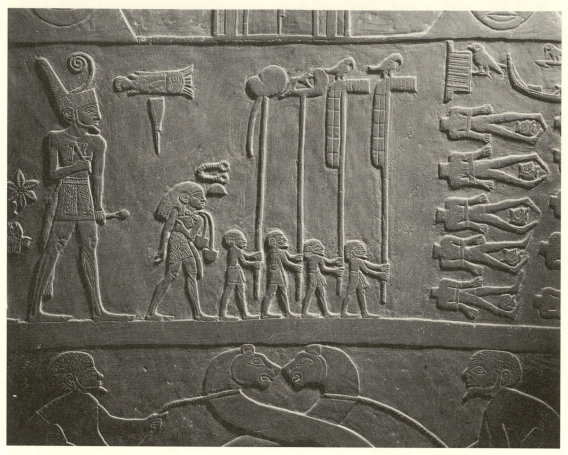

A detail of the Narmer Palette, ca. 3100 B.C., depicting a triumphal procession of King Menes, wearing the red crown of Lower Egypt at the temple of Horus, inspecting defeated enemies (The Art Archive/Egyptian Museum Cairo/Dagli Orti [A])

the century had revealed tombs attributed to the first pharaohs of the Dynastic period as well as the presence of extensive Predynastic cemeteries. The systematic investigation of the Abydos Predynastic cemeteries by Günter Dreyer during the 1980s and 1990s fully defined the scope of the Predynastic cemeteries that develop from north (Cemetery U dating to Nagada I through early Nagada III) to south (Cemetery B dating to the end of the Nagada III period). A marked growth in size and contents of certain tombs occurs with the beginning of the Nagada III period. The excavation of Tomb U-J, a multichambered tomb that still preserved some of its original contents, is likely the burial of a proto-king at the beginning of the Nagada III period. Significantly, Tomb U-J contained objects with early use of hieroglyphic signs for recordkeeping (including small inscribed dockets and ink la-

bels), demonstrating the use of writing was well advanced already at the end of Nagada II and beginning of Nagada III, ca. 3250 B.C.

The second half of the Nagada III period (Nagada IIIb, ca. 3150–3050 B.C.) is often called by archaeologists "Dynasty 0," referring to the fact that many of the central features of Dynastic Egypt are fully documented during this terminal phase of the Predynastic. A series of kings' names along with emergence of characteristic iconography of Pharaonic kingship characterize this period. From later Nagada III/Dynasty 0 we have a distinctive class of objects that suggest the final stages of state formation. These are commemorative stone maceheads and palettes (large decorated versions of the mudstone palettes and maceheads of the earlier phases of the Nagada culture). A cache of such commemorative stone palettes and maceheads was discovered in a deposit at Hierakonpolis by Quibell and Green in 1898. These objects may have originally been set up as dedicatory objects inside the early temple precinct of the god Horus at Hierakonpolis. The slate palettes are often decorated with scenes showing the defeat of chaotic forces, an important role of the pharaoh in Dynastic times. Some have scenes that are historical in nature. The most famous of these objects is the Narmer Palette, which depicts king Narmer defeating northern enemies. The Narmer Palette was long considered a record of the *Sema-Tawy* ("Unification-of-the-Two-Lands") by king Narmer (who thus has often been linked with Menes of Egyptian historical tradition). The majority of scholars now accept it as an object commemorating an important military victory of Narmer but not the actual Unification event. Other significant palettes and maccheads include the "Towns Palette," which bears city hieroglyphs associated with a series of different royal names, the "Scorpion Macehead," which has scenes of a king Scorpion possibly engaging in a foundation ceremony, and the "Narmer Macehead," which has scenes of king Narmer engaging in a royal religious ritual.

One widely discussed aspect of late Predynastic Egypt (Nagada II-III and Dynasty 0) is evidence for interaction with the contemporary culture of southern Mesopotamia. A number of late Predynastic (particularly southern Egyptian) objects display use of distinctively Mesopotamian artistic motifs (such as the Gilgamesh "hero" motif, serpent-headed quadrupeds, and boat scenes). These motifs occur on objects as diverse as the Hierakonpolis painted tomb (Tomb 100), the Narmer palette, and the ivory handle of a flint knife known as the Gebel el-Arak knife. It was long considered that Mesopotamian stimulus may have been a factor in Egypt's developing organization at the end of the Predynastic period. Most archaeologists working on Predynastic Egypt see this evidence as use of foreign artistic motifs by the developing elite of the Nagada III period, but do not see Mesopotamian inspiration as a prime catalyst in Egypt's developing complexity. The motivations behind contact between late Predynastic Egypt and Mesopotamia remain uncertain but may have included the trade for gold that occurred in the desert regions east of southern Egypt.

As archaeological work on Predynastic Egypt continues, in future years we can expect considerable new evidence that will further reshape our understandings of the rise of Egyptian civilization. The field is increasingly benefiting from the use of modern techniques such as remote sensing, physical dating, and analytical techniques. As the amount of evidence builds, the rise of complex civilization in the Egyptian Nile Valley during the crucial two millennia from 5000–3000 B.C. will become ever clearer.

Josef Wegner

See also Africa, Sahara; Caton-Thompson, Gertrude; French Archaeology in Egypt and the Middle East

References
Butzer, Karl W. 1976. *Early Hydraulic Civilization in Egypt.* Chicago: University of Chicago Press.
Hoffman, Michael A. 1979. *Egypt before the Pharaohs: The Prehistoric Foundations of Egyptian Civilization.* New York: Knopf.
Kemp, Barry. 1989. *Ancient Egypt: Anatomy of a Civilization.* London; New York: Routledge.
Rice, Michael. 1990. *Egypt's Making.* London and New York: Routledge.
Spencer, A. Jeffrey. 1993. *Early Egypt; the Rise of Civilization in the Nile Valley.* London: published for the Trustees of the British Museum by British Museum Press.
Trigger, Bruce. 1982. "The Rise of Egyptian Civilization." In Trigger et al. *Ancient Egypt, a Social History.* Cambridge and New York: Cambridge University Press.

Egypt Exploration Fund
See Egypt Exploration Society

Egypt Exploration Society
The Egypt Exploration Society is the principal British archaeological institute involved in excavations in Egypt. Before its founding in 1882, Amelia Edwards, an English novelist, visited Egypt in the winter of 1873–1874 and sailed the length of the Egyptian Nile. At that time, many of the ancient sites and monuments were

in need of preservation, and illicit excavations were regularly undertaken. Edwards was impressed by the places she visited and distressed by the lack of protection afforded them. On her return to England she wrote a book about her experience, *A Thousand Miles up the Nile* (1877), and devoted the rest of her life to the foundation and running of a society to excavate and preserve the antiquities of Egypt.

The Egypt Exploration Society was established (as the Egypt Exploration Fund) in 1882 with scholarly backing from Reginald S. Poole, keeper of coins and medals at the BRITISH MUSEUM in London. The society had the financial support of many private donors, chief of whom was Sir Erasmus Wilson, an eminent surgeon who had already defrayed the cost of the transport to London of the obelisk known as Cleopatra's Needle.

In the early years, the society concentrated on verifying biblical accounts of ancient Egypt. The first excavation it sponsored, was in 1893 at the site of Tell el-Maskhuta, which the excavator, the Swiss scholar EDOUARD NAVILLE, identified with the biblical city of Pithom. In 1894, the young WILLIAM MATTHEW FLINDERS PETRIE started work at Tanis, known as Zoan in the Bible. Naville and Petrie, the principal excavators for the society during the nineteenth century, were very different in character and in their approach to excavation and publication. Naville is probably best known for his clearance of the temples of Mentuhotep, Nebhepetre, and Hatshepsut at Deir el-Bahari, while Petrie excavated many sites for the society, the most important of which was ABYDOS, where he identified the tombs of the kings of the earliest dynasties. His work for the society at Diospolis Parva resulted in the invention of a system of sequence dates for the predynastic period that, with modifications, is still a basic tool for field workers today.

The newly formed society did not limit its activities to excavation. One of Edwards's main concerns was the damage inflicted on Egypt's standing monuments, and in 1889 the Society launched its Archaeological Survey to make facsimile copies, through nondestructive methods, of the scenes on the walls of temples and tombs.

The fine drawings and paintings, which were and still are produced by the Archaeological Survey, provide lasting records of the scenes and texts on the monuments. Another ongoing aspect of the society's work is that of the Graeco-Roman Branch, founded in 1895, which publishes Greek and Latin texts excavated by the society, particularly those from the site of Oxyrhynchus in Middle Egypt.

The main focus of the society's work has, however, been that of excavation in Egypt, and occasionally in the Sudan, and the publication of the results of this work. In the 1920s and 1930s, important excavations were undertaken at Abydos, Armant, and EL AMARNA, where a decade and a half of work established the plan of this last unique city established by the "heretic" pharaoh Akhenaten. In 1979, the society returned to el Amarna, with an expedition directed by Barry Kemp, to undertake a complete survey of the site and to carry out selective excavations and conservation work.

In the 1960s, the society participated in the UNESCO campaign to record and save the monuments of NUBIA before the construction of the Aswan High Dam. The temple and fortress of Buhen and the temples of Semna and Kumma in the Sudan were fully excavated and recorded. Work also began at the site of Qasr Ibrim on Egypt's southern frontier, as it was feared that Qasr Ibrim would be completely submerged by the rising waters of the lake. Fortunately, this proved not to be the case, and the excavation of the settlement Qasr Ibrim, currently directed by Mark Horton, has produced much interesting information about this site, which was continually occupied from 1500 B.C. to A.D. 1812.

Since World War II, much of the society's work has been concentrated in the region of SAQQARA, the cemetery of the ancient capital city at Memphis. BRYAN EMERY has excavated impressive tombs of the First Dynasty and the temples and labyrinthine galleries devoted to the cults of sacred animals in the late period, and the society has also engaged at Saqqara in a joint expedition with the Rijksmuseum van Oudheden of Leiden in the Netherlands, directed by Geoffrey T. Martin. Since 1975, this expedition has been clearing, recording, and conserving tombs of Memphis officials of the New Kingdom, including the tomb built for TU-TANKHAMUN's general Horemheb, who later became king himself.

In 1982, the society celebrated its centenary with a special exhibition at the British Museum and by launching a project, directed by David Jeffreys and Lisa Giddy, to survey and investigate the site of the capital city of Memphis. In recent years, a number of smaller-scale projects have been initiated, surveying sites such as the Wadi Abu Had in the eastern desert of Egypt and Gebel el-Haridi in Middle Egypt. In 1992, the society responded promptly to a call from the Egyptian Antiquities Organisation for archaeological assistance in recording sites in northern Sinai that were threatened by the construction of the El-Salaam Canal.

The results of the society's work in Egypt are published in various series of memoirs. The society also publishes the prestigious annual *Journal of Egyptian Archaeology* and, since 1991, a color magazine, *Egyptian Archaeology,* which presents articles on fieldwork and research in a more popular style.

The Egypt Exploration Society has offices and a library in London, and membership in the society is open to anyone with an interest in ancient Egypt. Lectures and social events are held in London and Manchester. In 1992, an office was opened in Cairo to provide support for field expeditions and an increased level of activities for members in Egypt.

Patricia Spencer

References

Dawson, W. R., and E. P. Uphill. 1972. *Who Was Who in Egyptology.* 3d ed. London: EES. 4th ed., 1995.

Edwards, Amelia B. 1877. *A Thousand Miles up the Nile.* London: Longmans. Paperback reprint, U.K.: Quentin Crewe, 1982.

James, T. G. H., ed. 1982. *Excavating in Egypt: The Egypt Exploration Society, 1882–1982.* London: British Museum Publications.

El Amarna

Tell El Amarna was a new city created during the eighteenth dynasty by the heretic pharaoh

Akhenaten, the pharaoh who built El Amarna (Ann Ronan Picture Library)

Akhenaten (1353–1337 B.C.) as a place of worship for the god Aten, and it was abandoned soon after Akhenaten's death. El Amarna was the site of significant excavations by SIR WILLIAM MATTHEW FLINDERS PETRIE between 1891 and 1892, and apart from a short period immediately prior to World War I, when the site was worked on by German archaeologist Ludwig Borchardt (1911–1914), El Amarna has seen three sustained campaigns by the EGYPT EXPLORATION SOCIETY.

Tim Murray

See also Egypt: Dynastic; Egypt: Predynastic

El Salvador

The first descriptions of archaeological sites in El Salvador were by nineteenth-century visitors from North America and Europe. Excavations of architectural centers, including Quelepa, Cihuatan, Tazumal, Campana San Andres, and Los Llanitos, went hand in hand with an interest in defining the spatial distribution of Maya-, Lenca-, and Nahua-speaking Pipil ethnic groups reported from the sixteenth century. Modern research has been concerned with clarifying the relations of the earliest sites with early Mesoamerican cultures, exploring the effects of volcanism and the possibility of migration out of and into the country following major eruptions, and the determination of distributions of ethnic or linguistic groups and of patterns of migration into the country throughout its history.

Archaeological sites in El Salvador were noted by a number of the visitors, including E. G. Squier and the Germans K. Sapper and S. Habel, who passed through the area in the mid- to late nineteenth century as commercial schemes were being developed in the newly independent Central American republics. The reports of these foreign visitors were followed by local explorations, and in 1944, archaeologist John Longyear noted that "to date, practically all the archaeological work in El Salvador had been carried on by private citizens of that country, notably the owners of estates containing ruins of various types." The collections amassed in this fashion were sufficient for Atilio Peccorini to publish a preliminary article in Spanish in 1913 on the general outlines of Salvadoran archaeology.

Attention from professional North American archaeologists quickly followed, and in 1915, H. J. Spinden published an English summary drawing on material in private collections. In keeping with his broad conceptual scheme for the development of civilization in Central America, Spinden classified remains as archaic, Mayan, and AZTEC. His archaic period was marked by solid, hand-modeled figurines and the pottery later named Usulutan resist. He identified as Mayan those pottery vessels painted with figural and glyphic motifs. He interpolated a third period of occupation between the Maya and Aztec occupations of the country, the latter identified with the Pipil people noted in sixteenth-century Spanish accounts. Later research by North American archaeologists in El Salvador, while modifying the terminology used by Spinden, essentially assumed the same scheme with its implication that the country was subject to periodic population displacements.

Stratigraphic support for both the general occupation sequence proposed by Spinden and the idea that populations had been displaced and replaced came from the documentation of volcanic ash separating different cultural deposits. The Salvadoran Jorge Lardé first reported this situation in 1924, and in 1926 he and Samuel K. Lothrop investigated the phenomenon at Cerro Zapote. There they described two layers of cultural material separated by volcanic ash. The lower corresponded to Spinden's archaic period while the upper included painted pottery classified as Maya, effigy vessels identified with the Pipil, and the pottery type Plumbate, which Spinden had identified as being typical of the intervening period. An admixture of archaic materials was also present in the upper layer. Lothrop's interpretation of the upper layer was that it indicated, at least in part, that all three of Spinden's periods overlapped each other. Lothrop's report paid no apparent attention to the possibility of stratification within the deposits sealed by the volcanic ash.

Field-workers who immediately followed directed their attention to exploring individual sites with obvious architectural remains and mounds in loosely arranged groups. On investigation, many sites proved to be constructed of materials that appeared anomalous when compared to the cut stone and plaster of the Mayan centers. Quelepa had been subject to early exploration by Peccorini, and in 1929, Antonio Sol, director of the Department of History of GUATEMALA, conducted the first government-sponsored excavations on the site of Cihuatan in central El Salvador. The cut stone architecture, pyramidal temple, ball court, and walled plazas conformed to patterns known from sites to the west and north. A decade elapsed before further professional fieldwork was initiated. In 1939, the Middle American Research Institute and the Carnegie Institution of Washington (CIW) expanded their programs of Mayan research into western El Salvador through excavations at the site of Campana San Andres directed by John Dimick, assisted by Stanley Boggs. Campana San Andres, according to Boggs (1950), was constructed of adobe with a thick cement facing, features he compared with the highland Maya site Kaminaljuyu recently excavated by the CIW. Boggs defined a series of four construction phases at the site, all associated with Mayan-style pottery, and argued for a short period of occupation at Campana San Andres and cultural identity with Maya-speaking peoples.

Further research on architectural centers in the country was carried out in 1941 and 1942 by John Longyear with funding from the Institute of Andean Research. Longyear produced an overview of Salvadoran archaeology, relying heavily on collections but also incorporating results of his own excavations at Los Llanitos and those of Stanley Boggs at Tazumal. Los Llanitos was at the time the easternmost architectural center known in the country. Longyear's excavations exposed buildings with rough stone walls, including a ball court complex with stone slabs lining the alley. Longyear later compared this ball court to one at Tenampúa in the Comayagua Valley of Central Honduras (Longyear 1966). He also identified the distinctive local polychrome pottery style at Los Llanitos, wrongly, with the Las Vegas pottery style of Comayagua. One of Longyear's concerns was to identify the Salvadoran sites with the ethnic groups reported in the sixteenth century. He regarded this task as "difficult in the central and western areas, where successive cultural and linguistic invasions spread over large territories," but achievable in the east, presumably not so frequently overrun. His equating Los Llanitos with Honduran sites advanced this goal by allowing him to identify the inhabitants of eastern El Salvador as part of the frontier with the Lenca population he attributed to central Honduras.

Boggs's excavations at Tazumal in extreme western El Salvador proved to be the initial season of a multiyear project, funded by the Salvadoran government, that ended in 1945. He identified construction techniques similar to those of Campana San Andres, and a series of burials encountered during the work served as the basis for a chronological sequence. Boggs suggested two major episodes of occupation separated by abandonment. The earlier episode was associated with pottery that suggested external affiliations with the Maya of Copan, Uaxactun, and Kaminaljuyu. The later construction episode was accompanied by plumbate pottery that Boggs recognized as following the classic Maya in time.

By 1950 Boggs, then chief of the Department of Archaeological Excavations of El Salvador, was able to summarize the chronological picture of the country, relying on his own work at Tazumal and Lothrop and Lardé's results from Cerro Za-

pote, as consisting of three major periods of occupation corresponding to Spinden's archaic, Mayan, and post-Mayan phases. He further subdivided the Mayan period into three phases of 100 or 200 years each based on construction sequence, superposition of burials, and the cross-dating of ceramics with Mayan sites to the west. He ended his review with an outline of a long-range systematic plan for addressing what he saw as major problems. These included gaps in the sequence, whether due to local abandonment of the sites dug or ignorance of a general emigration from the whole area, and the applicability of his proposed sequence to eastern El Salvador. Boggs's proposed strategy would have involved constructing chronologies for both western and eastern El Salvador by excavating at larger sites, which he presumed would be more likely to yield long sequences of occupation. This work would be complemented by the excavation of small sites in the area between these extremes to check for the presence and co-occurrence of traits diagnostic of the eastern and western sequences.

This goal had yet to be achieved when Longyear wrote a synthesis for the *Handbook of Middle American Indians* (1966). In it, Longyear asserted that the country was really divided into two regions by the Lempa River. Although he presented this division in geographic terms, the influence of Lothrop's (1939) definition of the Lempa as the location of the Mesoamerican frontier is obvious. The same idea, the notion of a cultural frontier between distinct eastern and western Salvadoran cultures, was implicit in Boggs's suggested strategy for Salvadoran archaeology. Longyear, as he had in his earlier monograph, supported the separation of these two regions through reference to sixteenth-century accounts of the distribution of ethnic groups in the country. The west he identified as the land of the Pokomam Maya, displaced shortly before the Spanish conquest by Pipil, and the Chorti Maya. East of the Lempa were the Lenca, a population that extended into Honduras to the north. Longyear presented his entire survey in terms of this fundamental division of El Salvador between two ethnic groups.

For western El Salvador, Longyear sketched a dynamic prehistory of population displacements marked by changes in pottery styles. He identified the preclassic pottery types with those of Copan and Kaminaljuyu in the highlands of Honduras and GUATEMALA and argued that the classic-period inhabitants of western Salvador were cut off from Kaminaljuyu when the latter site was Mexicanized and came under exclusive influence from the Mayan city of Copan. The classic Mayan-affiliated occupation of the area came to an end with the invasion of Mexican Pipil people after A.D. 1000. Longyear explicitly characterized western Salvador as an extension of other regions and portrayed changes in the archaeological record as responses to external influence. In his discussion of eastern El Salvador, he argued that little or no population displacement took place. From the preclassic period through to the classic, the region was comparable to central Honduras, and together they composed a Lenca archaeological culture.

Longyear's discussion raised one issue that crossed the two regions he defined: the status of the diagnostic preclassic pottery type Usulutan resist. The preclassic period was the focus of a number of tentative new projects in the 1950s, including excavations by Muriel Porter on ash-sealed deposits at Barranco Tovar, by William Coe in the El Trapiche group of Chalchuapa, and by Wolfgang Haberland at Atiquizaya and Acajutla, all in the western part of the country. The latter two projects were curtailed prematurely, and the archaeologists did not have access to their collections for publication. When large-scale archaeological work resumed in the 1960s, one of the major objectives of site-focused projects in both the east and the west was clarification of the preclassic occupation history of the country.

E. Wyllys Andrews V, excavating Quelepa in eastern El Salvador, drew on field notes from unpublished work by Pedro Armillas in 1949. Andrews conducted excavations of monumental architecture and a ball court and constructed a chronological sequence based on construction phases and changes in pottery that spanned the preclassic and classic periods, ending at the very beginning of the postclassic period. His preclassic pottery included abundant examples of Usulutan resist decoration. With the fuller data he

commanded on the associations of the Usulutan pottery, he was able to argue for strong connections with contemporary Honduran sites, reaffirming Longyear's alignment of eastern Salvador with the Lenca. Andrews explicitly identified uncertainty about the sixteenth-century inhabitants of the region as a problem in the interpretation of the archaeological record.

Robert Sharer carried out excavations at Chalchuapa in western El Salvador from 1966 to 1970, following up the unfinished work of his professor at the University of Pennsylvania, William Coe. Sharer's report expressed explicit concern about the application of scientific method as it was presented by "the new archaeologists." He discussed the potential bias in project results owing to the impossibility of carrying out probabilistic sampling, both because of financial limitations and because of constraints raised by the local sociopolitical context.

The Chalchuapa project introduced several methodological innovations in Salvadoran archaeology. In addition to traditional excavations in architecture, fine-grained stratigraphic deposits on an old lake shore were carefully excavated in natural levels, and Payson Sheets developed a behavioral model of stone tool production based on the presence of different types of debitage (the detritus that results from making stone tools) and finished products. Through experimental replication, the project produced pottery vessels with the appearance of Usulutan resist in a pioneering attempt to understand the technology of this pottery.

Results from the Chalchuapa and Quelepa projects formalized the separation between east and west that Longyear had begun. Sharer explicitly framed this differentiation as a question of the location and nature of the Mesoamerican frontier. He retrospectively presented the issue of the "frontier" of MESOAMERICA as one that had concerned earlier archaeologists. Sharer traced the original genesis of Coe's work at Chalchuapa to a survey by ALFRED V. KIDDER of the CIW in 1953 that had been designed to establish a chain of archaeological connectives from the Maya area through its southeastern periphery and into the non-Maya areas of lower Central America. He listed as his first objective in 1966 testing the basic validity of the frontier concept, although he noted that "the means for testing the proposition were not defined. Sharer's summary statement on the Chalchuapa project is a processual model of frontier dynamics beginning with the presence of an Olmec enclave from the Gulf of Mexico and ending with the invasions of the Pipil and Pokomam peoples in the postclassic period. In 1986, Arthur Demarest could open his report of work at Santa Leticia with the statement that Salvadoran archaeology has always been approached either explicitly or implicitly as the study of a frontier area. In practice, this meant that interpretive statements about the country's archaeology were concerned with the timing and nature of external contacts, preferably with Mesoamerican sites.

Demarest's own work exemplifies the way that this culture-historical concern has continued to pervade newer problem-oriented studies that followed the successful definition of anchoring sequences in eastern and western El Salvador by the Quelepa and Chalchuapa projects. Demarest identified four issues addressed in his research at the small western Salvadoran site of Santa Leticia: the location of the Mayan frontier; the origin and techniques of manufacture of Usulutan ceramics; late preclassic ceramic connections, invasions, and migrations; and the question of Olmec affinities for local stone sculptures labeled "potbellies." All four issues involved the degree and nature of contact between Salvadoran and Mesoamerican peoples. Demarest's project applied physical and chemical analyses to Usulutan ceramics to address the nature of the technology and reinforce the interpretation of stylistic similarities in ceramics. He also employed radiocarbon dating to help choose among various scenarios for connections between local stone carving traditions and those of Mesoamerica. But these and other innovations in methods were only applied to traditional concerns of linguistic or ethnic identity.

While Demarest sought to clarify the nature of preclassic relationships of Salvadoran archaeological sites with Mesoamerica, other contemporary researchers addressed the opposite extreme of the chronological sequence, the presumed intrusion of Mexican Pipil in the postclassic period. The presence of Nahua-speaking peoples in the country led early researchers to search for Mexican traits that would be diagnostic of the movement of these peoples from their presumed homeland. Haberland's definition of Marihua Red-on-Buff and comparison with Mexican ceramic types filled the requirement for a distinctive Pipil pottery style. Andrews, noting the presence in private collections from around Quelepa of wheeled figurines and the recovery from the site of ballgame sculptures, both better known from Veracruz, MEXICO, looked to that region for analogues to Quelepa's distinctive late-classic pottery styles. Later archaeology at the site of Cihuatan formalized the definition of a Pipil archaeological assemblage, drawing further comparisons with Veracruz and tracing the migration of Nahua speakers from Mexico to Nicaragua (Bruhns 1980; Fowler 1989; Kelley 1988). These migrations were viewed as culture-historical events, consequences of the collapse of the cities TEOTIHUACÁN or Tula in central Mexico.

The underlying assumption that the prehistory of El Salvador was marked by abrupt disjunctions had its origin in the volcanic stratigraphy first reported in the 1920s. The exploration of this phenomenon inspired the first systematic regional program of survey and test excavations in the country. As a member of the Chalchuapa project, Payson Sheets in 1970 collaborated with geologists on the identification of the source and dating of a layer of volcanic ash found at the site, and in 1975, he pursued the identification of the extent of the effects of this eruption. Between 1978 and 1980, Sheets directed a regional project in the Zapotitan Valley (including Campana San Andres) with an explicit processual concern with past human response to natural hazards and their effect on the local cultural ecology. He documented a series of volcanic eruptions that affected the region with varying intensity of impact on the local population. By assessing technological style, he was able to argue that resettlement of the area after the most extreme disaster came from neighboring Maya regions.

Sheets promoted the use of a wide range of specialized analyses to explore the environment and technologies of the Zapotitan basin. An unanticipated by-product of the focus on vulcanism was the discovery at Ceren of buildings and fields buried during eruption, preserving fragile organic remains and the relative contextual associations between items. Excavation and analysis of these materials, interrupted by the deepening of civil war in El Salvador in the 1980s, was resumed in the early 1990s.

Contemporary processual archaeology has greatly advanced the goal of establishing basic chronological control (see Sheets 1984). Projects have contributed valuable data on specific sites long noted as important, and they have introduced refined excavation techniques and a variety of specialized technical analyses. But other aspects of archaeology remain undeveloped. A focus on Mesoamerican contacts has limited the amount of attention directed to the eastern part of El Salvador, and data on this region are insufficient to begin to suggest models for interaction with neighboring Central American countries. Even in the better-studied western and central regions of the country, site-centered research and the often unique characteristics of sites limit the interpretation of internal developments.

Salvadoran archaeology continues to suffer from a lack of reliable regional data on settlement for most of the country. In addition to the Zapotitan basin, the Cerron Grande salvage project conducted in the valley of the Lempa River is the only major survey completed to date. The latter project is also notable in that it represents a national initiative following a period during which archaeology was primarily carried out by North Americans. Along with the end of civil war in El Salvador, the development of national archaeological programs may begin to address the existing gaps in Salvadoran archaeology.

Rosemary A. Joyce

See also Maya Civilization

References
Andrews V. E. W. 1976. *The Archaeology of Quelepa, El Salvador.* Middle American Research Institute, Publication 42. New Orleans: Tulane University.

Boggs, S. H. 1950. "Archaeological Excavations in El Salvador." In *For the Dean,* 259–276. Ed.

E. K. Reed and D. S. King. Tucson and Santa Fe: Hohokam Museums Association and Southwestern Monuments Association.

Bruhns, K. O. 1980. *Cihautan: An Early Postclassic Town of El Salvador.* Monographs in Anthropology, no. 5. Columbia: University of Missouri, Museum of Anthropology.

Demarest, A. 1986. *The Archaeology of Santa Leticia and the Rise of Maya Civilization.* Middle American Research Institute, Publication 52. New Orleans: Tulane University.

Fowler, W. R. 1989. *The Cultural Evolution of Ancient Nahau Civilizations: The Pipil-Nicarao of Central America.* Norman: University of Oklahoma Press.

Haberland, W. 1964. "Marihua Red-on-Buff and the Pipil Question." *Ethos* 1–2: 73–86.

Kelley, J. 1988. *Cihuatan, El Salvador: A Study in Intrasite Variation.* Vanderbilt University Publications in Anthropology, no. 35. Nashville: Vanderbilt University.

Longyear, J. M., III. 1944. *Archaeological Investigations in El Salvador.* Memoirs of the Peabody Museum of Archaeology and Ethnology, vol. 9, no. 2. Cambridge, MA: Harvard University.

———. 1966. "Archaeological Survey of El Salvador." In *Handbook of Middle American Indians,* 4:132–156. Ed. R. Wauchope, G. Ekholm, and G. Willey. Austin: University of Texas Press.

Lothrop, S. K. 1927. *Pottery Types and Their Sequence in El Salvador.* Indian Notes, vol. 1, no. 4. New York: Museum of the American Indian, Heye Foundation.

———. 1939. "The Southeastern Frontier of the Maya." *American Anthropologist* 41: 42–54.

Peccorini, A. 1913. "Algunos datos sobre arqueologia de la Republica del Salvador." *Journal de la Societe des Americanistes de Paris* 10: 173–180.

Sharer, R. J., ed. 1978. *The Prehistory of Chalchuapa, El Salvador.* 3 vols. Philadelphia: University of Pennsylvania Press.

Sheets, P., ed. 1983. *Archaeology and Volcanism in Central America: The Zapotitlan Valley of El Salvador.* Austin: University of Texas Press.

———. 1984. "The Prehistory of El Salvador: An Interpretive Summary." In *The Archaeology of Lower Central America,* 85–112. Ed. F. Lange and D. Stone. Albuquerque: University of New Mexico Press.

Spinden, H. J. 1915. "Notes on the Archaeology of El Salvador." *American Anthropologist* 17: 446–487.

Elgin, Lord (1766–1841)

Bruce Thomas Elgin was born into the line of the earls of Elgin and Kincardine in 1766, attended Harrow and Westminster schools, and studied at St Andrew's University in Scotland, and then in Paris. In 1771 he succeeded as earl on the death of his elder brother, and was a representative peer of Scotland from 1790 to 1807 and from 1820 to 1840.

Elgin's career began in the army in 1785; he became major-general in 1809 and general in 1837. He also became a diplomat. In 1790 he was appointed envoy in Brussels, and in 1795 envoy extraordinary in Berlin. But it was through his appointment in 1799 to the embassy of the Ottoman Porte of Constantinople (now Istanbul), that he was to become famous.

In this diplomatic position Elgin took the opportunity to more closely study and record the extant ancient Greek monuments and art within Greater TURKEY, which included what is now GREECE. Elgin was influenced and inspired by the great collector SIR WILLIAM HAMILTON, who had been impressing London with his Roman antiquities from POMPEII. At his own expense Elgin employed the painter Lusieri and several skilled draftsmen and modelers, who were sent to Athens to begin to record its monuments. In 1801 Elgin received permission from the Turkish administration to build a scaffolding around what they called the "temple of Idols" or the Parthenon in Athens, in order to make molded copies of the sculptures and re-

Lord Elgin (Hulton Getty)

liefs around its pediments. During this process the ongoing damage to the building and its detail by the Turks, as well as the French ambassador's interest in them, convinced Elgin that it would be safer to remove some of the Parthenon sculptures and other monuments from Athens in order to preserve them. As a result of this Elgin has been described as just another aristocratic antiquarian collector intent on pillaging the monuments of the Mediterranean—even for the best of reasons—for proof of his erudition, for the education of the upper

Tourists view the famous Elgin Marbles on display at the British Museum in London. (Reuters NewMedia Inc. / Corbis)

classes, and for filling the museums of western Europe.

Without the official permission of the Turkish government Elgin began to assemble what is now know as "the Elgin marbles," a collection of pedimental sculptures from the Parthenon and from the Athenian temple of Nike Aperos and various antiquities from mainland Greece and Asia Minor. Part of this collection was sent to England and shipwrecked in transit, taking three years and great expense to salvage. Other pieces continued to be smuggled out of Greece from 1803, when Elgin left his position in Constantinople, until at least 1812, when it is recorded that eighty cases of antiquities arrived in England.

Elgin displayed his collection initially in his London residence and later at Burlington House, where its acclaim by artists and scholars tended to overcome any qualms about its provenance. The English nation was gripped with a fervor for Greek art, which was soon to be replaced by a similar one for everything Egyptian, even though this time the French got there first. Initially criticized for the dubious methods of its procurement, the collection was soon deemed to be of such significance that the House of Commons recognized Elgin's ownership and purchased his marbles, at a greatly undervalued price, for the BRITISH MUSEUM, where they remain to this day—notwithstanding continued requests by the Greek government that they be repatriated.

Tim Murray

Emery, Walter Bryan (1903–1971)

Born in Liverpool, England, Emery was apprenticed to a firm of marine engineers when he decided instead to study Egyptology at the Institute of Archaeology in London (1921–1923). Between 1923 and 1924 he joined the EGYPT EXPLORATION SOCIETY's excavations at EL AMARNA. In 1924 he was appointed director of the Liverpool expedition to clear up and restore the New Kingdom tomb of Ramose and the tombs of other nobles in the necropolis at Thebes. It was during this task that Emery was able to visit the tomb of TUTANKHAMUN while it was being excavated.

In 1924, once more employed by the Egypt Exploration Society, he participated in the excavation of the Buchis bulls at Armant. In 1928 he was appointed by the Egyptian Antiquities Service to direct the Second Archaeological Survey of NUBIA. For six years he traveled all over southern Egypt excavating sites. These included the particularly rich site of Ballana near the border with Sudan. Here Emery found the fourth- to sixth-century A.D. royal burial mounds that became a significant part of the collections of the Cairo Museum. From 1935 until 1939 when he enlisted in the army, Emery excavated the 1st to 3rd Dynasty tombs at SAQQARA for the Egyptian government. He stayed in Egypt for the war, eventually becoming a lieutenant-colonel and director of military intelligence. Excavations at Saqqara resumed in 1945 until 1946, but then halted when he accepted a post as first secretary at the British embassy in Cairo.

In 1951 Emery was elected the Edwards Professor of Egyptology at University College, London, and in 1952 he returned to Saqqara with the Egypt Exploration Society once again, this time to complete the excavation of the tombs of the 1st Dynasty. After the Suez Crisis and in 1956, Emery and the Society began to work in the Sudan, excavating the Middle Kingdom fortress town of Buhen, which dated from 1970 B.C. He advised both the Egyptian and Sudanese Antiquities Services throughout the UNESCO campaign to save the monuments of Nubia and arranged for Buhen to be moved to Khartoum.

In 1964 Emery returned to Saqqara when he excavated the sacred animal necropolis of Memphis and its temple site—a rich hoard of animal mummies, bronze figures, temple furniture, and documents from the sixth to the first centuries B.C. He died in 1971 and is buried in Cairo.

Tim Murray

See also Egypt: Dynastic; Egypt: Predynastic

Emona

The Roman town of Colonia Iulia Emona in what is now Ljubljana, the modern capital of SLOVENIA, was founded on the site of a prehistoric settlement and situated on a highly important strategic point that controlled the main route from ITALY to the Balkans. Written sources for the period of the second and first centuries B.C. report that the first people to live there were members of the Celtic tribe Taurisci.

Roman Emona was situated on an important road coming from Aquileia, Poetovio, and Siscia and riverine routes on the river Sava, and the town fully exploited its strategic and commercial position. According to a construction inscription found in Ljubljana, Emona was founded between A.D. 14 and 15. For a long time, Emona was believed to have developed from the Roman legionary camp of the Legio XV Appolinaris, which was stationed in this area until around A.D. 14 when it was transferred to Carnuntum near Vienna. However, recent studies by J. ŠAŠEL have cast doubts on that thesis. One of the major arguments for the prior existence of the legion's camp is Emona's rectangular town plan. The town's walls measured 523 meters by 425 meters, and they were fortified with twenty-eight towers and four reinforced gates. An important early Christian complex was built in northwestern part of the town in the fourth century A.D.

The beginning of an interest in the antiquities of Emona (mainly epigraphic) can be traced to the fifteenth century. Rich epigraphic monuments and historical studies had long been the main focus of scholars from the seventeenth century and were published by German historian T. Mommsen, who was in charge of the "Limeskommission" set up in 1892 to investigate Roman remains. The establishment of the Provincial Museum in 1821 and the Museum Society in 1839 in Ljubljana gave an important impetus to the historical and archaeological research of the Roman town. In 1879, A. Mullner, the curator of the Provincial Museum, published a monographic study of Emona. In *Archaologische Studien aus Krain* he wrongly located Emona at Ig, a village some 10 kilometers south of Ljubljana. However, in 1898, Mullner started to excavate the Roman cemeteries in Ljubljana.

The first large excavations of the cemeteries began in the period between 1904 and 1907, and after almost 100 years of archaeological research and excavations, the Emona cemeteries are now among the largest excavated in the Roman Empire. Since 1635, when the first grave was reported, there have been more then 3,000 documented Roman graves in cemeteries situated outside the town and along the roads to Aquileia, Siscia, and CELEIA. Excavations of the settlement were initiated by the Provincial Museum, and between 1909 and 1912, almost one-third of the town was excavated. Walter Smid, the curator of the museum, published his results in *Jahrbuch fur Altertumskunde* in 1913.

The next large excavations were carried out by a city museum in the 1960s and 1970s as a result of extensive city development. The most important result of these excavations was the discovery of the early Christian center, comprising an administrative center, rich residential buildings, and town infrastructure.

Milan Lovenjak

References
Petru, S. 1972. *Emonske nekropole (odkrite med leh 1635–1960).* Ljubljana: Narodni Museum.
Plesnicar, L. 1972. *Severne emonske nekropole.* Ljubljana: Narodni Museum.
Šašel, J. 1955. *Vodnik po Emoni.* Ljubljana.
———. 1968. "Emona." In *Real Enciklopadie, Suppl. XI,* col. 540–578. Stuttgart.

Enkomi-Ayios Iakovos

Enkomi-Ayios Iakovos on the east coast of CYPRUS is the largest and most extensively excavated late–Bronze Age site on Cyprus. Early excavations by the BRITISH MUSEUM (1896) concentrated on the rich tombs, and it was subsequently recognized that they had been constructed within houses and open spaces inside the city walls. Additional work at the cemetery was undertaken by the Cyprus Museum by J. L. MYRES (1913), R. Gunnis (1927), and the Swedish Cyprus Expedition. Major excavations by PORPHYRIOS DIKAIOS (1947–1957) and a French team directed by Claude Schaeffer (1934, 1947–1974) concentrated on the settlement. The Turkish occupation of northern Cyprus has precluded further research at the site since 1974.

Extensive excavations revealed a large walled city laid out on a grid plan. There are numerous

Temple of Hadrian, Ephesus, Turkey (Ann Ronan Picture Library)

private and public building complexes, fortifications, and sanctuaries, including the Sanctuary of the Horned God and the Sanctuary of the Ingot God. Rich finds from both the settlement and the tombs include many high-status items imported from abroad or influenced by foreign prototypes. The latter include Mycenaean, Levantine, and Egyptian artifacts, as Cyprus was drawn into the international world of the eastern Mediterranean in the second half of the second millennium B.C. Processes of secondary state formation in Cyprus at the beginning of the late Bronze Age saw Enkomi develop as the earliest city on the island, and it maintained its preeminence when other polities developed later in the period.

David Frankel

References

Dikaios, P. 1969–1971. *Enkomi Excavations 1948–58.* 3 vols. Mainz: Verlag Philipp von Zabern.

Ephesus

Ephesus, an ancient city on the Ionian coast of TURKEY, was once a major port. It was famed in ancient times for the magnificent (and huge)

temple of Artemis, and after the original burned down in 356 B.C., it was replaced by an even more magnificent building, which became one of the Seven Wonders of the World. Because of its importance throughout Hellenistic and Roman times, Ephesus boasted many major buildings and was an important center for sculpture production. Although it continued to be important into the Byzantine era, the site was progressively reduced in size and significance until it was abandoned in the eleventh century A.D.

Archaeological excavation began in Ephesus under John Wood (between 1863 and 1874), and the English had the signal fortune of excavating the Artemision (the temple precinct) in 1904, a feat that involved D. G. HOGARTH. However, it has been the Austrians who have made the most significant impact on the site. Beginning in 1895, under the auspices of the Austrian Archaeological Institute, they have excavated there for over a century.

Tim Murray

References

Bean, G. E. 1966. *Aegean Turkey: An Archaeological Guide.* London: E. Benn.

Etruscan Archaeology

The Etruscans inhabited ITALY in the region known as Etruria (modern Tuscany, upper Latium, and parts of Umbria), from around 1000–900 B.C. into the first century B.C. Traditionally, Etruscan archaeology has been a multidisciplinary pursuit. Experts in the field seek to unite evidence on Etruscan language, history, society, religion, myth, art, and architecture with more strictly archaeological data concerning topography, settlement patterns, cemeteries, construction techniques, inscriptions, ceramics, and metalwork. The global approach is epitomized in the writings of Massimo Pallottino (d. 1995), who is universally acknowledged as the greatest of all Etruscan scholars.

Scholarship on the Etruscans began in the fifteenth and sixteenth centuries in connection with the pride and curiosity of Italians who were investigating the origins of their cities. They quickly recognized that many towns had Etruscan beginnings, and in some cases, they gave special emphasis to their own Etruscan ancestry—for example, the Medici of Florence (Cipriani 1980). Much of this research on the Etruscans was philological and art historical, drawing on Greek and Roman writers not only for Etruscan history but for such matters as the design of Etruscan temples, described by Vitruvius in the later first century B.C. (*De architectura* 4.7) or the nature of Etruscan terracotta sculpture and small bronzes, noted by Pliny the Elder in the first century A.D. (*Natural History* 33.158; 34.34). Pliny also gave a detailed account of the tomb of Lars Porsenna (*Natural History* 26.91), king of Etruscan Clusium (Chiusi).

Epigraphical evidence was recorded and evaluated in the Renaissance by Sigismondo Tizio of Siena (d. 1528), who compiled the first known Etruscan vocabulary list, and by Annio of Viterbo (d. 1502), who unfortunately was prone to enhance or even completely fabricate inscriptions in his home territory (Weiss 1988). Much more admirable scholarship is found in the report by the Renaissance artist and writer Giorgio Vasari on the discovery of the famed bronze Chimaera in 1553 in his native Arezzo (now in the Archaeological Museum in Florence). He concluded that the statue was Etr-uscan on the basis of the letters inscribed on its leg and was able to identify the beast through numismatic comparisons.

Some of the early scholars on the Etruscans were not Italians. The French savant Guillaume Postel, in *De Etruria regionis . . . originibus, institutis, religione, et moribus* (1551), lent his support to some of the more preposterous ideas of Annio, such as the notion that the Etruscans could be traced back to Noah. In the seventeenth century, the German archaeologist and antiquarian Athanasius Kircher visited an Etruscan tomb near Viterbo and left an amazing account of how he was told by a local guide that the stone-carved chambers and beds were actually made for underground cave dwellers. This misinterpretation can be forgiven in light of the scarce knowledge of Etruscan topography at the time.

The most important study of the Etruscans in the seventeenth century, by the Scotsman Thomas Dempster (Haynes 2000), was in fact written with little direct knowledge of archaeological sites. Dempster's famous *De Etruria regali libri septem* (Seven Books on Etruria of the Kings) is based on information from classical sources about the origins, customs, history, cities, and language of the Etruscans. Written for the Medici Cosimo II (d. 1621), the work was not published until over a century later by the English bibliophile Thomas Coke, who purchased the manuscript in Florence. The work appeared in 1726 (though the date of publication is listed as 1723–1724) and contains notes by the Florentine scholar Filippo Buonarroti (Galli 1986) and ninety-three illustrations. Buonarroti's archaeological commentary added immensely to the value of Dempster's work, including, for example, reports on some of his own systematic survey of tombs near Civita Castellana.

The publication of *De Etruria regali* was both a symptom and a cause of an absolute mania for the Etruscans that developed in the eighteenth century (de Grummond 1986, 39–40). On a fairly superficial level, this mania found its way into decorations of English country houses and provided the name "Etruria" for the neoclassical ceramics factory of Josiah Wedgwood in England. In Italy, a patriotic fervor for this Italian civilization emerged, and the Etruscans were

0   200 km

N

Bologna
Marzabotto

Fiesole
Firenze (Florence)
Volterra   Arezzo
Siena   Cortona
Murlo   Perugia
Populonia
Vetulonia   Chiusi
Roselle
Orvieto
Acquarossa
Vulci
Tarquinia   Falerii
Pyrgi   Veii
Cerveteri   Rome

Pithekoussai

Corsica

Sardinia

ADRIATIC SEA

TYRRHENIAN SEA

Sicily

Etruscan Archaeological Sites

credited with playing a leading role in developing ancient culture. The artist and antiquarian G. B. Piranesi created a polemic atmosphere by asserting the superiority of ancient Italy over Greece.

Of considerable significance was the founding in 1726 at Cortona of the Accademia Etr-

usca, which sponsored meetings, lectures, and publications on the Etruscans (Barocchi and Gallo 1985). The work of one of its members, Anton Francesco Gori (1691–1757), is remarkable in that he undertook purposeful excavation (1728 and following) at Volterra for the sake of knowledge rather than for the acquisition of antiquities, the usual motive for digging in the eighteenth century (Cristofani 1983; Giuliani 1987). Gori recorded in great and objective detail the finds of ash urns and pottery and included plans, elevations, and a topographical map of the location of the urns. Gori also initiated the publication of comprehensive works of Etruscan antiquities in collections.

The famous painted tombs of Tarquinia came under serious study in the eighteenth century with the activities of the English artist, dealer, and banker Thomas Jenkins (Haynes 2000). A member of the SOCIETY OF ANTIQUARIES OF LONDON, he reported to that body on his investigation of Etruscan tombs at Tarquinia made in 1761 and provided illustrations that were published in the *Philosophical Transactions of the Royal Society* in 1763. Jenkins was followed by the Scottish dealer, scholar, and guide James Byres (Ridgway 1989), for whom the Polish artist Franciszek Smuglewicz prepared illustrations of tombs Byres visited at Tarquinia in the 1760s. Like his countryman Dempster, Byres did not live to see his work published, for it did not appear until 1842, under the title *Hypogaei; Or, Sepulchral Caverns of Tarquinia, the Capital of Antient Etruria.*

Also in the eighteenth century, scholars began to pay increasing attention to pre-Roman Italy in general and to sort out the relationships between the Etruscans and their contemporaries. The ceramic vases found in Etruria in great numbers were now recognized as Greek, first by SIR WILLIAM HAMILTON, who collected such vases excavated on the Bay of Naples outside of Etruria proper, and later by Luigi Lanzi, who denied that the vases were Etruscan when he realized that their inscriptions were in Greek. Lanzi published a study of the Etruscan language in which he made comparisons with the languages of neighboring peoples such as Greeks, Oscans, Umbrians, and Romans.

The heroic age of the discovery of Etruscan tombs came in the first half of the nineteenth century (*Les étrusques et l'Europe* 1992, 322–337, 414–431). Between 1828 and 1833, some ten new painted tombs were identified in the Monterozzi necropolis at Tarquinia. Artists took great pains to record the paintings, with varying success in accuracy. Carlo Ruspi conceived the idea of making tracings as preparatory drawings for full-scale facsimiles, which he created for the new Museo Gregoriano Etrusco at the Vatican (founded 1837) and for the Pinakothek in Munich. In this same period were discovered "the Tut's tomb" of Etruscan archaeology, the spectacular Regolini-Galassi Tomb at Cerveteri (1836), which was named after its discoverers, a priest and a soldier, respectively. The finds from this seventh-century tomb group went to the new Vatican museum along with a nearly life-sized figure, identified as Mars, found at Todi in Umbria in 1835.

Also at Cerveteri, Marchese Giovanni Pietro Campana unearthed the richly sculptured Tomb of the Reliefs (1846–1847), and at Veii, he found the seventh-century Tomba Campana (1842–1843). The Hellenistic Tomb of the Volumnii, with its handsomely carved ash urns, was discovered at Perugia by G. B. Vermiglioli in 1840. A bit later (1857), Alessandro François and A. Noel des Vergers found the marvelous painted sepulcher at Vulci that became known as the François Tomb. Though most sites were funerary, Marzabotto near Bologna, excavated by G. Gozzadini in 1862–1863, was soon thought to be a habitation site with evidence of town planning.

These dramatic new finds were of interest to a widening circle of scholars and public alike. Especially active was a group of young men from northern Europe known as the Hyperboreans. The noblemen August Kestner and Otto Magnus von Steckelberg went out to Tarquinia to investigate painted tombs (the famous Archaic Tomb of the Baron is named for Kestner) and joined with Eduard Gerhard in planning Etruscan publications. Their association evolved into the international Instituto di Corrispondenza Archeologica (established in 1829), which became the German Archaeological Institute in Rome in 1871. This body was of the greatest importance because of its publications, such as the *Bullettino;* the *Monumenti inediti,* which was richly illustrated with the latest discoveries; and the *Annali.* Etruscan antiquities were frequently reported in these pages, and Gerhard also initiated systematic corpora such as the famous five-volume work on Etruscan mirrors, *Etruskische Spiegel* (1840–1897).

Entrance to the tomb of the Necropolis at Cerveteri (Ann Ronan Picture Library)

The British appetite for the Etruscans was whetted in these years by the opening of a show of Etruscan tombs in London (1836–1837) by the Campanari family, which had excavated extensively at Tuscania. A spate of publications in English on the Etruscans followed (Haynes 2000). First was Elisabeth Hamilton Gray's popular account, *Tour of the Sepulchres of Etruria in 1839,* a record of a visit to Italy that had been directly inspired by the Campanari show. Next Byres's *Hypogaei* (1842) appeared, but most significant of all was the work by George Dennis, an English government official who relieved the boredom of his assignments by travel and study in Italy and other countries.

Dennis's masterpiece, *The Cities and Cemeteries of Etruria,* appeared in three printings (1848; rev. eds., 1878 and 1883) and preserves an exceptionally good record of the sites of Etruria as they appeared in the 1840s when he visited them. Dennis described the topography of each locality, including the monuments and the important finds up to that time as well as relevant literary evidence. The book included illustrations by Dennis himself as well as a few by his

traveling companion, the painter Samuel James Ainsley, whose many drawings, now in the BRITISH MUSEUM, also record the condition of Etruria in the 1840s.

The collecting of Etruscan antiquities and the formation of museum displays became increasingly important. In 1838, the British Museum purchased much of the material from the Campanari show, and the Museo Gregoriano displayed Etruscan antiquities excavated by Vincenzo Campanari at Vulci in the 1830s (Buranelli 1992). The most sensational event in the distribution of Etruscan objects occurred with the sale of the vast collections of Marchese Campana beginning in 1858 (*Les étrusques et l'Europe* 1992, 350–361). After investigations revealed that Campana had embezzled funds from a bank he directed in Rome to sustain his collecting activities, officials seized his holdings. The material was sold off in lots to the British Museum, the Capitoline Museum in Rome, the Russian imperial collections at the Hermitage in St. Petersburg, and above all, the LOUVRE in Paris. Of the antiquities that went to Paris, of special interest were the painted archaic Campana plaques from

Cerveteri, a gold diadem from Perugia, and a painted archaic terracotta sarcophagus showing a couple reclining, also from Cerveteri.

Of course, the collections of the Medici and their successors, the dukes of Lorraine, were highly important. Having been assembled in the Uffizi Gallery in Florence by Luigi Lanzi, the collections were taken over by the Italian state soon after the unification of Italy in 1870. Magnificent pieces such as the Chimaera and the bronze orator (*Arringatore,* acquired by the Medici in 1566) were soon combined with objects recently excavated at numerous sites in Tuscany. In 1881, the Florence Archaeological Museum was established in the quarters it still occupies in the Via della Colonna. A spirited debate arose over how the material should be arranged and whether the criteria should be historical, topographical, or aesthetic. Under the direction of Luigi Milani, the Museo Topografico Centrale dell'Etruria was opened in 1897, and objects were displayed in a scientific, objective way according to their provenance and not their rank as art objects. Unfortunately, the great flood of Florence in 1966 wrecked the topographical museum, and the previous arrangement has never been regained.

The most important collection of Etruscan-Italian antiquities in the world is that of the Museo Nazionale di Villa Giulia in Rome. Instituted by decree in 1889 and housed in the historic villa of Pope Julius III (built 1551–1555), the museum was designated to house antiquities from sites in Latium in Italy. It began to function effectively in 1908 under the guidance of G. A. Colini and today boasts a successful topographical sequence of Etruscan, Faliscan, Latin, and Praenestine materials.

The question of the relationship between the Etruscans and other pre-Roman cultures became a central problem in the later nineteenth century. An acrimonious controversy arose after the discovery in 1853 at Villanova, near Bologna, of material that seemed to predate Etruscan culture as it was known at the time. "Villanovan" remains of the Italian Iron Age (1000 or 900–700 B.C.), characterized by the use of handmade ash urns and fibulae, were soon identified at other sites. Gozzadini, the owner of the land at Vil-

Etruscan amphora (Ann Ronan Picture Library)

lanova and original discoverer of the culture (Vitali 1984), believed that Villanovan was an early phase of Etruscan civilization. He was violently opposed by Brizio and others who upheld the long-cherished theory that the Etruscans came as invaders from the east and overwhelmed native cultures (the Greek historian Herodotus had stated that the Etruscans came from Lydia in Asia Minor). Brizio was opposed not only by Gozzadini but also by Luigi Pigorini, Wolfgang Helbig, and others who argued that the Etruscans arrived in Italy from northern Europe, having come across the Alps.

The lively debates on "the origin of the Etruscans," which had at stake nationalist pride along with various cultural and archaeological issues, led to a reexamination of existing evidence and a ferment of new ideas. In particular, scholars addressed the problem of the Etruscan language, which, they noted, defied classification with the Indo-European languages of an-

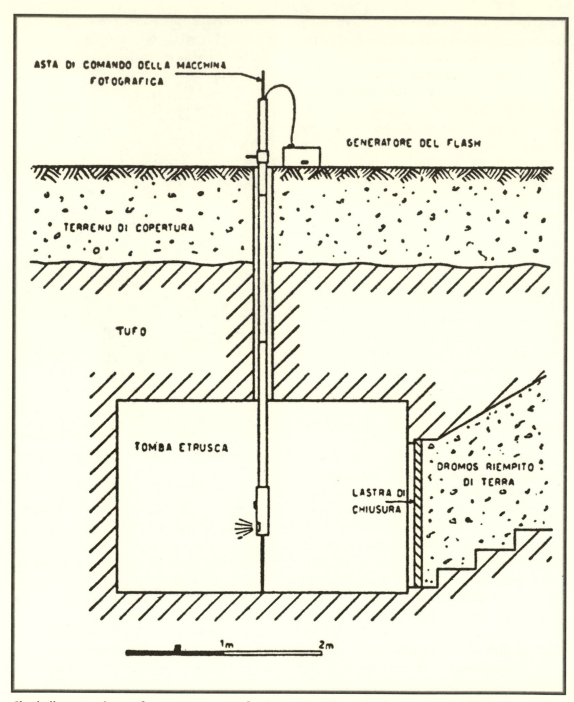

Sketch illustrating the use of an automatic camera for photographing the inside of an unexplored tomb (Courtesy of the New York Graphic Society)

cient Italy. This observation gave rise to the popular notion, now often repeated, that the Etruscans were "mysterious."

The debates over the origin and mystery of the Etruscans long ago turned sterile. Pallottino cleared the air in his *Etruscologia* (1st ed., 1952;

1st English ed., *The Etruscans,* 1955), in which he noted that the problem of Etruscan origin should not be focused on *provenance* but rather on the process of *ethnic formation.* Most other archaeologists have followed his lead and now study the Villanovan period as an early phase of a culture that evolved in Italy as Etruscan. The "orientalizing" wave of the seventh century is integrated into this evolution and is now viewed, not as a period of invasion, but as a period in which Italy opened up to Near Eastern and Greek trade, especially through the eighth-century B.C. Greek settlement at Pithekoussai (Ridgway 1988, 639).

Achievements in Etruscan studies in the twentieth century (Bonfante 1986; *Les étrusques e l'Europe* 1992, 458–461) cannot be easily summarized. Of key significance was the founding in Florence in 1925 of a Comitato Permanente per l'Etruria, spearheaded by A. Minto, which soon organized the First International Etruscan Congress, which was held in 1928. This meeting in turn led to the creation in 1932 of the principal organization for the study of the Etruscans, the Istituto di Studi Etruschi (later Istituto Nazionale di Studi Etruschi e Italici). The periodical it sponsors, *Studi Etruschi,* had already begun to appear in 1927.

Sensational individual discoveries have continued: the Apollo of Veii in 1916; the gold bilingual Pyrgi tablets (Etruscan and Phoenician) in 1964; the Tomb of the Blue Demons at Tarquinia in 1985. Of greater significance for the advancement of Etruscan science have been the long-term excavations that help to provide context and a sense of continuity in Etruscan history, society, and religion. Excavations by the University of Rome at Pyrgi, beginning in 1957 under the direction of Pallottino and continued by Giovanni Colonna, have revealed startling new information about Etruscan temples and sanctuaries. Habitation sites have been explored by the British School at Rome under J. B. Ward Perkins; by the Swedish Institute at Rome, with the participation of King Gustavus VI Adolphus (*Les etrusques et l'Europe* 1992, 462–467); and by a U.S. team from Bryn Mawr College under Kyle Phillips. The Italians have also made noteworthy discoveries in recent decades in the cities of Cerveteri (Mauro Cristofani) and especially Tarquinia (Bonghi Jovino 1999). In cemeteries, geophysical prospecting techniques used by the Lerici Foundation in 1955–1962 identified some 6,000 new tombs at Tarquinia, including some significant painted examples.

Enormous strides in the understanding of the Etruscans have been made in connection with a number of exhibitions and their catalogs as well as scientific meetings of the Istituto Nazionale and other bodies. The important show "Art and Civilization of the Etruscans" toured six European cities in 1955–1956 *(Mostra dell'arte e civiltà etrusca).* In 1985, proclaimed "the year of the Etruscans" in Italy, the Second International Etruscan Congress was held, and some eight different major exhibitions were mounted in Italy covering a wide range of topics, including sanctuaries, houses and palaces, metallurgy, inscriptions, the Romanization of Etruria, and the Etruscan legacy. Of more recent exhibits, the most significant for the study of the history of Etruscan archaeology was the splendid *Les étrusques et l'Europe* shown in Paris and Berlin in 1992–1993.

Nancy Thomson de Grummond

References

Barocchi, P., and D. Gallo. 1985. *L'Accademia etrusca.* Milan: Electa.

Bonfante, L. 1986. "Etruscan Studies Today." In *Etruscan Life and Afterlife: A Handbook of Etruscan Studies,* 1–17. Detroit: Wayne State University Press.

Bonghi Jovino, M. 1999. *Oltre le colonne d'Ercole: Etruscologia tra ricerca e didattica.* Bologna: Rastignano.

Borsi, F., ed. 1985. *Fortuna degli etruschi.* Milan: Electa.

Buranelli, F. 1992. *Gli scavi a Vulci della società Vincenzo Campanari: Governo Pontificio (1835–1837).* Rome: "L'Erma" di Bretschneider.

Cipriani, G. 1980. *Il mito etrusco nel rinascimento fiorentino.* Florence: L. S. Olschki.

Colonna, G. 1987. "Archeologia dell'età romantica in Etruria, i Campanari di Toscanella e la Tomba dei Vipinana." *Studi Etruschi* 46: 81–117.

Cristofani, Mauro. 1983. *La scoperta degli etruschi, archeologia e antiquaria nel '700.* Rome: CNR.

de Grummond, Nancy T. 1986. "Rediscovery." In *Etruscan Life and Afterlife: A Handbook of Etruscan Studies,* 18–46. Detroit: Wayne State University Press.

de Grummond, Nancy T., ed. 1996. *An Encyclopedia of the History of Classical Archaeology.* Westport and London: Greenwood.

Les étrusques et l'Europe. 1992. Paris: Editions de la Réunion des musées nationaux. German ed.,

Die Etrusker und Europa (Berlin, 1993; Italian ed., *Gli etruschi* (Milan: Bompiani, 1998).

Galli, D. 1986. *Filippo Buonarroti e la cultura antiquaria sotto gli ultimi Medici.* Florence: Cantini.

Giuliani, L. 1987. *Il carteggio di Anton Francesco Gori.* Rome: CNR.

Haynes, S. 2000. "Etruria Britannica." In *Ancient Italy in Its Mediterranean Setting: Studies in Honour of Ellen Macnamara,* 4: 319–325. Accordia Specialist Studies on the Mediterranean. London.

Pallottino, M. 1975. *The Etruscans.* Trans. J. Cremona; ed. David Ridgway. Rev. and enl. ed. Bloomington: Indiana University Press.

———. 1984. *Etruscologia.* 7th rev. ed. Milan: Hoepli.

Ridgway, D. 1988. "The Etruscans." In *The Cambridge Ancient History,* 4: 634–675. 2d ed. Cambridge: Cambridge University Press.

———. 1989. "James Byres and the Ancient State of Italy: Unpublished Documents in Edinburgh." In *Secondo Congresso Internazionale Etrusco. Firenze 26 maggio–2 giugno 1985,* 213–229. Rome: G. Bretschneider.

Vitali, D. 1984. "La scoperta di Villanova e il conte Giovanni Gozzadini." In *Dalla stanza delle antichità al Museo Civico: Storia della formazione del Museo Civico Archeologico di Bologna,* 223–237. Ed. C. Morigi Govi and G. Sassatelli. Bologna: Grafis.

Weiss, R. 1988. *The Renaissance Discovery of Classical Antiquity.* 2d ed. Oxford: Blackwell.

Europe, Medieval

See Medieval Archaeology in Europe

European Mesolithic

What Is the Mesolithic?

In 1932 GRAHAME CLARK defined the Mesolithic as the period "between the close of the Pleistocene and the arrival of the Neolithic arts of life" (J. G. D. Clark 1932, 5). This is the definition adhered to by the majority of those who study the period, and it is how the term will be used here. It is a deliberately loose definition, referring only to a somewhat imprecise period of time rather than to a rigorously defined cultural stage separate from what preceded and succeeded it. However, not all who study the period accept this definition. Some agonize about links with the Paleolithic and insist that

the period should be referred to as the Epipaleolithic (e.g., Rozoy 1989); others, mainly in eastern Europe, consider that ceramics and claimed sedentism mean that the later part of the period should be termed "Neolithic" (e.g., Dolukhanov 1979). The Mesolithic thus has the dubious distinction of being the only major period in European prehistory whose very name is a matter of dispute among its students.

The Place of the Mesolithic in European Prehistory

The Mesolithic was the last of the major periods in European prehistory to be named. CHRISTIAN J. THOMSEN'S THREE-AGE SYSTEM of Stone, Bronze, and Iron Ages was published in 1836. The first age was divided into the Paleolithic (of glacial age) and the Neolithic (of postglacial age) by Sir John Lubbock (later known as LORD AVEBURY) in 1865. The term *Mesolithic* was first used in 1872, but it was not systematically applied until the early years of the twentieth century (J. G. D. Clark 1980; Rowley-Conwy 1996).

That the period was not recognized for so long is rooted in the history of archaeology in the nineteenth century. Prior to 1858 prehistoric archaeology scarcely existed. After that date it emerged from a fusion of two distinct lines of study. On the one hand were geologists, who studied nonhuman aspects of the distant past; on the other were historical archaeologists, who studied material culture in the context of historically documented societies. Before 1858 these two groups had nothing in common: it was not believed that humans lived at the same time as the glacial deposits and bones of extinct animals that the geologists studied, so the geologists had nothing to say on the subject of early human societies. The historical archaeologists claimed the pre-Roman "Celtic" period but made little in the way of a systematic attempt to study it. WILLIAM PENGELLY'S excavations at BRIXHAM CAVE in 1858 demonstrated the contemporaneity of humans and extinct mammals in a glacial climate, a position generally accepted by 1863. This brought humans into the area studied by geologists, and most of the early Paleolithic specialists had a geological background. Meanwhile, the historical archaeologists were pushing their studies back in time, bringing postglacial farming societies within their domain (Van Riper 1993; Grayson 1983; Gräslund 1987).

Although formally united as "prehistoric archaeologists" after 1863, the two groups of researchers still had little in common because of their different temporal foci and methods, and to an extent the division persists to the present day. In the later nineteenth century the jewels in the crowns of the two groups were, on one side, caves, containing complex stratigraphic sequences, stone tools, animal bones, and (if the researchers were lucky) spectacular paintings, and, on the other side, beautiful items of metal and jewelry, much pottery, and many visible monuments.

It is thus understandable that the Mesolithic, being postglacial but preagricultural and producing neither cave paintings nor monuments and metalwork, belonged nowhere and therefore had a difficult birth. Its very existence was denied by scholars such as French archaeologist GABRIEL DE MORTILLET, whose "hiatus theory" claimed that Europe was unoccupied between the cave painters and the crop planters. This ignored events in DENMARK, where, as early as 1851, scholars recognized that certain shell heaps were the rubbish middens of a postglacial but preagricultural people (Steenstrup 1851); Havelse Mølle has the distinction of being the first recognized settlement of the period that would later be called Mesolithic.

Despite the repudiation of the hiatus theory, the Mesolithic period did not compare favorably to the Paleolithic and Neolithic periods. This was because of the Victorian evolutionary view that human progress moved through a series of ever higher "levels" of civilization. The hunter-painters of the Paleolithic were considered sufficiently impressive to be precursors to the agricultural barbarians of pre-Roman Europe. By contrast, the Mesolithic, with a simplified and diminutive technology and little or no art, looked like an uninteresting period of cultural retrogression. This view continued well into the twentieth century, not least of all in the dominating works of VERE GORDON CHILDE. In the first edition of The Dawn of European Civilization,

Childe wrote that "the contribution of [the mesolithic] to European culture is negligible. The hiatus is only recreated" (1925, 3). In the sixth and final edition of The Dawn, he was still writing of "cultures that are termed mesolithic because in time—but only in time—they occupy a place between the latest palaeolithic and the oldest neolithic cultures" (1957, 35).

The rest of this entry will examine the transformation of Mesolithic archaeology from the study of a retrogressive cultural stage into the study of hunter-gatherer adaptations in a diverse and changing landscape. Because of the extent of the change, the Mesolithic is arguably the best arena in which to examine changes in the theory and practice of European archaeology in the twentieth century.

From Hiatus to Behavior

The archetypal artifact of the Mesolithic is the microlith (the word simply means "small stone"). Larger items exist, but most Mesolithic sites contain numerous microliths, and many typological studies have been undertaken. Microliths amount to small blanks that may be mounted in a variety of tools. They are occasionally found as parts of arrowheads, such as the well-known example from Loshult in Sweden that used two, one as tip and one as barb (this item is widely illustrated, see, e.g., J. G. D. Clark 1975, fig. 12). Up to a dozen at a time are found mounted on larger spearheads or daggers (e.g., J. G. D. Clark 1975, fig. 43). None have been found in Europe mounted as sickles or other implements connected with plants, but their potential role in this connection has been stressed (J. G. D. Clarke 1976, fig. 2).

In 1932 Grahame Clark synthesized the British material in The Mesolithic Age in Britain, and he extended this to the mainland in The Mesolithic Settlement of Northern Europe (1936). He argued that the major Mesolithic event was the spread of the Capsian-derived Tardenoisian culture into a Europe peopled by local groups descended from different Upper Paleolithic cultures. The Mesolithic cultures were interpreted as peoples, and the history of the Mesolithic was the history of their interactions and developments (J. G. D. Clark 1932, 93 ff.). The axe-using Maglemosians occupied the lowlands of northern Europe, whereas the Tardenoisians had no axes and occupied sandy and hilly regions; the Maglemosians produced some art and made bone tools, whereas the Tardenoisians did neither (J. G. D. Clark 1936). The behavioral view that has replaced this argument derives from work in two main fields: archaeology and ecological anthropology. These will be examined in turn.

Archaeology

The upland-lowland cultural dichotomy came under strain in Britain during the 1960s. Radley and Mellars (1964) pointed out that microliths in the two zones were very similar and that axes were occasionally found in the uplands. On the mainland similar results were published (Geupel 1973; Newell 1973). Most would now see the differences as reflecting behavior and preservation rather than cultural variation. Acid conditions have destroyed bone at the upland sites. Varying proportions of artifacts are found in both upland and lowland areas, and these are thought to reflect varying activities. The rarity of axe/adzes in the uplands probably reflects the thinner woodland in these regions (J. G. D. Clark 1972, 1973; Jacobi 1978; Mellars 1976a).

A second element in the understanding of the Mesolithic was DATING. During the 1970s the radiocarbon revolution reached the Mesolithic, and the mainland Mesolithic was divided into three main technological phases. Phase 1 was characterized by a high proportion of obliquely blunted points among the microliths. This is conventionally thought to have started at the Pleistocene-Holocene boundary at 10,000 B.P. (see further discussion in later passages). Phase 2 began around 8800 B.P. and was typified by smaller microliths, such as triangular and lanceolate forms. Phase 3 began around 7850 B.P. and was marked by artifacts made on broader blades, among which trapeze-shaped microliths were the most numerous. This phase ended with the appearance of the Neolithic period (for major reviews, see Kozlowski 1975, 1976; Rozoy 1978).

Work in Britain identified an early phase corresponding to phase 1 on the mainland, charac-terized by the same microlithic forms and ending at the same time; the industries are termed "broad blade." Britain's later phase, termed "narrow blade," was similar to the mainland phase 2. The blade and trapeze industries of mainland phase 3, however, never reached Britain. By the time this phase appeared on the mainland, Britain had been isolated by the rising post-glacial sea, and the narrow gap was apparently sufficient to inhibit the spread of trapeze industries (Jacobi 1973, 1976; Mellars 1974, 1976b; Switsur and Jacobi 1979).

A third strand of relevant archaeological work has been spread over a much longer period and concerns organic remains of various kinds. This strand has been important in countering the early view that the Mesolithic was both technologically and artistically impoverished. The formation of peat bogs has led to superb conditions of preservation in some parts of Europe. The bows that shot the microlith-tipped arrows have turned up at several major settlements, including early-Mesolithic Holmegård in Denmark (illustrated in S. H. Andersen and Nielsen 1982, 22) and late-Mesolithic Ageröd V in SWEDEN (Larsson 1983a, figs. 32, 33). Barbed bone and antler points are common; major concentrations were found at Star Carr in England (nearly 200 points, see J. G. D. Clark 1954, figs. 47–64) and at Mosegården III in Denmark (over 300 points, see K. Andersen 1983). At Mosegården III they were found spread across an area about 1,000 by 300 meters, not directly associated with a settlement but on the bed of a former lake. Nearby settlements contain many fish bones, and some of the Mosegården III examples were found point downward, suggesting they were mounted as leisters and lost during fishing (K. Andersen 1983, 155–173). At Star Carr they were found concentrated in just a few square meters at the edge of the settlement, but the settlement produced no fish bones (J. G. D. Clark 1954, fig. 5); this suggests they were cached and intended for use against land mammals and would therefore have been mounted as spears (Legge and Rowley-Conwy 1988, 95).

Larger, more complex fish-catching items are also known. The famous seine from Antrea in Karelia was some 30 meters long and 1.5 meters high (J. G. D. Clark 1975, 223–224). Other nets are known, as well, such as those from Sventoji 2B in LITHUANIA (Rimantiené 1992, fig. 4) and Friesack in Germany (Gramsch 1987, pl. 25–26). Basket fish traps made of wickerwork are also known, for example, from Ageröd V in Sweden (Larsson 1983a, 62–69) and several sites in Denmark (Becker 1941). Larger fish traps made of fixed stakes are known from Tybrind Vig and Lystrup in Denmark (S. H. Andersen 1987a, fig. 155, and 1996, figs. 3 and 4) and Sventoji 1A in Lithuania (Rimantiené 1992, fig. 5). In addition, organic items for use in transport are known; these include canoes, one from Tybrind Vig in Denmark measuring 9.5 meters in length (S. H. Andersen 1987a, 275–276), and a ski fragment from Sarnate in LATVIA (Zvelebil 1979, 214). Such items have *not* survived from the Upper Paleolithic.

Among the organics are various items with artistic designs and motifs. Visibility of art thus covaries with the degree of organic preservation. Denmark probably has provided more artwork than any other country (J. G. D. Clark 1975; S. H. Andersen 1980). The site of Tybrind Vig must again be mentioned, as its decorated paddle blades are perhaps the finest Mesolithic designs known from Europe (S. H. Andersen 1987a and 1987b, fig. 165). Artistic work did, therefore, clearly continue in the Mesolithic, although not on cave walls—except in eastern SPAIN, where parietal art persisted into the postglacial period (e.g., Sieveking 1979, 193–195).

Ecological Anthropology

In European hunter-gatherer studies there is little effective contact between archaeologists and anthropologists. As a result concepts derived from ecological anthropology have tended to reach Europe via the works of North American scholars. Early influential examples include Meiklejohn (1978) and Price (1981). Such work made use of concepts such as the mating network of about 500 people (Wobst 1976). Price (1981) noted that the areas occupied by stylistically defined archaeological entities are frequently 100 to 200 kilometers in diameter, thus measuring about 8,000 to 31,000 square kilometers. If these represent mating networks

of 500 people, they imply population densities of 0.064 to 0.016 people per square kilometer (Price 1981, table 4). This is within the expected range and therefore supports the identification of these stylistic units as closed mating networks. Late-glacial stylistic units covered far larger areas; J. G. D. Clark (1975, 72–73) mentioned a range of 70,000 to 120,000 square kilometers. An area of 100,000 square kilometers would, if occupied by 500 people, imply a population density of 0.005 people per square kilometer—similar to that of some inland groups of caribou hunters in North America.

These concepts, derived from ecological anthropology and listed above, were rapidly adopted in Britain (Jacobi 1979), but it is perhaps accurate to say that they have made less impact in mainland Europe. Although these ideas are clearly very useful, some scholars have argued that more flexibility needs to be employed when applying them to coastal regions (Rowley-Conwy 1986). Price (1981, 227) stated that at normal population densities, Denmark might have contained three mating networks. Coastal productivity very much exceeded that of inland regions, however, and hunter-gatherer populations in favorable regions would have been much larger (Rowley-Conwy 1983; Zvelebil and Rowley-Conwy 1986). Some of the smallest stylistic entities in the European Mesolithic are in Denmark—those identified by Vang Petersen (1984, fig. 15). These are only some 50 kilometers across and are, furthermore, not circular because they are on the coast, so they are far smaller than others in the continental interior. *If* these are interpreted as semicircular mating networks, population density would have been in the order of 0.5 people per square kilometer. Territorial behavior was likely. In any event, favorable coastal regions were likely to have seen higher population densities and group sizes, arguably in conjunction with more complex social organizations (Renouf 1991; Rowley-Conwy 1983; Rowley-Conwy and Zvelebil 1989). This may be why agriculture was relatively slow to penetrate some of these coastal regions (Zvelebil and Rowley-Conwy 1986).

Anthropological concepts have been important in other areas, such as technology. Robin

Torrence demonstrated that technological complexity varied with latitude (1983, figs. 3.1, 3.2). She suggested that economic activities in higher latitudes were more likely to be "time stressed" because resource availability was concentrated into ever more limited periods as latitude and seasonality increased. The shorter the period a resource is available, the more specialized the technology must be to maximize procurement in the brief time available (Torrence 1983). When the Mesolithic is considered in this light, it is evident that a technology *less specialized* than that of the Upper Paleolithic would be expected because conditions changed from arctic to temperate. Arguably, this is what the microlith represents: an unspecialized blank capable of use in a wide variety of tools. Thus, anthropology provides an alternative to the view that the Mesolithic was a period of cultural retrogression: a less specialized technology can be seen as an adaptation to less time-stressed activities.

This section has sought to demonstrate the transition from a cultural to a behavioral perspective by European Mesolithic studies, and recent syntheses do indeed combine archaeology with anthropologically derived concepts (for a good example in the British context, see Smith 1992). The study of hunter-gatherers is perhaps the area of archaeology in which the behavioral perspective is most developed, and the Mesolithic certainly used to be regarded as the most retrogressive period in European prehistory. The changes described earlier therefore amount to probably the biggest shift in views anywhere in European prehistory.

Regional Perspectives

This section will present a discussion of work in various areas of Europe. In no sense can the presentations that follow be considered reviews; space permits the inclusion of only a few aspects of work and a small number of publications. The coverage is intended to emphasize variability.

The Mesolithic is sometimes thought of as a temperate forest phenomenon, but, although southern Scandinavia is indeed in the temperate zone, Iberia is mostly Mediterranean in climate, and the upper reaches of Norway lie far north of the Arctic Circle.

Southern Scandinavia

It is appropriate to begin with the region that has both the earliest work and the most complete record of any in Europe. Good reviews of the Danish and southern Swedish Mesolithic can be found in Brinch Petersen (1973), J. G. D. Clark (1975), and Price (1985).

The earliest phase of the Mesolithic is represented by only a few sites, such as Klosterlund. The second phase, characterized by lanceolate and triangular microliths (see the previous discussion), is the period of the Maglemose culture, falling in the eighth millennium B.P. Most sites lie on the banks of former lakes that have since filled with peat, creating excellent conditions for organic preservation. Many sites were discovered during peat cutting in the early years of the twentieth century, and some of these have been published, including Ulkestrup (K. Andersen, Jørgensen, and Richter 1982), Sværdborg I (Henriksen 1976), and Lundby (Henriksen 1980). The sites are all small, and sometimes they include the preserved bark floors of small dwellings (e.g., at Ulkestrup); the sites might have been occupied only once or multiple times over a certain period and involve material being dumped in the former lakes alongside the huts (Blankholm 1987, 1996; Grøn 1995).

Faunal remains consist of the "big five" land mammals of postglacial Europe, namely, red deer, elk (or moose), roe deer, aurochs, and wild boar. In addition, many fish bones, mainly of pike, are found on some settlements (see the earlier description of the Mosegården III fishing area), and hazelnut shells hint at the wide range of plant foods that must have been exploited. Most of the settlements are believed to have been occupied in summer (as was the similar site of Star Carr in Britain—see Legge and Rowley-Conwy 1988). The case has been made that a minority were occupied in winter (Grøn 1987), although the faunal evidence argues against this conclusion (Rowley-Conwy 1993; Blankholm 1996). At the time of occupation the sea level was appreciably lower than it is today; it may be that some winter settlements lie below the present sea level, for Maglemosian artifacts have been found by divers at depths of 10 to 15 meters in the now submerged area between Denmark and Sweden (Larsson 1983b).

In the earlier part of the third (blade and trapeze) phase of the Mesolithic, the sea was rising rapidly. The Kongemose culture belonging to this period (ca. 6800 to 6300 B.P.) is little known, but the succeeding Ertebølle culture (ca. 6300 to 5200 B.P.) has provided many settlements. In the north and east of Denmark, Ertebølle coasts are above present sea levels; on these raised beaches are the many SHELL MIDDENS for which this culture is renowned (Europe's first recognized Mesolithic settlement, Havelse Mølle, is one of these). Oysters usually predominate among the shellfish, but bones of land and sea mammals, birds, and fish are numerous, and these taxa probably provided most of the diet— the importance of plant foods again being unquantifiable. Analysis of C-13 content in human skeletons indicates that the Ertebølle diet was dominated by marine foods, probably to a greater extent than would be suspected from other lines of evidence, and that this changed abruptly to a terrestrially based diet at the start of the Neolithic period (Tauber 1982).

Many excavations have been published; in Jutland the eponymous site of Ertebølle has been the scene of renewed work (S. H. Andersen and Johansen 1986), and smaller shell middens such as Norsminde (S. H. Andersen 1989) and the inland site at Ringkloster (S. H. Andersen 1975) have also been recently excavated. Farther east oysters played a lesser part in the diet as salinity decreased, but sites were still large; examples include those around Vedbæk Fjord in Denmark (Price and Brinch Petersen 1987) and Segebro in Sweden (Larsson 1982). In southern Denmark the raised beaches run below present sea levels; the site of Tybrind Vig, excavated by divers, testifies to the continuation of the Ertebølle in this region (S. H. Andersen 1987a and 1987b).

Some of the larger shell middens were occupied year-round (Rowley-Conwy 1983). Other sites were seasonally occupied; Ringkloster, in the interior, was a winter-spring site. The sedentism suggested by evidence in the sites has given rise to discussions of possible social complexity (Rowley-Conwy 1983), although it has been stressed that the data are vague (Price 1985). The remarkable early Ertebølle cemeteries at Vedbæk in Denmark (Albrethsen and Brinch Petersen 1976) and Skateholm in Sweden (Larsson 1988) may indicate territorial behavior.

Iberia

Iberia is a large and diverse landmass, ranging from a cool, temperate north to a warm, oceanic southwest and a hot, Mediterranean south and east. Research has inevitably been somewhat patchy in so large an area, but enough has been done to identify Iberia as an area of key interest in the European Mesolithic.

The later Mesolithic of PORTUGAL was characterized by groups of substantial shell middens (for recent reviews, see Arnaud 1989, 1990; Lubell and Jackes 1988; Zilhão 1993). These date to around 7000 to 5500 B.P. and lie some way inland from the present seacoast, overlooking post-Mesolithic alluvial deposits. Those on the Muge River (a tributary of the Tagus) are comparatively well known. Moita do Sebastião is a major midden with traces of one or more structures and a large cemetery (Roche 1972a), and Arruda and Amoreira also both have cemeteries (Roche 1972b). Other shell middens lie farther south on the Sado River. Cabeço do Pez and Poças de São Bento are the two largest; these and several others have cemeteries (Arnaud 1989). Finally, a third group lies on or close to the Mira River (Arnaud 1990).

Although these shell middens do not consist of tightly packed oysters like the ones in Denmark, they have a more diffuse content of smaller marine and brackish-water shells and are sometimes a short distance from the contemporary shore. Animal bones are present in quantity in some middens, with those of red deer and wild boar being the most common. Fish bones tend to be less visible, although many were recovered at Arapouco at the seaward end of the Sado group. The species of fish in question indicate a summer occupation of this site, whereas Cabeço do Pez at the inland end may have been a winter site. This supports the suggestion that there was short-distance seasonal movement within at least the Sado middens, with groups spending summers near the seacoast and winters further inland (Arnaud 1989). The role of plant foods is difficult to determine; Arnaud (1989) stressed the potential importance of acorns and pine nuts, both available locally. Unusually for the European Mesolithic, the middens contain grindstones, which could have been used to prepare plant foods. Stable-isotope analysis indicates that Mesolithic populations had more marine foods in their diets than did Neolithic populations, but the break between the two is less abrupt in Iberia than in Denmark (Lubell and Jackes 1988).

The Asturian culture of the northern Spanish coasts has been relatively thoroughly researched (see, e.g., G. A. Clark 1983a; González Morales 1989). Many of the sites are shell middens with limpets as the main component, and some of these are found in caves—a major example being La Riera, where the Asturian midden overlies substantial Paleolithic deposits (Straus and Clark 1986). Among the animal bones those of the red deer predominate (G. A. Clark and Yi 1983). Less is understood of seasonality and settlement patterns in this area. It has been suggested that the Asturian sites may be seasonally complementary to Azilian sites inland, at least during the relatively short period of chronological overlap between the two—but longer-term coast-inland complementarity was likely (G. A. Clark 1983b, 1989).

Other areas of Iberia have received less scrutiny. One particular problem in this connection is the possible appearance of domestic sheep and/or goats and pigs in Mesolithic sites in eastern and southern Spain (Boessneck and von den Driesch 1980; Bernabeu, Aura, and Badal 1993; Ribé, Cruells, and Molist 1997; Zilhão 1993). The appearance of the bones of sheep, goats, and pigs in the data have recently come under criticism from two directions. First, the stratigraphic problems in the caves in question may have been underestimated, with the relevent bones ascribed to the wrong layers (Zilhão 1993); second, the distinction between wild and domestic pigs is problematic and may have been too rigidly applied (Rowley-Conwy 1995a). There are currently no compelling reasons to assume that domestic livestock were present in the Mesolithic of southeastern Spain.

Norway

The sheer size of the Scandinavian peninsula is not always appreciated: the distance from Copenhagen to the most northern cape of Norway equals the distance from Copenhagen to Naples, and most of this span is Norway, which extends to beyond 71° north latitude. In addition, the coastline is deeply indented, giving Norway a total coastal length of over 26,000 kilometers. Much of the country's terrain is steep and difficult, and organic materials usually do not survive in Norway's climate. Given such difficulties, it is a testimony to Norwegian colleagues that so much is known of the Norwegian Mesolithic period, one of the most interesting in Europe.

The central parts of the country are less well researched than the Arctic or southern parts (for a good review, see Nygaard 1989). A consensus is growing that agriculture did not appear at the start of the artifactual Neolithic. The first evidence in southeastern Norway may date to the middle Neolithic (mid-fifth millennium B.P.). Elsewhere it occurred substantially later: in southwestern Norway there is no agricultural evidence until the late Neolithic (Bjørgo, Kristoffersen, and Prescott 1992; Prescott 1991), and near the Arctic Circle stratigraphically early cereal grains from Stiurhelleren have been directly dated to as late as around 3200 B.P. (Johansen 1990). For more recent reviews, see Prescott (1996) and Peter Rowley-Conwy (1995b).

Early-Mesolithic groups are known as the Fosna culture in southern Norway and the Komsa culture in the Arctic (Nygaard 1989). Organic material is rare, and later periods are better known. In the south there was extensive late-Mesolithic/early-Neolithic hunter-gatherer settlement in the deeply dissected coastal zone (see, e.g., Mikkelsen 1978; Bang-Andersen 1996). The major settlement of Kotedalen lay on a strait rich in fish and was probably occupied all year (A. B. Olsen 1992). The large faunal sample showed a strongly marine orientation, dominated by fish (primarily from the cod family). The most common mammals were seals and otters, followed by red deer and pigs (Hufthammer 1992). Farther inland, in the inner fjord zone, remains at the cave site of Skipshelleren also contain many fish and seals, but there is a much larger proportion of land mammals (H. Olsen 1976). Whether Skipshelleren was utilized by groups from the outer coast on a seasonal basis remains unclear. Small sites in the Hardanger massif in the interior were probably seasonal reindeer-hunting stands (Bang-Andersen 1996).

Arctic Norway also presents a picture of maritime adaptations. Substantial house structures are known (Engelstad 1989). The best-surveyed area is Varanger Fiord, in the most northeastern part of the country. Substantial faunal remains have been recovered from some settlements there. Earlier models of long-range mobility based on recent ethnography have given way to models of restricted movement or sedentism based on the archaeological material: individual middens on the same site may indicate different seasons, but in all, they suggest year-round occupation (Renouf 1988, 1989).

Eastern Europe

The Mesolithic of eastern Europe is little known in the west, although recent years have seen an upsurge in contacts between east and west, and the coming years will surely see this increase still further. The best review of the whole region is Dolukhanov (1979). Various areas are of major interest.

The northeast Baltic contains many large settlements with excellent organic preservation. Archaeologists with command of the relevant languages have provided information about these (e.g., Zvelebil 1979), and some information about individual settlements, such as Sventoji in Lithuania (Rimantiené 1992), is becoming available. Claims are made for a small number of domestic cattle and pigs in some sites (see Dolukhanov 1979), but detailed zooarchaeological data are not available.

The Iron Gates Gorge, containing the Danube, separates ROMANIA from the former Yugoslavia. The gorge contains a number of major Mesolithic sites. The most famous is LEPINSKI VIR, which has substantial house remains and monumental sculptures (Sjrejovic 1972), but other sites are also substantial (see, e.g., Prinz 1987; Voytek and Tringham 1989). Fish, mainly

catfish and members of the carp family, apparently were a very important resource, accounting for over half the bones recovered from Lepinski Vir (Bökönyi 1970), Padina III (Clason 1980), and Icoana (Bolomey 1973). Faunal reports all conclude that these three settlements were occupied all year.

Continuity from the Later Upper Paleolithic

Historically, the Mesolithic has been described as a separate entity. However, much new work is now being done to bridge the gap between the Upper Paleolithic and the Mesolithic, and not surprisingly, there is substantial continuity. The two periods are now being studied largely by the same researchers, whereas in earlier years the division between Pleistocene and Holocene also formed a research division. This is particularly the case in the North European Plain, where human occupation ceased during the maximum extent of the last glacial period: the later Upper Paleolithic reoccupation is treated together with the Mesolithic as a single unit of study, albeit with recognition of rapid change through time. This renders irrelevant any question of whether we should actually call the postglacial period "Mesolithic" or "Epipaleolithic."

Climatic warming at the Pleistocene-Holocene boundary appears to have been extremely rapid. As a result, it took some centuries for plant communities to begin to adjust. There is a substantial similarity between the flint technology of this period and the immediately preceding later Upper Paleolithic, both on the mainland (Gob 1991) and in Britain (Barton 1991). Similarity in bone and antler artifacts is also attested (Smith and Bonsall 1991). One interesting recent development is the accelerator dating of a point recovered from the bed of the North Sea at a depth of 39 meters; the date is 11,740±150 B.P. (OxA 1950), which places the point firmly in the later Upper Paleolithic and emphasizes the large areas that have been submerged since the last glacial.

It was mentioned earlier that microliths may reflect a less specialized technology, as would be expected when climatic amelioration takes place. Can microlithization therefore be considered an adaptation to prevailing conditions? Much more work needs to be done on the late-glacial industries before this question can be answered, but some observations can be made at this point. Late-glacial environments are becoming better understood. The last millennium or so was characterized by very cold conditions (the so-called Dryas III, ca. 11,000–10,000 B.P.). Preceding this was a warmer interstadial period (the late-glacial interstadial, sometimes divided into the Bølling and Allerød interstadials, ca. 13,000–11,000 B.P.) in the North European Plain. Before 13,000 B.P. came the major period of last-glacial cold (Barton, Roberts, and Roe 1991, xii).

Microlithization varies with this in what is potentially a most interesting way. Later Upper Paleolithic industries in southern Europe showed a trend toward microliths (Gamble 1986, 220–221), which increased in the Azilian around the Pleistocene-Holocene boundary (Straus 1985). Remarkably, southern FRANCE for a time saw a chronological overlap between (1) groups hunting reindeer with Magdalenian technology and (2) groups hunting red deer with Azilian technology (Straus 1996). In northern Europe, the Hamburgian dates to the earlier part of the late-glacial interstadial period and is typified by the heavy, tanged points that were used to kill reindeer (Fischer 1991, 1996; Holm and Rieck 1992). Microlithization began in the second part of the late-glacial interstadial period (Rozoy 1989, 25). Cultural entities of this period in the North European Plain are variously termed Federmesser, Tjongerian, Arch Backed Piece, and so forth (Fischer 1991; Gob 1991; Schild 1976; Houtsma et al. 1996; Newell and Constandse-Westermann 1996). Large, tanged points continued in the northern edge of occupation, in the Brommian of Denmark (Fischer 1991), although some Federmesser elements are also known (Holm 1996). Ahrensburgian tanged points from the final cold spell in the Younger Dryas have been found across much of the North European Plain, again associated with reindeer hunting (Schild 1976; Fischer 1991). At the end of the Younger Dryas final Paleolithic industries continued until 9600 B.P. in POLAND, by which time the site of Frie-

sack in Germany had already "gone Mesolithic," although this phenomenon cannot yet be linked to ecological factors because no faunal remains survive (Schild 1996). This pattern could be consistent with (1) specialized reindeer hunting using tanged points and (2) more generalized hunting using smaller armatures, moving north and south as climate and resources fluctuated. More work is, however, needed on late-glacial industries and resources before this supposition can be substantiated.

Final Remarks

This essay has tried to show why the Mesolithic period in Europe is no longer regarded as a cultural hiatus or a retrogressive backwater. Variability has been stressed; in some areas hunter-gatherer economies were apparently a viable alternative to farming for centuries or longer. Thus, when farming spread across Europe, groups of people who lived at the Portuguese shell middens and the Iron Gates hunter-fisher sites continued to occupy them for centuries although surrounded by farmers; by contrast, the boundary between hunter-gatherers and farmers in southern Scandinavia and northern Germany was more or less stable for over a millennium.

It is heartening that many of the changes in views discussed here have come about not as theoretical changes divorced from the archaeological material but as the direct consequence of methodological and interpretational advances on the part of Mesolithic scholars all across Europe. An optimistic view of the future of Mesolithic studies thus stresses the importance of continued work: excavation, interpretation, reinterpretation, synthesis. It is from this process that a greater understanding will come in the years ahead.

Peter Rowley-Conwy

See also Britain, Prehistoric Archaeology
References
Albrethsen, S. E., and E. Brinch Petersen. 1976. "Excavations of a Mesolithic Cemetery at Vedbæk, Denmark." *Acta Archaeologica* 47: 1–28.
Andersen, K. 1983. *Stenalderbebyggelsen i den Vestsjællandske Åmose.* Copenhagen: Fredningsstyrelsen.
Andersen, K., S. Jørgensen, and J. Richter. 1982.

Maglemose Hytterne ved Ulkestrup Lyng (with English summary). Copenhagen: Det Kongelige Nordiske Oldskriftselskab.

Andersen, S. H. 1975. "Ringkloster: En jysk inlandsboplands med Ertebøllekultur" (with English summary). *Kuml 1973–1974:* 11–108.

———. 1980. "Ertebøllekunst: Nye østjyske fund af mønstrede Ertebølleoldsager" (with English summary). *Kuml:* 7–59.

———. 1987a. "Tybrind Vig: A Submerged Ertebølle Settlement in Denmark." In *European Wetlands in Prehistory,* 253–280. Ed. J. M. Coles and A. J. Lawson. Oxford: Clarendon.

———. 1987b. "Mesolithic Dug-outs and Paddles from Tybrind Vig, Denmark." *Acta Archaeologica* 57: 87–106.

———. 1989. "Norsminde. A Køkkenmødding with Late Mesolithic and Early Neolithic Occupation." *Journal of Danish Archaeology* 8: 13–40.

———. 1996. "Ertebøllebåde fra Lystrup" [Ertebølle canoes from Lystrup] (with English summary). *Kuml 1993–1994:* 7–38.

Andersen, S. H., and E. Johansen. 1986. "Ertebølle Revisited." *Journal of Danish Archaeology* 5: 31–61.

Andersen, S. H., and P. O. Nielsen. 1982. *Jæger og Bonde i Stenalderen.* Copenhagen: Lademann.

Arnaud, J. M. 1989. "The Mesolithic Communities of the Sado Valley, Portugal, in Their Ecological Setting." In *The Mesolithic in Europe,* 614–631. Ed. C. Bonsall. Edinburgh: John Donald.

———. 1990. "Le substrat mesolithique et le processus de neolithisation dans le sud du Portugal." In *Rubané et Cardial,* 437–446. Ed. D. Cahen and M. Otte. Etudes et Recherches Archéologiques de l'Université de Liège 39.

Bailey, G. N., ed. 1983. *Hunter-Gatherer Economy in Prehistory.* Cambridge: Cambridge University Press.

Bang-Andersen, S. 1996. "Coast/Inland Relations in the Mesolithic of Southern Norway." *World Archaeology* 27: 427–443.

Barton, N. 1991. "Technological Innovation and Continuity at the End of the Pleistocene in Britain." In *The Late Glacial in North-West Europe,* CBA Research Report 77, 234–245. Ed. N. Barton, A. J. Roberts, and D. A. Roe. London: Council for British Archaeology.

Barton, N., A. J. Roberts, and D. A. Roe, eds. 1991. *The Late Glacial in North-West Europe,* CBA Research Report 77. London: Council for British Archaeology.

Becker, C. J. 1941. "Fund af ruser fra Danmarks stenalder." *Aarbøger for Nordisk Oldkyndighed og Historie,* 131–149.

Bernabeu, J., J. E. Aura, and E. Badal. 1993. *Al Oeste del Eden: Las primas sociedades agrícolas en la Europa Mediterránea.* Madrid: Editorial Sintesis.

Bjørgo, T., S. Kristoffersen, and C. Prescott. 1992. *Arkeologiske Undersøkelser i Nyset-Steggjevassdragene 1981–87.* Historisk Museum, Universitetet i Bergen, Arkeologiske Rapporter 16.

Blankholm, H. P. 1987. "Maglemosian Hutfloors: An Analysis of the Dwelling Unit, Social Unit and Intra-site Behavioural Patterns in Early Mesolithic Southern Scandinavia." In *Mesolithic Northwest Europe: Recent Trends,* 109–120. Ed. P. Rowley-Conwy, M. Zvelebil, and H. P. Blankholm. Sheffield, England: Department of Archaeology and Prehistory.

———. 1996. *On the Track of a Prehistoric Economy: Maglemosian Subsistence in Early Postglacial South Scandinavia.* Aarhus, Denmark: Aarhus University Press.

Boessneck, J., and A. von den Driesch. 1980. "Tierknochenfunde aus vier Südspanischen Höhlen." In *Studien über frühe Tierknochenfunde von der Iberischen Halbinsel,* 7:1–83. Ed. J. Boessneck and A. von den Driesch. Munich: Institut für Palaeoanatomie, Domestikations- forschung und Geschichte der Tiermedizin der Universität München.

Bökönyi, S. 1970. "Animal Bones from Lepenski Vir." *Science* 167: 1702–1704.

Bolomey, A. 1973. "An Outline of the Late Epipalaeolithic Economy at the 'Iron Gates': The Evidence on Bones." *Dacia* 17: 41–52.

Bonsall, C., ed. 1989. *The Mesolithic in Europe.* Edinburgh: John Donald.

Brinch Petersen, E. 1973. "A Survey of the Late Palaeolithic and Mesolithic of Denmark." In *The Mesolithic in Europe,* 77–127. Ed. S. K. Kozlowski. Warsaw University Press.

Childe, V. G. 1925 [1957]. *The Dawn of European Civilization,* 1st ed. London: Routledge and Kegan Paul [6th ed., Saint Albans: Paladin].

Clark, G. A. 1983a. *The Asturian of Cantabria: Early Holocene Hunter-Gatherers in Northern Spain.* Tucson: Anthropological Papers of the University of Arizona 41.

———. 1983b. "Boreal Phase Settlement/Subsistence Models for Cantabrian Spain." In *Hunter-Gatherer Economy in Prehistory,* 96–110. Ed. G. N. Bailey. Cambridge: Cambridge University Press.

———. 1989. "Site Functional Complementarity

in the Mesolithic of Northern Spain." In *The Mesolithic in Europe,* 589–603. Ed. C. Bonsall. Edinburgh: John Donald.

Clark, G. A., and S. Yi. 1983. "Niche-width Variation in Cantabrian Archaeofaunas: A Diachronic Study." In *Animals and Archaeology,* vol. 1, *Hunters and Their Prey,* 183–208. Ed. J. Clutton-Brock and C. Grigson. BAR International Series 163. Oxford: British Archaeological Reports.

Clark, J. G. D. 1932. *The Mesolithic Age in Britain.* Cambridge: Cambridge University Press.

———. 1936. *The Mesolithic Settlement of Northern Europe.* Cambridge: Cambridge University Press.

———. 1954. *Excavations at Star Carr.* Cambridge: Cambridge University Press.

———. 1972. *Star Carr: A Case Study in Bioarchaeology.* Addison-Wesley Module in Anthropology 10. Reading, MA: Addison Wesley.

———. 1973. "Seasonality and the Interpretation of Lithic Industries." In *Estudios Dedicados al Professor Dr Luis Pericot,* 1–13. Ed. J. Maluquer de Motes. Publicaciones Eventuales 23. Barcelona: Barcelona University Press.

———. 1975. *The Earlier Stone Age Settlement of Scandinavia.* Cambridge: Cambridge University Press.

———. 1980. *Mesolithic Prelude.* Edinburgh: Edinburgh University Press.

Clarke, D. L. 1976. "Mesolithic Europe: The Economic Basis." In *Problems in Economic and Social Archaeology,* 449–481. Ed. G. Sieveking, I. H. Longworth, and K. E. Wilson. London: Duckworth.

Clason, A. T. 1980. "Padina and Starcevo: Game, Fish and Cattle." *Palaeohistoria* 22: 141–173.

Dolukhanov, P. 1979. *Ecology and Economy in Neolithic Eastern Europe.* London: Duckworth.

Engelstad, E. 1989. "Mesolithic House Sites in Arctic Norway." In *The Mesolithic in Europe,* 331–337. Ed. C. Bonsall. Edinburgh: John Donald.

Fischer, A. 1991. "Pioneers in Deglaciated Landscapes: The Expansion and Adaptation of Late Palaeolithic Societies in Southern Scandinavia." In *The Late Glacial in North-West Europe,* CBA Research Report 77, 100–121. Ed. N. Barton, A. J. Roberts, and D. A. Roe. London: Council for British Archaeology.

———. 1996. "At the Border of Human Habitat: The Late Palaeolithic and Early Mesolithic in Scandinavia." In *The Earliest Settlement of Scandinavia,* 157–176. Ed. L. Larsson. Acta Archaeo-logica Lundensia, 8th series, 24. Stockholm: Almquist and Wiksell.

Gamble, C. 1986. *The Palaeolithic Settlement of Europe.* Cambridge: Cambridge University Press.

Geupel, V. 1973. "Zur kenntnis des Mesolithikums im Süden der DDR." In *The Mesolithic in Europe,* 157–176. Ed. S. K. Kozlowski. Warsaw University Press.

Gob, A. 1991. "The Early Postglacial Occupation of the Southern Part of the North Sea Basin." In *The Late Glacial in North-West Europe,* CBA Research Report 77, 227–233. Ed. N. Barton, A. J. Roberts, and D. A. Roe. London: Council for British Archaeology.

González Morales, M. R. 1989. "Asturian Resource Exploitation: Recent Perspectives." In *The Mesolithic in Europe,* 604–606. Ed. E. Bonsall. Edinburgh: John Donald.

Gramsch, B. 1987. *Ausgrabungen auf dem mesolithischen Moorfundplatz bei Friesack, Berzirk Potsdam.* Veröffentlichungen des Museums für Ur- und Frühgeschichte Potsdam 21, 75–100. Berlin: Deutscher Verlag.

Gramsch, B., ed. 1981. *Mesolithikum in Europa.* Veröffentlichungen des Museums für Ur- und Frühgeschichte Potsdam 14–15. Berlin: Deutscher Verlag.

Gräslund, B. 1987. *The Birth of Prehistoric Chronology.* Cambridge: Cambridge University Press.

Grayson, D. K. 1983. *The Establishment of Human Antiquity.* New York: Academic Press.

Grøn, O. 1987. "Seasonal Variation in Maglemosian Group Size and Structure: A New Model." *Current Anthropology* 28: 303–327.

———. 1995. *The Maglemose Culture.* BAR International Series 616. Oxford: Tempus Reparatum.

Henriksen, B. B. 1976. *Sværdborg I: Excavations 1943–44.* Copenhagen: Akademisk Forlag.

———. 1980. *Lundby-Holmen: Pladser af Maglemose-Type i Sydsjælland* (with English summary). Copenhagen: Det Kongelige Nordiske Old-skriftselskab.

Holm, F., and F. Rieck. 1992. *Istidsjægere ved Jelssøerne* (with English summary). Skrifter fra Museumsrådet for Sønderjyllands Amt 5. Haderslev: Haderslev Museum.

Holm, J. 1996. "The Earliest Settlement of Denmark." In *The Earliest Settlement of Scandinavia,* 43–59. Ed. L. Larsson. Acta Archaeologica Lundensia, 8th series, 24. Stockholm: Almquist and Wiksell.

Houtsma, P., E. Kramer, R. R. Newell, and J. L. Smit. 1996. *The Late Palaeolithic Site of Haule V:*

From *Excavation Report to the Reconstruction of Federmesser Settlement Patterns and Land-Use*. Assen: Van Gorcum.

Hufthammer, A. K. 1992. "De osteologiske undersøkelsene fra Kotedalen." In *Kotedalen—En Boplass gjennom 5000 År*, vol. 2. Ed. K. L. Helle, A. K. Hufthammer, P. E. Kaland, A. B. Olsen, and E. C. Soltvedt. Bergen: Historisk Museum.

Jacobi, R. M. 1973. "Aspects of the 'Mesolithic Age' in Great Britain." In *The Mesolithic in Europe*, 237–265. Ed. S. K. Kozlowski. Warsaw University Press.

———. 1976. "Britain Inside and Outside Mesolithic Europe." *Proceedings of the Prehistoric Society* 42: 67–84.

———. 1978. "Northern England in the Eighth Millennium B.C.: An Essay." In *The Early Postglacial Settlement of Northern Europe*, 295–332. Ed. P. Mellars. London: Duckworth.

———. 1979. "Early Flandrian Hunters in the South-west." *Proceedings of the Devon Archaeological Society, Jubilee Conference* 48: 93.

Johansen, O. S. 1990. *Synspunkter på Jernalderens Jordbrukssamfunn i Nord-Norge*. Tromsø: University of Tromsø, Institute of Social Sciences.

Kozlowski, S. K., ed. 1973. *The Mesolithic in Europe*. Warsaw University Press.

———. 1975. *Cultural Differentiation of Europe from the 10th to 5th Millennium B.C.* Warsaw University Press.

———. 1976. "Les courants interculturels dans le mésolithique de l'Europe occidentale." *9th Congrès International des Sciences Préhistoriques et Protohistoriques, Nice,* Colloque 19: 135–160.

Larsson, L. 1982. *Segebro: En Tidigatlantisk Boplats vid Sege Ås Mynning* (with English summary). Malmö Museum, Malmöfynd 4.

———. 1983a. *Ageröd V: An Atlantic Bog Site in Central Scania*. Acta Archaeologica Lundensia, 8th series, no. 12.

———. 1983b. "Mesolithic Settlement on the Sea Floor in the Strait of Öresund." In *Quaternary Coastlines and Marine Archaeology: Towards the Prehistory of Land Bridges and Continental Shelves*, 283–30. Ed. P. M. Masters and N. C. Flemming. New York: Academic Press.

Larsson, L., ed. 1988. *The Skateholm Project I: Man and Environment*. Skrifter utgivna av Kungliga Humanistiska Vetenskapssanfundet i Lund 79.

Legge, A. J., and P. A. Rowley-Conwy. 1988. *Star Carr Revisited*. London: Centre for Extra-Mural Studies.

Lubell, D., and M. Jackes. 1988. "Portuguese Mesolithic-Neolithic Subsistence and Settlement." *Supplemento della Rivista di Antropologia* 66: 231–248.

Meiklejohn, C. 1978. "Ecological Aspects of Population Size and Growth in Late Glacial and Early Postglacial North-western Europe." In *The Early Postglacial Settlement of Northern Europe*, 65–79. Ed. P. Mellars. London: Duckworth.

Mellars, P. 1974. "The Palaeolithic and Mesolithic." In *British Prehistory*, 41–99. Ed. C. Renfrew. London: Duckworth.

———. 1976a. "Settlement Patterns and Industrial Variability in the British Mesolithic." In *Problems in Economic and Social Archaeology*, 375–399. Ed. G. Sieveking, I. H. Longworth, and K. E. Wilson. London: Duckworth.

———. 1976b. "The Appearance of 'Narrow Blade' Microlithic Industries in Britain: The Radiocarbon Evidence." *9th Congrès International des Sciences Préhistoriques et Protohistoriques, Nice,* Colloque 119: 166–174.

Mikkelsen, E. 1978. "Seasonality and Mesolithic Adaptation in Norway." In *New Directions in Scandinavian Archaeology*, 79–119. Ed. K. Kristiansen and C. Paludan-Müller. Studies in Scandinavian Prehistory and Early History 1. Copenhagen: National Museum of Denmark.

Newell, R. 1973. "The Postglacial Adaptations of the Indigenous Population of the Northwest European Plain." In *The Mesolithic in Europe*, 399–440. Ed. S. K. Kozlowski. Warsaw University Press.

Newell, R. R., and T. Constandse-Westermann. 1996. "The Use of Ethnographic Analyses for Researching Late Palaeolithic Settlement Systems, Settlement Patterns and Land Use in the Northwest European Plain." *World Archaeology* 27: 372–388.

Nygaard, S. E. 1989. "The Stone Age of Northern Scandinavia: A Review." *Journal of World Prehistory* 3: 71–116.

Olsen, A. B. 1992. *Kotedalen—En Boplass gjennom 5000 År*, vol. 1. Bergen: Historisk Museum.

Olsen, H. 1976. *Skipshelleren, Osteologisk Materiale*. Bergen: Zoological Museum.

Prescott, C. 1991. "Kulturhistoriske Undersøkelser i Skrivarhelleren." Historisk Museum, Universitetet i Bergen, Arkeologiske Rapporter 14.

———. 1996. "Was There *Really* a Neolithic in Norway?" *Antiquity* 70: 77–87.

Price, T. D. 1981. "Regional Approaches to Human Adaptation in the Mesolithic of the North

European Plain." In *Mesolithikum in Europa.* Veröffentlichungen des Museums für Ur- und Frühgeschichte Potsdam 14–15: 217–234. Ed. B. Gramsch. Berlin: Deutscher Verlag.

———. 1985. "Affluent Foragers of Mesolithic Southern Scandinavia." In *Prehistoric Hunter-Gatherers,* 341–363. Ed. T. D. Price and J. Brown. New York: Academic Press.

Price, T.D., and E. Brinch Petersen. 1987. "A Mesolithic Camp in Denmark." *Scientific American* 255, 3: 112–121.

Prinz, B. 1987. *Mesolithic Adaptations on the Lower Danube: Vlasac and the Iron Gates Gorge.* BAR International Series 330. Oxford: British Archaeological Reports.

Radley, J., and P. Mellars. 1964. "A Mesolithic Structure at Deepcar, Yorkshire, and the Affinities of Its Associated Flint Industries." *Proceedings of the Prehistoric Society* 30: 1–24.

Renouf, M. A. P. 1988. "Sedentary Coastal Hunter-Gatherers: An Example from the Younger Stone Age of Northern Norway." In *The Archaeology of Prehistoric Coastlines,* 102–115. Ed. G. Bailey and J. Parkington.

———. 1989. *Prehistoric Hunter-Fishers of Varangerfjord, Northeastern Norway.* BAR International Series 487. Oxford: British Archaeological Reports.

Renouf, P. 1991. "Sedentary Hunter-Gatherers: A Case for the Northern Coasts." In *Between Bands and States,* 89–107. Center for Archaeological Investigations, Occasional Paper no. 9. Ed. S. A. Gregg. Carbondale: Southern Illinois University.

Ribé, G., W. Cruells, and M. Molist. 1997. "The Neolithic of the Iberian Peninsula." In *The Archaeology of Iberia,* 65–84. Ed. M. Diaz-Andreu and S. Keay. London: Routledge.

Rimantiené, R. 1992. "Neolithic Hunter-Gatherers at Sventoji in Lithuania." *Antiquity* 251: 367–376.

Roche, J. 1972a. *Le Gisement Mésolithique de Moita do Sebastião, Muge, Portugal,* vol. 1, *Archéologie.* Lisbon: Instituto de Alta Cultura.

———. 1972b. "Les amas coquilliers *(concheiros)* mésolithiques de Muge (Portugal)" (with English summary). In *Die Anfänge des Neolithikums von Orient bis Nordeuropa VII: Westliches Mittelmeergebiet und Britische Inseln.* Ed. J. Lüning. Cologne: Böhlau.

Rowley-Conwy, P. 1983. "Sedentary Hunters: The Ertebølle Example." In *Hunter-Gatherer Economy in Prehistory,* 111–126. Ed. G. N. Bailey. Cambridge: Cambridge University Press.

———. 1986. "Between Cave Painters and Crop Planters: Aspects of the European Mesolithic." In *Hunters in Transition,* 17–32. Ed. M. Zvelebil. Cambridge: Cambridge University Press.

———. 1993. "Season and Reason: The Case for a Regional Interpretation of Mesolithic Settlement Patterns." In *Hunting and Animal Exploitation in the Later Palaeolithic and Mesolithic of Eurasia,* 179–188. Ed. G. L. Peterkin, H. Bricker, and P. Mellars. Archaeological Papers of the American Anthropological Association no. 4.

———. 1995a. "Wild or Domestic? On the Evidence for the Earliest Domestic Cattle and Pigs in South Scandinavia and Iberia." *International Journal of Osteoarchaeology* 5: 115–126.

———. 1995b. "Making First Farmers Younger: The West European Evidence." *Current Anthropology* 36: 346–353.

———. 1996. "Why Didn't Westropp's 'Mesolithic' Catch on in 1872?" *Antiquity* 70: 940–944.

Rowley-Conwy, P., and M. Zvelebil. 1989. "Saving It for Later: Storage among Hunter-Gatherers in Prehistoric Europe." In *Bad Year Economics: Cultural Responses to Risk and Uncertainty,* 40–56. Ed. P. L. J. Halstead and J. O'Shea. Cambridge: Cambridge University Press.

Rozoy, J-G. 1978. *Les Derniers Chasseurs,* 3 vols. (with English summaries). Bulletin de la Societé Archéologique Champenoise, special number.

———. 1989. "The Revolution of the Bowmen in Europe." In *The Mesolithic in Europe,* 13–28. Ed. C. Bonsall. Edinburgh: John Donald.

Schild, R. 1976. "The Final Palaeolithic Settlements of the European Plain." *Scientific American* 234, 2: 88–99.

———. 1996. "The North European Plain and Eastern Sub-Balticum between 12,700 and 8,000 BP." In *Humans at the End of the Ice Age,* 129–157. Ed. L. G. Straus, B. V. Eriksen, J. M. Erlandsen, and D. R. Yesner. New York: Plenum.

Sieveking, A. 1979. *The Cave Artists.* London: Thames and Hudson.

Sjrejovic, D. 1972. *Europe's First Monumental Sculpture: New Discoveries at Lepenski Vir.* London: Thames and Hudson.

Smith, C. 1992. *Late Stone Age Hunters of the British Isles.* London: Routledge.

Smith, C., and C. Bonsall. 1991. "Late Upper Palaeolithic and Mesolithic Chronology: Points of Interest from Recent Research." In *The Late*

Glacial in North-West Europe, 208–212. CBA Research Report 77. Ed. N. Barton, A. J. Roberts, and D. A. Roe. London: Council for British Archaeology.

Steenstrup, J. J. S. 1851. "Beretning om Udbyttet af nogle ved Isefjordens Kyster og i Jylland sidste Sommer anstillede geologisk-antiquariske Undersögelser angaaende Landets ældste Natur- og Cultur-Forhold." *Oversigt over det kongelige danske Videnskabernes Selskabs Forhandlinger,* 1–31.

Straus, L. G. 1985. "Chronostratigraphy of the Pleistocene-Holocene Transition: The Azilian Problem in the Franco-Cantabrian Region." *Palaeohistoria* 27: 89–122.

———. 1996. "The Archaeology of the Pleistocene-Holocene Transition in Southwest Europe." In *Humans at the End of the Ice Age,* 83–99. Ed. L. G. Straus, B. V. Eriksen, J. M. Erlandsen, and D. R. Yesner. New York: Plenum.

Straus, L. G., and G. A. Clark. 1986. *La Riera Cave: Stone Age Hunter-Gatherer Adaptations in Northern Spain.* Arizona State University, Anthropological Research Papers no. 36.

Switsur, V. R., and R. M. Jacobi. 1979. "A Radiocarbon Chronology for the Early Postglacial Stone Industries of England and Wales." In *Radiocarbon Dating,* 41–68. Ed. R. Berger and H. Suess. Berkeley: University of California Press.

Tauber, H. 1982. "Carbon–13 Evidence for the Diet of Prehistoric Humans in Denmark." *PACT* 7: 235–237.

Torrence, R. 1983. "Time Budgeting and Hunter-Gatherer Technology." In *Hunter-gatherer Economy in Prehistory,* 11–22. Ed. G. N. Bailey. Cambridge: Cambridge University Press.

Van Riper, A. B. 1993. *Men among the Mammoths: Victorian Science and the Discovery of Human Prehistory.* University of Chicago Press.

Vang Petersen, P. 1984. "Chronological and Regional Variation in the Late Mesolithic of Eastern Denmark." *Journal of Danish Archaeology* 3: 7–18.

Voytek, B., and R. Tringham. 1989. "Rethinking the Mesolithic: The Case of South-East Europe." In *The Mesolithic in Europe,* 492–499. Ed. C. Bonsall. Edinburgh: John Donald.

Wobst, H. M. 1976. "Locational Relationships in Palaeolithic Society." *Journal of Human Evolution* 5: 49–58.

Zilhão, J. 1993. "The Spread of Agro-pastoral Economies across Mediterranean Europe: A View from the Far West." *Journal of Mediterranean Archaeology* 6: 5–63.

Zvelebil, M. 1979. "Subsistence and Settlement in the North-eastern Baltic." In *The Early Postglacial Settlement of Northern Europe,* 205–241. Ed. P. Mellars. London: Duckworth.

Zvelebil, M., and P. Rowley-Conwy. 1986. "Foragers and Farmers in Atlantic Europe." In *Hunters in Transition,* 67–93. Ed. M. Zvelebil. Cambridge: Cambridge University Press.

Evans, Sir Arthur (1851–1941)

Arthur Evans was the eldest son of the famous geologist and antiquary SIR JOHN EVANS. The father's friendship with many notable archaeologists such as Sir John Lubbock (LORD AVEBURY), HUGH FALCONER, AUGUSTUS PITT RIVERS, and GUSTAF MONTELIUS must have had an impact on his son Arthur, and the death of his mother when he was six resulted in a close relationship between father and son. Arthur Evans attended Harrow School and Oxford University and graduated in history in 1874. Independently wealthy, Evans traveled to Germany to study for a year, and he then went to Bosnia, Herzegovina, FINLAND, and Lapland. He pursued independent research on the history and antiquities of the southern Slavic peoples and became an advocate of Illyrian independence from the Austro-Hungarian Empire. He returned to England in 1878 and married Margaret Freeman.

In 1883, Evans and his wife left for an extended tour of GREECE, meeting HEINRICH SCHLIEMANN in Athens and visiting his sites. Seeing preclassical Mycenean civilization captured and kept Evans's interest for the rest of his life. He returned to England to become keeper of the ASHMOLEAN MUSEUM in Oxford, restoring its collections and rehousing them in a new building. In 1894, a year after the death of his wife, Evans traveled to Crete for the first time.

His subsequent passion for Cretan archaeology was the result of his interest in the nature and extent of oriental influences on the cultures of early Europe. He returned to Crete in 1895 and 1896 and successfully negotiated the purchase of one-quarter of Kephala Hill at Knossos from its Turkish owner. He was able to purchase the rest in 1899 after the Turks had been driven from Crete as a reward for his public support of Greek independence.

Sir Arthur Evans holding a Cretan sculpture of a bull's head at an exhibition of relics from Knossos at the Royal Academy, London (Hulton Getty)

Evans and his colleage DAVID HOGARTH established a Cretan Exploration Fund, with links to the British School in Athens, and with Evans's private resources began to excavate. In the first year, the general plan of the Bronze Age palace of KNOSSOS was uncovered, and the "throne room" and "magazines" were revealed. Other finds included the first of the marvelous frescoes, traded items from Egypt and BABYLON, and tablets covered with linear script. Intensive excavation of the site continued for the next eight years and was largely financed by Evans, whose success at Knossos encouraged more excavations on Crete and in Greece proper.

Of equal importance to his excavations were Evans's self-funded efforts to restore the palace of Minos. Although Evans's motivations were to make the site comprehensible to others and to stabilize it, he was greatly criticized for compromising conservation in favor of restoration and worked at the site to that end until 1931. Between 1921 and 1936, Evans's most enduring legacy, the book *The Palace of Minos at Knossos,* was published.

Evans resigned from the Ashmolean in 1908 and worked for the Hellenic Society and the British Schools in Athens and Rome. He transferred all of his property on Crete to the British School in Athens, and during the Versailles Peace Conference after World War I, he tirelessly lobbied the British government to support an independent Yugoslavia. He was an accomplished draftsman, numismatist, collector, and excavator, and his artistic tastes were matched by his deductive flair. His development of the chronology of Knossos was a tour de force.

Tim Murray

References

For references, see *Encyclopedia of Archaeology: The Great Archaeologists, Vol. 1,* ed. Tim Murray (Santa Barbara, CA: ABC-CLIO, 1999), pp. 218–219.

Evans, Sir John (1823–1908)

Born in Buckinghamshire, England, and educated at his headmaster father's school, John Evans intended to go to Oxford but instead traveled to Germany. On his return in 1840, he joined his uncle's paper-manufacturing business, John Dickinson and Company, of which he became a partner in 1850. Although he was an excellent businessman, and did not retire from the company until 1885, he also pursued many interests that lay outside the field of his employment. These included geology and palaeontology, which led him to accompany geologist SIR JOSEPH PRESTWICH to France, as an assistant, to visit French palaeontogist JACQUES BOUCHER DE PERTHES and examine chipped flints from the Somme gravels.

Evans and Prestwich were convinced that the stone tools were indeed proof of human antiquity in western Europe, and Evans began to collect stone and bronze implements, to visit cave sites, and to publish his findings. Evans also collected and published on fossil remains of extinct animals and the provenance, typology, and distribution of medieval antiquities, Anglo-Saxon and Lombardic jewelry, posy-rings, bronze weapons, and ornaments. His real area of expertise was in numismatics, and his collections of ancient British money, Roman emperor gold coins, and Anglo-Saxon and English coins were unique. He also contributed more than a hundred items to the *Numismatic Chronicle* and the standard works on British coins.

Evans was elected a fellow of the Royal Society in 1864 and was the society's vice-president from 1876 to 1878 and then its treasurer from 1878 to 1898. He was president of the Geological Society from 1874 to 1876, and in 1880, he received the Lyell Medal for his services to geology, particularly post-tertiary geology, and for developing the relationship between archaeology and geology. At various times in his busy life, he was a member and president of the SOCIETY OF ANTIQUARIES OF LONDON, the Numismatic Society of London, the Anthropological Institute, the EGYPT EXPLORATION SOCIETY, the Society of Arts, the Paper-makers Association, and the British Association. He was also a trustee of the BRITISH MUSEUM and was awarded many academic honors in England and abroad, as well as being on one occasion high sheriff of Hertfordshire. He left his collections to his son SIR ARTHUR EVANS, who in turn presented portions of them to the ASHMOLEAN MUSEUM in Oxford.

Tim Murray

Falconer, Hugh (1808–1865)

Born in Scotland, Hugh Falconer graduated from Aberdeen University in 1826. Despite his interests in botany, geology, and paleontology, he went to Edinburgh University to study medicine. After graduating, and before taking up a position as surgeon with the East India Company, he spent a year in London working with the botanist Nathanial Wallich and with William Lonsdale, curator for the Geological Society of London. It was through these contacts that he finally traveled to India as a botanist rather than as a doctor.

Falconer eventually became superintendent of the East India Company's botanical gardens at Saharanpur in northern India, which allowed him to also pursue his interests in natural history in the nearby Siwalik Hills, which he dated to the Tertiary period. With the help of a military engineer, Falconer recovered a series of wonderful fossil mammals and reptiles from sites in the hills, for which he and the engineer were awarded the Geological Society of London's Wollaston Medal in 1837. Falconer's work in northern India stimulated his interest in the issue of human antiquity.

Because of illness, Falconer spent the years between 1838 and 1847 in London working on his collections at the British Museum. He returned to India and served as the superintendent of the Royal Botanic Gardens in Calcutta until 1855 when he retired from colonial service. Back in London, Falconer took up full-time paleontological research, examining fossil faunal assemblages from caves across Europe. In 1858 he met the Cornish archaeologist WILLIAM PENGELLY, and together they excavated BRIXHAM CAVE in Devon.

The results of these excavations had consequences for the extension of human antiquity, as they provided evidence for the coexistence of human beings with extinct mammals. It was with Falconer's support that geologist SIR JOSEPH PRESTWICH and the archaeologist SIR JOHN EVANS demonstrated the similarity of evidence from Brixham Cave with evidence from open sites in the Somme River valley found by the French paleontologist JACQUES BOUCHER DE PERTHES. In 1860, Falconer provided even more evidence for human antiquity through his discoveries of material at the Grotta di Maccagnone near Palermo, Sicily.

Falconer was also deeply involved in resolving the MOULIN QUIGNON controversy concerning the authenticity of human remains found France in 1863 and with the first description of the Gibraltar skull and site in 1864. He received the Royal Society's Copley Medal in 1864, was elected to the Royal Society in 1845, and was its vice-president when he died in London.

Tim Murray

Finland

The historical roots of antiquarianism and archaeology in Finland date from the era of Swedish rule, most notably from the seventeenth century when SWEDEN was a leading European power and the ideological potential of antiquities was recognized by the state. A royal decree of 1666 placed antiquities under the official protection of the state, listing ancient fortresses, earthworks, cairns, and rune stones to be protected *ad maiorem patriae gloriam,* and administration for this purpose was established. The clergy in both

Sweden and Finland were ordered to gather information on springs, groves, and stones known as sites, offerings, and sacrifices in addition to other historical data on their parishes. The early legislation and decrees had a "state-patriotic" basis—the antiquities were regarded as evidence of the glorious past of the realm.

Finland's first university, the Academy of Turku (the predecessor of the University of Helsinki), was founded in 1640. A larger number of minor published theses describing parishes and localities, prepared at the academy as part of the curriculum, regularly contained topographic information on historic sites and antiquities. The philologist and polymath Henrik Gabriel Porthan (1739–1804), professor of rhetoric (Greco-Roman literature) at the academy, was the first Finnish scholar to address the prehistory of Finland and the Finnish people with reference to the Finno-Ugrian family of languages and their speakers. Based on contemporary central European studies, Porthan presented the rudiments of the subsequently adopted "family-tree" model of the descent of the Finno-Ugrian languages and peoples, which in various forms was to define the general conception of Finnish prehistory well into the late twentieth century. Porthan was actively involved in the study of Finnish ethnography and history in addition to promoting the collection of antiquarian material.

Toward the close of the eighteenth century, clergymen in the then-province of Southern Ostrobothnia undertook excavations of prehistoric burial cairns. However, this activity did not have any broader scholarly purpose other than collection in the spirit of the Swedish botanist Carolus Linnaeus.

Finland was annexed into the Russian Empire in 1809, but as an autonomous grand duchy the country was allowed to have its own institutions of government and to keep its laws and statutes laid down during Swedish rule. With regard to prehistoric and historical antiquities, existing legislation provided for their protection, but there was no longer any official body that would handle the tasks of the former Swedish authorities. In 1827, the Academy of Turku was moved to the new capital, Helsinki, to become the University of Helsinki and the center of antiquarian and related interests well into the 1870s. This period of early national romanticism was marked by an avid collection of folk poetry and ethnographical and archaeological materials.

In the mid-nineteenth century, the archivist K. A. Bomansson undertook excavations of burial cairns in the Åland Islands to establish their cultural context, and the philologist M. A. Castrén sought to distinguish the antiquities of the Lapps (Sámi) from those of the assumedly later Finnish settlers. Castrén developed the philologically defined model of ethnic descent, suggesting that the original "home" of the Finno-Ugrians, prior to their dispersal and descent, was in the Minussinsk steppe region of western Siberia. On an expedition to Siberia in the 1850s, Castrén excavated a number of graves in Minussinsk.

Those ventures, however, were isolated. In 1863, parts of the prehistoric collections of the Museum of the University of Helsinki were published by the naturalist H. J. Holmberg in an illustrated catalog, and although Holmberg was familiar with the Scandinavian THREE-AGE SYSTEM, he had no grasp of stratigraphy, and his presentation of the material was purely theoretical—and inevitably mistaken. These isolated efforts, however, demonstrated the potential of antiquities and prehistoric artifacts as sources and promoted the adoption of systematic methods to establish a chronological basis. Working in this spirit, the historians Yrjö Koskinen and K. F. Ignatius excavated at two late–Iron Age cemeteries, dating the graves with coin finds and applying the results in a work on the early Middle Ages.

Johannes Reinhold Aspelin (1842–1915) is regarded as the founder of Finnish archaeology as a discipline in the modern sense. In response to the problems of ethnic identification of antiquities raised by his early investigations (1868–1869) of prehistoric burial cairns in Ostrobothnia, in western Finland, Aspelin undertook a study trip to Stockholm to investigate the archives and collections of the state historical museum there. In this connection, he also studied the new archaeological methods developed by OSCAR MONTELIUS and H. O. HILDEBRAND. Aspelin recognized the potential of the new methods and introduced them into the study of Finnish prehistory. At a later stage, he conducted studies in Copenhagen, making the acquaintance of J. J. A. WORSAAE and SOPHUS MÜLLER and experiencing important influences and impulses from the Danish museums and archaeological collections.

Between 1870 and 1890, Aspelin was actively involved in organizing Finland's archaeological museum collections, establishing an antiquarian administration, founding the Archaeological Society of Finland (later the Finnish Antiquarian Society), and engaging in archaeological fieldwork including expeditions to Russia. The Russian studies were primarily motivated by a quest for the "original home" of the Finno-Ugrians.

Although Aspelin was familiar, via Scandinavia, with the typological method and sought to establish chronology and a basic systematization of materials, these were not his prime concerns. The ethnic identification of materials—or the "ethnographic aspect" as it was called at the time—overrode typology and the analysis of the archaeological record in natural-scientific terms. Aspelin was no less inspired by the national-romantic paradigm of ethnic origin than his predecessors, but he managed to develop their amateur approaches into a serious scholarly inquiry corresponding to the standards of the day. Based on the work and theories of Castrén, Aspelin investigated the Ural-Altaic regions, establishing a basic chronological and spatial systematization for the area and its diverse antiquities and finds. Compared to contemporary Scandinavian scholarship, Finnish archaeology, with its linguistically defined agenda, laid claim to a far larger domain—the extensive northern Eurasian regions inhabited by the present Finno-Ugrians and their assumed ancestors. Aspelin's five-volume compendium *Antiquités du nord finno-ougrien* (1877–1884), was a monument to this concept of national prehistory.

That perspective also reflected in very practical terms Finland's political status as a grand duchy of the Russian Empire. Finland enjoyed a considerable degree of cultural and administrative autonomy that was not seriously curtailed until the "Russification" policies at the turn of the nineteenth and twentieth centuries. In principle, and often in practice, Finnish scholars were free to work and study in all parts of the vast Russian realm.

Archaeological research and antiquarian administration achieved organized forms during the last decades of the nineteenth century. The Archaeological Society of Finland was founded in 1870 to promote the official care and protection of antiquities, and in 1883, the predecessor of Finland's present Antiquities Act was passed, declaring prehistoric finds and antiquities to be the property of the state and falling under its automatic protection and the administration of the State Archaeological Commission, the predecessor of the present National Board of Antiquities. The head of the commission was known as the state archaeologist, and the first holder of this position was Aspelin. In 1893, the country's main archaeological and antiquarian collections were incorporated into a state historical museum, with separate departments for archaeological, ethnographic, and historical materials. It was later reorganized as the National Museum of Finland.

Although Aspelin held a supernumerary professorship at the University of Helsinki, there was no chair of archaeology in Finland until 1923. Finnish archaeology thus was predominantly a state concern, administered by a government office, organized into central state-owned collections, and regulated by antiquarian legislation that was among the strictest of its kind in all of Europe. This orientation was to survive almost intact until the 1970s, and it dictated the way archaeology was perceived by archaeologists and the general public alike—the culturally and nationally important work of an enlightened government. The only significant exception to this pattern of Finnish archaeologists in government service was AARNE MICHAËL TALLGREN, whose career is discussed later in this entry.

Aspelin was state archaeologist until his death, but after the early 1890s he concentrated on medieval research and left the field of archaeology to a younger generation. Hjalmar Appelgren-Kivalo (1853–1937) was his main successor. A specialist in Iron Age hill-forts and costumes, Appelgren-Kivalo became state archaeologist in

1915. He was also the founder of the journals *Suomen Museo* and *Finskt Museum.* Theodor Schvindt carried out significant studies on the Iron Age culture of Karelia, and Julius Ailio presented the first comprehensive systematization of the Stone Age in Finland.

The problem of ethnic origin as an element of national identity still dictated the theoretical orientation of Finnish archaeology. In 1905, Alfred Hackman published *Die Eisenzeit Finnlands,* a fundamental work on the Finnish Iron Age presenting a subsequently accepted model of the migration of the ancestors of the present-day Finns into western Finland from Estonia and other parts of the eastern Baltic area around the beginning of the Common Era. Hackman's colonization theory assumed the depopulation of Finland in the last centuries before the birth of Christ, with only bands of nomadic "Lapps" hunting and fishing in its wilderness regions. One of the reasons for the depopulation was a cooling of the climate. Hackman's theory also posited a gradual spread of the Finnish colonists, with the country pushing the Lapps further north in a manner analogous to the spread of European settlement into the western parts of North America. It also presupposed a "Gothic," i.e., eastern Baltic, influence on the Finnish language. Although Ailio disputed the theory, suggesting that the Finns were in fact descendants of the Stone Age population, Hackman's model remained the accepted explanation of Iron Age ethnic developments until the late 1960s and early 1970s.

With analyses and syntheses of northern Eurasian Bronze and Iron Age materials, Aarne Michaël Tallgren began his career by addressing the problems of archaeologically identifying and defining the "original" Finno-Ugrian culture. Tallgren's thesis of 1911 conclusively proved that Aspelin's original assumption of a Ural-Altaic Bronze Age culture, identifiable as Finno-Ugrian, was incorrect. Although Finnish archaeologists now rejected the straightforward interpretation of northern Russian and Eurasian archaeological cultures in terms of Finno-Ugrian ethnogenesis, the philological paradigm of ethnic prehistory dating back to Castrén and his predecessors persisted. The changing of perspective for archaeologists and prehistorians was also dictated by political developments. Finland gained its national independence in 1917, and the new Soviet Russia closed its borders to western researchers. With his encyclopedic knowledge and fruitful contacts, Tallgren remained the sole representative of the Eurasian orientation of Finnish archaeology.

During the years between the two world wars, newly independent Finland carried on the processes of cultural nation building that had been launched in the late nineteenth century. Although archaeology had a definite role within this broad paradigm, prevailing ideological trends were reflected only indirectly in scholarship and perhaps more in the general concerns and areas of interest than in specific content or conclusions.

Though practiced professionally on a full-time basis by only a very small group of experts, Finnish archaeology had developed into a full-fledged discipline by the 1920s. The University of Helsinki established a chair of archaeology in 1923, with Tallgren as its first holder. Tallgren was fundamentally a liberal who distanced himself from the narrow-minded nationalist sentiments that emerged in Finland in the 1920s and 1930s, and his influence was possibly instrumental in helping Finnish archaeology avoid the nationalist overtones that emerged in central Europe in the interwar years. Tallgren's *Suomen muinaisuus* [Antiquity of Finland], a general presentation of Finnish prehistory published in 1930, also reflected a sober attitude toward the nationalist fervor that surfaced in other fields. In general, archaeology in the 1920s and 1930s followed an explicitly antiquarian and typological line.

Aarne Äyräpää (1887–1971) was the leading Stone Age expert of the inter– and post–world war years. He applied the results of geological studies on shoreline displacement and land upheaval, based on the fact that the hunter-gatherer sites of the Stone Age were predominantly shore-bound and could thus be linked to ancient shorelines in a broad chronological system. Äyräpää's typological and stylistic classification of Comb Ware and other Stone Age pottery has remained largely valid to the present day. Äyräpää held a supernumerary (honorary) professorship in archaeology from 1938 until 1954.

Ella Kivikoski (1902–1990) began her career in the 1930s, and by the time she was appointed professor of archaeology at the University of Helsinki in 1948, she had become an undisputed expert on the Iron Age. Kivikoski was not drawn to broad theories or far-reaching conclusions; she stressed the importance of sound classification and typology as opposed to transient interpretations. Kivikoski's 1948 systematization of Finnish Iron Age materials (*Suomen Rautakauden kuvasto,* two volumes published in revised form as *Die Eisenzeit Finnlands* in 1973) have remained standard works. Kivikoski also published a prehistory of Finland in 1961.

Of Kivikoski's contemporaries, Ville Luho was a leading expert on the Mesolithic Stone Age, and C. F. Meinander succeeded Kivikoski in the chair of archaeology at the University of Helsinki. Meinander's doctoral thesis of 1954 was on the Bronze Age, and one of his main contributions was to revise the hitherto accepted view of depopulation, which preceded the assumed colonization by the ancestors of the Finns in the early Iron Age. With reference to the early–Iron Age ceramic traditions of southern Finland, Meinander argued that there had never been any interruption of settlement in the Bronze Age or early Metal Age. These suggestions were borne out by radiocarbon dates in the 1970s. Meinander's conclusions became the basis of a new "theory of continued settled" that replaced the older model of colonization formulated by Alfred Hackman in 1905.

The 1960s and 1970s witnessed growing collaboration between archaeology and the natural sciences. The introduction of radiocarbon dating was of prime importance, but the ongoing tradition of cooperation with palynologists and paleobotanists was also established. Cooperation with Quaternary geologists had been established since the late 1920s, and new chronological syntheses of data related to Stone Age settlements were presented in the 1970s by Ari Siiriäinen, who succeeded Meinander as professor of archaeology in Helsinki. Torsten Edgren's work includes classifications and syntheses of Stone Age materials, notably sub-Neolithic Jäkärlä Ware and Corded Ware pottery in Finland. Edgren has also published a basic general presentation of Finnish prehistory.

Iron Age research was carried on by Aarni Erä-Esko and Pirkko-Liisa Lehtosalo-Hilander, the latter conducting extensive excavations and material studies of the Luistari cemetery at Eura in southwestern Finland. Her publications of the Luistari finds in the 1980s and 1990s have become new standard works on Viking-age material culture. A leading younger expert on the Iron Age is Jussi-Pekka Taavitsainen, professor of archaeology at the University of Turku in southwestern Finland. His predecessor was Unto Salo, a specialist in the Bronze Age. The chair of archaeology at the University of Turku was established in the 1960s, and academic teaching in archaeology has also spread to the University of Oulu in northern Finland.

The 1980s and 1990s were years of diversification in Finnish archaeology. Along with its official legislated role of protecting and salvaging prehistoric and historic antiquities, and despite the vagaries of government funding, the National Board of Antiquities also carried out research projects related to specific goals, particularly in Iron Age studies. At the University of Helsinki, Meinander sought to introduce aspects of "the new archaeology" as opposed to the nontheoretical and traditionally typological orientation of the discipline. On the other hand, growing collaboration with the natural sciences introduced a strict positivist trend that left little room for syntheses of cultural history. Siiriäinen, in turn, established active international contacts and research projects abroad, particularly in the Third World, with particular emphasis on cultural ecology and related processual approaches. The 1980s also saw the advent of postprocessual developments, with a return to the goals of historiography and anthropology. A variety of new archaeological approaches also emerged at the universities of Turku and Oulu in the late 1990s.

Jüri Kokkonen

References

Kivikoski, Ella. 1954. "A. M. Tallgren." *Eurasia Septentrionalis Antiqua,* supplementary volume.

———. 1960. *Tehty työ elää: A. M. Tallgren 1885–1945.* Helsinki.

Kokkonen, Jüri. 1985. "Aarne Michaël Tallgren and Eurasia septentrionalis antiqua." *Fennoscandia Archaeologica* 2.

———. 1993. "Archaeology Goes Postmodern." *Fennoscandia Archaelogica* 10.

Nordman, C. A. 1968. *Archaeology in Finland before 1920*. History of Learning and Science in Finland 1828–1918. Helsinki.

Tallgren, A. M. 1936. "Geschichte der antiquarischen Forschung in Finnland." *Eurasia Septentrionalis Antiqua* 10.

Tommila, Päiviö, ed. 2000. Suomen tieteen historia 2. Humanistiset ja yhteiskuntatieteet. Porvoo-Helsinki-Juva.

Fleure, Herbert J. (1877–1969)

Born on the English Channel island of Guernsey, Herbert J. Fleure as a child was kept isolated and on the island by ill health until he was fourteen, and his interests in natural history and Darwinian theory were encouraged. In 1897, he won a scholarship to Aberystwyth University College in Wales where he read zoology, geology, and botany. In 1904, he took up a fellowship at the Zoological Institute in Zurich, SWITZERLAND, where he studied physical anthropology and marine biology. He returned to Aberystwyth to work as lecturer in geology, zoology, and geography, and in 1910, he became professor of zoology and a lecturer in geography.

In 1917, Fleure became professor of anthropology and geography at Aberystwyth, uniting these two disciplines to develop concepts of human physical and social evolution in diverse environments worldwide. At this time the study of geography was in its infancy, and Fleure realized and taught its full potential and popularized it in books such as *The Peoples of Europe* (1922).

Fleure was also influenced by physical anthropologist SIR GRAFTON ELLIOT SMITH's ideas about the Neolithic period and the invention of agriculture and by RAPHAEL PUMPELLY's "oasis hypothesis," which he wrote about with HAROLD PEAKE in *The Corridors of Time* (1927–1956), a widely read ten-volume series about prehistory.

In 1930, Fleure became professor of geography at Manchester University in England, between 1949 and 1950, he was professor at both Alexandria and Cairo Universities, and in 1946, he was made honorary lecturer at University College, London. He published his large *Natural History of Man in Britain* in 1951, a work that was to become a classic. He was the first professional geographer to be made a fellow of the Royal Society in 1936, and he was president of Royal Anthropological Institute and its Huxley Medallist and lecturer in 1937.

Tim Murray

Florida and the Caribbean Basin, Historical Archaeology in

The post-1492 history of the Caribbean Basin has been largely defined by colonialism. It has the longest colonial history in the Americas, with the first European colony in the region established in 1493 and the last European colonies and American commonwealths remaining there until 1995. This time depth is accompanied by a cultural diversity unparalleled elsewhere in the post-Columbian Americas. The Caribbean Basin is the only region in the hemisphere in which American Indian, Spanish, French, English, Danish, Dutch, African, and Euro-American people established societies and claimed political dominion during the colonial era. At least partly because of this complexity, relatively few historians and even fewer archaeologists have treated the circum-Caribbean area as a coherent unit (for one of a number of exceptions see Williams 1970). Instead, its written history—to which historical archaeology is inextricably linked—has been largely defined and organized by discrete episodes of European and North American intervention and involvement in the region.

Historical archaeology as used here refers to the archaeological investigation of sites occupied after 1492 for which both written documents and European technology are pertinent to interpretation. This endeavor has been largely a twentieth-century phenomenon not only in the Caribbean region but throughout the Americas as well. Both avocational and professional historical archaeologists in the Caribbean Basin and Florida have addressed questions related to an exceptionally diverse array of cultural and ethnic groups, time periods, site types, historical questions, and anthropological problems over the past century, during which changing social philosophies, national interests, and technologies have additionally affected the orientations and outcomes of archaeology (*see* Patterson 1991; Sued Badillo 1996). Despite recent criticism that historical archaeology in the region has been unfruitful and dominated by concerns defined by European hegemony (Sued Badillo 1992), twentieth-century historical archaeological research in Florida and the Caribbean has, in fact, addressed questions of internal development, indigenous American identity and colonialism for several decades.

The following discussion of the history of that work in the Caribbean and Florida is ordered in a general way by the chronology of archaeological research in the region; however, it should be emphasized that equally important organizational distinctions for historical archaeology in the Caribbean are provided by the dominant postcontact cultural distinctions of the region—that is, American Indian, African, Spanish, French, English, and Dutch—as well as by the traditional geographic distinctions—that is, the Lesser Antilles, the Greater Antilles, the Bahamas, Florida, and the mainland Caribbean coasts. These will be incorporated as necessary.

The chronology of circum-Caribbean historical archaeology is organized here for convenience by four somewhat artificial and overlapping periods, which nevertheless correspond roughly to paradigmatic and political developments in the region. These include: (1) the period before 1935 and the formalization of professional archaeology, (2) the years of ca. 1935–1970, (3) the period between ca. 1970 and 1990, and (4) the Quincentennial-dominated post-1985 period.

Historical Archaeology before 1935

A few essentially archaeological studies of post-Columbian sites took place in Florida and the Caribbean before 1930; however these were generally undertaken by historians or other non-specialists to commemorate the anniversary of a historic event or a famous European person. In 1767 for example, the French geographer Moreau de St. Mery attempted through survey and collection to locate and identify the site of La Navidad, the first fort that Columbus was forced to establish in Haiti after the wreck of the *Santa Maria* in 1492. In the process, he inadvertently identified the site of Puerto Real, a sixteenth-century Spanish town, as La Navidad (Moreau de St. Mery 1958; Hodges 1995). Another early archaeological effort to study Columbus was that commissioned by the North American Commission for the Observance of the Columbian Quadricentennial in 1891. The U.S. Navy vessel *Enterprise* was sent to the site of La Isabela in the Dominican Republic, which was the first settlement intentionally established by Christopher Columbus in the Americas. The site was surveyed, mapped, and described by Navy Lt. Colvocorresses (Thatcher 1903).

Little historical archaeology was attempted in Florida or the Caribbean Basin during the early twentieth century, and most information about postcontact archaeological sites was buried as footnotes or ancillary observation in studies of pre-Columbian sites (e.g., Hatt 1932). One notable exception to this was the work of William Goodwin in Jamaica. A businessman who went to the West Indies in 1915 to recover from nervous prostration, Goodwin began a long-term study of the early Spanish and English ruins of Jamaica, occasionally studying presumed Spanish ruins in Florida as a comparison (Goodwin 1946). Between 1911 and 1937 he mapped and excavated a series of colonial sites on the island, including what was probably the first underwater search for Columbus's caravel ships (Goodwin 1946, 46–55), and collaborated with local collectors and antiquarians to document many of Jamaica's historic colonial remains. It was not until after 1935, however, that the largely idiosyncratic interest in monumental sites and highly visible historical events manifested by nineteenth- and early-twentieth-century investigators coalesced into the discipline of archaeology in Florida and the Caribbean. From this time onward, historical archaeology was practiced consistently, if eclectically, in the region.

1935 to ca. 1970

Some of the earliest explicitly intentional historical archaeology in the Americas was carried out in Florida and the Caribbean during the 1930s and 1940s, most of it devoted to the Spanish colonial presence in the region, and much of it dominated by North American concerns. These projects reflect the diffuse nature of American historical archaeology at that time, both in the reasons for doing archaeology and in the people who did it. Avocational archaeologists, for example, played a central role during this period in the development of historical archaeology in the region.

A major emphasis was the study of monumental sites for purposes of historical interpretation, not only by archaeologists but often by historians or architects. Other concerns of the period addressed primarily by archaeologists were questions of artifact classification and chronology and of Spanish influence on, and the acculturation of, the American Indians of the region. All of these themes have endured as important emphases in the historical archaeology of Florida and the Caribbean to the present day.

Three developments in the United States at this time shaped the direction of historical (and pre-Columbian) archaeology. The establishment of the SOCIETY FOR AMERICAN ARCHAEOLOGY in 1935 marked the formalization of professional archaeology in the Americas. Although prehistory was the primary concern of the Society, its establishment focused professional consensus on appropriate archaeological questions and methodologies, which in 1935 were predominantly those of classification and chronology (see Dunnell 1986; Willey and Sabloff 1980, 73–74). This coincided with the establishment of the United States Works Progress Administration Program of the 1930s, which provided some of the first opportunities to develop and implement these archaeological methodologies on historic sites.

The end of this period was marked by the emergence of historical archaeology as a recognized discipline, signaled by the establishment of the Conference on Historic Sites Archaeology. This annual conference was first organized by Stanley South in 1960, and was held in conjunction with the Southeastern Archaeological Conference (see South 1994). Florida historical archaeologists John Goggin, John Griffin, Hale

Smith and Charles Fairbanks were particularly active in the conference, and the first four conference proceedings were published in the *Florida Anthropologist*. During the 1960s the conference was largely devoted to what Goggin called the "brass tacks" of historical archaeology, "to the kind of details that archaeologists deal with. In other words my feeling is that as archaeologists we deal with artifacts, and with few exceptions colonial artifacts have not been analyzed or classified by a method suitable for the archaeologists to handle" (South 1964, 34). Resolving this problem was to be one of the enduring themes of historical archaeology after 1960.

The Development of Enduring Themes:
Spanish Towns and Monuments
St. Augustine, Florida—the United States' oldest European settlement—was an early beneficiary of the U.S. Works Progress Administration program. A program of survey, excavation, and study of historical resources was undertaken jointly from 1935 to 1937 by the Federal Works Project Administration, the Carnegie Institution of Washington, D.C., and the St. Augustine Historical Society. The work was explicitly multidisciplinary, involving archaeologists, historians, and architects, and it emphasized monumental sites in its attempt to archaeologically study and partially reconstruct the Spanish defensive systems in the colony (Chatelaine 1941). The archaeological program initiated in St. Augustine during this period has continued to the present day, evolving to incorporate questions of Spanish acculturation and the development and recognition of colonial identity (see Cusick 1994; Deagan 1983; Deagan 1991).

Interest in monumental sites associated with early Spanish presence was sustained throughout the period, often in support of restoration and public interpretation of sites. The historical archaeology of the sites of forts and towns in Florida during this period was continued in St. Augustine at the Castillo de San Marcos in 1947 and 1953 and at several domestic sites in the town by Smith and Griffin (*see* Deagan 1991, xvi-xvii; xxv-xxiv). Elsewhere in Florida, investigation was initiated at other seventeenth- and

Drawing of St. Augustine, Florida (Ann Ronan Picture Library)

eighteenth-century Spanish frontier forts, including San Luis (Boyd, Smith, and Griffin 1951), Fort Pupo (Goggin 1951), and at San Marcos de Apalache on the Gulf coast (Smith 1956:76–77). The site of Santa Rosa Pensacola, Florida (1720–1752) was also located and studied during this period (Smith 1965).

Spanish forts and town sites were also among the first subjects of historical archaeology in the Caribbean. One of the first restoration-oriented Spanish colonial archaeological projects in the region was carried out in Puerto Rico by historian Adolfo de Hostos at the site of Caparra. The remains of the monumental stone structure and its associated artifacts were thought to be remnants of Ponce de Leon's palace, in which he lived as the first governor of Puerto Rico (Pantel et al. 1988). Thirty years later another large-scale excavation in San Juan was carried out at the fortress of El Morro by Smith, also in support of renovation and restoration (Smith 1962; Manucy and Torres Reyes 1973).

Excavations were conducted by C. S. Cotter, a plantation agent and avocational archaeologist

in Jamaica, at the site of Sevilla Nueva in 1937–38 (Cotter 1948; Goodwin 1946, 11). The site is exceptional for the architecture and ornate masonry work uncovered there, which manifests some of the earliest known American-European artistic syncretism (Cotter 1948). Investigations were continued by Cotter under the auspices of the Institute of Jamaica in 1953 (Cotter 1970; Woodward 1988), and a major program of excavation was carried out at the Sevilla Nueva between 1982 and 1990 by Spanish archaeologist Lorenzo Lopez y Sebastián.

Archaeological investigations (1515–1545) at the Spanish settlement of Nueva Cádiz, Venezuela, began in the late 1940s with the work of Alfredo Boulton and José M. Cruxent (Cruxent and Rouse 1958, 58–60), with excavations continuing sporadically into the 1960s (Willis 1976). Nueva Cádiz was established to take advantage of the rich pearl beds located in 1598 near the island of Margarita, off the coast of Venezuela. It was essentially a single-resource extractive community, to which large numbers of Caribbean Indians were relocated and enslaved. The archaeological work there provided one of the first materially based descriptions of the conditions under which Caribbean Indians were enslaved and exploited, and underscored the dramatic differences in the lives of the Spaniards and Indians inhabiting the city (Cruxent and Rouse 1958; Willis 1976). The materials from Nueva Cádiz also formed an important baseline resource for understanding the first half of the sixteenth century and for Spanish colonial material remains DATING.

One of the most intensive and long-lived programs of historical archaeology in Spanish town sites began in the Dominican Republic in the 1940s. Intermittent excavations continued at La Isabela through the period (Puig-Ortiz 1972), and investigation was begun at the early-sixteenth-century site of Concepción de la Vega (Palm 1952). Another building thought to be a residence of Ponce de Leon was later studied in the Higuey region of the Dominican Republic (Boyrie-Moya 1964).

Historical archaeology in the Dominican Republic became particularly active during the 1950s and 1960s, when a major program of investigation began in Santo Domingo, in support of restoration and interpretation efforts of the sixteenth-century section of the city. Excavations during this time contributed primarily to the mitigation of threatened sites, the interpretation of Spanish colonial presence to the tourist public, and the beginnings of the systematization of Spanish colonial material culture. The results of much of this work are summarized in a large and varied literature (*see* Nieves Sicart 1980; Ortega 1982; Pérez Montás 1984). Archaeology in Santo Domingo continued into the 1990s with much the same objectives, and was greatly stimulated in the 1980s by the observation of the Columbian Quincentenary (Veloz Maggiolo and Ortega 1992).

*Spanish-Indian Interaction
and Transculturation*

Not all of the historical archaeology in Florida and the Caribbean was oriented toward descriptive or restoration goals during this period. Several pioneers of American historical archaeology, including Griffin, Smith, Goggin, José Cruxent, Francisco Prat Puig and Fairbanks developed active programs in Florida and the Caribbean between 1940 and 1960. They were explicitly interested in the mechanisms and consequences of European-American Indian contact, primarily from the perspective of the American Indians (see Smith 1956).

Among the most important elements of these programs were the Florida missions, which provided the focus for some of the first anthropologically oriented historical archaeology in the United States. In 1934, a historic-period Indian burial ground was discovered on the grounds of the Fountain of Youth Park tourist attraction in St. Augustine by archaeologist J. Ray Dickson, and the site was identified by SMITHSONIAN INSTITUTION archaeologist Matthew Stirling as a probable Spanish mission. Archaeological and physical anthropological research at the mission site and surrounding areas has been carried out at the site intermittently since then for more than sixty years, not only focusing on the Timucua village associated with the mission, but also locating the original site of St Augustine (Chaney and Deagan 1989).

The focus of mission archaeology was explicitly defined by Griffin and Smith during the 1940s when they undertook the study of several seventeenth-century Spanish missions in order to better understand the responses of the Florida Indians to Spanish colonization and evangelization (Boyd, Smith, and Griffin 1951; Smith 1956). Recent assessments of this work, as well as syntheses of mission archaeology into the 1990s can be found in Thomas 1990, among others.

Questions of interaction and transculturation between Spaniards and American Indians in settings other than missions were the focus of considerable archaeological attention during the 1930s and 1940s, and were centered on Cuba, due largely to the influence of anthropologist Fernando Ortíz. Not only were a number of contact period Indian sites located and recorded, but some of the first explicit theoretical attention was paid to the processes of transculturation in the contact period (Ortíz 1983). This was largely owing to the activities of the Grupo Guamá, an organization of archaeologists committed to the archaeological investigation of Caribbean history, prehistory, and art. Organized and based in Cuba, the group also included archaeologists from the Dominican Republic, Venezuela, and North America, and sponsored projects and expeditions throughout the Caribbean Basin. The Grupo Guamá was active during the 1940s and 1950s, and during that time laid the groundwork for much subsequent Spanish colonial and contact-period Taino archaeology in the West Indies. This emphasis, too, has continued in Cuba to the present time (*see* Dominguez and Pantoja 1992; Fariñas Gutierrez 1992).

Tools of Chronology and Classification

A significant amount of pre-1970 historical archaeology in Florida and the Caribbean was undertaken specifically to develop classificatory and chronological tools. The most notable and broadly based of these efforts were Goggin's comprehensive studies of Spanish majolica (a tin-enameled earthenware pottery) and Spanish Olive Jars (storage containers) (Goggin 1960a, and 1958, respectively). Goggin not only drew from existing collections but also initiated surveys, surface collections, and excavations throughout Florida and the Caribbean between 1949 and 1957 in order to recover well-dated samples of majolica to use in a dated typological seriation (Goggin 1968). The result was a detailed classification of majolica using the then-standard North American Midwestern Taxonomic system. Despite criticism of his typological system, Goggin's majolica study has remained a reliable classificatory and dating system since its publication, with only minor revision (Deagan 1987).

Sunken Towns and Ships
Systematic underwater historical archaeology in Florida and the Caribbean began during the 1950s with a series of investigations loosely coordinated by Mendel Peterson of the Smithsonian Institution (see Peterson 1965, 5–17). Various shipwrecks, including those of the Spanish treasure fleets and British privateers sunk in Florida were studied; however the most important project of this period was at the sunken city of Port Royal, Jamaica. The British colonial city was plunged into the sea by an earthquake in 1692 and remained submerged as a seventeenth-century time capsule. Edwin and Marion Link, avocational archaeologists working with Peterson and a team of U.S. Navy divers, began investigation of the site in 1956 to identify sunken structures and recover evidence of life in seventeenth-century Port Royal (Link 1960).

Archaeological research at the site has continued to the present day under the auspices of the Jamaican government, carried out from 1965 to 1968 by Robert Marx (Marx 1973), and during the 1980s and 1990s by the Institute for Nautical Archaeology at Texas A&M University under the direction of Donald Hamilton (Hamilton 1992). Through Texas A&M's involvement, Port Royal became the site of one of the few academic field training programs in underwater archaeology in the Americas. Port Royal is also one of the few colonial sites in the hemisphere at which underwater and terrestrial excavations have been conducted simultaneously, in order to coordinate the study of submerged remains with those buried remains not drowned by the 1692 earthquake.

Meanwhile in Florida, developments in shipwreck excavation shaped a very different kind of trajectory for underwater archaeology in the state, which until recently was defined by the search for sunken treasure. The first organized treasure hunting consortium in Florida, Real Eight, was formed during 1959 and 1960 through the efforts of Kip Wagner and Mel Fischer. Real Eight received permits from the State of Florida to salvage several wrecks off the east coast, with 25 percent of the recovered value going back to the State of Florida. Archaeologists Goggin and William Sears provided oversight for both the projects and the division of remains, but by 1964 fiscal and contractual problems resulted in the appointment of Florida's first State Underwater Archaeologist, Carl Clausen (*see* Burgess and Clausen 1982; Wagner and Taylor 1972). The State Underwater Archaeologist was assigned to manage and oversee the study and salvage of Florida's marine resources, and the position as well as the permitting partnerships have been maintained since that time.

Once consequence of these early developments in Florida's marine archaeology program was the sustained interest of Goggin in underwater archaeology. Goggin and Fairbanks encouraged the incorporation of submerged archaeological data with terrestrial research in a way that has rarely been seen since that time. Goggin's early interest in underwater historical archaeology was focused on a variety of sites and materials submerged in rivers and springs, including isolated finds, mission refuse, Seminole materials, and abandoned settlements (Goggin 1960b; Fairbanks 1964).

Despite the level of activity and the diversity of interests in the historical archaeology of Florida and the Caribbean during the period from 1935 to 1970, the field was not formally recognized as a coherent school, specialty, or subdiscipline within the wider archaeological community until the 1960s. The Conference on Historic Sites Archaeology was organized by Stanley South and many of the Florida historical archaeologists (*see* South 1994), publishing its first several proceedings in the *Florida Anthropologist*. The primary professional organ for

Caribbean archaeology was not established until 1965 with the name "The International Congress for the Study of pre-Columbian Man in the Lesser Antilles," and the first congress paper with an explicitly historical-archaeological theme was not included in the Congress Proceedings until 1977 (Garcia Arévalo 1978b). In 1979 the archaeologists in the region decided to change the name of the congress to "The International Congress for Caribbean Archaeology" to reflect the broader temporal and geographical interests of archaeology in the Caribbean that developed after 1970.

Historical Archaeology, 1970–1990

Historical archaeology in both Florida and the Caribbean region expanded considerably in scope and in intensity after 1970 as a consequence of political and professional developments at both the international and regional levels. The decade of the 1960s was one of widespread political change in the Caribbean, with seven British colonial nations gaining independence between 1962 and 1974 and the communist revolution in Cuba in 1959. These events ultimately directed historical archaeology toward questions of colonialism and American cultural identity near the end of the period.

One of the most influential professional developments was the gradual formalization through the 1960s of American historical archaeology as a distinct discipline, with the expansion of the Conference on Historic Sites Archaeology, and the formal establishment of the SOCIETY FOR HISTORICAL ARCHAEOLOGY in 1967 (*see* South 1994). The latter event marked the advent of a conscious self-identification of historical archaeology as a social science distinct from both prehistoric archaeology and from history, with its own set of theoretical and methodological principles, and therefore a distinct set of guiding questions. One of the most important of these for historical archaeology in the circum-Caribbean was the explicit general recognition that the encounter between Europe and America—which first took place in this region—was one between literate and nonliterate people, and that systematic investigation of that world-changing process required both archaeo-

logical and documentary information. Historical archaeology was the only field that developed and articulated such an approach.

Archaeologists working in Cuba had been among the first to explicitly address these issues, as well as others that focussed on colonialism. The Cuban revolution of 1958 promoted active attention among Cuban historians and archaeologists toward questions of cultural origins and national identity. For much of the subsequent three decades, during which cold war politics dominated the globe, Cuban historical archaeology was relatively isolated from the rest of the Caribbean. Cuban archaeologists during this period continued to work on the questions of transculturation and social dynamics posed during the previous period by the Grupo Guamá, but their inquiries came to be informed by Marxist theory and a concern with the dialectics of property and class considerably before these paradigms emerged in mainstream American archaeology.

The formalization of historical archaeology coincided with the emergence and general acceptance of what came to be known as the new archaeology, which called for attention to dynamic cultural processes rather than to the structural culture histories that had dominated earlier periods (*see* Dunnell 1986). These concerns had a profound effect on the kinds of questions asked by historical as well as pre-Columbian archaeologists in Florida and in the Caribbean, and in the methods used to answer them. Subsistence strategies and environmental adaptations, for example, figured prominently in frameworks for investigation, and required the incorporation of multidisciplinary specialists in the natural sciences in addition to those in history and architecture. Although some interdisciplinary research, such as Elizabeth Wing's pioneering study of food remains from Nueva Cádiz (1961), had been carried out in the Caribbean and Florida before 1970 the involvement of multidisciplinary scholars did not become standard in the historical archaeology of the region until after about 1975.

A third important influence on historical archaeology throughout the Americas during this period was the increased consciousness of and legal attention to cultural resources management issues. This was particularly influential in those areas under formal U.S. government jurisdiction after the passage of the Moss-Bennett Bill in 1974, as well as in Cuba after the establishment of the Castro government. Although legislation mandating survey and mitigation of archaeological sites was not universal throughout the Caribbean, the management of cultural resources for the preservation of cultural patrimony and the potential for tourism was nearly so.

Serious attention was given to the definition of national identities and the management of historic sites, and this encouraged the development of programs throughout the region that were designed to recover information relevant to public interpretation.

Developments in marine archaeology during this period were closely tied to the management of historical archaeological resources on land. Research-oriented archaeology of shipwrecks evolved into an important, if controversial, emphasis in the historical archaeology of Florida and the Caribbean during the period from 1970 to 1990, paralleled by an even greater growth in treasure hunting and salvaging of shipwrecks for commercial reasons.

These developments directed the course of historical archaeology in Florida and the Caribbean after 1970 in several ways. One was by encouraging explicitly historical archaeological research unrelated to the specific concerns of prehistoric archaeology or of historic monument restoration, and by placing stronger emphasis on systemic questions of encounter and acculturation, colonialism, capitalism, and slavery, and less emphasis on chronology and classification. Archaeologists in general became more interested in cross-cultural studies as a way to address some of these questions, and increasingly turned archaeological attention to non-Spanish and postcolonial historic sites for the first time. This broadening of focus was also encouraged by the requirements of cultural resources management programs aimed at cultural patrimony in newly independent nations, which brought attention to bear on both non-Spanish and post colonial sites. This trend has been perhaps most notable in the initiation and rapid growth of effort devoted to African-American archaeology since 1970.

It should be noted that a number of programs continued research after 1970 to refine and enhance the understanding of historic material culture classification, chronology, and interpretation. Such efforts built upon and extended the work begun in the previous period (*see* Cruxent and Vaz 1975; Deagan 1987; Marken 1994).

The formalization of historical archaeology as an entity was reflected in both Florida and the Caribbean during this period in the training of archaeologists. Formal training in historical archaeology was provided at the state universities of Florida by Fairbanks, Smith, and Griffin and led to many of the historical archaeological programs ongoing in the Caribbean and Florida. Another training program with far-reaching influence on Caribbean historical archaeology was the *Curso de restauracion de bienes muebles especializado en ceramologia historica*. This program was established in Panamá in 1974 under the auspices of the Organization of American States and the Instituto de Cultura de Panamá, and continued for a decade under the direction of José M. Cruxent (Cruxent 1976, 1980).

Basic methods for excavation methodology and artifact classification—including those of historical archaeology—were taught in the program, which trained archaeological technicians from throughout Latin America and the Caribbean.

Cultural Resources Management
In some areas, such as San Juan, Santo Domingo, and St. Augustine, management programs built upon the studies of monumental sites that dominated the pre-1970 period, and were intensified by formal programs of cultural resources management. In other areas, programs of urban cultural resources management archaeology began during this period, including in Havana (Cuba), Pensacola (Florida), and Spanish Town (Jamaica). In all of these areas historical archaeologists are still attempting to accompany the rapid growth and development in these cities, to salvage sites, and to trace the cities' architectural and economic evolution.

The 1970s also marked the initiation of programs that concentrated on rural sites and regional landscapes in areas occupied by English, Dutch, African, and French colonists. The impetus for these efforts was often provided initially by historical architects in the region, working with international and national historic preservation organizations such as the International Council of Monuments and Sites (ICOMOS), the Organization of American States (OAS) and the United Nations Educational, Scientific and Cultural Organization (UNESCO). Between 1978 and 1982 historic preservation architects and archaeologists from throughout the Caribbean, coordinated by Eugenio Pérez Montás of the Dominican Republic, worked on the development of a region-wide plan for historic preservation. Plan CARIMOS (Plan for Monuments and Sites in the Wider Caribbean) was formalized at the University of Florida in 1982, with its seat established in Santo Domingo. Since that time, CARIMOS, working with the OAS, UNESCO, ICOMOS, and the University of Florida's Preservation Institute–Caribbean (PIC) has been an important force in the intensification and diversification of historical archaeology throughout the Caribbean. (For summaries of CARIMOS activities *see* Pérez Montás 1991.)

Underwater Archaeology
Much of the marine archaeology during the period from 1970 to 1990 also developed in the context of the management of resources for public interpretation and, with the exception of Port Royal, was dominated by shipwrecks of the Spanish treasure fleets and explorers (see Burgess and Clausen 1982; Borrell 1983; Marx and Marx 1993; Smith 1993). The necessity for protecting underwater resources and developing a broad base of public support for noncommercial marine archaeology led to programs of site protection and public interpretation throughout the region. In some areas, such as the Dominican Republic and Florida, a significant part of underwater archaeology was carried out through joint efforts between private salvers, recreational sport divers, and government archaeological agencies. The Comisión de Rescate Arqueólogico Submarino was established in the Dominican Re-

public in 1979 to oversee the management and study of the submerged historic resources of the Dominican Republic. The Comisión, coordinated by Pedro Borrell, worked closely with the Grupo de Investigaciones Submarinas, Inc., a group of professional and avocational divers and archaeologists, and the commercial firm of Caribe Salvage, Inc. to study and interpret many of the vast number of shipwrecks along the country's north coast (see Borrell 1983). This ongoing effort is still under way.

Florida during this period was the location of some of the earliest underwater historical archaeological parks in the region. The U.S. National Park Service established Fort Jefferson National Monument (today known as Dry Tortugas National Park) near Key West in 1935, and Biscayne National Park in southeast Florida in 1968. Underwater surveys were first undertaken at these sites in 1970 and 1975 by George Fischer of the National Park Service, and continue.

Shipwrecks in Florida were both studied and salvaged (often simultaneously) during this period. Although most of the shipwrecks were investigated by private salvage companies operating under permits issued by the state, academic and governmental research programs increased toward the end of the period. Unlike the initial days of public-private partnerships, the projects of the 1970s and 1980s, such as the excavation of the controversial *Atocha,* were often conducted by professional marine archaeologists working for private companies (Matthewson 1986). A heated debate over the conduct and ethics of underwater archaeology for commercial purposes was born during the 1970s, centering on the issues of professional methods and the ethics of selling artifacts. The debate remains vigorously unresolved.

The Institute of Nautical Archaeology (INA) at Texas A&M University, through the efforts of George Bass, Donald Keith, and Donny Hamilton, was also an important influence on the development marine archaeology in the Caribbean and in Florida during this period. Through the 1980s INA initiated a series of academic marine survey and study projects in the Caribbean that were intended to illuminate the evolution of ship architecture and maritime economy in the re-

Crewmen on a commercial salvage expedition lift a bronze cannon, believed to be from the galleon Atocha. *The* Atocha, *which sank in a hurricane in 1622, was believed to be carrying $100 million in gold and silver. (© Bettmann/Corbis)*

gion. Late-fifteenth and early-sixteenth-century ships of discovery and exploration provided a primary focus for the INA efforts, at least partly in anticipation of the 1992 Quincentenary of Columbus's voyages of exploration. Survey and testing were carried out in the Dominican Republic, Jamaica, the Bahamas, and Panamá.

Programs of marine archaeology were begun in several non-Spanish areas of the Caribbean toward the end of the period between 1970 and 1990 (*see* Bequette 1991), offering a systematic basis for international comparisons of circum-Caribbean maritime technology and economy.

Transculturation, Adaptation, and the Euro-American Experience

The emphasis on culture contact and interaction exhibited by archaeologists during the period from 1970 to 1990 had strong roots in the previous period, particularly in the research of the Grupo Guamá and the work in the Florida missions. Unlike historical archaeology in the earlier period, however, research on European-American contact and interaction after 1970 was concerned with adaptations in Euro-American as well as in Native American society. This interest corresponded in the Caribbean to the increasing influence of nationalism that pervaded the Caribbean after World War II and particularly through the 1960s (see Sued Badillo 1996; Williams 1970, 463–478).

Long-term multidisciplinary programs of historical archaeology were undertaken in several Spanish-American town sites, building on work begun in the previous period. While the pre-1970 projects had been devoted primarily to the excavation and reconstruction of monumental remains, the later projects were intended to better understanding of the adaptive processes and resulting Creole cultural forms of post-Columbian America (*see* Deagan 1988), and were often carried out by interdisciplinary teams of researchers. These have included Santo Domingo (1502–present) and Concepción de la Vega (1498–1562) in the Dominican Republic, Puerto Real in Haiti (1503–1578), Havana, Cuba (1511–present), St. Augustine, Florida (1565–1763), and Sevilla Nueva, Jamaica (1510–1535).

Research in these towns has concentrated on cultural interaction among Spanish, American Indian, and African residents and the resulting syncretic and newly developed *criollo* forms. In all of the excavations that have been so far reported from these sites, a pattern of differential adoption and incorporation of Amerindian and/or African traits along gender lines has been documented in Spanish households. The archaeological record suggests that this admixture included the incorporation of Amerindian elements in non–socially visible, infrastructural areas, such as diet and food preparation, while visible symbols of social identification remained rigidly Spanish. Even after the extinction of the native Taino and related Amerindian people in the Caribbean, Spanish colonists continued to incorporate non-European traits into their households, replacing Indian contributions with African.

Subsistence studies have been central to these interpretations. Faunal analysis in historical archaeology was pioneered during the 1970s by Elizabeth Wing (1961, 1989) and her students working in Florida and the Caribbean, notably Elizabeth Reitz (1979, 1990). Zooarchaeological analysis is now a standard part of historical archaeology throughout the region. The use of floral remains has been an even more recent development.

The Non-Spanish Caribbean
The attention to multicultural transculturation and integration that has pervaded the post-1970 historical archaeology of Spanish-occupied areas has not been as pronounced in the English, French, or Dutch colonial sites of the region. This is at least partly owing to the developmental histories of both Euro-American societies in these areas and the historical archaeology that occurred there. By the time many of the seventeenth-century English, French, and Dutch colonies were established, the resident Amerindian populations had been severely decimated, thereby reducing the opportunities for cultural exchange. The populations of these areas came quickly to be dominated by people of African origin, brought for the most part unwillingly to the Caribbean and Florida as slaves

(see Dunn 1972). The non-Spanish colonial occupations of the Caribbean and Florida Basin were furthermore dominated by dispersed plantation systems, in contrast to the more centralized towns that characterized the Spanish colonies, and this led to different approaches to the archaeological database.

Systematic historical archaeology first took place in these areas during the 1970s and 1980s and was informed by the methodological advances of cultural resources management that pervaded American archaeology in general. These advances emphasized regional settlement patterns and broad-scale surveys and were particularly appropriate for the problems related to plantation economies. Much of the initial work in these areas was thus devoted to survey and inventory, such as that done in Barbuda and Antigua (Clement 1995); St. Eustatius (Barka 1985); Montserrat (Goodwin 1982); Jamaica (Higman 1991); the Virgin Islands (Righter 1990) and Curacao (Haviser and Simmons-Brito 1991).

Although some archaeological attention has been devoted to European towns—most notably Spanish Towne and Port Royal, Jamaica, Oranjestad, St. Eustatius (Barka 1985), and more recently in the Guyanas to contact period Amerindian sites (Petitjean Roget 1991)—historical archaeology in the non-Spanish Caribbean has for the most part concentrated on plantations rather than on towns, with particular attention paid to slave settlements and to agricultural industrial systems.

Some of the earliest explicit archaeological attention to sugar production remains took place in Florida, with the study and excavation of the eighteenth-century Bulow sugar plantation. Intermittent projects in industrial archaeology took place at sugar installations in the Caribbean after that time; however, it was the advent of resource management surveys and historic preservation in the region after about 1980 that focused attention on industrial aspects of the Caribbean sugar plantations (*see* Eubanks 1993).

African Heritage
Some of the earliest historical archaeology in the hemisphere to explicitly address issues of African

American slavery was done in 1967 and 1968 by Fairbanks. His research at the Zephaniah Kingsley plantation in North Florida was designed to investigate questions of African-American lifeways under slavery and the extent to which African cultural survivals could be documented in the archaeological record (Fairbanks 1984). Although Fairbanks was unable to clearly define "Africanisms" in the material record, he was able to document a sufficiency of life for the slaves that was at odds with much documentary information about plantation slave life.

Shortly after this time Jerome Handler initiated the archaeology of Caribbean plantation with his work in Barbados, looking not only at the domestic lives of slaves (Handler 1972) but also at the physical anthropology and ritual behavior through the excavation of slave cemeteries (Handler and Lange 1978). Fairbanks's and Handler's early efforts gave rise to a vital and very active program devoted to the archaeology of slavery and plantations in both the United States and the Caribbean, which, in the 1990s, has evolved into an emphasis on the origins of African American society in general (see Fairbanks 1984, Posnansky 1983; Singleton 1985, 1995).

An influential role in this development was played by Merrick Posnansky of the University of California, Los Angeles. Posnansky, an Africanist archaeologist, encouraged a more systematic archaeological study of the African diaspora, and a more explicit integration of African social models, in the Caribbean (1983). Posnansky's exhortation has been implemented most vigorously in the plantation settings of the Caribbean, and information about early Afro-Caribbean architecture, diet and health, economic activities, craft production, ritual, and interethnic influence in the plantation setting has been recovered by historical archaeologists in Jamaica (Agorsah 1994; Armstrong 1990), Barbados (Handler and Lange 1978), Montserrat (Watters 1994), Antigua (Clement 1995), Curacao (Haviser and De Corse 1991), St. Eustatius (Heath 1988), and elsewhere.

Although most of the archaeological research into African American society in Florida and the Caribbean has concentrated on slave sites, there was a steady growth of interest through the pe-

riod in non-slave black settlements. The original impetus for this work was provided by historians working in the Caribbean during the 1960s and 1970s, who began to pay serious attention to the roles of free black colonists in the Caribbean and particularly to African resistance to slavery and the resulting cimarrón, maroon, and marron societies (terms used in Spanish, English, and French respectively to describe free black communities formed after rebellion by former slaves). Summaries of some of the influential work on the history of African resistance to slavery and free society for the Caribbean can be found in works such as Agorsah (1993), Price (1973), and Sued Badillo (1986).

One of the first archaeological studies of a free black settlement in the United States took place in Florida at the site of Fort Gadsden, a nineteenth-century fort manned largely by African American soldiers (Poe 1963). Explicit archaeological attention to colonial-era free African life, however, first took place in the Dominican Republic, where manieles (cimarrón settlements) were located and investigated by Bernardo Vega and subsequently by Juan Arrom and Manuel Garcia Arévalo. Few cimarrón sites have been located and studied archaeologically since that time in the Caribbean or Florida, owing at least in part to their concealed and isolated locations. One exception is the site of Nannytown, Jamaica, which is occupied today by descendants of the colonial-era maroons and which is being investigated through archaeology and oral history by Kofi Agorsah (1994). Another is the site of Fort Mose in Florida. Mose was an eighteenth-century fortified community near St. Augustine that was settled in 1739 by African slaves who escaped from the British colonies to the north and were granted freedom by the Spanish government in Florida. The site of Fort Mose was located and investigated in Florida during the 1980s (Deagan and McMahon 1995).

In Florida the archaeology of Seminole Indian sites was often thematically related to that of African cimarrónes. Fairbanks suggested that the name "Seminole" was an anglicized degeneration of "Cameroon," occasioned by the fact that the Seminoles were considered to be wild and rebellious Indians who fled from their settled towns in British-dominated areas to vacant lands in Florida (Fairbanks 1978, 171). The Seminoles furthermore formed close alliances and lived together with African runaways.

The archaeological study of Seminole sites was actually initiated before 1970 by Goggin, who incorporated Seminole archaeology into his overall schemes of cultural evolution and chronology in Florida and defined archaeological manifestations of Seminole culture for the eighteenth and nineteenth centuries (Goggin 1958). His colleagues and students subsequently became interested in aspects of Seminole-European interaction (Gluckman and Peebles 1974), and by the 1990s there was increased archaeological interest in Black Seminoles (Harron 1994). Archaeological work that took place between 1970 and 1990 to better understand Seminole cultural formation and development has been synthesized by Weisman (1989).

Much of the archaeological attention to African influence in the colonial Caribbean has focused on Afro-American ceramic traditions. One of the earliest inquiries into this question was that of Duncan Matthewson, who correlated locally made folk pottery in Jamaica with West African ceramic traditions. Since that time, African-Caribbean ceramic traditions have been studied in a number of areas, including Cuba (Dominguez 1980), Haiti (Smith 1986), Jamaica (Eubanks 1993), and the lesser Antilles (Heath 1988; Peterson and Watters 1988). Like those of Ferguson and others in the southeastern United States, these investigations concluded not only that African influence was considerably more pronounced in the material world of post-Columbian American society than has traditionally been acknowledged, but also that African contributions are most accurately understood through historical archaeology (rather than through history or archaeology alone). This has been especially relevant in the Caribbean region, where African influence in the Americas persists most visibly in the syncretic societies of the twentieth century.

Historical Archaeology in the 1990s
The 1990s in Florida and the Caribbean were marked by the convergence of nationalist ideol-

ogy in the Caribbean and by postmodernist thought ("postprocessualism") in historical archaeology. A focus for this convergence was provided by the 1992 Quincentenary of Columbus's first voyage, which marked the beginning of European colonialism in the Americas and provoked not only an enormous increase in attention to the Caribbean past but also a great deal of support for historical archaeology in the region.

Postprocessualism gained ascendancy as a major paradigmatic addition to historical archaeology in the 1980s, and in fact, much of the Quincentenary-related archaeological research informed by postprocessual thought was initiated and largely carried out in the 1980s. Postprocessualism of the 1980s objected to "reductionist" approaches designed to provide a generalized expression or description of cultural behavior (such as statistical correlations reflecting group characteristics), and especially to efforts to arrive at general statements or lawlike generalizations about past behavior. These activities were perceived essentially as masking the true internal diversity of a society as represented by the individuals who constituted it, and as inevitably communicating the prevailing dominant perspective while burying the roles of resistance and individual variation. Individual actions and decisions were seen as more important and influential than group norms or environmental variables in shaping societies and the archaeological records they leave. The postprocessualist approach is concerned with individual decisions and acts—rather than systemic processes or environmental factors—that reflect, mitigate, or enforce the unending cycle in societies of efforts by both individuals and groups to assert social dominance in some cases and to resist it in others (see Little 1994; Paynter and McGuire 1991; Schmidt and Patterson 1996).

Despite claims to the contrary by at least one Caribbean ethnohistorian (Sued Badillo 1992), the coincidence of the Quincentenary with the entry into the mainstream of postprocessual thought provoked many historical archaeologists throughout the Caribbean to turn attention toward questions of modern Caribbean cultural identity, the historical roles of non-European peoples after contact and the varieties of resistance to European hegemony. Most of this work built upon the work on acculturation and colonialism begun in the previous period, and much of it attempted to deconstruct the dominance ideology of the Quadricentennial centennial, and reconstruct the colonial arena from an American perspective. (For critiques of these efforts see Patterson 1991; Wilson 1990).

The meeting of the Society for Historical Archaeology was held in the Caribbean for the first time in 1992, in Kingston, Jamaica, and this event provided both a forum for Caribbean historical archaeology (Agorsah and Smith 1992; Barka 1992; Emerson 1992; Hamilton 1992; Luna 1992) and an opportunity for critical self-analysis by the archaeologists doing it (Scott 1992; Spencer Wood 1992). The meeting was dominated by sessions devoted to slavery, resistance to slavery, and the construction of post-Columbian ethnicity and cultural identity, and these concerns continued to direct research in the Caribbean and in Florida during the 1990s (see Hurry and Dinnell 1995).

The Quincentenary also generated a great deal of archaeological research at sites of early European contact and colonization in both Florida and the Caribbean. Although much of that work was initially conceived in support of historical tourism related to the Quincentenary, it also resulted in important advances in understanding the mechanisms of colonization, the forms of colonial interactions, and the ethnogenesis of Iberian-American society (Deagan 1988, 1996; Thomas 1990; Milanich and Milbrath 1989).

Archaeological work at Columbus-related sites was carried out intensively in the Caribbean, including interdisciplinary efforts to identify the landfall site of Columbus in the Bahamas (see Hoffman 1987). What was probably the most intensive archeological effort at Quincentenary-related sites took place in the Dominican Republic, where a massive program of tourism-related development was begun during the late 1980s (see Deagan and Cruxent 1993; Wilson 1990). Renewed study of La Isabela, the first American town established by Columbus, was undertaken by Dominican, Venezuelan, U.S.,

Spanish, and Italian researchers and led to the creation of a museum and an archaeological park at the site. The research also produced the first modern characterization of the late medieval—and ultimately unsuccessful—colonization strategy brought initially to the Americas by Columbus (see Cruxent 1990; Deagan and Cruxent 1993). A considerable amount of excavation also took place in Santo Domingo, including at the locations and study of the city's original 1498 to 1502 site.

La Navidad, Columbus's first fort established in Haiti in 1492, holds particular importance as the site of the first sustained encounter between the people of Europe and the Caribbean, one at which the Europeans were defeated and driven away. Archaeological work took place from 1983 to 1988 at the site believed to be the Indian town in which La Navidad was established, and concentrated on the impact of this brief encounter on the Taino Indians of the area.

The development potentials of the Quincentenary also provided impetus for a seven-year archaeological program at Puerto Real, Haiti, primarily orientated toward the adaptive and interactive processes that led to the formation of post-Columbian American society (Deagan 1995). Research with similar orientations took place in Cuba (Dominguez and Pantoja 1992) and St. Augustine, Florida (Cusick 1994).

In Florida the Quincentennial events stimulated archaeological research on the contact period, with particular emphasis on reconstructing American Indian social and demographic patterns by reassessing the accounts and archaeological remains of the earliest explorers—most frequently Hernando de Soto—in the region. Summaries of that work can be found in Milanich 1991, Milanich and Milbrath 1989, and Thomas 1990.

Marine archaeology in Florida and the Caribbean was also affected by the Quincentenary, most visibly in efforts to locate and study the ships of Columbus and other early Spanish explorers. Advances in these areas are summarized by Smith (1993). During the late 1980s and the 1990s, however, marine archaeology in Florida and the Caribbean also expanded dramatically both in its intensity and in the diversity of sites investigated (Luna 1992). In many cases, such as those of Dutch colonial shipwrecks in the Dominican Republic (Hall 1995), the Dutch Antilles eighteenth-century ships in Barbados, and the U.S. Civil War–period *Maple Leaf* in Florida, this happened through new partnerships between government agencies, private companies, academic programs, and recreational sport divers.

Under state underwater archaeologist Roger Smith, Florida established a series of underwater archaeological preserves that were intended to enhance public appreciation of and involvement in underwater site conservation and protection. The first of these was established in 1987 at the wreck site of the *Urca de Lima* (1715), and by 1995 there were five such underwater preserves in Florida.

As the twentieth century drew to a close, historical archaeology in Florida and the Caribbean was deeply concerned with a number of difficult issues. They included primarily those related to the conservation and protection of archaeological resources—both terrestrial and marine—in the face of escalating economic development and earth-impacting growth. In many parts of the region, however, such growth was welcomed by the local residents as an opportunity for economic well-being, while arguments against development were frequently put forth by archaeologists from outside the area (urban sectors of the country or state, or from outside the countries themselves). This issue was inextricably connected to another dominant dialogue that pervaded historical archaeology in the region, concerned with questions about who could most meaningfully, or rightfully, reconstruct the Caribbean and Floridian colonial past. "Ownership" of the past becomes an increasingly central issue in the use of history in nationalist ideology and political maneuvering, and particularly in attempts to establish a postcolonial identity in much of the Caribbean (*see* Patterson 1991; Sued Badillo 1996; Vargas Arenas 1996). This problem is underscored—and in part inspired by—the marked inequity in resource distribution between North American and Caribbean practitioners of archaeology, particularly in terms of access to public and pri-

vate funds for archaeology. The increasingly expensive requirements of what has become standard multidisciplinary archaeology—equipment, analytical techniques, consultants, libraries, collections, travel to meetings, and the like—exacerbate imbalances between many Caribbean and North American researchers.

Developing joint strategies to mitigate, if not eliminate, these imbalances, while at the same time acknowledging and respecting the national interest and local perspectives of Caribbean communities, is probably the greatest challenge facing archaeologists in the region at the beginning of the new millennium.

Kathleen Deagan

References

Agorsah, Kofi E. 1993. "Archaeology and Resistance History in the Caribbean." *African Archaeological Review* 11: 175–196.

———. 1994. *Maroon Heritage: Archaeological, Ethnographic and Historical Perspectives.* Kingston, Jamaica: Canoe Press.

Agorsah, Kofi, and Roger Smith. 1992. "Jamaica Archaeology on Land and Underwater." Symposium organized at the twenty-fifth annual meeting of the Society for Historical Archaeology, Kingston, Jamaica. Abstracted in *Program for the 25th Annual Conference on Historical and Underwater Archaeology: 500 Years of Change, Contact and the Consequences of Interaction,* ed. by Douglas Armstrong. Society for Historical Archaeology.

Armstrong, Douglas. 1990. *The Old Village at Drax Hall Plantation: An Archaeological Study of an Afro-Jamaican Settlement.* Chicago: University of Illinois Press.

Armstrong, Douglas, ed. 1992. *Program for the 25th Annual Conference on Historical and Underwater Archaeology: 500 Years of Change, Contact and the Consequences of Interaction.* Society for Historical Archaeology.

Arróm, J. J., and M. Garcia Arévalo. 1986. *Cimarrón.* Santo Domingo: Ediciones Fundación Garcia Arévalo.

Barka, Norman. 1985. "Archaeology of St. Eustatius, Netherlands Antilles: An Interim Report on the 1981–1984 Season." *St. Eustatius Archaeological Research Series # 1.* Williamsburg, VA: Department of Anthropology, College of William and Mary.

———. 1990. "The Potential for Historical

Archaeological Research in the Netherlands Antilles." *Proceedings of the Eleventh Congress of the International Association for Caribbean Archaeology:* 393–399. San Juan, P.R.

Barka, Norm, organizer. 1992. "Saving What Is Left: Disaster Management in Saint Maarten." Symposium organized at the 25th annual meeting of the Society for Historical Archaeology, Kingston, Jamaica. Abstracted in *Program for the 25th Annual Conference on Historical and Underwater Archaeology: 500 Years of Change, Contact and the Consequences of Interaction,* ed. Douglas Armstrong. Society for Historical Archaeology.

Bequette, Kathryn. 1991. "Shipwrecks of St. Eustatius: A Preliminary Study." *Proceedings of the Thirteenth Congress of the International Association for Caribbean Archaeology,* 787–800. Curacao.

Borrell, Pedro. 1983. *Arqueologia submarina en la Republica Dominicana.* Santo Domingo: Museo Casas Reales.

Boyd, Mark F., Hale G. Smith, and John W. Griffin. 1951. *Here They Once Stood: The Tragic End of the Apalachee Missions.* Gainesville: University of Florida Presses.

Boyrie-Moya, Emile. 1964. *La Casa de Piedra de Ponce de Leon en Higuey.* Santo Domingo, Dominican Republic.: Academia Dominicana de la Historia.

Burgess, Robert, and Carl Clausen. 1982 (1966). *Florida's Golden Galleons.* Stuart, FL: Florida Classics Library.

Chaney, Ed, and Kathleen Deagan. 1989. "St. Augustine and the La Florida Colony: New Life-Styles in a New Land." In *First Encounters: Spanish Exploration in the Caribbean and the United States, 1492–1570,* 166–182. Ed. Jerald T. Milanich and Susan Milbrath. Gainesville: University of Florida Press.

Chatelaine, Verne. 1941. *The Defenses of Spanish Florida, 1565–1763.* Publication 511. Washington, DC: Carnegie Institute.

Clement, Christopher O. 1995. "Landscapes and Plantations on Tobago: A Regional Perspective." Ph.D. dissertation, University of Florida.

Cotter, Charles S. 1948. "The Discovery of the Spanish Carvings at Seville." *Jamaican Historical Review* 1, no. 3: 227–233.

———. 1970. "Sevilla Nueva. The Story of an Excavation. *Jamaica Journal* 4, no. 2: 15–22.

Crahan, Margaret, and Franklin Knight, eds. 1979. *African and the Caribbean: The Legacies of a Link.* Baltimore: Johns Hopkins University Press.

Cruxent, José M. 1976. "Elementos decorativos en la majolica Panameña." In *Curso de restauración de bienes muebles especializado en ceramología historica,* 13–103. Panamá: Centro Interamericano Subregional de Restauración de Bienes Muebles, Instituto Nacional de Cultura.

———. 1980. *Notas ceramologiá: algunas sugerencias sobre la práctica de la descripción de cerámicas arqueológicas de la época indo-hispanica.* Coro, Venezuela: Ediciones Universidad Francisco de Miranda, Cuaderno Falconiano.

———. 1989. "Relación y noticias cerca de la Isabela." *Ysabela* 1, no. 1: 12–18.

———. 1990. "The Origin of La Isabela." In *Columbian Consequences,* 251–259. Vol. 2. Ed. D. H. Thomas. Washington, DC: Smithsonian Institution Press.

Cruxent, José M., and Irving Rouse. 1958. *An Archeological Chronology of Venezuela.* 2 vols. Pan American Union Social Science Monographs no. 6. Washington, DC.

Cruxent, José M., and Eduardo Vaz. 1975. "Determination of the Provenience of Majolica Pottery Found in the Caribbean Area Using Its Gamma-Ray Induced Thermoluminescence." *American Antiquity* 40, no. 1: 71–82.

Cusick, James. 1994. "Ethnic Groups and Class in an Emerging Market Economy: Spaniards and Minorcans in Late Colonial St. Augustine." Ph.D. dissertation, University of Florida (Anthropology). Ann Arbor, MI: University Microfilms.

Deagan, Kathleen. 1983. *Spanish St. Augustine: The Archaeology of a Colonial Creole Community.* New York: Academic Press.

———. 1987. *Artifacts of the Spanish Colonies: Florida and the Caribbean* Vol. 1. Washington, DC: Smithsonian Institution Press.

———. 1988. "The Archaeology of the Spanish Contact Period in the Caribbean." *Journal of World Prehistory* 2, no. 2: 187–233.

———. 1990. "Sixteenth Century Spanish Colonization in the Southeastern United States and the Caribbean." In *Archaeological and Historical Perspectives in the Spanish Borderlands East,* 225–250. Columbian Consequences Vol. 2. Ed. D. Thomas. Washington, DC: Smithsonian Institution Press.

———. 1996. "Colonial Transformations: Euro-American Cultural Genesis in the Earliest Spanish Colonies." *Journal of Anthropological Research* 52, no. 2: 135–160.

Deagan, Kathleen, ed. 1991. "America's Ancient City: Spanish St. Augustine 1565–1763." *Span-*

ish *Borderlands Sourcebooks.* Vol. 25. Gen. ed.
D. H. Thomas. New York: Garland Press.

———. 1995. *Puerto Real: The Archaeology of a
Sixteenth Century Spanish Town in Hispaniola.*
Gainesville: University Presses of Florida.

Deagan, Kathleen, and José Cruxent. 1993. "From
Contact to Criollos: The Archaeology of Spanish Colonization in Hispaniola." In *The Meeting
of Two Worlds: Europe and the Americas 1492–1650,*
67–104. Ed. Warwick Bray. Proceedings of the
British Academy no. 81. Oxford: Oxford University Press.

Deagan, Kathleen, and Darcie MacMahon. 1995.
*Ft. Mose: Colonial America's Black Fortress of Free-
dom.* Gainesville: University Presses of Florida.

Dominguez, Lourdes. 1980. "Cerámica de tran-
sculturación del sitio colonial Casa de la
Obrapia." *Cuba Arqueologica* 2. Santiago, Cuba:
Editorial Oriente.

Dominguez, Lourdes, and Alesis Pantoja. 1992.
"Procesos étnicos y transculturación en Cuba
en vísperas del encuentro entre el viejo y el
nuevo mundos." Paper prepared for the 25th
annual meeting of the Society for Historical
Archaeology, Kingston, Jamaica. Abstracted in
*Program for the 25th Annual Conference on Histori-
cal and Underwater Archaeology: 500 Years of
Change, Contact and the Consequences of Interaction.* Ed. Douglas Armstrong. Society for Historical Archaeology.

Dunn, John. 1972. *Sugar and Slaves: The Rise of the
Plantation Class in the British West Indies.*
Williamsburg, VA: Institute for Early American
Culture.

Dunnell, Robert. 1986. "Five Decades of American
Archaeology." In *American Archaeology, Past, Present and Future,* 35–99. Ed. D. Meltzer, D.
Fowler, and J. Sabloff. Washington, DC: Smithsonian Institution Press.

Emerson, Matt, organizer. 1992. "Locally Made
Pottery Traditions in the Colonial New World."
Symposium organized at the 25th annual meeting of the Society for Historical Archaeology,
Kingston, Jamaica. Abstracted in *Program for the
25th Annual Conference on Historical and Underwater Archaeology: 500 Years of Change, Contact and
the Consequences of Interaction.* Ed. Douglas Armstrong. Society for Historical Archaeology.

Eubanks, Thomas. 1993. "Sugar, Slavery and Emancipation: The Industrial Archaeology of the
West Indian Island of Tobago." Ph.D. dissertation, University of Florida, Gainesville
(anthropology).

Fairbanks, Charles. 1964. "Underwater Historic
Sites on the St. Mark's River. The Third Annual
Conference Historic Sites Archeology, 1962."
Florida Anthropologist 17, no. 2: 44–49.

———. 1978. "The Ethno-Archaeology of the
Florida Seminole." In *Tacachale: Essays on the
Indians of Florida and Southeastern Georgia During
the Historic Period,* 163–193. Ed. J. T. Milanich
and S. Proctor. Gainesville: University Presses
of Florida.

———. 1984. "The Plantation Archaeology of the
Southeastern Coast." *Historical Archaeology* 18,
no. 1: 1–14.

Fariñas Gutierrez, M. D. 1992. "Paralelismo y
transculturación en la religiosidad aborígen
antes y después de la conquista." *Revista Cubana
de Ciencias Sociales* 9: 102–122.

Garcia Arévalo, Manuel. 1978a. "La arqueologia
Indo-Hispano en Santo Domingo." In *Unidades
y variedades: Ensayos en homenaje a José M. Cruxent,*
77–127. Caracas: Centro de Estudios
Avanzados.

———. 1978b. "Influencias de la dieta Indo-
Hispanica en la cerámica Taina." In *Proceedings
of the Seventh International Congress for the Study
of the Precolumbian Cultures of the Lesser Antilles,*
263–277. University of Montreal: Centre des
Recherches Caraibes.

———. 1990. "Transculturation in Contact Period
and Contemporary Hispaniola." In *Archaeological
and Historical Perspectives in the Spanish Borderlands East,* 269–280. Columbian Consequences
Vol. 2. Ed. D. Thomas. Washington, DC: Smithsonian Institution Press.

Gartley, Richard T. 1979. "Afro-Cruzan Pottery—
A New Style of Colonial Earthenware from St.
Croix." *Journal of the Virgin Islands Archaeological
Society* 8: 47–61.

Gluckman, Stephen J., and Christopher Peebles.
1974. "Oven Hill (Di–15), A Refuge Site in the
Suwanee River. *Florida Anthropologist* 27:
21–46.

Goggin, John M. 1951. "Ft. Pupo: A Spanish Frontier Outpost." *Florida Historical Quarterly* 30:
139–192.

———. 1958. "Seminole Pottery." In *Prehistoric
Pottery of the Eastern United States.* Ed. James B.
Griffin. Anne Arbor: Museum of Anthropology,
University of Michigan.

———. 1960a. "The Spanish Olive Jar: An
Introductory Study." *Yale University Publication in
Anthropology* 62. New Haven: Yale University
Press.

————. 1960b. "Underwater Archaeology: Its Nature and Limitations." *American Antiquity* 25, no. 3: 348–354.

Goodwin, Conrad. 1982. "Archaeology on the Galways Plantation." *Florida Anthropologist* 35, no. 2: 251–258.

Goodwin, Walter. 1946. *Spanish and English Ruins in Jamaica*. Boston: Meador.

Griffin, John W. 1947. "Comments on a Site in the St. Marks National Wildlife Refuge, Wakulla County, Florida." *American Antiquity* 13: 182–183.

Griffin, Patricia, ed. 1996. *Fifty Years of Southeastern Archaeology: Selected Works of John W. Griffin*. Gainesville: University Presses of Florida.

Hall, Jerome L. 1995. "Seventeenth Century Dutch Ship Types in the Caribbean." Paper presented at the 28th annual meeting of the Society for Historical Archaeology, Washington, DC. Abstracted in *Program for the 28th Annual Conference on Historical and Underwater Archaeology: Archaeological perspectives on American pasts*. Ed. Silas Hurry and Katherine Dinnel. Society for Historical Archaeology.

Hamilton, Donald, organizer. 1992. "Port Royal: Its Past and Present." Symposium organized at the 25th annual meeting of the Society for Historical Archaeology, Kingston, Jamaica. Abstracted in *Program for the 25th Annual Conference on Historical and Underwater Archaeology: 500 Years of Change, Contact and the Consequences of Interaction*. Ed. Douglas Armstrong. Society for Historical Archaeology.

Handler, Jerome. 1972. "An Archaeological Investigation of the Domestic Life of Plantation Slaves in Barbados." *Journal of the Barbados Museum and Historical Society* 34, no. 2: 64–72.

Handler, Jerome, and Frederick Lange. 1978. "Plantation Slavery in Barbados: An Archaeological and Historical Investigation." Cambridge, MA: Harvard University Press.

Harron, Jordon. 1994. "Black Seminole Settlement Patterns." Unpublished M.A. thesis, University of South Carolina.

Hatt, Gudmund. 1932. "Notes on the Archaeology of Santo Domingo." *Saertryk af Geografisk Tidsskrift* 35: 1–8.

Haviser, Jay B., and Christopher DeCorse. 1991. "African-Caribbean Interaction: A Research Plan for Curacao Creole Culture." In *Proceedings of the Thirteenth Congress of the International Association for Caribbean Archaeology*, 326–337. Curacao.

Haviser, Jay B., and Nadia Simmons-Brito. 1991. "Sub-Surface Archaeological Testing in the Punda Area of Curacao, Netherlands Antilles." In *Proceedings of the Fourteenth Congress of the International Association for Caribbean Archaeology*, 380–407. Barbados, W.I.

Heath, Barbara. 1988. "Afro-Caribbean Ware: A Study of Ethnicity on St. Eustatius." Ph.D. dissertation, University of Pennsylvania. Ann Arbor, MI: University Microfilms.

Higman, B. 1991. *Jamaica Surveyed*. Kingston: Institute of Jamaica.

Hodges, William. 1986. *La Fortaleza de la Navidad: Further Considerations*. Typescript MS. Haiti: Musée de Guahabá Limbé.

————. 1995. "How We Found Puerto Real." In *Puerto Real: The Archaeology of a Sixteenth Century Spanish Town in Hispaniola*. Ed. K. Deagan. Gainesville: University Press of Florida.

Hoffman, Charles. 1987. "Archaeological Investigations at the Long Bay Site, San Salvador, Bahamas." In *Proceedings of the First San Salvador Conference: Columbus and His World*, 237–245. Ed. D. Gerace. San Salvador, Bahamas.

Hurry, Silas, and Katherine Dinnel, eds. 1995. *Archaeological Perspectives on American Pasts: Program for the 28th Annual Conference on Historical and Underwater Archaeology*. Washington, DC.

Kelly, Kenneth G. 1989. "Slaves No More: An Archaeological Comparison of Two Post-Emancipation House Sites on Drax Hall and Seville Estate, St. Annes, Jamaica." M.A. thesis, College of William and Mary, Williamsburg.

Kelly, Kenneth G., and Douglas V. Armstrong. 1991. "Archaeological Investigations of a 19th Century Free Laborer, Seville Estate, St. Ann's, Jamaica." In *Proceedings of the Thirteenth Congress of the International Association Caribbean Archaeology*, 429–435. Curacao.

Link, Marion. 1960. "Exploring the Drowned City of Port Royal." *National Geographic* 117, no. 2: 151–183

Little, Barbara. 1994. "People with History: An Update on Historical Archaeology in the United States." *Journal of Archaeological Method and Theory* 1, no. 1: 5–40.

Luna, Pilar, organizer. 1992. "Caribbean Underwater Archaeology: Past and Present." Symposium organized at the 25th annual meeting of the Society for Historical Archaeology, Kingston, Jamaica. Abstracted in *Program for the 25th Annual Conference on Historical and Underwater Archaeology: 500 years Of Change, Contact and the Conse-*

quences of Interaction. Ed. Douglas Armstrong. Society for Historical Archaeology.

Manucy, Albert, and Ricardo Torres-Reyes. 1973. *The Forts of Old San Juan.* Old Greenwich, CT: Chatham Press.

Marken, Mitchell M. 1994. *Pottery from Spanish Shipwrecks 1500–1800.* Gainesville: University Press of Florida.

Marx, Robert. 1973. *Port Royal Rediscovered.* Garden City, NY: Doubleday.

Marx, Robert, and Jennifer Marx. 1993. *The Search for Sunken Treasure.* Toronto: Key Porter Books.

Matthewson, Duncan. 1986. *Treasure of the Atocha.* New York: Pisces Books.

Milanich, Jerald T. 1995. *The Florida Indians and the Invasion from Europe.* Gainesville: University Press of Florida.

Milanich, Jerald T., ed. 1991. *The Hernando de Soto Expedition.* Spanish Borderlands Sourcebooks no. 11. Ed. David. H. Thomas. New York: Garland Publishing.

Milanich, Jerald T., and Susan Milbrath, eds. 1989. *First Encounters, Spanish Explorations in the Caribbean and the United States, 1492–1570.* Gainesville: University Press of Florida.

Moreau de St. Mery, J. 1958 (1767). *Description topographique, physique, civile, politique et historique de la partie Française de l 'Ísle Saint-Domingue.* Ed. Blanche Maurel and Étienne Taillemite. Paris: Société de l'Histoire de Colonies Françaises.

Nieves Sicart, Maria. 1980. "Piezas cerámicas conservadas en los depositos del Departamento de Ceramologia Historica del Museo Casas Reales." *Casas Reales* 11: 87–98. Santo Domingo.

Ortega, Elpidio. 1982. *Arqueologia colonial en Santo Domingo.* Santo Domingo: Fundación Ortega-Alvarez.

Ortíz, Fernando. 1983 (1940). *Contrapunteo cubano del tabaco y azúcar.* Havana: Ediciones Ciencias Sociales.

Palm, Erwin. 1952. "La Fortaleza de la Concepción de la Vega." *Memoria del V congreso historico municipal Interamericano* 2: 115–118.

Pantel, A. G., J. Sued Badillo, Aníbal S. Rivera, and Beatriz Pantel. 1988. "Archaeological, Architectural and Historical Investigations of the First Spanish Settlement in Puerto Rico, Caparra." Unpublished project report. San Juan: Foundation of Archaeology, Anthropology, and History of Puerto Rico.

Pantel, A. T., Iraida Vargas Arenas, and Mario Sanoja Obediente, eds. 1990. *Proceedings of the Eleventh Congress of the International Association for Caribbean Archaeology.* San Juan, P.R: Foundation of Archaeology, Anthropology, and History of Puerto Rico; the University of Puerto Rico; and the United States Department of Agriculture, Forest Service.

Patterson, Thomas. 1991. "Early Colonial Encounters and Identities in the Caribbean: A Review of Some Recent Works and Their Implications." *Dialectical Anthropology* 16: 1–13.

Paynter, Robert, and Randall McGuire, eds. 1991. *The Archaeology of Inequality.* Oxford: Basil Blackwell.

Pérez Montás, Eugenio. 1984. *República Dominicana: Monumentos Históricos y Arqueológicos.* Publication no. 380. Mexico City: Instituto Panamericano de Geografia e Historia.

———. 1991. "CARIMOS: Monumentos y sitios del Gran Caribe (Monuments and Sites of the Greater Caribbean)" *Casas Reales* 20. 2d ed. (in Spanish and English). Santo Domingo: Museo de Casas Reales.

Peterson, J. B., and D. R. Watters. 1988. "Afro-Monserratian Ceramics from the Harney Site Cemetery, Montserrat, West Indies." *Annals of the Carnegie Museum* 57, no. 8: 167–187.

Peterson, Mendel. 1965. *History under the Sea: A Handbook for Underwater Investigation.* Publication 4538. Washington, DC: Smithsonian Institution.

Petitjean Roget, Hugues. 1991. "La Grenouille Bleu de Dolph: Approache des Sites Amerindiens de la Baie de L'Oyapock a L'epoque des Premiers Contacts Europe-Guyane." In *Proceedings of the Thirteenth Congress of the International Association for Caribbean Archaeology,* 492–504. Barbados, W.I.

Poe, Stephen R. 1963. *Archaeological Excavations at Fort Gadsden, Florida.* Notes in Anthropology no. 8. Tallahassee: Florida State University Anthropology Department.

Posnansky, Merrick. 1983. "Towards an Archaeology of the Black Diaspora." In *Proceedings of the Ninth Congress of the International Association for the Study of Precolumbian Man in the Lesser Antilles,* 443–450. Montreal, Canada.

Price, Richard, ed. 1973. *Maroon Societies: Rebel Slave Communities in the Americas.* Baltimore: Johns Hopkins University Press.

Puig Ortíz, J. A. 1972. *Por la valorización historica de las ruinas de la Isabela, Primera Ciudad del Nuevo Mundo.* Santo Domingo, R.D.

Reitz, Elizabeth J. 1979. "Spanish and British Subsistence Strategies in St. Augustine, Florida and
Frederica, Georgia." Unpublished Ph.D. dissertation, University of Florida, Gainesville.
———. 1990. "Zooarchaeological Evidence for
Subsistence at La Florida Missions." In *Archaeological and Historical Perspectives on the Spanish
Borderlands East,* 543–554. Columbian Consequences, vol. 2. Ed. David Hurst Thomas.
Washington, DC: Smithsonian Institution Press.

Righter, Elizabeth. 1990. "Land Use History and
Environmental Management at Plantation
Zufriedenheit between A.D. 1683 and A.D.
1817." In *Proceedings of the Eleventh Congress of
the International Association for Caribbean Archaeology,* 472–485.

Rouse, Irving. 1952. "Porto Rican Prehistory." *New
York Academy of Sciences Scientific Survey of Porto
Rico and the Virgin Islands* 18, no. 3–4. New York.
———. 1992. *The Tainos: Rise and Decline of the
People Who Greeted Columbus.* New Haven: Yale
University Press.

Scarry, Margaret M. 1993. "Plant Production and
Procurement in Apalachee Province." In *Spanish
Missions of La Florida,* 357–375. Ed. Bonnie G.
McEwan. Gainesville: University Press of
Florida.

Schmidt, Peter, and Thomas Patterson, eds. 1996.
*Making Alternative Histories: The Practice of Archae-
ology and History in Non-Western Settings.* Santa
Fe, NM: School of American Research.

Scott, Elizabeth. 1992. "'Those of Little Note':
Gender, Cultural Diversity and Visibility in
Historical Archaeology." Symposium organized
at the 25th annual meeting of the Society for
Historical Archaeology, Kingston, Jamaica.
Abstracted in *Program for the 25th Annual Confer-
ence on Historical and Underwater Archaeology: 500
Years of Change, Contact and the Consequences of
Interaction.* Ed. Douglas Armstrong. Society for
Historical Archaeology.

Singleton, Theresa A. 1995. "The Archaeology of
the African Diaspora in the Americas." *Society
for Historical Archaeology, Guides to the Archaeological Literature of the Immigrant Experience in America* 2.

Singleton, Theresa A., ed. 1985. *The Archaeology of
Slavery and Plantation Life.* New York: Academic
Press.

Smith, Greg C. 1986. "A Study of Colono Ware
and Non-European Ceramics from Sixteenth-
Century Puerto Real, Haiti." M.A. thesis, University of Florida, Gainesville.

Smith, Hale G. 1956. "The European and the Indian: European-Indian Contacts in Georgia and
Florida." In *Notes in Anthropology* 2. Florida
Anthropological Society Publication 4.
Tallahassee: Florida State University Department of Anthropology.
———. 1962. "El Morro." In *Notes in Anthropology*
6. Tallahassee: Florida State University Department of Anthropology.
———. 1965. "Santa Rosa Pensacola." In *Notes in
Anthropology* 10. Tallahassee: Florida State University Department of Anthropology.

Smith, Roger. 1993. *Vanguard of Empire: Ships of
Exploration in the Age of Columbus.* Oxford:
Oxford University Press.

South, Stanley. 1964. "Preface to the Third Annual
Conference on Historic Sites in Archaeology,
1962." *Florida Anthropologist* 17, no. 2: 34.

South, Stanley, ed. 1994. *Pioneers in Historical
Archaeology.* New York: Academic Press.

Spencer Wood, Suzanne, organizer. 1992. "Cri-
tiques of Historical Archaeology." Symposium
organized at the 25th annual meeting of the
Society for Historical Archaeology, Kingston,
Jamaica. Abstracted in *Program for the 25th
Annual Conference on Historical and Underwater
Archaeology: 500 Years of Change, Contact and the
Consequences of Interaction.* Ed. Douglas Arm-
strong. Society for Historical Archaeology.

Sued Badillo, Jalil. 1992. "Facing Up to Caribbean
History." *American Antiquity* 57, no. 4: 599–607.
———. 1996. "The Theme of the Indigenous in
the National Projects of the Hispanic
Caribbean." In *Making Alternative Histories,*
25–46. Ed. P. Schmidt and T. Patterson. Santa
Fe, NM: School of American Research.

Thatcher, John Boyd. 1903. *Christopher Columbus:
The Life, His Works, His Remains.* New York.

Thomas, David H., ed. 1990. *Archaeological and
Historical Perspectives in the Spanish Borderlands
East.* Columbian Consequences Vol. 2. Washing-
ton, DC: Smithsonian Institution Press.

Vargas Arenas, Iraida. 1996. "The Perception of
History and Archaeology in Latin America: A
Theoretical Approach." In *Making Alternative His-
tories,* 47–68. Ed. P. Schmidt and T. Patterson.
Santa Fe, NM: School of American Research.

Veloz-Maggiolo, Marcio, and Elpidio Ortega.
1992. *La fundación de la villa de Santo Domingo.*
Serie História de la Ciudad no. 1. Santo
Domingo: Colección Quinto Centenario.

Wagner, Kip, and L. B. Taylor. 1972. *Pieces of Eight.*
New York: E. P. Dutton.

Watters, David R. 1994. "Mortuary Patterns at the Harney Site Slave Cemetery, Montserrat, in Caribbean Perspective." *Historical Archaeology* 28, no. 3: 56–73.

Watters, David R., and James Petersen. 1991. "The Harney Site Slave Cemetery, Montserrat: Archaeological Summary." *Proceedings of the Thirteenth Congress of the International Association for Caribbean Archaeology,* 317–325. Curacao.

Weisman, Brent. 1989. *Like Beads on a String.* Tuscaloosa: University of Alabama Press.

Willey, Gordon, and J. Sabloff. 1980. *A History of American Archaeology.* 2d ed. San Francisco: W. H. Freeman.

Williams, Eric. 1970. *From Columbus to Castro: The History of the Caribbean.* New York: Vintage Books.

Willis, Raymond. 1976. "The Archeology of 16th Century Nueva Cadiz." M.A. thesis (Anthropology), University of Florida.

Wilson, Sam. 1990. *Hispaniola: Caribbean Chiefdoms in the Age of Columbus.* Tuscaloosa: University of Alabama Press.

Wing, Elizabeth. 1961. "Animal Remains Excavated at the Spanish Site of Nueva Cadiz on Cubagua Island, Venezuela." *Nieuwe West-Indische Gids* 2: 162–165.

———. 1989. "Evidences for the Impact of Traditional Spanish Animal Uses in Parts of the New World." In *The Walking Larder,* 72–79. Ed. J. Clutton-Brock. London: Urwin Hyman.

Woodward, Robyn P. 1988. "The Charles Cotter Collection: A Study of the Ceramic and Faunal Remains." M.A. thesis, Texas A&M University, College Station.

Flowerdew Hundred Plantation, Virginia

Flowerdew Hundred Plantation is a working plantation and an archaeological park on the James River near Hopewell, Virginia. A 1,000-acre grant in 1617 to Governor George Yeardley was named for his wife, Lady Yeardley, née Temperance Flowerdew, and occupation has been continuous since 1619 despite numerous changes in ownership.

Excavations in the late 1960s by N. F. Barka of the College of William and Mary exposed a compound enclosing a large house of post construction, a stone foundation for a dwelling, its outbuildings, and other early- and later-seventeenth-century structures. William and Mary field schools in the 1970s explored both prehistoric and historical sites, and in the 1980s, J. F. DEETZ, with students from the University of California at Berkeley, initiated long-term research into the succession of plantation and settlement types from the early-seventeenth century through the mid-nineteenth century. Deetz synthesized the results in *Flowerdew Hundred* (1993).

Dates derived from measuring bore diameters of pipe stems recovered from eighteen sites indicated three groups: seven early-seventeenth-century sites, six late-seventeenth-century ones, and five mid- to late-eighteenth century sites. Deetz interpreted the evidence from each grouping in light of local, regional, and global factors influencing changes on the Chesapeake frontier of the British Empire, offering comparisons with British colonial sites in South Africa and elsewhere and assessing findings in light of contemporary debates in historical archaeology.

Evidence from Flowerdew indicates slave manufacture both of pottery and decorated clay pipes, products formerly assumed to be of Native American manufacture. Deetz saw Flowerdew as a microcosm for examining the emergence of a distinct American culture from a British colony.

Mary C. Beaudry

References

Barka, N. F. 1993. "The Archaeology of Piersey's Hundred, Virginia, within the Context of the Muster of 1624/5." In *Archaeology of Eastern North America: Essays in Honor of Steven A. Williams,* 313–355. Ed. J. B. Stoltzman. Special issue of the *Bulletin of the Eastern States Archaeological Federation.*

Deetz, J. 1993. *Flowerdew Hundred: The Archaeology of a Virginia Plantation, 1619–1864.* Charlottesville and London: University Press of Virginia.

Fontana, Bernard L. (1931–)

Bernard L. Fontana was born on 7 January 1931 in Oakland, California, where he spent his formative years. In 1948, he entered the anthropology program at the University of California, Berkeley, and graduated with a B.A. in

1953. After serving two years in the U.S. Army, he continued his education at the University of Arizona, where he entered the Ph.D. program in anthropology. He received his degree in 1960 and took a position as field historian with the University of Arizona Library. Two years later, he became an ethnologist at the Arizona State Museum. In 1977, Fontana once again became the library's field historian, a post he held until he retired in 1992. He continues to be active despite his official retirement.

Primarily as a result of a graduate archaeology seminar, Fontana became interested in historic sites. In 1958, while still a student, he and others began excavations at the eighteenth-century mission of San Xavier de Bac, outside Tucson, Arizona. This work was followed in 1962 with the publication of a book on Papago Indian pottery, a study that has achieved status as a regional classic and remains the only reliable source on this historic pottery. Also published in 1962 was the JOHNNY WARD'S RANCH report on the 1960–1961 excavations at a nineteenth-century site in southern Arizona. The ranch was the first non-Spanish period historic site to be excavated in Arizona, and the pioneering report received national recognition because it was the first to treat late-nineteenth-century interchangeable parts type artifacts seriously. The report remains a widely used classic.

Additionally, Fontana taught the first-ever regular historic sites archaeology course in the American Southwest from 1966 to 1972. This stimulating and innovative course served to encourage many students to pursue a career in the field.

Fontana's professional career, which has spanned thirty-five years, has been punctuated by contributions to historic sites archaeology in addition to those in ethnography, history, and related subjects. Despite the fact that archaeology was not his major field, Fontana undoubtedly will be best remembered for his contributions to historic sites archaeology at a time when historic sites were neither popular nor valued.

James Ayres

Foote, Robert Bruce (1834–1912)

Robert Bruce Foote was an officer of the Geological Survey of India employed mainly in the southern part of the country. He was deeply influenced by the Royal Society's acceptance of the geological antiquity of man in 1859. Both Neolithic stone tools and microlithic flakes and tools had been found in various parts of India, but it was Foote who discovered Paleolithic evidence in a gravel pit near Madras in 1863. He pursued his prehistoric interests for the rest of his working life, publishing a two-volume catalog of his collection in the Madras Museum (Foote 1914, 1916). He worked all over southern India and in Gujarat in western India. Many of the premises he developed, based on his study of the prehistory and protohistory of the areas where he worked, have been found to be substantially correct by modern researchers (see Chakrabarti 1979).

Foote's work symbolizes a vigorous phase of prehistoric discoveries in India during the second half of the nineteenth century. It was during this time that the basic significance and the general distribution and stratigraphy of prehistoric artifacts, and their association with extinct fauna in some cases, came to be well understood. Among his contemporary workers were Valentine Ball in east India, William King in south India, and A. C. L. Carlleyle and William Cockburn in central India. However, it must be emphasized that investigators during this period were concerned not only with stone tools but also with a wide ranges of "prehistoric" finds from southern Indian Iron Age megaliths to Neolithic sites. Rock paintings were discovered throughout central India.

Dilip Chakrabarti

References
Chakrabarti, D. E. 1979. "Robert Bruce Foote and Indian Prehistory." *East and West* 29: 11–26.
Foote, R. B. 1979. *Prehistoric and Protohistoric Antiquities of India.* Delhi: Leelader's Publications.

Ford, James Alfred (1911–1968)

James Alfred Ford was an outstanding American archaeologist from the 1930s to the late 1960s. He was born in Water Valley, Mississippi, on 12

February 1911, and perhaps because of that birth date took on a Lincolnesque appearance with dark black hair and a lean six-foot, four-inch height. He excavated and reported his results on sites from Point Barrow, Alaska, to the VIRU VALLEY in Peru, but he is best known for his work in the southeastern United States.

Ford received his B.A. degree from Louisiana State University in 1936, his M.A. degree in anthropology from the University of Michigan in 1938, and his doctoral degree from Columbia University in 1949. His passage through the formal requirements of academia was slowed by World War II and the pull of opportunities for fieldwork. His all-around skills in excavating and interpreting what he had found had created a market for his talents by the late 1930s. Later his position at the American Museum of Natural History enabled him to direct his own field program.

Ford and a high school associate, Moreau Chambers, worked for three summers, 1927–1929, doing survey work for the Mississippi Department of Archives and History, and they became closely associated with Henry B. Collins of the Smithsonian Institution at the excavation of sites in Yazoo County in 1929. Collins introduced them to northern Alaskan archaeology in 1930–1931, and he also sponsored Ford as assistant to Frank M. Setzler, also of the Smithsonian, who initiated the first labor relief program during the Great Depression at Marksville, Louisiana.

Ford is best known in the southeast United States for his excavations at Oculgee National Monument near Macon, Georgia; a group of Hopewellian mounds near Helena, Arkansas; and the Jaketown multicomponent site near Belzoni, Mississippi, in association with Philip Phillips and William G. Haag. He also coauthored reports on the early Marksville period Crooks site in LaSalle Parish, Louisiana, with GORDON R. WILLEY and on the Tchefuncte early Woodland period of southern Louisiana with George I. Quimby. A survey report in 1951 on the lower Mississippi Valley was coauthored with Phillips and JAMES B. GRIFFIN.

The 1951 landmark survey report was a major presentation of Ford's seriation of the pottery collections with the percentage computation of individual types per site, or site unit arranged stylistic inception, popularity, decline, and extinction. This methodology confirmed his concept of a uniform gradualistic ceramic change, and he became a convert to cultural determinism. He wanted to introduce quantitative and empirical methods to make archaeology a science, and he also employed the direct historical approach, diffusion, migration, and interareal relationships.

Ford was president of the SOCIETY FOR AMERICAN ARCHAEOLOGY in 1963–1964, received the Spinden Award in 1966 for outstanding accomplishments in theory, methodology, and chronology, and chaired a number of southeastern archaeological conferences. He did not like large gatherings or formal social events, and he was unhappy living in or large cities. He was very effective espousing his ideas to small groups of archaeologists, and he was a versatile and ingenious innovator and a probing theoretician. He was a living refutation of his belief that an individual does not make a difference in the pattern of cultural change, for he was a leader in changing the tenor of archaeological work in the southeastern part of the United States and in South America.

James B. Griffin

See also United States of America, Prehistoric Archaeology

References

For references, see *Encyclopedia of Archaeology: The Great Archaeologists, Vol. 2,* ed. Tim Murray (Santa Barbara, CA: ABC-CLIO, 1999), pp. 650–651.

France

The study of prehistory began in France. In the nineteenth century the worked stone tools that the customs officer JACQUES BOUCHER DE PERTHES collected in northern France were the oldest tools known anywhere in the world, even older than their discoverer had thought, since they dated back 700,000 years (Demoule 1990).

One hundred and fifty years later, in one of the two issues of *World Archaeology* devoted to "regional traditions of archaeological research,"

Françoise Audouze and ANDRÉ LEROI-GOURHAN (1981) called their contribution "France: A Continental Insularity," emphasizing how separate French research had been from that of other countries. Yet there was nothing original about the work done in France after the time of Boucher de Perthes. French archaeology has been unique only in that more than half of its professional archaeologists have excavated abroad. Most of the excavations within France were conducted by amateurs, and archaeology in France suffered as the result of a severe economic crisis (Chapelot et al. 1979; Querrien and Schnapp 1984). At the end of the 1970s French archaeology received only about one-tenth of the funding that its counterparts in equally affluent European countries did.

In fact, for a very long time in France, prehistoric and historic remains were given no protection whatsoever if they were not monumental (well known and associated with known historical events); the public authorities were not even interested in them. Archaeological research was entirely free from any government control or protection until 1941, when the Vichy government issued the first law relating to archaeology (endorsed in 1945), at a time when part of France was occupied by the Germans. Under the law, excavations required authorization, chance finds had to be declared to the authorities, and the land on which they were found was "frozen." This law was the first recognition of archaeology as a part of French heritage. However regional organizations, later established around a few "directors of antiquities," were given virtually no resources to protect or conserve archaeological sites. Nothing in dreams or reality gave any indication of the radical changes that were to occur in the last quarter of the twentieth century.

The Upheavals at the End of the Twentieth Century

The first signs of change in the French government's approach to archaeology came at the end of the 1960s, when two scandals, caused by clashes between archaeological authorities and powerful commercial interests, caused a considerable stir in Paris and Marseilles. These arguments reached the highest levels of government and the scandals had such an impact that a report was commissioned from Jacques Soustelle in 1974. On Soustelle's advice, the Fonds d'Intervention pour l'Archéologie de Sauvetage (Intervention Fund for Rescue Archaeology) was established. In 1977, an article was added to the urban planning regulations stipulating that a building permit could be refused or issued subject to restrictions if the project threatened the conservation or enhancement of archaeological remains. But nothing was stipulated about how and by whom the costs of excavation or conservation were to be met.

In 1981, a "Department of Archaeology" was finally created to study, protect, conserve, and promote archaeological sites. Then, in 1996, France ratified a European Union convention (the Malta Convention) intended to "protect the archaeological heritage as a source of the European collective memory and as an instrument of historical and scientific study." In ways that no one had foreseen, the number of excavations in France rose—from 720 in 1964 to 3,410 in 1995. France made up for lost time, and whole areas of national heritage were preserved.

The number of staff employed by the state to supervise excavations multiplied by 25 in 25 years (increasing from 10 in 1964 to 255 in 1988). Local authorities, who had not hired an archaeologist before 1971, employed 120 archaeologists in 1988. In 1989 there were 160 researchers working on French archaeological topics employed either by the national funding body for academic research, the Centre National de la Recherche Scientifique (CNRS), or by the universities. During the 1980s, significantly, major politicians began claiming a personal interest in archaeology. Heritage issues, often rather ambiguous ones—tied up with the effects of globalization on the national consciousness—came to play a key role in the budgets allocated by state and private enterprise to rescuing the archaeological remains that they were destroying. French president François Mitterrand, like the emperor Napoleon III and Marshal Pétain before him, started making references to the mythical ancestors of the French, the Gauls. In September 1985, he made a speech on this theme at the top of Mont Beuvray—where Vercingetorix had been proclaimed "leader" of the uprising against Julius Caesar. At the same time, he granted the site, which had been dug in the nineteenth century by JOSEPH DÉCHELETTE, more generous funds for excavation and improvement than ever before in French research. The complete refurbishment of the LOUVRE Museum, including the building of a glass pyramid in the center of the main courtyard, was another of the principal cultural endeavors of the Mitterrand presidency.

However, public authorities had to operate in a total legal vacuum as they attempted to force developers to contribute to the costs of rescue archaeology, amounting to 400 million francs per year nationally. This contribution was exacted on each occasion in return for the release of the land in question, following bargaining (which might be described as racketeering) based on the extent of the threat that the plans posed to the national heritage, and the legal obligation of the developers to preserve it. The funds were collected from the developers, with the backing of the Ministry of Finance, by a voluntary organization: the Association pour les Fouilles Archéologiques Nationales (Association for National Archaeological Excavations), better known by its acronym, AFAN. Between 1985 and 1989, AFAN's budget increased from 30 million francs to 130 million. In 1990, it had more than 1,300 archaeologists working under contract, that is, many more than in all French research institutions put together.

Thus, in a country that had for so long refused to recognize that remains under the ground constituted part of its heritage, rescue archaeology made steady progress at the end of the twentieth century. It is estimated that, in the last twenty-five years of the century, it was the source of 90 percent of the data produced by French archaeology.

Archaeologists Resort to Public Demonstrations

By the end of the 1990s, in the absence of any law on funding rescue digs and of resources allocated by the state to its own services, devel-

opers were becoming less and less inclined to pay for excavations. Furthermore, since developers' contributions were limited to releasing the land, analysis studies and publications of the archaeological material could not keep up. It looked as if there would be an inevitable division into two opposing types of archaeology. On the one side, field archaeology (de terrain) with abundant material and means but with little time to think about their findings, and on the other side, laboratory archaeology with little material and few facilities but with plenty of research time. This split deeply affected a professional community with a short institutional past. The archaeologists working on French sites—who had acquired their status only twenty years earlier—were still full of the utopian dreams and dynamism that drives any first generation of conquerors. It was at this point, in 1998, that the Ministry of Finance recommended that rescue archaeology be privatized and subject to financial competition. Archaeologists went on strike, occupied government buildings, opened museums and invaded television studios. In the end, more than a thousand archaeologists (over two-thirds of the archaeological community) demonstrated noisily in the streets of Paris against the government's policy.

To deal with this crisis, an emergency committee with three members, including archaeologist Jean-Paul Demoule, was set up by the Ministry of Culture. A parliamentary bill on the funding of rescue archaeology and the creation of a new public agency were proposed, and the bill was passed into law and the agency created in 2001. At the start of the second millennium, French archaeology—both scheduled archaeology and rescue archaeology—is still united, employs 2,000 people, and at long last has the modern resources that it requires.

Nevertheless some questions remain: Why was there so little hurry to professionalize archaeology in France, and why has the country never felt a lasting need to investigate its origins? The answer lies in the vision that France has always had of its citizenship and culture, having for years looked for its past in the Parthenon or the Capitol rather than in the huts of "our ancestors the Gauls." In any case, in a country with a large immigrant population, it was thought absurd to wish to show all the nation's children that their ancestors were Gauls.

Why Has France Never Felt a Lasting Need to Investigate Its Origins?

France is the source of the modern concept of the nation-state, based on the ideals of the French Revolution. It is also the most complete example of a nation-state in that, for longer and more strongly than elsewhere, the central government in France has asserted its supremacy over all other democratic institutions. The continuity of the structures of the state is indeed usually taken—now, as for several centuries past—to be identical with the unity of the country.

Nevertheless, the Revolution and the upheavals of the eighteenth century that affected Europe's sense of space, identity, time, and history led in France to the profound questioning of the concepts of society and nation. During that period the medieval myth of the Germanic and Trojan origins of the aristocracy was replaced by a different social and national model, in which the history of the nation was driven by historical, ethnic, and social forces that pitted the winners—the Franks—against the losers—the Gauls (Olivier 1999). Given the attitude toward social emancipation propounded by the Revolution and following in the philosophical tradition of the Enlightenment, the Frankish racial ancestry claimed by the aristocracy became socially indefensible. The nation henceforth was to be made up of the whole of society, meaning all those—whatever their origins—who had chosen to live together, and anyone who supported the values of the Republic was deemed to be a citizen.

However, conjuring away the racial ancestry allegedly bequeathed by the Franks to the minority of their noble descendants in favor of the cultural inheritance from the Gauls and Romans (supposedly the prerogative of the majority) gave rise to a pernicious notion of the French nation and its citizenship. As French archaeologist Laurent Olivier argues, these notions are both political (all those who support the values of the Republic are citizens) and ethnic (all those who live within the national frontiers are French). This ambiguity was to reemerge every time that the structural legitimacy of the state or the country's frontiers were challenged: in the reign of Napoleon III, after the defeat of 1870, and during the Second World War under the Vichy régime. Appeals were made to archaeology on each occasion because, on each occasion, the myth of "our ancestors the Gauls" was revived. This myth, by supporting the idea of the continuous existence of the nation ever since the very beginning (and France or the Republic being taken as its expression), made it possible—very briefly—to give legitimacy to the coincidence of the state, the frontiers, and the nation.

It is therefore logical that in 1996, at a time of increasing Americanization and when socially productive relationships were being affected by globalization, France did not hesitate to sign the Malta Convention, which advocated the protection of archaeological heritage as a source of European collective consciousness. It is also easy to understand why the French archaeological community shifted in a couple of decades from "universal" interests to curiosity about questions of identity, unconsciously based on a return to the values of a "national" past.

Low Priorities: Theoretical Models and Epistemological Curiosity

For many years the second feature peculiar to French archaeology was its rejection of theoretical models and its lack of epistemological curiosity. During the 1970s and 1980s, this trend was contradictory to those in the rest of society because French philosophy was emerging from one of its most productive periods, with figures like Sartre, Merleau-Ponty, Lévi-Strauss, Ricœur, Lacan, Goldmann, Lefèvre, Braudel, Althusser, Foucault, Barthes, Piaget, and later Vernant, Godelier, Bourdieu, Baudrillard, Derrida, and others making contributions. The paradox was even odder in that Anglo-American postmodern (or "postprocessual") archaeology borrowed most of the terms for its concepts from French.

It must be borne in mind, however, that French archaeologists were still few in number, and their institutions lacked, to put it mildly, coherence and policies. They had ludicrously tiny resources, and as a result theoretical models were not among their top priorities. Furthermore, at the time when French metropolitan archaeology was at last becoming established, modernity and grand explanatory paradigms were no longer in fashion. Besides, the individuality and proliferation of "postmodernist" ideas, which have continued to spring up ever since, were unable to gain widespread acceptance. French intellectuals grow up in a Cartesian deductive tradition, captured in the famous phrase *cogito, ergo sum.* In other words, their ability to think is their prime certainty. Their "reason" is not a faculty for epistemological questioning but a means of acquiring a direct grasp of the way things are. By following the logic of *cogito, ergo sum,* the intellectual can come to know and understand this reality purely through deduction.

Consequently, unlike their British or North American counterparts (who grow up in a system of empiricism), French researchers are not tempted to throw out the old paradigms and replace them with new ones that appear better suited to the problems of the moment. Instead, old and new concepts are combined as necessary into a general intellectual approach that cannot easily be labeled. This is why, for instance, structuralism in France has never been considered to be a theory or a school of thought, but simply a working method. Moreover, although nowadays young French archaeologists are familiar with epistemological concepts and ideas, they have difficulty in believing that there could be archaeological theories. The French indeed observe that archaeological data have never been used directly as the basis of a theory, when theory is defined as an explanatory system that works for data *other than* those used originally to generate the theory.

Archaeology, French Style

We have seen that, despite several crises of national legitimacy, French archaeology developed without the impetus of necessity. Local archaeology from the northern shores of the Mediterranean was never very interesting or contentious in France because of its inability to ever match up with the vision of excellence of Greco-Roman "civilization." This notion of archaeology as distinct from any idea of civilization is extremely important for an understanding of the situation of archaeological research in a country where the intelligentsia has always held a dominant position.

Yet everything began well. The fifteen volumes of *L'Antiquité expliquée en figures* by the Benedictine scholar BERNARD DE MONTFAUCON (published 1719–1724), which brought to public notice the antiquities attributed to the Gauls, and the *Recueil d'antiquités égyptiennes, étrusques, grecques, romaines et gauloises* by the COMTE DE CAYLUS (1752–1757), which emphasized the new notion of a typology, are evidence of the birth and growth of archaeological knowledge well able to take its place among the other humanities (Schnapp 1993). Admittedly, Montfaucon and Caylus were antiquaries, representatives of a style of archaeology that was mainly object-based and concerned only with monuments. But Caylus was not content merely with using antiquities for "illustrative" purposes. He wanted the study of antiquities to be one particular means of learning about the past, to interpret them using ethnographic comparisons, and to establish stylistic rules that would make it possible to assign a date and a place of origin to every object. Hence the care taken to collect the objects, describe them, and publish them formed the basis of a technical knowledge that, in the hands of men like Auguste Millin (1826) and later Solomon Reinach, was extremely important for French classical archaeology.

However, this prestigious tradition was eclipsed in the first half of the nineteenth century by the rise of German archaeology. In Germany, the *Altertumswissenschaft* revolution was under way, in which philology was given pride of place. It carried along with it German classical archaeology, which acquired a position in academe well before archaeology elsewhere in Europe was accorded similar status. Admittedly, the discoveries in France and the immense prestige of J.-F. CHAMPOLLION and, later, P. E. BOTTA contributed to the creation of outstanding schools of Egyptology and Assyriology. But Orientalism developed in Europe more as a cultural phenomenon than as a branch of archaeology. The philological research of scholars like Champollion or SIR HENRY RAWLINSON mattered more at that time than did the work of explorers like Botta or AUSTEN LAYARD. But the years 1830 to 1850 were decisive for the French study of prehistory quite independently of these other developments (Laming-Emperaire 1964). Prehistory in France grew out of anthropology, which had utterly different philosophical roots.

Despite his literary interests and his general culture, which were influenced by the Enlightenment, Boucher de Perthes helped create a type of prehistoric archaeology that owed little to the antiquaries of the eighteenth century. The natural history of mankind—as it developed in the second half of the nineteenth century, and to which the anthropological school of physical anthropologist Paul Broca made a substantial contribution—was very much a branch of natural science that devised its methods by analyzing remains directly in the field. It turned to experimentation and ethnological comparison for the same assistance that classical archaeology derived from aesthetics. This major difference still divides the field of archaeology and explains why prehistory and classical archaeology have had such dissimilar fates in France. Men like Jacques Boucher De Perthes, ÉDOUARD LARTET, and GABRIEL DE MORTILLET never had positions in the French academic system. And although Lartet was appointed late in life to the Museum of Natural History (where he did not have time to take up his chair) and de Mortillet was given a curatorship at the Museum of National Antiquities, French prehistorians were doubly excluded from academe until the 1950s, barred from both arts and science faculties. At the very time that French prehistory was making an impact on the study of archaeology worldwide, thanks to the wealth of finds in France and to de Mortillet's abilities as an organizer and theoretician, it was completely lacking in resources for action. Within France, nevertheless, de Mortillet's nomenclature and his typological definition of LITHIC industries were adopted as the frame of reference for the study of prehistory. But although the discipline was magnificently equipped to investigate Paleolithic periods, it had to look elsewhere—to Scandinavia, Britain, Germany, and Central Europe—for the elements it needed in order for the study of French protohistory to develop beyond its earliest stages. Despite the work of Déchelette, prematurely ended by his death in the First World War, French protohistorical archaeology never raised itself to the same standard as archaeology in Scandinavia or Central Europe. Excavations were few in number and depended entirely on private funding, and although OSCAR MONTELIUS's methods were acknowledged and adopted, they never generated original extensions.

A Long Period in the Wilderness

After the First World War, the Durkheim "school" of sociology, under its director, anthropologist Marcel Mauss, resumed its work. Faithful to the universalist traditions of the Enlightenment, it broadened its approach to include linguistics, comparative studies (*comparatisme*), and Orientalism. However, the archaeology of France itself did not seem able to develop, or to raise much interest. The state continued to exist, in conjunction with national unity, and in contrast to what happened in Germany nationalist claims were still not sufficiently intense to generate the idea of a foundation myth and a national archaeology. There had never needed to be any appeals to the origins, prehistory, and protohistory of France in order to legitimize anything. Consequently, while the human and social sciences started to grow around the journal *Année sociologique* and as Lucien Febvre and Marc Bloch launched *Les Annales,* the most influential French historical journal, French prehistorians and archaeologists were nowhere in sight.

Henri Hubert, curator at the Museum of National Antiquities, and Marcel Mauss worked together to initiate some fascinating studies of the expansion of Celtic culture. Classical archaeology, based on the French Schools in Athens and Rome, continued to develop slowly, and the ABBÉ HENRI BREUIL offered a first synthesis of the cultural prehistory of Europe. But the only courses of study available to anyone interested in prehistory were those of the Institute of Human

Standing stones in Carnac, France (Corel)

Paleontology, where men like Raymond Vaufrey and Henri Vallois maintained the tradition, rather than helping to train the key professionals in an expanding discipline. From that time onward the choice was straightforward: between orthodoxy (superbly represented by the Abbé Breuil and FRANÇOIS BORDES) or heterodoxy, inevitably shaped by the ideas of people who were self-taught. The institutional marginality and creativity of someone like André Leroi-Gourhan reaped their own reward in this setting.

André Leroi-Gourhan and Prehistoric Ethnology

After Gabriel de Mortillet, André Leroi-Gourhan was undoubtedly the person who made the greatest contribution to shaping French prehistory. Like de Mortillet, he was self-taught and he brought the same passionate interest to understanding technical systems as the former did to defining the laws of evolution (Leroi-Gourhan 1943, 1945). By laying the foundations of comparative ethnography and drawing on anthropology and Orientalism, he established prehistory as a field in its own right.

His approach to prehistory was completely different from the typologies of Breuil, which François Bordes later brilliantly developed and transformed (Bordes 1973). Whether with regard to the techniques of human labor, hominization, the interpretation of wall paintings, or excavation finds, the work of Leroi-Gourhan provided a frame of reference, an area of debate as vital for prehistoric archaeology as the work of Gordon Childe for protohistory. Against the disciplinary approach of traditional archaeology, which was primarily concerned with culture and classification, Leroi-Gourhan argued in favor of synthesis, combining anthropology and semiology in "prehistoric ethnology."

Leroi-Gourhan's approach—which had similarities with oriental archaeology—seemed well placed to win the day. But because it stayed deliberately marginal to both traditional prehistory and established ethnology, the work of Leroi-Gourhan was for a long time a matter of disappointment rather than development. It is important to realize that the questions raised by Leroi-Gourhan were discussed, then accepted or rejected. But the repercussions for archaeology were patchy rather than fully assimilated, and details, rather than the whole approach, were adopted. Excavation techniques were used when necessary, as was the criticism of ethnographic analogy when trying to establish a different analogy (Leroi-Gourhan 1985). Nevertheless by the end of the 1990s and at the beginning of the third millennium, his overall view of the process of hominid development—which raises the question of what it is to be human—was at last put into perspective, and his analysis of post-Neanderthal epiphylogenesis became part of the cognitive sciences. The visionary postulate of his book *Le Geste et la parole* (1964, 1965) and the logic underlying *Mécanique vivante* (1983), written in 1954, appear now to be remarkably relevant and epistemologically inspiring, compared with the debates on the origins of modern humans that stir up and cause futile clashes between researchers from all parts of the world.

Stumbling Blocks on the
Way Out of the Wilderness

Etudes archéologiques, the wide-ranging volume by several authors edited by Paul Courbin in 1963, was uninspiring and made no impact outside professional circles. But some of the papers (such as the one by Courbin himself on stratigraphy) were critical of French archaeology abroad, which had long been accustomed to clearing the most renowned sites around the Mediterranean in a somewhat cavalier fashion. Other papers, such as those of André Leroi-Gourhan and Jean-Claude Gardin, set out the program of work for the future. For this reason, these two authors were to be among the few French role models for a whole generation.

Almost all archaeological attention in the 1960s and 1970s concentrated on the technical aspects of observation and recording. As prehistoric archaeology emerged from the wilderness of a lack of public and government support, essential improvements in excavation methods quickly became an ideological stumbling block: for classical archaeologists, stratigraphic excavation was an end in itself, whereas prehistoric archaeologists always and everywhere excavated using the delicate tools of dentist's spatula and

fine brush. Consequently, when in 1971 Bohumil Soudsky started excavating at Cuiry-les-Chaudardes and other sites in the Aisne valley by machine-stripping, which he had perfected twenty years earlier in Bohemia, this use of this innovation—which was generally accepted everywhere else in Europe—caused outrage. And when, also in the Aisne valley, the first report appeared in 1973 listing all the sites threatened with destruction and suggested the idea of "selecting" which should be given priority on the basis of urgency, available funding, and scientific interest, the same violent reaction was unleashed. At that time in France there was no middle way between excavating inch by inch and total destruction. Methods based on physics and chemistry ("ARCHAEOMETRY") that had begun to be used by archaeologists were another stumbling block. The ability to obtain data and generate results using scientific apparatus and statistical techniques opened up the possibility of dispensing with philosophy, or the under-picture, which gave physicists—themselves just as much novices in this new collaboration—an unwarranted feeling of absolute power. Disillusionment was, however, painful when the first assessments were made in the early 1980s and these substitutes for clear thinking were found lacking. Documentation, data-processing, and interpretation encountered the same problems. Leroi-Gourhan's seminar at the Collège de France was devoted to developing a "temporary terminology" that was not just descriptive but also provisional. The creation of archaeological databases and expert systems as proposed by Gardin (1970) suffered from the same generalizing and self-defeating tendencies. In fact, the difficulty of creating a list of standardized generally applicable terms, required in order to computerize data, was an obstacle to creating a completely formal scientific discipline in the manner prophesied by Gardin (1979). Instead, two disparate kinds of study developed: nonspecialist documentary studies using a highly simplified descriptive vocabulary and individual, narrowly specialized research projects using incompatible complex descriptive terms. In studies of prehistory, the "analytical typology" of Laplace was unlikely to be adopted because its formal approach was much more difficult to put into practice than François Bordes's synthetic lists, and its criteria were not relevant to the questions that could now be addressed by analyzing the technologies of prehistoric tools.

For most people, the problems were intellectual, institutional, and financial; for others, the stumbling block was conceptual. Those who tried to echo the discussions about the "new archaeology" (Cleuziou et al. 1980; Schnapp 1980) were obliged to begin with the fundamentals, which meant becoming directly involved in the reform of institutions. This commitment was all the more necessary because archaeology was disastrously lacking in resources. The journal *Nouvelles de l'Archéologie,* launched in 1979, was a particularly effective weapon in this regard. A similar strategy, though less political, if not actually apolitical, was adopted by Gardin, who was the main architect of what he saw as a general reorganization of archaeology in France with the creation of a national archaeological institute, the Centre de Recherches Archéologiques. Thus it was that some members of the younger generation of the time, imbued with the utopian visions of 1968 and exceptionally united, tried—first via a systematic survey of the resources of French archaeology—to make the decision-makers fully aware of the discipline's chronic lack of funding (Normand and Richard 1974; Chapelot et al. 1979). This group worked tirelessly for more than twenty years to reshape university teaching, to create a unified discipline, to define policies for research, and to get funds earmarked, but also to adapt the techniques and strategies of excavation to the realities on the ground and the academic issues involved.

Consequently contacts with the inspiring new ideas of the "new archaeology" were real but anecdotal and personal. A notable exception was the debate between François Bordes and LEWIS BINFORD on the meaning of the different Mousterian *faciès,* which the former interpreted in terms of different cultures whereas the latter saw them as reflecting different functions. Ironically, the more "conservative" position (that of Bordes) was probably the more relevant. Thanks to the interest of American scholars in the Perigord, Bordes's work was soon translated and became popular in the United States, as he did himself. By contrast, the studies of Leroi-Gourhan (which should have generated even more interest) remained unknown to the English-speaking public until the 1990s.

The Special Characteristics of French Archaeology in Its Early Phases

It is noteworthy that archaeology played only a tiny role in the *Annales* school of history, in spite of the efforts of Lucien Febvre and Marc Bloch and Fernand Braudel's interest in "material civilization." Prehistory and "new history" came into contact only rarely (Brun 1987), and then with regard to material culture (Coudart and Pion 1986). It is true that *Annales* was the victim of its own success. Swept along by the growth of publishing and the media and affected by the European disenchantment with the models of economism and Marxism, the journal ultimately switched its focus to the history of *mentalités,* of cultural areas and "micro-history" rather than history over long periods (*de la longue durée*). Nevertheless, the studies undertaken by the Center for Historical Research at the École des Hautes Études en Sciences Sociales (EHESS) helped to develop the history of deserted villages and the social investigation of the rural world in the Middle Ages. It was a medieval historian and an archaeologist, then teaching at the EHESS, who produced the fullest survey of the medieval village (Chapelot and Fossier 1980). Today, other fields are proving equally fruitful. Excavations and work on the Bronze and Iron Ages are shedding new light on the role and situation of the Bronze Age and Celtic inhabitants of the temperate regions of Europe. The archaeology of Western Europe now faces vast ethnic and historical questions that so far have barely been addressed.

As for the school of Jean-Pierre Vernant and Pierre Vidal-Naquet, which brings together history, the history of religions, and anthropology, the focus there has been on framing questions of social and economic history and examining the role of images in ancient Greece (Vernant and Bérard 1984; Durand 1986; Schnapp 1993). This approach—the result of combining a structuralist analysis of the Greek tradition with an analysis of iconography—has been highly revealing and has helped to demonstrate the need for an hermeneutics of archaeology. This kind of history should now be deriving new material from the excavations in urban areas that have been under way in France since the 1980s. These major sites (the most famous is at the Louvre) are totally transforming the knowledge of daily life in medieval and postmedieval cities.

The French have also developed particular expertise in the specialized field of technological culture. This tradition arose from the conjunction of three things. The first is ethnology proper, starting with the work of pioneers such as André-Georges Haudricourt and André Leroi-Gourhan, who were followed by Charles Parain, Bertrand Gille, Robert Cresswell, François Sigaut, and most recently Pierre Lemonnier. Second is Leroi-Gourhan's ethnological approach to the study of prehistory. Last are the experiments in the technology of stone tools conducted by Jacques Tixier and the team he established. The anthropological study of technologies and technical systems, which has been particularly strong and is well illustrated by the group producing the journal *Techniques et culture,* is at present of greater interest to archaeologists than to ethnologists. The former are hoping that it will yield theories about the relationship between artifact and cognition, between material culture and society. But it is above all in the field of stone tools that archaeological experimentation in France has developed a wide range of resources—instruments for observing and monitoring movements of lithic raw materials (Tixier et al. 1980, 1984), "*chaînes opératoires*" (operating sequences) for producing tools, theories on the technical and cognitive capacities of *Homo erectus,* etc. Technology was therefore the direction taken by what may be called the "ethno-archaeological strategy" in the 1980s (Pétrequin 1984; Pétrequin and Pétrequin 1984). But the use made of ethnology has been both prudent and highly empirical, whether with regard to vernacular architecture in the Middle East, pottery-making in India, the dynamics of lake-settlements in Bénin, processing skins in western North Amer-ica, the lifestyles of Arctic peoples, or tool-making in New Guinea. This research taken as a whole has, however, yielded a substantial quantity of data and fresh ideas.

At the Beginning of the Twenty-first Century: Every Reason for Optimism

Only with the creation in 1979 by Fernand Braudel's Maison des Sciences de l'Homme of the journal *Les Nouvelles de l'Archéologie,* an academic journal also concerned with policies and information, did conceptual thinking about archaeology acquire coherence in France. At the same time, as we saw earlier, rescue archaeology was radically overhauled—a development that the editors of the journal were to follow and sustain with interest. The idea of an excavation plan became indispensable in the context of the large-scale rescue operations, and at the same time it led to the development of practical thinking about prospecting, sampling, and quantitative methods. Salvage excavations and regional programs to support them and bring together all available methods were put into place, and proved effective in the Aisne valley in Picardy and on Lakes Clairvaux and Chalain in the Jura. Nevertheless it took the revolt of the archaeologists in 1998 (the third of its kind since 1989) and the appointment of Catherine Trautmann as minister of culture for this growth at last to be restructured through reform, law, and the creation of a public body responsible for excavation and research that would look after rescue archaeology, and indeed archaeology in general (*Les Nouvelles de l'Archéologie* 1999–2000, 73–79).

As is clear from the catalogue for the 1989 Paris exhibition (Mohen 1989), and in spite of the work of people like Jacques Cauvin (1994) or the 30- and 40-year-olds who received less media coverage, French archaeology in the 1990s was still committing the same sins as before. Thus most archaeologists continued to be skeptical about building social and cultural models, following in the tradition of people like Bordes, Leroi-Gourhan (his position in the 1970s and 1980s, at least), Courbin, Gardin, and some others. This skepticism led them to deal in notions that are all the more dangerous

The ruins of Glanum, a Roman city near St. Remy de Provence, France (Spectrum Colour Library)

because they are not stated explicitly. For instance, the arsenal of techniques drawn from the natural sciences has often given rise to oversimplified determinist environmental models. At the same time, the appearance from time to time of British or North American scholars in France has encouraged the development of antidiffusionist approaches—frequently based on an excessive use of radiocarbon dating, with its imprecise measurements that can give a false impression that objects are contemporary—that do not always appear to fit the facts. Similarly, certain postprocessual works have been read by people without enough background and this has led to ahistorical interpretations at variance with the facts or lacking in any determinism. By contrast, in a completely different field, diffusionism has been much used in France by a group of extreme right-wing intellectuals, "the New Right," in order to account for the Indo-Europeans and to demonstrate the superiority of European civilization. In passing, it should be pointed out that archaeology alone certainly would not provide a simple answer to this intriguing question; rather, the solution would require the close collaboration of archaeologists, linguists, and experts on ethnology and myth to produce new theoretical models (Demoule 1980, 1999).

At the beginning of the twenty-first century, the quantity of data being assembled and the number of professional archaeologists in post were infinitely greater than in the past. Whereas barely a dozen professional archaeologists were working on French sites in the early 1960s, in 2001 there were almost 1,500. Thus, at the beginning of the twenty-first century, the expansion being experienced at last by French archaeology, in terms of both people and institutions, offered the prerequisites for making good the lack of epistemological questioning, theories, and interpretations. Work is under way to rethink the sociological models of the Neolithic period, the Bronze and Iron Ages, and the Gallo-Roman period, addressing the transformation of mentalities and the role of symbolism in the development of the Neolithic; the role of material culture, of animals, the environment and spatial organization in the construction, reproduction and transformation of social relationships and cultural identities; and trying to identify the factors involved in the transformations of landscape, the development of the Neolithic, and the emergence of statehood.

Lastly, one of the remarkable features of French archaeology is the position of women. During the slow development of the field, the few key posts were held by men. But since the 1990s, most of them have been occupied by women, as if it was not until the job had become a proper profession that it opened up to both sexes. For example, the directors of the two most important archaeological laboratories, the CNRS (Center for Archaeological Research, closed down in 1997), and the team "Archéologies et sciences de l'antiquité," created the same year, were women; the head of the largest collection in France of archaeological publications (the Documents d'archéologie française) is a woman; the editor of the most emblematic archaeological journal, *Gallia,* is a woman; as are the editors of the only international journal, *Paléorient,* and of the journal devoted to opinions and policy issues in archaeology, *Les Nouvelles de l'Archéologie* (and, as such, symbolic of a peculiarly French trait).

In 1998—a quarter-century after the creation of what was intended to be a top-quality institution (the moribund National Center for Archaeological Research disappeared in 1997 without causing much reaction) and a few months before the publication of the parliamentary bill that would establish the first public agency responsible for rescue archaeology and archaeological research—for the first time in France, a laboratory was set up bringing together about 200 prehistorians, protohistorians, classical archaeologists, historians, and paleo-environmentalists. Admittedly, French archaeology had taken 150 years to become united and to acquire an institutional base, but today there is every reason for optimism.

Anick Coudart

See also Africa, Francophone; French Archaeology in the Americas; French Archaeology in Egypt and the Middle East; French Archaeology in the Classical World

References

Journals: *Bulletin de la Société préhistorique française; Gallia; Les Nouvelles de l'Archéologie; Paléorient; Techniques et Cultures.*

Audouze, F., and A. Leroi-Gourhan. 1981. "France: A Continental Insularity." *World Archaeology* 13, no. 2: 170–189.

Bordes, F. 1973. "On the Chronology and the Contemporaneity of Different Paleolithic Cultures in France." Pp. 217–226 in *The Explanation of Culture Change. Models in Prehistory.* Ed. C. Renfrew. London: Duckworth.

Brun, P. 1987. *Prince et princesse de la Celtique.* Paris: Errance.

Cauvin, J. 1994, 1998. *Naissance des divinités, naissance de l'agriculture. La révolution des symboles au néolithique.* Paris: CNRS Editions, and Flammarion (coll. Champs).

Caylus, Anne Claude François (de). 1752–1757. *Recueil d'antiquités égyptiennes, étrusques, grecques et romaines.* 7 vol. Paris.

Chapelot, J., and J. Fossier. 1980. *Le village et la maison au moyen âge.* Paris: Hachette. (1985. *Village and House in the Middle Ages.* London: Batsford.)

Chapelot, J., A. Querrien, and A. Schnapp. 1979. "L'archéologie en France. Les facteurs d'une crise." *Le Progrès scientifique* 202: 57–110.

Cleuziou, S., and J.-P. Demoule. 1980. "Situation de l'archéologie théorique." *Nouvelles de l'Archéologie* 3: 7–15.

Coudart, A., and P. Pion. 1986. *L'archéologie de la France rurale. De la préhistoire aux temps modernes.* Paris: Belin.

Déchelette, J. 1931. *Manuel d'archéologie préhistorique, celtique et gallo-romaine.* Paris: Picard.

Demoule, J.-P. 1980. "Les Indo-européens ont-ils existé?" *L'Histoire* 28: 108–20.

———. 1990. *La France de la Préhistoire. Mille millénaires, des premiers hommes à la conquête romaine.* Paris: Nathan.

———. 1999. "Ethnicity, Culture and Identity: French Archaeologists and Historians." *Antiquity* 73, no. 279: 190–198.

Durand, J.-L. 1970. *Archéologie et calculateurs: problèmes mathématiques et sémiologiques.* Paris: CNRS.

———. 1986. *Sacrifice et tabou en Grèce ancienne. Essai d'anthropologie religieuse.* Paris: La Découverte.

Gardin, J.-C. 1979. *Une archéologie théorique.* Paris: Hachette. (1979. *Archaeological Constructs. An Aspect of Theoretical Archaeology.* Cambridge: Cambridge University Press.)

Laming-Emperaire, A. 1964. *Origines de l'archéologie préhistorique en France, des superstitions médiévales à la découverte de l'homme fossile.* Paris: Picard.

Leroi-Gourhan, A. 1943. *Évolution et techniques: L'homme et la matière.* Paris: Albin Michel. (Reprint 1971.)

———. 1945. *Évolution et techniques: Milieu et techniques.* Paris: Albin Michel. (Reprint 1973.)

———. 1964. *Le geste et la parole I. Technique et langage.* Paris: Albin Michel.

———. 1965. *Le geste et la parole II. La mémoire et les rythmes.* Paris: Albin Michel.

———. 1983. *Mécanique vivante. Le crâne des vertébrés du poisson à l'homme.* Paris: Fayard (Le Temps des sciences).

———. 1985. *Le fils du temps. Ethnologie et préhistoire (1935–1970).* Paris: Fayard.

Millin, A. L. 1826. *Introduction à l'étude de l'archéologie.* Paris: Chez Girard.

Mohen J.-P. 1989. *Archéologie de la France. Trente ans de découvertes.* Paris: Réunion des Musées nationaux.

Montfaucon, B. de. 1719–1724. *L'antiquité expliquée et représentée en figures.* 15 vols. Paris.

Normand, F. and A. Richard. 1974. "L'archéologie française en crise." *La Recherche* (Septembre): 754–762.

Olivier, L. 1999. "The Origins of French Archaeology." *Antiquity* 73, no. 279: 176–183.

Pétrequin, A.-M., and P. Pétrequin. 1984. *Habitat lacustre du Bénin. Une approche ethnoarchéologique.* Paris: ERC.

Pétrequin, P. 1984. *Gens de l'eau, gens de la terre. Ethnoarchéologie des communautés lacustres.* Paris: Hachette.

Querrien, A., and A. Schnapp. 1984. "Second rapport sur la politique de la recherche archéologique en France." *Nouvelles de l'Archéologie* 16: 7–61.

Schnapp, A. 1980. *L'archéologie aujourd'hui.* Paris: Hachette.

———. 1993. *La conquête du passé. Aux origines de l'archéologie.* Paris: Editions Carré.

Tixier, J., M.-L. Inizan, and H. Roche. 1980, 1984. *Préhistoire de la pierre taillée 1 (Terminologie et technologie), 2 (Economie du débitage laminaire).* Paris: Editions du CNRS.

Vernant, J.-P., and P. Bérard. 1984. *La cité des images.* Paris and Lausanne: LEP-Nathan; Princeton, NJ: Princeton University Press.

Frankfort, Henri (1897–1954)

Born in Amsterdam, Henri Frankfort served in the army of the NETHERLANDS during World War I and later studied history at the University of Amsterdam before transferring to University College, London, to work on his M.A. with SIR WILLIAM MATTHEW FLINDERS PETRIE. From 1925 until 1929, Frankfort directed excavations for the EGYPT EXPLORATION SOCIETY at Tell EL AMARNA, ABYDOS, and Armant. He received a Ph.D. from the University of Leiden in 1927.

In 1929, Frankfort was invited by the great American ancient historian Henry Breasted to be field director of the University of Chicago's ORIENTAL INSTITUTE's Iraq Expedition at Diyala, a position he held until 1937. In 1932, he was appointed Research Professor of Oriental Archaeology at the Oriental Institute of the University of Chicago and concurrently held the position of extraordinary professor in the history and archaeology of the ancient Near East at the University of Amsterdam. During World War II, Frankfort lived in Chicago and concentrated on research, publications, and teaching, and during the war and afterward he influenced a generation of U.S. student archaeologists and anthropologists.

Frankfort published fifteen books, among which are the seminal *Studies in Early Pottery of the Near East* (1924–1927), *Cylinder Seals* (1939), *Ancient Egyptian Religion: An Interpretation* (1948), *Kingship and the Gods* (1948), and *The Art and Architecture of the Ancient Orient* (1954). He also wrote over seventy-three journal articles and as many book reviews.

In 1949, he accepted the directorship of the Warburg Institute in London and a professorship in the history of preclassical antiquity at the University of London. He last visited the Near East in 1952 as a Guggenheim fellow to research and write *The Art and Architecture of the Ancient Orient.*

Tim Murray

References
Frankfort, Henri. 1924–1927. *Studies in Early Pottery of the Near East.* London: Royal Anthropological Institute of Great Britain and Ireland.

———. 1939. *Cylinder Seals; a Documentary Essay*

on the Art and Religion of the Ancient Near East. London: Macmillan.

—. 1948a. *Ancient Egyptian Religion: An Interpretation*. New York: Harper & Row.

—. 1948b. *Kingship and the Gods: a Study of Ancient Near Eastern Religion as the Integration of Society & Nature*. Chicago: University of Chicago Press.

—. 1954. *The Art and Architecture of the Ancient Orient*. Harmondsworth, UK: Penguin Books.

French Archaeology in the Americas

As might be expected, French archaeological research in the New World began only at the start of the nineteenth century, when the independence of the United States put an end to Spanish colonial rule. The same is, of course, mostly true for other European countries, if one does not take into account the early years of archaeological investigation in the United States and the Moundbuilders controversy. In their *History of American Archaeology* (1974), GORDON WILLEY and Jeremy Sabloff called the period from discovery until 1840 the time of witnesses and armchair historians. IGNACIO BERNAL GARCIA, in his *History of Mexican Archaeology* (1980) differed somewhat, considering the discovery of the Calendar Stone in MEXICO in 1792 and its study by Alzate and Leon y Gama as the starting point for the next period of early study. In fact, the first four decades of the nineteenth century were a period of intense activity—but mainly due to local, French, or English investigators. The publication of JOHN STEPHENS and FREDERICK CATHERWOOD's *Incidents of Travel in Central America, Chiapas and Yucatán* in 1840 was the culmination of this early interest.

From 1840 to 1914 the explorations and descriptions of archaeological sites in the Americas were intensive, but by the end of the nineteenth century there was more of a tendency toward institutional and scientific research. During this period French explorers were quite active, but 1914 marked the end of an era, and this date has a deep significance for the whole of Americanist research. Specific events, such as the Mexican Revolution and its consequences and World War I in Europe, generated a rare strain of European field research that was to last for several decades

and, therefore, an Americanization of archaeological investigation that would continue until the end of World War II. The year 1914 also brought strong changes in archaeological theories and methods. The development of new techniques, such as the stratigraphic revolution, and the establishment of new institutions in Mexico and the United States, such as the Carnegie Institution, accompanied a complete transformation in the ideological background of archaeology, under American anthropologist Franz Boas's influence.

The aftermath of World War I resulted in a nearly total absence of French investigators the Americas for many years. French anthropological research fared slightly better in the 1930s, but the political situation prevented the acceleration of this trend, and it is not possible to discern French involvement in the Americanization process until the 1950s. By the time French investigators and archaeologists once again became active in this field, American archaeology had undergone a complete and autonomous growth, to which the Europeans had to adapt themselves. In the 1950s those working in the field of archaeology experienced turmoil and dissatisfaction, partly because of their own results but also because of the introduction of new techniques (aerial photography, radiocarbon dating). This occasioned a change in theoretical approaches toward functional and contextual preoccupations, which in turn paved the way for the "New Archaeology." Many Latin American countries began to organize archaeological research on an institutional basis and to promote the legal protection of sites and their national patrimony. Renewed French archaeological research had to adapt to these many changes: ultimately, it took several years to put together the scientific and institutional basis that gave birth to the new French Americanism, which is still very active today.

Thus, the history of French Americanism does not fit within either Willey and Sabloff's or Bernal's proposed chronological frameworks, as exemplified in the accompanying table (see page 536). If 1492 is taken as a starting point, the first period—the period of discovery and history—would last until 1824–1834, ending

	Willey-Sabloff American research	Bernal Mexican research	French archaeology Proposed chronology
1492	Discovery Witnesses and historians	Discovery Armchair studies	Discovery Historians and collectors
1792		First archaeological discoveries in Mexico	
1834			Publication of *Antiquités Mexicaines*
1840	Publication of Stephens and Catherwood's book		
1860	Explorers	Explorers	French Scientific Commission in Mexico Explorers
1914	Start of the stratigraphic revolution The classificatory period	Mexican Revolution and Archaeological School of Mexico	World War I: the end of the explorers
1940– 1950		The institutionalization of archaeological research	The collapse of French Americanism
1960	The first dissatisfactions The beginning of New Archaeology		Starting anew: a rebirth of French archaeology in America

with the publication of *Antiquités Mexicaines*. The next decades, up to 1860, continued this early start, and from 1860 until 1914 France took an active role in the exploration and registration of archaeological sites in the Americas. The first half of the twentieth century saw a collapse of French archaeological research in the Americas, and it is only after 1960 that this complex history resulted in actual scientific and systematic studies of the American past.

From Discovery to Antiquités Mexicaines

It took France some time to become interested in the discovery of the Americas. Like Great Britain, France was deeply entangled in its struggle against the Spanish king Charles V in Europe, and the existence of a new continent aroused only slight interest in intellectual circles, mostly among writers and artists. Writers such as Michel Eyquem de Montaigne or François Rabelais sometimes referred to the inhabitants of the New World; this interest did not amount to more than a mere curiosity for exotics and new artifacts.

As its political situation improved, France slowly paid more attention to the American continent. While corsairs plundered colonies and attacked Spanish fleets in the south, the arrival of Jacques Cartier in CANADA in 1534 marked the beginning of French colonial enterprises in that part of the world. Canada quickly became a French stronghold and would remain so for several centuries, but French settlements in Florida and Brazil did not succeed, and only a few scattered settlements in the West Indies were permanently occupied. These territories proved themselves, in many respects, much less attractive than Mesoamerica or Peru, and France quite naturally turned its attention toward the exploitation of economic resources, rather than Indian civilizations. Very few artifacts were taken away to be featured in the Wunderkammer, or Cabinets de Curiosités (collections of strange objects and precursors of museum collections), in France. Those that were featured there, as Pascal Riviale (1993) demonstrated, were usually classified as "naturalia" or "artificialia," rather than works of art. From the very beginning American artifacts in France were assigned to the realm of natural history.

This does not mean that French Cabinets de Curiosités were entirely devoid of American objects. Their presence was acknowledged, the most important instance being the *Codex Telleriano-Remensis,* the collection of artifacts given to the Royal Library by Archbishop Le Tellier at the beginning of the eighteenth century. A few Peruvian ceramics were also taken back to France by smugglers from Saint Malo, with the help of French residents in Lima, such as Dr. Leblond. In addition, there was a great desire to acquire larger collections, as was made obvious in documents such as the instructions issued to the Jussieu–La Condamine and Dombey expeditions to PERU, which directed the teams to try to collect artifacts from Chancay and Pachacamac. But the whole collection amounted to little more than a few items, and the American past was more likely to be the subject of speculative or literary activity.

As Keen amply demonstrated (1971), from the end of the sixteenth century until 1820, the Americas and the Amerindian civilizations became the focus of a growing interest. The pioneering books of De Belleforest in 1572 and Thevet, a geographer in the court of King Henri II, were quickly translated into many languages. Discussions of the Americas became contentious as time went by, and most well-known eighteenth-century philosophers, such as Buffon, Voltaire, and Prevost, took sides in these controversies. The Americas even provided a source of inspiration for poetry, theater, and opera. This general interest for American civilizations was part of an increasing tendency to dwell on humankind's past. As Schnapp recently demonstrated, archaeology—or at least scholarly activity in archaeology—was establishing itself as a scientific discipline, and discoveries in southern Italy quickly led to the systematic study of ruins. The kings of SPAIN promoted this research and sent explorers to the Mayan ruins of PALENQUE (Baudez 1987). In Mexico the chance discovery of AZTEC sculptures in 1792 prompted national investigations by scholars such as Alzate and Leon y Gama. The Bonaparte expedition to Egypt stands out as the most famous example of early French studies in archaeology. The American continent was not entirely neglected, as evidenced by the travels of Humboldt and Bonpland in South and Central America in 1810. The French concept of the American past was anthropological in nature, expressing a natural historical approach rather than an interest in American art, and French research focused mainly on human diversity, not just upon archaeological remains. The end of Spanish rule in Latin America provided opportunities that France and other countries seized immediately.

The breakthrough for French Americanism came in 1834, six years before Stephens and Catherwood's book, with the appearance of *Antiquités Mexicaines.* This book included the manuscripts of Galindom Del Rio and Juarros, as well as articles by Humboldt, Warden, Jomard Baraère, and even Chateaubriand, but it failed to attract much attention. The French public had to wait 150 years to be able to read Stephens and Catherwood's book in translation. This situation symbolizes perfectly the original inadequacy of French Americanism in the nineteenth century—too little and too late.

A Century of Exploration
For the whole of the nineteenth century (or, more precisely, from 1824 to 1914), American archaeology in France remained restricted to a small circle of explorers and scholars, who succeeded in obtaining the backing of official institutions but failed to raise public interest. French explorers and adventurers, though few in number, *were* able to organize associations and committees to raise funds for their travels. The French Ministry for Public Instruction was the most prominent sponsor, especially after the creation of the Mission Service, but the Natural History Museum and the Navy also played useful roles. For example, in 1836, the ship *La Venus,* commanded by Dupetit-Thouars, was instructed by Brongniart to collect Peruvian ceramics for the Musée de Sèvres. Societies such as the Geographical Society in Paris created prizes and medals, published reports, and organized conferences, and they succeeded in attracting investigators from other countries, such as the American antiquarian Ephraim Squier and naturalist Alexander von Humboldt, as corresponding members.

An aerial view of ruins in the Mayan settlement at Tonina, Mexico (Danny Lehman/Corbis)

But this state-directed exploration was inevitably dependent upon political events. The ultimate failure of the French Scientific Expedition to Mexico (1861–1865) was followed by the failure of French intervention in the Mexican Revolution. In the next century World War I brought an end to the era of exploration. The official backing was a part of national ideological tendencies, and French explorers were deeply influenced by the ideology of colonialism, with strong undertones of Eurocentrism. The scholars' belief in progress and positivism influenced their studies and hypotheses toward a general evolutionary approach to American civilizations. These theoretical bases would isolate the French scholars from the other investigative currents that were to culminate in the making of American archaeology.

However, prior to 1850, the contribution of French explorers to the knowledge and study of ancient civilizations of the Americas was tremendous. The pioneer expedition of Humboldt and Bonpland at the beginning of nineteenth century (1810–1816) generated great interest. Many books on American Indian civi-

lizations were translated, among them those of Bullock, Pionsett, Hall, and Beltrami. The identification of Mayan writing by Raginesque provoked Champollion's attention. In 1819 an archaeological expedition was sent to El Tajin, in Central Veracruz, and three French explorers—Sussanet, Naudin, and Castillon—were accepted as members of the team. Between 1822 and 1836 no fewer than forty articles on Mexico were published in the *Geographical Society Bulletin.* Meanwhile, the preparation of *Antiquités Mexicaines* brought together new scholars. In 1828 Baradère took Dupaix's manuscripts, drawings, and numerous artifacts from Mexico back to France. Waldeck was sent to London to copy Armendaris's illustrations, which is how he became involved in Mayan archaeology. He spent many years in Palenque (Baudez 1993), thus earning his nickname, "The Last of the Pioneers" (Stuart 1992). At the same time, Nebel, a German architect sponsored by French funds, worked in Xochicalco, El Tajin, and La Quemada. The list of known Mexican sites grew constantly, and to the ones already mentioned can be added Mitla, MONTE ALBÁN, Uxmal, Tonina, Cholula, and, of course, TEOTIHUACÁN. At the same time in Mexico, Joseph Marie Aubin started collecting pictorial manuscripts, which he took back to Paris before selling them to Eugène Goupil. These were the basis for Boban and Ternaux-Compan's studies. One of the richest collections outside Mexico, they remain in the Bibliothèque Nationale.

Andean civilizations received much less attention at this time than their Mexican counterparts. However, Alcide d'Orbigny traveled extensively through Peru and BOLIVIA between 1826 and 1833, and the results of his expedition, as recorded in his journal, were on a par with discoveries in Mexico.

By the time of Stephens's travels, France was deeply involved in the discovery of American antiquities, and several of the most famous French explorers had already completed their research. Stephens and Catherwood's book contributed to a renewal of interest in the Americas and to the appearance of the second generation of explorers, such as Charnay and Brasseur de Bourbourg. A short lapse of twenty years separated their contributions from those of their predecessors, and during the interim only Castelnau's travels in South America in 1843 are worth mentioning. In France itself official structures designated to strengthen field research were set up. The Mission Service of the Ministry for Public Education was established in 1842 to provide funds for exploration, and several societies conceived a corpus of instructions to direct and orient investigations to fill in the blanks of knowledge about past American civilizations. Linguistics, physical anthropology, ethnology, and archaeology were included in these objectives. Now, for the first time, American objects found their way into French museum collections. At the LOUVRE Longperier gathered together over 1,000 American artifacts—an improvement when compared to the few items available at the end of eighteenth century but also proof that French knowledge of the Americas was still scanty.

From 1860 on, explorations tended to become more systematic and coordinated; this was true for every country and all the more so for France. Under the auspices of recently established institutions, research grew steadily, and during the last four decades of the nineteenth century thirty-two expeditions were sent to America (Riviale 1991):

Peru:	10 missions	Chile:	2 missions
Mexico:	9 missions	Argentina:	2 missions
Bolivia:	5 missions	Costa Rica:	1 mission
Brazil:	4 missions	Salvador:	1 mission
Guatemala:	3 missions	Venezuela:	1 mission
Panama:	3 missions	Central America:	1 mission
Paraguay:	3 missions	South America:	1 mission
Ecuador:	2 missions		

One must remember, of course, that this total represents only 6.5 percent of all the official missions, for France's greatest activities were directed toward its areas of colonial interests in Africa, the Middle East, and the Far East. However, the preceding list does include almost the whole of the Americas. Among explorers and adventurers, several scholars were included, such as Charnay, Génin, Brasseur de Bourbourg, or Pérogny in Mexico; Crevaux in Guyana; Pinart in Alaska; and Wiener, Ber, Vidal-Senèze, and Créqui-Montfort in the Andes. Americanist research attracted greater public attention, as exemplified by the inclusion of exhibits in the Universal Expositions of 1867 (with Méhédin's reconstitution of the Xochicalco pyramid) and 1878 (with Wiener's collections).

The work of the French Scientific Commission in Mexico, founded by Napoleon III at the time of French intervention in Mexican politics, though still underestimated, stands as a great French achievement. Mexico's victory and the subsequent fall of the French empire obliterated much of what it accomplished. The commission was directed by men such as Aubin, JEAN DE QUATREFAGES, Larrey, Longpérier, and Daly; in Mexico scholars such as Charnay, Brasseur, and Guillemin-Tarayre and Mexican archaeologists such as Garcia Cubas and Ramon Almarez participated in its activities. Successes of the commission include the first excavations at Teotihuacan by Méhédin and Almaraz, ill-fated research in Uxmal by Brasseur, and Remi Simeon's identification of the Aztec system of numeration. The political failure of this commission did not prevent further archaeological research.

In North America explorers were less numerous, but some of them made important contributions to archaeology. In the Mississippi Valley Lesueur excavated some mounds, and Pinart's research on the northwest Pacific Coast is still significant. The most important contribution was made by Cessac, whose lithic collections in the Chumash area still form the basis of the history of California.

MESOAMERICA attracted most investigators. There, Charnay used photographs for the first time to register monuments. He also identified the mythical Tollan as Tula, and he conducted the first excavations of that site. Diguet's contribution to the archaeology of northwestern Mexico still awaits proper evaluation, and in the Mayan areas, Périgny discovered the Rio Bec site and style. The Swiss investigator De Saussure published a unique article on the site of Cantona, now for the first time the subject of a vast archaeological project. But his main contribution lay in the study of glyphs, with his publication of *Codex Becker*.

The study of Mesoamerican writing systems constituted a special branch of archaeology in which French scholars participated during the nineteenth century. Brasseur's discovery of Landa's Relacion de las Cosas de Yucatan and of the Popol Vuh and then the Codex Tro-Cortesianus were essential landmarks in the field of epigraphy. Despite the intervention of scholars such as Charencey and Rosny later on, epigraphical studies were quickly left to German or American specialists (Seler, Förstemann, Scwellhas, Maler, Maudslay, and Goodman).

South American civilizations were somewhat neglected but not ignored by French archaeologists: Wiener is known for having brought back 2,500 artifacts from his two-year stay in Peru, many of them characteristic of previously unknown styles such as Recuay. The Créqui-Montfort expedition to the South Andes benefited from the help of specialists such as GABRIEL DE MORTILLET and Boman, and it brought into focus little-known aspects of South American civilizations, including the Diaguites. A special mention must be made of Ber, who, though still neglected, insisted for the first time upon the need for a contextual approach to collecting Peruvian remains. This list of researchers is far from exhaustive: one could add many other names, among them Nadiallac, Crevaux, and Colpaert in Peru and Pector in Central America.

This intense activity rested, as already mentioned, on a fragile theoretical basis, but it led to some outstanding results, including the organization of the first International Congress of Americanists in Nancy, France, in 1875. This meeting proved to be such a success that three more congresses were held in Paris before 1900. The Société des Américanistes recruited old hands such as Rosny, Hamy, Lejéal, and Nadaillac, as well as newcomers such as Cordier, Capitan, Rivet, and even Maspéro, and the duke of Loubat. The duke sponsored field research, either by French or foreign scholars (Seler, Holmes, and Saville), and he created the first academic position, at the Collège de France, where Lejéal and Beuchat had a chance to teach. Unfortunately, these changes came too late, and in the field, French explorers were confronted with trained archaeologists from other countries such as MAX UHLE, Alfred Tozzer, and MANUEL GAMIO. Exploration gave way to scientific research, and at the creation of the first school of archaeology in Mexico in 1910, only one Frenchman was involved—Enguerrand, who stands as the perfect symbol of this new situation. French explorers lost touch with current trends and the study of the Americas was no longer deemed fashionable. When World War I exploded in 1914, most French scholars in archaeology were either dead or retired, and the Americanization of American studies was on its way.

1914–1960: A Collapse?

If we follow Willey and Sabloff's chronological scheme, the period between 1914 and 1960 was characterized by the stratigraphic revolution. Everywhere in America, chronologies were sought after, excavations were conducted by huge teams, and at the end of the period, the use of new techniques such as aerial photography and radiocarbon DATING allowed for the elaboration of secure aereal chronological charts. Although similar progress occurred in France itself, with some influence on this evolution, French archaeologists were not in the field in the Americas. French research was limited to a short-lived grant allowance that enabled young students in anthropology to spend some time in the field (such as Soustelle Ricard, Gessain, Stresser-Péan), and to the field intervention of a few trained investigators such as d'Harcourt, Beuchat, and Rivet. Their most important achievement lay in the creation of the Musée de l'Homme, in Paris, the third stronghold of French American studies.

The public perception of American Indian art, at the same time, went through a significant change under the influence of both artists (e.g., the surrealists) and antiquarians. Along with African and Far Eastern civilizations, the peoples of Mesoamerica and the Andes were at last recognized as art producers. Several exhibitions and numerous articles and catalogs were devoted to the popularization of native art from the Americas, which had finally found a place in French art history.

World War II suppressed this renewed interest. The turmoil of war and political instability caused many European anthropologists, among them Armillas Palerm and Wittfogel, to emigrate to the American continent. But only Rivet in COLOMBIA contributed to the establishment of scientific research. French-trained archaeologist Reichel-Dolmatoff migrated as well, and his synthesis of Colombian archaeology stands out among the few general publications of the 1950s. In CHILE Emperaire conducted field research on the Alakaluf, a neglected area, and some other archaeologists kept working, including Flornoy in Peru and Lehmann in GUATEMALA. But ethnology and general anthropology were the dominant interests, and the French contribution to the archaeology of the Americas remained small. One must nonetheless mention Soustelle's books on the Aztecs, which, though closer to ethnohistory, showed that French American studies were not to be underestimated.

By the end of the 1950s the economic situation in France had improved, and French research, which was supported by the firmly established structures of the Société des Américanistes, the Musée de l'Homme, and the International Congresses, could begin again.

Institutional Research: The Flowering of French Activity

French Americanists sought official backing from the French government's secretary for foreign affairs, who was called on to create the equivalent of the Athens or Rome schools of archaeology in the Americas. This caused the birth of the Institut Français d'Etudes Andines (IFEA) in Lima and the Mission Archéologique et Ethnologique Française (MAEFM, now known as CEMCA) in Mexico, both of which were devoted to anthropological investigation in the Andes and Mesoamerica. The MAEFM was established in 1961, and the IFEA in Peru was part of a general cooperational governmental agreement in 1970 between Mexico and France, on a permanent basis. There is some justification for the existence of such centers, despite their being characteristic of a French state-oriented mentality. They provide stability and financial or technical help to French investigators, and they encourage an interdisciplinary approach that suits the present needs of scientific research.

It is too early to judge recent research in the Americas, but this history of French Americanist archaeology would be incomplete if it did not include the results of the IFEA and MAEFM. French archaeology in the Americas has grown steadily. In 1971 these institutions directed three archaeological projects; by 1990 fifteen projects were under way in nine different countries.

Thanks to the help and efficiency of P. Guillemin, director of the department who manages IFEA and MAEFM at the secretary for foreign affairs, the IFEA and the MAEFM consolidated their local position, and simultaneously in France, specialized sections at the Centre National de la Recherche Scientifique (CNRS) and at various universities were organized. Archaeological research also started up in French territories—that is, in Guyana and some islands in the West Indies, an area that had previously been neglected.

These institutional and governmental structures were also strengthened by French investigators living in the Americas, and French-trained archaeologists and French Canadians began to get involved: Paul Tolstoy and Louise Paradis in Canada, A. Nelken Terner, C. Niedergerger, and P. Gendrop in Mexico, and A. Ruz

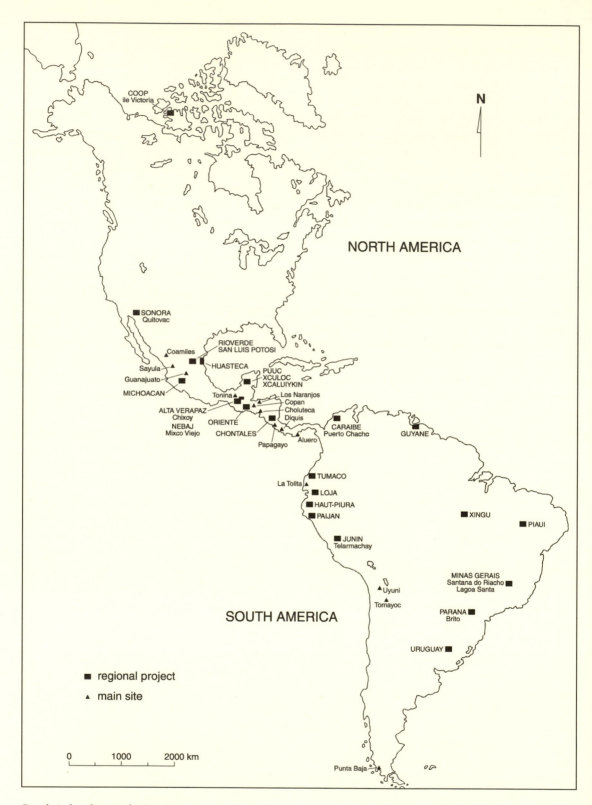

N

COOP
ile Victoria

NORTH AMERICA

SONORA
Quitovac

RIOVERDE
SAN LUIS POTOSI
Coamiles
HUASTECA
Sayula
PUUC
Guanajuato
XCULOC
XCALUIYKIN
MICHOACAN
Tonina
Los Naranjos
Copan
Choluteca
ALTA VERAPAZ
Diquis
Chixoy
ORIENTE
NEBAJ
CHONTALES
Mixco Viejo
CARAIBE
Papagayo
Puerto Chacho
GUYANE
Aluero

TUMACO
La Tolita
LOJA
HAUT-PIURA
PAIJAN
XINGU
PIAUI
JUNIN
Telarmachay

MINAS GERAIS
Santana do Riacho
Uyuni
Lagoa Santa
Tomayoc
PARANA
Brito

SOUTH AMERICA
URUGUAY

■ regional project
▲ main site

Punta Baja

0   1000   2000 km

French Archaeology in the Americas

Lhuillier, who helped create a teaching department for archaeology in Paris, are only a few examples. Meanwhile, the European Community has generated cooperative archaeological projects in Spain, Germany, England, BELGIUM, and Holland (with whom France shares some interest in the West Indies) and in northwestern Mexico (research by Hers and Daneels, for instance).

Although far from numerous, comprising less than a dozen structured teams, French archaeologists are quite active everywhere from the Arctic to Tierra del Fuego. Major activity is centered on Mesoamerica and Central America and the Andes, but a policy of working with national and local authorities has led to French intervention in BRAZIL, Uruguay, ARGENTINA, Nicaragua, and the CARIBBEAN. The Piaui project with N. Guidon in Brazil and the Tomayoc project with D. Lauallee in Argentina are recent examples of this cooperation. This contractual attitude of such research can be criticized, since it apparently fosters dispersed work devoid of scientific cohesion. But current research, as a matter of fact, is less rigid and much more pragmatic than former research, thus allowing more flexibility. And since the number of active teams is quite reduced, it is up to the researchers themselves to give these projects their scientific orientation.

One can easily identify the main lines of thought along which these research studies are organized. The main themes remain, of course, the study of High Civilization, that is, the culture of the Andean area (D. Lavallee, J. F. Bouchard in Tumaco, Loja, Piura, Junin) and the Maya area (P. Becquelin, C. F. Baudez, A. Ichon in Copan, Tonina, the Guatemala highlands, and the Puuc area), in direct connection with the IFEA and the CEMCA. But alongside these "geographical-cultural" aspects, there is an interest in frontiers. In Mesoamerica, the northern frontier has generated several projects in the Huasteca (Stresser, Pean, Michelet) Rio Verde and San Luis Potosi, Michoacan (Michelet, Arnauld), Guanajuato, Coamiles (Soustelle). The Central American civilizations and their connections and relationships with Mesoamerica were the focus of several projects (C. F. Baudez in Los Naranjos, Papagayo, Diquis, the Chontales area, and the Azuero peninsula). In South America, the same is true with regard to the Tumaco–La Tolita project (J. F. Bouchard).

These projects developed naturally into a preoccupation with contacts between the High Civilizations and their neighbors and thus led to excavations in peripheral zones (in Mexico, the Sonora project, led by Rodriguez); in South America (the Xingu and Uruguay projects); in the Caribbean area (excavations in Guyana, Martinique, and Guadeloupe). The Arctic and Tierra del Fuego field research fit in with this approach as well, but it can also be regrouped with the main thrust by which French archaeologists can make the best use of prehistoric archaeology—that is, the Neolithic processes in the Americas. Research studies in this respect have mostly been conducted in South America (in Jujuy, Telarmachay Piaui, Paijan, Puerto Chacho, and Minas Gerais); in Mexico some French archaeologists took part in the Tehuacan or Zohapilco excavations.

French archaeology in the Americas may seem dispersed, but this perception actually stems from the discipline's scientific approach rather than from a lack of cohesion. Clearly, the current policy, which combines existing official backing with a more pragmatic attitude, corresponds more closely with the needs of a scientific approach and with the evolution of research structures in the Americas.

Eric Taladoire

See also United States of America, Prehistoric Archaeology

References

Baudez, C. F. 1987. *Les cités perdues des Mayas.* Paris: Découvertes Gallimard no. 20.

———. 1993 *Jean Frédéric Waldeck, peintre: Le premier explorateur des ruines mayas.* Paris: Hazan.

Becquelin, P., and D. Lavallee. 1985. "Amérique." In *L'Archéologie française à l'étranger: Recherches et découvertes,* 340–403. Paris: Edition Recherche sur les Civilisations.

Bernal, I. 1980. *A History of Mexican Archaeology: The Vanished Civilizations of Mesoamerica.* London: Thames and Hudson.

Dossiers: 1990. "Les Amériques de la préhistoire aux Incas." *Les Dossiers d'Archéologie,* no. 145 (February). Dijon.

Gerber, F., C. Nicaise, and F. Robichon. 1992. *Un aventurier du Second Empire, Léon Mehédin (1828–1905)*. Bibliothèque Municipale de Rouen. France.

Keen, B. 1971. *The Aztec Image in Western Thought.* New Brunswick, NJ: Rutgers University Press.

Monchal, M. 1987. "Les Français et l'étude du Mexique préhispanique: Autour d'un ouvrage français: *Antiquités Mexicaines, 1934–36*." Manuscript. Centre de Recherches en Archéologie Précolombienne, University of Paris.

Mongne, P. 1987. *Désiré Charnay: Le Mexique 1858–1861—Souvenirs et impressions de voyage.* Paris: Ed. Du Griot.

Riviale, P. 1991. "Les Français à la recherche des antiquités du Pérou préhispanique au XIXème siècle (1821–1914): Les hommes et les institutions." Ph.D. dissertation, University of Paris.

———. 1993. "Les antiquités péruviennes et la curiosité en France sous l'Ancien Régime." Histoire de l'Art no. 21–22: *Collections et collectionneurs,* pp. 37–45. Paris.

Shavelzón, D. 1984. "Francia: Arquelogía y americanismo en Mexico (1810–1918)." Manuscript. Centre de Recherches en Archéologie Précolombienne, Université de Paris and Centre d'Études Mexicaines et Centre-Américaines, Mexico.

Stuart, G. 1992. "Quest for Decipherment: A Historical and Biographical Survey of Maya Hieroglyphic Investigation." In *New Theories on the Ancient Maya,* 1–64. E. C. Damien and R. J. Shearer (eds.). University Museum Monographs no. 77. Philadelphia: University of Pennsylvania.

Willey, G. R., and J. Sabloff. 1974. *A History of American Archaeology.* London: Thames and Hudson.

Zavala, S. 1983. "American en el expiritú frances del siglo XVIII." *El Colegio Nacional.* Mexico.

French Archaeology in the Classical World

France was not in the forefront as a founder of archaeological science. In the fifteenth and sixteenth centuries, it was the Italians, such as CYRIAC OF ANCONA and Pirro Ligorio, who were the pioneers in the field, which was only to be expected given the abundance of antiquities on Italian soil. Meanwhile in France, as elsewhere in the western world, the climate of the Renaissance and the spread of humanism sparked an interest in antiquity. The humanists were concerned primarily with the writings of earlier authors and the discovery of new manuscripts; archaeology took second place to philology. Mention should be made of the collections of King Francis I (1494–1547) of France and the casts he commissioned of Roman remains.

In the seventeenth century, however, the presence of the French was very significant in the field of classical archaeology. Nicolas-Claude de Fabri, seigneur of Peiresc, was typical of the new breed of French antiquarian. He was a councilor at the parliament of Aix-en-Provence and was interested in law and sciences as well as archaeology. His cabinet of curios, one of the most famous in Europe, testified to his eclectic tastes: antiques were displayed alongside works of art and natural curiosities. For him, an artifact was not merely a sign of prestige but also an object of study that led to knowledge of antiquity. Although he never published any of his research, he had a considerable influence on scholars through the network of connections he established in Europe. Yet his influence had its limitations; even though he had done the grand tour of Italy, he remained more interested in collectable objects than in historical monuments, more interested in written works than in sites to be explored.

In the second half of the seventeenth century, a new spirit of inquiry appeared as the result of voyages by both scholars and ambassadors accompanied by artists and men of letters. In 1674, the marquis of Nointel, the French ambassador at the Turkish court, visited Athens and had drawings made of the sculpted marble of the Parthenon—pediments, frieze, and metopes—thus preserving a record of the state of the temple before it was badly damaged by the Venetians in 1687. One sign of the new way of thinking was that antiquarians began to concede a greater importance to material sources, which they saw as being more reliable records than the printed word. They were particularly interested in inscriptions and coins found at the sites where they had been made.

Jacques Spon may be seen as the best example of this new type of antiquarian. He was a doctor from Lyon and played a leading role among the scholars who contributed to the origins of archaeology, and he was the first to use the term in the preface to his collection of inscriptions, the *Miscellanae eruditae antiquitatis,* published in the late eighteenth century. He believed that classical philology alone was not enough to develop the historical sciences; it was imperative to go back to other sources, too, such as inscriptions and incised monuments. Antique remains were books "whose stone and marble pages were written with hammer and chisel." Systematic use of inscriptions and ceaseless comparison of texts and observable data on site were the rules of Spon's critical method. He applied his method, not only as he studied the antiquities of Lyon, but also during his travels in ITALY, Dalmatia, GREECE, and TURKEY (1674–1675). Spon's great originality was to have discovered and shown that "the soil is a history book."

In the eighteenth century, the vogue for antiquities spread in France at an incredible rate, reflecting the mood of the times. The philosophy of the Enlightenment was guided by two dominant ideas, nature and reason, and it was admitted once and for all that both were the prerogative of antiquity. There was, therefore, a return to the antique and its aesthetic and moral values. This enthusiasm was only in part the result of the movement of ideas, for travel to Italy, and then to Greece and Asia Minor, became a mark of social distinction among the European elites. Simultaneously, travel writing bloomed: engravings, descriptions, and commentaries on monuments appeared in lavish publications, such as *Le voyage pittoresque de Naples et de Sicile* by the Abbé of Saint-Non (1781–1786) and *Le voyage pittoresque en Grece* by the ambassador Choiseul Gouffier (1782); the latter corresponded with the French consul in Athens, Louis Fauvel, who was commissioned to collect antiques for Gouffier, becoming one of the foremost connoisseurs of the sites in Athens. Another work that was very popular was by the Abbé Barthelmy, *Le voyage du jeune Anacharsis en Grece,* even though it described a fictional journey and was a literary version of Greece.

The whole approach to ancient history underwent a radical change in the eighteenth century. Interest in antiquities became less theoretical, and philology became less popular, especially in France, even though the Académie des Inscriptions et Belles Lettres was still sending out expeditions to bring back medals and manuscripts. The study of material remains began to be taken into proper account, linked as it was with the interest of the Encyclopédie (the movement within the Enlightenment to record and know everything possible) in materials, tools, and techniques.

BERNARD DE MONTFAUCON (1655–1741) exemplified the transition between the seventeenth and the eighteenth centuries. He was a Benedictine monk and a philologist, a scholar of the written word but fascinated, too, by visual images, and he published the first collections of antiquities in an attempt to illustrate historical monuments as faithfully as possible. A generation later, the COMTE DE CAYLUS, Anne-Claude-Philippe de Pestels de Lévis de Tubières-Grimoard (1692–1765), broke with the philological tradition and inaugurated a new era in archaeology. He gave priority to studying and examining objects, even those used in daily life, and his method must be considered progress, archaeologically speaking, compared to the seventeenth century approach, which was concerned, above all, with coins and inscriptions. In an encyclopedic vision of culture, he wrote *Recueil d'antiquités égyptiennes, étrusques, grecques, romaines et gauloises* (1752–1758). He was the first to classify these antiquities and to draw up a typology that would bring out geographical and historical distinctions.

In the eighteenth century, there were the spectacular but unscientific excavations of cities buried by Vesuvius (HERCULANEUM and POMPEII), excavations supported by the Bonapartes of Naples, and also a systematic search for Greek antiquities in southern Italy and Sicily. French architects contributed significantly to the knowledge of monuments and sites. Soufflot surveyed and drew the ruins of Paestum around 1750, and Hittorff later demonstrated the polychromy of Greek architecture by studying the temples in Sicily. David Le Roy brought back from his travels to Greece drawings that were more picturesque than scientifically exact (they were published in 1758) and then tried to impose Greek architecture as a model in Paris, just as James Stuart and Nicholas Revett were doing in England at the time.

In the nineteenth century, circumstances governing the knowledge of antiquity changed: more became known, and the information began to be organized differently. Archaeology became more obviously the pawn of politics and was now part of any plan by the great powers aimed at the occupation of the Mediterranean basin; there was rivalry between France and England in Greece and then between France and Germany after 1870. The French government was anxious to support any undertaking that would enhance France's prestige. In this context, one should mention the great scientific expeditions, the creation of the French schools in Athens and Rome, and the competition to lead the most prestigious excavations. Simultaneously, although slightly more slowly than in Germany, archaeology developed as an academic subject in France through the creation of university chairs and specialized courses.

The link between politics and archaeology can be clearly seen in the scientific expedition to Morea that took place from 1829 to 1831 when French troops were in the Peloponnese to take part in the liberation of Greece. It was a multidisciplinary expedition (physical sciences, archaeology, architecture), and though it could not be counted a great success on the archaeological level, its members did oversee excavations at Olympia, where the site of the temple of Zeus was plotted, and they brought back metopes for the LOUVRE museum. The conquest of Algeria in 1830, followed by the establishment of the French protectorate in Tunisia in 1881, yielded a vast field of research for French archaeologists. This research, inspired partly by curiosity and partly by scientific interest, was also the result of a desire to justify the conquest by and the superiority of European culture. Other smaller-scale expeditions, of a nonmilitary nature but driven by the political will of successive French governments, were led by Philippe Le Bas to Greece and Asia Minor in 1843 to bring back inscriptions, and by Leon Heuzey, who set off in 1861, at the request of

Napoleon III, to visit the ancient battle sites in the north of Greece. The latter discovered the archaeology of Macedonia, excavated the royal Hellenistic palace at Palatitsa, and carried back the stone parts (door and bed) of a royal tomb to the Louvre.

In the nineteenth century, France founded two institutions that played a crucial role in archaeological research in the Mediterranean. It was felt that a loss of political influence had to be compensated for by a win in the cultural and scientific spheres. This sentiment was true for the French School of Athens, whose creation in 1846 was justified by the necessity to spread the French language, customs, and influence, and it was even truer for the School of Rome, which was born after the defeat of France in 1870 by Germany. In Rome in the first half of the nineteenth century, the French and Germans had helped to found the Institute of Archaeological Correspondence (1829), the ancestor of all the Roman scientific institutes. This particular institute, which had the aim of publishing all the archaeological discoveries in the Mediterranean region, had a French section headed by several famous amateur antiquarians and scholars. The institute lost its international character after 1870 and became entirely German. Finding itself without any scientific institution in Italy, France sent out a young scholar trained in Athens, Albert Dumont, to establish a branch of the institute, which became autonomous in 1875.

The two pillars of French archaeology abroad were in place, and the evolution of those two institutions reflect French activity in Italy and Greece up to the present day. The scientists using these schools for running expeditions or publishing their finds have long held all the university chairs of ancient history. Unlike the situation in the eighteenth century, archaeology was no longer the preserve of enlightened amateurs and artists; it was now the domain of professionals and academics. At the Collège de France, a chair of Latin epigraphy was created in 1861 and a chair of Greek epigraphy was created in 1874; at the Sorbonne, G. Perrot held the first chair of Greek archaeology in 1876. However in France there were fewer positions than the sixteen chairs of archaeology in Germany at the same time.

In the second half of the nineteenth century, excavations and publications proliferated. The French conducted various activities in Greece and Asia Minor as well as more extensive work at the major sites, Delos (1873) and Delphi (from 1892), which yielded a rich harvest of monuments, inscriptions, and sculptures. Even though the main publications, such as the *Corpus* for inscriptions, were in the hands of the Germans, the French were certainly present in the field of epigraphy, architecture, and sculpture. In the twentieth century, and especially after World War I, archaeological investigation spread to Crete and the Minoan question (at the site of Malia) and to the northern Aegean at the site of Thasos. The results of these excavations were published in the *Bulletin de correspondance hellenique,* which was launched in 1874, and also in works specific to each site. The part played by the architects resident at the Villa Medicis in Rome in all this archaeological activity in Greece should be noted, for it was they who had to draw and reconstruct the ancient sites and monuments discovered by the archaeologists, especially the French.

Whereas the French School of Athens had been almost exclusively a school of archaeology since the 1870s, the School of Rome did not follow the same pattern. From its foundation, it was defined as a school of history and archaeology and included medievalists as well as ancient historians. The ancient history section was not allowed to take part in excavations on Italian soil, with the exception of the Etruscan site of Vulci. The French were equally as interested in Rome as they were in Etruria, and Jules Martha wrote the first *Manuel d'archéologie etrusque et romaine* in 1884.

Archaeology in Africa followed in the wake of military conquest and it was either members of the army (such as Captain Delamare in Algeria) or the church (Father Delattre in Carthage) who were the first to start excavating in these new French territories. Then scholars from the School of Rome carried the torch: Stephane Gsell worked tirelessly in the field in Algeria, organized museums, and wrote a history of Roman Africa. The interest in Africa by French archaeology lasted until decolonization in the 1950s and 1960s.

The structures that were set up in the nineteenth century still survive today and have left their mark on the landscape of French archaeology. Contemporary classical archaeology in France is strong in traditional disciplines (epigraphy, architecture, sculpture), although there is a renewal of centers of interest, and for a long time, the French were slow to apply technical or technological innovations (stratigraphy, analysis of materials, use of statistical methods), even though this gap has now been filled. Since the 1980s French archaeologists have been receptive to debates on archaeological theories, even though the profusion of research on these topics in the United States and England has been slow to spread to France.

French classical archaeology is the province of a great number of organizations, which, to a certain extent, are proof of its richness, and above all multiple sources of finance. There are three administrations involved: first, the Ministère des Affaires Etrangères, which supports the Commission des Fouilles and institutes such as those in Istanbul, Damascus, and Beirut, which also recruit archaeologists. Then there is the Education Nationale, which supports the schools in Athens and Rome and the Casa Velasquez in Madrid, and last, there is the Centre National de la Recherche Scientifique (CNRS), which supports teams working on projects. Research in the field is not directed or organized by an archaeological institute or the universities: the initiative is left up to academics or CNRS researchers to find financial support from the institutions listed above.

Just as there are several funding bodies, there are several training institutions. The universities play a crucial role, but other centers, such as the Collège de France, the Ecole Pratique des Hautes Etudes, and the Ecole du Louvre, also offer training in classical archaeology. This very diversity helps to give France a high profile in all archaeological disciplines and, in the classical field, a broad geographical presence extending throughout the Mediterranean basin, from Portugal and Morocco to Syria and Afghanistan.

In Greece, French archaeology is still concerned with the traditional sites mentioned previously. The School of Athens plays a decisive role, though no longer an exclusive one. The harvest is very rich and covers the different fields of history, especially Hellenistic (thousands of epigraphic texts have been published and analyzed, more than 2,000 for Delos alone). Also of interest is the evolution of the great sanctuaries—their organization and monumentalization—most notably Delos and Delphi, and the history of art, painting, and sculpture plays a role—the excavation of Delphi made a huge contribution to the field of archaic art. Since 1990 research perspectives have changed in accordance with general movements in field archaeology toward landscape archaeology and submarine archaeology, excavations of farms, and studies of workshops. The School of Athens is extending its center of interest to the Balkans, and France also has bases in TURKEY at the Greek and Roman sites of Xanthos and Claros.

Since World War II, new impetus has come as much or even more from digs at Greek settlements in the peripheral zones, such as Ai Khanoum in Afghanistan, or Greek colonies in the West (southern Italy and Sicily, to say nothing of the work of French archaeologists in southern Gaul and Marseilles). The School of Rome has played a major role in this domain by excavating the site at Megara Hyblaea on the east coast of Sicily and by participating in numerous ventures that have helped lead to a better understanding of colonial Hellenism in the West. Issues such as regular town planning, contact with the "natives" and acculturation phenomena, and types and forms of exchange have all been investigated by French archaeologists. The School of Rome was also responsible for the Etruscan dig at Bolsena. Even though there is no university course in Etruscan studies, the French school dealing with this subject is a very vigorous one (CNRS, Louvre, Aix-en-Provence).

France is represented in different capacities in numerous Roman and Greek sites around the Mediterranean. Of particular note is a strong presence in SPAIN and PORTUGAL, in North Africa (especially in Tunisia, where the French are still working on traditional sites such as Bulla Reggia

and Carthage), the upkeep of a mission in Libya, sustained activity in Syria and JORDAN, and, of course, the French School's excavation in Rome. More recently, France has been taking part in the archaeological opening up of the eastern bloc countries. The work, done by the Service Archéologique National en France, deserves recognition as its specially commissioned digs and emergency conservation digs have contributed data and given rise to numerous syntheses. One of the most striking features of contemporary French archaeology is that France, which until World War II favored the pursuit of classical archaeology abroad in Italy and Greece, has developed a national archaeology that, richly endowed (largely by developers) and using the most modern of techniques, has become one of the leading exponents of experimental research even in classical antiquity, as the excavations of Greek and Roman Marseilles illustrate so magnificently.

Roland and Françoise Etienne;
translated Judith Braid

See also Society of Dilettanti
References
Dondin-Payre, Monique. 1988. *Un siècle d'epigraphie classique: Aspects de l'oeuvre des savants français dans les pays méditerranéens.* Paris: Centre National de la Recherche Scientifique.
Etienne, Roland, and Francoise Etienne. 1990. *La Grece antique: Archéologie d'une decouverte.* Paris: Gallimard.
Gras, Michel. 1986. "Les Etrusques." *La Recherche* 182: 1310–1320.
Hubert, Emmanuelle. 1982. "Un precurseur de l'archéologie: N. Claude Fabri de Peiresc." *Archeologia* 170: 73–76.
Radet, Georges. 1901. *Histoire et oeuvre e l'Ecole Française d'Athenes.* Paris.
Schnapp, Alain. 1975. *L'Ecole française de Rome 1875–1975: Exposition organisee a l'occasion de son centenaire.* Paris: Archives de France.
———. 1982. *Paris-Rome Athenes: Le voyage en Grece des architectes français aux XIXe et XXe siècle.* Paris.
———. 1985. *L'archéologie française a l'etranger: Recherches et decouvertes.* Paris: Edition Recherches sur les Civilisations.
———. 1992. *La redecouverte de Delphes, Ecole Française d'Athenes.* Paris.

———. 1993. *La conquête du passé, aux origines de l'archéologie.* Paris: Editions Carre.

French Archaeology in Egypt and the Middle East

By the end of the eighteenth century, France began a political extension toward the Oriental world. Simultaneously, far from its national borders, it entered into archaeological research, first in Egypt, then in the Near East (i.e., the Asiatic possessions of the Ottoman Empire that came into existence as nations after World War I), and lastly in Persia (modern IRAN). Considering the importance of the archaeology undertaken by France in those countries, it is not feasible to catalogue or sum up nearly two hundred years of its archaeological work in this article. However it should be understood that the prestige of French archaeology lies less in the great width of its activities than in the simple fact that, more than once, these stand as landmarks in the history of the archaeological studies of the Ancient Near East.

The first contact between France and Eastern civilization happened in a rather striking way. In 1798, for intricate political, scientific, and ideological reasons, Napoleon Bonaparte decided to have scholars and engineers join his army in a military expedition to Egypt. His science crew's mission was to obtain and collect all the information they could about Egypt, both ancient and modern.

Although the works and facts recorded about Coptic and Islamic monuments proved to be the most remarkable achievements of this expedition, the greatest immediate influence was the investigation of Pharaonic relics from antiquity. For instance, the knowledge of Upper Egyptian sites, so far virtually unknown, increased considerably. Vivant Denon was the first author to publish accounts of the expedition, in his *Voyage dans la Basse et la Haute-Egypte, Pendant les Campagnes du Géneral Bonaparte en Egypte.* This very successful work was the result of the first investigations of Upper Egypt in 1798, when Denon followed General Desaix, who was pursuing Mourad-Bey and his followers on their retreat south.

Edouard de Villiers and Prosper Jollois, two young engineers, made important additions to Denon's accounts. Both men were members of a commission departing for Upper Egypt in early 1799 with numerous tasks, one of which was to draw the outlines of the Nile Valley. Fascinated by the monuments they encountered, of their own accord they made thousands of drawings and notes of them. With the full cooperation of the other members of the expedition, who had concentrated on the monuments of Lower Egypt, this vast collection of data was published in the monumental multivolume work *Description de l'Égypte* in late 1799. This exceptional work not only comprises the largest and most comprehensive collection of documents ever to have been published on Egypt in those days, but it is still referred to, and is seen as all the more precious as many of the sites it recorded no longer exist. The scientific achievements of the different expeditions constitute the most lasting and least questionable gain of Napoleon Bonaparte's adventures in Egypt.

During a military expedition, on the eve of the land battle of Aboukir (1799), Captain Bouchard, as a consequence of prebattle trenching at Rosette, came across the famous "Rosetta" stone bearing inscriptions in two languages and three kinds of writing: hieroglyphic, demotic, and Greek. The importance of this find was immediately understood by scholars. England confiscated the stone after the Eastern Army surrendered to them, and however unfortunate this loss was for French scholars, it was no hindrance to JEAN-FRANCOIS CHAMPOLLION. Working from a copy of the stone, in 1822 he established the foundations for deciphering hieroglyphic writing.

The exciting years at the close of the Age of Enlightenment at the end of the eighteenth century and those at the beginning of the nineteenth century mark the beginning of scientific Egyptology. France became involved in the protection of monuments and laid the foundations for its future research at these sites. AUGUSTE MARIETTE, the excavator of Memphis Serapeum, was prominent in the creation of the "Service des Antiquités," an organization that policed and protected archaeological sites, and the first museum in Egypt. A few years prior to this, between 1828 and 1829 when Champollion led the Franco-Tuscan expedition, he realized that many of the monuments he had seen during his first visit had disappeared. He tried to convince Mehemet Ali that there was an urgent need to halt such destruction. But it was not done until 1858, when the Turkish Viceroy Saïd Pacha decided to act and appointed Mariette "Directeur des fouilles," that is, chief engineer for excavations. Under Mariette's leadership intensive archaeological research began in Upper Egypt and in Memphis, in Lower Egypt, eventually reaching as far as Sudan.

It was not until 1880 that the involvement of France in the archaeology of Egypt was, thanks to Gaston Maspero, definitely settled. Succeeding Mariette, Maspero had no easy task. He was in charge of creating a permanent French archaeological foundation in Cairo, similar to those already established in Athens and Rome. The aims of the new research foundation (known in the beginning as the Ecole Française du Caire) were the survey and perusal of the history and philology of Egyptian antiquities and, later, of Oriental antiquities as well. This latter integration of the archaeology of the Near East into the foundation's research work originated in 1898, and the institute was renamed the Institut Français d'Archéologie Orientale du Caire (IFAO), a designation that remains unchanged to the present day. The foundation of the institute in Cairo fulfilled Mariette's ambitions and confirmed the place of French archaeology in Egypt. The bonds between the Egyptian Service des Antiquités and the French Institute (IFAO) became stronger as the French foundation was the source, for many years, of the Egyptian civil servants of the Service des Antiquités—with one exception when Jacques De Morgan was head of the Service from 1892 to 1897. But until the Egyptians could directly and permanently manage and staff their entire civil service, almost all of the surveyors and curators appointed in Egypt were ancient "pensionnaires" of the IFAO. Thus, all during the second half of the nineteenth century, French archaeology in Egypt was predominantly organized around the IFAO, and to this day it remains the center of French archaeological research in Egypt.

In the rest of the territories of the Ottoman Empire in Asia, the growth of archaeology was entirely different. During the seventeenth and eighteenth centuries France and other countries were passionately involved in investigating and collecting antiquities. By the middle of the nineteenth century, France had started excavating in MESOPOTAMIA, due to the establishment of a French consulate in Mossoul in 1842. Mossoul stands beside the remains of Quyundjik, believed since the Middle Ages to be those of the ancient city of NINEVEH. French scholars encouraged diplomat PAUL-EMILE BOTTA to begin excavating the site, which led to the revival of an interest in Assyrian civilization and was the starting point for French archaeological research in Mesopotamia. However the results were disappointing and in 1843, Botta abandoned the site and moved on to excavate the "tell" of Khorsabad. Here he was certain that he had at last found Nineveh. This was confirmed in 1847 with the decipherment of cuneiform epigraphy that he had excavated from the palace of Sargon II at Dûr Sharrûkin. Botta's excavations from 1842 to 1844 not only endowed France with the first Assyrian collection in a museum in Europe but also provided archaeologists with important data concerning Assyrian epigraphy and monuments, published in 1849–1850 as the *Monuments de Ninive*. Botta was transferred to a minor diplomatic post, interrupting French research at the original site and leaving it free for the English archaeologist AUSTEN HENRY LAYARD to excavate. His success incited France to resume Mesopotamian archaeology.

In Botta the duties of consul were united with the work of an archaeologist, which inaugurated a tradition in French archaeology in the area—it remained a consular activity during all of the nineteenth century. Thus in 1852 the French government encouraged Victor Place, also a consul at Mossoul, to resume the research of his predecessor at Khorsabad—and he quite successfully did. Unfortunately, in May 1855 the rafts carrying the material discovered during the expedition were attacked by Bedouins, and the greatest part of them sank. This great loss put an end to the first period of French archaeological investigation in Mesopotamia.

Twenty years later, the French vice-consul at Bassorah, Ernest de Sarzec, began to excavate the site of Tello in Southern Mesopotamia, and excavations continued under Captain Gaston Cros until 1909. These investigations confirmed the existence of Sumerian civilization, which philologists had assumed had existed but had been unable to prove. Despite its distinguished past record, on the eve of World War I France was no longer working in Mesopotamian archaeology. Immediately after the war foreign archaeological missions were able to begin to excavate once more because of favorable conditions created by the British mandate over Iraq. But France was hampered by its political responsibilities in Syria and therefore could only take a late and brief part in the excavations. In 1928, the excavation of Tello began again under the direction of Abbé Henri de Genouillac and ANDRÉ PARROT and continued until 1933. André Parrot led the investigation of the site of Larsa in 1933. New regulations about antiquities were passed and the clauses pertaining to the sharing of finds with their country of origin made excavations by foreigners less attractive. Consequently, France decided to concentrate on work in Syria. It was not until 1967, when the diplomatic circumstances were more propitious, that France and André Parrot resumed their research in Iraqi archaeology at Larsa. Ten years later, in an attempt to settle and develop the archaeological effort in Iraq, the Delégation Archéologique Française en Iraq (DAFIQ) was established. The new institution served as a framework within Iraq, with several teams of archaeologists, both French and Iraqi, cooperating at least until Iraq invaded Kuwait in the 1990s. Not only did France continue its investigations at Larsa, but it also took part in other excavations, especially in association with Iraq's hydraulic plans, which necessitated the rescue of several sites in Upper-Mesopotamia.

In Syria and Lebanon the bulk of French archaeological research took place between the two world wars. However Palestine, Syria, and Lebanon experienced sporadic and occasionally brilliant French archaeological investigations before 1914. During this period, Félicien de Saulcy and Melchior de Vogüe dedicated themselves to the study of biblical archaeology at sites on the Jordan River. Most of de Vogüe's work was on the monuments of Central Syria. Charles de Clermont-Ganneau was another great specialist in the archaeology of the monuments of Palestine, Phoenicia, and Syria. However the most outstanding scholar was Ernest Renan, who began the archaeological investigation of Phoenicia. The Emperor Napoleon III was very interested in all of the wondrous archaeological adventures he supported, and in 1861 established archaeological missions in Macedonia under the direction of Léon Heuzey and in Galatia under Georges Perrot.

In 1860, France sent a military force to Lebanon to help the Maronite Christians, whom the local Druse people were slaughtering. The military presence was seen by the emperor as both a protection of Maronites and a help for the establishment of another archaeological mission. He appointed Renan as official consul in Palestine and Syria. Even though Renan only investigated ground-level remains, his research is impressive—at Ruad, Tortose, Amrit, Byblos, Sidon, and Tyr. Renan gathered a considerable amount of information, and published it in the *Mission de Phoénicie,* between 1864 and 1874. Renan's work stands as the foundation of Phoenician archaeology.

However, except for the Jesuit activities of the Université Saint-Joseph de Beyrouth on the eve of World War I, France did not participate in the archaeology of Syria and Lebanon. Palestinian studies existed only in the form of the Dominicans at the Ecole Biblique in Jerusalem. After World War I, with changed circumstances, France tried to make its archaeological research profit by its newly acquired political status. Through the Service des Antiquités, created between 1919 and 1920, and under the Haut-Commissariat, successively directed by Joseph Chamonard, Charles Virolleaud, and Henri Seyrig, France, the mandated power in Syria and Lebanon, organized, developed, and controlled the whole archaeological research of this region and worked in permanent and close scientific cooperation with the Académie des Inscriptions et Belles Lettres in Paris. René Dussaud, curator of the Département des Antiquités Orientales in the Musée du Louvre and a member of the institute (Académie des Inscriptions et Belles Lettres), became famous through his work in Syria. Dussaud intervened in the appointment of responsible operators in the Service des Antiquités and in the choice of the leaders of important missions, such as Maurice Dunand at Byblos, Claude Schaeffer at Ras Shamra, and André Parrot at Mari. During this period, which lasted until World War II, great projects were launched. Some are still going on today, directed by France either alone or in close cooperation with other countries, for example at Doura, Europos, and Antioch. In addition to excavations, Baalbeck and Palmyre and the Kreak des Chevaliers were cleaned up and restored. With the end of World War II came the end of the French mandate over Syria. France abandoned the Service des Antiquités, but Seyrig maintained French influence by settling the French Institute of Archaeology in Beirut in 1946 and leading it until 1967. In 1977, it became the Institut Français d'Archéologie du Proche Orient (IFAPO), and it includes and manages permanent sections at Damas, Beirut, and Amman.

In the area of Islamic studies, French archaeology is present in the form of the Institut Français des Etudes Arabes (IFEAD) at Damas, founded in the first years of the mandate. Excavations at the medieval sites of Meskené-Balis and Meyadin were undertaken under its patronage.

France's purpose was to extend its sphere of archaeological action over the whole territory of the ancient Ottoman Empire, especially in Palestine, even if it remained under British mandate, and in TURKEY itself. But in these last two countries since the end of the nineteenth century, archaeological regulations did not favor foreign archeological missions, and France's activities there have been limited. The Ecole Biblique et Archéologique Française de Jérusalem, created in 1920 out of the Dominican Ecole Biblique founded by le Père Lagrange, is involved, for the most part, in Palestinian archaeology. Le Père Vincent (because of his works at Bethlehem, Hebron, Emmaus, and especially at Jerusalem) and le Père de Vaux (because of his excavations at Khirbet Qumram,

where the Dead Sea Scrolls were found) dominated the archaeology of this school.

In spite of French efforts in Turkey, French archaeological activity there remained small in scale. The great explorations led by Charles Texier at the beginning of the nineteenth century, the above-mentioned mission in Galatia of Georges Perrot, and various preliminary surveys by the members of the Ecole Française d'Athènes at the end of the nineteenth century are worth mentioning, but are not as significant as the results of other nations, such as Germany. No notable changes in this situation occurred after the end of World War I. However, the Institut Français d'Istanbul was created in 1930 by Albert Gabriel. In 1975 it became the Institut Français d'Etudes Anatoliennes (IFEA) and it has made notable contributions to the exploration of Phrygia and to the understanding of Turkish monuments and of Greco-Roman cities. The monumental excavations at Xanthos, successful as they have been, are an isolated example of French archaeological work on a larger scale.

In Persia (modern Iran) the situation was entirely different. As early as 1897 the Délégation Française en Perse was created, because of an agreement signed in 1895 by Nasir al-din Shah that conferred the monopoly of all excavations in the whole of Persia to France. Until then archaeological activity by France, or by any other country, had been almost nonexistent in this region. The one important event prior to this was a diplomatic mission (1839–1842) directed by the Comte de Sercey and including architect Pascal Coste and artist-designer Eugène Flandin, to draw plans of Persian monuments. Between 1884 and 1886 the Palace of Darius at the site of Susa was excavated under the direction of Jane and Marcel Dieulafoy. When France began negotiations with the Persian government in 1895, its purpose was to protect so promising a site from foreign archaeological competitors. France had no wish to repeat its experience at Nineveh. And so a chance conversation at the convention of 1895, reinforced in the summer of 1900 by the final agreement signed in Paris by Muzzafar-al-din Shah, gave France not only the site of Susa but also the entire collection and results of excavations undertaken in Susiana, as well as control over the whole archaeology of Persia. The Délégation lasted fifteen years, from 1897 to 1912, and its prestige was due to the character of Jacques De Morgan. A prehistorian by training, De Morgan's great knowledge of Iran was the result of extensive travel between 1889 and 1891, from the Caucasus into and around Northern Persia, then over the whole country, and finally to Susa. When the French government appointed him to a position in Persia, he had already successfully managed the Service des Antiquités in Egypt.

De Morgan's plans were initially very ambitious, with the whole of the archaeological wealth of Persia under his control. But De Morgan believed that the urgent work at Susa had to come first before all other projects and should never be sacrificed for the sake of hazardous ventures. So, facing a financial situation that did not allow him to diversify his research unless he jeopardized the studies at Susa, his efforts and those of the Délégation were essentially devoted to the Susa site. His important work at Susa greatly benefited both the LOUVRE Museum and other scholars, and in the long term it seems that Jacques De Morgan was right about his priorities. However, he was criticized about his research choice and attacked by fellow workers, and by then his long, hardworking years in the Middle East had exhausted him. In 1912, De Morgan resigned, and with this the Délégation Scientifique Française en Perse came to an end.

The agreement that founded the Délégation was not repealed until 1927, and France's archaeological interests were maintained by the Direction des Antiquités under command of André Godard until 1960 and the Institut Français de Recherche en Iran (IFRI). But while the Délégation ceased to exist after De Morgan's departure, the excavations at Susa continued. After World War I, when France diversified its archaeological research into the Iranian plateau and along its borders, Susa and Susiana remained the center of its activity. Roland de Mecquenem until 1946, then Roman Ghirshman, and finally Jean Perrot from 1968 have been successively responsible for the work in this area.

Nothing less than two world wars and, in 1979, the Islamic Revolution in Iran, could interrupt nearly a century of French research in Susania.

The archaeological activity of France in most of the Near East goes back to the nineteenth century. Due to scientific concerns, politics, and economics other areas have been opened to research more recently. In Arabia France is presently engaged in numerous archaeological projects. Twice interrupted by world wars, and then, occasionally, by the repercussions of political events, the archaeological activity of France in the Near East and Egypt has carried on for two centuries and, as much as circumstances will allow it, it continues.

Nicole Chevalier

See also Egypt: Dynastic; Egypt: Predynastic; Israel; Syro-Palestinian and Biblical Archaeology

Frere, John (1740–1807)

John Frere was born in Norfolk, England, and graduated from Caius College, Cambridge. An antiquary and a member of the local upper-middle class, Frere was also high sheriff of Suffolk in 1766, was elected to Parliament for Norwich in 1799, and became a fellow of the Royal Society in 1771.

In 1797, Frere reported to the SOCIETY OF ANTIQUARIES OF LONDON that he had found stone tools (what are now described as Acheulean hand axes) in the same levels as the bones of long-extinct animals—four meters down—in undisturbed Pleistocene deposits in a brickpit at Hoxne, Suffolk. He argued that the overlying strata, which included evidence of a rise in sea level and half a meter of deposit, could only have been laid down over a very long period and that the stone tools and animal deposits had to be over 6,000 years old. *Archaeologia* in 1800 included a description of the find, a stratigraphic description, and a section of the deposit. Frere and his publication were politely ignored by the scientific establishment mainly because the conclusions seriously challenged the accepted date for the creation of human beings, which had been established in 1650 by Bishop JAMES USSHER, based on biblical calculations, as occurring on the evening of 22 October 4004 B.C. At the beginning of the nineteenth century, most scientists were still reluctant to challenge this widely accepted theological dogma.

However more human artifacts and extinct animals kept turning up in sealed and undisturbed layers of stratigraphy in caves in Europe and England, providing more evidence that human beings must have been around at the same time as the accompanying and long-vanished mammals. But it was not until the mid-nineteenth century that many scientists were prepared to believe, and more important to publicly state, that the world was probably a lot older than Genesis and Ussher had determined. By then, many people had forgotten that fifty years previously John Frere had linked archaeological and paleontological evidence to argue for a greater human antiquity.

Tim Murray

G

Gabrovec, Stane (1920–)

Stane Gabrovec is a Slovenian archaeologist and a specialist in the Bronze and Iron Ages of central and southwestern Europe. He graduated in archaeology and classical philology from Ljubljana University in 1948, specialized in prehistoric archaeology at the University of Tübingen in Germany, and received his Ph.D. from the University of Zadar in Croatia. He was curator of prehistory at the National Museum in Ljubljana after World War II (1948) and after 1956, head of the Prehistory Department at the same institution. From 1969 to 1989, he taught prehistory at the University of Ljubljana. Gabrovec became a member of the Slovenian Academy of Arts and Sciences and a correspondent member of the Bavarian Academy of Sciences in Munich.

Gabrovec has dedicated most of his scientific work to solving problems of chronology and cultural definition in the Bronze and Iron Age cultures of the southeastern Alps and Caput Adriae, the area comprising SLOVENIA, AUSTRIA, northeastern ITALY, western Hungary, and northern Croatia. His most important and highly influential work on Slovenian prehistoric archaeology and beyond, i.e., on the establishment of the chronology for the late–Bronze and early–Iron Ages in Slovenia, was published in *Halstatska kultura v Sloveniji* [Hallstatt Culture in Slovenia], *Arheoloski vestnik* (Ljubljana) 15–16 [1964–1965]: 21–63. In those studies, he defined five regional groups within the Slovenian Hallstatt culture: the Dolenjska (lower Carniola) group in central Slovenia, the Sveta Lucija (St. Lucia) group in western Slovenia, the Notranjska (inner Carniola) group in southwestern Slovenia, the Gorenjska (upper Carniola) group in north-

western Slovenia, and the Stajerska (Styria) group in northeastern Slovenia and southeastern Austria. Gabrovec incorporated these groups into the cultural and chronological schemes of southeastern and central Europe, and he also demonstrated that the process of transition from the late Bronze Age to the early Iron Age is characterized to a great extent by cultural and ethnic continuity from the "Urnfield culture" and by the presence of the early Iron Age elements originating from the Balkans. He demonstrated a similar phenomena of ethnic and cultural continuity in the LA TÈNE period in Slovenia, when several cultural groups continued their development from the early Iron Age while CELTS populated only parts of central and eastern Slovenia in the middle La Tène period.

Gabrovec also published an extensive and updated synthesis of the late Bronze Age and early Iron Age in Slovenia. Among the numerous sites excavated by Gabrovec, the most important is the famous princely hill fort at STIČNA. This large barrow was excavated between 1960 and 1964, and part of the settlement was excavated between 1967 and 1974. Besides studies of the Bronze and Iron Ages, his work includes the history of Slovenian archaeology, prehistoric topography, and prehistoric art.

Methodologically, Gabrovec's approach can be described as part of the so-called Gero von Merhart historical school, developed in the 1940s and 1950s at the University of Marburg in Germany. This approach is based on a detailed analysis of material culture, its chronological sequence and development, and its geographical distribution, and such analysis is applied to the definition of the different cultural regions, the identification of cultural groups, and their social structure, historical, and ethnic adherence.

Predrag Novakovic

See also Kastelic, Jožef
References
Gabrovec, S. 1966. *Srednjelatensko obdobje v Sloveniji* [Middle La Tène Period in Slovenia]. *Arheoloski vestnik* 17, 169–242. Ljubljana.
———. 1970a. *Dvozankasta locna fibula.* Doprinos k problematiki zacetka zelezne dobe na Balkanu in v jugovzhodnih Alpah [Two-looped bow fibula].
———. 1970b. *Godisnjak Centra za balkanoloska ispitivanja* 8, 5–65. Sarajevo.
———. 1983–1987. *Praistorija jugoslavenskih zemalja* [Prehistory of the Yugoslav Lands]. Vols. 4–5. Sarajevo.
———. 1994. *Sticna I.,* Catalog and monograph no. 28. Ljubljana: Narodni Museum.
Kastelic, J. 1980. "Ob sestdesetletnici" [Sixtieth Anniversary of Stane Gabrovec]. *Situla* (Ljubljana) 20–21: 5–8. Contains bibliography.

Gallatin, Albert (1761–1849)

Albert Gallatin was born in Geneva, SWITZERLAND, into an aristocratic family. He studied classical and modern languages, geography, and mathematics and became a follower of the French philosopher Jean-Jacques Rousseau and European Romanticism. He left Geneva for the United States in 1789, where he briefly taught French at Harvard College before purchasing land on the then-frontier in western Pennsylvania. He was not a successful farmer or frontiersman and soon became involved in politics. He was elected to the state legislature between 1790 and 1791 and then served as a senator in the federal government, becoming a friend of THOMAS JEFFERSON, Henry Adams, James Madison, and Alexander Hamilton. He married into New York society, served in Congress, and was secretary of the Treasury from 1801 to 1814. He then served as a diplomat, traveling to Russia and Belgium, and was a representative for the government of the United States in Paris from 1816 to 1823 and in London from 1826 to 1827.

Gallatin left government service and returned to New York City, where he and John Jacob Astor founded a bank and he became one of the founders, and the first president of the council, of the University of the City of New York in 1831. During his years in FRANCE, Gallatin had shared his long-term interest in philology with Alexander and Wilhelm von Humboldt and in 1823 had contributed an essay to their book on American Indian languages. It was this latter interest that now absorbed most of his time and earned him the title "father of American ethnology."

In 1826, Gallatin's book *A Table of Indian Languages in the United States* was published, and it included the first map of tribal languages and the first attempt at designating language groups through the comparative method. This work was followed in 1836 by "A Synopsis of Indian Tribes . . . in North America," an extended version of the Humboldt essay. In 1843, Gallatin was instrumental in the founding of the American Ethnological Society and became its first president. His "Notes on the Semi-Civilized Nations of Mexico, Yucatan, and Central America" and "Introduction to Hale's Indians of North-West America and Vocabularies of North America" were published in volumes one and two of the *Transactions of the American Ethnological Society.* Although he was most proud of these publications, and judged them to be the most important he wrote, Gallatin is far more widely known for all of the annual and special reports he wrote as secretary of the Treasury, for his diplomatic notes and correspondence, and for his numerous pamphlets on finance, public lands, the Oregon question, and the Mexican War written during his years in government.

Tim Murray

Gamio, Manuel (1883–1960)

Manuel Gamio was born in Mexico City and studied mining until 1903, when his father sent him to administer a family plantation. While engaged in that work, he had contact with the indigenous Nahua people, learned their language, and was appalled by their poverty. Returning to Mexico City in 1906, Gamio studied anthropology and archaeology at the National Museum for two years. His first archaeological excavations were of the site of Chalchihuites, Zacate-

Temple of the Feathered Serpent at Teotihuacán, the subject of Manuel Gamio's major archaeological project in the 1920s (Photo by Kay A. Read)

cas, on which his thesis was based. He also made some preliminary nonstratigraphic excavations at Azcapotzalco in western MEXICO, where he tried to associate the materials he obtained with indigenous groups from the fifteenth and sixteenth centuries.

In 1909, Gamio received a scholarship to study anthropology at Columbia University in New York City, where the anthropologist professor Franz Boas was to become his friend and collaborator on a number of archaeological and anthropological programs. In 1912, Gamio returned with his M.A. to Mexico City and began working with the newly founded International School of American Archaeology and Ethnography, excavating once more at Azcapotzalco. His exploration of the mound at San Miguel Amantla in 1913 was the first stratigraphic excavation in North America, and the culture sequence of archaic (formative)/TEOTIHUACÁN/AZTEC that he identified was correctly ordered (if incomplete), as has been demonstrated by subsequent stratigraphic work in the basin of Mexico. In 1914, Gamio described the stratigraphic technique in the manual "Methodology

Concerning the Investigation, Exploration, and Conservation of Archaeological Monuments" published in the *Anales* of the National Museum. In the same year, he published a report on his excavations of the main plaza of TENOCHTITLÁN, the Aztec capital, in the center of Mexico City.

In 1916, Gamio became the director of the International School of American Archaeology and Ethnography, and there he produced important studies in archaeology, ethnology, and linguistics. In the same year, he also published an influential collection of essays on the political and social problems of Mexico, *Founding the Fatherland,* which included proposals for improving the lives of indigenous peoples. The work inspired many revolutionary intellectuals and political leaders, including two presidents of Mexico, Venustiano Carranza (1911–1914) and Alvaro Obregon (1920–1924). During the subsequent civil war, Gamio openly supported Emiliano Zapata, the revolutionary leader most concerned with the problems of Indian groups, an unpopular stance to take in Mexico City, where Gamio was surrounded by politicians and generals who did not share his views.

In 1917, Gamio founded and was the first director of a federal department of anthropology and, despite political upheavals, received sufficient resources to set up several research programs. One of these was the first multidisciplinary anthropological program in the Americas—work on the population of the Teotihuacán Valley. This program lasted five years (1917–1922), involved investigations by over twenty scholars, and combined ethnographic and archaeological studies. The five-volume report that resulted is still an indispensable reference source for central Mexican anthropology and history. Gamio also wrote a doctoral dissertation for Colombia University based on this research.

Other projects initiated by Gamio during the 1920s included investigations into the early sedentary archaic (formative) cultures in the basin of Mexico, the excavation of Copilco and other sites, and supporting a project by Byron Cummings at an early urban center of Cuicuilco. Gamio also founded and edited the journal *Ethnos* (1920–1925), which published influential reports and essays by Gamio and others concerning the archaeology, ethnology, and contemporary problems of the indigenous peoples of Mexico.

Between 1924 and 1925 Gamio had a brief political career as undersecretary of public education, but after denouncing government corruption in Mexico City newspapers, he had to flee the country. He spent over two years in exile in the United States and GUATEMALA, during which time he began his famous studies of Mexican immigrant laborers in the United States, which became classic in sociology and applied anthropology. After his return to Mexico and for the rest of his life, Gamio was primarily concerned with the direction of several key government and international institutes devoted to improving the living conditions of indigenous groups. He founded and then directed (1942–1960) the Inter-American Indian Institute, and his work still exercises a profound influence on contemporary Mexican anthropology.

Roberto Cobean and
Alba Guadalupe Mastache Flores

References
For references, see *Encyclopedia of Archaeology: The Great Archaeologists, Vol. 1*, ed. Tim Murray (Santa Barbara, CA: ABC-CLIO, 1999), pp. 331–333.

Garbology: The Archaeology of Fresh Garbage

Gold cups, jade beads, mummies, temples lost in rainforests—to me, these were the essence of archaeology. Oh, how I longed to become an archaeologist and journey back to the days of our ancient ancestors by following the breadcrumb trails of the artifacts they left behind. In 1954, when I was nine, that was the archaeology I dreamed about as I drifted to sleep beside my dog-eared copy of *The Wonderful World of Archaeology* (Jessup 1956).

Fourteen years later I found myself in graduate school immersed in the stifling smell of dusky potsherds punctuated every so often by the thunderous explosions of 200–300 broken pieces of pottery being poured out of linen bags onto masonite laboratory tables. These potsherds had become my path to ancient lives. By this time, I had learned enough of archaeology's arcane secrets that I fully appreciated the stories that could be told by potsherds and other commonplace discards about a society's rise and fall and its day-to-day existence. I was, in fact, literally excited to be systematically and scientifically analyzing the vast expanse of discards to discover replicated patterns of human behavior that we can still recognize today. At the time, I believed I was about to add my own small piece to understanding the puzzle of the classic Maya collapse (Rathje 1971, 1973). In 1968, that was the archaeology I dreamed about when I dozed off late at night on top of my well-worn copy of *Uaxactun, Guatemala: Excavations of 1931–1937* (Smith 1950).

Today, more than three decades years later, I look back on my past dreams of archaeology with a bemused smile on my face, my hands full of fresh garbage, and my mind dancing with thoughts of the calories from fat in our diet or of the recyclables mixed into garbage instead of separated for curbside collection. And instead of dreams, I peruse an Environmental Protection Agency (EPA) report entitled *Characterization of Municipal Solid Waste in the United States: 1995 Update* (Franklin Associates 1996).

My visions of archaeology, as diverse as they appear, have always been the same: to come to understand some basic threads in the fabric of humanity—which our ancestors wove into us and which we are likewise weaving into our descendants—by touching as a person and by measuring as a scientist the artifacts humans make and leave behind. With this personal preamble as background, I now attempt to describe what I can of the history, nature, and public benefits of a type of archaeology called *garbology,* which I believe is currently adding one small piece of understanding to solve the puzzle of the human enigma.

"BURIED ALIVE: The Garbage Glut" was the cover headline of *Newsweek,* 27 November 1989, and "Are We Throwing Away Our Future with Our Trash?" had been the title of the "American Agenda" segment of *ABC Evening News with Peter Jennings* on 2 December 1988. In the late 1980s, the amount of garbage the United States generated had reached crisis proportions for the media and the public. The vast majority of refuse was sent to landfills, and those landfills were filling up and closing down. Where was the garbage to go?

Concerned citizens, convinced that action had to be taken without delay, quickly identified the garbage culprits among the discards that visibly shocked them everyday—litter. Editorials in prestigious newspapers, such as the *New York Times,* echoed popular perceptions that fast-food packaging, disposable diapers, and plastic grocery bags were singularly responsible for "straining" our landfills, and public officials in communities nationwide proposed banning the accused perpetrators. In the meantime, into what kinds of holders were responsible folks to put their unwanted burgers, hot coffee, and groceries? Oddly enough, the answer was not clear because in all the commotion there had been few facts presented about what actually was in the garbage and thus the landfills. It was at this point that a new kind of archaeologist, a garbologist, one who studies fresh garbage, was able to unearth a few relevant facts that began to fill the information vacuum that surrounded our discards.

Workers around the country were regularly digging into landfills to install methane vents, but no one paid much attention to the refuse that was exhumed in the process. After all, it was just smelly, disgusting garbage. The smell and look of discards were not deterrents to archaeologists, who always expect to get their hands dirty, and in fact, to archaeologists, contemporary garbage is a gold mine of information. No society on earth has ever discarded such rich refuse, much of it packaging that identifies the contents it once held by brand, type, cost, quantity, ingredients, nutrient content, and more. Yielding to this temptation, between 1987 and 1997 archaeologists from the Garbage Project at the University of Arizona systematically excavated, hand-sorted, weighed, measured for volume, and recorded thirty-five tons of material from sixteen landfills located across North America—from California to Toronto and from the deserts of Arizona to the Everglades of Florida. The information that resulted from these digs was unexpected (see Rathje 1986, 1991, 1996; Rathje and Murphy 1992a, 1992b).

In contrast to all of the concern directed at fast-food packaging and disposable diapers, the archaeological data demonstrated that both items *together* accounted for less than 2 percent of landfill volume in refuse deposited over the previous ten years. Even more surprisingly, because of industry-wide "light-weighting"—that is, making the same form of an item but with less resin—plastic grocery bags had become thinner and more crushable to the point that 100 plastic bags consumed less space inside a landfill than 20 paper bags. If all three items at the center of public concern had been banned and were not replaced by anything, the garbage archaeologists were certain that landfill managers would not have noticed the difference.

At the opposite end of the spectrum of contents were materials that occupied large portions of landfill space but received little public attention. Construction/demolition debris (C/D) was one. Because of definitional issues, C/D was not even included in the EPA's national estimates of the refuse that goes to MSW (municipal solid waste, or standard community refuse) landfills. Nevertheless, C/D accounted for 20 percent or more of excavated refuse by volume and was the second-largest category of discarded materials recovered by the Garbage Project from MSW landfills.

The largest category occupying MSW landfill space was paper. This was true for refuse buried in the 1980s as well as for refuse dating as far back as the 1950s, because in most landfills, paper seemed to biodegrade very slowly. As a result, by volume, nearly half of all of the refuse excavated by the Garbage Project consisted of newspapers, magazines, packaging paper, and nonpackaging paper such as computer printouts and phonebooks.

Not long after the Garbage Project's first reports following its landfill digs, the energy directed at passing bans was largely redirected toward curbside recycling. A number of communities began placing emphasis on reuse and recycling programs for C/D, and paper recycling promotions started stressing the need to keep paper out of landfills because it did not biodegrade as quickly as most people had once hoped. An association of state attorneys general determined from dig data that several products that claimed to be "biodegradable," including some brands of disposable diapers and plastic garbage bags, did not biodegrade in landfills, and the false advertising of these products was eradicated. All of this was evidence that some crucial views of garbage held by policy planners, the media, and the public had changed—and that garbology had been validated as a new kind of archaeology, one that could make an immediate public contribution.

The Rationale for Garbage Archaeology

For as long as there have been archaeologists there have been jokes, cartoons, and stories that guess what it would be like for an archaeologist to dig through our own refuse (Macaulay 1979). Although often humorous, such speculations are, in fact, based on a serious rationale: if archaeologists can learn important information about *extinct* societies from patterns in ancient garbage, then archaeologists should be able to learn important information about *contemporary* societies from patterns in fresh garbage. The pieces of pottery, broken stone tools, and cut animal bones that traditional archaeologists dig out of old refuse middens provide a surprisingly detailed view of past ways of life, just as all the precisely labeled packages, food debris, and discarded clothing and batteries in modern middens reveal the intimate details of our lives today.

During the summer of 1921, the great American archaeologist ALFRED V. KIDDER seemed to understand this fact when he took the trouble to observe the artifacts that were coming out of a trench being cut for a sewer line through a "fresh" garbage dump in Andover, Massachusetts. From at least this point on, archaeologists have studied contemporary urban refuse informally and sporadically as class exercises and methodological experiments. A variety of subspecialties—ethnoarchaeology, historic sites archaeology, industrial archaeology, and experimental archaeology—have been edging ever closer to analyzing what citizens of the industrialized world discarded last year, last month, and even yesterday. In fact, all archaeologists are aware that it is inevitable that contemporary rubbish will be studied by traditional archaeologists in the same manner they now study the middens of ancient Troy and Tikal—that is, in a hundred or so years from now.

If there are useful things to learn from an archaeological study of our garbage—things that can enrich human lives and minimize the undesirable environmental consequences of the industrialized world—why wait until we (and I literally mean you and I) are all dead and buried to find them out? At least, that is what a group of students and I thought when we founded the Garbage Project at the University of Arizona in the spring of 1973. Today, all of us who are a part of the project, including codirector Wilson Hughes who was one of the founding students, are still thinking along these same lines (Rathje 1996).

After nearly two and a half decades of sorting, recording, and interpreting MSW, garbology, or the archaeological study of contemporary urban refuse, has become a recognizable subspecialty within archaeology and other behavioral sciences (see American Heritage Dictionary Editors 1992; Fagan 1985, 1991a, 1991b; Oxford Dictionary Editors 1995; Podolefsky and Brown 1993; Rathje 1996; Thomas 1979; Turnbaugh, Jurmain, Nelson, and Kilgore 1996). Perhaps the defining characteristic of all garbology "*digs*" is that they combine traditional concerns of archaeological method and theory to produce results that are immediately relevant to understanding and mitigating current social dilemmas (Rathje 1996). The highly publicized "garbage crisis" of the 1980s literally had the Garbage Project's name on it and made it relatively easy to convince the public at large that the study of contemporary refuse provided a significant contribution to society. The "crisis," however, was not given great media coverage until the *Mobro 4000* garbage barge, which took garbage out to sea, sailed in 1987. During its first fourteen years, the Garbage Project studied problem areas that were less literally "archaeological" in nature.

The Garbage Project's first data collection format, called "the regular sort," was designed to sample and record household pickups of fresh refuse (a "pickup" is all of the materials placed out by a single household on one regular refuse collection day). From the beginning, project procedures have rigorously protected the anonymity of the households that discarded the refuse that was sampled.

Solid waste managers have been characterizing wastes by material composition (paper, plastic, glass, etc.) and weight since the 1880s. To these traditional measures, the Garbage Project added a series of innovations, including records from package labels (brand, cost, solid weight or fluid volume of original contents, specific type of contents, packaging materials) and more detailed breakdowns of refuse categories, such as "food waste"—separated into "once-edible food" versus "food preparation debris" and both identified by specific food item—(Hughes 1984). Because of their exacting level of detail, the regular-sort data files that document residential refuse are ideal for analyzing the role of specific household behaviors in generating wastes. Today, the Garbage Project's fresh refuse records, compiled from the long-term ongoing

study in Tucson, Arizona, and short-term studies in five other cities, form a one-of-a-kind database that in the year 2000 encompassed twenty-seven years of time depth.

Garbage Project studies of fresh refuse have consistently documented a few basic patterns in the way we interact with the material world around us: First, what people say they do and what they actually do are often different. For example, while respondents rarely report to interviewers that they waste any food at home, two decades of Garbage Project studies have documented that households generally waste about 15 percent of the solid food they buy (Fung and Rathje 1982; Rathje 1976, 1986). Such misreports characterize a broad range of household behaviors. In other words, people who are interviewed or fill out surveys do not accurately report how much food they waste, what they eat and drink, what they recycle, or the household hazardous wastes they throw away (Rathje and Murphy 1992a, 1992b).

This discovery, of course, is not a great surprise. It is common knowledge among behavioral scientists that any methodology that depends upon the accuracy of answers given to interviewers or in surveys suffers from problems of informant bias (Webb, Campbell, Schwarts, and Sechrest 1966). Respondents may not be able to accurately and quantitatively recall specific behaviors, such as how many ounces of green beans they ate the day before or how often they discard a half-full container of pesticide, and even if respondents can accurately recall behaviors, such as beer drinking or changing the oil in their cars, they may not want to admit to the specifics.

At this point it should be noted that systematic sorts of garbage avoid informant biases. Refuse data, like virtually all archaeological data, are quantitative: packaging and commodity wastes can be weighed, measured for volume, and chemically analyzed, and their labels can be read for further information, all without relying upon the memory or honesty of respondents. When refuse is identified by specific household (versus recording only the generating household's census tract), the Garbage Project obtains permission from the discarders.

Even under these conditions of self-awareness, project analyses show that discards generally adhere to the same patterns found in garbage collected anonymously at the census tract level (Ritenbaugh and Harrison 1984).

Although independent of informant-based distortions, refuse analysis is susceptible to other forms of bias. The most obvious one is garbage disposals, and the Garbage Project has conducted studies, not unlike those of ethnoarchaeologists, to develop correction factors for ground up food (Rathje and McCarthy 1977). Other biases include people who carry recyclables to drop-off buy-back centers and the fact that behavior can be characterized only at the household level, not on the individual level.

Overall, the advantages of garbage sorting as both an alternative and a quantitative measure of behavior outweigh its limitations, and the first pattern identified—that self-reports differ from refuse records—has opened up a broad new research area.

The second conclusion drawn from refuse analysis is that there is a clear patterning in the differences between what people report they do and what they actually do. This conclusion was drawn from a number of Garbage Project studies that were designed to verify consumer responses to various kinds of diet questionnaires by comparing self-reports about food use against packaging and food debris in fresh refuse. One specific self-report/refuse pattern the Garbage Project has documented is "the good provider syndrome": a female adult reporting for a household as a whole has a tendency to overreport everything the household uses by 10 to 30 percent or more. Another pattern is "the surrogate syndrome": to find out how much alcohol is consumed by household members, do not ask a drinker; drinkers consistently underreport their alcohol consumption by 40 to 60 percent. Instead, ask a nondrinker, as people in this category report accurately what drinkers drink (Dobyns and Rathje 1987; Johnstone and Rathje 1986). The second conclusion is again no real surprise.

Unlike the first two, the third conclusion was full of surprises. The differences between respondent reports and the material remains in refuse frequently indicate directly opposed behaviors; to be more specific, respondents normally report rational behaviors while their actual behaviors often appear irrational. One of the best examples of this kind of counterintuitive relationship between self-reports and refuse occurred during the highly publicized "beef shortage" in the spring of 1973. At that time, when consumers were complaining bitterly about high prices and the erratic availability of beef, the Garbage Project was recording the highest rate of edible beef waste it has ever documented (Rathje and McCarthy 1977).

Several other instances of this kind of counterintuitive report/refuse pattern have been documented. In 1977, the Garbage Project gave "meat fat" its own separate category. Using a long-term database, the Garbage Project determined that in 1987 people began cutting off and discarding much larger than normal quantities of the separable fat on fresh cuts of red meat and, at the same time, they also bought less fresh red meat. Both actions seemed to be responses to a 1986 National Academy of Science study that was widely reported in the media and which identified fat from red meat as a cancer risk factor. There was just one problem. The consumers studied replaced the fresh red meat in their diet with processed red meat—salami, bologna, sausage, hotdogs, etc., which contained large quantities of hidden fat—so the level of fat intake in the diet did not fall; instead, it stayed the same or increased (Rathje and Ho 1987).

A third case involved household hazardous wastes (see Rathje, Wilson, Hughes, and Herndon 1987). In 1986, Marin County in California sponsored a Toxics Away! Day to collect household hazardous wastes such as used motor oil and unused pesticides. The Garbage Project recorded residential refuse two months after the collection day and compared it to household discards sorted before the collection day. The results were completely unexpected: there were nearly two times more potentially hazardous wastes recorded in the refuse *after* the collection day than there had been before. The data clearly demonstrated that all of the increase in hazardous wastes was owing to the discard of large quantities of items from only a few households (such as three or four half-full cans of paint or several full containers of pesticide in just one pickup). The Garbage Project's interpretation was that the media surrounding the collection day made people aware of the potentially hazardous commodities in their homes, but for those who missed the collection day, no other appropriate avenue of discard had been identified. As a result, some residents disposed of their hazardous wastes in the only avenue available to them—their normal refuse pickup. The same pattern was verified in subsequent studies in Phoenix and Tucson (Rathje and Wilson 1987). The lesson learned: communities that initiate hazardous waste collection days should inform residents of future collection times or of other avenues for appropriate discard.

Such counterintuitive interview/refuse patterns indicate that consumers may not be aware of how much their reported behaviors differ from their actual behaviors and that the Garbage Project is beginning to document a previously unmeasurable phenomenon between what people think is happening and what is really going on. Such studies have already led to some general principles of the differences between people's awareness of their behavior and their actual behavior (Rathje 1996).

The Garbage Project's contribution to a better understanding of the relationship between what people report they do and what they actually do (Rathje 1996; Rathje and Murphy 1992a) relies heavily on the use of archaeological methods and theory to quantitatively document actual behaviors from refuse. This is the grist of any archaeologist's mill, and the validity of the Garbage Project's data records and interpretations is based upon 100 years of previous archaeological studies that have analyzed refuse to reconstruct behavior.

For the same period of time, archaeologists have also been studying refuse in an attempt to count the number of people who lived within particular sites or regions at particular times. The Garbage Project has now done the same thing at the request of the U.S. federal government. The U.S. Census Bureau has long been aware of the criticism that its interview-survey methods lead to a significant undercounting of ethnic minorities, especially young adult males who may be undercounted by 40 percent. In 1986, the Quality Assurance Branch of the Census Bureau funded a study to answer the question, Could the Garbage Project count people based on the types and quantities of residential refuse they generate? The answer was yes (Rathje and Tani 1987). For any unit of time in any given neighborhood, the overall weight of total refuse discarded (minus yard wastes, which vary markedly between suburbs and inner cities) varies directly according to the number of resident discarders. The Garbage Project converted quantities of refuse thrown out per week to numbers of people by using "per person" generation rates documented in test areas. Overall, a series of garbage-based estimates of population were within 5 percent of the actual number of residents. The Garbage Project now stands ready to cross-verify census counts with a method that does not violate the subjects' anonymity.

Ongoing Research

Since 1980, the Garbage Project has worked on a large number of specialized topics similar to the census study, and all of them are the focus of continuing inquiry. Landfill excavations, for example, are gauging the impact of recycling programs on the volume of wastes that reach landfills. The first reported results estimated that metropolitan Toronto's "blue box" curbside recycling program has conserved some 20 percent of landfill space in the metropolitan area since 1982 (Tani, Rathje, Hughes, Wilson, and Coupland 1992).

The recovery of 2,425 datable, readable newspapers from the project's excavations dramatically changed the view that biodegradation is commonplace in landfills. To better understand why biodegradation does and does not occur in landfill environments, the Garbage Project has so far conducted four cooperative digs that have involved microbiologists and environmental engineers from the University of Arizona, University of Oklahoma, University of Wisconsin–Madison, Argonne National Laboratories, and Proctor and Gamble's Environmental Laboratory (Suflita et al. 1993). In this same mode, the Garbage Project excavated and examined samples of refuse from a ten-year-old "bioreactor" landfill in Sandtown, Delaware, one designed to enhance biodegradation. According to the project's evaluation, after ten years of burial, the Sandtown refuse exhibits some indications of increased biodegradation but nothing conclusive (Rathje 1999). The next Sandtown dig is scheduled for 2008.

The Garbage Project has also initiated several studies that integrate its fresh and landfill data on hazardous wastes in MSW. The heavy-metal assays of finds are being compared with detailed item-by-item lists (such as two lightbulbs, one drain opener can, two newspapers, etc.) of the refuse identified within each 150 pounds of landfill sampled. The goal is to determine the rate of movement of heavy metals in commodities and inks and other hazardous wastes from refuse into the landfill matrix (Rathje, Hughes, et al. 1992).

Garbage Project Students and Staff

The Garbage Project does not consist of only systematic records compiled by a hands-on sorting of household garbage; it also consists of the sorters and project staff attached to the hands. Although many people find the results of project data studies interesting, most of them also find the sorting process itself revolting. In fact, a few market researchers realized in the 1950s that household refuse contained useful information but after repeated experiments they found they could not pay people to sort refuse. Those hired either quit quickly or kept sloppy records. Who would possibly be willing to rummage through someone else's smelly trash and keep accurate records of its contents?

The answer is a matter of public record. *Rubbish!* (Rathje and Murphy 1992b, paperback 1993) contains a list of more than 900 university students and others who sorted refuse for the Garbage Project between 1973 and 1991. The intimate archaeological view these and subsequent sorters have had of the materials that are discarded from households much like their own has provided them with a unique perspective, and while they do not preach to others, they are enthusiastically dedicated to providing

everyone possible with the same insights they have drawn from their own hands-on sorting of residential refuse.

In attempting to share results, the Garbage Project has focused most directly on schools, museums, and other avenues of access to students. The rationale is that the archaeology of our own society will mean the most to the young people who can do the most with archaeological insights. Currently, the project is especially proud of two endeavors. The first is the compilation of *WRAP (Waste Reduction Alternatives Program) Resource Manual* (Dobyns and Hughes 1994), which has been distributed to schools throughout Arizona and the United States. The manual is designed to help both students and teachers learn how their individual behavior can produce significant quantities of garbage and how they can each make changes that will greatly decrease that amount of garbage. The second endeavor resulted in "The Garbage Dilemma," an interactive video on permanent display in the Hall of Science in American Life at the Smithsonian's National Museum of American History. The video was the product of cooperation among the Garbage Project staff, the Smithsonian's design staff, and the Chedd-Angier Production Company. Schools and museums—not landfills—provide the kinds of environments where the Garbage Project hopes all of its results will eventually come to reside.

Garbology in the Twenty-first Century

What has set the archaeologists of the Garbage Project apart from other behavioral science researchers is that all of their studies have been grounded in the hands-on sorting of quantifiable bits and pieces of garbage instead of collecting data through interview surveys, government documents, or industry records. In other words, the Garbage Project is studying consumer behavior directly from the material realities that are left behind rather than from self-conscious self-reporting.

The exhaustive level of detail Garbage Project student sorters use to record data has also set the project's studies apart from other data sources. Many local plans by engineering consultant firms and even by solid waste managers are based on national characterizations of solid waste generation that involve the questionable validity of using government and industry records of production, together with an untold number of untested assumptions, to estimate residential and other discards. Even if the national estimates are accurate, they are available only at the level of categories of material composition—so much plastic, glass, aluminum, paper, steel, and so on. But how can anyone plan on the basis of such data? Most of the materials come from the packaging that people buy at stores, but no one goes shopping for five ounces of glass, three ounces of paperboard boxes, and eight ounces of aluminum cans. Instead, they shop for a jar of Best Foods mayonnaise, a box of Cap'n Crunch cereal, and a twelve-pack of Bud Light beer. This brings the project back full circle to its item-by-item regular sorts of fresh refuse. In other words, in contrast to virtually all other sources of information, the Garbage Project looks at refuse the way all archaeologists do—as the material result of human behavior.

Ultimately, the contribution of the Garbage Project comes down to one simple component: in order to understand and mitigate important problems, we have to, first, become aware of the problems and, second, measure their impact. This difference in approach can mean a considerable difference in results.

Since 1987, communities everywhere have been promoting recycling, reuse, source reduction, and everything else they can to decrease the amount of refuse being discarded. At the same time, to cut collection costs and reduce worker injuries, many communities have converted to automated systems that depend on standard-sized garbage containers. The containers that most families bought for themselves were usually sixty-gallon containers, about what one person could carry a short distance. The new standardized containers have wheels and can hold ninety gallons, one-third bigger, to accommodate the needs of the largest families. By all accounts, the results of these changes have been that recycling is increasing and on-the-job injuries are down.

The Garbage Project's hands-on sorting, however, adds another dimension—a darker side that

is rarely mentioned (Rathje 1993). When the Garbage Project first studied residential refuse in the city of Phoenix, that city, unlike Tucson, already had an automated system, and Garbage Project personnel were surprised to discover that Phoenix households discarded nearly double the refuse thrown out by households less than 100 miles away in Tucson. The mystery was greatly clarified when Tucson switched to the automated system and its household refuse generation rate increased by more than one-third. At this point, the Garbage Project identified a "Parkinson's Law of Garbage" with implications for every city's solid waste management strategy (Rathje 1993).

The original Parkinson's Law was formulated in 1957 by C. Northcote Parkinson, a British bureaucrat who concluded, "Work expands to fill the time available for its completion." Parkinson's Law of Garbage similarly states, "Garbage expands to fill the receptacles available for its containment."

Parkinson's Law of Garbage is really quite simple. When people have small garbage cans, larger items—old cans of paint, broken furniture perpetually awaiting repair, bags of old clothing—do not typically get thrown away. Rather, these materials sit in basements and garages, often until a residence changes hands. But when homeowners are provided with plastic minidumpsters, they are presented with a new option. Before long, what was once an instinctive "I'll stick this in the cellar" becomes an equally instinctive "I'll bet this will fit in the can."

The Garbage Project has compared the components of Tucson residential refuse collected before and after mechanization. Solid waste discards went from an average of less than fourteen pounds per biweekly pickup to an average of more than twenty-three pounds. The largest increase was in the yard waste category, followed by "other" (broken odds and ends), food waste, newspapers, and textiles. The first pickup of the week was substantially heavier than the second, reflecting the accomplishment of weekend chores, and the discards in that first pickup were loaded with consistently larger quantities of hazardous waste than the Garbage Project had come to expect in a typical load. These findings suggest that the introduction of ninety-gallon containers should be of concern for three reasons.

First, the increase in discarded newspaper suggests that one counterproductive result of the larger containers may be a lower participation rate in any form of recycling. For people who find separating out recyclables a bother, the ninety-gallon bin is a no-penalty way of circumventing the issue. Likewise, the increase in "other" materials and textiles could indicate an alternative to the "donation avenue," in which unwanted resources go to the Salvation Army and other charities, or even to yard sales.

Second, the substantial increase in the amount of hazardous waste indicates that the large bins are a convenient alternative to storing toxic items until used up at home or until the next household hazardous waste collection day. Third, at the same time that all-out recycling programs are being implemented to decrease the flow of garbage, collection techniques are being installed that unwittingly may be increasing the overall flow of garbage at an even higher rate.

The evidence for Parkinson's Law of Garbage is not yet conclusive. The only way to know whether it is a behavioral pattern is hands-on garbology archaeology. This archaeological research question is important to answer for the method and theory of archaeology, for culture history, and for our cities' immediate economic and environmental future. Garbologists, grab your gloves and facemasks. The results of your efforts may be enough to one day convince everyone to pay attention to their own discards—and then recycle them.

W. L. Rathje

References

American Heritage Dictionary Editors. 1992. *The American Heritage Dictionary of the English Language.* 3d ed. Boston: Houghton Mifflin.

Dobyns, S., and W. W. Hughes. 1994. *The WRAP (Waste Reduction Alternatives Program) Resource Manual.* Final Report to the Reduce, Reuse, and Recycle Grant Program, Arizona Department of Environmental Quality.

Dobyns, S., and W. L. Rathje, eds. 1987. *The NFCS Report/Refuse Study: A Handbook of Potential Dis-* *tortions in Respondent Diet Reports.* 4 vols. Final Report to the Consumer Nutrition Division. Washington, DC: U.S. Department of Agriculture.

Encyclopædia Britannica. 1996. *Yearbook of Science and the Future.* Chicago: Encyclopædia Britannica, Inc.

Fagan, B. M. 1985. *The Adventures of Archaeology.* Washington, DC: National Geographic Society.

———. 1991a. *Archaeology: A Brief Introduction.* 4th ed. New York: HarperCollins.

———. 1991b. *In the Beginning.* 7th ed. New York: HarperCollins.

Franklin Associates. 1996. *Characterization of Municipal Solid Waste in the United States: 1995 Update.* Publication no. 530-R-96-001. Washington, DC: Environmental Protection Agency.

Fung, E. E., and W. L. Rathje. 1982. "How We Waste $31 Billion in Food a Year." In *The 1982 Yearbook of Agriculture,* 352-257. Ed. J. Hayes. Washington, DC: Department of Agriculture.

Hughes, W. W. 1984. "The Method to Our Madness." *American Behavioral Scientist* 28, no. 1: 41-50.

Jessup, R. 1956. *The Wonderful World of Archaeology.* Garden City, NY: Garden City Books.

Johnstone, B. M., and W. L. Rathje. 1986. "Building a Theory of the Difference between Respondent Reports and Material Realities." Paper presented at a symposium, Different Approaches to Using Food Consumption Data Bases for Evaluating Dietary Intake, at the Institute of Food Technologists Annual Meeting, Dallas, Texas.

Macaulay, D. 1979. *Motel of the Mysteries.* Boston: Houghton Mifflin.

New York Times. 1988. "Serious about Plastic Pollution." In "Topics of the *Times.*" 8 January.

Oxford Dictionary Editors. 1995. *Oxford Dictionary and Usage Guide to the English Language.* Oxford: Oxford University Press.

Podolefsky, A., and P. J. Brown, eds. 1993. *Applying Anthropology: An Introductory Reader.* 3d ed. Mountain View, CA: Mayfield Publishing Company.

Rathje, W. L. 1971. "The Origin and Development of Lowland Classic Maya Civilization." *American Antiquity* 36, no. 3: 275-285.

———. 1973. "Classic Maya Development and Denouement." In *Classic Maya Collapse,* 405-454. Ed. T. P. Culbert. Albuquerque: University of New Mexico Press.

———. 1976. *Socioeconomic Correlates of Household*

Residuals: Phase 1. Final Report to the Program for Research Applied to National Needs. Washington, DC: National Science Foundation.

———. 1986. "Why We Throw Food Away." *Atlantic Monthly* 257, no. 4: 14–16.

———. 1991. "Once and Future Landfills." *National Geographic* 179, no. 5: 116–134.

———. 1993. "A Perverse Law of Garbage." *Garbage* 4, no. 6: 22–23.

———. 1996. "The Archaeology of Us." In *Encyclopaedia Britannica's Yearbook of Science and the Future—1997,* 158–177. Ed. C. Ciegelski. New York: Encyclopaedia Britannica.

———. 1999. "Landfill Biodegradation at Sandtown." *MSW-Management* 9, no. 3: 78–83.

Rathje, W. L., and E. E. Ho. 1987. "Meat Fat Madness: Conflicting Patterns of Meat Fat Consumption and Their Public Health Implications." *Journal of the American Dietetic Association* 87, no. 10: 1357–1362.

Rathje, W. L., W. W. Hughes, D. C. Wilson, M. K. Tank, G. H. Archer, R. G. Hunt, and T. W. Jones. 1992. "The Archaeology of Contemporary Landfills." *American Antiquity* 57, no. 3: 437–447.

Rathje, W. L., and M. McCarthy. 1977. "Regularity and Variability in Contemporary Garbage." In *Research Strategies in Historical Archaeology,* 261–286. Ed. S. South. New York: Academic Press.

Rathje, W. L., and C. Murphy. 1992a. "Beyond the Pail: Why We Are What We Don't Eat." *Washington Post,* 28 June.

———. 1992b. *Rubbish! The Archaeology of Garbage.* New York: HarperCollins. Paperback, 1993.

Rathje, W. L., and M. K. Tani. 1987. *MNI Triangulation Final Report: Estimating Population Characteristics at the Neighborhood Level from Household Refuse.* 3 vols. Final Report to the Center for Survey Methods Research. Washington, DC: Bureau of the Census.

Rathje, W. L., and D. C. Wilson. 1987. "Archaeological Techniques Applied to Characterization of Household Discards and Their Potential Contamination of Groundwater." Paper read at a conference, Solid Waste Management and Materials Policy, New York City.

Rathje, W. L., D. C. Wilson, W. W. Hughes, and R. Herndon. 1987. *Characterization of Household Hazardous Wastes from Marin County, California, and New Orleans, Louisiana.* Report no. EPA/600/x–87/129. Las Vegas: U.S. EPA Environmental Monitoring Systems Laboratory.

Ritenbaugh, C. K., and G. G. Harrison. 1984. "Reactivity and Garbage Analysis." *American Behavioral Scientist* 28, no. 1: 51–70.

Smith, A. L. 1950. *Uaxactun, Guatemala: Excavations of 1931–1937.* Publication no. 588. Washington, DC: Carnegie Institution.

Suflita, J. M., G. P. Gerba, R. K. Ham, A. C. Palmisano, W. L. Rathje, and J. A. Robinson. 1993. "The World's Largest Landfill: Multidisciplinary Investigation." *Environmental Science & Technology* 26, no. 8: 1486–1494.

Tani, M. K., W. L. Rathje, W. W. Hughes, D. C. Wilson, and G. Coupland. 1992. *The Toronto Dig: Excavations at Four Municipal Solid Waste Disposal Sites in the Greater Toronto Area.* Toronto: Trash Research Corporation.

Thomas, D. H. 1979. *Archaeology.* New York: Holt, Rinehart and Winston.

Turnbaugh, W. A., R. Jurmain, H. Nelson, and L. Kilgore, 1996. *Understanding Physical Anthropology and Archeology.* 6th ed. Minneapolis/St. Paul: West Publishing Company.

Webb, E. J., D. T. Campbell, R. D. Schwarts, and L. Sechrest. 1966. *Unobtrusive Measures: Nonreactive Research in the Social Sciences.* Chicago: Rand McNally.

Garrod, Dorothy (1892–1968)

Born in London the daughter of Sir Archibald Garrod (who became Regius Professor of Medicine at Oxford University), Dorothy Garrod studied history at Newnham College, Cambridge. During World War I, in which all three of her brothers were killed, she worked for the Ministry of Munitions and then for the Catholic Women's League in FRANCE. Convalescing in Malta toward the end of the war, where her father was director of war hospitals, she first became interested in archaeology.

After the war, Dorothy Garrod began to study anthropology at Oxford under R. R. Marret, one of the excavators of the Paleolithic site of La Cotte de St. Brelade on the Channel island of Jersey. By the time she graduated, Garrod had become fascinated by Paleolithic archaeology, and Marret sent her to study in Paris under the great French paleontologist HENRI BREUIL. There she gained valuable practical experience, excavating Upper Paleolithic cave sites at La

Quina, Les Eyzies, Isturitz, and Correge in central France, and she also became familiar with the French system for the classification of sites.

After returning to Oxford, Garrod applied her detailed knowledge of the French sequence to classifying all available Upper Paleolithic material from sites in Great Britain, which during the late Pleistocene age, had been no more than a marginal extension of France. Breuil encouraged this work and also suggested she excavate in Gibraltar, where in 1926 Garrod recovered remains of Neanderthals in association with a Mousterian culture, thus linking a particular fossil hominid with a particular technology and a plentiful residue of contemporary fauna.

Also in 1926, the remains of a Neanderthal in the context of Mousterian culture were found Zettupeh in what was then Palestine— the most eastern discovery of such material. Garrod was invited by Grant McCurdy, founder and director of the American School of Prehistoric Research, which was responsible for the discovery at Zettupeh, to find out just how much further east Mousterian culture had extended. Garrod made a preliminary visit to the Kirkuk region in Iraq and was able to demonstrate that the Mousterian culture had reached as far as northeastern Iraq. Excavations at the cave of Hazar Merd in Iraq not only confirmed the presence of the Mousterian but revealed an overlying Upper Paleolithic period, and other excavations at Zarzi confirmed the presence of an Upper Paleolithic level succeeded by microlithic industry.

Between seasons in Iraq Garrod began to dig in Palestine, and in the cave of Shukbah in the Wady en-Natuf she found a microlithic industry that was distinctive because it covered an eroded breccia containing a Levallois-Mousterian industry. This find demonstrated that there had been continuous occupation and local development of technology and inaugurated the excavation, with Theodore McCown, from 1929 to 1934 of the Mount Carmel caves. Garrod went on to prove that the French system of classification of the Paleolithic period was only valid for restricted parts of western Europe— that the Paleolithic period had different cultural manifestations in different parts of the world.

She also demonstrated that the Solutrean and the Magdalenian phases in stone-tool production were the only ones indigenous to Europe— and that all the rest, such as the Chatelperronian, the Aurignacian, and the Gravettian, had originated outside Europe and spread to that continent.

In 1939, Garrod was elected to the Disney Chair of Archaeology at Cambridge, the first holder of that chair to be a prehistorian. During World War II, from 1942 to 1945, she was a member of the Women's Auxiliary Air Force and interpreted air photographs of bomb damage for an intelligence unit. After the war, she worked at integrating prehistory and fieldwork, the history of archaeology, and world prehistory into the university curriculum.

She retired in 1952 and lived in France, continuing to excavate the rock shelter at Angles-sur-Anglin, Vienne, until 1963. She resumed excavations in the Near East in 1956, testing the stratigraphy of the Abri Aumoffen in southern Lebanon with the English archaeologist Diana Kirkbride. This work confirmed the presence of a stone-blade toolmaking industry, the Amudian (between the Acheulean and the Middle Paleolithic), underlying a Jabrudian (late Amudian) deposit with racloirs and bifaces. Two years before she died, Garrod summarized the Paleolithic archaeology of Egypt and southwestern Asia for the *Cambridge Ancient History*. The chronicle of southwestern Asian archaeology was, with a few exceptions, largely the outcome of her own fieldwork and her collaborations. More important, Garrod's researches in southwestern Asia had shown that prehistory had to be pursued over widespread territories, indeed on a worldwide scale.

Based on an essay by
the late Sir Grahame Clark

References

For references, see *Encyclopedia of Archaeology: The Great Archaeologists, Vol. 1*, ed. Tim Murray (Santa Barbara, CA: ABC-CLIO, 1999), pp. 410–412.

Garstang, John (1876–1956)

Born in England, John Garstang was educated at Blackburn Grammar School and owing to his excellence in mathematics, won a scholarship to Jesus College, Oxford, in 1895. He became interested in archaeology while he was still at school and after excavating the Roman camp of Bremetennacum at Ribchester, he published his findings in 1898. Garstang spent his undergraduate vacations excavating, and after he graduating with third-class honors in mathematics, he took up archaeology full time, joining SIR WILLIAM MATTHEW FLINDERS PETRIE at ABYDOS in Egypt and discovering and excavating the tomb of Beyt Khallaf.

Garstang was appointed reader in Egyptian archaeology at Liverpool University in 1902 and led expeditions to Negadah, Hierakonpolis, Esneh, and Beni Hassan in Egypt over the next two years. By then his interests in the Hittites had been aroused, and in 1904, he traveled to Asia Minor and received permission to excavate the Hittite capital of BOĞAZKÖY, TURKEY. In 1907, at the personal request of the Kaiser of Germany, this site was instead given to German archaeologists to excavate.

From 1907 until 1941, Garstang was professor of the methods and practice of archaeology at Liverpool University where he contributed to the establishment of the Institute of Archaeology and the journal *Annals of Archaeology and Anthropology*. In 1908, he returned to Asia Minor, excavating the late Hittite site of Sakje-Geuzi in Turkey; in the winter, he returned to Abydos in Egypt to continue excavating there. His topographic study of Hittite monuments, *The Land of the Hittites,* was published in 1910.

From 1909 to 1914, Garstang excavated at Meroe in the Sudan, the site of the capital of Meriotic civilization from early third century B.C. to the early fourth century A.D. He served with the Red Cross in France during World War I, and in 1919, he became head of the newly created School of Archaeology in Jerusalem (serving in that post until 1926) and working as director of the Department of Antiquities in Palestine (1920–1926). Among his many achievements during this time was the discovery of the site of Hazor in ISRAEL, an important

Canaanite town. He published *Joshua Judges* in 1931 and *The Heritage of Solomon* in 1934, and from 1930 until 1936, he excavated Jericho until the political situation made it impossible to continue.

In 1936, Garstang returned to Turkey to survey the Cilician plain, and he excavated the site of Yumuk Tepe near Mersin until the outbreak of World War II. He returned to complete this work in 1946, published in *Prehistoric Mersin* (1953), and to help establish the British Institute of Archaeology at Ankara in 1948, becoming its first director. He received honorary degrees from Aberdeen University, received the Legion of Honour in 1920, and became a Commander of the British Empire in 1949.

Tim Murray

Geoffrey of Monmouth (ca. 1100–1154)

It is thought that Geoffrey of Monmouth was born in Monmouth, Wales, at the beginning of the twelfth century. The son of the family priest of William, earl of Gloucester, an influential aristocrat of the time, Geoffrey was brought up by his paternal uncle Uchtryd, archdeacon and later archbishop of Llandaff, Wales. Geoffrey attended Oxford University where he met another archdeacon, Walter Calenius, from whom he was supposed to have obtained the material for his monumental book *Historia Regum Britannia*. This book was widely available in some form by 1139, because it was reported on and examined by Henry of Huntingdon in Normandy on his way to Rome with Theobald, the archbishop of Canterbury. Geoffrey of Monmouth became a Benedictine priest at the age of fifty in 1152, was consecrated as a bishop by Theobold that same year, and was buried in Llandaff two years later.

Geoffrey of Monmouth was a significant medieval scholar and historian whose great knowledge of both older and contemporary writers was evident from the acknowledged sources in his book, although he was criticized in his day for his bad Cymric (Welsh) and vulgar Latin. Victorian scholars dated the surviving edition of the *Historia Regum Britanniae* as the last 1147 edition, which comprises Geoffrey of Monmouth's translations and retelling of ancient British legends from written Cymric and Breton sources into medieval Latin. The Breton language, used by the inhabitants of Brittany in FRANCE, and Cymric, or Welsh, were almost identical at the time that Geoffrey of Monmouth was working on his book and up until the reign of Henry I, when substantial differences between the two languages occurred.

Geoffrey's sources for his work included manuscripts from the tenth century, such as the Latin "Nennius," which is extant, and a book of Breton legends, which has since vanished. The latter was the source of the story of the descent of British princes from the fugitives of Troy, a legend that is also common in stories about the origins of the Franks in Gaul; the story seems to have become popular in both countries after the invasion of the Teutonic tribes in the sixth century. Although the legends were not recorded by the historian Bede in his eighth-century chronicle, they were part of written history by the ninth century.

The publication of *Historia Regum Britanniae* marks a milestone in the literary history of Europe. Within fifty years of its completion, stories about the Holy Grail, Lancelot, Tristan, Perceval, and the Round Table had appeared, and Merlin and Arthur had become as popular in Germany and Italy as they were in England and France. The book was later translated into Anglo-Norman, and 100 years later into English. The material was then used by a long line of famous British storytellers and historians such as Robert of Gloucester, Roger of Wendover, Holinshed, Shakespeare, Milton, Dryden, Pope, Sir Thomas Malory, Wordsworth, and Tennyson.

As important as its long-term impact on European civilization was the book's short-term influence on the people of England, which included a large part of France at the time. The popularity of the work's legends and stories helped to defuse racial animosities among Welsh, Breton, British, French, and Teuton, and the various groups became more politically unified through their mutual belief in a shared origin.

Tim Murray

Geographic Information Systems
Historical Background
Archaeologists, like geographers, think spatially, and both make sense of their data by referring to its spatial dimension. Archaeology—particularly European archaeology—has been closely linked to geography and has borrowed from it methodological principles to develop its own theoretical tenets. This close association with geography dates from the formal mapping methods of attributes and artifacts developed by the Austro-German school of "anthropogeographers" of the 1880s and 1890s. However it is with the Cambridge School of New Geography, and in particular with Peter Haggett's *Locational Analysis in Human Geography* (1965), Richard Chorley and Peter Haggett's *Models in Geography* (1967), and Michael Chisholm's *Rural Settlement and Land Use* (1968) that the otherwise implied sway of geography toward archaeology was formalized. This influence is best reflected in the archaeologists Claudio Vita-Finzi's and ERIC HIGGS's 1970 site catchment analysis of Mount Carmel, Ian Hodder and Clive Orton's *Spatial Models in Archaeology (*1976), and DAVID CLARKE's *Spatial Archaeology* (1977).

More recently, geography is once more leaving its mark on the theoretical development of archaeology. The emergence of landscape archaeology, a derivation of geography's landscape theory, has re-ignited interest in the spatial associations between archaeological sites and their physical environment on both sides of the Atlantic. Within this context, the application of geographic information systems (GIS) has been hailed as the new paradigm. But just how much can the application of GIS assist in the interpretation of the archaeological data? Before attempting to answer this question a brief review on the development of GIS is necessary.

Development of GIS
Reflecting about the complexity of archaeological data, David Clarke declared in 1977 that the analysis of the spatial relationships of artifact and site distribution could no longer be done by intuitive methods such as simple visual inspection, or "eyeballing." The challenge, then, was to develop the methodological tools that would

make the analysis of enormous amounts of data feasible. With the advent of the personal computer as an affordable, fast, and user-friendly analytical tool, it is now possible to process in a very short period of time amounts of data that otherwise would have taken days or even weeks to process.

The sheer size of the databases that archaeologists have to work with, which include archaeological and environmental data, made it extremely difficult, if not virtually impossible, to integrate all the material into a spatial-temporal framework. The best archaeologists could hope for was that through the production of accurate maps of site or artifact distribution, a meticulous visual inspection would reveal any spatial pattern.

Traditionally, maps have been an indispensable tool for archaeology and related disciplines. The basic geographic features are displayed using various visual artifices, such as diverse symbols or colors or text codes, which are explained in the legends. Naturally, the most important limitation these maps have is the amount of information they can effectively communicate, if more information is needed, it would have to be included in another form.

Map production, however, is a very expensive and time-consuming activity. As our scientific knowledge of the earth advances, new information needs to be charted almost immediately, but the effective and prompt assessment of natural resources, meteorological phenomena, and urban growth requires that maps be produced expediently and at low cost.

The demand for detailed map information has put pressure on for the development of better mapping techniques, and naturally, computer applications such as computer assisted design (CAD) and computer assisted mapping (CAM) have been instrumental in meeting this demand. Still, these advantages in map production and the ability of computer applications like CAM or CAD to identify spatial patterns between the mapped features—points, lines, and polygons—are very limited, because they are not linked to a relational database. It is only with the advent of GIS that we are able, for the first time, to link the geographic position of the mapped features with the qualitative and quantitative information that describes them and make queries about them.

In essence, GIS is a spatially referenced database that allow us to store great amounts of data, retrieve it with ease, manipulate it mathematically, and visualize the results within its spatial context. Hence, the core of the analytic power of GIS lies in its ability to handle digital maps to create new information from the pre-existing data.

To fully understand this advantage we need to take a closer look at the conceptual changes in maps as a result of the insertion of GIS. Prior to this insertion, the study of the spatial distribution of natural resources and human and plant populations was approached in a qualitative way. The principal aim was to produce inventories of these data, and the enormous amount of information produced forced the cartographer to rely on qualitative methods of classification and mapping.

Consequently, quantitative descriptions were hindered mainly because of a lack of the appropriate mathematical tools needed to describe the spatial variations. With GIS, however, maps underwent a critical transformation because spatial variations could now be rendered as digits. Therefore, maps are no longer conceived as simplified pictorial depictions of the real world but as numbers. This is a major conceptual leap since throughout the approximately 8,000 years of mapmaking, maps have been primarily *descriptive,* which has limited their application to showing the exact location of things. Increasingly, however, maps are becoming *prescriptive,* containing the data necessary to assist us in making decisions.

Applications of GIS in Archaeology

GIS technology is relatively recent as the first operational GIS was developed in Canada in 1972, around the same time that the first text on GIS was published. It was not until the 1980s, however, that archaeologists begin applying GIS to their field of study. In 1982, the study of the settlement patterns in relation to the seasonal availability of natural resources in western Arizona was approached using GIS.

Database management and cultural resource management (CRM) applications began in the mid-1980s, and toward the latter part of the decade, GIS was being used in site prediction models.

By enabling the management of extensive spatially related databases, GIS has provided archaeologists with a powerful analytical tool, one that can lead to the discovery of the various levels of spatial patterns in the archaeological record. This in turn can lead to a more in-depth analysis of the underlying principles of those spatial patterns. There are three broad categories into which all spatial modeling done using GIS fall: data mining, predictive modeling, and dynamic simulation. The first two are perhaps the more common forms applied in archaeology.

Data mining consists of the retrieval of specific data items or a combination of items in relation to their spatial/temporal location. The settlement pattern studies in western Arizona mentioned above, and the study of the potential impact on known archaeological sites owing to works of infrastructure, e.g., the construction of a dam or a road, constitute good examples of this type of model.

Predictive modeling in GIS differs from simple mathematical models in the sense that it interpolates the field data into mapped variables, thus providing us, in addition to a hard figure, with the spatial location of the relevant variables. Predictive modeling is frequently used in CRM when dealing with the potential effects to unknown archaeological sites from the aforementioned infrastructure works. There are also various examples in the American Southwest where site prediction has been used in the study of settlement patterns, and its potential in assisting in the design of the archaeological survey strategies has just been tapped.

Only recently has the third category begun to be explored in connection with archaeological problems. Its most promising feature is that it enables the user to interact with the spatial model by allowing for change in the variables in order to track alternative behavioral patterns. A fine example of this type of modeling is Kohler and Carr's swarm-based modeling of prehistoric settlement systems in the American Southwest. Swarm is an object-oriented model designed to ease the process of simulating large numbers of interacting agents, and traditional GIS modeling was combined with this object-oriented model to explore and refine models of settlement behavior in the Mesa Verde region of Colorado. The initial GIS approach was limited to the data mining and prediction models mentioned above, which resulted in statistical measures of strength and significance of association of sites with the relevant environmental variables. In the case of Mesa Verde, the agents were represented by the prehistoric households, which were "released" onto the paleo-productivity landscapes generated with the GIS, and the Swarm model was run to observe their locational solutions to making a living on those landscapes.

It has become apparent that the application of GIS to archaeological issues has assisted archaeologists in addressing more complicated questions on the nature of the interaction between human societies and their landscapes and that it can ultimately help in obtaining a better understanding as to how the factors involved in the formation of the archaeological record interact. More and more, through the application of GIS, archaeologists are enable to address not only questions such as, Where is? or How many? but also questions such as, What if?

Armando Anaya Hernández

References

Allen, Kathleen M. S., Stanton W. Green, and Ezra B. W. Zubrow, eds. 1990. *Interpreting Space: GIS and Archaeology.* London, New York, and Philadelphia: Taylor and Francis.

Berry, J. K. 1995. *Spatial Reasoning for Effective GIS.* Fort Collins, CO: GIS World Books.

Kvamme, K. L. 1992. "Geographic Information Systems in Archaeology" In *Computer Applications and Quantitative Methods in Archaeology 1991*, 77–84. Ed. Gary Lock and Jonathan Moffett. BAR International Series S577. Great Britain.

German Archaeological Institute
See Deutsches Archäologisches Institut

German Classical Archaeology

The first scientific approaches to classical archaeology in Germany date back to the so-called antiquaries, who were active from the sixteenth century on and who—due to their systematic classification of the material estate of Antiquity—were often and rather unjustly called ignorant. The *Thesaurus Brandenburgicus selectus,* written by Lorenz Beger (1653–1705) and published in three volumes between 1696 and 1701, may be regarded as the most significant opus of an antiquary in Germany. The intensity of the antiquaries' influence, especially that which they exerted on following generations of classical scholars, characterized particularly in Germany by the factual and substantial organization of manuals and, above all, of corpora.

Even JOHANN JOACHIM WINCKELMANN (1717–1768), who vehemently opposed the antiquaries, followed an antiquarian pattern in the draft of his *Monumenti antichi inediti,* published in 1772. Winckelmann's hermeneutic method (i.e., his explanation of antique monuments mainly by means of Greek mythology) and his aesthetic approach built on the achievements of the antiquaries. A significant difference, however, can be noted in his observation that the art of antiquity, until that time regarded as an absolute entity, could be given a chronology. In this observation he was partially influenced by concepts taken from the late-Hellenistic period, although Winckelmann's judgment was predominantly influenced by the aesthetic criteria of his time. His discovery of the possibility of differentiating the various stages of the development of antique art by means of stylistic analyses enabled him to subdivide that art into several periods, a classification that is more or less still valid today. In his *Geschichte der Kunst des Altertums* (1764) he distinguished between the *Alterer Stil* (Older Style) of the first half of the fifth century B.C., the *Hoher Stil* (Grand Style) of the period of Phidias, the *Schoner Stil* (Beautiful Style) of Praxiteles, Lysipp, and Hellenistic works of art, and the *Stil der Nachahmer* (Style of the Imitators) of the classicist period. The time of the Roman Empire was defined as an era of decay and the complete decline of art.

Winckelmann's aim was to discover the Wesen der Kunst (nature of art) and define the use of beauty and verity, distinctive to a particular work of art. Both of these values he regarded as fulfilled in the Hoher Stil and the Schoner Stil. He also wanted to develop a model of general (as in a universal) validity: "The history of art should teach the origin, the growth, the change, and the decline of art, as well as the different styles of peoples, periods, and artists and to prove this to the greatest possible extent by means of those works of Antiquity left over" (Winckelmann 1764).

In this way Winckelmann prepared the basis for a developmental approach to art, which is still influential today. This model of development of a comparative art history almost necessarily implied a concentration on each and every work of art, as well as an understanding of its contents and its value (despite this being often determined subjectively). Winckelmann's influence on successive generations of scholars was considerable and his passionate and refined language, used to describe such monuments as the outstanding statutes Laocoon and the Apollo of Belvedere, was also influential. Both the study of art, according to his model, and his literary attainments can be regarded as strange contrasts to the intended delineation of art-historical contexts. Winckelmann's subjective idealization and, above all, mystification of Greek art and his intention to deduce aesthetic rules and standards from it was inherently contradictory to an interpretation striving for historical facts.

Christian Gottlob Heyne (1729–1812), the realistic, dispassionate archaeologist who was also enthusiastic about Greek beauty, was Winckelmann's counterpart. Heyne was greatly important to the development of archaeology as an academic discipline, primarily because of his "Academic Lectures on the Archaeology of the Art of Antiquity," which he had given since 1767 at the University of Gottingen. His work "Introduction into the Study of Antiquity, or Draft of a Guide to the Knowledge of Ancient Works of Art," published in 1772, was also very significant and pioneering because he was a philologically determined classical scholar. On the one hand he proceeded methodically according to his profession; on the other hand he recognized the need to meticulously register the monuments. To this end Heyne made his own instructive collection of plaster casts.

Philological methods determined German archaeological research in the nineteenth century, whose central subject was the visual art of classical antiquity. The scholar Eduard Gerhard (1795–1867) described his scientific position with these words: "Research concerning the monuments of classical antiquity is obliged to begin with its literary knowledge, on which is based, in a narrower sense, the so called philology; its monuments are studied on a philological basis by the archaeologist; to achieve this aim various friends of Antiquity have to explore the material for him; artists will have to judge and examine it" (Gerhard 1853). Gerhard considered philological methods as indispensable to archaeological research as much as the profound knowledge of antique monuments. To fulfill this latter requirement, he founded journals and corpora. Gerhard's greatest contribution to the institutionalization of archaeology as a scientific discipline was the foundation of the Instituto di Corrispondenza Archeologica in Rome in 1829 as an international institute of research. In 1859 the Prussian state took over its funding, and it was from this henceforth national institution from which the German Archaeological Institute (DEUTSCHES ARCHÄOLOGISCHES INSTITUT—DAI) emerged in 1874, a substantial establishment for German archaeology as a whole. The Instituto di Corrispondenza Archeologica's primary functions were to publish new archaeological discoveries and to promote the exchange of discoveries in the various disciplines of classical science.

Philologically oriented archaeology led to several important scientific discoveries and effective achievements, such as the sober, systematic, and precisely formulated works of Karl Otfried Muller (1797–1840) and the work of Otto Jahn (1813–1869), who planned a corpus of antique sarcophagus reliefs, a project taken over by the German Archaeological Institute. The development of archaeology initially as a historical and later a positivist determined science also encouraged a discipline whose aim sometimes comprised the presentation of material rather wider in scope than in content.

Emerging from a philologically determined archaeology but still under its auspices, the scholar Heinrich Brunn (1822–1894), whose main work was *Geschichte der griechischen Kunstler* (1859) (History of Greek Artists), became the next pioneer of a new archaeological method. Brunn wrote: "A philologist explaining an author must know the language grammatically and lexically. In the same way an archaeologist explaining a monument must, above all, be profoundly familiar with the language of art, its forms and syntactical connections, with its constant types and their connection to artistic motifs, and must first try to explain a monument out of itself. It is only on this basis that he will succeed in making use of the written sources of our knowledge . . . an archaeologist cannot renounce a philological basis for his studies. But the philologist is not an archaeologist and without special archaeological training he will often, by his philological knowledge, run the risk of clouding his view, and closing his eyes to the evidence" (Brunn 1857–1859). Adolf Furtwangler (1853–1907), Brunn's pupil and successor to the chair of archaeology at the University of Munich, continued Brunn's work with his respectively formal and analytic, and stylistic and critical approach to archaeology.

Beginning in the 1870s great archaeological monuments and discoveries increased in quantity and variety due to a series of unsystematic explorations and excavations by HEINRICH SCHLIEMANN (1822–1890) at the Homeric site of Troy. In 1875 German excavations directed by ERNST CURTIUS (1814–1896) began at Olympia. The researchers' aim was the exploration of groups of Greek monuments in their original context. Extant sources of knowledge were to be augmented by means of a widely determined cultural-historical concept, whose validity was recognized only gradually. Other great German excavations at Pergamon and Miletus were guided by equivalent, almost exclusively historical aims.

World War I not only changed the external conditions under which classical archaeology developed in Germany as a positivist scientific discipline but also marked a fundamental change in terms of the field's aims and research methods. Prior to 1914 archaeology had endeavored to give new significance to the study of antique monuments, to keep looking for Winckelmann's aesthetic successions, and to find new criteria with which to judge and classify antique art. Now archaeology began to look for a connection to the contemporary science of art; it treated the question of form in antique art as theoretical, and it demanded structural research. Contrary to Winckelmann's development of stylistic analyses, structural research concentrated on the search for the principle of the inner organization of form as Guido Kaschnitz von Weinberg (1890–1958) defined it—*Struktur* (structure). This recognized forms as unchangeable, nonindividual, everlasting, with considerable factors that are bound to concrete cultures, to search for their descent, and to separate from those factors and traces in the work of art, which originates in the individuality of the artist. The result of this method was that historical aspects of the judgment of antique works of art were thrust into the background. It became possible, for the first time, to look afresh at the peculiarities and values of the different periods of antique art, especially Roman art, and to do that without the restrictions caused by a developmental approach based on the theory of inherent laws of form, detached from historical context. This far-reaching theoretical explanation of the science of art influenced the study of archaeology, which tends to an abstract schematism, and was opposed to irrational-mystical ideas concerning the interpretation of hardly understandable artistic forms. The subjective impression of the individual scholar, as a personality, was allowed.

The endeavors of Ernst Buschor (1886–1961) and his spontaneous experience of antique art removed from its historicity must be viewed in that context. This scholar, endowed with an extraordinary ability to recognize artistic forms, cultivated a refined scientific prose of a late-expressionistic type. He judged his own interpretation of antique art an almost congenial artistic achievement, transformed into an adequate language. It was a highly individual, most effective view of things, claiming that the development of Greek sculpture was an evolution, the life history of an individual, and that the history of ancient art was a sequence of different attitudes toward the reality of the visible world. In this sense he talked about the *Ahnungswelt* (presentimental world) of the geometric period, the *Wirklichkeitswelt* (world of reality) of the Archaic period, the hohe Schicksalswelt (world of grand fate) of the classical time, the Bild- un Scheinwelt (world of pictures and appearance) of the Hellenistic period, the Kunstwelt (artificial world) of the first century B.C. to the third century A.D., and the Zeichenwelt (world of signs) of late Antiquity.

The scientific achievements of German classical archaeology in the 1920s and 1930s reflected the problems experienced at that time by the discipline of archaeology as a whole. There were reservations regarding the discussion of theoretical questions, which went along with a preference for factual research, such as fieldwork-based interpretations with exemplary, careful publications of extensive complexes of monuments.

Recent publications have been concerned with understanding antique monuments more as historical sources than as works of art, with estimating their cultural-historical and intellectual-historic. These publications have also examined minor monuments, in their historic context, and considered the social and economic conditions under which both customers and artists' workshops interacted. This methodical approach argued that the inclusion of the material culture of Antiquity and its social, economic, and political context (i.e., the inclusion of circumstances independent of art) in the analyses of works of art would lead to new knowledge and even to changes in form and in the history of style. This more recent approach, however, has run the risk that "nonartistic" factors can easily be transformed into determinative ones. Consequently, monuments, interpreted for a certain reason, are only used to illustrate knowledge, already gained by other sources. Solid results can only be achieved when monuments are examined both from the viewpoint of the science of art and from a historical perspective, that is, when different approaches are used for a reciprocal control.

This limitation on the role of monuments is echoed in Adolf Heinrich Borbein's recent request for a model of interpretation that comprises the artistic form as an upholder of significance, those external circumstances by which the latter is influenced, different kinds of contemporary artistic expressions, political, social, and cultural phenomena, and the question of the relation of each of these factors to the other and for their mutuality in substance. In this view, visual art provides the concrete idea of the "spirit of time" or of its contemporary and intellectual tendencies, even more so than historical facts. By extension, artistic farsightedness may influence or anticipate future developments in other social fields.

This concept, which integrates historical context and aims to describe the historical position of monuments, allows new access to the comprehension of Roman art, an area to which German archaeology has recently been devoted. Tonio Holscher's 1960 treatise *Roman Picture Language as a Semantic System* must be understood in this way. Proceeding on the assumption of a pluralism of styles in Roman art, formulated earlier, Holscher demanded that monuments must begin to be observed within an overall cultural-historical context, before a single aspect of Roman visual art and its significance can be commented on. Furthermore, he propounded the substantial thesis that in Roman art for different allied subjects and different patterns from different epochs of Greek art were selected. These established patterns were reused throughout Roman art, unaffected by contemporary stylistic tendencies. On the basis of examples he succeeded in demonstrating that the choice of Greek stylistic forms followed a system, or semanticization of styles. Holscher argued that by Augustan times there was an established canon of representational modes and picture types, that is, a more or less constant picture language, and this semantic system did not undergo serious changes during the first and second centuries A.D. With regard to the relation of picture language and style, he made clear that style "as an expression of general taste and habit" represents a variable factor, in contrast to the more likely static character of the picture language. This picture language submitted to the semantic system does not exclude stylistic changes, that is, different modes and types of representation. In the historical dimension of his examinations Holscher showed that a systematic, static picture language was advantageous for the conveyance of messages and general communication in the Roman Empire. He also pointed out that the tendency to set up norms, observed in a section of art, was generally characteristic of Roman imperial culture. Holscher's theoretical analyses of Roman art characterized the position of German classical archaeology today: to practice archaeology as both a science of art and a historical discipline.

E. Thomas

See also German Prehistoric Archaeology

References

Beger, L. 1696–1701. *Thesaurus Brandenburgicus selectus* 1–3, Colln.

Brunn, H. 1857–1859, 1889. *Geschichte der griechischen Kunstler* 1–2, Stuttgart.

Buschor, E. 1939. Wesen und Methode der Archaologie, in: Otto, W. (Hrsg.), *Handbuch der Archaologie* I, Munchen 3–10.

Furtwangler, A. 1893. *Meisterwerke der griechischen Plastik.* Kunstgeschichtliche Untersuchungen, Leipzig/Berlin.

Gerhard, E. 1853. *Grundriß der Archaologie.* Fur Vorlesungen nach Mullers Handbuch.

Holscher, T. 1987. *Romische Bildsprache als semantisches System, Abhdlgn.* Akad. d. Wiss. Heidelberg.

Kaschnitz von Weinberg, G., Rezension: Riegl, A. 1929. *Spatromische Kunstindustrie,* Wien 1927, Gnomon 5, 195–213.

———. 1937. Ancora la "struttura," Critica d'Arte 2, 280–284.

———. 1965. *Kleine Schriften zur Struktur,* Ausgewahlte Schriften I, Berlin.

Winckelmann, J. J. 1764. *Geschichte der Kunst des Altertums.* Dresden.

———. 1767–1772. *Monumenti antichi inediti I-III,* Rom.

German Prehistoric Archaeology

Germany, like other European nation states, has a long tradition of prehistoric research, but prehistoric archaeology was first taught in the uni-

NORTH SEA

BALTIC SEA

Haithabu

Hamburg

Feddersen
Wierde

NETHERLANDS

Seddin

Salzwedel

Eberswalde

POLAND

Berlin

Hanover

Detmold

Münster

Vettersfelde

Neanderthal

Göttingen

Helmsdorf

Köln-Lindenthal

Rössen

Aldenhovener
Platte

Leubingen

Marburg

Gönnersdorf

Jena

Dresden

Glauberg

Frankfurt a. M.

Mainz

**CZECH
REPUBLIC**

N

Heidelberg

Nuremberg

Kleinaspergle

Hochdorf

Manching

FRANCE

Tübingen

Heuneburg

Federsee

Munich

Unteruhldingen

Zurich

0   100 km

SWITZERLAND

AUSTRIA

Hallstatt

● sites mentioned in the text   ○ other cities

German Prehistoric Sites

versities at a relatively late date, at the beginning of the twentieth century. Although German archaeologists have done important work abroad, the following short overview will concentrate on research conducted in Germany itself and ignore the work of German archaeologists elsewhere in the world. No mention will be made of such important sites as Olympia, Tiryns, Pergamon, Troy, Boğazköy, Babylon, Kamid el Loz, or Merimde and the scholars who devoted much time to their excavation, analysis, and interpretation. Some of these men and women originally were trained in prehistoric archaeology.

Germany as a political unity—from a historical perspective—is a relatively recent and unstable structure. The German Empire was founded in 1871, and the last division of Germany ended in 1989. Therefore it makes no sense to limit the discussion of "German" prehistoric archaeology to the area within the actual political boundaries of the Federal Republic of Germany. Rather, it is necessary to include in this survey all the regions of central Europe where German is spoken today, including areas in AUSTRIA and SWITZERLAND. Despite all the political conflicts the regions connected by the German language during the last two centuries shared a common culture. This is especially true in the academic field, where intense contacts often existed regardless of political boundaries.

Research undertaken in Austria and Switzerland contributed much to the development of prehistoric archaeology, as the publications of the Viennese Anthropological Society and the Antiquarian Society of Zurich clearly show. Sites such as Austria's Willendorf, with its famous Upper Paleolithic Venus statue, or Hallstatt, with its large Iron Age cemetery—which gave its name to a whole period—have become landmarks in the development of our knowledge of European prehistory. This is also true for the famous lake-dwellings in northeastern Switzerland, which were first discovered in the winter of 1853–1854. In Germany itself the Neanderthal skeleton found in 1856 in a Neolithic cemetery at Rössen, the rich chieftains' graves from the Bronze and early Iron Ages at Leubingen, Helmsdorf, Seddin, and Kleinaspergle, the deposits of golden objects at Vettersfelde (today Witaszkowo, POLAND) and Eberswalde, the Roman limes (armed frontiers) and Slavic hill-forts from the eastern part of the country have all dominated our knowledge and understanding of the distant past in the early phases of the development of prehistoric archaeology.

In the twentieth century large-scale excavations of prehistoric settlements have greatly added to this knowledge. These sites include the

The Venus of Willendorf (Francis G. Mayer / Corbis)

early-Neolithic village of Köln-Lindenthal, the late–Bronze Age wetland settlement at Buchau in the Federsee area, the early–Iron Age hillfort "Heuneburg," the Celtic oppidum (fortified town) at Manching, and the settlements of the period from the Roman to the Viking ages in the coastal areas of northern Germany. Along with these settlements many cemeteries and graves have also been excavated, such as the famous Iron Age princes' graves (Fürstengräber) found in 1978 near Hochdorf and in 1994 at the foot of the Glauberg hill-fort.

The cultural and intellectual life of the German-speaking areas, unlike that of other strongly centralized polities, was not concentrated in one capital but dispersed over a number of regional centers. This federal structure is mirrored in the large number of local and regional museums and associations devoted to the study of antiquities. On the one hand, this situation provides a varied and fascinating picture; on the other hand, it is sometimes difficult to see the connections between what happened in different parts of central Europe at certain points of time. This situation is further complicated by significant differences within the archaeological record itself. Roman and Celtic antiquities are concentrated in the south and west of Germany and in Switzerland and Austria, but in the eastern and northern parts of Germany, Germanic (and partly Slavic) antiquities dominate. In the past this was a permanent source of conflict for the discipline. Nevertheless, it is possible to uncover some common themes in its development.

The name traditionally used by institutions that deal with research on human prehistory in Germany, Austria, and Switzerland is *Vor- und Frühgeschichte* (or *Ur- und Frühgeschichte*). This is most aptly translated as "pre- and proto-history" and refers to those periods from which written sources are unknown or, at best, rare. The German term *Archäologie* (archaeology) has long been virtually reserved for the archaeology of classical antiquity (*Klassische* archaeology). Only in the last few years has it become customary among prehistorians to use the term *Archäologie* or, more accurately, *Ur- und Frühgeschichtliche Archäologie* (pre- and proto-historic archaeology).

Toward a History of Prehistoric Archaeology in Germany

The history of prehistoric archaeology has been a topic of interest within the discipline of archaeology in Germany for a long time. In 1938 Hans Gummel published a thick volume on the history of German prehistoric archaeology from the seventeenth century until the 1930s. In retrospect the early date chosen for the beginning of this synthesis seems somewhat surprising. The first ordinary chair for prehistoric archaeology at a German university was established only in 1927, at the University of Marburg. Before that time prehistory at German universities was taught by extraordinary professors or by lecturers and scholars from other disciplines. The first extraordinary chairs were established at the turn of the twentieth century at the Universities

of Vienna (assumed by Moritz Hoernes in 1900) and Berlin (occupied by GUSTAF KOSSINNA in 1902), and as early as 1874 RUDOLF VIRCHOW had expressed doubts as to whether prehistory would ever become an independent discipline. Under these circumstances, why was such an early date given for the history of archaeology in Gummel's work? From the historical context it is clear that Gummel's synthesis must be seen in relation to contemporary attempts to transform prehistoric archaeology into what could be regarded as a mature discipline. Due to political circumstances the success of this initiative remained limited.

Gummel's efforts to promote the necessity of a continued reflection on the history of prehistory were not very successful. Despite his own early monograph and other early contributions to this topic, especially by Ernst Wahle (1951), research on the history of prehistoric archaeology even today remains underdeveloped in central Europe, and critical assessments of the history of prehistoric archaeology have only become available since the mid-1990s (Härke 2000). Many of the more recent attempts focus on the role of prehistoric archaeology during the Third Reich (Leube 2000), a topic that was dealt with earlier by historians (Bollmus 1970; Kater 1974). Older periods of the history of prehistoric archaeology are still only seldom written about, and apart from publications that deal with single aspects of the subject in Germany, only one recent overview is available today (Kossack 1999; also see Kossack 1992 and Kühn 1976). In that overview author Georg Kossack drew on his own long experience within German prehistoric archaeology and not only gave valuable information on important scholars, excavations, methods, and ideas but also described the political background of twentieth-century prehistoric archaeology.

A Short Outline of the Development of Prehistoric Archaeology in Germany

The history of prehistoric archaeology in central Europe is closely linked with the political history of the relevant countries. This is especially true in Germany. The main crises and resolutions in German history during the nine-

The Hermannsdenkmal (Arminius Monument) near
Detmold was erected in 1875 to commemorate the Roman
defeat by Germanic tribes in the Teutoburg Forest in A.D.
9. (Photograph by Ulrich Veit)

in the establishment of a number of nationwide
institutions that became influential in the development of prehistoric archaeology during the
next phases. These include the Germanic National Museum (Germanisches Nationalmu-
seum) at Nuremberg and the Roman-Germanic
Central Museum (Römisch-Germanisches Zen-
tralmuseum) at Mainz, both of which were
founded in 1852. According to its founder, LUD-
WIG LINDENSCHMIT (1809–1893), the aim of the
latter institution was to unite the most important archaeological objects under one roof. Since
it was not possible to get enough important
original finds, Lindenschmit, who was an artist,
developed the idea of making exact copies of all
famous antiquities and exhibiting them in his
museum. This allowed visitors to make broad
comparisons on a scale that was not possible in
earlier times.

The Hermannsdenkmal (Arminius Monument) near Detmold remains a symbol of romantic nationalism. This huge statue commem-
orates the German victory over the Romans
under Varus in A.D. 9 in the dark forests of Ger-
mania. The monument, designed by Ernst von
Bandel, shows Arminius raising his sword after
his victory. Its foundation stone was set in
1838, but the monument was not finished until
1875, four years after the foundation of the
German Reich.

This first phase in the development of prehistoric archaeology was followed by a period of
further institutional consolidation and development, which coincided with the so-called Gün-
derzeit, the years after the foundation of the
German Reich in 1871. From that point forward associations such as the Berliner
Gesellschaft für Anthropologie, Ethnologie und
Urgeschichte, founded in 1869, were the most
important institutions for the development of
knowledge about prehistory. Rudolf Virchow
(1821–1902) was the leading figure in prehistory during this period. Mainly known as a
pathologist, physical anthropologist, and politician, Virchow also devoted much of his time to
the organization and promotion of prehistoric
research in Germany. He advocated the integration of archaeology into a comprehensive "prehistoric anthropology" that would include all

teenth and twentieth centuries (in 1871, 1918,
1933, 1945, and 1989) also represent crises and
resolutions within prehistoric archaeology.
Since the beginning of the nineteenth century
we may distinguish a minimum of five major
phases in prehistoric archaeology's development.

The first phase of development (1800–1871)
was characterized by a growth of interest in prehistoric remains mainly on local or regional
bases. About fifty new associations that dealt
with antiquities of prehistoric and other ages
were founded in the first decades of the nineteenth century. The first more systematic excavations took place—for example, the work in
Hallstatt (from 1846 to 1864). This increased interest was the result of a growing romantic nationalism, reached its climax in the years before
the German Revolution in 1848. It culminated

neighboring disciplines, such as physical anthropology, ethnology, and prehistory. In accordance with the positivistic thinking of his time Virchow fought for a methodology that combined the careful analysis of skeletal remains with artifacts, linguistic evidence, and written sources. Ironically, Virchow is now best remembered for his failure to recognize the antiquity of the Neanderthal skeleton in 1856; he argued that it was not greatly different from those of modern humans.

The German Archaeological Institute (DEUTSCHES ARCHÄOLOGISCHES INSTITUT, or DAI) was actually founded in 1829 in Rome (under the name Instituta di Corrispondenza Archaeologica) but based itself in Berlin from 1832 onward, with a focus on classical antiquity and Mediterranean archaeology. In 1892 a special commission was established to investigate the Roman limes (frontiers) of central Europe (Reichslimeskommission). The research executed by this commission under the direction of the historian Theodor Mommsen also included fieldwork at various sites. These investigations became the basis for the establishment of a commission for Roman and Germanic studies (Römisch-Germanische Kommission, or RGK) within the DAI at Frankfurt in 1902. This event marked the beginning of regular research on the prehistory of central Europe, especially on the Bronze and Iron Ages, within the DAI.

The year 1902 was important for German prehistoric archaeology, not only because of the foundation of the Commission at Main but also because it was the year that Virchow died, bringing about the end of his universal and interdisciplinary concept for prehistoric research. What followed was a period in which—under the influence of growing nationalism and racism—the classical culture-historical paradigm of prehistory was developed and applied to the available archaeological finds on a large scale. Archaeological cultures, as visible on distribution maps, were equated with peoples. As a consequence of these developments prehistoric archaeology began to be taught at universities. The appointment of Gustaf Kossinna (1858–1931) as professor at Berlin University in 1902 best exemplified this approach.

Kossinna believed that Germans and Aryans, represented physically as blond and blue-eyed Nordic types, were the pinnacle of creative humanity and had their homeland in southern Scandinavia, from whence they spread over Europe. His idea of prehistory as "a predominantly national science" would later become fundamental to the development of Nazi prehistory. Nevertheless, it is not possible to simply equate Kossinna's ideas with those of Nazi archaeology. Although his publications are evidence of his strong nationalist and, indeed, racist thinking, Kossinna also tried to give prehistory a sound methodological basis, and his "settlement-archaeological method" (*Siedlungsarchäologische Methode*) became influential both in Germany and abroad. The early publications of VERE GORDON CHILDE, for example, reveal the strong influence of Kossinna's methodology.

After the National Socialist Party (NSDAP) was elected in 1933 German prehistory formally became part of the cultural policy of the Third Reich, terminating any scientific freedom. From that point forward the party effectively controlled all important new posts in major institutions, including universities. As only party members were allowed to occupy high offices, scholars of Jewish descent were dismissed. In this situation the representatives of the prehistory discipline had to choose between collaboration, resistance, or exile. The spectrum of possibilities can be illustrated by the biographies of four influential prehistorians of the time: Hans Reinerth, Herbert Jankuhn, GERHARD BERSU, and Gero von Merhart.

Hans Reinerth (1900–1990) was a lecturer in the late 1920s at Tübingen University and was well known for his excavations in the Federsee region in southwestern Germany. He joined the National Socialist movement early on and became an adherent of the new ideology. This enabled him to become a professor at Berlin in 1934. At the same time Reinerth became a leading figure in the "Rosenberg office" (Amt Rosenberg—named after Alfred Rosenberg, Hitler's chief ideologist), whose task was to prevent deviations from National Socialist ideology. Herbert Jankuhn (1905–1990), who began his career in 1930 with the excavation of the Viking age settlement of Haithabu, also joined the party and shared the new ideology; he became head of the prehistory section of the SS-Ahnenerbe, an association founded in 1935 by members of the Nazi secret police (Schutzstaffel, or SS) with the aim of studying the German past.

The situation for Gerhard Bersu (1899–1964) and Gero von Merhart (1886–1959) was very different. In 1935 Bersu was removed from his post as first director of the RGK because of his Jewish background. He left Germany in 1937 and spent the war years in England, where his excavations at Little Woodbury contributed to the development of British field archaeology. Gero von Merhart, a professor at Marburg University, was accused of not complying with the demands of the new regime by party members (including Reinerth) and was forced to retire.

Despite such cases of open discrimination, however, the Nazi influence on prehistoric archaeology was probably not as effective as it could have been. From the beginning there were conflicts between leading opponents of the new ideology, especially between scholars working in the Rosenberg office and those in the SS-Ahnenerbe. Both sections struggled for influence within Germany and, after the beginning of the war, within the countries that Germany occupied, where they confiscated whole museum collections and transported them back to their homeland. In the end Jankuhn's SS-Ahnenerbe proved to be more successful, and Reinerth and his adherents came under pressure during the war.

Looking at these developments, it comes as no surprise that after Germany lost the war in 1945, the reputation of its prehistoric archaeology was diminished. As a consequence of the misuse of archaeological knowledge for political reasons, the discipline's central paradigm was suspect, and the prospect of Germans writing a prehistory of European peoples seemed illusory. No alternative paradigms had been developed over the Nazi period. From an organizational point of view, however, the structure of the discipline was kept intact despite changes in personnel.

When Bersu returned to office and reorganized the work of the RGK in Frankfurt, Reinerth was banned from holding a publicly funded

post in West Germany. He became director of the Lake Village Museum (Pfahlbaumuseum) at Unteruhldingen on Lake Constance, a private institution. But Reinerth was the only person eliminated from public service. Despite their membership in the SS many other prehistorians eventually held high positions within the discipline. Jankuhn, for example, ultimately became the director of the University Institute at Göttingen, continuing his research on the social and economic problems of pre- and proto-historic communities of northern Germany and directing large archaeological projects on the coastal region of northwest Germany.

With the partition of Germany into two opposing political systems—the capitalist Federal Republic of Germany (FRG) and the socialist German Democratic Republic (GDR)—cold war prehistoric archaeology also became paradigmatically divided into two camps. In West Germany a traditional culture-historical approach still dominated, but in East Germany a small group of archaeologists lead by Karl-Heinz Otto (and later Joachim Herrmann) tried to develop a specific Marxist approach to prehistory. Although a large number of publications were produced, this project ultimately proved unsuccessful. In practice most East German archaeologists continued to adhere to the traditionalist, culture-historical outlook.

Apart from these ideological battles, the post–World War II period, especially the decades between 1960 and 1990, was characterized by the major development of state archaeological services, in both the FRG and the GDR. In the short time since German reunification in 1990, there has been a reorganization of institutions, and some attempts have been made to achieve a paradigmatic renewal of German archaeology. Because it is too early to speculate about the outcome of these efforts, the main contributions of the German tradition to the development of prehistoric archaeology will be summarized in the following section.

Main Contributions of the German Tradition of Prehistoric Research

From a long-term perspective at least four central aspects characterize the archaeology of German-speaking countries: field archaeology, chronology, culture-history, and settlement archaeology.

From the beginning field archaeology was one of the great achievements of prehistoric archaeology in Germany. In this context HEINRICH SCHLIEMANN (1822–1890) was legendary. Although he was certainly not a good excavator in a modern sense, he nonetheless indirectly contributed greatly to the development of field archaeology. His successors, such as Carl Schuchhardt (1859–1943), undertook outstanding fieldwork in the early twentieth century in northern and eastern Germany. Schuchhardt was followed by scholars such as Gerhard Bersu and Werner Buttler. New fieldwork methods were developed in northern Germany before and after World War II in the course of investigating large wetland settlements along the coast, including the sites of Haithabu and Feddersen Wierde (see p. 584). Another specialized tradition within archaeological fieldwork, which connected prehistoric archaeology with other disciplines such as geology, botany, and zoology, was the outcome of the investigations of lake-dwelling sites in Switzerland and southern Germany. Pioneering work was undertaken in this area in the 1920s and more recently since 1970.

The second constant concern of German prehistory has been chronology. Although the Danish archaeologist C. J. THOMSEN has to be acknowledged as the founder of the THREE-AGE SYSTEM, German scholars were expressing similar ideas very early on. This is especially true of Johann Friedrich Danneil (1783–1868), a teacher in Salzwedel, Altmark, and Friedrich Lisch (1801–1883), the director of the antiquities collection of the grand duke of Mecklenburg. Although the three-age system was rejected by the German scholars Ludwig Lindenschmit (1809–1893) and Christian Hostmann (1829–1889), by the end of the nineteenth century Otto Tischler (1843–1891) at Königsberg (East Prussia) and Paul Reinecke (1872–1958) at Mainz were successful in developing a periodization of the Bronze and Iron Ages of central Europe; the fundamentals of this periodization are still used today. The comparative chronology of the European Neolithic developed by Vladimir Milojcic (1918–1978),

professor at Heidelberg in the 1940s, was equally influential. His system provided common ground for scholars working on the European Neolithic until the "radiocarbon revolution" of the 1960s. Unfortunately, Milojcic himself refused to accept this dating innovation, and because his influence persisted even after his death, innovations within German archaeology were hindered for some time.

The third aspect characterizing German prehistory, especially during the first half of the twentieth century, was the attempt to identify ancient peoples from their material remains. The concept of "archaeological cultures" became central and can be traced back to Gustav Kossinna (1858–1931) and his settlement-archaeological method. This method gave rise to broad discussions, which continue today. Major early contributions to these discussions came from Karl-Hermann Jacob-Friesen (1886–1960), Ernst Wahle (1889–1981), and Hans-Jürgen Eggers (1906–1975). They were especially concerned with questions of source criticism with developing attempts to establish the quality of the data being used by archaeologists.

An approach that differed somewhat from that of Kossinna and his followers was represented in the writings of Oswald Menghin (1888–1973), a professor at Vienna. Adopting ideas from the *Kulturkreislehre,* a paradigm developed by German ethnologists Wilhelm Schmidt and FRITZ GRAEBNER at the beginning of the twentieth century, Menghin, in the 1930s, postulated a number of primary cultures and tried to detect their later interaction from archaeological evidence. His final aim was an integration of archaeological and ethnological knowledge into a universal history of early mankind. This approach ended with the rejection of Kulturkreislehre within ethnology in the 1950s.

The fourth important concern is closely related to the first. The execution of well-organized excavations of large settlements, combined with scientific analyses of the materials uncovered, enabled German scholars to investigate not just settlements but whole settlement systems. From this basis Herbert Jankuhn developed a broad settlement-archaeological method (not to be confused with Kossinna's method,

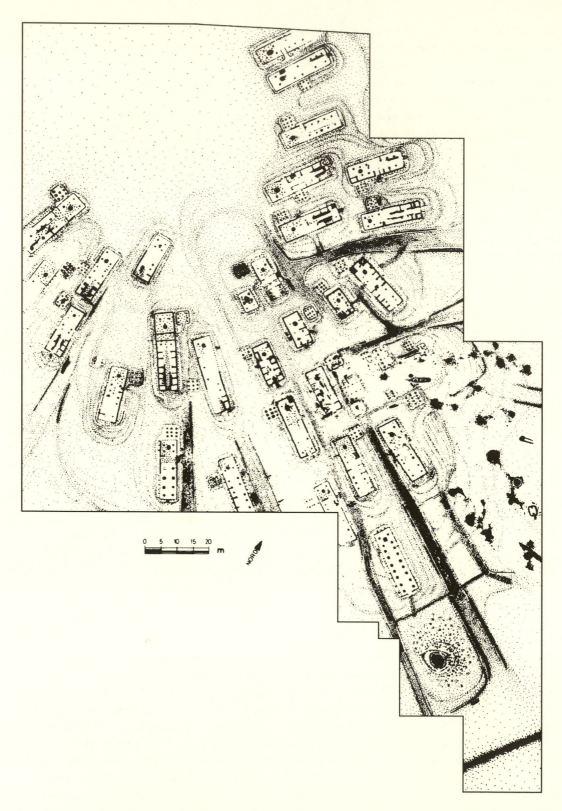

Excavations at the settlement of Feddersen Wierde near Bremerhaven, 1955–1963: map of Layer 5 with twenty-three farmsteads (third century A.D.) (after W. Haarnagel). From H. Jankuhn, Einführung in die Siedlungarchäologie *(Berlin: de Gruyter, 1977), fig. 44, p. 119.*

also known by that name) with the aim of clarifying the settlement history of selected areas. This approach has been improved by a number of projects since 1970 such as the Aldenhovener Platte, where the settlement system of the early Neolithic period could be reconstructed.

Today German prehistoric archaeology is appreciated worldwide for its solid and meticulous work on primary evidence, for its careful source criticism, and for its prolific publications. It would be unfair, however, to limit the acknowledgment of German scholarship to these points alone. In the past more abstract ideas played an important role, especially with regard to the concept of writing history by archaeological means and, even more concretely, writing the history of prehistoric peoples.

Ulrich Veit

See also German Classical Archaeology; Lindenschmidt, Ludwig

References

Arnold, B. 1990. "The Past as Propaganda: Totalitarian Archaeology in Nazi Germany." *Antiquity* 64, no. 244: 464–478.

Bollmus, R. 1970. *Das Amt Rosenberg und seine Gegner: Zum Machtkampf im nationalsozialistischen Herrschaftssystem.* Stuttgart: Deutsche Verlagsanstalt.

Gummel, H. 1938. *Forschungsgeschichte in Deutschland: Die Urgeschichtsforschung und ihre historische Entwicklung in den Kulturstaaten der Erde.* Berlin: de Gruyter.

Härke, H., ed. 2000. "Archaeology, Ideology and Society: The German Experience." *Gesellschaften und Staaten im Epochenwandel* 7. Frankfurt: Lang.

Kater, M. H. 1974. *Das "Ahnenerbe" der SS 1935–1954: Ein Beitrag zur Kulturpolitik des Dritten Reiches.* Stuttgart: Deutsche Verlagsanstalt.

Kossack, G. 1992. "Prehistoric Archaeology in Germany: Its History and Current Situation." *Norwegian Archaeological Review* 25, 2: 73–109.

———. 1999. *Prähistorische Archäologie in Deutschland im Wandel der geistigen und politischen Situation. Sitzungsber.* Bayer. Akad. Wiss. München, Phil.-Hist. Kl. 1999, H. 4. München: Verl. Bayer. Akad. Wiss.

Kühn, H. 1976. *Geschichte der Vorgeschichtsforschung.* Berlin and New York: de Gruyter.

Leube, A., ed. 2000. *Die mittel- und osteuropäische Ur- und Frühgeschichtsforschung zwischen 1933 und 1945.* Dresden: Synchronverlag.

Veit, U. 1985. "Gustaf Kossinna und V. Gordon Childe. Ansätze zu einer theoretischen Grundlegung der Vorgeschichte." *Saeculum* 35: 3–4, 326–364.

———. 1989. "Ethnic Concepts in German Prehistory: A Case Study on the Relationship between Cultural Identity and Archaeological Objectivity." In *Archaeological Approaches to Cultural Identity,* 35–65. Ed. S. Shennan. One World Archaeology 10. London: Unwin Hyman.

Wahle, E. 1950–1951. "Geschichte der prähistorischen Forschung." *Anthropos* 45: 487–538 and 46: 49–112.

Wiwjorra, I. 1996. "German Archaeology and Its Relation to Nationalism and Racism." In *Nationalism and Archaeology in Europe,* 164–188. Ed. M. Díaz-Andreu and T. Champion. London: University College.

Getty Museum

The J. Paul Getty Museum was established in 1953 to make Getty's personal collections of Greek and Roman antiquities, French decorative arts, and European paintings available to the public. Located first in one wing of a ranch house in a Malibu Canyon in California, the museum moved in 1974 into a Roman-style villa built on the same site. Designed with the assistance of Norman Neuerburg, the plans for the building were adapted from the ground plans of the original Villa dei Papirii in HERCULANEUM in ITALY, which has not yet been fully excavated; various other Roman villas in POMPEII and Herculaneum provided the inspiration for the building's elevations and interior and exterior architectural details and wall paintings.

Although the museum as an institution has never participated in archaeological excavations, it has served as a resource and sponsor for archaeological and archaeometric research. Its collections now include over 25,000 ancient objects in various media; most represent the cultures of GREECE and Rome, though some examples of the arts of CYPRUS, Persia, and Egypt are also included. The primary collections include Cycladic sculpture and terracottas, Greek and Roman sculptures in stone and bronze, Greek and southern Italian vases, Greek and

Roman intaglios, and carved ambers. There are also small but significant collections of Greek and Roman jewelry, vessels in precious metals and glass, Roman wall paintings, mosaics, lamps, and inscriptions.

To encourage and support research and publication of the museum's extensive collections, the Departments of Antiquities and Antiquities Conservation each year invite a number of guest scholars and conservators to study the materials on exhibition and in the collection. In addition to the original *Catalogue of Ancient Art in the Getty Museum* by C. C. Vermeule and N. Neuerburg (1973), the collection catalogs *Roman Funerary Sculpture* (G. Koch, 1988), *Ancient Gems and Finger Rings* (J. Spire, 1992), and *Metalwork from the Hellenized East* (M. Pfrommer, 1993) have been published. Four fascicles, or parts (of the thirteen planned) of the *Corpus vasorum antiquorum* are also in print, and articles on both the art history and scientific aspects of individual antiquities in the collection appear regularly in the annual *Getty Museum Journal* together with a list of all recent acquisitions. In addition to the journal, the museum also publishes *Occasional Papers on Antiquities,* edited by the Antiquities Department, a series dedicated to the publication of recent research on objects in the collection.

In 1985, the museum sponsored its first international symposium, "The Amasis Painter and his World," held in conjunction with an exhibition of the same title organized by the Toledo Museum of Art and displayed in Los Angeles at the Los Angeles County Museum of Art. Subsequently, the Getty Museum has organized five other international meetings on ancient topics: "Marble: Art Historical and Scientific Perspectives on Ancient Sculpture" (1988); "Small Bronze Sculpture from the Ancient World" (1989); "Chalcolithic Cyprus" (1990, in collaboration with the Antiquities Department of Cyprus); "Ancient and Historical Metals" (1991); and "The Getty Kouros," held in Athens in 1992 (in collaboration with the Nicholas P. Goulandris Foundation and Museum of Cycladic Art) and in Alexandria in 1993. Volumes of the proceedings of each meeting have been published.

One of the Getty Museum's strongest commitments is to education, and the Departments of Antiquities and Antiquities Conservation have explored new ways to make the ancient collections more accessible to the diverse public that the institution serves. Each year, the departments host a number of seminars, lectures, and at least one lecture series on archaeological topics. The museum developed and installed one of the first truly interactive video disc programs, *Greek Vases,* in 1985, and object conservation was the subject of a special exhibition in 1992, "Preserving the Past," which gave clear demonstrations of the techniques of analysis, cleaning, restoration, and installation of ancient artifacts. The larger issue of site conservation was the subject of the exhibition "In the Tomb of Nefertari: The Conservation of the Wall Paintings" held in 1992–1993. Dedicated to the preservation of sites and monuments around the world, the Getty Conservation Institute completed six years of conservation work on Nefertari's great tomb in 1992, and the exhibition explored the complex problems presented by this monument, the meticulous studies undertaken before decisions were made on the conservation solutions, the implementation of those solutions, and the development of a plan for future protection of the site.

As part of its public programs, the museum inaugurated a series of dramatic performances in 1992 that were intended to complement the ancient collections with "The Wanderings of Odysseus." A new translation of parts of the *Odyssey* was prepared by Oliver Taplin specifically for this presentation, and the production was staged at the museum in conjunction with the Mark Taper Forum of Los Angeles.

Although the museum itself does not sponsor archaeological excavation, staff members of both the Departments of Antiquities and Antiquities Conservation do participate in fieldwork and archaeological-conservation training programs. Conservators have worked on mosaic conservation and site-management training courses organized by the Getty Conservation Institute at PAPHOS on Cyprus, and curatorial staff members have worked on excavations at Marion on Cyprus and Torone in northern Greece and on the publication of excavated material from the Athenian Agora.

Marion True

Ghosh, Amalananda (1910–)

Along with Indian archaeologist HASMUKH D. SANKALIA, Amalananda Ghosh was the most important archaeologist of postindependence India. From 1953 to 1965 he was the director general of the Archaeological Survey of India, which he had joined in the 1930s, and a tremendous surge of work that was initiated all over the country, covering virtually all phases of cultural development, occurred as a result of his leadership and guidance.

Ghosh's early work was in Bihar in eastern India, where he surveyed early historic Asur sites on the Ranchi plateau and the Buddhist city site of Rajgir. English archaeologist MORTIMER WHEELER supervised Ghosh's fieldwork at Taxila, India, and earlier Ghosh had been involved in the Archaeological Survey of India's excavations at Ahichchhatra in India. Soon after independence in 1948, Ghosh surveyed the Ghaggar Valley in the former Bikaner state of Rajasthan, which resulted in the discovery of a large number of Indus sites in that part of India. On the assumption of the office of the director-general of the survey, which greatly expanded in size under him, Ghosh had little time to be in the field for prolonged periods, but it was he who finally recommended sites for excavation and edited the reports of the survey's officers.

After retirement in 1965, Ghosh worked briefly in Indonesia and elsewhere and wrote a thoughtful volume, *The City in Early Historical India* (1973). The two volumes of the *Encyclopaedia of Indian Archaeology* (Ghosh 1989), which he painstakingly edited, carry, for those who knew him, the unmistakable stamp of his intimate familiarity with all the ways and byways of ancient Indian historical and archaeological scholarship. These include entries on Sanskrit and epigraphy, which were the foundations of his academic career. He established a school of archaeology in the survey to train staff, and it has served its purpose well.

Dilip Chakrabarti

References

Ghosh, A. 1973. *The City in Early Historical India.* Simla: Indian Institute of Advance Study.

Ghosh, A., ed. 1990. *Encyclopaedia of Indian Archaeology.* Delhi, Leiden, and New York: E. J. Brill.

Gjerstad, Einar (1897–1979), and the Swedish Cyprus Expedition

Einar Gjerstad first traveled to CYPRUS in 1924 to undertake postgraduate research. His *Studies on Prehistoric Cyprus* (1926) presented a summary of all known Bronze Age sites, and a critical evaluation of past research was presented alongside the results of his pioneering excavations of settlement sites. The typological and chronological systems he developed at this time and later remain fundamental to Cypriot research. After completing his doctoral work, Gjerstad conceived and organized the Swedish Cyprus Expedition.

There are few projects in the history of archaeology that match the scale and professionalism of the Swedish Cyprus Expedition. Together with the other three members of the expedition (Alfred Westholm, John Lindros, and Erik Sjoqvist—and their families), Gjerstad spent the years 1927–1931 surveying and excavating a series of twenty-five sites of all periods across the island. The expedition's professional approach to excavation, recording, analysis, and publication resulted in the efficient production of the first three volumes of very substantial detailed site reports in 1934, 1935, and 1937 (*The Swedish Cyprus Expedition*). Six further volumes, containing syntheses and overviews, were published over the next thirty-five years. One of these, volume four, published in 1948, was Gjerstad's own study of the Cypro-geometric and Cypro-archaic periods. The Swedes set new, and very high, standards of efficiency, quality, and thoroughness for Cypriot archaeology, and the data they collected and the frameworks they developed continue to structure approaches to research on the island.

In 1935, Gjerstad turned his attention to the archaeology of early Rome following his appointment as director of the Swedish Institute there, but he maintained a continuing involvement in Cypriot archaeology.

David Frankel

References

Åström, P., E. Gjerstad, R. S. Merrillees, and A. Westholm. 1994. *"The Fantastic Years on Cyprus": The Swedish Cyprus Expedition and Its Members.*

Studies in Mediterranean Archaeology Pocket-book no. 79. Jonsered: Paul Åströms Forlag.

Gjerstad, E. 1980. *Ages and Days in Cyprus*. Göteborg, Sweden.

Winbladh, M.-L., ed. 1997. *An Archaeological Adventure in Cyprus: The Swedish Cyprus Expedition 1927–1931, a Story Told with Contemporary Photographs and Comments.* Stockholm: Medelhavsmuseet.

Gladwin, Harold Sterling (1883–1983)

Harold Sterling Gladwin was born in New York City and educated in England. After returning to the United States in 1901, he became a stockbroker until 1922 when he moved to California and became associated with the Santa Barbara Museum of Natural History. Although his first scientific interest was with butterfly mutations, Gladwin also developed an interest in the prehistory of California, and that interest soon excluded any other and expanded to include the archaeology of the Americas with a particular interest in theories of migrations from Asia.

By 1924, Gladwin had become a friend of the great American archaeologist ALFRED V. KIDDER and a research fellow in archaeology of the Southwest Museum in Los Angeles. Gladwin began to excavate the ruins of the CASA GRANDE in Arizona, where he used occupation refuse to develop a chronology and identify the prehistoric Hohokam culture. His work revived archaeological interest in southern Arizona, which had been neglected since Frank Cushing's work twenty years earlier. In 1928, Gladwin and his wife-to-be, Winifred MacCurdy, established the Gila Pueblo Archaeological Foundation outside Globe, Arizona, and that foundation became the research center for Southwestern prehistory for the next thirty years. In 1951, Gila Pueblo was given to the University of Arizona, and its collections were transferred to the Arizona State Museum.

Gladwin created a number of new field methods, such as a method of archaeological surveying that allowed for extensive but economic data collection. The result was the establishment of records of 10,000 ruins and habitation sites across a huge area of the United States—from Montana to MEXICO and from California to the Mississippi River—and these records were the basis for ongoing research. His greatest contribution was in the area of cultural reconstruction, mapping large data sets over long time periods, and he was an early convert to the use of dendrochronology in archaeology. Gladwin's best known publications were *Men out of Asia* (1947) and his popular synthesis, *A History of the Ancient Southwest* (1957).

Tim Murray

Godwin, Sir Harry (A. J. H.) (1901–1985)

A. J. H. (Harry) Godwin was born the son of a grocer, attended a local grammar school, and won a scholarship to Clare College, Cambridge, in 1918. Godwin studied both botany and geology, and he was influenced by the ecological work of the botanist Sir A. G. Tansley. Godwin obtained first-class honors at Cambridge and went on to study for a Ph.D. in plant physiology. He began teaching at Cambridge in 1923, moving from junior university demonstrator in botany to research fellow at Clare College in 1925, college fellow from 1934 to 1968, and professor of botany from 1960 to 1968, when he retired.

In 1923, Godwin began the systematic study of Wicken Fen, in Cambridgeshire, applying methods of pollen analysis to the deep deposits of peat in this fen (or swampland) to establish a long history of changes in its vegetation. Godwin proved the relationship between pollen zones and peat stratigraphy based on the identification and relative abundance of pollen grains of different trees in different strata—which helped define the ecology of the area during prehistoric times, i.e., its climate, forest composition, and agricultural practices. These data and their interpretation were published in *The History of British Flora* (Godwin 1950).

Godwin became a global leader in ecological thought and practice. He was president of the British Ecological Society in 1942–1943 and joint editor of the *New Phytologist* from 1931 to 1961. In 1948, he was founding director of the subdepartment of quaternary research within the School of Botany at Cambridge University.

Holding this position until 1966, he contributed to the uses of radiocarbon DATING, to the geological history of changes in land and sea levels, and to the archaeological implications of this work. He was elected fellow of the Royal Society in 1945, received the Prestwich Medal from the Geological Society of London in 1951, the gold medal of the Linnean Society in 1966, and was knighted in 1970.

Tim Murray

Golson, Jack (1926–)

A native of Yorkshire, England, famed as a cricketer as well as an archaeologist of great skill and wisdom, Jack Golson studied archaeology at the University of Cambridge in the late 1940s and early 1950s. Originally intending to pursue research in medieval archaeology (he had embarked on graduate fieldwork at the abandoned English village of Wharram Percy in 1953), Golson soon emigrated to New Zealand to take up a position as the first prehistoric archaeologist appointed to the University of Auckland. His relocation to New Zealand lent great impetus to the development of prehistoric archaeology in that country and in the developing field of Pacific archaeology. Moving to the Australian National University (ANU) in 1961 to assume a founding position in prehistory, Golson set about conducting fieldwork in tropical northern Australia and encouraging the earliest of the thirty-nine graduate students who would earn Ph.D. degrees under his supervision.

Golson's role at the ANU (which concluded with his retirement in 1991) has marked him as one of the most significant archaeologists in Australia. However, it was his excavations in the western highlands of Papua New Guinea, particularly at the site of Kuk, that brought him considerable international fame due to the site's association with evidence of early agriculture in the region. A past president of the WORLD ARCHAEOLOGICAL CONGRESS, Golson is an inspiring educator and scientist whose strong political and ethical principles have done much to establish the special character of Australian and Oceanic archaeology.

Tim Murray

See also Mulvaney, John; New Zealand: Prehistoric Archaeology; Papua New Guinea and Melanesia

Gorodcov, Vasiliy Alekeyevich (1860–1945)

Vasiliy Alekeyevich Gorodcov was born in the Russian province of Riazan. The son of a village sexton, he initially studied to become an Orthodox priest but instead joined the army, serving as an officer from 1880 until 1906. Gorodcov's interest in archaeology was inspired by his reading of Anuchin's Russian translation of John Lubbock's (LORD AVEBURY'S) *Prehistoric Times,* and he began to undertake field surveys in the areas where his military unit was stationed.

In 1887, Gorodcov attended the Seventh Archaeological Congress and reported on some Neolithic sites he had found, but it was not until the following congress in Moscow that prehistoric archaeology, with the support of the geographer and anthropologist Anuchin and the geologist Inostrantsev, became part of the congress agenda. In response to the interest in prehistoric sites and the need for archaeological mapping, Gorodcov mapped the Neolithic settlements of the Oka River and began to excavate the dunes. In 1901, when he was transferred to the southern part of the Russian Empire, he excavated burial mounds in the Donets River basin and organized excavations in the Izium district of Kharkov; in 1903, there were more excavations in the Bakhmut district of Yekaterinoslav Province. In 1905 and 1907, in the monumental transactions of the Twelfth and Thirteenth Archaeological Congresses, Gorodcov published the full reports of all of these excavations, including summary tables for the distribution of grave materials and photographs that were a model of archaeological reporting for their time.

The scope of Gorodcov's fieldwork was extraordinarily wide, but he also became interested in the theoretical and methodological analysis of archaeological material. In a paper of 1902 entitled "Russian Prehistoric Ceramics," he attempted to create a universal classification system for pottery that was even more rigorous than the Linnaean system for biology. He based it on his classification for fragmentary Neolithic ceramics, from which he could define territorial and chronological boundaries of groups as well as contacts and influences, a system more useful for diffusionists than for evolutionists. Between 1908 and 1916, Gorodcov published his analyses of pre-Scythian burial mounds—a quantum leap for prehistoric archaeology in RUSSIA, taking it from antiquarianism to twentieth-century science through his delineation of pit, catacomb, and timber graves and the Indo-European origins of their occupants.

In 1907, after his retirement from the army, Gorodcov began to teach archaeology at the Moscow Archaeological Institute. In 1908 he published the first part of his lectures as *Prehistoric Archaeology,* and in 1910 the second part, *Everyday Archaeology,* appeared. Both served as basic manuals and reference books for decades in RUSSIA. In 1919, Gorodcov became professor at Moscow University and in 1923 head of the Archaeological Department of the Russian Association of Scientific Research Institute of Social Sciences (RANIION).

An active school of archaeology formed around Gorodcov, and many Russian archaeologists of the second half of the twentieth century were taught and influenced by him. In 1933, some of his work on classification was translated into English and influenced the North American archaeologists Clyde Kluckhohn and IRVING ROUSE. He survived the Stalinist political upheavals of the early 1930s, and the radicalism of Marxist archaeology, and received an honorary doctoral degree in 1934.

Leo Klejn

References

For references, see *Encyclopedia of Archaeology: The Great Archaeologists, Vol. 1,* ed. Tim Murray (Santa Barbara, CA: ABC-CLIO, 1999), pp. 261–262.

Graebner, Fritz (1877–1934)

Fritz Graebner was born and studied history in Berlin, where by chance he became a research assistant in the Royal Museum of Ethnography in 1899. By the time he graduated from Berlin University a year later, Graebner had become fascinated by ethnographic problems and had begun working with the museum ethnographer Bernard Ankermann. In 1904, Graebner and Ankermann founded *Kulturkreislehre* ("study of culture circles," or "cultural-historical ethnology") within the Berlin Society for Anthropology, Ethnology, and Prehistory. Stimulated by the work of anthropologist Leo Frobenius and the geographer FRIEDRICH RATZEL, Graebner and Ankermann lectured on *Kulturkreise* ("culture circles") and *Kulturschichten* ("culture strata") in Oceania and Africa, rejecting the then-dominant biological-evolutionary concepts of ethnography.

In 1907, Graebner moved to Cologne to work at the new Rautenstrauch-Joest-Museum where he was able to research the museum's collections and continue his work on theoretical issues. The result of was his book *Die Methode de Ethnologie* [The Method of Ethnology] in which he argued for an epistemology of "culture-historical" research, emphasizing the importance of culture-historic connections for the interpretation of data and the understanding of development sequences. With the museum's director, Willy Foy, Graebner founded the museum's publication *Ethnologica.*

Graebner's area of fieldwork was the South Pacific, and he published wide culture-historical-based work concerning that area. In 1914, while trying to leave Australia after a conference, he was arrested and interned for the duration of World War I.

After his return to Germany, he studied for his Ph.D. at the University of Bonn and became a professor there in 1921. He succeeded Foy at the museum in Cologne in 1925 and became a professor at the University of Cologne in 1926. Ill health caused his early retirement in 1928, and he moved back to Berlin. Graebner's studies of Oceania are still relevant today, but his culture-historical theories, which greatly influenced researchers in Vienna, central Europe, and Scandinavia until the middle of the twentieth century, are today regarded as crudely reducing cultural variation to a few key geographic influences.

Tim Murray

Great Zimbabwe

Great Zimbabwe stands at the top of a granite hill in the modern nation of Zimbabwe, in the center of the Victoria District. The site consists of a stone-walled settlement composed of enclosures, towers, portals, and staircases, occupying both the hilltop and the valley below. Great Zimbabwe existed for over 500 years as a bustling center of trade and commerce, and it politically dominated the surrounding valley and plateaus. At its peak, around A.D. 1200, it was probably the largest settlement in sub-Saharan Africa (Ndoro 1994). Built by ancestors of the present Shona people, Zimbabwe derived its name from the Shona word for "houses of stone." In 1980 Rhodesia was renamed Zimbabwe in recognition of the country's cultural heritage.

First documented by Portuguese explorers in the sixteenth century, the site was noted for its carvings and sophisticated architecture. From the beginning of colonial contact in the nineteenth century, the city's origins were a focus of controversy. Europeans were unwilling to recognize a connection between the impressive ruins and the indigenous Shona people of the area. Instead, explorers and excavators proposed a range of sources for Great Zimbabwe, suggesting, for example, that it was a palace of the Queen of Sheba or King Solomon or a monument built by the Phoenicians, south Indians, or Arabs. These attempts to strip the local African people of their archaeological past persisted well into the twentieth century and served as a tool in the recession efforts of the white Rhodesia Front government in the 1960s (Mahachi and Ndoro 1997).

The ruins were looted repeatedly beginning in the late 1800s in an effort to find the legendary gold of King Solomon and to carry away ornamental stonework and artifacts. Richard Hall was appointed curator of the site in 1902 and conducted large-scale, unscientific excavations that resulted in the destruction of almost all culture-bearing deposits in the stone enclosures. Later archaeologists, such as GERTRUDE CATON-THOMPSON who excavated in the 1930s, argued that the site showed evidence of local African development and had clearly been built by indigenous inhabitants. Such views were largely ignored, however, in favor of sensationalist foreign-origin theories. Recent research supports the African Iron Age provenance of the site, and current investigations are being conducted by Zimbabwean archaeologists such as Kundishora Tungamirai Chipunza and students eager to reclaim their history.

Inhabited from A.D. 900 to 1450, Great Zimbabwe occupied an important trade position between the Zimbabwean plateau and the Indian Ocean coastline. Its wealth was derived from control of local gold and ivory production and trade of the resulting goods with Arab and Swahili merchants. The city functioned as a marketplace and trade emporium, importing such exotic items as cotton cloth, Persian glass beads, and Chinese porcelain. The political influence of the Great Zimbabwe complex extended as far as Mozambique, Botswana, and South Africa; other important contemporary sites of this Zimbabwe Tradition include Khami, Nalatale, Danamombe, and Tsindi (Chipunza 1997).

Inhabitants raised cattle, cultivated sorghum and millet (Callahan 1998), and depended on food tribute from surrounding farming communities. The center declined with the degradation of the local environment (including depletion of the soil and exhaustion of firewood sources), due to the demands of a dense urban population. The Shona inhabitants had largely abandoned the area by 1500, only to be forced back by European settlement of the more fertile and productive high plains areas during the colonial period. The widespread distribution of the Shona language over this area today gives support to the idea that a powerful trading empire was based at Great Zimbabwe in the past (Callahan 1998).

The stone walls of the hilltop complex delineate a classic African village design, containing groups of wattle-and-daub huts within each stone-walled enclosure. These would have been occupied by elite family groups associated with the settlement's leader (Callahan 1998). The ruler lived in the uppermost enclosure, removed from the common people and proclaiming his or her power through the visible manifestation of stone walls and towers (Pwiti 1996). Architectural similarities found in other

The ruins of Great Zimbabwe (Ann Ronan Picture Library)

ruins on the Zimbabwe plateau indicate that Great Zimbabwe had established hegemony over a network of trading centers and gold and ivory production sources. This dominance may have been achieved by installing members of the royal family as local leaders in the outlying sites.

The permanent population in the surrounding valley numbered between 3,000 and 6,000 people; at its height, Great Zimbabwe itself may have had a population between 12,000 and 15,000 people (Ndoro 1997). The site occupies about 1,800 acres and consists of three main parts—the Hill Complex, the Great Enclosure, and the Valley Ruins (Ndoro 1997). The stone walls, rising up to 11 meters, were not constructed according to a preconceived plan. Instead, workers built and expanded walls as the need arose, creating an organic settlement plan.

The Hill Complex occupies the top of the granite hill that dominates the site. This area was inhabited dating to the early Iron Age, before the use of dry stone walling. Sophisticated engineering techniques were employed to stabilize the walls in the complex on the uneven granite boulders that were incorporated into the architecture. The Great Enclosure is located in the valley and includes a 178-meter-long outer wall and an interior conical tower, decorated with stones in a chevron-and-checker pattern. The Valley Ruins are located between the Hill Complex and Great Enclosure and consist of several individual enclosures with parallel passages connecting them (Ndoro 1997).

Erosion has been a problem at the site since Hall's excavations in 1902, when large soil deposits were removed without backfilling, and it has been made worse by reconstruction efforts that entailed the removal of earthen structures and archaeological deposits surrounding the stone walls. In the 1950s all wooden structural elements were removed for carbon dating, resulting in further damage. Future efforts at the site include the preservation of fragile stone architecture, a more accurate restoration of material remains, and the integration of the Shona's historical beliefs into the official literature interpreting the site for visitors (Ndoro 1994).

Thalia Gray

References

Callahan, B. 1998. "Early African History through the Era of the Slave Trade." Image Archive. Available at http://www.virginia.edu/~history/courses/fall.98/hiaf201/imagearchive/zimbabwe.html.

Chipunza, K. T. 1997. A Diachronic Analysis of the Standing Structures of the Hill Complex at Great Zimbabwe, pp.125–142. In *Caves, Monuments and Texts: Zimbabwean Archaeology Today.* Ed. Gilbert Pwiti. Studies in African Archaeology 14. Uppsala, Sweden.

The Lost City of Zimbabwe. 1993. Princeton, NJ: Films for the Humanities and Sciences. (Distributed by Devillier/Donegan Enterprises.)

Mahachi, G., and W. Ndoro. 1997. The Socio-Political Context of Southern African Iron Age Studies with Special Reference to Great Zimbabwe, pp. 89–108. In *Caves, Monuments and Texts: Zimbabwean Archaeology Today.* Ed. Gilbert Pwiti. Studies in African Archaeology 14. Uppsala, Sweden.

Ndoro, W. 1994. "The Preservation and History of Great Zimbabwe." *Antiquity* 68: 616–623.

———. 1997. The Evolution of a Management Policy at Great Zimbabwe, pp. 89–124. In *Caves, Monuments and Texts: Zimbabwean Archaeology Today.* Ed. Gilbert Pwiti. Studies in African Archaeology 14. Uppsala, Sweden.

Pwiti, G. 1996. "Let the Ancestors Rest in Peace? New Challenges for Cultural Heritage Management in Zimbabwe." *Conservation and Management of Archaeological Sites* 1: 151–160.

Greece

The astonishing wealth of archaeological material found in Greece over the last 300 years has provided something of interest to virtually everyone that has seen it, and the precise nature of that interest has varied greatly according to the culture and personality of the viewer. Art historians from Enlightenment Europe, intellectuals from a newly independent Greece, U.S. university professors between the two world wars, and the local schoolchildren and foreign tourists of today have all looked for different archaeologies of Greece, and so far, Greece has always been able to provide them.

The history of archaeology in Greece has often been told from the point of view of the

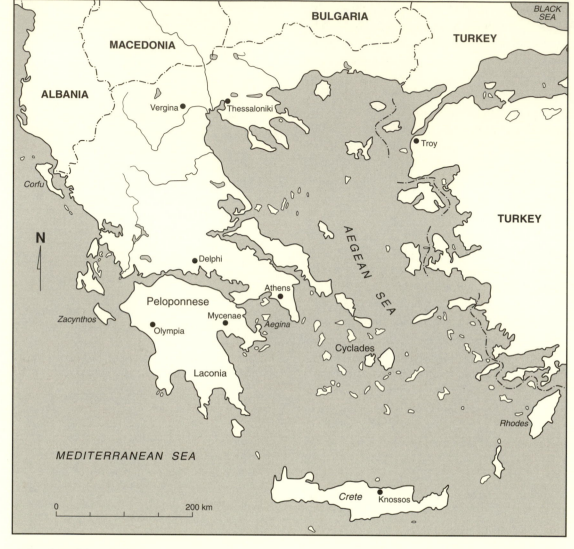

Archaeological Sites in Greece

great foreign excavators who made such an impact on sites, on the local inhabitants, and on the development of archaeological practice: the story is often dominated by big names such as HEINRICH SCHLIEMANN, ARTHUR EVANS, and CARL BLEGEN. Their importance is undisputed, although there are other big names to be added to the list, names such as CHRISTOS TSOUNTAS, Georgios Oikonomos, and Spyridon Marinatos. But this concentration on the "great men of history" draws attention away from the social importance of archaeology in Greece over the last 200 years. Countless women and men have worked as skilled or unskilled laborers on excavations, had careers in the Greek Archaeological

Service, and passed on the results of research to schoolchildren, students, and tourists. Knowledge and interest in archaeology, thanks mainly to its importance within the education system, are much wider even than that and have been since the nineteenth century.

On a broader level, archaeology in Greece—as elsewhere—has been closely bound up with changing cultural and political conditions. People's interests and interpretations depend to a large extent on prevailing intellectual fashions and can often be influenced by political pressure or social position. The Parthenon in the nineteenth century, for example, was variously a link with the great Hellenic past, a model of perfection to revive western European art, and a convenient location to house a military garrison. To understand the history of archaeology in Greece, we need to investigate a wide range of participants and place them within their social and political contexts.

Art, Enlightenment, and Statue Smuggling

During the eighteenth century, the aristocrats of western Europe were educated in the classics, and part of a young man's education was to go on "the grand tour" of classical sites. They first went mainly to Italy, the home of western Christianity and the Renaissance and thus more relevant to European culture. Gradually their destination changed, as the Enlightenment encouraged reason, logic, and a belief in human progress as opposed to an unquestioning acceptance of a universal order imposed by God. The relics of Christianity became irrelevant, and the search for the origins of Europe led to the art and architecture of ancient Greece.

As the new values became prevalent, painters and architects were dispatched to Greece to record this first flowering of European civilization and thereby rejuvenate the art of their own more decadent times. In 1751, for example, a prestigious London dining club called the SOCIETY OF DILETTANTI sent the painter James Stuart and the architect Nicholas Revett to Athens to paint and record the ruins there. Their meticulous work was marred only by minor inaccuracies in recording the higher parts of the temples, owing mainly to a chronic shortage of ladders. The four volumes of *The Antiquities of Athens* published between 1762 and 1816 were intended entirely for a British audience and provided models for the then-current craze for Greek architecture and ornament. The Ottoman governors of Greece, when it suited them, were happy to gain credibility with the European powers by allowing their painters and architects to record apparently valueless ruins. As for the local inhabitants, they only appeared as small and stereotypical figures in the paintings to provide local color and a scale for the architecture of their ancestors.

By 1800 the shift in European intellectual fashion from Italy and Christian origins to Greece and European origins was complete and was further heightened by the Napoleonic Wars, which prevented easy travel to Italy. There was yet another intellectual change. Eighteenth-century art historians, particularly the Prussian JOHANN JOACHIM WINCKELMANN, had used ancient texts to elucidate the Greek spirit that lay at the origins of European civilization. Thanks partly to the efforts of Stuart and Revett and their successors, there was, by the early nineteenth century, a firm interest in the monuments and masterpieces themselves.

When LORD ELGIN was appointed British ambassador to Constantinople in 1799, he originally intended only to make casts of the Parthenon sculptures for the inspiration of British artists. Ottoman gratitude for British help in removing the French from their province of Egypt gave him the opportunity to go further, however, and between 1801 and 1804 he was able to remove and export the actual pieces. The removal was not without criticism. The British architect Robert Smirke, watching Elgin's men extracting the sculptures, commented on his feelings: "a strong regret" as they were being taken "as a sort of signal of the annihilation of such interesting monuments."

Smirke's reservations were amply confirmed by the activities of European architects and agents in Greece during the first two decades of the nineteenth century. Not content with painting and measuring, they competed with each other in finding and removing statuary and even whole buildings for their various collections and national museums. If they could not gain permission, then perhaps the local governor could be bribed; if not, they could smuggle the statues out of the country by night. In 1811, for example, the English architect Charles Cockerell managed to send his newly discovered statues from the Temple of Aphaea on the island of Aegina to Athens with the help of a bribe to the pasha of the islands. From there they were smuggled out from a small fishing village to the island of Zante (now Zákinthos or Zacynthos), which was then under British occupation. At an international auction for the pieces the next year, the BRITISH MUSEUM representative was misdirected to Malta, and the statues were snapped up by the agent of Prince Ludwig of Bavaria for £6,000. Like the scramble for colonies in the later part of the century, western powers scrambled for Greek statuary to inspire their artists and bring prestige to their museums and their countries.

Archaeology and Hellenism in Independent Greece

Five years before the auction of the Aegina Marbles, the leading intellectual of the Enlightenment in Greece, Adamantios Koraïs, had called for the protection and preservation of Greek antiquities. The year after the auction, in 1813, a group of Greek intellectuals formed the Philomousos Eteria, or Society of Lovers of the Arts. Their aim was to discover antiquities and display them in a museum, originally intended to be the Erechtheum in Athens, for the benefit of the people of Greece in general and the country's youth in particular. Under Ottoman rule little progress could be made, but a revolution in 1821 and the eventual independence of the southern part of Greece under a Bavarian monarch in 1832 changed the situation. Even in 1825 the temporary government had protested the looting of antiquities and proposed setting up a museum in every school to teach future generations the importance of their ancestors.

One of the earliest laws that the new government passed concerned the archaeological heritage of the Greek nation. This law, passed in May 1834, declared that all antiquities were "national heritage" and "state property" and could not therefore be exported. Excavations could be carried out only with a permit. The foundation of the Greek Archaeological Service the next year provided the personnel and infrastructure to carry out excavations in the new state and marked a major shift toward Greek-run projects.

The reason for the major emphasis on archaeology lay in the ideology of the new kingdom and its need to create a new and widely accepted identity. Previously the inhabitants of this relatively unimportant Ottoman province had called themselves *Romei* ("Romans") and Orthodox Christians; they were ruled by Ottoman governors and by local chiefs and aristocrats who had attained some measure of autonomy—all of which hardly made them members of a modern European nation. Thanks to the European Enlightenment, however, they could appropriate their own classical past and identify themselves with "the Hellenes," the originators of European civilization. To do so required knowledge and control of the classical past, discovery of the tangible monuments of that past, and appropriate education of the people now to be called Hellenes.

The most famous symbol of the Hellenic past was the Acropolis, but the four classical structures that can be seen there today—the Parthenon, the Erechtheum, the Propylaea, and the Temple of Athena Nike—had been converted, respectively, into a mosque, an armory, a fortress, and a bastion. Visually, they were dominated by a tall Frankish defensive tower beside what had been the Propylaea and were surrounded by a warren of small houses and alleys. The task of the new Archaeological Service was to purify this morass of different periods and peoples. Under the directorship of Kyriakos Pittakis, conservator of antiquities from 1836, the mosque and minaret within the Parthenon were demolished, the Venetian and Turkish defenses were removed, the various houses and streets were destroyed, the blocks of the Temple of Athena Nike were discovered and reconstructed, and the Erechtheum porches were restored. This work of cleaning and restoring continued into the 1860s when the Acropolis Museum was built, and finally, in 1874, the Archaeological Society of Athens, with financial help from the archaeologist Heinrich Schliemann, demolished the Frankish tower. The Acropolis was thus returned to its original "pure" classical form with all its barbarian accretions removed.

There were dissenting voices. Not everyone, including some Greek intellectuals, agreed with the removal of all traces of later periods. King Otto, the son of the same Ludwig of Bavaria who had so eagerly acquired the Aegina Marbles, was wholeheartedly in favor of Greek classicism, but he and his advisers also favored the Byzantine period, which was a better symbol of stable autocracy than the warring democracies and oligarchies of the classical city-states. In

The western end of the Acropolis in Athens as seen from the pediment of the Parthenon ca. 1801. The Frankish tower stands in the center. Drawing by Sir William Gell. (British Museum)

1837, Otto passed a royal decree protecting Byzantine monuments as Greek archaeologists were happily destroying them in their enthusiasm for the classical antiquities that lay beneath. Greek archaeology, however, was firmly launched on a classicist agenda, and that agenda culminated in 1889 with the completion of the National Museum, an imposing Greek Revival structure designed to display the national heritage in suitable classical grandeur.

The Foreign Missions

The Greek state and the growth of the Greek Archaeological Service did not, of course, mean an end to foreign participation in archaeology in Greece. As archaeological methods improved during the nineteenth century, teams from Germany, Great Britain, the United States, France, and elsewhere were keen to excavate major classical and prehistoric sites. The difference was that foreign projects were now carefully controlled and they were entirely at the mercy of the Greek government, which often gained considerable prestige and power from the situation.

A good example of the need for control was Heinrich Schliemann's work at Mycenae in 1874. He brought with him from his excavations at Troy in northwestern Anatolia a reputation for smuggling gold artifacts out of the country without the knowledge of the Ottoman authorities and generally for trying to get round his permit in any way possible. The Greek government had actually given the permit to excavate at Mycenae to the Greek Archaeological Society, but as often happened, it was short of funds and asked Schliemann to excavate on its behalf and at his expense.

The government was decidedly wary of Schliemann but finally agreed to his excavation on condition that he was supervised by Panayiotis Stamatakis, on behalf of both the society and the government, and that all the finds would belong to Greece. The gold masks and jewelry that Schliemann's excavations uncovered in the sixteenth-century B.C. shaft graves are well known. Less well known are the briefness of Schliemann's visits to the site, his impatience with the classical and Roman material that interfered with his search for Agamemnon, and the constant difficulties of Stamatakis, who was actually running the excavation but with every obstruction put in his way by Schliemann and his Greek wife, Sophia.

It was clearly easier for the Greek government to deal with respected foreign institutions such as universities and museums. It was also easier for the foreigners to have representatives of their countries permanently in Athens to carry on the often complex negotiations with the government. The first foreign school of

Aerial view of the ruins of Mycenae (Image Select)

archaeology to be set up in Athens was that of the French, established in 1846 partly as an artists' colony. During the 1870s and 1880s this school was joined by German, American, British, and Italian schools of archaeology. Today there are seventeen such schools in Greece.

The government had much to gain in terms of international prestige by encouraging these schools; the Americans and British, for example, were both given state land for their institutions. On occasion, negotiations between governments was directed more by political considerations than by archaeological ones. In 1892, for instance, the French were given a permit for major excavations at the prestigious site of Delphi on condition that they pay for the removal of the village that had grown up on the site; more to the point, perhaps, the French had won the permit over their U.S. rivals by removing their import duty on Greek currants. In 1911, while the Greek Archaeological Service was excavating the Temple of Artemis on Corfu, the Kaiser of Germany visited the site. He was so impressed that he asked if Germany could take over the site, and the Greek government gave

him the rights to excavate. Just two days later Greece formally asked Germany and the other western powers to put political pressure on Turkey concerning its treatment of Greeks living within its borders. The excavation, in other words, was merely a bargaining tool in international politics, and the feelings of the Greek archaeologists who had already invested so much time and money in the site were ignored.

The position of the Greek government was often a difficult one. It certainly gained prestige and a measure of political power by granting or withholding excavation permits to foreigners, but it was also important that it should be Greek archaeologists who excavated the great sites. Unfortunately, the foreigners often had more money. During his first season at Knossos, Arthur Evans was able to employ up to 300 men and women, with bonuses for good work or the discovery of an important find. The funds came almost entirely out of his own (and his father's) pocket, and they had a considerable impact on local employment and prosperity.

Often it was hard for the various Greek societies and institutions to match foreign funding. A

Part of Arthur Evans's workforce in the Hall of the Double Axes at the Palace of Knossos in 1901 (Ashmolean Museum)

new law in 1928 limited the foreign schools to three excavation permits each. But with the economic problems of the late 1920s and early 1930s, the Greek Archaeological Service was almost bankrupt. For this reason, one of the potentially most exciting sites in Athens, the Athenian Agora, had to be given to the Americans. Between 1927 and 1940, they lavished on the site $1 million donated by John D. Rockefeller alone, quite apart from other sources. Much of the money went for expropriating the land from the several thousand refugees from Asia Minor who had inhabited it since 1922. In spite of gaining independence and control over its own archaeology, Greece could not quite escape the influence of the western archaeological powers.

The Advance of Method and Chronology

As early as 1852 the German archaeologist ERNST CURTIUS began raising money for a new type of excavation at Olympia, one that would not remove archaeological material to other countries but one that would systematically record and analyze this important site. It was only after Schliemann's more dramatic, if less systematic, work at Mycenae and elsewhere that the Germans (and others) began to appreciate the need for large-scale, well-funded projects. Curtius finally won his funding in 1875, and a

treaty was signed between Germany and Greece allowing the German Archaeological Institute (DEUTSCHES ARCHÄOLOGISCHES INSTITUT—DAI) to undertake systematic exploration at Olympia, on condition, of course, that all finds remained in Greece. Stratigraphy and particular find spots were carefully recorded, structures underwent architectural analysis, and the Olympia excavations became a model of the new systematic, scientific excavation methods.

Another result of Schliemann's massive self-publicity was a sudden interest in the prehistoric period. The key figure here is Christos Tsountas, who followed Schliemann at Mycenae and worked there over a period of more than two decades as well as at numerous other Bronze Age and earlier sites all over the mainland and islands of Greece. Unlike his predecessor, Tsountas set out, not to prove a myth, but to investigate material culture and the development of human society. He achieved his aims partly by remarkable finds, such as an undisturbed fifteenth-century B.C. princely tomb at Vapheio in Laconia, which he excavated in 1889, complete with weapons, jewelry, and gold cups. More pertinently, through the meticulous excavation of a broad range of sites, particularly cemeteries, and the careful comparison of their materials, he was able to put together a broad picture of the development of prehistoric Greece. *The Mycenaean Age,* written by Tsountas and J. Irving Manatt and published in 1897, was the first great synthetic work of Aegean prehistory, and the book made the subject the major branch of Mediterranean archaeology that it has been ever since.

Improvements in excavation techniques were accompanied by a general systematizing of the analysis of artifacts, particularly pottery, the basis of most archaeological dating. Before and after World War I, the Englishman Alan Wace and the American Carl Blegen complemented Tsountas's work by producing a coherent and precise chronology of pre-Mycenaean pottery. In the field of classical archaeology, the first half of the twentieth century was characterized by connoisseurship. Archaeological knowledge was ordered and classified, with artifacts being sorted and pigeonholed into vast corpora of inscriptions, coins, potsherds, figurines, lamps, and so on. The ultimate analysis was that of Greek vases by the Oxford art historian JOHN BEAZLEY. By identifying characteristic stylistic traits and mannerisms, as well as using the occasional signatures, he managed to detect the "hands" and "workshops" of individual ancient painters. Classical archaeology remained subservient either to art history, with statues, vases, and buildings being taken out of context as works of art, or to textual history, where the objects merely illustrated the accounts of Thucydides, Euripides, and the other classical writers.

Further changes came to archaeological methods and interpretations in the 1960s with the advent of scientific techniques and processual archaeology. Prehistorians such as Colin Renfrew led the way in modeling the influences and processes that had caused social change in the past. Most classical archaeologists remained firmly entrenched within their empiricist and descriptive traditions until the 1970s and 1980s when scholars such as Anthony Snodgrass began using the contextual analysis and theories of social change that are more normally associated with prehistory to question the rich range of data from the Iron Age and classical period.

Another striking change in archaeological methodology in Greece during the last two decades of the twentieth century was a rapid growth in the popularity of archaeological survey and landscape archaeology. These involved the use of a very different technique than that used in the exploration and site-hunting by earlier archaeologists. Teams of field-walkers covered large areas of landscape systematically and intensively, recording and sampling the surface material they found. This allowed an examination of small rural sites such as farmsteads and hamlets and when combined with geomorphological mapping and other disciplinary studies, enabled investigators to study the development of agriculture, ancient soil management, and a host of other off-site activities.

Because such survey projects found material of all periods, especially the late post-Roman period, they sparked an important interest in the archaeology of medieval and Ottoman Greece, in striking contrast to the classical purists of the nineteenth century. In 1988, the Greek government amended the antiquities law to allow each school to run three surveys and three excavations each year, and Greece now leads the eastern half of the Mediterranean in the field of archaeological survey.

The Archaeology of the Greek Nation

"Hellenic archaeology, gentlemen, is not a profession but a sacred mission." So spoke Georgios Oikonomos, secretary of the Archaeological Society of Athens, during preparations for the society's centenary in 1937. Ever since the War of Independence, in the first third of the nineteenth century, archaeology had been something greater than a job or an interest. Classical antiquities were considered to be almost sacred relics that expressed the innermost spirit of the Hellenic nation, which, above all, was the reason why the Greek state was determined to keep control over all artifacts and excavations and why it worked so hard from as early as the 1820s to educate future generations about the importance of the classical past.

The precise nature of this belief, of course, varied according to occasion and individual and developed in accordance with changing ideological and political conditions. Christos Tsountas, for example, was interested in the Mycenaeans for their own sake as they had an important and fascinating culture. But he also felt it was important to refute the views of his foreign colleagues who declared that the Mycenaean civilization was non-European and certainly non-Greek. To Tsountas, the Hellenic spirit could appear at different times in different forms, and the rich culture of late Bronze Age Mycenae was one of those manifestations. He was proved right in a very literal sense in 1952 when the British architect Michael Ventris deciphered the Linear B tablets from the palace archives of the late Bronze Age and discovered that they were written in an early form of Greek.

In 1833, newly independent Greece encompassed only a fraction of its current area, and as new areas were gradually acquired, they had to be incorporated into the state. Archaeology played a vital role in this process of nation building. When Macedonia (that is, the current Greek province of Macedonia) became part of Greece after the Balkan wars of 1912–1913, a Greek Archaeological Service of Macedonia was immediately set up, and numerous excavation projects were organized. It was initially rather awkward that the area lacked much of the classical architecture and artwork of southern Greece, and as a result, there was a strong focus on the much richer Byzantine culture of the region. In the mid-nineteenth century, the Byzantine period had been considered unimportant or even shameful, a time when Greece was ruled by an outside empire. Now it was incorporated into the Hellenic heritage, and the Byzantine churches of Thessaloníki that had been converted into mosques were restored to their original "pure" form.

Archaeology in Macedonia, and its role within the Hellenic nation, received a major boost in 1977 when Manolis Andronikos discovered a rich fourth-century-B.C. tomb at Vergina in Macedonia. Quite apart from the elaborate wall paintings, armor, and silver vessels, a gold ossuary within a marble sarcophagus contained bones wrapped in gold and purple cloth that were identified as those of Philip of Macedon, father of Alexander the Great. The outer chamber of the tomb also contained a gold box holding cremated ashes and was embossed with a star burst, or "star of Vergina," a symbol of the Macedonian kings. This archaeological discovery was widely believed to be a direct link with the Hellenic past. Macedonia was suddenly flooded with up to forty archaeological projects a year, and a wealth of publications appeared, both academic and popular. The star of Vergina became the national symbol of Greece in 1993, and when Andronikos died in 1992, he was given a state funeral and the honor of being the first Greek archaeologist to be depicted on a postage stamp.

The importance of archaeology to Greek national identity has, of course, led to disputes with other groups making rival claims to the past. One was with the former Yugoslav Republic of Macedonia, which also claimed the star of Vergina as a state symbol. Most well known is the dispute over the Parthenon (or Elgin) Marbles, which became a major national issue in the 1980s owing to the hugely popular ex-actress and minister of culture, Melina Mercouri. The campaign for the restitution of the sculptures by the British Museum is inspired above all by an almost religious belief in their centrality to Hellenic culture and identity. Manolis Andronikos, in a 1983 newspaper article, declared that "these sculptures belong to the most sacred monument of this country, the temple of Athena, which expresses the essence of the Greek spirit and incorporates the deepest nature of the Athenian democracy."

Conclusions

Greek archaeology has never been static or monolithic. Nor is its history a mere list of discoveries and acquired facts. The antiquities of Greece and the societies that produced them were major players in the European Enlightenment, the development of western art, the new academic discipline of archaeology, and above all in the formation of the identity and character of an independent Greek nation. Such is Greece's archaeological wealth and variety that there is still material to satisfy all new trends in archaeology, from scientific techniques of dating and analysis to an interest in the entire landscape of a region to the recent growth in underwater archaeology. New trends will arise, but Greece will always have the material to satisfy their pursuits.

Although there has been great variety in the last 300 years of archaeology in Greece, some general themes are common to much of the period. The wealth of material has not always been beneficial, attracting treasure hunters and allowing academics to slide into mere description rather than the questioning and analysis of material. The balance between local and foreign participation has swung to and fro depending on the international relations of the time, but cooperation has always been to the benefit of all parties. Even the Cockerells and Schliemanns inspired important developments in the history of archaeology in Greece.

The most striking aspect of Greek archaeology is its unique double association with a national identity and an international culture. The antiquities of Greece do indeed lie at the heart of western culture, through the artistic and intellectual revolutions of classical Athens, their rebirth in the Renaissance, and the craze for neoclassicism in the eighteenth and nineteenth centuries, but they are also the inspiration and symbol of one of the proudest national identities in Europe. The history of archaeology in Greece reflects the tension between the two sides of this paradox, as locals and foreigners alike focus on a heritage that is both universal and uniquely Greek.

Michael Given

See also Linear A/Linear B

References

Brown, A. 1983. *Arthur Evans and the Palace of Minos.* Oxford: Ashmolean Museum.

Clogg, R. 1986. *A Short History of Modern Greece.* 2d ed. Cambridge: Cambridge University Press.

Ferguson, A. C. S. 1986. "British Architects in Athens 1800–1850." *Architect* July: 20–25.

Hamilakis, Y., and E. Yalouri. 1996. "Antiquities as Symbolic Capital in Modern Greek Society." *Antiquity* 70: 117–129.

———. 1999. "Sacralising the Past: Cults of Archaeology in Modern Greece." *Archaeological Dialogues* 6: 115–135, 154–210.

Kotsakis, K. 1998. "The Past Is Ours: Images of Greek Macedonia." In *Archaeology under Fire: Nationalism, Politics, and Heritage in the Eastern Mediterranean and Middle East,* 44–67. Ed. L. Meskell. London: Routledge.

McNeal, R. A. 1991. "Archaeology and the Destruction of the Later Athenian Acropolis." *Antiquity* 65: 49–63.

Morris, I. 1994. "Archaeologies of Greece." In *Classical Greece: Ancient Histories and Modern Archaeologies,* 8–47. Ed. I. Morris. Cambridge: Cambridge University Press.

Perowne, S. 1974. *The Archaeology of Greece and the Aegean.* London: Hamlyn.

Snodgrass, A. M. 1987. *An Archaeology of Greece: The Present State and Future Scope of a Discipline.* Sather Classical Lectures, vol. 53. Berkeley: University of California Press.

Traill, D. 1995. *Schliemann of Troy: Treasure and Deceit.* London: John Murray.

Green, Roger Curtis (1932–)

Born in New Jersey, from an early age Green was interested in archaeology, and first studied anthropology at the University of New Mexico. He moved to Harvard to study for his doctorate in 1955, and was deeply influenced by Professor GORDON WILLEY's settlement pattern approach to archaeology. Green was also influenced by JULIAN STEWARD and Clyde Kluckhohn, but it was Douglas Oliver who steered him firmly away from the archaeology of the Southwest and Central America and toward the archaeology of the Pacific.

In 1958 Green took up a Fulbright Fellowship in New Zealand, based in the anthropology department at the University of Auckland. Here he worked with social anthropologist Ralph Piddington and British archaeologist JACK GOLSON. Green excavated a coastal midden at Tairua on the Coromandel Peninsula that was a landmark for its careful interpretation of all the material recovered, and for Green's use of what Golson has characterized as the "ecological approach."

Green then undertook major fieldwork projects in French Polynesia, Samoa, and the Solomon Islands based on settlement pattern study and ethno-historic approaches, which established him as a major figure in the relatively new field of Polynesian archaeology. From 1961 to 1967 Green taught at the University of Auckland and carried out a number of small excavations and surveys to provide training and opportunities for students. He served a term as president of the New Zealand Archaeological

Association and played an important role in the early effort to establish protection for archaeological sites. He produced a major synthesis of the prehistory of the Auckland province and a revision of the Fijian sequence. Green also taught at the University of Hawaii.

Despite his activity in New Zealand, Green's major interest lay in tropical POLYNESIA, and with support of the Bishop Museum in Honolulu, the U.S. National Science Foundation, and other institutions in New Zealand and Fiji, he returned to Western Samoa between 1963 and 1967 as part of the Polynesian Prehistory Program. From 1968 until 1970 Green undertook the Makaha Valley Historical Project in Hawaii, a major contract investigation funded entirely by private sources, which also made major contributions to the professional literature. Green also began his long collaboration with New Zealand ethnobotanist Douglas Yen at this time.

Green returned to New Zealand as the first Captain James Cook Fellow at the Auckland Institute and Museum and began a major fieldwork project in the southeast Solomons, co-directed by Yen and involving participants from New Zealand, Hawaii, and Australia. The major outcome of the project was the discovery of a number of sites containing Lapita pottery on the Santa Cruz and Reef Islands. This became the focus of his subsequent work. Green had been an important contributor to the definition of Lapita and other pottery in the central Pacific; now he was to become influential in defining the Lapita cultural complex in the western Pacific as well. The second phase of the southeast Solomons project during the late 1970s, again directed by Green and Yen, was concerned with Lapita sites on the Santa Cruz group.

During the 1970s Green wrote influential papers on the chronology of Oceanic languages, reviewed what was known about the Lapita cultural complex, and developed his ideas about Near and Remote Oceania. In the 1980s Green, along with archaeologist Dimitry Anson, undertook the reinvestigation of Lapita sites on Watom Island as part of the multi-institutional Lapita Homeland Project organized by Jim Allen, then of the Australian National University. The ongoing analysis of Lapita material from this project

and from the Santa Cruz and Reef Islands absorbed Green over more than a decade.

In 1973 Green was appointed to a personal chair in the anthropology department at Auckland University, which he held until his retirement in 1992, and he then became professor emeritus. He has continued to exert an influence through his teaching and the supervision of numerous theses. He has played a major role in the growth of Pacific archaeology, and his culture historical approach has been influential. He has served on the council of the Royal Society of New Zealand and he was elected a Fellow of the Royal Society of New Zealand in 1975 and a member of the American Academy of Sciences in 1984.

Janet Davidson

See also New Zealand: Historical Archaeology; New Zealand: Prehistoric Archaeology; Papua New Guinea and Melanesia

References

For references, see *Encyclopedia of Archaeology: The Great Archaeologists,* Vol. 1, ed. Tim Murray (Santa Barbara, CA: ABC-CLIO 1999), pp. 835–849.

Griffin, James Bennett (1905–1997)

Griffin was born in Kansas, the son of a railway worker who eventually settled his family in Illinois. Griffin originally studied law and business at the University of Chicago but changed to anthropology. In 1930 he received his M.A. and began his long-term association with the Hopewell culture, digging the Morton site near Lewiston, Illinois. In 1931 he excavated late Algonkian and historic Delaware sites in Pennsylvania. In 1932 Griffin began a doctorate in American archaeology at the University of Michigan and became one of the founding members of the National Society for American Archaeology. In 1936 he received his doctorate for his dissertation that focused on the ceramics from the Norris basin in Tennessee.

From 1936 to 1941 Griffin was a research associate and associate curator in charge of the Ceramic Repository in the Museum of Anthropology at the University of Michigan. With this responsibility he began his lifelong investigation of eastern archaeology, characterized by specimen study and frequent travels to conferences and museums. In 1937 he helped to found the Southeastern Archaeological Conference in conjunction with JAMES A. FORD, then a graduate student at Michigan. He also formulated the preliminary synthesis that became the intellectual background for his seminal paper on "Cultural Continuity and Change," delivered at the American Anthropological Association meeting in 1941. Griffin's goals were always larger than mere cultural-historical integrations, although his forays into that realm were very influential. He was interested in cultural process. From early on he also repeatedly examined the connection of prehistoric remains to the historically recorded tribal units—*ethno-historic* concerns, as they are now termed. The cardinal rule of his investigations was to obtain as much firsthand knowledge of the sites and artifacts as he could, and in his search for broad expertise he traveled extensively. He was also open-minded about new methods of analysis. He helped to pioneer the use of Carbon 14 DATING in North America and to establish the radiocarbon-dating laboratory in Ann Arbor, which would serve as a major source of New World dates for nearly twenty years.

During the war he taught economic and political geography to soldiers. In 1945 he was finally made an associate professor of anthropology with regular teaching responsibilities, and his title at the museum was upgraded to director in 1946. In 1941 Griffin had teamed up with James Ford at Louisiana State University and Philip Phillips of Harvard's PEABODY MUSEUM to undertake extensive field survey and archaeological testing in the Lower Mississippi Valley that continued during the war, resulted in a major and influential monograph, and was representative of his interest in spatial expanses and interareal interactions.

Over the next twenty-five years, until he retired in 1975, Griffin continued to build his record of accomplishments from his base in Ann Arbor. He became a full professor in 1949, and his teaching and extensive involvement with graduate students increased as the Museum of Anthropology and the department became one of the principal training grounds for North American archaeologists in the country. Griffin was president of the SOCIETY FOR AMERICAN AR-

CHAEOLOGY from 1951 to 1952, and in 1957 the society awarded him the Viking Fund Medal for Archaeology for his achievements. He was made a member of the National Academy of Science in 1968.

Griffin's legacy to American archaeology was significant. His strong published record of basic research totaled more than 260 items. He affected the personal and intellectual lives of scores of students and scholars—by 1975 he had guided more Ph.D. candidates through their degrees than anyone else in the department. He had a fine-tuned ability to evaluate new data and new ideas critically. All serious students of the archaeology of eastern North America must acknowledge Griffin's contribution, whether their area is woodland influences on the western plains or on the mid-Atlantic coast or the question of Iroquoian origins in the Great Lakes region. Griffin covered an unequaled range of subjects in space and time.

Stephen Williams

See also United States of America, Prehistoric Archaeology

References
For references, see *Encyclopedia of Archaeology: The Great Archaeologists*, Vol. 1, ed. Tim Murray (Santa Barbara, CA: ABC-CLIO, 1999), pp. 451–458.

Guatemala

Guatemala is one of the five independent republics of Central America and comprises a major part of what is defined in archaeology as the Mesoamerican region. The population today is approximately 12 million, over half of whom are Indians of Maya ancestry. Some twenty-two Maya dialects have been identified since the Spanish conquest, as well as Pipil (Nahuat) and Xinca, which are currently nearing extinction. Today the predominant Maya language groups in Guatemala are the Quiche, Cakchiquel, Tzutujil, Kekchi, Pokomam, and Mam.

Two major geographic-ecological regions have affected cultural evolution through time: the tropical lowlands and the temperate highlands. The lowlands area includes the Pacific coast and piedmont zone and the entire northern part of the country known as Petén. The highlands area is the mountainous and volcanic region that lies between the Pacific piedmont and Petén.

The history of Guatemala begins with its conquest in 1524 by Pedro de Alvarado, a trusted captain under Hernán Cortés in the conquest of Mexico. However, the area of Petén, occupied by groups such as the Maya Itzá, was not subdued until 1697. The country remained a Spanish colony until it gained independence, along with the rest of Central America, in 1821.

Precursors to Archaeological Exploration

Various letters and reports of the Spanish conquerors (e.g., Pedro de Alvarado and Bernal Diaz del Castillo) and early chroniclers described the Cakchiquel capital of Iximche and the Quiche capital of Utatlan in the highlands. Cortés wrote of various villages, such as Tayasal in Petén and Nito around Lake Izabal, on his march through the lowlands en route to Honduras in 1524 and 1525. All of these centers were abandoned by the inhabitants shortly thereafter. A few documents written by the Quiches and Cakchiquels in the early colonial period survive, including the *Popol Vuh* and the *Memorial de Tecpan Atitlan,* and these provide important information regarding these peoples' pre-Columbian history, their early migrations to Guatemala, and their worldview in general. Early land titles also contained references to events prior to the conquest. Reports by the clergy often provided valuable descriptions of native life, among them those by Bartolome de Las Casas in the 1550s, Bartolome de Fuensalida, and Juan de Orbita (1618–1619), and Andres de Avendaño y Loyola (1695–1696), as well as reports by the clergy to the various religious orders, such as those by Francisco Ximenez at the end of the seventeenth century.

The native population declined rapidly after the Spanish conquest, largely due to exposure to European diseases and the harsh conditions imposed by heavy labor in construction and agriculture. Christianization was achieved rapidly, and the influence of Christianity was seen in the native writings. These often reflected the biblical notions of the Spanish regarding the origins of the Americans, including the idea that they were descendants of one of the Lost Tribes of Israel. One exception was the work of Francisco Antonio Fuentes y Guzman who, writing in the 1700s, used the native documents and maps of the ancient centers to highlight the achievements and illustrious past of the former inhabitants and to show that the Guatemalan Indians of his day were descendants of those people (Fuentes y Guzman 1933, 2: 211, 3: 199).

The Enlightenment of the eighteenth century was reflected in Guatemala by a new interest in archaeological remains. The inclusion of Naples, Italy, in the Spanish domain during the reign of Carlos III awakened this interest and inspired the colonial authorities in Guatemala to carry out the first archaeological explorations on record. Between 1784 and 1789 three investigations were carried out in PALENQUE and Chiapas, which today are part of MEXICO but at that time were still part of Guatemala. The reports, maps, and drawings from the third expedition were published in London in 1822 and circulated among the intellectuals of the era. The first museum in Guatemala, exhibiting both natural and archaeological specimens, was established by the Sociedad Economica in 1797. It functioned until 1801, when it was closed by the Spanish government on the pretext that it was involved in political movements toward independence from Spain (Lujan 1972, 354, 360).

Guatemala succeeded in obtaining its independence in 1821, along with the rest of Central America. In 1832, after a period of turbulence and civil wars, the government of Guatemala under Mariano Galvez organized an investigation of the archaeological sites of Utatlan and Iximche in order to put together an atlas and recapitulation of the history of the country. Galvez also reinstalled the Sociedad Economica and ordered that a new archaeological museum be established under its aegis (Lujan 1972, 364).

With independence from Spain, Guatemala experienced heightened interaction with the outside world, including the United States, England, France, and other European countries. During the time of the Federal Republic of Central America, organized in 1823 and lasting until 1839, numerous archaeological explorations were carried out by Europeans and others. In 1839 and again in 1841 JOHN L. STEPHENS, a New Yorker, and the Englishman FREDERICK CATHERWOOD traveled to Mexico and Central America and visited Maya sites such as Tonina, Palenque, and Uxmal in Mexico, Quirigua, Utatlan, and Iximche in Guatemala, and Copan in Honduras. Subsequently Stephens published his account of the trips, along with drawings by Catherwood, and this helped to call the attention of the world to the subject of Maya archaeology.

The Beginnings of Archaeological Investigation in the Nineteenth Century

The second half of the nineteenth century witnessed increasing archaeological explorations in the Peten both by Guatemalans and by foreigners. In 1848 Ambrosio Tut, a Guatemalan, discovered the ruins of TIKAL. He reported these to the governor of Petén, Modesto Mendez, who published information on the find in the local newspapers and in the journal of the Academia de Geografía e Historia de Guatemala. In the next few years he found more sites in the general area of Petén (Lujan 1972, 364). Toward the end of the century further exploration was encouraged by the interest of U.S. companies in obtaining chicle from the forest for the manufacture of chewing gum.

Between 1881 and 1894 the Englishman Alfred P. Maudslay discovered and systematically issued reports on archaeological sites and monuments, all accompanied by excellent photographs and maps, which stimulated the first studies of Maya hieroglyphs. Slightly later the Austrian Tobert Maler discovered and photographed a number of sites along the Usumacinta River, and the results of his work were published by the PEABODY MUSEUM of Archaeology and Ethnology of Harvard University. The inception of coffee cultivation in Guatemala brought a number of Germans and other Europeans to the country to establish plantations, especially in the highlands. Karl Sapper, Otto Stoll, and Erwin Dieseldorff made important studies on the local ethnography and archaeology, especially in the region of Alta Verapaz.

Carved monolithic head from Monte Alto (Image Select)

The organization of liberal governments at the end of the nineteenth century promoted interest in pre-Columbian archaeology as a way of reconstructing national history. For this purpose Manuel García Elgueta, considered by some to have been the first Guatemalan archaeologist, carried out excavations in the highland sites of Xolchun and Chalchitan (Lujan 1972, 368). In celebration of the fourth centennial of the discovery of America in 1892, President José Maria Reyna Barrios ordered molds of monuments to be made and presented, along with archaeological objects, at the Columbian Exposition in Chicago and at another exhibition in Seville, Spain. During this endeavor the site of Ceibal in Peten was discovered by Federico Artes (Morley 1937–1938, 80). President Reina Barrios was the first government official to design laws to protect archaeological goods in the country, prohibiting the illegal excavation and exportation of these materials to other countries. The laws, however, were ignored during the following decades (Rubin de la Borbolla and Cerezo 1953, 13).

Professionalizaion of Archaeological Investigation in the First Half of the Twentieth Century

With the twentieth century came a new era in archaeological investigation in Guatemala, carried out by professional, trained archaeologists and financed by prestigious institutions abroad. The Peabody Museum of Archaeology and Ethnology, continuing to pursue its interest in the Maya region, organized twelve archaeological expeditions between 1892 and 1915. It also financed excavations at Altar de Sacrificios between 1958 and 1963 and at Ceibal between 1962 and 1966. In addition to the information that was recovered, these investigations amassed a large corpus of hieroglyphic texts (Morley 1937–1938, 83).

In the 1920s there was a growing curiosity on the part of Guatemalans regarding the pre-Columbian era and native traditions. In 1922 and 1925 the government issued new regulations concerning archaeological projects and trafficking in antiquities. In 1927 J. Antonio Villacorta and his son Carlos published, in Guatemala, a volume describing archaeological sites in the country. Adrian Recinos, a Guatemalan historian, translated and published the important Quiche document, the *Popol Vuh,* the Cakchiquel history known as the *Memorial de Solola* (also known as *The Anales de los Cakchiqueles*), and other native chronicles and land titles. Also furthering public interest, in 1931 the Guatemalan government inaugurated one section of the National Museum that was to be devoted to archaeology and designed to house the artifacts and monuments being discovered by the projects directed by U.S. institutions (Chinchilla 1999, 110–111).

One of the major groups with an interest in prehispanic Guatemala was the Carnegie Institution of Washington, which intensively explored archaeological sites in Peten and Yucatán from 1915 to 1937 under the direction of SYLVANUS G. MORLEY. Uaxactun, a site near Tikal, was a principal focus of interest because the earliest dated inscriptions known up to that time had been found there. The new stratigraphic methods of excavation that had been devised by then were meticulously applied in this work, ultimately providing the basic chronological outline for the Maya lowlands— known today as the preclassic, classic, and postclassic periods. The Guatemalan artist Antonio Tejeda was hired to copy the murals of Uaxactun for publication (Morley 1937–1938, 86–97). He later copied the murals of BONAM-

PAK', as well as paintings of vessels recovered from numerous excavations. In addition, TATIANA PROSKOURIAKOFF was employed to make reconstruction drawings of most of the sites that had been investigated by the Carnegie Institution in the Petén and Guatemala highlands. From 1936 to 1942 and again in 1952 the Carnegie Institution financed salvage operations at Kaminaljuyu, an important highland center that was being destroyed by the expansion of the modern capital, Guatemala City. Under the direction of ALFRED V. KIDDER, two publications resulted from the work, and these remain the basic references on the site.

The Department of Middle American Research at Tulane University contributed to archaeological explorations in Guatemala by sending an expedition in 1928. The expedition covered the entire Maya area and drew up the first archaeological site map of the region. From 1931 to 1937 the UNIVERSITY OF PENNSYLVANIA MUSEUM made an extensive survey of the site of Piedras Negras. On the basis of this work Proskouriakoff made a momentous breakthrough in epigraphy, showing that hieroglyphic texts were historical, relating important events during the reigns of the different kings, and not devoted solely to calendrical or astronomical records as had been believed.

Unfortunately, in spite of the careful excavating methods used in the first half of the twentieth century, excavations were often left without backfilling, and no attempt was made to restore ancient architecture. This was partly due to the difficulties involved in traveling to most of the sites, especially in the Petén area, and also to a lack of regulations requiring restoration; moreover, it was not anticipated that the sites would become tourist attractions (Chinchilla 1999, 111). However, following the political revolution that overthrew Gen. Jorge Ubico in 1944, the government initiated social reforms, founded new institutions, and formulated new laws for the protection of national patrimony. The National Museum of Archaeology and Ethnology was reorganized, and the Institute of Anthropology and History was established for the protection, registration, and investigation of archaeological and colonial national patrimony.

Summary of Archaeological Projects in Guatemala, 1970s to the Present

Site	Location	Institutional Sponsor	Date	Purpose
Rio Chixoy	Northern highlands	French-Guatemalan Archaeological Mission	1970s	Salvage
La Lagunita	Northern highlands	French-Guatemalan Archaeological Mission	1977, 1984	Salvage
Sakajuy and Porton	Northern highlands	University of Pennsylvania	1970–1974	Research
Kaminaljuyu	Central highlands	Pennsylvania State University	1969–1970	Research
Kaminaljuyu San Jorge	Central highlands	Instituto de Antropologia e Historia	1983–1987	Salvage
Kaminaljuyu Miraflores	Central highlands	Instituto de Antropologia e Historia	1995–1997	Salvage
Agua Tibia	Western highlands	Spanish Cultural Mission	1977–1978	Research
Site survey	South coast	University of San Carlos	1980–1990	Research
Monte Alto	South coast	Smithsonian Institution	1969–1971	Research
Cotzumalguapa	South coast	Universities of Valle and Carlos	1986, 1993 to present	Research
La Blanca	South coast	University of California, Berkeley	1985–1986	Research
El Mesak	South coast	Vanderbilt University	1987–1988	Research
Abaj Takalik	South coast	Guatemalan government	1989 to present	Research
Pacific littoral	South coast	Vanderbilt University and University of Valle	1990s	Research
Tikal and Uaxactun	Petén	Guatemalan government	1970 to present	Restoration
Yaxha, Nakum, Naranjo	Petén	Guatemalan government	1990s to present	Restoration
El Mirador	Petén	New World Archaeological Foundation	1980s	Research
Nakbe	Petén	University of California, Los Angeles	1988 to present	Research
Atlas of Peten	Petén	Guatemalan government	1988 to present	Survey
Peten lakes	Petén	National Science Foundation	1979–1999	Research
Peten caves	Petén	University of California, Los Angeles	1982–1988	Research
Rio Azul	Petén	University of Texas	1984–1988	Research
Petexbatun	Petén	Vanderbilt University	1989–1995	Research
Piedras Negras	Petén	Universities of Brigham Young and del Valle	1997 to present	Research
Cancuen	Petén	Vanderbilt University	1999 to present	Research
Joyanca	Petén	French-Guatemalan Archaeological Mission	1999 to present	Salvage
Lake Izabal	Izabal	University of San Carlos	1979–1980	Research
Sansare	Eastern Guatemala	University of San Carlos	1980s to present	Research

New Trends in
Archaeological Investigations

Beginning in the late 1940s and continuing into the present, the Guatemalan government has focused on using archaeological sites to attract tourists. The first of such project was the restoration of the site of Zaculeu, the ancient Mam capital in the northwest highlands, financed from 1946 to 1949 by the United Fruit Company. The French Archaeological Mission carried out a similar project (1959–1974) at Iximche, the Cakchiquel capital in the central highlands at the time of the Spanish conquest, and another at Jilotepeque Viejo (formerly known as Mixco Viejo). The Tikal Project (1956–1969) was undertaken with the idea of developing it as a national park in the Peten, sponsored by the Museum of the University of Pennsylvania; with the cooperation of the Guatemalan government, almost $1 million was obtained for this project from various foundations in the United States (Rainey 1970, 3). In 1970 the project was taken over by the Instituto de Antropologia e Historia, and the investigations continue under Guatemalan direction at the present time, more recently with cooperation from Spain.

In the 1950s the Rockefeller Foundation funded an educational program in archaeology at the Universidad de San Carlos, the national university in Guatemala City, to train professionals in the field. The program was short-lived, but some of the students were able to continue their field training by participating in the Tikal Project. By 1967 the university established a formal program in archaeology in the form of a regular curriculum to obtain a professional degree. From this time forward archaeological field projects increased significantly in all regions in Guatemala. In 1981 the Universidad del Valle initiated its Department of Archaeology, where the Madeleine and Alfred V. Kidder Chair was inaugurated in 1986, providing the funds for student training.

The guerrilla warfare that disrupted Guatemala beginning in the 1960s and continued for the next thirty years seriously interfered with archaeological investigation. The conflicts causing this unrest were settled by the Peace Accords of 1998, which included new regulations concerning rights and public access to "sacred places," often synonymous with pre-Columbian sites. Another public concern in Guatemala is the issue of national identity, and for this theme archaeological, historical, and ethnohistorical information is essential and is receiving more attention. The ethnohistorical studies of the Quiche by Robert Carmack in the 1970s are a good example of the type of work being done in this area. The recently published *Historia General de Guatemala* is helping to incorporate the archaeological, historical, and ethnohistorical information into the educational system at all levels.

A law issued in Guatemala in the early 1980s requires construction companies to finance at least a year of excavation on the land on which they wish to build, especially if it is suspected that archaeological remains are present. The law has facilitated archaeological research in many areas, especially on the south coast and at Kaminaljuyu, located on the southwestern fringe of the modern capital of Guatemala City. Nevertheless, although more public attention is being drawn to archaeological information through education and the media, investigation is being seriously hampered by urban expansion and rampant looting.

The accompanying table presents a summary of some of the archaeological projects carried out in Guatemala since the 1970s.

Matilde Ivic de Monterroso and
Marion Popenoe de Hatch

See also French Archaeology in the Americas
References

Chinchilla, Oswaldo. 1999. "Historia de la investigación arqueologica en Guatemala." In *Historia general de Guatemala,* vol. 1. Guatemala City, Guatemala: Asociación de Amigos del País.

Fuentes y Guzman, Francisco Antonio de. 1933. "Recordacion Florida." *Biblioteca "Goathemala,"* vols. 1, 2, 3. Guatemala: Sociedad de Geografia e Historia.

Luján Muñoz, Luis. 1972. "Historia de la arqueología en Guatemala." *América Indígena* (Instituto Indigenista Americano, México) 32, 2.

Morley, Sylvanus G. 1937–1938. "The History and Modern Exploration of the Department of Petén, Guatemala." In *The Inscriptions of Petén,*

Guatemala. Carnegie Institution of Washington Publication no. 437. Washington, DC.

Rainey, Froelich. 1970. "Tikal: A Fourteen Year Program Now Completed." In *Expedition* (12)2. University Museum of the University of Pennsylvania.

Rubín de la Borbolla, Daniel, and Hugo Cerezo. 1953. *Guatemala: Monumentos históricos y arqueológicos.* Mexico: Instituto Panamericano de Geografía e Historia.

Guo Moruo (1892–1978)

President of the Chinese Academy of Sciences from 1950 until his death in 1978 and Chinese Minister for Culture, Guo Moruo (or Kuo Mojo) was a famous writer, a poet, a cofounder of the literary Creation Society, and a radical who had communist leanings. In 1927 he escaped from CHINA and Chiang Kai-shek's anticommunism to Japan, where he lived in exile for ten years. During his exile he wrote several influential books, *A Study of Ancient Chinese Society* (1930), *A General Outline of Bronze Inscriptions of the Western and Eastern Chou Dynasties* (1932), *A General Study of Oracle Inscriptions* (1933), and *An Illustrated Catalogue of Bronze Inscriptions of the Western and Eastern Chou Dynasties* (1934), which established him as an important scholar of ancient China and some of which remain indispensable reading. Guo was not a field archaeologist, but his first book *A Study of Ancient Chinese Society* (1930) was the first attempt to write a Marxist history of China and was influential in archaeological circles. Both Guo's periodization of ancient Chinese history and production as the basis of society became fundamental to the writing of history and archaeology after 1949, when Marxism became the national and party doctrine.

Tim Murray

See also China

H

Halaf
See Mesopotamia

Hallstatt
See Austria; Switzerland

Hamilton, Sir William (1730–1803)

Hamilton was born into the British aristocracy, becoming an equerry to his foster-brother, the Prince of Wales, later King George III. After serving in the army in Holland, he married a wealthy wife and was briefly a member of Parliament until 1764. At that time he was appointed the British envoy extraordinary and plenipotentiary at the court of Naples in southern ITALY. He was popular at the court, and with little diplomatic work spent most of his time pursuing his interests in volcanoes and antiquities.

Hamilton was elected a fellow of the Royal Society in 1766. He published his observations on volcanoes and presented a collection of volcanic earths and minerals to the BRITISH MUSEUM. Nonetheless, his interest in geology gradually gave way to his passion for the Greek and Roman antiquities of southern Italy. He purchased the outstanding Porchinari family collection in Naples, which he sold to the British Museum in 1772, founding the museum's department of Greek and Roman antiquities. Hamilton also published inventories and pictures of other collections of artifacts, helping to create the fashion for collecting the antiquities of GREECE and Rome among the English and European aristocracy and wealthy middle classes during the late eighteenth and early nineteenth centuries.

Sir William Hamilton (Image Select)

Hamilton spent almost forty years in Naples assembling collections and then selling them. He never saw himself as an antiquarian or an archaeologist. Instead, he valued antiquities as models for modern artists, which also justified his funding of the excavation and plunder of cemeteries, and of Roman sites such as POMPEII and HERCULANEUM. His second collection was sent to England in 1798, and a third was partially lost when the ship carrying it went down. These collections greatly influenced the styles and fashions of the day—from architecture and furniture to fashion and fine arts, with Josiah Wedgwood reproducing elements from them

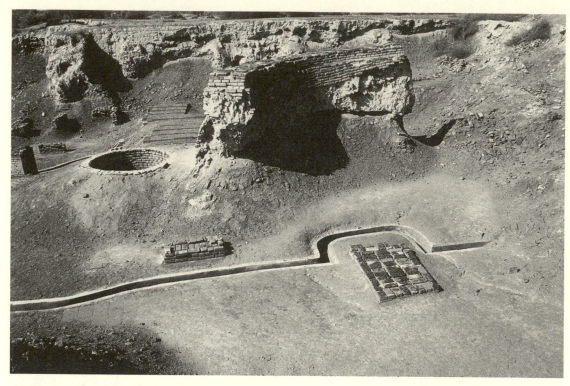

Ancient ruins of Harappa in Pakistan (Corel)

on his "Etruscan" ware in Staffordshire. Hamilton survived the French invasion of Italy and retired to England in 1800, spending his last years living with his second wife, Emma, and her lover, Lord Horatio Nelson.

Tim Murray

See also Britain, Classical Archaeology

Harappa

The type site of the Harappan (INDUS) civilization, Harappa is a major city located in the Punjab, SOUTH ASIA, and is thought to have been at its height between 2500 and 2000 B.C. Harappa was recognized as an archaeological site in 1826, but research had to wait for nearly a century when, between 1920 and 1921, Rai Bahadur Daya Ram Sahni of the Archaeological Survey of India began to explore the site. M. S. Vats continued the work during the time before the beginning of World War II, and after the war, SIR MORTIMER WHEELER, during his time at the Archaeological Survey of India, dug for a season in 1946. Another long hiatus in activity

was broken in 1986 when George Dales began excavations here.

Tim Murray

References
Vats, M. S. 1974. *Excavations at Harappa.* Varanasi: Bhartiya.

Harrington, Jean Carl (1901–1998)

Jean Carl Harrington, known to his colleagues as J. C. or Pinky Harrington, was one of the founders of HISTORICAL ARCHAEOLOGY in the United States. He was the prime builder behind the discipline both with regard to fieldwork and methodology and in the first attempts to intellectually define and position this new type of archaeology. Like all of his contemporaries, Harrington was trained in North American prehistory, specifically under Fay Cooper Cole at the University of Chicago (1932–1936), although he was somewhat unusual in having a formal grounding in architectural engineering and some prior contact (in 1924) with historic sites in the Southwest.

J. C ("Pinky") Harrington in 1940 examining prehistoric artifacts at Jamestown (Courtesy of the National Park Service, Colonial National Historical Park)

In 1936, the Great Depression drew Harrington toward historic sites when the National Park Service hired him, because of his architectural-archaeological background, to direct a new excavation project at JAMESTOWN, VIRGINIA, the first permanent English colony (1607) in North America. Between 1936 and 1941, when World War II halted most excavations in the United States and CANADA, Harrington at Jamestown and his colleagues at other famous sites across the continent experimentally developed basic field techniques, laboratory procedures, and intellectual perspectives for the study of historic Euro-American sites. This emphasis on early and famous individual sites continued after the war when Harrington, with the professional support of his wife, Virginia Sutton Harrington, went on to explore the locations of some of the most recognized events in American history. His site-specific orientation is also seen in his first attempts to name the new field "historic site archaeology."

Although he returned to Jamestown to excavate the glasshouse site in 1949, his next major project involved Sir Walter Raleigh's sixteenth-century fort in North Carolina, which Harrington explored between 1947 and 1950 and published the results in 1962 as "Search for the Cittie of Raleigh" (Harrington 1962). Two years later in western Pennsylvania (1952–1953), he explored a much later colonial site, Fort Necessity, a battlefield during the French and Indian Wars in North America in the middle of the eighteenth century. Harrington's *New Light on Washington's Fort Necessity* (1957) is one of the first professional reports produced in the United States on a Euro-American site, and it stands to this day as a benchmark in the combining of archaeological and archival sources.

Although Harrington worked at many other national sites, including Fort Frederica, West Point (Constitution Island), the Appomattox Courthouse, and the great Mormon nineteenth-century city of Nauvoo on the Mississippi River, he gave equal attention to historic artifacts and assemblages. His "Dating Stem Fragments of Seventeenth and Eighteenth Century Clay Tobacco Pipes" (Harrington 1954) created a new absolute DATING technique with global application.

Outside the laboratory and away from the field Harrington was equally a pioneer. He wrote the first survey of North American historical archaeology in 1952, and the article "Archaeology as an Auxiliary Science to American History" (Harrington 1955) initially defined the field and its relationship to history and the social sciences. He also carried the message of this new area of scholarship to the public in a number of popular articles. He was the first historical archaeologist named in the *National Geographic Magazine* (1942), and his well-written booklet *Archaeology and the Historical Society* (Harrington 1965) was widely distributed.

By January 1967, Harrington was fully retired from his thirty-year career in the National Park Service, but he was still a key player in the founding of the SOCIETY FOR HISTORICAL ARCHAEOLOGY at its organizational meeting that year in Dallas, Texas. That society, in turn, honored Harrington in 1981 when it established the J. C. HARRINGTON MEDAL IN HISTORICAL ARCHAEOLOGY, the highest and most prestigious award given worldwide within the discipline.

Robert L. Schuyler

References

Harrington, J. C. 1954. "Dating Stem Fragments of Seventeenth and Eighteenth Century Clay Tobacco Pipes." *Quarterly Bulletin of the Archaeological Society of Virginia* 9, no. 1: 10–14.

———. 1955. "Archaeology as an Auxiliary Science to American History." *American Anthropologist* 37, nos. 3–4: 181–188.

———. 1962. "Search for the Cittie of Raleigh." *Archaeological Research Series* no. 6. Washington, DC: National Park Service.

———. 1965. *Archaeology and the Historical Society*. American Association for State and Local History.

Hassuna

Tell Hassuna is a prehistoric site found on the Tigris River in northern Iraq. It was first exca-

vated by Seton Lloyd and Fuad Safar during World War II, when Lloyd was an adviser to the Iraq Department of Antiquities. The site is late Neolithic in age (about the sixth millennium B.C.) and is the type site of the Hassuna cultural complex, which features Hassuna, Samarran, and Halaf styles.

Tim Murray

See also Mesopotamia

Haua Fteah

A large cave in Cyrenaica (Libya) excavated by CHARLES MCBURNEY during the 1950s and subsequently extensively published by him. Rich deposits span the Upper Paleolithic (earliest dates on this site from around 47,000 B.C.) to the Holocene. The lowest levels of the site have not been excavated but the complex sequence of stone tool industries defined by McBurney from this site mark it as the most complete in North Africa.

Tim Murray

See also Maghreb

Hawes, Harriet Ann Boyd (1871–1945)

Harriet Hawes was born into a wealthy manufacturing family in New England and graduated from Smith College in 1892. Four years later, inspired by recent excavations on Crete, she joined the AMERICAN SCHOOL OF CLASSICAL STUDIES AT ATHENS. Discovering that female students were unable to participate in the school's excavations and encouraged by English archaeologists SIR ARTHUR EVANS and DAVID HOGARTH, Hawes decided to use her fellowship money to finance her own excavations. She chose a site at Kavousi in eastern Crete, where she excavated early–Iron Age houses and tombs.

The results of her excavations were published in 1897 in the *AMERICAN JOURNAL OF ARCHAEOLOGY* and were the basis of her master's thesis, which she completed at Smith College in 1901. That same year Hawes began to excavate Gournia, a Bronze-Age town that is still the only well-preserved urban Minoan site on Crete. This time, however, she was sponsored by the American Exploration Society of Philadelphia for a number of seasons—1901, 1903, 1904—and the results of her work were published in 1908. Harriet Hawes was not only the first woman to direct an excavation, she was also the first woman to publish her results.

Between 1900 and 1906 Hawes taught archaeology, epigraphy, and modern Greek at Smith College. She married and had two children and continued to publish and teach, first at the University of Wisconsin and then at Dartmouth College (1910–1917). After World War I she became assistant director (from 1919 to 1924) and then associate director (from 1924 to 1934) of the Museum of Fine Arts in Boston. She taught at Wellesley College until 1936. In her later years she was more involved with international and U.S. politics than with archaeology, becoming an active New Dealer in Boston in the 1930s.

Tim Murray

Hawkes, Christopher (1905–1992)

Hawkes was educated at Winchester and New College, Oxford. In 1928 he began working with the Department of British and Medieval Antiquities at the BRITISH MUSEUM as an assistant keeper. This position allowed him to develop an extensive overview of, and familiarity with, a wide range of material and artifacts. Hawkes was one of the national secretaries for the first International Congress for Pre- and Protohistoric Sciences (a forerunner of the International Union of Prehistoric and Protohistoric Sciences) held in London in 1932, publishing, with archaeologist THOMAS D. KENDRICK, *Archaeology in England and Wales 1914–31* and annual summaries of prehistoric research in Britain for the *Archaeological Journal*.

Hawkes came to archaeology through fieldwork, starting with SIR MORTIMER WHEELER in Wales, and then from 1924 to 1928 at St. Catherine's Hill, Winchester, both excavating the chapel and establishing the Iron-Age date of the fortifications. He also worked at Wroxeter, and directed the excavations at Alchester, a small Roman town north of Oxford. From 1930 to 1931 he participated in the excavation of the Iron Age

oppidia (or fortified town) of Camulodunum at Sheepen Hill, Colchester. Hawkes's publication of this work firmly established his expertise in late Iron Age studies. In 1932 Hawkes joined the Fenland Research Committee, the first truly modern prehistoric project in terms of its interdisciplinary scope. He later endorsed GERHARD BERSU's principles of excavation as practiced at Little Woodbury, and rejected Wheeler's overreliance on section/sequence evidence, allying himself with the sociological school of open-area plan-recovery excavations.

Primarily concerned with the problems of protohistoric Europe, Hawkes's archaeology was removed from the pure prehistory practiced by contemporaries GRAHAME CLARK, STUART PIGGOTT, VERE GORDON CHILDE, and GLYN DANIEL. Situated at the cusp of history/prehistory, it was formulated with an awareness of the impact of past migrations, ethnic pluralities, comparative philology, and social stratification. For many, it was the weight given to the historic that ultimately limited Hawkes's prehistory. His book *The Prehistoric Foundations of Europe, to the Mycenean Age* (1940) was both influential on, and comparable to, Childe's *Dawn of European Civilization*, but he was entirely overshadowed by Childe. By the 1960s his advocacy of invasion theory and diffusionism was considered dated.

During World War II Hawkes worked in the Ministry of Aircraft Production. In 1946 he was appointed Oxford University's first professor of European Prehistory. He was elected to the British Academy of Science in 1948. Hawkes established the Oxford Department of Archaeology and, in 1955, its Research Laboratory for Archaeology and the History of Art. Fluent in both French and German, along with Childe, Hawkes was one of the most "continentally" influential British prehistorians and was responsible for the integration of much British material with core European sequences. He retired in 1972.

Christopher Evans

See also Britain, Roman
References
For references, see *Encyclopedia of Archaeology: The Great Archaeologists, Vol. 1,* ed. Tim Murray (Santa Barbara, CA: ABC-CLIO, 1999), pp. 476–479.

Hensel, Witold (1917–)

One of the most eminent Polish archaeologists after World War II, Hensel studied prehistory at the University of Poznan under archaeologist JÓZEF KOSTRZEWSKI, historian Kazimierz Tymieniecki, and ethnographer Eugeniusz Frankowski. While still a student, Hensel took part in excavations conducted by Kóstrzewski at BISKUPIN, and he also participated in research on early Polish medieval sites in Gniezno, Klecko, and Poznan.

Hensel was one of the most important initiators of a huge archaeological and historical research project realized in connection with the commemoration of the anniversary of the millennium of the Polish state and the baptism of Prince Mesco I in A.D. 966. In a 1946 article entitled *Potrzeba przygotowania wielkiej rocznicy* (Need for Preparation of a Great Anniversary), Hensel outlined the main objectives of this research project. He actively participated in the activities of the Management of Studies of the Beginnings of the Polish State, which was changed in 1949 into the Institute of the History of Material Culture, Polish Academy of Sciences. His main scientific interests were focused on the problems of early medieval period, especially issues related to settlement studies, technology, contact, trade and exchange, and the process of creating the proto-classic societies and their transformation into the classic societies of early Piasts. These were western Slavic tribes who united to form small states between A.D. 800 and 960, and came to be ruled by the Piast dynasty, whose descendents ruled greater POLAND from A.D. 1047 until 1386.

Hensel was one of the founders of Slavonic archaeology, as he created the background that was fundamental for the development of the modern discipline in relation to the previous traditions of Polish archaeology. Additionally, that field of interest was one of the most important areas of contact between archaeologists from the former Soviet Union and the Slavonic former socialist countries. He contributed to the origin of a new journal, *Slavia Antiqua,* founded chiefly for the sake of these problems, and became its first and longstanding editor. Hensel also was the first director of the Department of Slavonic Archae-ology at the University of Warsaw, and he contributed very effectively to the dynamic development of Slavonic archaeology in other Slavonic countries. He was one of the main initiators and organizers of the International Congress of Slavic Archaeology, held in 1965 in Warsaw, and he was elected the first president of an International Union of Slavic Archaeology.

After World War II, Hensel advocated the introduction of Marxist methodology into Polish archaeology. This methodology was to serve as a platform for an integrated archaeology of Poland, including classical archaeology and ethnography within the history of material culture. Hensel was also interested in the periodization of Polish prehistory as he wished to reconcile traditional archaeological chronological divisions with the general divisions of history originated by Friedrich Engels and LEWIS HENRY MORGAN. He devoted a great deal of time to the history of archaeology, and to the methodology of archaeological enquiry, and in the latter area he was to initiate microregional analysis.

Hensel was an active supporter of international cooperation in historical archaeology, and he was an active organizer. In 1953, he became a member of as organizational committee to establish the Institute of the History of Material Culture at the Polish Academy of Sciences. From 1954 to 1989 he was director of the institute, which was the central, largest, and the most important archaeological institution in POLAND, and under his supervision, the institute became the center for Polish archaeology. His other duties included working at and then becoming director of the Department of Archaeology at the University of Poznan (1945–1954). He was director of the Department of Slavonic Archaeology from 1956 to 1965 and director of the Department of Prehistoric and Early Mediaeval Archaeology at the University of Warsaw from 1965 to 1970.

He is a full member of the Polish Academy of Sciences; editor of the archaeological journals *Slavia Antiaqua, Archaeologia Polona, Polskie Badania Archeologiczne* (Polish Archaeological Research), and *Swiatowit;* and a member of editorial committees for other Polish and foreign journals. Hensel remains an active member of

Excavation leading to the remains of Herculaneum (Ann Ronan Picture Library)

many societies and institutions both scientific and social, for example, the International Union of Pre- and Protohistorical Sciences and the International Committee of Slavists, and he was a president of Archeologia Urbium.

Hensel has been one of the most productive Polish archaeologists of the postwar period, and has excavated in Poland (e.g., Czersk, Kruszwica, Poznan) and abroad (e.g., Algiers, Algeria; Styrmen, BULGARIA; St. Jean-le-Froid, FRANCE; Cappacio Vecchia, and ITALY).

Arkadiusz Marciniak

Herculaneum

Herculaneum, like POMPEII, was a Roman town in the Bay of Naples, destroyed by the eruption of Vesuvius in A.D. 79. The eruption followed a slightly different course at Herculaneum, where a final flow of volcanic mud buried the site much more deeply than Pompeii (over 20 meters deep in places). This has made excavation much more difficult but often more rewarding, since carbonized perishable material is much better preserved at Herculaneum.

The site was discovered during the digging of a well in 1709. But lime burners seeking marble for their kilns displayed more interest in the find than did archaeologists, and systematic excavations only began in 1738, at the command of the Bourbon king Charles III. The theater and basilica were discovered in these early excavations, which were made by tunneling. The most sensational find came in 1750 in the form of the Villa of the Papyri (upon whose design the J. PAUL GETTY MUSEUM in Malibu, California, is based). The villa was packed with bronze sculptures, including a number of portraits of philosophers. Even more remarkable were the hundreds of papyrus scrolls, found carbonized but largely legible. They are mainly works by the Epicurean philosopher Philodemos. The villa may originally have been owned by the father-in-law of Julius Caesar, L. Calpurnius Piso, a patron of Philodemos.

Karl Weber might be considered the first semiprofessional archaeologist to work on the buried Roman cities around Vesuvius. A Swiss military engineer who had enlisted as a mercenary in Naples in 1743, he was in charge of the excavations at Herculaneum (as well as Pompeii and Stabiae) between 1750 and 1764. He oversaw the excavation of the Villa of the Papyri and produced detailed and accurate plans and other documentation. In this period of treasure hunting for the royal collections, Weber was unusual for his interest in the archaeological context of his discoveries. The Academia Herculanensis was founded in 1755 for the discussion and publication of the finds. The eight volumes of *Le antichità di Ercolano esposte,* published between 1757 and 1792, had a dramatic effect on contemporary taste in Europe and the United States.

The foul air in the tunnels may have hastened Weber's death, and work was halted on the Villa of the Papyri in 1764 because of the fumes. Herculaneum was at that time beginning to be overshadowed by the finds at Pompeii and other sites buried by Vesuvius. Excavation has been rather fitful since that time, characterized by long breaks—for example, between 1780 and 1828 and 1876 and 1927.

Excavation in open trenches began in 1828 and was carried out on a large scale by Amadeo Maiuri between 1927 and 1958. The picture of Herculaneum that emerged was not of a prosperous commercial and industrial town like Pompeii but rather of a seaside resort. Public buildings were few and large, luxurious houses were restricted to the seafront. Dozens of skeletons (otherwise rare in Herculaneum) have recently been discovered on the ancient shoreline in front of the town, but generally excavation since the 1960s has been conducted on a modest scale. There is enthusiasm in some quarters for continuing the excavation of the Villa of the Papyri after a break of almost 250 years. The recovery of further papyri bearing ancient literature that otherwise has been completely lost is a very strong lure. The cost, however, would be enormous, and the project has been opposed by many who believe that state funds would be better spent on restoration and conservation. The excavation may proceed with private funding from the United States.

Ted Robinson

References

Grant, M. 1971. *Cities of Vesuvius: Pompei and Herculaneum.* New York: Macmillan.

Parslow, C. C. 1995. *Rediscovering Antiquity: Karl Weber and the Excavation of Herculaneum, Pompeii, and Stabiae.* New York: Cambridge University Press.

Hewett, Edgar Lee (1865–1946)

A pivotal figure in U.S. archaeology in the early part of the twentieth century, Edgar Lee Hewett is best known for his political influence and dominating personality. Although largely ignored by recent historical syntheses, his influence on the character of archaeology in the American Southwest was far reaching.

Hewett was born in 1865 in Warren County, Illinois, and received a bachelor's degree from Tarkio College in Missouri and a master's degree in pedagogy from the Colorado State Normal School in 1898. His initial experience in archaeology was avocational, acquired while traveling by wagon through the Southwest on summer holidays in the 1890s. His appointment as first president of the New Mexico State Normal School in Las Vegas in 1898 provided an institutional base for fieldwork as well as for the establishment of relationships with a number of prominent important political figures in New Mexico Territory.

While serving in that position, Hewett established a reputation as an advocate for archaeological work, which until that time had largely been conducted by expeditions from eastern universities and museums. His attempts to establish local control over excavations in the region, such as those at CHACO CANYON, brought him into conflict with those institutions. On a national level, Hewett became allied with cultural nationalists and nontraditional scholars such as Charles Lummis and Alice Fletcher, heralding splits within the archaeological community along regional and class lines that became more evident following 1900.

Hewett's early field research concentrated on the Pajarito Plateau of northern New Mexico, an area that had been explored earlier by Adolph Bandelier, and some of the important sites in the region were subsequently preserved by the creation of Bandelier National Monument in 1916. Small-scale soundings may have been conducted in the region as early as 1895, and in the subsequent twenty years, excavations were conducted at the major prehistoric pueblos of Puye, Tyounyi, Yapashi, Long House, Tsankawi, and several smaller sites.

When his term of office at the New Mexico

Tiered cliff dwellings at Bandelier National Monument (© Michael T. Sedam / CORBIS)

Normal School was not renewed, Hewett enrolled in graduate studies at the University of Geneva and received his doctorate from there in 1908. The following ten years were the most influential period of his life. Hewett was one of the major architects of the Antiquities Act of 1906, which for the first time provided federal legislative means for the protection of prehistoric remains. His lobbying efforts on behalf of the bill successfully brought together disparate elements of the scholarly community, and a fellowship from the American Institute of Archae-

ology (AIA) was awarded to Hewett in 1906, which allowed him to conduct his political negotiations, popular lectures, and peripatetic field research. For the next several years he appears to have been the principal arbiter of archaeological research in the southwestern region of the United States.

In 1907, Hewett overcame considerable resistance on the part of several prominent archaeologists and was named as the first director of the AIA's School of American Archaeology (later renamed the School of American Research). Resentment over this appointment affected Hewett's relationship with his peers for decades. The school was installed in the Palace of the Governors in Santa Fe, New Mexico, where Hewett maintained a base for the rest of his life. The school's essential function was the training of students in archaeological field methods. The related Frijoles Canyon field school, which functioned between 1908 and 1913, was one of the first of its kind in the United States, and it served as an educational and intellectual center for archaeology in the region. Several future leaders of the discipline, such as ALFRED VINCENT KIDDER, SYLVANUS MORLEY, Neil Judd, and Jesse Nusbaum, participated in its activities. Hewett subsequently conducted field schools through the University of New Mexico in the Jemez region and in Chaco Canyon in the 1920s and early 1930s.

Throughout his career, Hewett demonstrated a talent for amassing institutional appointments. These included the directorship of the Museum of New Mexico from 1909 until his death; director of exhibits for the Pan-American Exhibition in San Diego, California (1911); and faculty positions at the State Teacher's College in San Diego, California (1922), University of New Mexico (1927), and the University of Southern California (1932). He was also closely involved with popular archaeological journals of the day, such as *Art and Archaeology,* and traveled a strenuous lecture circuit.

With its emphasis on regional, rather than national, institutions and on the importance of building a popular constituency for the conduct of archaeology, Hewett's philosophy ran counter to broader trends within the discipline, which was evolving from a broadly defined community with avocational roots into a smaller, professional cadre based in major universities and museums. Ultimately, Hewett's establishment of the School of American Research, the Museum of New Mexico, and several departments of anthropology created the institutions from which much of the archaeology in the Southwest has subsequently been conducted. It is this work that is his principal legacy.

James Snead

References

Bloom, Lansing B., ed. 1939. *So Live the Works of Men.* Festschrift volume; includes a complete bibliography. Albuquerque: University of New Mexico Press.

Chauvenet, Beatrice. 1983. *Hewett and Friends: A Biography of Santa Fe's Vibrant Era.* Albuquerque: Museum of New Mexico Press.

Hewett, E. L. 1946. *Two Score Years.* Albuquerque: University of New Mexico Press.

———. 1993. *Ancient Communities of the Southwestern Desert.* Albuquerque: Archaeological Society of New Mexico.

Hinsley, Curtis M., Jr. 1985. "Edgar Lee Hewett and the School of American Archaeology in Santa Fe, 1906–1912." In *American Archaeology Past And Future,* 217–236. Ed. David J. Meltzer, Don L. Fowler, and Jeremy A. Sabloff. Washington, DC: Smithsonian Institution Press.

Lee, Ronald F. 1970. *The Antiquities Act of 1906.* Washington, DC: National Park Service, Office of History and Historic Architecture, Eastern Service Center.

Mathien, Joan. 1991a. "Glimpses into the History of the 1908 Fieldwork at Yapashi, Bandelier National Monument." In *Puebloan Past and Present, Papers in Honor of Stewart Peckham,* 121–132. Ed. Meliha S. Duran and David T. Kirkpatrick. Papers of the Archaeological Society of New Mexico no. 17.

———. 1991b. "Three Months on the Jemez Plateau: An Account of Edgar Lee Hewett's 1905 Field Season." In *Clues to the Past: Papers in Honor of William M. Sundt,* 185–202. Ed. Meliha S. Duran and David T. Kirkpatrick. Papers of the Archaeological Society of New Mexico no. 16.

Rothman, Hal. 1988. *Bandelier National Monument: An Administrative History.* Southwest Cultural Resources Center Professional Papers no. 14. Santa Fe, NM: National Park Service.

———. 1989. *Preserving Different Pasts: The American National Monuments.* Urbana: University of Illinois Press.

Hieroglyphics

See Champollion, Jean-François; Maya Epigraphy

Higgs, Eric (1908–1976)

Eric Higgs did not take up archaeology as a full-time career until the age of 47. He had a degree in agricultural economics from London University, and had worked as a professional card player, builder, and farmer. In 1954 Higgs began a two-year postgraduate program in prehistory at Cambridge University, studying with GRAHAME CLARK and CHARLES MCBURNEY, who fostered his interests in the Paleolithic and the economic approach to prehistory.

Higgs participated in the final season of excavations at the cave of HAUA FTEAH in Libya with McBurney in 1955, becoming a research assistant in the Department of Archaeology and Anthropology, senior assistant in 1963, and assistant director of research from 1968 until 1972, when he retired. Higgs founded the Cambridge "Bone Room," which was the nearest that the university came to having archaeological laboratory facilities in the 1960s and 1970s. This provided the main focus for undergraduate teaching in practical work for many generations of students.

Between 1962 and 1967 Higgs carried out major fieldwork in the Epirus region of northwest GREECE that encouraged the development of paleo-geographic and paleo-economic approaches to the archaeological record. From 1967 to 1976 Higgs was director of the "Early History of Agriculture Project," housed in the Department of Archaeology, which consumed most of the funds then available for what was later to become known in Britain as "science-based archaeology." In his role as advocate of a more science-based methodology, he also edited jointly with Don Brothwell *Science in Archaeology,* one of the earliest comprehensive texts on the use of scientific methods in archaeology. Eric Higgs was a provocative and influential colleague and teacher, whose impact, despite only twenty years in archaeology, is still evident.

Geoff Bailey

References

For references, see *Encyclopedia of Archaeology: The Great Archaeologists,* Vol. 1, ed. Tim Murray (Santa Barbara, CA: ABC-CLIO, 1999), pp. 558–565.

Hildebrand, Bror Emil (1806–1884)

Swedish numismatist Bror Emil Hildebrand was a graduate of Lund University, the center for scientific archaeology in SWEDEN during the first half and middle of the nineteenth century. Hildebrand first worked on the collections in the museum at Lund, and then was appointed chief custodian of National Antiquities in Stockholm in 1837. His expansion of the national collection during the 1840s and 1850s was the result not only of both agricultural land reclamations and methodical excavations, but also of his intention to create a national and scientific archaeological collection. As early as 1850 Hildebrand consulted Danish archaeologist CHRISTIAN JÜRGENSEN THOMSEN and reorganized the archaeological collections at Lund and Stockholm based on Thomsen's THREE-AGE SYSTEM.

By the 1860s the Stockholm archaeological collection was remarkable for its quality and breadth—both of which were to influence the research of the next generation of Swedish archaeologists such as OSCAR MONTELIUS and B. E. Hildebrand's son, HANS HILDEBRAND. Because Sweden did not have the Roman monuments that absorbed the archaeological interest of much of the rest of Europe, its attitude to, and care of, prehistoric material were exemplary. The homogeneity of prehistoric cultures in Sweden also meant that its collections provided an overall picture of source material and evidence of local variations. So both general and typical artifact features were easily traced, and were in fact were more accessible than ever before—as greater proportions of collections of artifacts were on exhibition during the nineteenth century than they ever have been since then.

Hildebrand's achievements in museology were more than well matched by his abilities as an outstanding numismatist. In fact he may not have been as effective in his museum role had he not had a numismatic background. In this area, once again Hildebrand was influenced by Thomsen, classifying coins in Copenhagen under Thomsen's personal supervision in 1830 and completing his doctoral thesis *Numismata Anglo-Saxonica* (Anglo Saxon Coins) based on work by one of Thomsen's students. Hildebrand also realized the value of coins for dating native artifacts and ancient remains from the Iron Age that were found with them. In his early numismatic works on Roman coins found in Scandinavia, Hildebrand argued that the silver denarii must have been deposited before the third century A.D., and that the coins, like other Roman products, must have reached the north via direct or indirect trade with Roman territories and not by any other means. The grouping of the different flows of imported coins during the Iron Age became an important starting point for determining Iron Age chronology. Hildebrand completed a preliminary classification of the more important groups of coins, and went on to classify Scandinavian coin finds into four main detailed classes—the basis for later Swedish archaeologists' development of a chronology for the Iron Age.

Tim Murray

See also Evans, Sir John

Hildebrand, Hans (1842–1913)

Archaeologist, numismatist, historian, museum curator, and director, and very much like his father, BROR EMIL HILDEBRAND, Hans Hildebrand graduated from the University of Uppsala in 1865 and received his doctorate in 1866. Hildebrand studied botany, geology, mineralogy, mathematics, and astronomy as well as the humanities at university, and was an early member of the Natural Science Society. He was also interested in geology and paleontology—contentious subjects in Europe at the time of his graduation. In 1862 he accompanied his father and the anthropologist Gustaf Retzius to London and visited HENRY CHRISTY, English banker and partner of the French archaeologist ÉDOUARD LARTET. The three Swedes examined the newest Paleolithic finds of Britain and FRANCE and borrowed literature on the subject from Christy. With his father Hans had visited Paris the year before, where they had no doubt heard the debates about JACQUES BOUCHER DE PERTHES's stone tool finds at Abbeville. He returned to SWEDEN with a strong interest in the earliest history of humanity.

Hans Hildebrand was introduced to numismatics at an early age by his father, and his doctoral thesis *The Swedish People in Heathen Times* (1866) was on Iron Age coins. He was unique in his knowledge of both numismatics and archaeological data from the field and in the museum context. Between 1865 and 1866 Hans and OSCAR MONTELIUS helped B. E. Hildebrand reorganize the Iron Age exhibition in the National Antiquities Museum in Stockholm.

Hans Hildebrand is known as the originator of archaeological "typology." Unlike his colleague, the great Swedish typologist Oscar Montelius, Hildebrand was not interested in using typology to further chronological research and methodology. He was interested in the methodology of classifying prehistoric material culture. In his essay *The Early Iron Age in Norrland* (1869), Hildebrand used numerous typological descriptions of artifacts and proposed their DATING via their find contexts. He also used analogies with other artifacts from coin and bog sites from other parts of Scandinavia to create a descriptive typology. In *Towards a History of the Fibula* (1871) Hans Hildebrand argued, on the basis of descriptive typology, that the Hallstatt and LA TÈNE complexes were two successive horizons at the end of the Bronze Age and the beginning of the Iron Age in central and northern Europe. In 1874, as General Secretary of the International Archaeological Congress in Stockholm, he went on to suggest that both the Hallstatt and La Tène complexes were chronological and cultural concepts.

Like his father, Hildebrand was an advocate for the central and national collection of archaeological material in SWEDEN, the subject of *Scientific Archaeology, Its Task, Requirement and Rights* (1873), written on his return from his second Grand European Tour. In this pamphlet Hildebrand introduced the term *typology* into archaeology and stressed the importance of central museums for the development of scientific archaeology and the typological method. Other European countries such as England, France, and, later, Germany did not have national collections, and Hildebrand understood that they were one of the main reasons that Sweden dominated and led the development of prehistoric archaeology during the nineteenth century.

Hans Hildebrand used the term and concept of archaeological typology in the first section of his great book *The Prehistoric Peoples of Europe* (1873–1880). But it was his great knowledge and synthesis of anthropology, paleontology, geology, and Paleolithic prehistory in this book that was probably more remarkable—it was one of the first examples of a modern European prehistory.

In 1879 Hildebrand succeeded his father as the King's Custodian of Antiquities and director of the National Museum, a position he held until 1906. His book *Medieval Sweden* (1879–1903) remains essential reading today.

Tim Murray

Hissarlik

See Blegen, Carl William; Dorpfeld, Wilhelm; Schliemann, Heinrich; Turkey

Historical Archaeology

Historical archaeology as the archaeology of the modern world involves the excavation of sites and analysis of assemblages dating from approximately the last half millennium of human cultural history. Ironically, two of its distinctive hallmarks, its worldwide scope and the interconnected nature of its subject matter, are shared only with Paleolithic archaeology. This topical unity derives from three overlapping phases of modern world history: the early emergence and spread of major cultural innovations across Europe, Asia, and North Africa between A.D. 1400 and 1600; the subsequent creation of the first truly global world system, primarily a product of European expansion between A.D. 1500 and 1800; and the transformation of this planetary cultural system as a result of the Industrial Revolution (A.D. 1800 to the present).

Because the formation of the modern world spans six centuries and occurred at different times in different places, historical archaeology currently has a number of distinct subfields: postmedieval archaeology in Europe, archaeology of the colonial period in the New World (and by extension elsewhere), industrial archaeology in Europe and North America, and the exploration of post-1400 shipwrecks and submerged sites by underwater archaeologists around the world. Potential new subfields, such as Ottoman archaeology and archaeology of the twentieth century, are on the horizon.

Like its subject matter, historical archaeology arrived late in the sequence, and thus its professional history is limited to the twentieth century. Geographically, it is most developed in North America, with a continuous history extending back to the Great Depression of the 1930s; in western Europe and Oceania (Australia), it appeared only in the 1960s. Outside of Europe, in other regions of ancient Old World civilizations, it is almost nonexistent. With the exception of early work in the West Indies, the field is visible but only now developing in Latin America and parts of sub-Saharan Africa. A discussion of this discipline must therefore concentrate on North America.

Disciplinary Roots

In North America, historical archaeology has two separate but interrelated origins: the excavation of historic contact–Indian sites and the study of the archaeological record left by Europeans and other Old World peoples in the New World. Numerous encounters with both types of sites, and in a few instances excavation of historic sites, occurred in North America during the seventeenth, eighteenth, and nineteenth centuries. After the Pilgrims arrived in 1620, they dug into local burial mounds and found combinations of aboriginal artifacts and European trade goods. After the American Revolution and the closing of the colonial period, a British boundary commission in 1796 excavated the 1604 site of the du-Monts and Champlain colony in CANADA on the St. Croix River in an attempt to set the border between the new United States and British Canada. Examples of such work on historic sites increased in the nineteenth century, and in 1856, John Hall, a civil engineer, scientifically excavated the foundation of Myles Standish's house in Duxbury, Massachusetts. Hall not only made a site plan and noted stratigraphy but also plotted the location of individual artifacts.

Such incidents, although numerous and as yet poorly researched, were still isolated and disconnected. One of the two traditions behind the rise of historical archaeology, the excavation of contact sites, began to be carried out continuously in regions like the Southwest in the later nineteenth century, but it was not until the first half of the twentieth century that researchers influenced by the direct historical approach and the rise of ethnohistory were significantly drawn to historic Native American sites and the study of European trade goods. WILLIAM DUNCAN STRONG and his colleagues on the Great Plains, JAMES A. FORD in the Southeast and, slightly earlier, ALFRED V. KIDDER in New Mexico began to examine historic contact sites in an attempt to link known ethnographic groups with prehistoric sequences. Nevertheless, although there were rare exceptions—like Arthur Woodward, who in 1927 started a lifelong study of historic trade goods and industries—few of these excavators gave primary attention to the historic period. Investigation of contact situations would have likely remained a footnote appended to North American prehistoric studies except that in 1930 a major crisis in world society transformed American archaeology.

The Great Depression of 1930 through 1941 and the following post–World War II years massively expanded the number and, more important, the variety of historic sites being excavated by professional archaeologists in North America, and for the first time, the second origin of the field, work on famous European and Euro-American historic sites, rapidly assumed centrality in the creation of an autonomous discipline. Earlier events helped to set the stage. Passage of the 1906 Antiquities Act, which protected historic as well as prehistoric sites, and the 1916 establishment of the National Park Service (NPS) put key elements in place. A few locally or privately organized projects that included archaeology were already under way, such as John D. Rockefeller's 1927 funding of the restoration of colonial WILLIAMSBURG, but it was the 1932 election of the Franklin D. Roosevelt administration, its numerous programs to combat the Great Depression, and the related 1935 Historic Sites Act that opened the door to historical archaeology.

Significant federal funding of some government programs, including the Civilian Conservation Corps, Works Progress Administration, and the Tennessee Valley Authority, and a desire to reemphasize national heritage in the development of national (and some state) parks and monuments meant that a growing number of archaeologists began to work on historic sites across the United States. These researchers shared a set of common traits: they were professionally trained archaeologists, they were specialists in North American prehistory, they had been educated within an anthropological tradition, and they lacked prior knowledge of historic artifacts and architecture. Because of this common background and new institutional sponsorship supplied by the NPS, which was assigned a central role in organizing projects, these archaeologists formed a small but integrated community of professionals.

As prehistorians they spent the two decades before and after World War II inventing American historical archaeology from whole cloth. The excavation of famous and nationally significant Euro-American sites began, such as G. Hubert Smith's 1936 work at Fort Ridgely in the Midwest, A. R. Kelly's 1933 excavation of the Macon Trading Post in the Southeast, Harvey R. Harwood's 1934 exploration of La Purisima Mission on the West Coast, and Preston Holder's 1941 testing at Appomattox Courthouse in Virginia. Some of the archaeologists did one or two projects and then returned to prehistoric research, but a small number made an exclusive commitment to the historic period.

Harrington at Jamestown

One of the converts, JEAN CARL HARRINGTON (1911–1998), can be considered the founder of historical archaeology in the United States. He was similar to his colleagues in that he had trained in prehistoric archaeology and anthropology under Fay Cooper Cole at the University of Chicago but dissimilar in that he had a prior background in architectural engineering and one season of undergraduate experience in the restoration and recording of historic missions in the Southwest. When offered an NPS position at JAMESTOWN, where a project started in 1934

A 1938 photograph of J. C. Harrington and his wife, Virginia Sutton Harrington, explaining the foundations of Structure 83, Jamestown, to visitors to Virginia's seventeenth-century colonial capital. Virginia Harrington was the first woman park ranger in the National Park Service, and she was instrumental in opening the Jamestown excavations (1936–1941) to the public. (Courtesy of the National Park Service, Colonial National Historical Park)

was floundering because of conflicts between excavators and architectural historians, Harrington was at first reluctant to be assigned to such a "recent" site, but once he took command in 1936, he started a thirty-year-long building of American historical archaeology.

Between 1936 and 1941, as Harrington conducted extensive excavations at Virginia's first colonial capital (1607–1698), he developed basic field techniques for exploring historic sites with belowground architectural remains. He also started the difficult process of gaining knowledge of historic artifacts and tried to bring the results of the Jamestown project to the public through popular publications. His *Field and Laboratory Guide for Recording Archaeological Data* (1940) was a starting point for later NPS projects—for instance, it was adopted by Thomas R. Garth in his 1947 excavations at the Whitman Mission (1836–1847) near Walla Walla, Washington.

Work at Jamestown and other sites across North America halted in 1941 with the coming of war, but after World War II Harrington carried out excavations on a number of equally famous sites. Between 1947 and 1950 he skillfully excavated Sir Walter Raleigh's earthen fort (1585) on the coast of North Carolina, and between 1952 and 1953 he uncovered the small but nationally significant French and Indian War site of Fort Necessity (1754) in western Pennsylvania. His 1957 *New Light on Washington's Fort Necessity* was a classic site report that skillfully combined archaeological and documentary sources to fully reconstruct the fort on paper and on the ground. His research on historic artifacts including glass, tiles, and bricks parallels his advances in fieldwork, and in 1954, he published an innovative article on clay pipe chronology that allowed a worldwide DATING of seventeenth- and eighteenth-century sites.

Harrington's pioneer position went far beyond his fieldwork and material culture studies, for he defined and synthesized historical archaeology as a recognized intellectual endeavor. His article "Archaeology as an Auxiliary Science to American History" (Harrington 1955) established the importance of such research as a contribution to both history and science. Harrington viewed the field as properly centered on Euro-American, not contact-Indian, sites and most naturally tied into the specificity of history although he did recognize its anthropological potential. His suggested name for this new specialization, "historic site archaeology," highlights his theoretical position.

By the early 1950s, Harrington and his colleagues, including among others Louis Caywood in the Northwest, Arthur Woodward in the Southwest, John W. Griffin and Hale G. Smith working for the Florida Park Service in the Southeast, and Carlyle Smith on the Great Plains, had created historical archaeology as an established area of research. Work on historic Indian sites continued as an important theme, for example, George I. Quimby's study of trade goods in the Great Lakes region and the excavation of sites like the Hopi historic pueblo and mission of Awatovi between 1935 and 1939. KENNETH E. KIDD's 1941 excavations on a famous Jesuit mission site (1639–1649) in Ontario and his subsequent 1949 publication of *The Excavation of Ste Marie I,* probably the first site report in the field issued in book form, launched historical archaeology in Canada.

1960–1970: A Decade of Transition

By 1960 historical archaeology had been established as a research topic, but it was not yet professionally set off as a specialty. Ten years later it was a successfully organized, separate, publicly visible, and rapidly expanding, if small, discipline within anthropology. Four developments during the 1960s brought about this transformation: new institutional housing for the field, expansion of its subject matter, entrance into the academic world (which allowed formal training and education in the field), and professional autonomy with the founding of several scholarly associations.

After 1960, historical archaeologists found new positions in federal agencies outside the NPS in the United States and the newly active National Historic Sites Service in Canada, and individual states, such as Florida, California, and Texas, entered the field. In Texas, for example, the Office of State Archaeologist was established in 1965, and the Texas Historical Survey (after 1972 the Texas Historical Commission) had started exploring land and underwater sites by the end of the decade. Perhaps more significant, the field was brought into the academic world, as is exemplified by the career of JOHN L. COTTER (1911–1999). Like his predecessors, Cotter had a long worked on prehistoric, including Paleo-Indian, sites before he was assigned by the NPS to direct the second major project at Jamestown (1954–1956). By 1960, he was at the NPS office in Philadelphia, and that year, at the request of the Department of American Civilization at the University of Pennsylvania, he taught the first class in the United States to carry the title "Historical Archaeology." Within the next few years, other courses were introduced at Arizona by Arthur Woodward, Harvard by Stephen Williams, University of Florida by Charles Fairbanks, Illinois State University by Edward B. Jelks, University of California–Santa Barbara by JAMES DEETZ, and University of Idaho by Roderick Sprague.

The subject matter of historical archaeology began to expand in the same decade. Excavators began to move beyond famous national heritage sites and limiting archaeology to restoration functions at such prominent locations. A telling example of this enlargement is the work of BERNARD L. FONTANA and his colleagues at JOHNNY WARD'S RANCH in Arizona. These adobe ruins were originally selected as possibly being one of the oldest Jesuit sites in the area, but when the structure turned out to be a late American ranch house (1858–1903), the project was not abandoned but its purpose and goals were changed. Publication of "Johnny Ward's Ranch: A Study in Historic Archaeology" (1962) marked one of the first reports on a common type of Anglo-American site in the West, and the detailed analysis of the recovered assemblage became a classic guide for later-nineteenth-century artifacts.

Another influence transforming historical archaeology, and its selection of sites, during the 1960s and 1970s was culture theory. This field had emerged between 1930 and 1960 when the culture-history paradigm dominated anthropological archaeology. Historical archaeologists easily worked within this perspective, and their emphasis on discrete events and famous sites, attention to specific questions derived more from history than from anthropology, and their successful attempts to chronologically place artifact types and date historic assemblages matched similar goals among prehistorians.

In the mid-1960s, just as historical archaeology was achieving separate professional standing, the impact of the "new" or processual archaeology radically changed all American archaeology. The relationship between historical archaeology and this fundamental paradigm shift was complex and somewhat misleading. The study of historic sites seemed to play a central role in the movement—even LEWIS BINFORD, the founder of processual archaeology, had dug at Fort Michilimackinac (1959) and had attempted to refine Harrington's pipe-stem dating system—and in the middle of the decade, "new archaeology" was thought to have two equally innovative coconsuls: Lewis Binford and James J. F. Deetz.

That perception was erroneous and is clarified when the orientations of Deetz and an equally important contemporary, Stanley South, are contrasted. South, who had known Binford as a fellow student, converted to processualism, and his development of pattern recognition and his advocacy of quantitative methods reflected a desire to make historical archaeology more scientific and processual. He advanced this goal at a number of archaeological forums he organized in the late 1960s and explicitly outlined it in his book *Method and Theory in Historical Archaeology* (1977).

Deetz, by contrast, was never a processualist. His 1960 Ph.D. dissertation, published as *The Dynamics of Stylistic Change in Arikara Ceramic* (Deetz 1965), corresponded to, and probably predated, attempts by Binford's students in the Southwest to reconstruct prehistoric social organization from archaeological remains. His prominent research on New England gravestone seriation and the evolution of mortuary art also seemed processual in its quantitative nature and potential for testing specific hypotheses and models. Nevertheless, Deetz's theoretical orientation, unlike that of Binford and South, and his interpretative, cultural, and humanistic perspective more accurately foreshadowed the postprocessual archaeology of the 1980s and 1990s than did Binfordian positivism.

During the 1960s and 1970s, the field practices and concepts of most historical archaeologists more closely matched the view of IVOR NOËL HUME, an English archaeologist at colonial Williamsburg, as outlined in his book *Historical Archaeology* (Hume 1969). Those archaeologists were, and are to this day, historicalist and particularistic in practice and theory. A few visible figures, such as Stanley South, Charles Cleland, and James Fitting, were explicitly processual, but a more dynamic veneer of symbolic-structuralist interpretation, created by Deetz, his students, and a few colleagues, especially the folklorist Henry Glassie, highlighted the field and brought it to the attention of general anthropologists.

Historical archaeologists were not only studying past social organization and behavior in the 1960s, they were also socially organizing themselves. In 1960, Stanley South founded the very active if somewhat informal Conference on Historic Site Archaeology, which met from 1960 to 1982. Its *Conference Papers* and organized forums were the intellectual center of the field across the decade and well into the 1970s. The conference was national in scope but regionally based in the Southeast, and in 1966, a more clearly regional group, the Council for Northeast Historical Archaeology, was initiated in New York State.

In January 1967, in Dallas, Texas, historical archaeology was finally given an autonomous and viable base. At the invitation of Edward B. Jelks, almost all the leading figures in the field, constituting a "committee of fifteen," came together at Southern Methodist University and successfully organized the SOCIETY FOR HISTORICAL ARCHAEOLOGY (SHA). For the next thirty years this international association, clearly separate from the SOCIETY FOR AMERICAN ARCHAEOL-

OGY and its domination by prehistorians, served as the crucial organization in nurturing and building the discipline. The SHA was soon joined by the smaller Society for Post-Medieval Archaeology (1966–1967) in Europe, the Society for Australian Historical Archaeology (1970) in Oceania, and more-specialized associations such as the Society for Industrial Archaeology (1972) in America.

1970–2000

American historical archaeology entered the 1970s as an organized and expanding discipline but still clearly secondary to prehistoric studies. The influence of anthropology and various cultural themes initiated in the previous decade now greatly enriched the field and its public appeal, and entirely new topics were added to its subject matter. The study of ethnicity and "peoples without history" began with the work of Charles Fairbanks and his graduate students on mestizo sections of St. Augustine, Florida, and slave plantations of the Old South, and their excavations created a distinct topical specialization on the archaeology of African Americans. Roberta Greenwood and her colleagues started to explore overseas Chinese sites, and urban archaeology, traceable to the early work of Arnold Pilling in Detroit and John Cotter in Philadelphia, now spread to other cities on the East Coast (New York City; Alexandria, Virginia; Paterson, New Jersey; and Lowell, Massachusetts) and in the West (Tucson, Arizona; Ventura and Sacramento, California).

Topical additions to subject matter occurred as the result of a general debate, begun in the late 1960s, concerning the merits of a "historicalist" versus an anthropological framework for the growing discipline; by the end of the 1970s, the debate was clearly decided in favor of anthropology. In 1977, Deetz published *In Small Things Forgotten: The Archaeology of Early American Life*, the first book on the subject to achieve substantial public sales, and in 1978, the first source book for the field, *Historical Archaeology: A Guide to Theoretical and Substantive Contributions*, reprinted thirty-five classic papers and served as a text or supplementary text throughout the 1980s.

During the 1980s and 1990s, new topics—the archaeology of gender, class, race, and labor—were added to continuing work on sites ranging from the contact period to the industrial age. Historical archaeology played a secondary but again quite visible role in the rise of postprocessual archaeology, and many overly speculative interpretations of this countermovement to processual archaeology were at least understandable and sometimes testable in a documented context.

Yet it was not the new research topics, or even the general theoretical debates, that most fundamentally altered historical archaeology after 1970 but the hard realities of politics and economics. In 1966 Congress passed the National Historic Preservation Act, and it was followed by Executive Order 11593 in 1971 and the Archaeological and Historic Conservation Act in 1977. These and related bills created the National Register of Historic Places and State Historic Prevention Office (SHPO) offices on the state level, and soon most large-scale building projects in the United States were required to carry out exploratory archaeology and, if required, mitigation (completely digging the site). Massive public and private funding soon moved both prehistoric and historical archaeology into the maelstrom of the general marketplace, and although universities tried to incorporate these new funding opportunities, they were mostly replaced by private companies practicing cultural resource management (CRM).

On 26 April 1976, the Society of Professional Archaeologists (SOPA) was incorporated to meet the changing environment for archaeology in the United States. Interestingly its first president, Edward B. Jelks, was a leading historical archaeologist, and both anthropologists Charles Cleland and Bert Salwen served on its board. SOPA was only partially successful, drawing just over 700 practicing archaeologists into its membership during its short existence, and in 1998 it was restructured as the larger and growing Registry of Professional Archaeologists (RPA). Again, historical archaeologists took a leading role with William B. Lees acting as transitional president (SOPA-RPA) and Donald L. Hardesty as the first elected RPA president.

Excavations of the Telco Block Site in the South Street Seaport Historic District in New York City in 1981, directed by Diana Rockman [Wall], produced both colonial and nineteenth-century deposits. This site's legal and environmental setting—the dense urban section of Lower Manhattan and CRM funding under federal laws—is typical of many large historic projects after 1970. (David Barnet)

Theoretical fragmentation and the complexity caused by the decline of processualism and the rise and opening decline of postprocessualism have been paralleled by an equally complex sequential and overlapping series of occupational housing for the discipline. CRM rapidly elevated historical archaeology into the most commonly practiced and massively funded type of archaeology in North America, far surpassing prehistoric archaeology, but the primacy of New World prehistory and other traditional forms of archaeology artificially persevere in universities and the museum world. Historical archaeology is still not taught in the majority of American and Canadian universities, and the field is denied the true status it should have because of its professional size and theoretical importance.

Equally potential internal strains caused by the continuing academic intellectual leadership within historical archaeology have been, at least to the present, defused by the Society for Historical Archaeology's long tradition of drawing researchers equally from governmental, and now CRM, sources to fill its highest offices and the organization's successful appeal to all historical archaeologists irrespective of employment.

By the year 2000, the SHA, with 2,000 individual members, was the second-largest association of anthropological archaeologists, and historical archaeology was the most commonly practiced type of archaeology in North America. Its professional history, covering only six to seven decades, had passed through three major phases, intellectually arising from anthropology and socially derived from the national histories of the United States and Canada and world economics. From 1936 to the mid-1960s, it was historicalist in orientation and primarily supported by governmental agencies; during the 1960s and 1970s, it continued to be historicalist but with some influences from processual archaeology and quite different but simultaneous experiments in idealist interpretations. Sponsorship was still mostly governmental, but there was a small and important branch growing in the academic world. After 1980, historical archaeologists, like their counterparts in prehistory, became eclectic in their theory or they only implicitly discussed theory and left the intellectual stage empty for a few equally eclectic but highly visible idealist performers. As essentially practitioners of fieldwork, historical archaeologists moved massively, and probably permanently, into CRM.

Historical archaeology is currently also globally building up an internal disciplinary history, especially in Europe and Oceania and embryonically in Africa and Latin America. Interest in the history of this type of archaeology, however, is only now emerging, even in North America. There has been one historiographic discussion (Schuyler 1998) and two major books dedicated to disciplinary development. South (1994) uses a biographical set of chapters to cover all of North America, and Kidd (1969) surveys Canada. In 1999, Maria-Teresa Penna, a graduate student at the Sorbonne, did her Ph.D. dissertation on the subject, but her thesis has to date only been published in French (Penna 1999).

Robert L. Schuyler

See also Individual countries

References

Deetz, James J. F. 1965. *The Dynamics of Stylistic Change in Arikara Ceramics.* Urbana: University of Illinois Press.

———. 1977. *In Small Things Forgotten: The Archaeology of Early American Life.* New York: Doubleday.

Fontana, B. "Johnny Ward's Ranch: A Study in Historic Archaeology." 1962. *Kiva* 28, nos. 1–2.

Harrington, Jean Carl. 1955. "Archaeology as an Auxiliary Science to American History." *American Anthropologist* 37, nos. 3–4: 181–188.

Hume, Ivor Noël. 1969. *Historical Archaeology.* New York: Knopf.

Kidd, Kenneth E. 1969. "Historical Site Archaeology in Canada." *National Museum of Canada Anthropological Papers* 22. Ottawa.

Penna, Maria-Teresa. 1999. *L'archéologie historique aux Etats-Unis.* Paris: C.T.H.S.

Schuyler, Robert. 1998. "History of Historical Archaeology." *Bulletin of the History of Archaeology.* November, no. 2: 7–17.

Schuyler, Robert L., ed. 1978. *Historical Archaeology: A Guide to Theoretical and Substantive Contributions.* New York: Baywood Publishers.

South, Stanley. 1977. *Method and Theory in Historical Archaeology.* New York: Academic Press.

South, Stanley, ed. 1994. *Pioneers in Historical Archaeology: Breaking New Ground.* New York: Plenum Press.

Historiography

Historical works dealing with archaeology have been written to entertain the public, commemorate important archaeologists and research projects, instruct students in the basic concepts of the discipline, justify particular programs or ideas, disparage the work of rivals, and, most recently, try to resolve theoretical problems. These studies have taken the form of autobiographies, biographies, accounts of the development of the discipline as a whole, investigations of specific institutions or projects, and examinations of particular theories and approaches. They have used the analytical techniques of intellectual and social history and sought to treat their subject objectively, critically, hermeneutically, and polemically. Over time, historical studies have become more numerous, diversified, and sophisticated. Histories of archaeology are being written for all parts of the world, and in a growing number of countries, a large amount of material is being produced at local as well as national levels. There is no end in sight to the growing interest in this form of research.

The history of archaeology has been written mainly by professional archaeologists, who have no training in history or the history of science, and by popularizers. Only a small number of works have been produced by professional historians. Archaeology has attracted little attention from historians of science, despite its considerable interest to philosophers of science. This lack of interest is hard to understand since the difficulties inherent in inferring human behavior from archaeological evidence make archaeology an ideal discipline for addressing many of the issues of objectivity that are currently of interest to historians of science.

Early Histories of Archaeology

The earliest use of the history of archaeology appears to have been for didactic purposes. In the mid-nineteenth century, the physicist Joseph Henry, the first secretary of the SMITHSONIAN INSTITUTION, sought to purge American archaeology of useless speculation and to encourage an interest in factual research. To do this, he commissioned Samuel F. Haven, the librarian of the American Antiquarian Society, to write a critical historical review of studies of American prehistory titled *Archaeology of the United States* (1856). To improve the quality of American archaeology, Henry also published reports on developments in the discipline in the *Annual Report of the Smithsonian Institution,* which was widely distributed in North America. The most successful of these was "General Views on Archaeology" (1861), the translation of a paper by the Swiss geologist and amateur archaeologist Adolf Morlot, which summarized major developments over the previous fifty years in European prehistoric archaeology, especially in Scandinavia and SWITZERLAND. This article did much to encourage the adoption of a scientific approach to archaeology in eastern North America.

Popular Histories

For the next century, most histories of archaeology were popular accounts of archaeological discoveries, and they emphasized the romance of exploration and the most spectacular discoveries. As a result, they generally concentrated on the archaeology of ancient civilizations and important Paleolithic finds. One of the most widely read works dealing with the history of archaeology was the rather superficial *Gods, Graves, and Scholars* (1951), written by the Czech journalist C. W. Ceram (pseudonym for Kurt Marek). The continuing demand for works of this type is demonstrated by the success of Brian Fagan's *The Rape of the Nile* (1975).

Some popular histories of archaeology have sought to do more than entertain. Stanley Casson's *Progress of Archaeology* (1934) attempted to provide a balanced survey of the development of archaeology while the Assyriologist Seton Lloyd's *Foundations in the Dust* (1947; 2d ed., 1981) recounted the history of Mesopotamian archaeology in a manner that was of interest to professional archaeologists as well as to the general reader. Both Geoffrey Bibby's *The Testimony of the Spade* (1956), which dealt with European archaeology, and Michael Hoffman's *Egypt before the Pharaohs* (1979) sought not only to provide regional histories of archaeological research but also to explain to readers how archaeology was carried out. The Egyptologist John Wilson's *Signs and Wonders upon Pharaoh* (1964) was a celebration of American contributions to Egyptian archaeology and Egyptology, while Jeremy Sabloff's *The New Archaeology and the Ancient Maya* (1990) sought to explain to nonarchaeologists how processual archaeology has provided more superior insights into the ancient MAYA CIVILIZATION than did culture-historical archaeology.

In England, there has long been a receptive audience for popular biographies of archaeologists. These stress personal life and social contacts more than the intellectual context and scholarly contributions of their subjects. One of the earliest and best of these was Joan Evans's *Time and Chance* (1943), which recounted the lives of her father, JOHN EVANS, and her brother ARTHUR EVANS. More recent examples include Jacquetta Hawkes's *Mortimer Wheeler, Adventurer in Archaeology* (1982), H. V. F. Winstone's *Woolley of Ur* (1990), and, from the United States, J. J. Thompson's *Sir Gardner Wilkinson and his Circle* (1992). Personal and professional disputes are aired in autobiographies such as W. M. F. PETRIE's *Seventy Years in Archaeology* (1931) and MARY LEAKEY's *Disclosing the Past* (1984). Popular anthologies of archaeological literature include Edward Bacon's *The Great Archaeologists* (1976), a collection of articles from the *Illustrated London News* describing major finds between 1842 and 1970, and Jacquetta Hawkes's two-volume *The World of the Past* (1963), which contains excerpts from the publications of archaeologists who had worked around the world arranged geographically.

A final genre is the history of archaeological institutions pioneered by Joan Evans's *A History of the Society of Antiquaries* (1956) and exemplified more recently at its best by *The Scottish Antiquarian Tradition* (1981), a history of the SOCIETY OF ANTIQUARIES OF SCOTLAND edited by A. S. Bell.

The principal characteristic of popular histories of archaeology is their emphasis on spectacular discoveries. The archaeologists who feature prominently in them include many individuals, such as HOWARD CARTER, who made celebrated discoveries but contributed little to the intellectual development of archaeology. On the other hand, archaeologists whose ideas played a major role in shaping the discipline, such as OSCAR MONTELIUS, VERE GORDON CHILDE, and GRAHAME CLARK, are rarely mentioned in such works. To take account of the contributions of such individuals required the development of a more strictly professional history of archaeology.

Intellectual Histories

The modern scholarly history of archaeology began in England in the late 1930s, as a growing awareness of generational differences among professional archaeologists and the accumulation of a corpus of essential literature revealed changes in the conceptual basis of prehistory. A few far-sighted prehistoric archaeologists became convinced that knowing the reasons for the decline of evolutionary explanations of the past and their replacement by culture-historical ones was essential for understanding what was happening in their discipline. Following a lull during World War II, this sort of investigation has since increased exponentially and has spread around the world.

The original studies tended to be strongly influenced by British intellectual historians who, inspired by such works as Christopher Hussey's *The Picturesque* (1927) and Kenneth Clark's *The Gothic Revival* (1928), sought to relate changes in a literary and artistic fashion to shifts in the broader history of ideas. Many of these historians stressed rationalism and romanticism as alternating views of reality that influenced the understanding of human behavior. Historians of archaeology were also strongly influenced by the philosopher R. G. Collingwood's subjectivism, which denied that there could be any definitive version of the past since the past existed only as it was relived in the minds of individual historians and their readers. This idea encouraged the archaeological historians, like the historians who were disciples of Leopold von Ranke, to believe that the core of their discipline was the data they collected and that the interpretation of these data was little more than an expression of personal opinion. Many of these pioneering studies also surveyed their subject matter on a grand scale.

The first major study was Stanley Casson's *The Discovery of Man* (1939), which was written to justify an already moribund evolutionary archaeology. Casson sought to trace how from earliest times humanity had struggled against ignorance and superstition in an effort to understand itself more objectively. This struggle reached a new and definitive stage in the nineteenth century when evolutionism transformed and unified the study of human beings. Although only archaeology could trace humanity's physical and cultural development, it depended heavily on ethnology for an understanding of human behavior. Although Casson maintained that both disciplines were influenced by broader intellectual trends, he defined these trends vaguely. They often amounted to little more than a zeitgeist, such as the spirit of intellectual freedom that allegedly arose from the discovery of the New World.

The systematic study of the history of archaeology was initiated and for several decades guided by GLYN DANIEL. His work *The Three Ages* (1943) launched research that culminated in *A Hundred Years of Archaeology* (1950; 2d ed., 1975), the most comprehensive history of archaeology until recently. Daniel maintained that changes in archaeology occurred gradually and largely adventitiously. He accorded great importance to the expanding database and to the role played by new scientific techniques, especially radiocarbon DATING, in shaping the development of archaeology. Yet he maintained that archaeological interpretation was mainly influenced by randomly shifting intellectual fashions and therefore refused to assign absolute validity to any theory that purported to explain the past. The main lesson to be learned from studying the history of archaeology was that "the final truth" of any given period breaks down as new facts accumulate and new explanations are developed. Still, the main theme of his book was the rise and decline of evolutionary interpretations and their replacement by a culture-historical perspective.

Daniel clearly favored a culture-historical orientation, arguing that without it archaeology would decline into a new object-oriented antiquarianism. Although he sought to write a general history of European archaeology, his main emphasis was on the period from 1840 to 1900. He felt less confident about his ability to view the twentieth century objectively, and his account of it remained largely a catalog of discoveries.

Earlier phases in the history of British archaeology were studied by SIR THOMAS KENDRICK, whose *British Antiquity* (1950) interpreted the development of antiquarianism during the Tudor period as a triumph of renaissance over medieval thought, and Michael Hunter, whose *John Aubrey and the Realm of Learning* (1975) sought to demonstrate how AUBREY's archaeological research was shaped by the Baconian principles being promoted by the Royal Society of London. STUART PIGGOTT, in his magisterial *William Stukeley* (1950; 2d ed., 1985), argued that a general shift from rationalism to romanticism among British intellectuals accounted for what he saw as that antiquarian's abandonment of sober analytical studies in favor of Druidical fantasies. All of these works sought to relate changes in British antiquarian research to the broader history of ideas.

Another major contribution to the emerging intellectual history of archaeology was Annette Laming-Emperaire's *Origines de l'archéologie préhistorique en France* (1964), which traced the development of archaeology from medieval times until it achieved "essentially its modern form" in the late nineteenth century. Laming-Emperaire sought to account for the divisions of theory, method, organization, and attitude within modern French archaeology, especially those that differentiated the study of the Paleolithic period from that of more recent ones. Paleolithic archaeology was seen as having been created in the nineteenth century as a result of the combined influences of geology, paleontology, physical anthropology, and ethnology, which in turn promoted the development of a widespread interest in biological and cultural evolution. Paleolithic archaeology was seen as maintaining close links to the natural sciences while the study of later prehistory remained more closely aligned with history. Laming-Emperaire's book was distinguished by her careful examination of how structures of teaching and research, professional associations, and journals reflected and shaped the development of archaeology.

In the United States, the modern scholarly history of archaeology began, rather inauspiciously, with WALTER TAYLOR's *A Study of Archaeology* (1948). In the first part of that book, Taylor offered a savage critique of what he believed to be the theoretical inadequacies and resulting methodological shortcomings that had characterized the work of leading American archaeologists over the previous several decades. The frosty reception given this work may have inhibited the publication of more histories of archaeology for the following two decades.

Although the history of archaeology was often surveyed in graduate courses and brief discussions of it appeared in histories of anthropology, it was not until the general upheaval produced by "the new archaeology" of the 1960s that works devoted exclusively to the history of American archaeology began to appear. It was argued that the critical self-appraisal going on in American archaeology required a review of the development of the discipline and its concepts. Not surprisingly, in view of the positivism that was pervasive throughout the social sciences in the United States at the time and played a major role in new (or processual) archaeology, the study of the history of archaeology took a more positivist turn in the United States than it had in Britain or FRANCE. American archaeology was seen as following a logical and ultimately inevitable pattern, which, in the absence of political interference or social anomalies, would describe the development of archaeology everywhere. This course was thought to be shaped largely by the role played by evidence in confirming and refuting existing theories.

The first substantial contribution was Douglas Schwartz's *Conceptions of Kentucky Prehistory* (1967) in which he argued that American archaeology had been characterized by three successive approaches: a speculative one, followed after 1850 by an empirical trend and after 1950 by an explanatory one. Although each new trend was treated as supplementary to, rather than replacing, earlier ones, the overall effect was to transform archaeology in an irreversible manner.

The first comprehensive treatment of New World archaeology was GORDON WILLEY and Jeremy Sabloff's *A History of American Archaeology* (1974), which first appeared in Glyn Daniel's World of Archaeology series and has gone through two major revisions (2d ed., 1980; 3d ed., 1993). Willey and Sabloff divided their history into four periods: speculative (1492–1840), classificatory-descriptive (1840–1914), classificatory-historical (1914–1960), and explanatory (1960–present). In the third edition, the last stage is invidiously referred to as the modern period. Each division was defined as a specific unit of time, not as a overlapping trend, on the premise that the concept of "period" was more appropriate than that of "trend" for the purposes of historical analysis. Thus, Willey and Sabloff adopted a stratigraphic view of archaeological development.

A History of American Archaeology offered a historical legitimation of processual archaeology and its close relations with anthropology and at the same time criticized what were regarded as some of its theoretical excesses. Like Daniel and other intellectual historians of archaeology, Willey and Sabloff stressed the value of relating changes in archaeology to the intellectual tenor of the period; to theoretical developments in other fields such as ecology, systems analysis, and art history but above all to ethnology and social anthropology; to the availability of new analytical techniques such as radiocarbon dating and computers; and to changing patterns of funding. They blamed the failure of American archaeologists to adopt an evolutionary perspective prior to the 1960s at least partly on the influence of Boasian anthropology. Yet, by claiming that in the long run the development of archaeology was controlled by the discovery of new evidence and the utilization of sounder methods for evaluating data, Willey and Sabloff provided processual archaeology with a considerably more predetermined pedigree than Daniel had accorded culture-historical archaeology or Casson had provided for evolutionary archaeology.

The view that the history of archaeology consisted of a sequence of well-defined stages was shared by various contributors to James Fitting's *The Development of North American Archaeology* (1973), which consisted of a series of individually authored regional archaeological histories. This view, which contrasted with Daniel's gradualist vision of change, invited comparison with Thomas Kuhn's concept of scientific revolutions, and this comparison was made explicit by Eugene Sterud in a paper titled "A Paradigmatic View of Prehistory" (in Colin Renfrew, ed., *The Explanation of Culture Change* [1973]).

Sterud posited two successive paradigms: the THREE-AGE SYSTEM of the nineteenth century and processual archaeology. Using different terminology, the English archaeologist DAVID CLARKE argued that the preparadigmatic stage had lasted until the advent of critically self-conscious processual archaeology (1973). Yet, unlike Kuhn, these archaeologists viewed successive periods in a positivist fashion, as a logical and largely inevitable sequence of development. Only Fitting chose to follow Kuhn's *The Struc-*

ture of Scientific Revolutions (1962) and stress the socially determined nature of paradigms as well as to reject the cumulative character of archaeological understanding. Fitting regarded science as basically irrational and maintained that "prerevolutionary science is neither more nor less scientific than postrevolutionary science" (290).

Perhaps the most sophisticated product of the positivist approach to the history of archaeology produced so far is Donald Grayson's *The Establishment of Human Antiquity* (1983), which traces the steps that made possible the recognition in 1859 that human beings had inhabited the earth for much longer than the traditional biblical chronology implied. Although Grayson acknowledges that religious beliefs and social factors inhibited the recognition of this antiquity, he concludes that, ultimately, recognition was accomplished by providing irrefutable evidence of a human presence in geological contexts that were demonstrably more than 6,000 years old. The positivist approach is not limited to North America. The Swedish archaeologist Bo Graslund's *The Birth of Prehistoric Chronology* (1987) stresses the empirical nature of the Scandinavian research that laid the basis of seriation dating. He also emphasizes that this was a project almost completely internal to archaeology. Both of these books provide evidence not only of a positivist outlook but also of an internalist approach, which concentrates on delineating the changing understanding of a particular problem by archaeologists. The two approaches are conceptually closely aligned.

The first intellectual biography of an archaeologist, Stuart Piggott's *William Stukeley,* was rooted in intellectual history, as was Michael Hunter's study of John Aubrey. R. B. Woodbury's *Alfred V. Kidder* (1973) and Bruce Trigger's *Gordon Childe* (1980) utilized a similar intellectual approach, although they related their subjects' work more specifically to its archaeological and anthropological context. Robert Cunnington's *From Antiquary to Archaeologist* (1975), a biography of his ancestor WILLIAM CUNNINGTON, delineates Cunnington's understanding of successive discoveries and provides insights into the sophistication that was possible in the late eighteenth century, as well as the limitations of inferences based on only a narrow range of excavated material. On the other hand, the historian Gerald Killan's *David Boyle: From Artisan to Archaeologist* (1983) paid considerable attention to the social as well as the intellectual milieu that shaped the career of that nineteenth-century Ontario archaeologist. One encounters in archaeological biographies a similar range of approaches to that found in other studies relating to the history of the discipline.

Despite the influence of relativists such as Collingwood, Australian archaeologist Tim Murray has rightly suggested that "much of the history of archaeology reads as an account of the slow journey out of the darkness of subjectivity and speculation towards objectivity, rationality, and science" (1989, 56). One might have expected that such an approach would have appealed to processual archaeologists, yet, in general, processual archaeologists rejected and trivialized the history of archaeology, even though they welcomed Willey and Sabloff's historical charter. In his *Behavioral Archeology* (1976), Michael Schiffer pronounced that "graduate courses should cease being histories of thought" and concentrate instead on communicating the established principles of the discipline and indicating future lines of inquiry (p. 193). If carefully formulated techniques of analysis and an expanding corpus of data can produce increasingly accurate approximations of the past and more accurate theories, the history of archaeology is irrelevant to its past or future practice. If, on the other hand, the relativists are correct, facts constitute the core of archaeology while interpretations amount to little more than a history of personal opinions.

Social Histories

In Britain, the 1970s witnessed the development of the history of archaeology in the direction of social history. Both social and intellectual history share a relativist view of knowledge, but social history is concerned with how economic, political, and social conditions influence the interpretation of archaeological data. Because of this focus on the relationship between archaeological understanding and the sociocultural context in which archaeology is practiced, social history is more broadly externalist than intellectual history, which at most seeks to understand how archaeological interpretations relate to the contemporary intellectual milieu. Thus, social history stands at the opposite extreme from an internalist approach, which aims to delineate only the changing understanding of a problem by archaeologists. The distinction between externalist and internalist approaches is the same one that an older generation of historians drew between intellectual history and the history of ideas.

The social history of archaeology developed as an unforeseen consequence of Daniel's efforts to promote the study of the history of archaeology around the world, for such studies drew archaeologists' attention to the very different conditions under which archaeology was practiced. Ole Klindt-Jensen's *A History of Scandinavian Archaeology* (1975) and IGNACIO BERNAL GARCIA's *A History of Mexican Archaeology* (1980) were both commissioned for Daniel's World of Archaeology series. Each author traced the successive impacts of renaissance, rationalist, romantic, and positivist thought on the development of archaeology in a different part of the world. Klindt-Jensen went further, however, and delineated the political conditions that he believed had promoted the development of antiquarianism and the beginnings of scientific archaeology in Scandinavia. In tracing subsequent developments, he stressed the impact that changing political and economic circumstances had on archaeology in each Scandinavian country.

Partly inspired, although he only grudgingly admitted it, by Benjamin Keen's superb history of *The Aztec Image in Western Thought* (1971), Ignacio Bernal examined in detail the differing attitudes toward the study of pre-Columbian MEXICO adopted by Spanish officials and Creoles prior to Mexico's independence, liberals, and conservatives during the nineteenth century, and the Mexican government between 1920 and 1950. He also demonstrated how the institutional setting of Mexican archaeology was molded by political events and how it, in turn, influenced the character of Mexican archaeology. Bernal has perhaps gone further than any other historian of archaeology in delineating the influence of international scholarly trends; foreign scholarship; internal social, political, and economic conditions; and institutional structures for teaching and research on the development of archaeology in a single country.

The comparative, and hence the socially oriented, study of the history of archaeology was further stimulated by an international conference on the history of archaeology held in Aarhus, DENMARK, in 1978, the proceedings of which were published as *Towards a History of Archaeology* (1981), edited by Glyn Daniel. *Antiquity and Man* (1981), a festschrift edited in Daniel's honor by John Evans, Barry Cunliffe, and Colin Renfrew, as well as two successive issues of *World Archaeology* titled "Regional Traditions of Archaeological Research" (1981–1982), edited by Bruce Trigger and Ian Glover, also contained studies of the history of archaeology in various parts of the world. These studies, despite a shared corpus of methods, the questions archaeologists asked, and the answers they were predisposed to accept, varied widely from one society to another. The studies confirmed Klindt-Jensen's and Bernal's observations that the cultural patterns of individual societies and the expectations of particular social groups within them have influenced the practice of archaeology, as have the formal organization of the discipline and levels of funding available to carry out research.

Many historians of archaeology have begun to examine the impact of social, political, and economic conditions on the practice of archaeology. Karel Sklenár's *Archaeology in Central Europe* (1983) emphasizes how over a 500-year period prehistoric archaeology has been used by diverse ethnic groups and by particular social classes within those groups to pursue their own social, political, and economic agendas. Such agendas have encouraged and suppressed various archaeological projects and favored radically different interpretations of archaeological data. Kenneth Hudson's *A Social History of Archaeology* (1981) consists of a series of essays that attempt to relate the practice of archaeology in Britain during the nineteenth and twentieth centuries to the social conditions of the times and to "see how money, the educational

and political system and the class structure have determined both the selection and ambitions of archaeologists and the way in which they have set about their work" (1). Specific topics examined include the class affiliations of Victorian archaeological societies and the impact of the development of the railways on such bodies. Similar topics have been explored in Philippa Levine's *The Amateur and the Professional* (1986) and in some of Piggott's essays in his *Ruins in a Landscape* (1976).

In the United States, the first example of a social approach to the history of archaeology was Robert Silverberg's *Mound Builders of Ancient America* (1968), which explored the link between the nineteenth-century belief in the Mound Builders as a civilized, non-Indian people who had inhabited North America in prehistoric times and the denigration of aboriginal peoples that accompanied the spread of European settlement. The general impact of racism on North American archaeology was explored in Bruce Trigger's "Archaeology and the Image of the American Indian" (*American Antiquity,* 1980), and how it influenced the practice of archaeology at the Smithsonian Institution is discussed in Curtis Hinsley, Jr.'s, *Savages and Scientists* (1981) and David Meltzer's "The Antiquity of Man and the Development of American Archaeology" (*Advances in Archaeological Method and Theory* 6: 1983). In *The Davenport Conspiracy* (1970), Marshall McKusick documented the disorder that could occur in the small scientific clubs that flourished in the United States during the nineteenth century and the widespread antagonism between such organizations and "the big science" that was being sponsored by the Smithsonian Institution.

Neil Silberman's *Digging for God and Country* (1982) and *Between Past and Present* (1989) trace the impact of European colonialism and local nationalism on the archaeology of the Middle East. He demonstrates how archaeologists' loyalties determine what questions are and are not investigated. For example, western archaeologists have systematically ignored or misinterpreted evidence they have excavated that demonstrates that western European reorientations of world trade rather than the Turkish oc-

cupation were responsible for the economic decline of Cyprus and Palestine in recent centuries. In the historical sections of *Black Athena*
(1987), Martin Bernal has argued that since the
Napoleonic period, as a result of racism and
ethnocentrism, European archaeologists have
systematically ignored evidence of historical ties
between ancient Greece and Egypt.

The Impact of Postmodernism
In the 1980s, externalism was fueled by a growing postmodernist emphasis on subjectivity and
relativism, an emphasis that has influenced archaeology no less than it has the other social sciences. Central to this approach is a radical idealism that views understanding as being
determined by individual presuppositions
rather than by evidence and therefore mini-
mizes the possibility of objective knowledge.
This approach has been embraced by many archaeologists who wish to eliminate colonial,
gender, and class biases from archaeology or to
disempower the discipline as an elite discourse.
Basic to this approach is the radical relativist
claim that it is impossible to judge any one version of the past as being more right or wrong
than any other. Inherent in this nihilistic approach to archaeology is the belief that its main,
and perhaps only, legitimate role is to become a
vehicle for encouraging political action by calling accepted beliefs into question.

The principal influence of postmodernism
on the history of archaeology has been to encourage more radical externalism that seeks to
correlate specific changes in archaeological interpretation with particular social movements
of varying durations and degrees of specificity.
This approach is reflected in stimulating, but
highly controversial, papers such as R. R. Wilk's
"The Ancient Maya and the Political Present"
(Wilk 1985) and Thomas C. Patterson's "The
Last Sixty Years: Toward a Social History of
Americanist Archeology in the United States"
(Patterson 1986).

Although virtually all histories of archaeology agree that every interpretation of archaeological evidence is influenced to some degree by
personal or social biases, there is little agreement concerning the distortions produced by

bias. The more positivistic see these biases overcome, in either the short or the middle term, by
archaeological evidence. At the other extreme
are those who are inclined to accept Michael
Shank's and Christopher Tilley's denials that it is
possible for evidence to contradict presuppositions. Positivists such as Colin Renfrew have
countered such claims by demanding to know
on what basis any externalists claim to link archaeological interpretations to the social milieu.

Other historians of archaeology have attempted to determine empirically to what extent and under what circumstances archaeologists have been able to achieve insights that are
objective in the sense that they have been able to
withstand the double test of new evidence and
changing social circumstances. This was the main
objective of Bruce Trigger's *A History of Archaeological Thought* (1989). Trigger documented the
wide range of subjective factors that have influenced the interpretation of archaeological data
but at the same time offered evidence that the
"resistance" of archaeological evidence had produced certain irreversible changes in the understanding of human history and human nature.
Moreover, it appears that in general, as the archaeological increases, the ability of subjective
factors to distort the interpretation of archaeological evidence is curtailed. Using the history of
archaeology to address such theoretical issues
and to understand archaeological practice makes
the history of archaeology more of an essential
part of the theoretical core of the discipline.

Methodological Developments
Over the years there have been marked improvement in the technical quality of scholarly
studies of the history of archaeology. Early histories were based largely on scanning published
works and sometimes on secondary sources.
This practice continues, especially in large-scale
syntheses, but is gradually being replaced by
more varied and sophisticated methods.

The American archaeologist Robert Heizer
encouraged the critical reading of archaeological publications by publishing two volumes of
original papers that he judged had been crucial
for the development of archaeological method
and theory: *The Archaeologist at Work* (1959) and

Man's Discovery of His Past (1962). Ezra Zubrow ("Environment, Subsistence and Society: The Changing Archaeological Perspective," *Annual Review of Anthropology,* 1972) pioneered the application of a formal thematic analysis to archaeological publications, and Eugene Sterud was the first to employ citation analysis.

Over the years, historians of archaeology such as McKusick, Hinsley, Grayson, and Meltzer have made increasingly effective use of archival sources. More recent works strongly influenced by archival materials include Mark Bowden's biography of *Pitt Rivers* (1991); Ian Jenkin's *Archaeologists and Aesthetes* (1992), a study of the conceptual basis for the changing displays in the sculpture galleries of the BRITISH MUSEUM between 1800 and 1939; and Ronald Ridley's *The Eagle and the Spade* (1992), a study of archaeology in Rome during the Napoleonic era. Historians of archaeology gradually are becoming more aware of the need to record the recollections of older archaeologists and to preserve field notes, films of excavations, drawings and photographs, speeches, old artifact collections, and institutional records as sources of information about the history of the discipline. At least one important early manuscript source has been published in a scholarly fashion by J. A. Brongers *1833: Reuvens i Drenthe* (1973), a Dutch antiquarian's account of his researches in a northern province of the Netherlands.

This growing concern with the method and theory of studying the history of archaeology resulted in a conference on the subject at Southern Illinois University in May 1987. The proceedings, edited by the organizer, Andrew Christenson, were published as *Tracing Archaeology's Past* (1989). This first work to examine problems related to studying the history of archaeology constitutes a milestone in the development of the field. The conference also stimulated the professionalization of the history of archaeology in other ways. In 1987, a committee on the history of archaeology was established within the SOCIETY FOR AMERICAN ARCHAEOLOGY and charged with identifying, preserving, and making documentary material more accessible, as well as with promoting an interest in the history of the discipline. In 1988, a series of annual symposia

on the history of archaeology was initiated, which now alternates between the annual meetings of the American Anthropological Association and the Society for American Archaeology. Some of the papers from the first two of these conferences were published in *Rediscovering Our Past* (1992), edited by Jonathan Reyman. Finally, the *Bulletin of the History of Archaeology,* edited by Douglas Givens and appearing since 1991, contains short articles, bibliographies, book reviews, and notices of activities and events relevant to the study of the history of archaeology around the world.

Tentative steps are currently being taken to promote the study of the history of archaeology in the United Kingdom, and more studies relating to the history of archaeology are being published in Europe, Latin America, Australia, RUSSIA, and elsewhere. Among the most substantial of these works is Dilip Chakrabarti's *A History of Indian Archaeology from the Beginning to 1947* (1988). Heightened interest in the history of archaeology is also leading to the production of illustrated histories, biographical compendiums, and encyclopedias aimed at an international market.

Some professional historians are interested in the history of archaeology, but they generally study happenings prior to the twentieth century whereas archaeologists tend more often to be interested in developments closer to the present. This difference has lessened the incentives for archaeologists and historians to learn from one another. Such lack of contact is particularly regrettable since the skills that each group brings to such research are generally complementary.

Nevertheless, the growing number of people studying the history of archaeology is stimulating useful controversies. Some of these concern specific issues, others relate to the general nature of the history of archaeology and the goals and methods that are appropriate for its study. It is being questioned, for example, whether the emphasis currently being placed on the contributions of "great archaeologists" may not be distorting our understanding of the development of archaeology. It is suggested that there are still too few studies of the institutional structures of the discipline, of the impact of funding on archaeological theory and practice, of how archaeology has defined itself as a field, and of other sociological aspects of the production of archaeological knowledge. These debates are raising the self-consciousness of the people who study the history of archaeology and must contribute, in the long run, to improving the standard for such studies.

Conclusions

With a declining adherence to positivism and a lessening belief in a culture-free methodology for explaining human behavior, the history of archaeology has ceased to be regarded as marginal to archaeology and is assuming a more central position in the discipline. Its study provides a matrix for evaluating established theories and is calling current dogmas into question. The field also provides a basis for discussing epistemological questions in terms that are familiar to archaeologists. The history of archaeology is therefore coming to play a major role in both the understanding and the application of archaeological knowledge.

Bruce G. Trigger

References

To date little has been written about the study of the history of archaeology. Items include:

Clarke, David. 1973. "Archaeology: The Loss of Innocence," *Antiquity* 47: 6–18.

Murray, Tim. 1989. "The History, Philosophy, and Sociology of Archaeology: The Case of the Ancient Monuments Protection Act (1882)." In *Critical Traditions in Contemporary Archaeology*, 55–67. Ed. V. Pinsky and A. Wylie. Cambridge: Cambridge University Press.

Patterson, Thomas C. 1986. "The Last Sixty Years: Toward a Social History of Americanist Archeology in the United States." *American Anthropologist* 88: 7–26.

Pinsky, Valerie. 1989. "Introduction: Historical Foundations." In *Critical Traditions in Contemporary Archaeology*, 51–54. Ed. V. Pinsky and A. Wylie. Cambridge: Cambridge University Press.

Sterud, Eugene. "Changing Aims of Americanist Archaeology." *American Antiquity* 43: 294–302.

Trigger, Bruce G. 1980. "Archaeology and the Image of the American Indian," *American Antiquity* 45: 662–667.

———. 1985. "Writing the History of Archaeology: A Survey of Trends." In *Objects and Others: Essays on Museums and Material Culture*, 218–235. History of Anthropology, no. 3. Ed. George W. Stocking, Jr. Madison: University of Wisconsin Press.

———. 1989. *A History of Archaeological Thought*. Cambridge: Cambridge University Press.

———. 1994. "The Coming of Age of the History of Archaeology." *Journal of Archaeological Research* 2.

Wilk, R. 1985. "The Ancient Maya and the Political Present." *Journal of Anthropological Research*. 43: 307–321.

For a preliminary classification of correlations between archaeological interpretations and different types of social movements, see Gero, Joan M. 1985. "Socio-politics and the Woman-at-Home Ideology." *American Antiquity* 50: 342–350. Discussions of method are also found in Christenson, Andrew, ed. 1989. *Tracing Archaeology's Past*. Carbondale: University of Southern Illinois Press, and in successive issues of the *Bulletin of the History of Archaeology*. Daniel, Glyn. 1975. *A Hundred and Fifty Years of Archaeology*. 2d ed. London: Duckworth provides a comprehensive list of histories of archaeology written before 1975.

Hogarth, David George (1862–1927)

Hogarth was born in Lincolnshire and educated at Winchester School and Magdalen College Oxford. He studied classics and won a Craven traveling fellowship to pursue his interests in archaeology. In 1887 and 1890 he traveled with the epigraphist Sir William Mitchell Ramsay in Asia Minor. In 1888 he excavated at the site of PAPHOS on CYPRUS. Hogarth spent three seasons in Egypt in the early 1890s working for the EGYPT EXPLORATION SOCIETY at Deir-el-bahri, Alexandria, and the Fayum, where he perfected his excavation techniques, but he preferred classical to Egyptian archaeology. He was as excellent a writer as he was an archaeologist, publishing a number of popular travel books.

In 1897 Hogarth became a correspondent on Crete for *The Times* newspaper to cover its fight for independence from TURKEY, and later in Thessaly (northern GREECE) to report on the Greco-Turkish war. At the end of this year he became director of the British School of Archaeology in Athens. During his three years as

David George Hogarth (Image Select)

fice and was sent first to Athens and then to Cairo where he became director of the Arab Bureau. In this position and with the help of T. E. Lawrence and GERTRUDE BELL, Hogarth was able to encourage and support the Arab rebellion against Turkey, which was to be decisive in the war in the Middle East.

In 1917 Hogarth received the gold medal from the Royal Geographic Society and in 1925 he became its president. After the war he was a member of the British delegation at the Peace Conference at Versailles and he returned to the Ashmolean Museum and Oxford. He was awarded a D.Litt. from Oxford in 1918 and a Litt.D. from Cambridge in 1924.

Tim Murray

See also Britain, Classical Archaeology; Mesopotamia

director he excavated at the site of Phylakopi on Melos, and at Naucratis. In 1900 Hogarth left the British School and joined SIR ARTHUR EVANS in his first season on Crete, which saw the beginning of the excavation of KNOSSOS.

In 1903 Hogarth spent another season excavating at Naucratis, and in 1904 and 1905 he excavated the temple of Artemis at EPHESUS on behalf of the BRITISH MUSEUM. In 1908 he visited the upper Euphrates River surveying the sites of Carchemish and Tell Bashar. In 1908 he became Keeper of the ASHMOLEAN MUSEUM in Oxford, and to began to excavate Carchemish with the young archaeologists LEONARD WOOLLEY and T. E. Lawrence, both of whom would later become more famous than their mentor.

The Ashmolean Museum prospered under Hogarth—becoming especially important for its Cretan and Hittite archaeological collections, the later of which was Hogarth's primary interest. In 1915 he offered his linguistic, geographic, and historic expertise on Asia Minor and the Eastern Mediterranean to the War Of-

Holmes, William Henry (1846–1933)

William Henry Holmes was the preeminent figure in American archaeology around the turn of the last century. With the careful eye of an artist, he pioneered material culture studies, particularly the understanding of ceramic form, function, and design, and lithic technology. His analysis of collections at the SMITHSONIAN INSTITUTION (where Holmes was affiliated for nearly sixty years), replicative experiments, and excavations at prehistoric quarries enabled him to reconstruct in unprecedented detail the process and products of ceramic and stone tool manufacturing.

Studying stone tools revealed that what many people thought were primitive, ancient artifacts—indicators of an American Paleolithic period comparable in age to the Paleolithic of Europe—were merely rejects of the manufacturing process. Armed with that realization and the expertise developed in years of geological fieldwork in the western part of the United States, Holmes spearheaded the highly successful rout of the American Paleolithic. For several decades, Holmes, his geologist colleagues, and a protégé, the physical anthropologist ALES HRDLICKA, critically evaluated all purported claims of Pleistocene humans in North America. Although they correctly rejected those claims, the Folsom discovery in 1927 ultimately showed that human antiquity on the North American continent reached back to the late Pleistocene period.

Holmes's work was particularly valued by his peers because of his scientific approach, which entailed the considerable rhetoric on the proper conduct of science that was symptomatic of the growing professionalism of late-nineteenth-century archaeology, and Holmes's own explicit efforts to highlight the stark contrasts he saw between his efforts and the "old archaeology." Science to Holmes meant a commitment to empirical observation and measurement and a strong sense of order and method.

The method of choice, reflecting his geological background, was an archaeological uniformitarianism in which the past was understood in terms of the ethnographic present. Holmes was well aware, in principle, that traces of specific ethnographic groups could only be followed a short distance into the past, but, in practice, he often slighted that principle, attaching ethnographic labels to archaeological phenomena. He did so in the belief—partly rooted in his rejection of the American Paleolithic—that American prehistory was shallow. As a result, when he organized the archaeological record, it was along geographical lines and into cultural areas; temporal units were largely absent.

At the same time, however, Holmes was a confirmed evolutionist who followed anthropologist LEWIS HENRY MORGAN's general cultural evolutionary scheme and envisioned "the pathways of progress" from savagery to barbarism to civilization as being driven by human volition. Progress for Holmes was the axis and measure of evolutionary change, and he embarked on his ambitious effort to show through different classes of material culture "human progress from the point of view of material culture." But he ultimately came to realize that progress was not always evident in the small details, however clear on the larger scale.

Holmes was a key figure in Washington, D.C., museums and research bureaus when those were at the center of science in the United States. But in the twentieth century, that center shifted into the university system, and that caused a change in the theoretical compass of American archaeology. Holmes's brand of evolutionary theory was no longer fashionable, and the next generation of archaeologists—armed with stratigraphy and seriation and needing to fill the chronological gap created by Folsom—moved beyond his geographical archaeology into culture history.

David J. Meltzer

See also United States of America, Prehistoric Archaeology

References

For references, see *Encyclopedia of Archaeology: The Great Archaeologists, Vol. 1,* ed. Tim Murray (Santa Barbara, CA: ABC-CLIO, 1999), pp. 188–191.

Honduras; Honduran Institute of Anthropology and History

See Instituto Hondureño de Antropología e Historia

Hrdlicka, Ales (1869–1943)

Hrdlicka was born in Bohemia, in what is now the CZECH REPUBLIC, and immigrated with his family to the United States in 1881. He studied medicine at the New York Eclectic Medical College, and practiced in New York City while continuing to study at the New York Homeopathic College. In 1894 he became a junior physician at a homeopathic hospital for the insane and consequently became interested in anthropometry. In 1896 he was invited to join a multidisciplinary research team at the newly founded Pathological Institute in New York City. Prior to taking up this appointment Hrdlicka attended classes in Paris at the Ecole d'Anthropologie, and studied anthropometric techniques in the Laboratoire d'Anthropologie at the Ecole Pratique des Hautes Etudes.

In 1899 he resigned from the institute and became an unsalaried field anthropologist for the American Museum of Natural History in New York City, where he worked under anthropologist FREDERIC WARD PUTNAM from Harvard University. From 1899 until 1902 Hrdlicka undertook anthropometric surveys of the Indians of the American Southwest and northern MEXICO.

The Moche Pyramid at Huaca del Sol (AAA)

In recognition of this field experience and the publication of his results he was appointed head of the new Division of Physical Anthropology at the National Museum of Natural History, SMITHSONIAN INSTITUTION, Washington, D.C., in 1903.

During the next forty years in this position Hrdlicka built his department into a major research center, based on one of the best human osteological collections in the world. He founded the *American Journal of Physical Anthropology* in 1918 and the American Association of Physical Anthropologists in 1930. Hrdlicka's primary research interest focused on the origins and antiquity of Native American Indians. He studied all of the skeletal material claimed to be evidence of early human beings in America, and argued that it did not predate the postglacial period. He also undertook fieldwork in the Kodiak and Aleutian Islands off Alaska in the 1930s as part of a project to test the thesis that indigenous Americans had originally come from Asia. Hrdlicka was also interested in the origin of modern humans and argued that Neanderthals were the direct ancestors of modern humans, presenting the Huxley Memorial Lecture in 1927 on "The Neanderthal Phase of Man."

Tim Murray

Huaca del Sol

A large platform mound in the Moche Valley of PERU, Huaca del Sol (Shrine of the Sun), along with its companion mound Huaca del Luna (Shrine of the Moon), forms the heart of the Moche kingdom. Construction began around the time of Christ, and the site was intensively occupied for a period of 600 years prior to being devastated by floods around A.D. 560. Although the site was rebuilt, it was eventually abandoned owing to the encroachment of sand dunes, which had previously destroyed arable land in the vicinity. Huaca del Sol and its companion pyramid were two of the largest adobe edifices ever constructed in South America. It has been estimated that 143 million bricks were required to construct the stepped pyramid of massive dimensions (2,175,120 cubic meters) and that the rulers of the city employed a system of corvée labor to complete the task.

Tim Murray

References

Alva, Walter, and Christopher B. Donnan. 1993. *Royal Tombs of Sipán*. Los Angeles: Fowler Museum of Cultural History, University of California.

Hume, Ivor Noël (1927–)

Ivor Noël Hume was born in 1927 in London, educated in England, and initially entered the profession as the Guildhall Museum archaeologist (1949–1957) exploring the exposed remains, including postmedieval deposits, of postwar London. However, it was not until he crossed the Atlantic in 1957 to assume command of archaeology at another capital, colonial WILLIAMSBURG in Virginia, that he embarked on a career of over forty years that helped to transform historical archaeology.

With the support of his wife and professional colleague, Audrey Noël Hume (1927–1993), he continuously built the field within three spheres: fieldwork, public education, and scholarly publication. As a result of his English archaeological training, he introduced the tradition of tightly controlled stratigraphic excavations to colonial sites within and around Williamsburg. Site reports soon followed, but of equal importance were the articles and monographs reflecting the accumulating knowledge of both of the Humes on recovered archaeological assemblages. In 1970, Noël Hume published *A Guide to Artifacts of Colonial America,* a work that revolutionized understanding of seventeenth- and eighteenth-century archaeology in English North America and, by extension, the world. It stands to this day as the only general source for the field.

Noël Hume was set off from his American colleagues not only because he was not an anthropologist but also because of his ability to handle and appreciate primary archival sources—he produced a fully *historical* archaeology. As early as 1966 he authored *1775: Another Part of the Field,* which made him one of the few archaeologists in the United States to publish straightforward history. His archaeological publications have been equally grounded on documentary as well as belowground data. In 1977, the spectacular discovery and areal excavation of the early-seventeenth-century site at Wolstenholme Town in Martin's Hundred on the James River in Virginia made him equally an expert on the seventeenth as well as the eighteenth century. His 1982 popular *Martin's Hundred* and the full site report have given scholarship one of the best-excavated and most fully explored early-seventeenth-century sites (1620–1622) in the world.

Accomplished as a researcher and scholar, Hume has been an equally important advocate for public education. Numerous lectures, articles (see Hume 1979), and well-received books such as *Here Lies Virginia* (1963) and *Historical Archaeology* (1969) have vividly and invitingly brought the romance of historical archaeology to the general public. Unlike many of his colleagues, Noël Hume can write clear and readable English. Perhaps no single contribution better combines his efforts in field archival research, careful scholarship, and public presentation than *The Virginia Adventure: Roanoke to Jamestown, an Archaeological and Historical Odyssey* (1994), one of the most widely read books in the field. He used a combined archaeological-archival approach in this volume to correctly predict the survival and the location of the original JAMESTOWN Fort (1607–1620s), which has since been discovered and is being excavated by William Kelso.

Hume's English training and perspective initially separated him from his U.S. anthropological colleagues, but his productive and insightful scholarship has helped to bridge the Atlantic divide. In January 1967, he was an important participant in the organizational meeting in Dallas, Texas, that created the SOCIETY FOR HISTORICAL ARCHAEOLOGY (SHA) and at which he urged an internationalist-global perspective for the new discipline. His membership on the SHA board of directors and vice-presidency of the parallel Society for Post-Medieval Archaeology in Europe helped to link these two organizations in their founding years. Ivor Noël Hume has received many awards, including being made an Officer of the British Empire (1991) for his work in Virginia, and in 1991, the SHA presented him with the highest honor achievable in historical archaeology, the J. C. HARRINGTON MEDAL.

Robert L. Schuyler

References

Hume, Ivor Noël. 1963. *Here Lies Virginia: An Archaeologist's View of Colonial Life and History.* New York: Knopf.

———. 1966. *1775: Another Part of the Field.* New York: Knopf.

———. 1969. *Historical Archaeology*. New York: Knopf.

———. 1970. *A Guide to Artifacts of Colonial America*. New York: Vintage Books.

———. 1979. "First Look at a Lost Virginia Settlement." *National Geographic Magazine* June.

———. 1982. *Martin's Hundred*. New York: Knopf.

———. 1994. *The Virginia Adventure: Roanoke to Jamestown, an Archaeological and Historical Odyssey*. New York: Knopf.

Inca

The Inca empire, which controlled much of the Andes of South America, was overthrown as a result of the Spanish conquest in 1532. As they did to the AZTEC civilization in MESOAMERICA, the Spanish exploited local political divisions to bring about a swift collapse of imperial authority. The Inca had, themselves, only recently achieved such political and military dominance, with their expansion out of the region of Cuzco beginning only about a century earlier.

In one sense, the Inca were the clear successors of earlier cultures, such as the MOCHE and the CHAVÍN, but in terms of political organization, the Inca system of imperial control, which (where possible) allowed for the retention of local religions and power structures, was a unique development. Major sites such as Machu Picchu and Cuzco and their extensive network of roads and bridges, irrigation systems, and terracing demonstrate the Inca's abilities as engineers and builders, but their material culture (particularly in textiles) was also of the finest order.

Tim Murray

See also Ecuador; Peru
References
Rostworowski, de Diez Canseco, Maria. 1999.
History of the Inca Realm. Translated by Harry B. Iceland. Cambridge: Cambridge University Press.

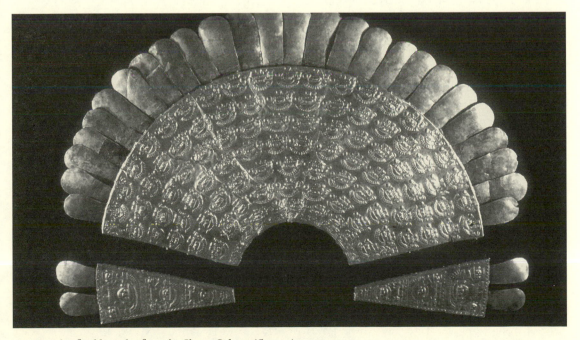

An example of gold jewelry from the Chimu Culture (Gamma)

India

See Indus Civilization; South Asia

Indo-Pacific Prehistory Association

The Indo-Pacific Prehistory Association (IPPA) has had several names since its inception in Batavia (at that time the capital of the netherlands Indies) in 1929 and its first congress in Hanoi in 1932. At first it was known only through the names of its congresses. The Hanoi congress was known as the First Congress of Far-Eastern Prehistorians; the second, held in 1935, was titled the Second Congress of Far-Eastern Prehistorians; and the third, held in 1938, was called the Third Congress of Prehistorians of the Far East. At the fourth congress, held after World War II, the name came to be the Far-Eastern Prehistory Association (FEPA). That name continued until 1975 when the organization adopted its final and present name, the Indo-Pacific Prehistory Association.

The beginning came about as a result of the Fourth Pacific Science Congress and the interest of Herbert E. Gregory, founder of the Pacific Science Association. In the preliminary organization of the Batavia Pacific Science Congress (1929), Gregory included a prehistory section and asked P. V. van Stein Callenfels to organize it. Among those taking part in this section, besides van Stein Callenfels, were Davidson Black, SIR GRAFTON ELLIOT SMITH, Sir Richard Winstedt, Victor Goloubew, and HENRY OTLEY BEYER. This group agreed to start an organization to promote research in prehistory in the Far East and settled on Hanoi for its first congress, to be hosted by the government of French Indo-China.

George Coedes was the organizing chairman of the congress, Paul Rivet was president, and Paul Mus acted as secretary. Other local organizers were Victor Goloubew and Madeleine Colani; other members were van Stein Callenfels from Java, Beyer from the PHILIPPINES, Richard Winstedt of Singapore, Ivor H. N. Evans of Taiping in what was then the Federated Malay States, Prince Rajadabhisek and Luang Boribal Buribhand of Thailand, Joseph Shellshear of Hong Kong, C. Haguenauer from JAPAN, and Henri Parmentier of CAMBODIA. The pro-

ceedings of the congress were published as *Praehistorica Asiae Orientalis* in Hanoi in 1932. The second congress was to have been in Bangkok in early 1935, but because of troubled conditions there in 1934, the congress was shifted to Manila. At that congress, there were sixteen delegates and nine associates representing eight different countries. Proceedings of this congress were never published, although a few of the papers presented were published later (Solheim 1957, 8).

The president of the third congress, held in Singapore in 1938, was W. Linehan, and he was assisted by F. N. Chasen and M. W. F. Tweedie. There were twenty-seven delegates and six associates, and in addition to the countries represented before, institutional delegates and associate members came from Australia, New Zealand, and CHINA—from Australia, D. A. Casey and FRED D. MCCARTHY and from China, Lin Huisiang (the founder of the first Anthropology Department in China and a former student of Beyer). Chasen and Tweedie (1940) edited the proceedings.

The fourth congress was to be held in Hong Kong in 1941, but the threatening international situation caused its postponement. It was finally held, jointly with the Eighth Pacific Science Congress, in Manila in 1953, organized by Beyer, in Batavia, with the prompting of H. E. Gregory. This was much larger than the previous congresses and included representatives from many Pacific islands as well as those from countries that had attended previously. Eighteen countries were represented with official delegates, and there were sixty-three members and delegates as well as seventeen associates and observers, with many more Asian participants.

The Far-Eastern Prehistory Association was organized at the final business meeting of the fourth congress. Eleven council members were elected to carry on FEPA business between congresses, and Beyer was elected as honorary chairman. Council members were McCarthy (Australia), LI CHI (China), Alexander Spoehr (Hawaii and the United States), F. S. Drake (Hong Kong), Bernard P. Groslier (Indochina), H. R. van Heekeren (INDONESIA), Ichiro Yawata (Japan), C. A. Gibson-Hill (Malaya), ROGER

DUFF (New Zealand), E. Arseno Manuel (Philippines), and Prince Dhani Nivat (Thailand). From these members, an executive committee of five was selected: Groslier as permanent president, Duff as permanent secretary, Li, Drake, and van Heekeren. Among other instructions, the executive committee was to sponsor future congresses, encourage the formation of branches in member countries or areas, prepare for member institutions and countries a semiannual report on prehistoric and other anthropological activities, and receive and administer funds.

Solheim was elected president of FEPA and was asked to write a constitution—up to this time, the organization had been without a constitution or bylaws. At each meeting, Solheim would propose incorporation, and Duff would counterpropose a vote of confidence in Solheim and that the organization should continue informally with Solheim doing all of the work. Duff always won. In 1972, Solheim started editing *The Far-Eastern Prehistory Association Newsletter* and continued to do so until 1975 when R. J. Lampert of Australia took over. The newsletter was replaced by the *Bulletin of the Indo-Pacific Prehistory Association* in 1980, edited by Peter Bellwood, who continues as editor.

A major congress was held in Nice, FRANCE, in 1975 in conjunction with the Eleventh Congress of the International Union of Prehistoric and Protohistoric Sciences. At this congress, a constitution was accepted, and it resulted in a reorganization and the change of the name to the Indo-Pacific Prehistory Association (Solheim 1977, 172–175). Solheim was elected president, and JACK GOLSON became vice-president, to assume the office of president in 1980. Rajendra Misra took over as president of IPPA in 1985 at the group's first independent congress, the twelfth, held at Penablanca, Cagayan Province, Philippines. Proceedings of a portion of this congress appeared in *Asian Perspectives* (Bellwood and Solheim 1984–1985). The second independent congress, the thirteenth, was held in Osaka and Tokyo in 1987, and the fourteenth congress took place in Yokyakarta, Indonesia, in 1990, with ROGER GREEN assuming the office of president. The fifteenth congress was held in Chiang Mai, Thailand, in January 1994 where R. P. Soejono took over as president and the sixteenth conference was held in Malacca, Malaysia, in 1999.

Wilhelm G. Solheim II

References

Bellwood, P., and W. G. Solheim II. 1984–1985. "Introduction." *Asian Perspectives* 26, no. 1: 15–17.

Chasen, F. N., and M. W. F. Tweedie. 1940. *Proceedings of the Third Congress of Prehistorians of the Far East.* Singapore: Government Printing Office.

Praehistorica Asiae Orientalis. 1932. Hanoi.

Solheim, W. G., II. 1957. "The Far-Eastern Prehistory Association." *Asian Perspectives* 1: 6–12.

———. 1977. "Reorganization of the Indo-Pacific Prehistory Association and the IXth Congress of the International Union of Prehistoric and Protohistoric Sciences." *Asian Perspectives* 20, no. 1: 172–178.

Indonesia

The growth of archaeology in Indonesia from an amateur activity to a science can be divided into five phases of development. The first phase comprises the intensive registration of ancient remains without the coordination and supervision of any authorized archaeological organization and occurred during the eighteenth and nineteenth centuries. The second phase, from 1900 to 1950, saw the institutionalization of archaeological activities, the consolidation of archaeological work, the emergence of new data, and the formulation of hypotheses across many different fields of archaeology. During the third phase, from 1950 to 1956, little archaeology was undertaken due to disruption by the struggle for political independence from Holland. Between 1956 and 1975 the study of archaeology of Indonesia by Indonesians was consolidated. From 1975 until the present archaeology in Indonesia has come of age.

Prior to the eighteenth century, knowledge of ancient objects and monuments was acquired through local and descriptive exploration, sometimes accompanied by classification based on their historical background but more often partly mythological and based on the beliefs of the local people. This kind of descriptive activity was carried out during the peak of the Majapahit kingdom in the middle of the fourteenth century by Npu Prapanca, as affirmed by several cantos of the Nagara Krtagama [Book of Royal Ode/Hymn] (Krom 1920, 1926, 1, 2, 47; Pigeaud 1960–1963, vol. 3).

The Eighteenth and Nineteenth Centuries

Descriptions of ancient objects and remains increased with the arrival of European powers in Indonesia. Many merchants, scholars, soldiers, civil servants, naturalists, travelers, priests, etc. (Koentjaraningrat 1958, 15–48) wrote about their experiences and Indonesia's curiosities as they explored the Indonesian archipelago (Rumphius 1705). Their descriptions included not only local traditions, history, and the economic situation but also prehistoric remains. Some descriptions, particularly during the eighteenth century, were in the form of reports and were later supplemented with more accurate observations of archaeological objects, such as the measurement of the Prambanan Temple by F. van Boeckholtz in 1790. The foundation of the Bataviaasch Genootschap van Kunsten en Wetenschappen (Batavian Society of Arts and Sciences) in 1778 had a great impact on research into the history, traditions, and archaeological remains of Indonesia.

During the nineteenth century, there was an increase in activity in several archaeological domains. Apart from more extensive observations, particularly of Hindu Buddhist temples (or candis), methods of dealing with the problems posed by ancient remains became more advanced. Archaeological activities were primarily of a documentary nature, with particular emphasis on candis, and they took the form of drawings (by H. Cornelius, H. N. Sieburgh, C. J. van der Vlis, F. C. Wilsen), photographs (by J. van Kinsbergen), inventories (by F. Junghuhn), restorations (e.g., of Mendut), and excavations (such as the temples on the Dieng Plateau). Systematic surveys and documentation (by J. F. G. Bramund, C. Leemans, W. P. Groeneveldt, R. D. M. Verbeek, J. Crawford, T. S. Raffles, etc.) are still important sources of information about Indonesia's past. Other European methods of site recording, such as the making of glass negatives of the Borobudur monument by A. Shaefer in 1845, were used with little success in Indonesia.

Other activities in prehistory undertaken during this century (Soejono 1969) included the grouping or classification of rectangular axes (C. N. Pleyte and others), a great interest in megalithic remains (H. E. Steinmetz and others), and the provenance of bronze kettledrums (JENS JACOB WORSAAE, A. B. Meyer, and others). By far the most significant achievement in prehistory during the nineteenth century was the discovery of *Pithecanthropus erectus* (Java Man) by EUGENE DUBOIS at Trinil, on the island of Java, in 1891.

Interest in Indonesia's Islamic past and observations and recordings of Islamic remains were minimal during this period. However, some fieldwork in this area included reports on the discovery of ancient gravestones in Aceh (1884) and a plan for the documentation (drawings, photographs, rubbings) and restoration of Islamic remains (Tjandrasasmita 1977). Many observers of ancient remains such as *candis*, megaliths, and bronze artifacts concluded that they were Hindu in origin. This observation was often the consequence of British archaeological activity in India and the structural resemblance between temple complexes and statues of deities or gods in Indonesia and those in India.

The increase of interest in ancient relics led to some attempts to establish a specific organization concerned with field archaeology, such as the Commissie tot het Opsporen, Verzamelen, en Bewaren van Oudheidkundige Voorwerpen (Commission for the Discovery, Collection, and Conservation of Ancient Objects) in 1822, but such attempts were unsuccessful. The private sector attempted to assist in archaeological research by founding the Archaeologische Vereeniging (Archaeological Society) in 1885, chaired by the engineer J. W. Ijzerman. He succeeded in exposing the basement of the Borobudur Temple decorated with Karmawibangga reliefs, which is, at present, covered by the lower terrace.

The foundations for the development of archaeology as a discipline in Indonesia were created by the Dutch in the fields of documentation, restoration, excavation, and interpretation.

These activities paralleled similar developments in Europe (Daniel 1950), as did all advances in archaeology in Indonesia during this period. By the middle of the nineteenth century, European principles of archaeology, such as the application of the THREE-AGE SYSTEM to ancient objects, diffusion, homotaxis, typology, the comparative method, synchronization techniques, and stratigraphic excavation, were being applied to sites and data in Indonesia. However, only a few of these, such as diffusion, typology, and homotaxis, were successfully applied. The reason may be that the archaeological practitioners in Indonesia were primarily amateurs and unable to fully grasp the development of the European methods of research, which had turned archaeologists there into professionals (such as CHRISTIAN J. THOMSEN, AUSTEN H. LAYARD, HEINRICH SCHLIEMANN, and others).

1900–1950

The focus on Hindu-Buddhist monuments continued into the twentieth century, indeed, until World War II. The Commissie in Nederlandsch Indie voor Oudheidkundig Onderzoek op Java en Madura (Commission in the Dutch East Indies for Archaeological Research in Java and Madura) was established in 1901, and its name reveals its limited powers and limited research scope. Behind its establishment was concern for the neglected state of Javanese antiquities, which had received little careful, detailed, or systematic examination, and the political necessity of creating a specialist archaeological organization similar to such organizations already in existence in Indochina and India. The commission survived until 1913 when the chairman of its board, J. L. A. Brandes, died. Then the Oudheidkundige Dienst (or OD, Archaeological Service) was created by the government of the Dutch East Indies, and N. J. Krom was appointed as its director. The OD's tasks, authority, and staff were extended in order to ensure better results.

The establishment of those two organizations was an important step in the development of archaeology in Indonesia. For the first time, a variety of archaeological activities was undertaken, and there was a center for the planning and direction of archaeology, which led to many improvements in archaeological practice in Indonesia (Soekmono et al. 1977). For the first time the results of archaeological research were published in the *Rapporten van de Oudheidkundige Commissie* (or *ROC* [Report of the Archaeological Commission]), which later continued as *Oudheidkundig Verslag van de Oudheidkundige Dienst in Nederlandsch Indie* (*OV;* Archaeological Report of the Dutch East Indies Archaeological Service). Archaeological schedules were proposed for every part of Indonesia, not just Java and Madura, and the technical support for the implementation of these plans was increased. H. L. Leydie Melville, P. J. Perquin, and J. J. de Vink were employed in the areas of inventory and documentation.

The restoration of Javanese temples received special attention, but it was not without controversy. There were arguments for a limited restoration of the remains of extant monuments, arguments for reconstructions of them on paper only (Krom), and arguments for the restoration of monuments, as far and as much as possible, by reconstruction. While F. D. R. Bosch was in charge of the OD, in 1916, there was conspicuous progress in temple restoration in Java. These restoration activities resulted in the formation of a permanent technical staff for this specialist restoration work located at Prambanan.

As the OD matured, there was more interest in other fields of archaeology such as Islamic remains (P. J. Moquette), prehistoric remains (P. V. van Stein Callenfels), and the more recent historic remains of the Portuguese and the Dutch East India Company (V. I. van de Wall). The investigation of inscriptions, pioneered in the previous century by R. M. Th. Friederich, Cohen Stuart, H. Kern, and others, increased, and archaeological investigations took place in Sumatra, Kalimantan, Sulawesi, Bali, the Lesser Sunda Islands, and the Moluccas.

Archaeological activities were also supported financially by prominent people outside the OD, such as civil servants, experts from other government institutions, and private individuals. The position of archaeology in Indonesia became even more stable after the Dutch East Indies government promulgated the Monumenten Ordonnantie (Ancient Monuments

Conservation Act) in 1931, which protected ancient remains and sites against damage, removal, and destruction.

The improvement in research, restoration, and recording led to the development of theories and hypotheses regarding the creation; distribution; styles; cultural, social, and religious significance; and history of Indonesia's antiquities. Bosch argued for the Indonesian people's greater involvement in the construction of their temples (Bosch 1919), counter to some opinions that Indians were the architects of these buildings and Indonesians only the laborers. These Indonesia-centric theories were supplemented more and more by the views of other scholars (Krom, W. F. Stutterheim, etc.). Other archaeological landmarks of this period include the publication of basic books on the Jago, Singasari, and Penataran monuments by Brandes (1904, 1909); Borobudur by Krom (1920) and Krom and van Erp (1920–1931); and Krom's work on Hindu-Javanese history (1926; Krom and van Erp 1920–1931) and Hindu-Javanese architecture. There was also growth in scientific archaeological activities when the OD was led by W. F. Stutterheim in 1936, but fieldwork declined owing to a shortage of staff and the economic crisis of the 1930s.

Although institutional and scientific archaeology was productive in Indonesia until the outbreak of World War II in East Asia, only a cadre of Dutch professionals were active in it. The OD was not large, and it was staffed by a core of Dutch archaeologists who worked across extensive regions. Archaeology stagnated in Indonesia during the Japanese occupation and the fight for independence from the NETHERLANDS after 1945. Only the technical staff at Prambanan was able to keep on with restoration and excavation during the Japanese occupation.

In 1945, during civil dissidence against the Dutch army, many documents that had been collected in Jakarta since the beginning of archaeological activities in Indonesia (such as archives of photographs, drawings, and books and a collection of research objects) were destroyed or disappeared. In 1947, the Dutch army, which had reoccupied Jakarta, set up and reorganized the OD.

This time the organization had technical branches in Ujung Pandang (South Sulawesi) and Gianyar (Bali). During the period of the struggle for independence, between 1947 and 1949, the prehistorian H. R. van Heekeren excavated in South Sulawesi, particularly at Maros, the cave-painting area, and at Kalumpang, a Neolithic settlement site. During this same period, J. C. Krijgsman was actively involved in the restoration of the ancient Hindu-Buddhist monuments of Bali.

1950–1956

In 1950, the Dinas Purbakala R.I. (Archaeological Service of the Republic of Indonesia) was established, with headquarters in Jakarta and A. J. Bernet Kempers as its head. Technical staff from Ujung Pandang were recalled to reinforce the staff at headquarters, and district offices called Seksi Bangunan Dinas Purbakala R.I. (Building Section of the Archaeological Service of the R.I.) were established. It was clear that the Republic of Indonesia urgently needed more support to become effective archaeologically as its scientific and technical staffs were inadequate.

In 1953, the Dinas Purbakala R.I. was placed under the charge of R. Soekmono, which meant that for the first time in the history of archaeology in Indonesia, the responsibility for Indonesia-wide archaeological work was under the supervision of an Indonesian archaeologist. Dutch archaeologists such as V. R. van Romondt, H. R. van Heekeren, J. G. de Casparis, M. J. van den End-Blom, and J. C. Krijgsman continued to work in Indonesia until 1960. Important work was accomplished in prehistory (Heekeren 1957), the Hindu-Buddhist or classical period (Bernet Kempers 1959), the Islamic period, and epigraphy (Casparis, 1950; Goris, 1954).

The last issues of *OV* (1941–1947, 1948, 1949) were published, and the journal was replaced by *Laporan Tahunan Dinas Purbakala* [Annual Reports of the Archaeological Service], which was published from 1950 to 1955. These publications contained general descriptions of the activities of the various branches of archaeology. The archaeological journal *Amerta,* a popular analysis of archaeological research in Indonesia, was also published at this time, and a more scientific analysis of data could be found in the series *Berita Dinas Purbakala* [Newsletter of the Archaeological Service]. More Indonesian scholars became involved in prehistoric, classical, and Islamic archaeology, and staff in the building sections were supplemented with Indonesian personnel and placed under Indonesian management. Professional courses for Indonesian archaeologists began at the Universities of Jakarta, Yogyakarta, and Denpasar, ensuring an ongoing Indonesian participation in the discipline.

When Dutch archaeologists returned to Holland after Indonesia's political independence, archaeological activities slowed down because of a shortage of appropriate Indonesian personnel. Although the operating budget for archaeology was minimal, Indonesian archaeologists, charged with the task of continuing the work of the OD, remained committed to the importance of Indonesian archaeology. Ironically, just at the time when more Indonesian archaeologists were beginning fieldwork and the science of archaeology was advancing rapidly, political circumstances in Indonesia made their lives and work difficult. Much effort was expended to fill gaps in the archaeological record and, with limited resources, to try to keep up with the many changes in archaeology and within the archaeological profession at an international level. Contact with international circles was maintained by means of regional and international conferences, publications in international media, and participation in joint archaeological programs with foreign teams.

Dutch archaeologists made significant contributions to the archaeology of Indonesia, and they were responsible for the establishment of Indonesia as an important area of archaeological research in Southeast Asia. In spite of many shortcomings, Dutch archaeologists laid the foundations for the further development of archaeology in Indonesia. Their most significant oversight was their failure to educate a cadre of Indonesian archaeologists to succeed them. (This was the case in many other ex-colonies in Southeast and SOUTH ASIA as well.) At independence, there was no leadership and little expertise in archaeology among the Indonesian peo-

ple. Dutch archaeologists had concentrated on developing technical staff to support their interests and fieldwork, and it was only these staff members who had received any education or training. Consequently, the archaeological infrastructure and focus bequeathed by the Dutch to Indonesia was outside the capabilities and interests of the Indonesian people.

It is important to note that prior to World War II, the Dutch discovery of Indonesian archaeological evidence contributed to the development of an Indonesian identity and to Indonesian nationalism, and Dutch archaeological literature and research remain important parts of Indonesia's archaeology. In 1956, the small number of Indonesian archaeologists left to shoulder the archaeological burden of the country found it almost impossible to carry out administrative and organizational tasks and also to conduct field and scientific research. Funding, facilities, and resources for archaeology declined to levels below those provided for it before World War II.

1956–1975

During this period, although archaeology in Indonesia remained complex and vast, and despite a lack of resources, the discipline matured and produced professional and high quality results. The Lembaga Purbakala dan Peninggalan Nasional (National Institutes of Archaeology and Antiquities, the former Archaeological Service) was set up with four field or branch offices. The provision of minimal facilities and funding, for both the central and the branch offices, meant that planned archaeological fieldwork, such as surveys, excavations, and restorations, was difficult to accomplish. Between 1956 and 1975, little fieldwork took place, and documentation, registration, reports, and scientific article writing all stagnated. Factors such as the system of government, politics, and socioeconomics, and the small higher-education system, meant that archaeology in Indonesia continued to develop slowly.

But there were some achievements, including the designation and restoration of the Borobudur Temple as a national project supported with special funds, the implementation

One of the ornate temples at Borobudur, Indonesia (Corel)

of joint programs with teams of foreign archaeologists, and the sending of Indonesian archaeologists abroad to further their education in both the technical and the theoretical fields. The last two achievements have increased Indonesia's ability to carry out restorations with the support of laboratories, technology, and the appropriate surveys and excavations.

1975–

A military coup of 1975 and the rule of the Suharto regime until 1999 drastically affected the organization of archaeology in Indonesia. The state organization for archaeology was divided into two special units, each with its own function and tasks (Soejono 1987). Archaeological activities were divided into two categories, administrative and scientific. The organization in charge of the administrative functions became the Direktorat Sejarah dan Purbakala (Directorate of Archaeology and History), and the organization in charge of the scientific activities was the Pusat Penelitian Purbakala dan Peninggalan Nasional (Center of Archaeological Research and National Monuments). These names

have been changed and are now the Direktorat Perlindungan dan Pembinaan Peninggalan Sejarah dan Purbakala (Directorate for Protection and Development of Historical and Archaeological Remains) and the Pusat Penelitian Arkeologi Nasional (National Research Center of Archaeology).

This division is significant for two reasons. First, each division concentrates on its respective area and tackles problems separately. There had been too many and complex administrative and organizational problems for a joint organization to resolve. Second, the division has created more opportunities for scientific work. The division of archaeology has been unified and coordinated with a large and qualified staff, a broad organizational structure, and a sufficiently large infrastructure. It is possible to avoid overlapping activities, and the two official divisions work to develop a national plan of priorities for monuments and archaeology.

National short- and long-term development programs now support a wide range of archaeological projects. These programs have improved conditions for archaeology, and their outcomes will greatly influence the advancement of archaeology as a science in modern Indonesia. Archaeology in Indonesia has now achieved a structure and level of organization within a framework of government that should lead to an increase in all areas—fieldwork, restoration, protection and conservation, and publication, all supported by the national development program. The education of archaeological cadres is now being provided by Indonesian universities.

Within two decades of the separation of archaeology into two specialized divisions, there was a great increase in archaeological fieldwork, scientific research, and restoration across almost all of the Indonesian archipelago. It has been a remarkable achievement given the huge area covered and the enormous amount of archaeological data involved. The preservation and research of prehistoric, classic (Hindu-Buddhist), Islamic, and colonial sites and artifacts have been carried out despite inadequate funding and personnel.

Discoveries comprise: fossil remains of early hominids in Java; bronze kettledrums, and prehistoric ceremonial objects in South Sumatra, West Kalimantan, Java, Bali, and East Nusa Tenggara; prehistoric burial complexes in Java and Bali; and Hindu-Buddhist temples on Java and Bali. Restoration and preservation have been undertaken at prehistoric megalithic sites and include objects in Sumatra and Java; Hindu-Buddhist temple complexes on Java, Sumatra, and Bali; ancient mosques and tombs of the Islamic period in Sumatra, Java, Sulawesi, and East Nusa Tenggara; and colonial buildings and fortresses in Sumatra, Java, Sulawesi, and East Nusa Tenggara. These discoveries and the results of research from both divisions have been published in professional and popular journals and reports.

Workshops and seminars on archaeology are annually organized at national and international levels. Field museums at several important archaeological sites like Trinil, Sangiran, Trowulan, and Banten, all located on Java, have been completed, and many archaeological artifacts are now in provincial museums. The Act of Preservation of Cultural Property, with particular reference to archaeological artifacts and sites, was implemented in 1992 to prevent illegal excavation and the export and sale of archaeological artifacts. Exhibitions and public lectures on archaeology are given frequently in the provincial capitals.

R. P. Soejono

See also Island Southeast Asia

References

Bernet Kempers, A. J. 1959. *Ancient Indonesian Art.* Amsterdam: Van der Peet.

Bosch, F. D. R. 1919. "Een hypothese omtrent den oorsprong der Hindoe-Javaansche kunst." In *Handelingen van het le Congres voor Je Taal-, Land-Volkenkunde van Java.*

Brandes, J. L. A. 1904. "Beschrijving van de ruine bij de desa Toempang, genaamd Tjandi Djago, in de residentie Paseeoeroean." *Batavia: Uitgave Koninklijk Instituut en Bataviaasch Genootschap.*

————. 1909. *Beschrijving van Tjandi Singasari; en de wolkentoneelen van Panataran.* Batavia: Uitgave Koninklijk Instituut en Bataviaasch Genootschap.

Casparis, J. G. de. 1950. *Inscripties uit de Cailendratijd: Prasasti Indonesia.* Vol. 1. Bandung and Jakarta: Dinas Purbakala R.I.

Daniel, G. E. 1950. *A Hundred Years of Archaeology.* London: Duckworth.

Goris, R. 1954. Prasastii Bali I-II. Bandung: Lembaga bahasa dan budaja, University of Indonesia.

Heekeren, H. R. van. 1957. *The Stone Age of Indonesia.* Verhandelingen Koninklijk Instituut voor Taal-, Land- en Volkenkunde, vol. 21. The Hague: Nijhoff. Rev. ed., 1972, vol. 61.

————. 1958. *The Bronze-Iron Age of Indonesia.* Verhandelingen Koninklijk Instituut voor Taal-, Land- en Volkenkunde, vol. 22. The Hague: Nijhoff.

Koentjaraningrat, R. M. 1958. "Beberapa metode anthropologi dalam penjelidikan-penjelidikan masjarakat dan ke-budajaan di Indonesia (Sebuah ikhtisar)." Ph.D. dissertation, University of Jakarta.

Krom, N. J. 1920. *Inleiding tot de Hindoe-Javaansche Kunst.* 2 vols. Verhandelingen Koninklijk Instituut voor Taal-, Land- en Volkenkunde. The Hague: Nijhoff.

————. 1926. *Hindoe-Javaansche Geshiedenis.* Verhandelingen Koninklijk Instituut voor Taal-, Land- en Volkenkunde. The Hague: Nijhoff. 2d rev. ed., 1931.

Krom, N. J., and T. van Erp. 1920–1931. *Beschrijving van Bara-budur.* 2 vols. The Hague: M. Nijhoff.

Pigeaud, Th. G. 1960–1963. *Java in the 14th Century.* 5 vols. Koninklijk Instituut voor Taal-, Land- en Volkenkunde, Translation Series no. 4. The Hague.

Rumphius, G. E. 1705. *D'Amboinsche Rariteitkamer.* Amsterdam: Fr. Halma.

Soejono, R. P. 1968–1969. "Reprospect and Prospect of Archaeology in Indonesia." *Journal of the Oriental Society of Australia* 6, nos. 1–2: 114–121.

———. 1969. "The History of Prehistoric Research in Indonesia to 1950." *Asian Perspectives* 12: 69–91.

———. 1983. *Syarat dan ruang lingkup pengembangan Arkeologi di Indonesia* [On the Conditions and Scope of the Development of Archaeology in Indonesia]. Seminar Arkeologi, Cibulan, 2–6 February 1976. Jakarta: Pusat Penelitian Arkeologi Nasional. pp. 35–53.

———. 1987. "Archaeological Research in Indonesia." *Journal of Southeast Asian Studies* 18, no. 3: 212–216.

Soekmono, R., et al. 1977. *Lima puluh tahun lembaga purbakala dan peninggalan nasional 1913–1963.* Jakarta: Departemen Pendidikan dan Kebudayaan.

Tjandrasasmita, U. 1977. "Riwayat penyelidikan kepurbakalaan Islam di Indonesia." In R. Soekmono et al., *Lima puluh tahun lembaga purbakala dan peninggalan basional 1913–1963,* 107–135. Jakarta: Departemen Pendidikan dan Kebudayaan.

Indus Civilization
First Phase (1924–1946)

On the basis of excavations in what is now Pakistan by D. R. Sahni at HARAPPA in 1920–1921 and by RAKAL DAS BANERJI at Mohenjo Daro in 1921–1922, JOHN MARSHALL, the then-director general of the Archaeological Survey of India, made the first formal announcement of the discovery of this civilization in 1924 (Marshall 1924). Both of these sites were known earlier, however. In 1911–1912, D. R. Bhandarkar had visited Mohenjo Daro to report on a Buddhist stupa there; in 1876, ALEXANDER CUNNINGHAM had published some seals and antiquities from Harappa; and "Indus" material from the site of Sutkagendor along the western part of the Makran coast in Baluchistan, much to the west of the Indus Valley, had been illustrated by W. T. Blandford in 1877. However, the Bronze Age character of these sites was not understood earlier (Chakrabarti 1988, 156–164; Deva 1982; Pande 1982; Possehl 1982).

Before MORTIMER WHEELER (1947), a successor of John Marshall, reexcavated the citadel mound at Harappa in 1946 and began a new phase of Indus studies, the work on that civilization had proceeded in the following directions. Mohenjo Daro in the lower Indus Valley, or the province of Sind, was excavated until 1927 under Marshall's supervision. It was further excavated in 1927–1931 by E. Mackay who, although an outsider to the survey, was engaged for the purpose because of his experience at the large and more or less contemporary Mesopotamian site of Kish. In 1935, Mackay excavated Chanhudaro, another Indus site in Sind. In both north and south Baluchistan, some Indus sites were reported by AUREL STEIN (1929, 1931) after exploring the region in 1927. Information about more of the sites in Sind were published by N. G. Majumdar (1934) and M. S. Vats (1938). In Gujarat in western India, an Indus site was identified by Vats (1937) at Rangpur. Sahni excavated Harappa in the upper Indus Valley, or Punjab, in 1920–1921 and 1923–1925, but between 1926 and 1934, the site was excavated by Vats (1940) who reported another site near Harappa in addition to pointing out the Indus character of Kotla Nihang Khan in the Simla foothills of northern India. In 1942, Stein (1942) reported Indus sites in Bahawalpur in what is now Pakistan.

Thus, in the first phase of its study, the distribution of the Indus civilization was known to have extended from the Makran coast to the Simla foothills and from northern Baluchistan to Gujarat. Its extensive distribution in Sind and in the dried-up Ghaggar-Hakra drainage system of Bahawalpur was also understood during this period. More significantly, the classical excavation reports on Mohenjo Daro (Mackay 1938; Marshall, ed. 1931), Harappa (Vats 1940), and Chanhudaro (Mackay 1943) were published.

The first and most significant statement

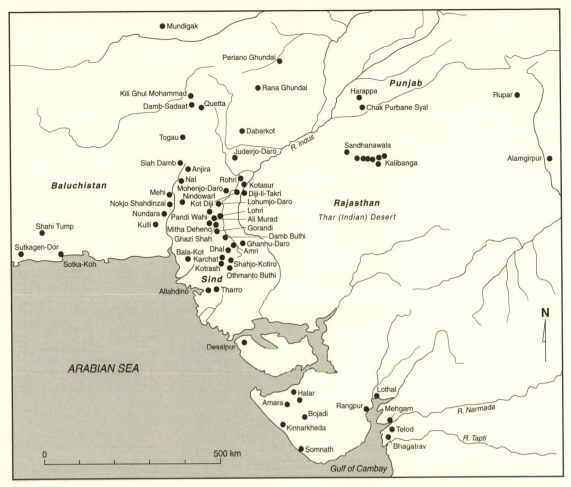

Indus Valley Civilization Archaeological Sites

about the Indus civilization during this period was made by Marshall (Marshall, ed. 1931). First, the civilization was roughly contemporary with the Sumerian antiquities of MESOPOTAMIA and as distinctive of the Indus as the civilization of the Pharaohs was distinctive of the Nile. Second, the civilization had deep roots in the soil. Third, it showed the earliest evidence of grid planning in the world, although in detail its civic planning was reminiscent of the austere character of British industrial cities. Fourth, in many ways, especially crafts, religion, and sculpture, this civilization preempted many features of the historic civilization of India. From this point of view, Hinduism was the oldest living faith in the world. Fifth, the civilization was pre- and non-Vedic in its relationship with the "Vedic period," which was the starting point of ancient India until this civilization was discovered. As far as the

last hypothesis is concerned, Marshall depended on the opinion of one of his own survey officers, R. P. Chanda (1926, 1929), who went to the extent of arguing that the civilization was destroyed by Aryan invasions, thus preempting what Wheeler (1947) wrote much later.

Further, Mohenjo Daro was supposed to have had three main periods: early, intermediate, and late. The early levels could not be fully excavated, but the buildings on the western mound at Mohenjo Daro were found to have stood on an artificial platform of the early intermediate period. It was also found that the city as a whole suffered a marked decline in civic standards during the late period. On the basis of his work at Amri, Ghazi Shah, Pandi Wahi, Jhukar, and Lohumjodaro in Sind, Majumdar (1934) postulated early, later, and late phases for the civilization as a whole.

Seals of the Indus Valley culture (Image Select)

Second Phase (1947–1963)

The second phase of Indus studies began in 1947 when Wheeler published the results of his excavations at the western mound of Harappa in 1946. The main achievement of this work was that a major Indus civilization site came to be bracketed between earlier and later occupations. Wheeler also argued that the Indus civilization was ruled by "priest-kings," had a military character in the form of defense walls, and eventually fell to the Aryan invaders whose archaeological evidence he claimed to have found in Cemetery H ware at the site. In 1950, in his new capacity as the archaeological adviser to the government of Pakistan, Wheeler outlined the fortification wall of the western mound of the site and argued for the presence of a granary among its building complexes.

In 1953, Wheeler published the first edition of *The Indus Civilization,* a work that in two major ways marked a significant departure from the earlier analysis of the civilization by Marshall. First, its chronology was brought down to

2500–1500 B.C. Assuming that evidence of its contact with Mesopotamia went back only to the Sargonic period (c. 2300 B.C.) and that its end coincided with the assumed date of Aryan invasions to India around 1500 B.C., the Indus civilization, instead of being roughly a contemporary of the Sumerian antiquities of Mesopotamia, as in Marshall's analysis, became one of its late contemporaries. Second, Wheeler argued that the idea of civilization in the Indus Valley was derived from Mesopotamia. This idea was a complete turnaround from those of Marshall's days and marked the beginning of a trend that has only been reinforced by the writings of a large number of Western scholars who have recently worked between IRAN, the Gulf, and the Indus.

In India, this phase was marked by a great number of discoveries in the Ghaggar-Drishadvati system in Rajasthan-Haryana and Gujarat. This was also the time when the easternmost point in the distribution of Indus sites was traced at Alamgirpur in Uttar Pradesh near

Delhi. Among the excavations in India undertaken or begun during this period were those at Rupar in Punjab, Alamgirpur in the Doab, Rangpur and Lothal in Gujarat, and Kalibangan in the dried-up Ghaggar Valley in Rajasthan (Pande 1982, 397–398). In Pakistan, the major breakthrough at Kot Diji led to the premise of a continuity between the earlier Kot Diji culture and the later Indus civilization level at the site, and at Amri, there were further elaborations of Majumdar's work during the preceding phase. Some miscellaneous work in Baluchistan highlighted the early character of village farming communities in the region. Along the Makran coast, the "port" character of the Indus site of Sutkagendor was highlighted, especially in the context of new discoveries in the Gulf area throwing light on its contact with the Indus civilization (annual volumes of *Pakistan Archaeology*, a government publication from 1964 onward).

Third Phase (1964–1984)

Beginning in about 1964, the third phase lasted up to the mid-1980s. This phase perhaps began with G. F. Dales's publication on the mythical massacre at Mohenjo Daro (Dales 1964), in which the improbability that the city fell to Aryan invaders was argued graphically. The excavations at Kalibangan in Rajasthan (Lal 1979) continued through the 1960s, and excavations began during this period at Surkotada in Kutch in northwestern India (Joshi 1990) and at Banawali (Bisht 1982, 1987) in Haryana. In Pakistan, this phase witnessed the beginning of a massive structural and other documentation project at Mohenjo Daro, including an intensive surface survey to locate craft-activity areas (Jansen and Urban 1984, 1987). A late level of the civilization was identified at Daimabad (Sali 1986) in the Godavari Valley of Maharashtra, and a mature form of the civilization was located at Shortughai, around the Indus River in India (Francfort 1989).

In Pakistan, the discovery of a large number of sites from the presumably fifth millennium B.C. Hakra ware phase to the late "Harappan/Indus" horizon of the second millennium B.C. in the dried-up Hakra drainage system in Bahawalpur (Mughal 1982) was a major event. In India, it was found that the entire area between

the Ghaggar course in Rajasthan (known as the Hakra in Pakistan) and Saharanpur in the Doab was dotted with early, mature, and late sites. Another major discovery was that of the Ganeshwar-Jodhpura culture in the Sikar district of Rajasthan, a culture contemporary with the early phase of the civilization. The northernmost extension of the Indus sites in India was found at Manda in Jammu, and in Gujarat, too, there were major discoveries during this phase, notably in Kutch (Joshi, Bala, and Ram 1984).

Ideas regarding the origin and decline of the civilization took some specific forms during this period. On the basis of earlier work at Amri and Kot Diji and the ongoing work at Kalibangan, A. GHOSH (1965) argued in favor of a homogeneous pre-Harappan substratum in the entire Harappan distribution area. Other scholars also favored such a hypothesis, which was put on a more solidly documented basis by R. Mughal (1971). However, the reason for the transformation from the early to the mature Harappan was not explained, which left scope for factors such as long-distance trade and proto-Elamite influence to be invoked as catalytic factors in the genesis of the Indus civilization. Radiocarbon chronology was applied to this civilization in the early 1960s (Agrawal 1964), but so far it has not been able to dislodge the Wheeler bracket of 2500–1500 B.C., an attempt at calibration (Brunswig 1975) and evidence of pre-Sargonic contact with Mesopotamia (Chakrabarti 1982) notwithstanding. The quest for Aryans is not yet over (cf. Hiebert and Lamberg-Karlovsky 1992).

On the whole, however, there was no difficulty at all in visualizing the late phase of the Indus civilization as transformation into an essentially nonurban form that developed regional characters in all the relevant areas. Subsistence (Vishnu-Mittre and Savithri 1982; Weber 1991), trade (Chakrabarti 1990; Lahiri 1992, 67–144; Ratnagar 1981; Shaffer 1982), metallurgy (Agrawal 1971), script (Mahadevan 1977), miscellaneous craft behavior such as the manufacturing of shell bangles and beads (Hegde, Karanth, and Sychanthavong 1982; Kenoyer 1984), etc., began to be subjected to detailed study. In the early 1980s, the "Neolithic" discovery at Mehrgarh in the Bolan Val-

Lower city with well shaft at Mohenjo Daro, Pakistan (AAA)

ley alluvium of Baluchistan provided a very long rural antecedent to the development of civilization in the Indus region.

Current Phase (1985–)

Since the mid-1980s, the study of the Indus civilization has been in its fourth and current phase. In India, this phase is likely to be dominated by the ongoing excavations at Dholavira in Kutch (Bisht 1991), which have already added new features to Harappan planning, water management, stonemason's work, etc. The discovery of a few large script signs, made of carefully cut crystalline material and presumably set on a wooden board, has also led to a fresh appreciation of the extent of Harappan literacy. This site has also shown the entire archaeological sequence of this civilization in Kutch, including its early and later phases. In Pakistan, this is the phase of prolonged excavations at Harappa, especially in its eastern sector, and the stratigraphic and cultural details that have already emerged (Dales 1992) help us to understand this civilization, as at Dholavira, as an integral part of a deep-rooted cultural development and its subsequent transformation.

On the theoretical side there is now a marked contrast between an approach centered on western Asia and an approach that favors an indigenous framework of development and transformation. The first approach favors a short chronology for the civilization and restricts it, by implication, to the status of being a mere episode in the history of SOUTH ASIA. Second, this approach puts an inordinate amount of emphasis on external trade with various areas in western and central Asia. For instance, western archaeologists who work in Oman argue that Oman was the main supplier of copper to the Indus civilization, despite the very large presence of copper on the subcontinent. In contrast, the indigenous approach argues for a long chronology, cites ethnographic data to argue that the civilization's external trade was not characteristically different from the trade that continued well into the twentieth century in this region overall, and provides a scheme that helps to understand the civilization as an integral part of the total process of Indian history and culture.

Basically, there were apparently two major variables in the emergence of the Indus civilization. First, the sites in the Indus Valley shift to the floodplain proper only with the emergence of the Indus civilization, which means that the behavior of the Indus was understood and controlled before this period. In the premodern period, the river could be used in the otherwise arid landscape of Sind for agriculture because of an irrigation system based on artificially dug flow channels that moved from the higher level of the riverbed to the lower level of the adjacent plain. It has been argued that this system came to be devised in the early Harappan period, possibly first in the Ghaggar-Hakra drainage in the Bahawalpur sector. I believe that because of its lesser gradient and also because of its origin in the outer Himalayan arc, and not in the snow-fed region, this drainage system was far easier to control than the Indus in full flow. There is also a study based on remote-sensing techniques and micromorphological studies that shows that early Harappan and later sites in Haryana were linked to irrigation canals, which thus gives the present hypothesis added credibility.

The second variable is in the shape of the singularly copper-rich Ganeshwar culture, of which more than fifty sites exist to the east of the Ghaggar-Hakra system. It has been argued that the development of a very rich copper metallurgical tradition with demonstrably close links to the early Harappan level was likely to have led to the intensification of metallurgical and other craft activities at this level. This process could be the key second variable in the emergence of the Indus civilization.

Regarding the end of the Indus civilization, it has been argued that when the central system of the civilization collapsed, there emerged some regional cultures covering a large number of mostly small sites. The distribution maps suggest a steady movement of "late Harappans" to the Doab on the one hand and to Deccan and Malwa on the other. One of the major factors of collapse was possibly the increasing drying up of the Ghaggar-Hakra drainage, which in the Bahawalpur sector was indeed the core area of the development of the civilization. Another probable factor was the archaeologically demonstrable fact that even though a considerable part of its distribution lay outside the core area, the Indus civilization was imposed on an essentially hunting-and-gathering economy. Therefore, it was much easier for the civilization to revert to a rural form once the central system collapsed. It has further been argued that the Harappans in general and the late Harappans in particular interacted with the advanced Mesolithic hunter-gatherers of inner India, which led to the growth of Neolithic-Chalcolithic communities in various parts.

At the grassroots level, the history of India is the story of absorption of regional hunter-gatherers within the fold of a plow-based agricultural system, and it is obvious that the indigenous approach outlined above enables one to visualize the beginning of this process as early as the period of the Indus civilization. The facts that the Bahawalpur area was the core area of development of the Indus civilization and that, toward the end, this civilization merged with the cultural process of inner India have been made clear by the work in Bahawalpur in Pakistan and the work in India from near that sector to the Doab on the one hand and from Kutch to Maharashtra and Malwa on the other.

Dilip Chakrabarti

References

Agrawal, D. P. 1964. "Harappa Culture: New Evidence for a Shorter Chronology." *Science,* 28 February, 1–3.

———. 1971. *The Copper-Bronze Age in India.* New Delhi: Munshiram Manoharlal.

Bisht, R. S. 1982. "Excavations at Banawali: 1974–77." In *Harappan Civilization,* 113–124. Ed. G. L. Possehl. New Delhi: Oxford & IBH in collaboration with American Institute of Indian Studies. Hereafter cited as *HC.*

———. 1987. "Further Excavation at Banawali: 1983–84." In *Archaeology and History,* 1:135–156. Ed. B. M. Pande and B. D. Chattopadhyay. Delhi: Agam Kala Prakashan.

———. 1991. "Dholavira: A New Horizon of the Indus Civilization." *Puratattva* 20: 71–82.

Brunswig, R. H. 1975. "Radiocarbon Dating and the Indus Civilization Calibration and Chronology." *East and West* 25: 111–145.

Chakrabarti, D. K. 1982. "Long Barrel-Cylinder Beads and the Issue of Pre-Sargonic Contact between the Harappan Civilization and Mesopotamia." In *HC,* 265–270.

———. 1988. *A History of Indian Archaeology from*

the Beginning to 1947. New Delhi: Munshiram Manoharlal Publishers.

———. 1990. *The External Trade of the Indus Civilization*. New Delhi: Munshiram Manoharlal Publishers.

———. 1995. *The Archaeology of Ancient Indian Cities*. Delhi : Oxford University Press,

Chanda, R. P. 1926. *The Indus Valley in the Vedic Period*. Calcutta: Government of India, Central Publication Branch.

———. 1929. *Survival of the Prehistoric Civilization of the Indus Valley*. Calcutta: Govt. of India, Central Publication Branch.

Dales, G. F. 1964. "The Mythical Massacre at Mohenjodaro." *Expedition* 6: 36–43.

———. 1992. "Recent Excavations at Harappa." *Eastern Anthropologist* 45: 21–38.

Deva, K. 1982. "Contributions of Aurel Stein and N. G. Majumdar to Research into the Harappan Civilization with Special Reference to Their Methodology." *HC*, 387–393.

During-Caspers, E. C. L. 1971. "Etched Carnelian Beads." *Bulletin of the Institute of Archaeology* 10: 83–98.

Francfort, H-P. 1989. *Fouilles de Shortughai*. 2 vols. Paris: Mission archéologique française en Asie centrale : Diffusion de Boccard.

Ghosh, A. 1965. "The Indus Civilization." In *Indian Prehistory*, 113–156. Ed. V. N. Misra and N. S. Mate. Poona, India: Deccan College Postgraduate & Research Institute.

Hegde, K. T. M., R. V. Karanth, and S. P. Sychanthavong. 1982. "On the Composition and Technology of Harappan Microbeads." *HC*, 239–243.

Hiebert, F. T., and C. C. Lamberg-Karlovsky. 1992. "Central Asia and the Indo-Iranian Borderlands." *Iran* 30: 1–15.

Jansen, M., and G. Urban, eds. 1984. *Interim Reports, Vol. I*. Aachen: German Research–Project Mohenjo-Daro.

———. 1987. *Interim Reports, Vol. II*. Aachen: German Research–Project Mohenjo-Daro.

Joshi, J. P. 1990. *Excavations at Surkotada and Exploration in Kutch*. New Delhi: Archaeological Survey of India.

Joshi, J. P., M. Bala, and J. Ram. 1984. "The Indus Civilization: A Reconsideration on the Basis of Distribution Maps." In *Frontiers of the Indus Civilization*, 511–530. Ed. B. B. Lal and S. P. Gupta. New Delhi: Published by Books & Books on behalf of Indian Archaeological Society jointly with Indian History & Culture Society.

Kenoyer, J. M. 1984. "Shell-working Industries of the Indus Civilization: A Summary." *Paleorient* 10: 49–63.

Lahiri, Nayanjot. 1992. *The Archaeology of Indian Trade Route*s. Delhi; New York: Oxford University Press.

Lal, B. B. 1979. "Kalibangan and the Indus Civilization." In *Essays in Indian Protohistory*, 65–97. Ed. D. P. Agrawal and D. K. Chakrabarti. Delhi: Published on behalf of the Indian Society for Prehistoric and Quaternary Studies [by] B. R. Pub. Corp.

Mackay, E. 1938. *Further Excavations at Mohenjodaro*. Delhi: Delhi, Manager of publications

———. 1943. *Chanhudaro*. New Haven.

Mahadevan, I. 1977. *The Indus Script: Texts, Concordance, and Tables*. New Delhi: Archaeological Survey of India.

Majumdar, N. G. 1934. *Explorations in Sind*. Delhi: Manager of Publications.

Marshall, J. 1924. "First Light on a Long-Forgotten Civilization." *Illustrated London News,* 20 September, 528–532, 548.

Marshall, J., ed. 1931. *Mohenjodaro and the Indus Civilization*. Delhi: Indological Book House.

Mughal, R. 1971. *The Early Harappan Period in the Greater Indus Valley and Northern Baluchistan*. Ann Arbor, MI.

———. 1982. "Recent Archaeological Research in the Cholistan Desert." *HC*, 85–96.

Pande, B. M. 1982. "History of Research on the Harappa Culture." *HC*, 395–413.

Ratnagar, S. 1981. *Encounters*. Delhi and New York: Oxford University Press.

Sali, S. A. 1986. *Daimabad*. New Delhi: Archaeological Survey of India, Government of India.

Shaffer, J. G. 1982. "Harappan Commerce: An Alternative Perspective." In *Anthropology in Pakistan,* 166–210. Ed. S. Pastner and L. Flam. Karachi: Indus Publications.

Stein, A. 1929. *An Archaeological Tour in Waziristan and Northern Baluchistan*. Calcutta : Govt. of India, Central Publication Branch.

———. 1931. *An Archaeological Tour in Gedrosia*. Calcutta : Government of India, Central Publication Branch.

———. 1942. "A Survey of Sites along the 'Lost' Sarasvati River." *Geographical Journal* 102: 193–227.

Vats, M. S. 1937. "Trial Excavations at Rangpur Limbdi State, Kathiawar." *Annual Report, Archaeological Survey of India 1934–1935*, 34–38.

———. 1940. *Excavations at Harappa.* Delhi: Manager of Publications.

Vishnu-Mittre and R. Savithri. 1982. "Food Economy of the Harappans." *HC,* 205–221.

Weber, S. 1991. *Plants and Harappan Subsistence.* Boulder, CO: Westview Press.

Wheeler, M. 1947. "Harappa 1946: The Defences and Cemetery R-37." *Ancient India* 3: 58–130.

———. 1953. *The Indus Civilization.* London.

Industrial Archaeology

A systematized means of utilizing artifacts, images, structures, sites, and landscapes in the investigation of the industrial past, industrial archaeological studies are making significant contributions to historical understanding. There are learned societies, journals, and publications on the subject in most western European countries, in North America, in JAPAN, and in Australia. Industrial heritage is receiving increasing attention in RUSSIA and in Latin America and is beginning to be recognized in most other countries.

An international organization, the International Committee for the Conservation of the Industrial Heritage (TICCIH), was formally constituted at a conference at Grangärde, Sweden, in 1977 after preliminary meetings at Ironbridge, England, in 1973 and Bochum, Germany, in 1975. TICCIH holds conferences, usually at three-year intervals, and each result in a volume of reports on developments in the industrial heritage of particular countries in addition to the conference proceedings (CEHOPU 1992; CILAC 1981, 1985; Cossons 1975; Georgeacopol-Winischhofer, Swittalek, and Wehdorm 1987, 1990; Kroker 1978; Nisser 1978, 1981; Nisser and Bedoire 1978; Vanderhulst 1992; Victor and Wright 1984; Wright and Vogel 1986). TICCIH also encourages the establishment of national organizations for promoting the study of the industrial heritage, and its council and officers are elected by the accredited representatives of such bodies.

In England, the expression *industrial archaeology* is sometimes used to imply that it is a social activity, and, in other European countries, terms meaning industrial heritage—*patrimoine industriel* or *industrieel erfgoed,* for example—are similarly comprehensive, encompassing such activities as the conservation and operation of railways and canals, the collection of steam road vehicles, and the adaptive reuse of industrial buildings. The term *industrial archaeology* is best used in a more narrow academic sense to describe research into past industrial societies based on the scientific analysis of physical remains, whether these are artifacts, images, structures, sites, or landscapes, and industrial archaeology is a subsector of the broader field of investigation defined as archaeology.

The Portuguese polymath Francisco de Sousa Viterbo (1845–1910) first used the term *arqueologia industrial* in 1896 in a study in which he argued that much could be learned from study of the physical remains of past manufacturing activities and from the memories of people who had been involved in the production process (Sousa Viterbo 1896/1986). The value of artifacts in the study of industrial history was acknowledged by the founders of the great national museums of technology like the Musée National des Techniques, Paris; the Science Museum, London; and the Technisches Museum für Industrie und Gewerbe, Vienna. Historians of industry in the first half of the twentieth century nevertheless made sparse use of archaeological evidence, and some standard works on the British Industrial Revolution show a remarkable ignorance of the most basic technological processes and scarcely any awareness of the most important manufacturing complexes. The only outstanding archaeological study of industry in England in this period was by an amateur scholar (Straker 1931).

Industrial archaeology was reborn in the 1950s. The Belgian scholar René Evrard (1907–1963), founder of the Museum of Iron and Coal in Liège, was using the term *archéologie industrielle* by 1950. The first recorded use of the English term in print was by Michael Rix (1913–1981) of the University of Birmingham in an article published in 1955 (Rix 1955), although supposedly it was used by scholars in the Department of Economic History at the University of Manchester before that date. Kenneth Hudson (1916–), journalist, broadcaster, and subsequently museum critic, was the author of the first book in English on industrial archaeology (Hudson 1963) and editor of the first journal on the subject, whose object was to draw attention to the surviving monuments of our industrial past, which also appeared in 1963.

Industrial archaeology flourished in Britain in the latter part of the 1960s and the early 1970s. Some important museums and other conservation projects were established during the period, including the North of England Open Air Museum at Beamish, the Ironbridge Gorge Museum in Shropshire, the Gladstone Pottery Museum in Stoke-on-Trent, and the Morwellham Quay Open Air Museum. Many books, particularly the series *The Industrial Archaeology of the British Isles* published by David and Charles of Newton Abbot, England, documented those monuments of the British industrial past that could readily be recognized, while a parallel series examined the evolution of canals and railways on a regional basis. A succession of books (Buchanan 1972; Butt and Donnachie 1979; Cossons 1988; Falconer 1980; Minchinton 1984; Raistrick 1972) surveyed the subject from a national perspective.

Renewed interest in the monuments of industrial history was part of a wider revival of concern in Britain with aspects of the nation's past, which had been disparaged in the decades of imperial pomp between the 1870s and World War II. The interest was paralleled by new serious concerns about the history of local communities, the history of landscapes (Beresford 1957; Hoskins 1955), and buildings such as dissenting chapels and railway stations that had been ignored by historians of architecture who had concentrated instead on country houses and Anglican churches.

The beginnings of this movement can be traced to before World War II and were exemplified in some of the poems of John Betjeman (1906–1984) who wrote with affection about London suburbs; in the work of officially commissioned war artists, among them John Piper (1903–), who painted the Iron Bridge and the Coalbrookdale ironworks; and in the school of documentary filmmakers who produced such masterpieces as Basil Wright's (1907–1987) *Night Mail* in 1936 and Humphrey Jennings's

(1907–1950) *Diary for Timothy* in 1945. Two of the leading figures of the documentary movement directly influenced the development of industrial archaeology: Jennings, as an anthologist of descriptive writing of the Industrial Revolution (Jennings 1985), and Sir Arthur Elton (1906–1973), a collector of images of industrialization.

The new attitudes were exemplified in the series of guidebooks *About Britain* published for the Festival of Britain in 1951 and edited by Geoffrey Grigson, who wrote:

> The Festival shows how the British people, with their energy and natural resources, contribute to civilisation. So the guidebooks as well celebrate a European country alert, ready for the future, and strengthened by a tradition which you can see in its remarkable monuments and products of history and even prehistory. If the country includes Birmingham, Glasgow or Belfast, it includes Stonehenge. If it contains Durham Cathedral, it contains coal mines, iron foundries and the newest of factories devising all the goods of a developing civilisation (Hoskins 1951).

The growing concern for industrial history in Britain was fostered by university adult education classes and summer schools and the Association for Industrial Archaeology, a national organization that was founded in 1973 as a result of a series of conferences held at the University of Bath. Interest in the subject was sustained by the success of preservation societies that brought back traffic to derelict canals and rivers and reopened steam railways as tourist attractions (Mackersey 1985; Rolt 1953, 1977; Squires 1983; Winton 1986). Such schemes owed much to the spirit of community service that had flourished during World War II, in which, as in the Home Guard or the Women's Voluntary Service movement, volunteers had been organized under "expert" leadership.

In industrial archaeology, as in the voluntary conservation organizations, there was a tendency to reject professional expertise and to delight in amateurism. L. T. C. Rolt (1910–1974), a pioneer in industrial archaeology as well as in railway preservation and waterways restoration, remarked, "If canals are left at the mercy of economists and scientific planners, before many years are past, the last of them will become a weedy, stagnant ditch" (Rolt 1944). Raistrick was not displeased that professional historians from the University of Birmingham did not become involved in the establishment of the museum at Coalbrookdale in 1959 (Raistrick 1980), and Buchanan thought that the development of industrial archaeology as an academic discipline was retarded because "it offers something to everybody" and was too closely associated with leisure-time pursuits (Buchanan 1972). By the mid-1970s, the people responsible for the "public face" of industrial archaeology—that is, the presentation of the subject to the paying public—were increasingly aware of the need for professional standards in such areas as visitor facilities, retailing, marketing, and curatorship.

Parallel concerns for the industrial heritage developed in most western European countries. In Belgium, the subject was fostered by Jan Dhondt (1915–1972) of the Department of Contemporary History at the University of Ghent. In FRANCE, the historian of technology Maurice Daumas launched a national survey of industrial monuments in 1975. In Germany, the first inspector of ancient monuments with specific responsibility for industrial buildings was appointed in 1973 in North Rhine–Westphalia. In most European countries, there are now provisions in conservation legislation for the protection of industrial monuments. The Project-bureau Industrieel Erfcoed (Institute for Industrial Heritage) in the NETHERLANDS is the most ambitious state-backed scheme to collect and disseminate information about Dutch industrial heritage. In North America, the Society for Industrial Archaeology was established in 1972, with a membership drawn from both the United States and CANADA.

During the 1980s, industrial archaeology in Great Britain became an increasingly professional concern. An Institute for Industrial Archaeology (subsequently, as its concerns were broadened, renamed the Ironbridge Institute) was established at Ironbridge in Shropshire, England, in 1980 by the University of Birmingham and the Ironbridge Gorge Museum. Since 1982,

the institute has provided postgraduate programs in industrial archaeology, which have attracted students from Australia, Canada, DENMARK, GREECE, Japan, the Netherlands, New Zealand, and South Africa as well as from Britain. The institute's research publications, many of them produced for English Heritage, a major British government heritage organization, have helped to establish new research methodologies (Alfrey and Clark 1993), and the first encyclopedia of industrial archaeology was edited at the institute and published in 1992 (Trinder 1992a).

Increased attention has also been paid to industrial archaeology within the conservation and recording agencies in Britain as individuals who had learned to appreciate its value were promoted. Industrial buildings and structures have been among the prime concerns of relisting projects and of the Monuments Protection Program undertaken by English Heritage. Royal commissions in England, Scotland, and Wales have produced some distinguished publications (Baker 1991; Calladine and Fricker 1993; Douglas and Oglethorpe 1993; Giles and Goodall 1992; Hughes 1988, 1990; Williams 1992). There has been an increasing concern in Britain about twentieth-century industrial buildings and about the archaeology of industries like food processing and road transport that were neglected in the first generation of national and regional surveys.

During the 1970s, there was a considerable debate about the objectives and scope of industrial archaeology and about its relationship to other disciplines. In Britain, some came to regard it post-postmedieval archaeology, the study of all types of physical evidence of the period since 1750, the declared period of interest of the Post-Medieval Archaeology Society (Crossley 1990). Raistrick (Raistrick 1972) was prominent among those who argued that industrial archaeology should be concerned more narrowly with manufacturing processes of all periods from the prehistoric onward. There now appears to be a consensus in Britain and elsewhere that industrial archaeology is a period-based discipline and that studies of such topics as weaving or the smelting of metals, which extend over many centuries, are best regarded as part of the history of technology, a discipline that has generated more interest in the United States than in Britain. Decisions on the chronological limits of industrial archaeology tend to be made on an ad hoc basis, for example, when museum displays, books, or academic courses are being planned. In most countries, the focus is likely to be on the period when factory-based production methods were introduced.

The relationship between industrial archaeology and other disciplines varies from country to country, which affects the subject scope of the discipline. Nowhere is industrial archaeology regarded literally as the study of *all* the physical remains of the recent past. Agricultural structures, polite architecture in the form of churches, public buildings and the houses of the rich, and military fortifications are usually, by convention, left to other specialists. The main areas of argument concern housing and communal buildings, which in countries like Great Britain and SWEDEN, in which many of the practicing industrial archaeologists have training in social history, are seen as an integral part of the industrial landscape. In the United States, industrial archaeology tends to be more narrowly focused on processes and structures, reflecting the role of historians of technology in the development of the discipline, and the activities of specialists in the parallel studies of historical archaeology and material culture. Some industrial archaeologists, particularly in Sweden, have argued that those engaged in the discipline should show more concern for the people who were employed in manufacturing and for the experience of work (Hudson 1980; Lindquist 1978; Sillen 1977).

Some common patterns can be observed in the literature of industrial archaeology in most countries. The first books on the subject tended to be general studies describing the obvious industrial monuments of a particular country and attempting to set agendas (Hudson 1963; Van den Abeelen 1973). Subsequent national surveys have either introduced more discussion of technology (Cossons 1975, 1992) or have been more detailed and site specific, in some cases because

they have been based on preliminary national surveys (Daumas 1980; Falconer 1980; Hume 1976–1977; Slotta 1975–1988; Viaene 1986). From national surveys, regional inventories have developed. The study of the Mohawk-Hudson area of New York State in 1969 (Vogel 1973) had a strong influence on the development of industrial archaeology in the United States, and there have been several parallel studies of other regions (Bluestone 1978; Thomas 1975). Notable regional surveys have been published in Great Britain, Germany, BELGIUM, ITALY, and SPAIN (Cleere and Crossley 1985; Fehl, Kaspari-Kuffen, and Meyer 1991; Genicot and Hendrickx 1990; Gomez, Ezkerra, and Llanos 1988, 1990; Hume 1974; Mioni et al. 1981–1983).

From general surveys, thematic studies of particular regions developed, like the surveys of ironmaking in the Ardennes, blast furnaces in Normandy, and slate quarries in the Loire region (André, Belhoste, and Bertrand 1987; Belhoste et al. 1991; Kéroutan 1988); Watson's work on textile mills in Dundee (Watson 1990); and the surveys of pottery works and textile mills by a royal commission in England (Baker 1991; Calladine and Fricker 1993; Giles and Goodall 1992; Williams 1992); and national surveys of particular industries such as motorcar factories in Britain, heavy clay products in Scotland, and textile mills in Canada (Collins and Stratton 1993; Douglas and Oglethorpe 1993; McCullough 1992). Methodologies have also been developed for analyzing particular manufacturing sites, whether ironworks, textile mill complexes, or food factories (Belhoste, Bertrand, and Gayot 1984; Cartier and Jantzen 1994; Stratton and Trinder 1988; Trinder 1992b; Trottier 1980). The Royal Commission in Wales has set high standards for the surveying of linear features like canals and railways, and a different but equally stimulating approach has been developed for the analysis of the archaeology of roads by material culture specialists in North America (Hughes 1988, 1990; Schlereth 1985). Some large-scale works that try to achieve an element of synthesis within the discipline appeared in the early 1990s (Gordon and Malone 1993; Trinder 1992a).

One of the first considerations of the

methodology of recording industrial structures was published by a royal commission in Scotland (Hay and Stell 1986), but a more recent guide based on the practice of the Historic American Engineering Record took a more comprehensive approach (Burns 1989). In the same way, industrial archaeologists are taking an increasingly scientific approach to the analysis of landscapes, using plot-based databases in addition to the literary sources that were the foundation of the pioneering study of this aspect of the discipline (Alfrey and Clark 1993; Trinder 1982).

Rix emphasized in 1955 that industrial monuments could be beautiful, and the representation of industrial structures as artifacts meriting admiration has been a continuing tradition within industrial archaeology, especially in Germany. The publications of the photographers Bernd and Hilla Becher and Manfred Hamm have stimulated new ways of looking at water towers, railway stations, and textile mills, bringing order to what are often confused contexts and highlighting beauty in unexpected settings (Becher and Becher 1988; Binney, Hamm, and Föhl 1984; Föhl and Hamm 1985, 1988; Hamm 1992) while the Royal Commission on Historic Monuments in England and the Historic American Engineering Record have published books that demonstrate the value of photography as a means of recording (Lowe 1986; Thornes 1994). The importance of historic photographs of industrial subjects was also demonstrated at an exhibition in London in 1986 (Davies and Collier 1986).

The most influential study of the iconography of the Industrial Revolution was the publication in 1968 of a reworking of Francis Klingender's pioneering study, which first appeared in 1947, but there have been subsequent studies of particular industries and regions (Gray and Kanefsky 1982; Klingender 1968; Smith 1979; Wright 1986) and of some of the classic sources of industrial iconography (Prescher and Wagenbreth 1993). Graphic images have been used with skill in some of the publications of *L'Inventaire* in France, and elsewhere industrial archaeologists have shown a growing interest in the images conveyed in such ephemera as advertisements and labels (Campigotto and Curti 1992).

Archaeological studies of industrial artifacts are as yet comparatively rare, although this is an area in which there are many overlaps between the interests of industrial archaeologists and the interests of such specialists as collectors of pottery and restorers of vintage motorcars or steam locomotives. Evidence concerning clay tobacco pipes from many countries and many sources has been anthologized in Britain (Davey 1979). Metallurgical techniques that were used in prehistoric and medieval archaeology have not as yet been extensively employed in investigating the industrial period (Tylecote 1986). There are, for example, no published works that provide ready guidance to the identification of slags and other residues of metallurgical processes. Nor have advanced techniques from the materials sciences yet been employed to a significant extent in the study of such historic machines as the first generation of mechanized textile machines and the earliest railway locomotives.

The construction of replicas or large-scale working models is proving an effective means of investigating both the technology of early industrial machines and the ways in which the machines were deployed in factories. This technique was pioneered in Bologna, ITALY, where a half-size model of a seventeenth-century silk-throwing machine has been built (Comune di Bologna 1980). In Great Britain, full-scale replicas have been constructed of a Newcomen engine at the Black Country Museum and of two of the first steam locomotives, both designed by Richard Trevithick, one at the Welsh Industrial and Maritime Museum in Wales and the other at the Ironbridge Gorge Museum. Anglo-German cooperation has produced full-scale replicas of carding machines and water frames for the restored mill at Cromford, Ratingen, in Germany, where Johann Brügelmann established the first water-powered cotton mill in continental Europe in 1784.

Most university teaching in industrial archaeology in Europe and North America is done in programs principally concerned with historical archaeology, geography, anthropology, or conservation architecture. There are specialist master's degree programs at the Ironbridge Institute and at the Michigan Technological University, and the subject is an element in a postgraduate program at l'Université Panthéon-Sorbonne, Paris I, and the Ecole des Hautes Etudes en Sciences Sociales in Paris. There is an undergraduate program in industrial archaeology at l'Université de Haute-Bretagne, Rennes-II, from which have emerged two of the best popular works on the subject (Andrieux 1991, 1992). Other European universities specializing in the discipline include those at Coimbra in PORTUGAL; Bologna and Milan, Italy; Cologne and Bonn, Germany; and Stockholm, Sweden.

The techniques used by industrial archaeologists—the phased recording of buildings, ground survey, excavation, the analysis of artifacts—are those used by all other archaeologists. The theoretical basis of the discipline is that which pertains in the study of Roman civilization, the Middle Ages in Europe, the colonization of the Americas, or of any other historical period for which there is written evidence. Industrial archaeology is not a facile means of obtaining new and fashionable evidence in support of existing theories, nor is it an esoteric study, isolated from the concerns of researchers whose prime sources are accounts, maps, patents, or newspapers. It is a means of allowing the study of artifacts, images, structures, sites, and landscapes to stimulate new questions and new hypotheses.

Barrie Trinder

References

Alfrey, J., and C. Clark. 1993. *The Landscape of Industry: Patterns of Change in the Ironbridge Gorge.* London: Routledge.

Andre, L., J-F. Belhoste, and P. Bertrand. 1987. *La métallurgie du fer dans les Ardennes* [Ironmaking in the Ardennes]. Paris: L'Inventaire Général.

Andrieux, J-Y. 1991. *Les travailleurs du fer* [The Ironworkers]. Paris: Gallimard.

———. 1992. *Que sais-je? Le patrimoine industriel* [What Do I Know about Industrial Heritage?]. Paris: Presses Universitaires de France.

Baker, D. 1991. *Potworks: The Industrial Architecture of the Staffordshire Potteries.* London: Royal Commission on the Historical Monuments of England.

Becher, B., and H. Becher. 1988. *Water Towers.* Cambridge, MA: MIT Press.

Belhoste, J-F., et al. 1991. *La métallurgie normande XIIe–XVIIe siècles: La révolution du haut fourneau* [The Norman Metal Industry from the Twelfth to the Seventeenth Century: The Revolution Brought about by the Blast Furnace]. Paris: L'Inventaire Général.

Belhoste, J-F., P. Bertrand, and C. Gayot. 1984. *La manufacture de Dijonval et la draperie sedanaise 1650–1850* [The Dijonval Manufactory and the Sedan Cloth Industry 1650–1850]. Paris: Ministère de la Culture.

Beresford, M. W. 1957. *History on the Ground.* London: Lutterworth.

Binney, M., M. Hamm, and A. Föhl. 1984. *Great Railway Stations of Europe.* London: Thames and Hudson.

Bluestone, D. M. 1978. *Cleveland: An Inventory of Historic Engineering and Industrial Sites.* Washington, DC: National Park Service.

Buchanan, R. A. 1972. *Industrial Archaeology.* Harmondsworth, Eng.: Penguin.

Burns, J. A. 1989. *Recording Historic Structures.* Washington, DC: American Institute of Architects Press.

Butt, J., and I. Donnachie. 1979. *Industrial Archaeology in the British Isles.* London: Paul Elek.

Calladine, A., and J. Fricker. 1993. *East Cheshire Textile Mills.* London: Royal Commission on the Historical Monuments of England.

Campigotto, A., and R. Curti. 1992. *Il sole qui non Tramonta* [The Sun that Does Not Go Down]. Bologna: Grifis Edizioni.

Cartier, C., and H. Jantzen. 1994. *Noisiel: La chocolaterie menier, Seine—et—Marne.* Paris: L'Inventaire.

CEHOPU. Comisión de Estudios Históricos de Obras Públicas y Urbanismo. 1992. *Industrial Heritage '92: National Reports: The 8th International Conference of the Conservation of the Industrial Heritage.* Madrid: CEHOPU.

CILAC. 1981. *ICCIH 1981: The Fourth International Conference on the Conservation of Industrial Heritage.* Paris: CILAC.

———. 1985. *L'étude et la mise en valeur du patrimoine industriel: 4è conférence internationale Lyon-Grenoble, Septembre 1981.* [The Study and Value of the Industrial Heritage: The Fourth International Conference, Lyon and Grenoble, September 1981]. Paris: Centre National de la Recherche Scientifique.

Cleere, H., and D. W. Crossley. 1985. *The Iron Industry of the Weald.* Leicester, Eng.: Leicester University Press.

Collins, P., and M. Stratton. 1993. *British Car Fac-*

tories from 1896: A Complete Historical, Geographical, and Technological Survey. Godmanstone, Eng.: Veloce.

Comune di Bologna. 1980. *Machine, scuole industria* [Mills: The Origins of Industry]. Bologna: Comune di Bologna.

Cossons, N. 1975. *Transactions of the First International Congress on the Conservation of Industrial Monuments, Ironbridge, 19 May to 5 June 1975.* Telford, UK: Ironbridge Gorge Museum.

———. 1988. *The BP Book of Industrial Archaeology.* 2d ed. Newton Abbot, UK: David and Charles.

Crossley, D. W. 1990. *Post-medieval Archaeology in Britain.* Leicester, UK: Leicester University Press.

Daumas, M. 1980. *L'archéologie industrielle en France.* Paris: PUF.

Davey, P. M. 1979. *The Archaeology of the Clay Tobacco Pipe.* Oxford: British Archaeological Reports.

Davies, S., and C. Collier. 1986. *Industrial Image.* London: Photographers' Gallery.

Douglas, G., and M. Oglethorpe. 1993. *Brick, Tile, and Fireclay Industries in Scotland.* Edinburgh: Royal Commission on the Ancient and Historical Monuments of Scotland.

Falconer, K. 1980. *Guide to England's Industrial Heritage.* London: Batsford.

Fehl, G., D. Kaspari-Kuffen, and L-H. Meyer. 1991. *Mit Wasser und Dampf: Zeitzeugen der frühen Industrialisisierung im Belgisch-Deutschen Grenzraum* [With Water and Steam: Evidence of Early Industrialization in the Borderland between Belgium and Germany]. Aachen, Ger.: Meyer and Meyer.

Föhl, A., and M. Hamm. 1985. *Die Industriegeschichte des Wassers* [The Industrial History of Water]. Düsseldorf: VDI-Verlag.

———. 1988. *Die Industriegeschichte des Textils: Technik, Architektur, Wirtschaft* [The History of the Textile Industry: Its Technology, Architecture, and Economics]. Düsseldorf: VDI-Verlag.

Genicot, L-F., and J-P. Hendrickx. 1990. *Wallonie-Bruxelles: Berceau de l'industrie sur le continent Europeen* [Brussels and Wallonia: Birthplace of Industry in Continental Europe]. Louvain-la-Neuve, Belgium: a.s.b.l. Patrimoine Industriel Wallonie-Bruxelles.

Georgeacopol-Winischhofer, U., P. Swittalek, and M. Wehdorn. 1987. *TICCIH: Industrial Heritage, Austria 1987: Transactions I, National Reports.* Vienna: Federal Office for the Protection of Monuments.

———. 1990. *TICCIH: Industrial Heritage, Austria 1987: Transactions II, Conference Papers and Results.* Vienna: Federal Office for the Protection of Monuments.

Giles, C., and I. Goodall. 1992. *Yorkshire Textile Mills 1770–1930.* London: HMSO.

Gomez, M. I., A. S. Ezkerra, and M. Z. Llanos. 1988. *Arqueologia industrial en Bizkaia* [Industrial Archaeology in Bizkaia]. Bilbao, Spain: University of Deusto.

———. 1990. *Arqueologia industrial en Gipuzkoa* [Industrial Archaeology in Gipuzkoa]. Bilbao, Spain: University of Deusto.

Gordon, R. B., and P. M. Malone. 1993. *The Texture of Industry: An Archaeological View of the Industrialization of North America.* Cary, NC: Oxford University Press.

Gray, D., and J. Kanefsky. 1982. *Coal: British Mining in Art 1680–1980.* London: Arts Council of Great Britain.

Hamm, M. 1992. *Archetypen der Utopie: Industriebauten der Jahrhundertwende* [Archetypes of Utopia: Industrial Buildings of the Twentieth Century]. Berlin: Galerie Georg Nothelfer.

Hay, G., and G. P. Stell. 1986. *Monuments of Industry: An Illustrated Historical Record.* Edinburgh: Royal Commission on the Ancient and Historical Monuments of Scotland.

Hoskins, W. G. 1951. *About Britain: Chilterns to Black Country.* London: Collins.

———. 1955. *The Making of the English Landscape.* London: Hodder and Stoughton.

Hudson, K. 1963. *Industrial Archaeology.* London: John Baker.

———. 1979. *World Industrial Archaeology.* Cambridge: Cambridge University Press.

———. 1980. *Where We Used to Work.* London: John Baker.

Hughes, S. 1988. *The Archaeology of the Montgomeryshire Canal.* 3d ed. Aberystwyth: Royal Commission on Ancient and Historical Monuments in Wales.

———. 1990. *The Archaeology of an Early Railway System: The Brecon Forest Tramroads.* Aberystwyth: Royal Commission on Ancient and Historical Monuments in Wales.

Hume, J. R. 1974. *The Industrial Archaeology of Glasgow.* Glasgow: Blackie.

———. 1976–1977. *The Industrial Archaeology of Scotland.* London: Batsford.

Jennings, H. 1985. *Pandemonium 1660–1886: The Coming of the Machine as Seen by Contemporary Observers.* London: Deutsch.

Kèroutan, J-L. 1988. *Les ardoisières en Pays de la Loire* [The Slate Quarries of the Pays de la Loire]. Paris: Ministère de la Culture.

Klingender, F. 1968. *Art and the Industrial Revolution*. Ed. Sir Arthur Elton. London: Paladin.

Kroker, W. 1978. *SICCIM: The Second International Conference on the Conservation of Industrial Monuments: Transactions*. Bochum, Ger.: Deutsches Bergbau-Museum.

Lindquist, S. 1978. *Gräv där du star* [Dig Where You Stand]. Stockholm: Geber.

Lowe, J. 1986. *Industrial Eye*. Washington, DC: Preservation Press.

McCullough, A. B. 1992. *The Primary Textile Industry in Canada: History and Heritage*. Ottawa: Environment Canada.

Mackersey, I. 1985. *Tom Rolt and the Cressy Years*. Cleobury Mortimer, UK: Baldwin.

Minchinton, W. 1984. *A Guide to Industrial Archaeology Sites in Britain*. London: Paladin.

Mioni, A., et al. 1981–1983. *Archeologia Industriale in Lombardia* [Industrial Archaeology in Lombardy]. Milan: Mediocredito Lombardo.

Nisser, M. 1978. *The Industrial Heritage: The Third International Conference on the Conservation of Industrial Monuments: Transactions I: National Reports: Europe except Scandinavia, North America, Japan*. Stockholm: Nordiska Museet.

Nisser, M., ed. 1979. *Industriminnen, en bok om industri- och teknik-bebyggelselsmiljöer* [Industrial Monuments: A Book on the Environments of Industry and Technology]. Stockholm: Arkitekturmuseet.

———. 1981. *The Industrial Heritage: The Third International Conference on the Conservation of Industrial Monuments: Transactions III*. Stockholm: Nordiska Museet.

Nisser, M., and F. Bedoire. 1978. *The Industrial Heritage in Scandinavia: The Third International Conference on the Conservation of Industrial Monuments: Transactions II: Scandinavian Reports*. Stockholm: Nordiska Museet.

Prescher, H., and O. Wagenbreth. 1993. *Georgius Agricola: Seine Zeit und ihre Spuren* [Georgius Agricola: His Life and His Legacy]. Leipzig: DVG.

Raistrick, A. 1972. *Industrial Archaeology: An Historical Survey*. London: Eyre Methuen.

———. 1980. "The Old Furnace at Coalbrookdale, Shropshire." *Industrial Archaeology Review* 4, no. 2: 117–134.

Rix, M. 1955. "Industrial Archaeology." *Amateur Historian* 2, no. 1: 225–229.

———. 1967. *Industrial Archaeology*. London: Historical Association.

Rolt, L. T. C. 1944. *Narrow Boat*. London: Eyre and Spottiswoode.

———. 1953. *Railway Adventure*. London: Constable.

———. 1977. *Landscape with Canals: An Autobiography*. London: Allen Lane.

Rubio, M. G., and J. V. Vicente. 1991. *Arquelogia industrial en Sagunto* [Industrial Archaeology in Sagunto]. Valencia, Spain: Edicons Alfons el Magnanim.

Schlereth, T. J. 1985. *US40: A Roadscape of the American Experience*. Indianapolis: Indiana Historical Society.

Sillen, G. 1977. *Stiga vi mot ljuset* [We Rise toward the Light]. Stockholm: Geber.

Slotta, R. 1975–1988. *Technische Denkmaler in der Bundesrepublik Deutschland* [Technical Monuments in the Federal Republic of Germany]. Bochum, Ger.: Deutsches-Bergbau Museum.

Smith, S. B. 1979. *A View from the Iron Bridge*. London: Thames and Hudson.

Sousa Viterbo, F. 1896. *Arquelogia industrial Portuguesa: Os moinhas* [Industrial Archaeology in Portugal: The Mills]. Reprint 1986: Guimarães, Port.: Muralha.

Squires, R. W. 1983. *The New Navvies: A History of the Waterways Restoration Movement*. Chichester, UK: Phillimore.

Straker, E. 1931. *Wealden Iron*. London: Bell.

Stratton, M. 1987. *Interpreting the Industrial Past*. Telford, UK: Ironbridge Institute.

Stratton, M., and B. Trinder. 1988. "Stanley Mill, Gloucestershire." *Post-Medieval Archaeology* 22, no. 2: 143–180.

Thomas, S. 1975. *Delaware: An Inventory of Historic Engineering and Industrial Sites*. Washington, DC: National Park Service.

Thornes, R. 1994. *Images of Industry: Coal*. London: Royal Commission on the Historical Monuments of England.

Trinder, B. 1982. *The Making of the Industrial Landscape*. London: Dent.

———. 1992a. *The Blackwell Encyclopedia of Industrial Archaeology*. Oxford: Blackwell.

———. 1992b. "Ditherington Flax Mill—A Reevaluation." *Textile History* 27, no. 2: 189–114.

Trottier, L. 1980. *Les forges: Historiographie des forges du Saint-Maurice* [The Forges: The Historiography of the Forges of Saint-Maurice]. Montreal: Boréal Express.

Tylecote, R. F. 1986. *The Prehistory of Metallurgy in the British Isles*. London: Institute of Metals.

Van den Abeelen, G. 1973. *L'archaeologie industrielle*. Brussels: Éditions Creatif.

Vanderhulst, G. 1992. *Industry, Man, and Landscape:
The International Committee for the Conservation of
the Industrial Heritage—Belgium 1990*. Brussels:
TICCIH-Belgium.

Viaene, P. 1986. *Industriele archaeologie in Belgie* [In-
dustrial Archaeology in Belgium]. Ghent: Museum voor Industriele Archaeologie en Textiel.

Victor, S., and H. Wright. 1984. *Industrial Heritage
84, National Reports: The Fifth International Conference on the Conservation of the Industrial Heritage*. Washington, DC: Society for Industrial
Archeology.

Vogel, R. M. 1973. *A Report of the Mohawk-Hudson
Area Survey: A Selective Recording Survey of the
Industrial Archaeology of the Mohawk and Hudson
River Valleys in the Vicinity of Troy, NY, June–
September 1969*. Washington, DC: Smithsonian
Institution Press.

Watson, M. 1990. *Jute and Flax Mills in Dundee*.
Tayport, UK: Hutton Press.

Williams, M. 1992. *Cotton Mills in Greater Manchester*. Preston, UK: Carnegie.

Winton, J. 1986. *The Little Marvel: 150 Years of the
Festiniog Railway*. Rev. ed. London: Michael
Joseph.

Wright, H. 1986. "The Image Makers: The Role of
the Graphic Arts in Industrialization." *Industrial
Archeology* 12, no. 2: 5–18.

Wright, H., and R. Vogel. 1986. *Industrial Heritage
84: Proceedings of the Fifth International Conference
on the Conservation of Industrial Heritage*. Washington, DC: Society for Industrial Archeology.

Instituto Hondureño de Antropología e Historia

Founded in 1952, the Instituto Hondureño de
Antropología e Historia (IHAH, Honduran Institute of Anthropology and History) is the legal
guardian of the archaeological patrimony of
Honduras and publishes the journal of Honduran anthropology and history entitled *Yaxkin*.
Through its function in approving research proposals, it shapes the course of Honduran archaeology. The institute has sponsored significant
programs of research, trained Hondurans in archaeological methods, and fostered the development of archaeology as a career in the country.

According to Honduran archaeologist Ricardo Agurcia, the earliest Honduran government action directed toward preservation of the
archaeological record was legislation passed in
1845 to control exploration of the ruins of classic Mayan Copán and place the responsibility for
their protection in the hands of local authorities. Nonetheless, Agurcia notes that in the
1890s, legally approved expeditions from Harvard University's PEABODY MUSEUM and the
BRITISH MUSEUM removed large quantities of archaeological remains from the site. These actions led to new legislation in 1900 prohibiting
the exportation of material from Copán and
also from other ruins in the country. The legislation explicitly allowed exploration, including
excavation, with prior permission by the executive branch of the government. In 1946, the
first legislation authorizing a governmental
body charged with exploration and protection
of the archaeology, ethnography, and history of
the country was produced, laying the groundwork for IHAH.

The founding of IHAH in 1952, according to
Honduran archaeologist Vito Veliz, owed much
of its impetus to Jesus Nuñez Chinchilla, an archaeologist trained in mexico in the 1940s.
Nuñez Chinchilla conducted excavations at
Copán, and during its early years, IHAH emphasized this site. New legislation in 1968
legally established IHAH as an autonomous institution, and this legal status gave IHAH control over its personnel and facilities and effectively allowed it to function as an investigative
unit. According to Agurcia, this new status
reached fruition in 1975 when IHAH began its
modern history of aggressively fostering archaeological research.

All archaeology conducted in Honduras
since the last date has taken place under permits
issued by IHAH. Even in the 1960s and 1970s,
the scope of projects proposed by outside researchers extended far beyond Copán to en-
compass a broad corridor extending south from
the Ulua Valley through Lake Yojoa, Comayagua,
and the Gulf of Fonseca and extending east
along the north coast. In addition to reopening
research in these areas by its approval of outside
projects, beginning in the 1970s IHAH initiated
its own programs of archaeological inventory

Mayan ruins at Copán (Corel)

and management. In 1979, IHAH created the Proyecto Arqueológico Sula (PAS), with Honduran and North American investigators working to assemble a site inventory for the lower Ulua River where the residential and industrial growth of San Pedro Sula had placed archaeological resources at risk. The lower Ulua Valley had been known since at least the 1890s as a center of substantial archaeological remains, and the immediate precedent for PAS was a series of salvage excavations of Travesía, a major center destroyed in 1975. In association with PAS, IHAH founded a regional center for archaeology on the north coast in the town of La Lima.

In the same year, IHAH organized the Proyecto Arqueológico El Cajón (PAEC), the first cultural resources management initiative in Honduras. PAEC was funded as part of an internationally financed hydroelectric project, and it represented a subtle, but significant, shift in IHAH activity. Although PAEC was dedicated, like pas, to the salvage of sites doomed by economic development, the area covered by PAEC had no previously known archaeological remains. The requirement for a survey, rather than resting on the destruction of already known sites, was predicated on the need to establish what kinds of cultural resources would be destroyed and to mitigate that destruction.

IHAH has been limited in its ability to initiate research both by low funding and by the still-small number of trained archaeologists in the country. Since 1979, much of its resources has gone to the supervision of projects proposed by researchers from other countries. IHAH has used its influence to encourage the extension of research to areas that either were previously little studied or had never received archaeological attention. The internationally funded work authorized by IHAH in the 1980s and early 1990s has included projects in the hinterlands between Copán and the lower Ulua Valley, survey and excavation in the Comayagua Valley, and research east of the Ulua-Comayagua corridor reaching as far as the Mosquito area on the Nicaraguan border. IHAH has recruited collaborators for projects aimed at both the very earliest stages of occupation and the post-Columbian period, both largely ignored by previous researchers. Most important, through the permit process

Stele B from Copán (Image Select)

and periodic conferences, IHAH has begun the development of standards crucial to coordinating research, which in recent decades has involved archaeologists from FRANCE, Germany, Great Britain, JAPAN, Australia, CANADA, the United States, and Mexico and Hondurans trained in European, North American, and Latin American traditions.

Rosemary A. Joyce

References

Agurcia, R. 1984. "La defensa del patrimonio cultural en Honduras: El caso de la arqueología." *Yaxkin* 7, no. 2: 83–96.

Veliz, V. 1983. "Síntesis histórica de la arqueología en Honduras." *Yaxkin* 6, nos. 1–2: 1–8.

———. 1984. "La ley Patrimonio Cultural de la Nación." *Yaxkin* 7, no. 2: 123–140.

International Union of Prehistoric and Protohistoric Sciences

The creation in La Spezia, Italy, in September 1864 of the Congres Paleoethnologique International (CPI) during a meeting of the Societa Italiana di Scienze Naturali marks the de facto beginnings of the International Union of Prehistoric and Protohistoric Sciences. In 1867, the CPI changed its name to Congres International d'Anthropologie et d'Archéologie Prehistoriques (CIAAP), and that organization can be described as the direct ancestor of the contemporary union. The origins of the present organization therefore go back some 130 years. The prime movers in this international initiative were Giovanni Capellini (president of Societa Italiana di Scienze Naturali) and the French archaeologist GABRIEL DE MORTILLET.

Between 1866 and 1912, fourteen international congresses were organized (a Permanent Council was created during the Lisbon session of the CIAAP in 1880), but World War I put a stop to these fruitful and constructive meetings. The Institut International d'Anthropologie (IIA), founded in 1921 after the war, tried to bring archaeologists and anthropologists together again, but this group was almost totally French inspired and dominated (all five members of the executive committee were French). It was also totally different from the CIAAP in two essential ways: its main emphasis was on "anthropology" in its widest sense (as the study of living human communities, comparative religion, folklore, etc.), with prehistoric archaeology forming a smaller section than had previously been the case; and scholars belonging to the "vanquished nations" were excluded from the activities of the IIA. For both of these reasons, numerous prehistorians and anthropologists did not choose to join or belong to the IIA, and several (such as MARCELLIN BOULE, R. Verneau, HUGO OBERMAIER, and P. Bosch-Gimpera) tried to continue the real international tradition of the prewar CIAAP.

After several efforts at collaboration between members of the Permanent Council of the CIAAP and the Executive Committee of the IIA, it was finally decided that the fifteenth session of the CIAAP and the fourth session of the

IIA would meet together in Portugal in 1930 under the joint name Congres International d'Anthropologie et d'Archéologie Préhistorique. Not many prehistorians took part in this consolidation, however, because most were still unhappy about what they considered to be the still minor role allocated to prehistoric archaeology.

Later in 1930, the so-called committee of five (archaeologists GERHARD BERSU, R. Lantier, Obermaier, W. Unverzagt, and Bosch-Gimpera as secretary) met in Berlin to discuss the organization of international congresses devoted exclusively to prehistoric archaeology, which would convene on a truly international level and without any exclusions whatsoever. This idea was finalized in Bern, Switzerland (27–29 May 1931), and the new organization took the name Congres International des Sciences Prehistoriques et Protohistoriques (CISPP).

Some 500 scholars attended the first congress of the CISPP in London in August 1932 under the presidency of Sir Charles Peers. A. W. Brogger and JOHN L. MYRES were both secretaries-general of the CISPP, and VERE GORDON CHILDE, CHRISTOPHER F. C. HAWKES, H. S. Kingsford, and C. A. Ralegh Radford were secretaries of the organizing committee. Archaeologists from thirty-five different countries formed a new Permanent Council.

The second congress was organized in 1936 in Oslo. Again, some 500 archaeologists attended its meetings, but the political climate of the time made for some unpleasantness. The proposal to hold the third congress in Budapest in 1940 was accepted, but the beginning of World War II intervened. After an abortive attempt to hold the congress in Budapest in 1949, the third congress finally met in Zurich in 1950. The absence of scholars working in eastern Europe undoubtedly explained why only some 250 prehistorians attended. On this occasion, the Executive Committee was created, with E. Vogt as its (provisional) secretary. In 1952, he was replaced by S. De Laet as secretary-general of the Executive Committee.

In 1954, the fourth congress took place in Madrid, and once again some 500 prehistorians attended, with colleagues from fifty-one countries being elected to the Permanent Council. It was decided that adherence to the Conseil International de la Philosophie et des Sciences Humaines (CIPSH) would make it possible to obtain financial help from the United Nations Educational, Scientific, Cultural Organization (UNESCO) for some of the scientific initiatives proposed by the congress. This affiliation to CIPSH (September 1955) made it necessary once more to change the name of the organization, this time to Union Internationale des Sciences Prehistoriques et Protohistoriques (UISPP, International Union of Prehistoric and Protohistoric Sciences).

The next congresses all saw a steady growth in the number of participants—which reached a peak in Nice of some 3,500 in 1976—and a corresponding growth in the number of members elected to the Permanent Council, which today has some 250 scholars working in nearly 100 countries. The next congress venues were as follows: fifth congress (1958), Hamburg; sixth (1962), Rome; seventh (1966), Prague; eighth (1971), Belgrade (this congress was the first to be organized five years after the previous one in accord with UNESCO's five-year rule for major international congresses); ninth (1976), Nice; tenth (1981), Mexico City; eleventh (1987), Mainz.

The original venue in 1986 (Southampton-London) was changed to Mainz by a vote of the Permanent Council because the executive of the United Kingdom organizing committee had decided in late 1985 not to allow scholars active in South Africa to participate in the congress. This decision could not be accepted as it was contrary to the statutes and the tradition of the UISPP. Also, the decision was made without consulting either the Permanent Council, the Executive Committee, or the secretary-general of the UISPP. The meeting in Southampton took place under the title WORLD ARCHAEOLOGICAL CONGRESS (a change of name that had also been decided without any previous consultation with the UISPP executive), and this meeting repeated the error of the ill-fated Institut International d'Anthropologie, which in 1921 refused, for purely political reasons, to admit to its meetings scholars from Germany, Austria, etc. The decision by the Permanent Council and the

Executive Committee of the UISPP not to recognize the Southampton meeting was communicated to the CIPSH, and it was confirmed by the General Assembly of the CIPSH and by the UNESCO representative at that General Assembly, emphasizing that the UISPP is the only scientific organization active in the study of prehistory and proto-history that is officially recognized by those bodies. (Recently, the UISPP was recognized by with the Scientific Committee of the Council of Europe, which gave it official status as observer.)

Another political matter that for some months threatened to interfere with the organization of the twelfth congress (which took place in 1991 in Bratislava) was the change in the political structure of what had been Czechoslovakia. Fortunately, thanks to the goodwill of the Czechoslovakian colleagues, all difficulties were overcome in time. During the Bratislava meeting it was decided to hold the thirteenth congress in Forli, Italy, in 1996, and 2001 will be held in Belgium.

The guiding principle of the organization over all the years has been the fervent wish of prehistorians from many countries to meet and discuss prehistory and to collaborate as much as possible in any number of international projects. The administrative organization of the UISPP continues to reflect this wish, as is shown by the most recent revision of the statutes adopted by the Permanent Council in Dublin in 1989. On that occasion, some twenty-five scientific commissions were officially integrated into the organization of the UISPP.

The present-day structure of the UISPP is as follows: First is the General Assembly, which consists of all persons who have paid their participation fee to the international congress of the UISPP; second is the Permanent Council, the main body of the UISPP, which consists of a maximum of four members per country, one delegate per associated international organization, the president of each special committee, and the president of each scientific commission. The members of the Permanent Council are elected in their personal capacity as scientists, and they are elected by a simple majority vote. The council meets during the congresses of the

UISPP and once between congresses and archaeologists working in some 100 countries are members of the Permanent Council. The council elects during each congress the president and the organizing secretary of the next congress. This president is automatically the president of the organization and head of the General Assembly, the Permanent Council, and the Executive Committee for five years. The Permanent Council also elects the secretary-general of the council and the Executive Committee; it demands no financial contribution from its members.

The third structural body is the Honorary Committee, which is made up of members of the Permanent Council who for statutory reasons can no longer form a part of that council. The Permanent Council can elect to the Honorary Committee any person it judges to have played an important role in prehistoric research or to have helped the UISPP in any significant way.

Fourth is the Executive Committee, which is elected by the Permanent Council. It meets every year and consists of fifteen voting members, the president of the UISPP being one. The secretary-general has no vote, and a number of scholars who are invited to the meetings of the Executive Committee also do not vote. They are the presidents and organizing secretaries of the previous congresses, the previous secretaries-general of the UISPP, the presidents of the special committees and the scientific commissions, the delegates of the affiliated international organizations, and the organizing secretary of the next congress. Members of the Executive Committee are elected for a term of five years and may serve a second term.

Fifth is the Bureau, which consists of the president and the secretary-general, who meet whenever necessary. Sixth, the secretary-general is elected from the members of the Permanent Council for a period of five years, and this mandate is always renewable. During this mandate, the secretary-general ceases to be a member of the Permanent Council. The secretary-general sends out the invitations to the several meetings of the Permanent Council and the Executive Committee and reports to both bodies. The secretary-general runs the day-to-day business of the UISPP.

Seventh, members of the National Organizing Committee serve for five years and are responsible for organizing the next international congress. The Permanent Council elects the secretary of the National Organizing Committee, and its members are the Permanent Council members of the country hosting the next congress.

Over the years, a number of special committees have been created to organize projects of international importance, and many of them still continue. Several of these special committees have built up an imposing group of specialists and are responsible for a long list of publications. In addition, some twenty scientific commissions have been incorporated into the organization of the UISPP to coordinate research in specific areas of pre- and proto-history, which can be thematic, regional or interregional, chronological, interdisciplinary, etc. Finally, several international associations have become affiliated with the UISPP, through which they have access to the CIPSH. All of the special committees, scientific commissions, and other organizations meet regularly during congresses and in symposia, colloquiums, and conferences, and the results of their work are generally published, sometimes in multivolume proceedings, sometimes in less ambitious collections of papers.

To conclude, I quote part of the Preamble to statutes of the UISPP, in which the international union clearly proclaims its scientific aims and philosophical convictions:

> The U.I.S.P.P. is an international association of scholars; the universality of Science is the philosophical basis of its activities. Its aim being the collaboration of the scholars from all countries to help advance prehistoric and protohistoric studies, it proclaims its total attachment to academic freedom.
>
> Knowledge of Humanity concerns all present-day societies. For this reason, the U.I.S.P.P. is in total opposition to any form of discrimination based upon the concepts of race, ethnic group, geographical unit, philosophical conviction, nationality, sex, language or any other; such discrimination being, by its intolerance and its very definition, the negation itself of any form of co-operation. The U.I.S.P.P. excludes

no bona fide scholar from its scientific activities. (Bulletin of the XIII Congress of the International Union of the Prehistoric and Protohistoric Sciences, Forli, Italy, 1996, 34–38).

Jacques Nenquin

Iran

No comprehensive history of archaeology in Iran exists though there are a few summaries about specific aspects (e.g., Amiet, Chevalier, and Carter 1992; Dyson 1968; Moorey 1972; Young 1986) and a few autobiographies (Dieulafoy 1888, 1890; Ghirshman 1970; Goff 1980). There are also important recent syntheses and collections of articles (Hole 1987; Olszewski and Dibble 1993; Smith 1986; Voigt and Dyson 1992), a basic bibliography for the prehistoric periods (Voigt and Dyson 1992), virtually exhaustive bibliographies for all periods (Van den Berghe 1966, 1979; Van den Berghe and Haerinck 1981), and an archaeological tour of Iran (Matheson 1972).

Historical Overview

Archaeology in Iran has developed unevenly in terms of periods and regions studied. The earliest archaeological investigations, from the late nineteenth century onward, concentrated on western and southwestern Iran, and this pattern has largely persisted. This emphasis is primarily owing to the facts that these areas had the strongest interaction with MESOPOTAMIA; they were the homeland of historically important civilizations such as Elam and Achaemenid Persia, which were of greatest interest to western scholars; and access to them was relatively easier. In addition, the discipline has been compartmentalized chronologically, and with some exceptions, researchers fall into one of three groups: those few who have studied the relatively neglected Paleolithic period, the majority who have focused on the Neolithic to the Achaemenid periods, and another smaller group of people who have concerned themselves with the post-Achaemenid and Islamic periods.

Late-nineteenth- and early-twentieth-century archaeology in Iran can be reasonably characterized as museum-driven, object-oriented research. Throughout this period, FRANCE had a monopoly on archaeological research in the country, and they concentrated almost entirely on the great Elamite and Achaemenid site of Susa in Khuzistan. There was no expansion of archaeological research in Iran immediately after the hiatus caused by World War I because the French retained their monopoly for several more years and western archaeologists had much easier access to Iraq, Syria, Lebanon, and Palestine, which had all become foreign mandates. In 1927, Reza Shah's government radically revised the antiquities regulations, and the French monopoly was finally broken. The scope of archaeological research widened greatly thereafter as other international expeditions finally gained access, and there was also some general improvement in field methods, which, hitherto, had been primitive. Because of the pronounced geographical and environmental regionalization of the country, the main thrust of Iranian archaeology from then on has been the establishment of regional sequences.

World War II brought another hiatus in fieldwork, but after it, the discipline continued to improve, especially from the late 1950s onward with the launching of many major new projects and the first impact of "the new archaeology." In addition to elaborating regional sequences, there was a strong focus on sophisticated regional surveys and on achieving a more comprehensive investigation of the entire country. All work came to an abrupt halt as a result of the 1979 revolution, and it is only recently that fieldwork, conducted by the Iranians themselves, has resumed in a very limited manner.

Knowledge of Iran's Past Prior to the Late Nineteenth Century

By the end of the Sassanian period (A.D. 651), knowledge of the preceding Achaemenid (550–331 B.C.), Hellenistic/Seleucid (331–175 B.C.), Parthian (175 B.C.–A.D. 224), and Sassanian (A.D. 224–651) periods was virtually lost within Iran itself. Alexander the Great was (and still is) remembered in oral tradition and the Iranian national epic, the *Shahnameh* [Book of Kings]—but as the half-brother of Darius III.

The advent of Islam in the mid-seventh century A.D. effectively discouraged any scholarly or popular interest in a pagan past. Only under the Qajar shahs in the nineteenth century did Iran experience a revival of concern with the Achaemenids and their successors. Although there was no systematic research, it became fashionable to copy Achaemenid reliefs for architectural decoration and to carve new reliefs in an archaic style. Indirect knowledge of Achaemenid Iran was preserved in Europe through the Old Testament and classical Greek sources, especially Herodotus (though he never visited the country) and Xenophon. Reports from other ancient Greek travelers and mercenaries and the testimony of expatriate Persian refugees in GREECE provided additional detail.

From the fourteenth century onward, European travelers brought back descriptions of the great ruined cities of PERSEPOLIS and Pasargadae, though their true identity remained unknown until the beginning of the seventeenth century. From the seventeenth to the nineteenth centuries, an increasing number of European travelers, diplomats, and scholars—mostly French, British, and Dutch—reported in greater and greater detail about the standing monuments of Iran (Sancisi-Weerdenburg and Drijvers 1991; Wright 1977).

The first excavations occurred in 1825 when Colonel Stannus, the East India Company resident at Bushire, dug at Persepolis and made the first set of molds of sculptures along the north facade of the Apadana. Colonel Macdonald, head of a mission to Iran, also excavated at the site shortly afterward. In 1835, HENRY CRESWICKE RAWLINSON, a former officer in the Indian army who had studied Persian, Arabic, and Hindustani, was posted to Kermanshah as a military adviser, and by 1837, he had produced fairly accurate copies of the trilingual (Old Persian, Akkadian, and Elamite) cuneiform relief carved by Darius I in about 520 B.C. on a rock face at Bisitun (Behistun). In the subsequent decade, Rawlinson unraveled the Old Persian and Akkadian texts. In 1840–1841, AUSTEN HENRY LAYARD, later distinguished by his work at the great Neo-Assyrian capitals of NINEVEH and NIMRUD, traveled throughout western Iran and vis-

Royal bodyguard, relief from the palace of Darius I in Susa, ca. 500 B.C. of the Persian Kings (Image Select)

ited Susa. In a report to the Royal Asiatic Society in 1850, he suggested that excavations be conducted at the great mound of Susa for the express purpose of discovering more bilingual inscriptions, and he persuaded the British prime minister, Lord Palmerston, to provide a parliamentary grant of 500 pounds for further explorations of the site.

Beginnings of Sustained Archaeological Research in Iran

The first scholarly excavations in Iran were those of the British geologist, William Kennett Loftus, a member of a commission formed by the British and Russian governments to arbitrate the delineation of the frontier between Persia and Turkey. In 1850, Loftus and another member of the commission, Henry A. Churchill, visited Susa intending to excavate. Because of local resentment, the visit was brief. The two returned in 1851 along with Colonel W. F. Williams, the commandant of the frontier commission, and they planned the site, identified it through inscriptions as the Susa of the Old Testament, and established the presence of Sassanian, Achaemenid, and earlier (Elamite) levels.

The French at Susa

During a trip across Persia in 1881–1882, Marcel-Auguste Dieulafoy, a French engineer, soldier, and architectural historian, visited Susa with his wife, Jane, and upon their return to France, Dieulafoy persuaded the national museums to provide modest financing for excavations. Unlike most of his contemporaries, Dieulafoy was more interested in architecture than museum-quality objects. Thus, from 1884 to 1886, the Dieulafoys worked exclusively on the columned Apadana (Audience Hall), previously identified by Loftus, from which they retrieved spectacular Achaemenid remains. These antiquities became the core of the LOUVRE's extensive Susa collection.

In 1886, Nasir el-Din Shah (1848–1896), who was aware that the local population was still discontented with the excavations, shut them down, and almost a decade passed before the French legation in Tehran felt it could re-open the matter. In 1895, the French ambassador, Rene de Balloy, finally persuaded the shah to sign a treaty that granted the French an exclusive concession for archaeological research throughout Persia. In Mesopotamia, then under Ottoman control, considerable rivalry between

French and British archaeologists had existed for several decades, and the French undoubtedly wished to ensure that the British could not exercise prior rights to Susa because of the work done by Loftus. In 1897, the French government created the Délégation Scientifique Française en Perse and provided it with funding unprecedented in the history of archaeology. The fifteen-year history of the Délégation Scientifique is inseparable from the career of Jacques Jean Marie de Morgan.

The son of a Welsh mining engineer, Jack or Jacques Jean Marie de Morgan followed in his father's footsteps and graduated from the French Ecole des Mines. Although his geological work took him around the world, he also nurtured a childhood passion for prehistory (his paternal uncle was a Parisian antiquities dealer) and indulged it whenever his professional activities permitted. After a visit to the Caucasus, de Morgan explored northern Persia between 1889 and 1891, eventually arriving at Susa. In 1891, he was appointed director of the Cairo Museum, and from 1892 to 1897, he served as director-general of the Service of Antiquities in Egypt. De Morgan was appointed director of the Délégation Scientifique in 1897 and set up camp at Susa at the end of the year.

The situation was insecure as pillaging tribes frequently crossed the Ottoman-Persian border to raid Khuzistan, so in 1898, in order to protect his staff, de Morgan began the construction of a residence and headquarters on the north side of the Acropolis. Made entirely of bricks recovered from the Susa excavations, the building was constructed in the form of a fortified medieval chateau. The original team included some of de Morgan's colleagues from Egypt. Although de Morgan had published a book on field methods in archaeology, in Egypt he had incurred the scorn of SIR WILLIAM MATTHEW FLINDERS PETRIE for the poor standard of his excavations, and the techniques employed at Susa continued to be extremely crude.

De Morgan not only tunneled but at times employed over 1,000 men to excavate a 100-meter-long *grande tranchee* ("large trench"), which he took down in 5-meter levels. The returns were staggering, but activity was not restricted to Susa. Between 1899 and 1902, de Morgan investigated numerous prehistoric sites in Mazandaran, Gurgan, Azerbaijan, and the Talish regions; in 1902–1903, the Délégation Scientifique worked at Tepe Musyan, northwest of Susa; and in 1909, de Morgan was involved in the survey of the plain of Varamin near Tehran and dug at the prehistoric site of Rayy.

The original objectives of the Délégation Scientifique were not exclusively archaeological, as de Morgan had every intention of conducting other scientific research, especially in geography, geology, and natural history. However, even though the funding for the Délégation was the envy of every other contemporary archaeologist, it was insufficient to support such varied research. Despite the uninterrupted flow of treasures back to the Louvre and despite the many volumes published by the Délégation, de Morgan was severely criticized by some of his colleagues for pursuing only archaeological investigations. Exhausted by these attacks, worn down by the great length of time he had spent in Egypt and Persia, and bristling from accusations of stealing, de Morgan resigned from the Délégation in 1912 and was succeeded by de Mecquenem, who retained the directorship until 1946.

The 1895 agreement stipulated that all jewelry and other objects of gold and silver were the property of the Iranian government but that the French could buy half at a reasonable price and had first option on the other half if the government chose to dispose of it. The French were also permitted to take half of all other archaeological materials, including engravings, statues, and inscriptions. Despite these generous conditions, de Morgan was dissatisfied and, with the help of the French legation, worked to secure even more. In 1900, a definitive version of the treaty was signed in Paris during a state visit by Muzaffar el-Din Shah (1896–1907), and the new treaty gave de Morgan all archaeological material from Susa. The 1900 treaty also stipulated that any request by another foreign expedition to excavate at any other site in Iran required the approval of the French government. Meanwhile, legal and illegal excavations by Iranian antiquities dealers flourished. One American missionary who vis-

Griffin-lion shown in tiled relief, from a royal site (probably Persepolis or Susa), fourth century B.C. (Image Select)

ited Hamadan (the ancient Median capital, Ecbatana) in the late nineteenth century reported that excavation for antiquities in large areas in and around the city was a systematic industry farmed out by the government for revenue. There was also a thriving production of fake antiquities, mostly coins, for the European market.

The modernizing reforms of Nasir al-Din, the most able of the Qajar shahs, brought about his assassination in 1896. His successors were either ineffectual or despotic, and the period leading up to World War I was one of great internal turmoil that culminated in the invasion of northern and southern Iran by Russia and Britain, respectively. In 1911, members of the first Majlis (National Assembly) introduced a bill designed to cancel the French archaeological monopoly, but by 1913, the French ambassador had successfully arranged for the bill to be shelved. The war brought excavations to an end though SIR AUREL STEIN conducted a survey in Seistan in 1915–1916. De Mecquenem remained in Iran until the end of the war to protect French archaeological interests.

The Interwar Period

French control of archaeology continued until 1927 when it was finally abolished by Reza Shah Pahlavi (1925–1941). As a concession, the shah established an archaeological museum and library in Tehran and appointed a French director-general of antiquities responsible for establishing an archaeological service, making an inventory of historic monuments, and carrying out necessary restorations. The position was taken in September 1927 by a French architect, Andre Godard, who held it until 1960. Godard's achievements were considerable: he created the necessary administration, the Iranian Archaeological Service (IAS), and established the Muze Iran Bostan (now the National Museum of Iran) and oversaw its construction in Tehran between 1935 and 1937. He also conducted important work on Islamic architecture and supervised the restoration of historic buildings, especially in Isfahan. In 1931, when the antiquities market was being flooded by Luristan bronzes from illegal excavations in central-west Iran, Godard wrote what became the standard text on the bronzes. He was also vigorous in the popularization of Iranian art and archaeology on an international level. Laudable as these achievements were, they were largely self-serving, and there was virtually no provision for the training of Iranians who could conduct independent archaeological research, staff museums, or educate the next generation.

Throughout most of Godard's tenure, the only Iranians involved in excavations were those working for antiquities dealers and, up until the 1950s, only three Iranians (Mahdi Bahrami, Issa Behnami, and Mohsen Moqaddam) managed to obtain doctorates in Iranian art and archaeology from French universities. Some excavations initiated by the IAS (e.g., Hasanlu and Khurvin) were, from an Iranian point of view, arbitrarily transferred to foreign projects. There was also a vigorous illegal trade in antiquities, and much material ended up in the BRITISH MUSEUM, the Louvre, and numerous other museums and private collections. In 1959 alone, the Louvre bought 500 Luristan bronzes from Jacques Coiffard, the French ambassador in Tehran—the question of provenance was never raised.

Other Foreign Projects

In 1931, the ORIENTAL INSTITUTE of the University of Chicago (OIC) began a major archaeological project in Fars with the Achaemenid capital of Persepolis as the main focus and headquarters. Excavations at Persepolis and neighboring sites were directed by Ernst Herzfeld (1931–1934) and Erich Schmidt (1934–1939). The OIC subsequently undertook other projects, including aerial and ground surveys, in the mountains of Luristan and elsewhere in Iran between 1935 and 1937. Brief excavations were made at over a dozen sites. Also in 1931, the UNIVERSITY OF PENNSYLVANIA MUSEUM (UM) began two important projects in the little-explored northeastern part of Iran.

During the 1930s, there were few foreign expeditions apart from those of the major players, the French and the Americans. Aurel Stein (Harvard University and the British Museum) made four trips between 1932 and 1936 visiting and testing numerous sites in southeastern (Kerman, Baluchistan, and Fars) and western Iran, and he identified numerous ancient sites,

such as Hasanlu, that subsequently became archaeologically famous. A Swedish expedition led by T. J. Arne investigated Shah Tepe in the Gurgan Plain in 1933. Although the situation in the 1930s can be described as considerably improved, there was no coordination of international efforts, excavation methods remained fairly crude, and programs of excavation, while sometimes sustained, were not at all systematic. The decade of research prior to World War II threw isolated and random shafts of light on the development of Iran from the Neolithic to the Achaemenid period, and in no region was there anything approaching a complete sequence.

However, great strides had been made. For example, Herzfeld's 1934 Schweich Lectures on the archaeological history of Iran, over 100 pages in length, devoted only 8 pages to the pre-Median and pre-Achaemenid eras (Herzfeld 1935). Seven years later, D. C. McCown (1942) needed over 60 pages to synthesize the comparative stratigraphy of the prehistoric periods of north-central, western, and southwestern Iran even though some areas were still relatively unexplored. The prehistory of northwestern Iran was disposed of in a single page, and southeastern Iran was not mentioned. World War II and internal conditions in Iran brought a second hiatus in foreign fieldwork.

The Post–World War II Period: 1945–1979

The accidental discovery of the fabulous early-first-millennium-B.C. golden hoard at Ziwiyeh in northern Kurdistan in 1947 gained widespread international interest, but foreign fieldwork still recommenced rather slowly after World War II. The French returned to Susa promptly enough in 1946 under a new director, Roman Ghirshman, who held the post until 1967 when he was succeeded by Jean Perrot (1967–1990), who introduced modern stratigraphic methods there. The British returned to the field in 1948, and the IAS was increasingly active following the completion of work at Persepolis. The IAS were joined by a Japanese team led by Norio Egami (Tokyo University) in 1956, and in 1957, Robert Dyson, Jr., led a UM team back to Iran.

In the two decades between 1959 and 1979, archaeology flourished in Iran perhaps more vigorously than anywhere else in western Asia. There was a virtual explosion of international activity with expeditions from Britain, the United States, CANADA, West Germany, France, SWEDEN, ITALY, JAPAN, BELGIUM, and DENMARK. In 1976, for example, there were seventeen archaeological surveys and thirty excavation projects. By 1978, the number of foreign expeditions in Iran had risen to over fifty, the majority of them being major projects. For the first time, some balance was achieved in chronological coverage, at least in western Iran, and other previously neglected areas began to be explored.

Though some important achievements occurred in Paleolithic studies, this subfield continued to lag. Iran's great environmental diversity and complex geography of deserts, mountain valleys, and coastal plains are reflected in the numerous cultural adaptations in prehistory. For this reason, archaeologists have eschewed syntheses of larger areas and time periods in favor of constructing prehistoric regional sequences (see Voigt and Dyson 1992). This period also saw the introduction of modern excavation standards and close attention to stratigraphy, so necessary when dissecting complex mound settlements, and, by the mid-1960s, the impact of the theoretical and methodological innovations of "the new archaeology." In addition, there was a rapid and intense development of surface survey strategies, perhaps more so than anywhere else in western Asia. This was inspired by GORDON WILLEY's VIRÚ VALLEY project in PERU in 1953 and the extensive surveys conducted in both Iraq and Khuzistan by ROBERT MCCORMICK ADAMS.

Survey data were used to identify administrative hierarchies; stylistic, functional, and chronological variability; trading networks; population dynamics; and so forth through the employment of such methods as gravity modeling, rank size indexing, cluster analysis, multidimensional scaling, and statistical analysis. A number of important ethno-archaeological projects were also conducted, especially Patty Jo Watson's and Carol Kramer's separate studies of two villages in central-west Iran. There was a notable increase of fieldwork done by the IAS as well as an increase in the number of Iranians be-

ing trained not only in Iran but also in Europe and North America. In 1958, Ezatollah Negahban, himself a graduate of the OIC, created the Institute of Archaeology at the University of Tehran. The institutional framework was further strengthened with the appearance of the Iranian Centre for Archaeological Research (ICAR), directed by Firouz Bagherzadeh, and also the National Organization for Restoration of Historical Monuments. By 1961, both the British Institute of Persian Studies and a German institute had been opened in Tehran, and the American Institute of Iranian Studies was opened soon afterward. Specialized journals appeared, especially *Iran* (1962), *Iranica Antiqua* (1965), *Archaologische Mitteillungen aus Iran,* new series (1967), and *Cahiers de la Délégation Archéologique Française en Iran* (1971), and in addition, numerous international colloquia, symposia, conferences, and exhibitions were organized.

History of Paleolithic Research in Iran

Because of the relative lack of overlap between Paleolithic research and that of later periods, the history of Paleolithic archaeology in Iran is most effectively dealt with separately. Compared to other areas of western Asia, Paleolithic research in Iran was very late to develop. Stone tools were recovered from a Pleistocene context near the Caspian Sea in the late nineteenth century by de Morgan, and further discoveries were reported from river terraces in Seistan. De Morgan's belief that, during the Pleistocene, the mountains and plateaus of Iran would have been uninhabitable possibly dissuaded further interest. Indeed, much of the country is at such a high altitude that it is likely that the entire Paleolithic sequence of Iran will be consistently marked by hiatuses around glacial maxima.

DOROTHY GARROD's pioneering research in southern Iraqi Kurdistan in 1928 documented Lower, Middle, and Upper Paleolithic occupations at the surface site of Chemchemal and in the caves of Zarzi and Hazar Merd near Sulaimaniya, and it was expected that similar evidence would be discovered in Iran. In 1934, Middle Paleolithic flints were recovered near Shiraz in Fars Province, and Herzfeld, in the first published synthesis of Iranian archaeology, emphatically endorsed a Paleolithic occupation of the entire country, though he could say nothing beyond that (Herzfeld 1935, 1). It was not until 1949 that the U.S. physical anthropologist Carleton S. Coon (UM) conducted the first excavations with the objective of discovering the western Asian antecedents to the European Upper Paleolithic. Coon excavated in Hunter's Cave at Bisitun (Kurdistan), Tamtama Cave near Rezaiyeh (Azerbaijan), and the Khunik rock shelter (southern Khorasan near the Afghan border), all of which contained only Middle Paleolithic deposits. In Belt Cave (Ghar-I Kamarband) on the Caspian foreshore and in nearby Hotu Cave, Coon found evidence of Mesolithic, Neolithic, and later occupations.

In the 1960s and 1970s, there was a brief flurry of activity in Paleolithic research with projects emanating from Britain, Canada, Denmark, France, Italy, and the United States. For example, in 1959 and 1960, ROBERT BRAIDWOOD (OIC) conducted a survey and excavated several Middle and Upper Paleolithic sites in the region of Kermanshah. Between 1962 and 1964, CHARLES MCBURNEY (University of Cambridge) investigated Mesolithic levels in the cave of Ali Tappeh near Beshshahr (1964) and Middle Paleolithic deposits in Mazandaran (1963). In 1969, McBurney also surveyed a number of rock shelters in the Zagros and a Middle Paleolithic rock shelter (Houmian) in Luristan and as well as several caves in the mountains around Mashad, including a very large one at Moghan. Frank Hole (Rice University) and Kent Flannery (University of Michigan) identified a Middle Paleolithic "main component" at Kunji Cave in the Khorramabad Valley, central-west Iran, in 1963. In the 1960s and 1970s, Paleolithic research concentrated in the Zagros region, but SHANIDAR cave (Iraqi Kurdistan), with its rich Mousterian sequence, is still the preeminent site for the general area. Notwithstanding considerable foreign activity, interest in the Paleolithic among Iranian archaeologists has been virtually nonexistent.

Achievements to 1979

One person's periphery is another person's center. By the end of the period from 1959 to 1979 it had become apparent that, far from being pe-

ripheral to the development of civilization in western Asia, Iran had played an important part in the Neolithic transition, the development of agriculture and pastoralism, and the development of urbanism. Western and southern Iran had generated polities that had brought about the collapse of the once-mighty Assyrian empire and had gone on to conquer much of western Asia under the Achaemenids, the Parthians, and the Sassanians. In addition, it was now possible to construct a prehistoric chronology for Iran based primarily on internal evidence rather than on parallels to Mesopotamia and other adjacent areas.

Post-Achaemenid Archaeology in Iran

Limited references thus far to the work of Iranian archaeologists belies their overall contribution since much of their work has focused on the post-Achaemenid period. For the Parthian period alone, major excavations have been conducted in the Parthian cemetery at Hamadan (M. Azarnoush, ICAR), in the Anahita temple complex at Kangavar (Sayfollah Khambakhsh-Fard, ICAR), and in the city of Bishapur (Ali Akbar Sarfaraz, IAS). Also worthy of note is the extensive survey of Mazanderan and associated excavations at Qal'eh-i Kharab Shar in the late 1970s by M. Y. Kiani (ICAR).

There have also been several major foreign projects that have focused on the post-Achaemenid period. These include excavation of Shahr-i Qumis (ancient Hecatompylos), occupied in the Parthian, Sassanian, and Islamic periods; a Sassanian fire temple at Takht-i Sulaiman; the sprawling elite Sassanian complex at Qal'eh-i Yazdegird; Sirjan, the late Sassanian and early Islamic capital of Kirman Province and largest city in southern Iran by the tenth century A.D.; Islamic Ghubayra; Siraf, the famous medieval seaport on the Gulf, south of Bushire, with trade connections to India, CHINA, and the eastern Mediterranean; and the rich Islamic site of Tepe Dasht-i- Deh.

Postrevolutionary Archaeology in Iran

Archaeological fieldwork came to a virtual standstill in the decade following the Islamic Revolution. In the early 1990s, work resumed on a moderate scale under the supervision of the Cultural Heritage Organization directed by Serajuddin Kazerouni. Reports have been published in *Guzarishha-yi bastanshinasi* [Archaeological Reports] and *Majalleh-ye Bastanshinasi va Tarikh* [Journal of Archaeology and History], but little has appeared in international journals. The focus of research seems heavily weighted to the Islamic period, but this is hardly a break with earlier patterns, and excavation of both prehistoric and early historic sites has also occurred.

Important projects have been conducted on the citadel mound of the ancient Median capital of Ecbatana at Hamadan (Muhammad Sarraf); at Ziwiyeh (Nosratollah Motamedi); on the Apadana mound at Susa (Mir-Abedin Kabuli); at Shahdad (Kabuli); at the Sassanian site of Borazjan on the Persian Gulf (Ehsan Yaghmaei); in prehistoric mass graves in Luristan (Alireza Farzin); at Tepe Mil, a prehistoric, Sassanian, Seljuk, and Islamic site near Rayy (Zarintaj Sheibani); and in the important Sassanian complex at Kuh-i Khwaja in eastern Seistan. In 1995, the governments of Iran and Germany signed an accord on scientific and cultural cooperation, but assistance on the archaeological front was limited to educational exchanges. Although foreign scholars may visit and study in Iran, foreign archaeological projects remain prohibited.

Stuart Brown

See also French Archaeology in Egypt and the Middle East

References

Amiet, P., N. Chevalier, and E. Carter. 1992. "Susa in the Ancient Near East." In *The Royal City of Susa*. Ed. P. O. Harper, J. Aruz, and F. Tallon. New York: Metropolitan Museum of Art.

Dieulafoy, Jane. 1888. *A Suse: Journal des fouilles, 1884–1886.* Paris: Phoebus.

———. 1890. *At Susa, the Ancient Capital of the Kings of Persia.* Philadelphia: Gebbie.

Dyson, Robert H., Jr. 1968. "Early Work on the Acropolis at Susa: The Beginnings of Prehistory in Iraq and Iran." *Expedition* 10, no. 4: 21–31.

Ghirshman, Tania. 1970. *Archéologue malgré moi: Vie quotidienne d'une mission archéologique en Iran.* Neuchâtel: A. Le Baconniere.

Goff, Clare. 1980. *An Archaeologist in the Making.* London: Constable.

Herzfeld, Ernst. 1935. *Archaeological History of Iran.*
Schweich Lectures 1934. London: British Academy.

Hole, Frank. 1987. *The Archaeology of Western Iran.* Washington, DC: Smithsonian Institution.

McCown, D. E. 1942. *The Comparative Stratigraphy of Early Iran.* Oriental Institute Studies in Ancient Oriental Civilization no. 23. Chicago: University of Chicago Press.

Matheson, Sylvia. 1972. *Persia: An Archaeological Guide.* London: Faber.

Moorey, P. R. S., Ed. 1972. *Excavations in Iran: The British Contribution.* Oxford: Organizing Committee of the Sixth International Congress of Iranian Art and Archaeology.

Olszewski, Deborah I., and Harold L. Dibble, eds. 1993. *The Paleolithic Prehistory of the Zagros(c) Taurus.* Philadelphia: University Museum, University of Pennsylvania.

Sancisi-Weerdenburg, H., and J. W. Drijvers, eds. 1991. *Through Travellers' Eyes: European Travellers on the Iranian Monuments.* Achaemenid History 7. Leiden: Nederlands Instituut voor het Nabije Oosten.

Smith, P. E. L. 1986. *Palaeolithic Archaeology in Iran.* Philadelphia: University Museum, University of Pennsylvania for the American Institute of Iranian Studies.

Van den Berghe, L. 1966. *Archéologie de l'Iran Ancien.* Leiden: Brill.

———. 1979. *Bibliographie analytique de l'archéologie de l'Iran ancien.* Leiden: Brill.

Van den Berghe, L., and E. Haerinck. 1981. *Bibliographie analytique de l'archéologie de l'Iran ancien, Supplement 1: 1978–1980.* Leiden: Brill.

Voigt, M. M., and R. H. Dyson. 1992. "Iran." In *Chronologies in Old World Archaeology,* 1: 122–178, 2: 125–153. Ed. R. W. Ehrich. Chicago: University of Chicago Press.

Young, T. C. 1986. "Archaeology, Pre-Median: History and Method of Research." *Encyclopedia Iranica* 2, no. 3: 281–288.

Wright, Denis. 1977. *The English among the Persians during the Qajar Period, 1787–1921.* London: Heinemann.

Iraq

See Mesopotamia

Isaac, Glyn Llywelyn (1937–1985)

Born in South Africa, Isaac went to Cambridge University, received his Ph.D. in 1961, and became a protégé of LOUIS LEAKEY. During the 1970s Isaac helped DESMOND CLARK establish the University of California, Berkeley, as a center for the study of African archaeology. In 1983 he transferred to Harvard University.

Isaac became one of the most significant prehistoric archaeologists of his generation as a result of his brilliant excavation of major sites in East Africa such as OLORGESAILIE, Naivasha, and Peninj and his novel and challenging interpretations of hominid behavior occurring millions of years ago. From 1970 until his early death he was codirector with Richard Leakey of the East Turkana Research Project, which contributed a great deal of new information about fossil hominids and the environments in which they lived. He was also responsible for educating, encouraging, and working with a new generation of African archaeologists from African nations. Isaac died at a tragically young age, very much at the height of his powers.

Tim Murray

References

Isaac, G. U. 1977. *Olorgesailie: An Archaeological Study of a Middle Pleistocene Lake Basin in Kenya.* Chicago: University of Chicago.

———. 1989. *The Archaeology of Human Origins.* Papers by Glyn Isaac. Ed. B. Isaac. Cambridge: Cambridge University Press.

Island Southeast Asia

This essay includes both prehistoric and historical archaeology. The definition of Island Southeast Asia depends on the distinction between Island Southeast Asia and Mainland Southeast Asia. This definition was made at the Eleventh Pacific Science Congress, held in Tokyo in 1966, and was approved as Resolution 2.2 of the Congress (Solheim 1967a, 2). This resolution presented, for the first time, the terms *Mainland Southeast Asia* and *Island Southeast Asia*. The ad hoc committee of the Anthropology Division of the Congress that submitted this resolution, first to the Anthropology Division and then to the Council of the Pacific Science Association, further presented tentative boundaries as follows: "Mainland Southeast Asia would extend from the thirtieth parallel of latitude (approximately the Yangzi River) to the south as far as Singapore, and from the Irrawaddy River to the South China Sea; Island Southeast would include all the islands off the coast of Mainland Southeast Asia, from Formosa around to the Andaman Islands" (Solheim 1967a, 3; 1967b, 896). As presented and as used here, both terms are capitalized. For the record, the ad hoc committee that developed these terms was made up of Tom Harrisson, R. P. Soejono, and the author.

There was little communication between historical and prehistoric archaeologists working in Southeast Asia until recently. Historical archaeologists have been interested primarily in monumental architecture and art (stone and bronze sculpture in particular) and have done very little excavation. An attempt to bring historians, historical archaeologists, and prehistoric archaeologists together on the transition from prehistoric to historic times in Southeast Asia was the "London Colloquy on Early South East Asia" held in 1973 (Smith and Watson 1979). Until recently, historical archaeologists depended primarily on ancient Chinese records for the interpretation of their finds previous to European contact in the area.

Art history has been an important approach to historical archaeology but, unfortunately, there has also been little communication between archaeologists involved in prehistoric archaeology and art historians. In an attempt to bring art historians and archaeologists together, a symposium on "Early Chinese Art and its Possible Influence in the Pacific Basin" was organized by the Department of Art History and Archaeology of Columbia University (Barnard 1972). While art historians were saying that Chinese art styles, primarily of late Chou times, were an important influence on Pacific Basin art, in part by way of the spread of Dongson art through Indonesia into the Pacific, archaeologists were pointing out that virtually all of the specific examples presented were earlier in Southeast Asia than in CHINA and that the influence was Southeast Asian rather than Chinese. There was little communication between the two different approaches.

It is not possible to establish a universal periodization for this history as to some extent each country (and even each portion of a country as large as INDONESIA) has a different history. The one thing that all these countries share is that the first stage of archaeological study for each was initiated and carried out by foreigners. Only gradually did the original inhabitants of the countries become involved and finally take over, through archaeology, the study of their own past. There is one other element of this history that is shared by all the countries of Island Southeast Asia, and that is that World War II marked the end of the total domination of archaeological research by foreigners. Following the war there was a short period of adjustment when a few new foreigners entered the field and quickly started training local archaeologists. As these countries, except for Brunei and, to a lesser degree, Taiwan, are developing countries, they do not have big budgets for archaeological research. While they are able to locally train archaeologists needed for the jobs available, they need an increase in trained archaeologists to keep up with development and to start covering the whole area of their countries.

Island Southeast Asia is treated here country by country, within three very generalized time periods: pre–World War II, the short adjustment period following the war, and the last thirty-five years of the twentieth century, when local archaeologists became the primary research force.

Colonial Archaeology, 1700–1942

Indonesia

The first archaeological research in Island Southeast Asia, as elsewhere, was the making and recording of surface collections. For Southeast Asia, this continued to be the major source of archaeological data until after World War II. In Island Southeast Asia, as in much of the rest of the world, it was, and still is, widely believed that polished stone artifacts are supernatural objects of extraterrestrial origin, brought to earth through thunder and/or lightening. As a result these ancient stone tools, when discovered, were kept by the finders as amulets for protection against fire started by lightening, for protection of crops in the fields, and for personal protection. Much of the early collections was created by purchasing these artifacts from

local farmers and villagers. The earliest-known such collector in Indonesia, who published data on his collections, was G. E. Rumphius (1705; Soejono 1969, 68–69; Solheim 1969a, 31–32).

Soejono (1969, 70–73) lists a number of collectors who published on polished adzes, bronze drums and weapons, megalithic and cave sites, human skeletal remains, and ancient beads during the nineteenth and early twentieth centuries. (See Soejono 1969, 70–73 for details on this work.) Heine-Geldern (1945, 129) states that "the first systematic excavation of a prehistoric site ever to be undertaken in the Archipelago . . . was that of the Toala Caves in Southwest Celebes by Paul and Fritz Sarasin in 1902." A major event was the discovery of the *Pithecanthropus* skull cap in Trinel, Java, by EUGENE DUBOIS in 1891. Between 1907 and 1908 a follow-up German expedition, led by Frau L. Selenka, searched in Trinel but found nothing else. Soejono also said:

> During the first quarter of the twentieth century, intensive studies were done in cave cultures, kettledrums, and the Megalithic culture. . . . It was suggested that the megalithic tradition was introduced by peoples of the Mediterranean; differing racial groups were assumed to be the producers of the different cave cultures; and ancient beads were thought to have an interconnection with regions in Asia and the Mediterranean. The Archaeological Service, . . . however, did not pay much attention to drums, caves, megaliths, or beads, as its greatest concern was the survey and preservation of "Hindu-Javanese" movements. The existence of a prehistoric stage preceding the Hinduized cultural level was still a matter of obscurity. (1970, 12–13)

Historical archaeology had its beginnings almost as early as prehistoric archaeology, but in the form of written references to historic sites rather than collections of artifacts. In 1733 a Dutch official mentioned the Prambanan temples, which he had visited, in his diary, and toward the end of the eighteenth century F. von Boekholz described them in detail. In 1805 J. H. Cornelious was ordered by the Dutch administrator to explore them (Soekmono 1969, 93).

Organized recording of historical sites and monuments was started by Sir Stamford Raffles during the British interregnum in Java, and he made several visits to some of these sites. He included a chapter on antiquities in his two-volume work on the history of Java. In 1822, following the departure of Raffles, a Commission for the Exploration and Conservation of Antiquities was founded, but there is no indication that anything was done by this body. By the middle of the nineteenth century most of Java's historic sites were known through the efforts of a variety of travelers, some connected with the Batavia Society of Arts and Sciences. An archaeological society was founded in 1885 in Yokyakarta and its Chairman, J. W. Ijzerman, in the same year discovered the hidden foot of Borobudur. A report was made on an excavation of the Prambanan temples in 1887 by the Yokyakarta society. W. P. Groeneveldt published a catalog of the Jakarta Museum archaeological collection in 1887. In 1885 a catalog of Javanese antiquities in the Leiden Museum in Holland was published by C. Leemans, and in 1891 R. D. M. Verbeek published a list of descriptions of field antiquities in Java (Soekmono 1969, 94).

With prodding from W. P. Groeneveldt, H. Kern, L. Serrurier, and G. P. Rouffaer, the Dutch government organized the "Commission in the Netherlands Indies for Archaeological Research in Java and Madura." Under the direction of J. L. A. Brandes several monuments were studied and annual reports (*Rapporten van de Commissie Nederlandsch Indie voor Oudheidkundig Onderzoek op Java en Madoera*) were issued. Unfortunately Brandes died in 1905 and the only important work that continued was registration of antiquities and the restoration of Borobudur by T. van Erp. During this period Indonesian monuments were thought to be Hindu in origin, and this view continued until the second quarter of the twentieth century (Soejono 1970, 11–12; Soekmono 1969, 94–95).

In 1913 the Archaeological Service in the Netherlands Indies was established. With N. Krom as its director, a permanent staff, and the expansion of its duties, at this point it had become a truly professional body. Krom was followed in 1915 by F. D. K. Bosch, who continued as the head of the Archaeological Service for twenty years and expanded coverage to include all of Indonesia. Islamic archaeology became a part of the program under R. de Vink in Acheh, northern Sumatra. Under Bosch it was recognized that the monuments and associated art were not simply a transplanted Hindu tradition but had been reinterpreted to combine Javanese elements.

Bosch introduced the reconstruction (anastylosis) of monuments against the opposition of Krom, who felt this should be done only on paper. A special commission was organized to examine this question. Only after many years did this commission finally agree with Bosch. With this principal established, reconstruction of the main temple at Prambanan was begun in 1918, and "became a permanent branch of the Archaeological Service's activities and led to the establishment of a special architectural division at Prambanan" (Soekmono 1969, 95).

W. F. Stutterheim followed Bosch in 1936 as the director, and in 1937 the full reconstruction of the main temple at Prambanan was started. With the entry of JAPAN into World War II all archaeological activity in Indonesia came to a halt, except for the gradual anastylosis of the Prambanan main temple. Stutterheim died in 1942, in a Japanese prison camp. While the Archaeological Service was under the direction of Bosch a special branch on prehistory was started, due to the urging of P. V. van Stein Callenfels, who became its first director.

From 1923 until the Japanese invasion of Indonesia during World War II is the period most thoroughly covered by prehistoric archaeology. This article uses primarily seven sources for this period: Heine-Geldern 1945; Van Heekeren 1957, 1958a, 1958b, and 1972; and Soejono 1969 and 1970.

Soejono called this the period of systematic prehistoric research. Although, relative to what was being done before, the research could be called systematic, there does not appear to have been any overall plan made or direction established. "This period was marked by efforts to synthesize work in both small and large scale projects toward understanding the framework of prehistoric Indonesia, and to extend researches to fill in the framework using collected data acquired during the previous period of research. Researches and excavations to find items from successive cultural stages were carried out cooperatively in order to build a prehistoric chronology" (Soejono 1970, 13).

Only one of the archaeologists working during this period, W. J. A. Willems, had been trained in prehistoric archaeology and he was not active for long, nor did he publish very much. Many of the discoveries and resulting short reports were done by amateurs who were not employed by the Archaeological Service. Van Stein Callenfels was originally a historical archaeologist, and though he advocated what could be called "scientific" archaeology in the field he did not make use of it in published reports; instead of making use of the stratigraphic position of excavated artifacts that he advocated his interpretation was based primarily on typology.

> Brief reports concerning van Stein Callenfels's investigations as well as information announced by him in newspapers or magazines remind us of the steady work of this energetic scholar. Many sites of the Toalian culture, the fertile Kalumpang Neolithic settlement [both in Sulawesi], and the Bali bronze-age sarcophagi were excavated during the years before his sudden death in 1938, and it is regrettable that van Stein Callenfels did not publish full reports on the results of these important investigations. (Soejono 1969, 75)

P. V. van Stein Callenfels was considered by his contemporaries the leading archaeologist in Southeast Asia. He was certainly a leader in the field. He organized the First Congress of Prehistorians of the Far East, held in Hanoi in 1932, which led to the founding of the Far-Eastern Prehistory Association and the INDO-PACIFIC PRE-HISTORY ASSOCIATION. He also saw to the establishment of the division of prehistory at the Museum of the Koninklijk Bataviaasch Genootschap in 1933, which later became the National Museum of Indonesia.

H. R. van Heekeren was one of the most serious amateurs doing archaeological fieldwork before World War II, concentrating primarily on excavations of rock shelters at Besuki, in Java,

and in southern Sulawesi. Several of his books (1957, 1958a, 1958b) were the first extensive and detailed reviews of Indonesian prehistory and were based primarily on the research done before World War II. In a review of one of these books the reviewer referred to it as a "laundry list" (Smith 1959, 335). Others argue that this was not van Heekeren's fault as practically all the data in published reports could be considered as coming from surface finds (Solheim 1975a, 115).

Research on Pleistocene fossil man and Paleolithic cultures has been a strong element of Indonesian archaeological research. Following Dubois, the primary searchers for fossil man were C. Ter Haar, W. F. F. Oppenoorth, and G. H. R. von Koenigswald. Their finds were made in central Java at such sites as Trinil, Patjitan, and Ngandong. Koenigswald recovered a considerable number of stone tools and interpreted them as a part of traditional European typology. American H. L. Movius reinterpreted these tools as a part of his Chopper/Chopping Tool Tradition, a Southeast and East Asian typological tradition. Unfortunately the stone tools have not been found in association with fossil finds. To add to the chronological problem the geological stratigraphy of the finds is very complex, and remains controversial.

Finds were made of a number of apparently different cultures from the early and middle Holocene. The first excavations by van Stein Callenfels, in northern Sumatra, were of kitchen middens with artifacts of the Hoabinhian stone industry. No dating has been done on these sites. While Hoabinhian-like stone tools were also found in West Kalimantan, in Java in Gua Lawa by van Stein Callenfels, in caves of Besuki by van Heekeren, and in other caves in Java, it is generally considered that the only true Hoabinhian sites in Indonesia are those in Sumatra. Numerous cave sites, apparently of this general time period, were investigated in East Java, Sulawesi, Timor, and Roti; several of those in East Java contained Hoabinhian-like tools but also glade and flake artifacts, a large number of shell tools, and bone implements. Some of these sites, including the Toalian sites of South Sulawesi excavated by van Stein Callenfels, had projectile points of a form very similar to points found in Early Holocene Japan and Korea. A different flake/blade industry was found in Sumatra (Van der Hoop 1940) and West Java.

Sites identified as Neolithic have been unusually rare. From central Sulawesi, Cense excavated at Sikendeng in 1933 and van Stein Callenfels excavated at Kalumpang in 1933. In East Java Heekeren excavated at Kendeng Lembu in 1941. Unfortunately no reports on these sites were published, although van Stein Callenfels reported on Kalumpang at the Third Congress of the Far-Eastern Prehistory Association in Manila in 1935, the report of which was finally published in 1951.

Megaliths of a variety of forms, including cist graves, were reported and in some cases excavated in considerable number beginning in the 1920s. In the 1920s it was not realized that many of these were prehistoric, but by the 1930s it was recognized that the earliest were probably Neolithic in origin, and that they continued to be erected until the present day in some areas. They were found primarily on the larger islands of Sumatra, Java, Sulawesi, and Kalimantan, but some were found on islands in the Lesser Sundas.

Early Metal-Age finds include bronzes, iron artifacts, glass, and other kinds of beads and urn burials. These objects are often associated with megalithic burials. Both the megaliths and metal age artifacts were studied in comparison to similar artifacts in Mainland Southeast Asia, the PHILIPPINES, and Taiwan. It was noted that many of the early bronze finds were similar to bronze artifacts from the mainland, and in particular from the site of Dongson in Vietnam.

Due to van der Hoop's keen observations of the Pasemah remains in 1931, a prehistoric bronze culture that seemed to have existed contemporaneously with the megalithic culture became discernable. "Shortly thereafter, a bronze culture, later designated by Heine-Geldern (1936) as the Dongson civilization and much later (1945) designated the Dongson culture by the same scholar—formally assumed its proper place in the chronology of Indonesian prehistory. It was settled that the Dongson finds dated from the Han period and included specimens that dated from the first centuries A.D." (Soejono 1969, 82).

The earliest form of large bronze drums (Heger I) were found in Sumatra, Java, Bali, Salajar, Sangean, Roti, Luang, Leti, and the Kei Islands. Referring to the Dongson elements of decoration, van Stein Callenfels "stated that the oldest pattern of ornamentation on the continent dated from 600 to 500 B.C. and that the southward move of this bronze tradition took place at 400 to 300 B.C. bringing with it ornaments of more degenerate types. At the same time, Heine-Geldern came to an almost similar conclusion" (Soejono 1969, 84). It is now known that Dongson bronzes, although not the large kettledrums, were being made in Vietnam by 800 B.C. and probably earlier, and that many elements of what had been considered the Dongson art style originated much earlier than the Dongson civilization in both Thailand and Vietnam and entered both the Philippines and Indonesia before 1000 B.C.

In Alor, Bali, East Java, and Central Java distinct variants of the Dongson bronze drum, called the moko type, were discovered and found to be locally manufactured. Discoveries by van Stein Callenfels and van der Hoop showed that bivalve molds were used for casting bronze artifacts.

Urn burials were discovered in South Sumatra, East Java, Central and South Sulawesi, Salajar, and Sumba starting in 1922. DATING at first was a problem but as more were found many jars contained or had associated bronze and iron artifacts and glass, indicating Early Metal Age dating for most. A few sites had stone tools and no metal, suggesting possible Late Neolithic. Examination of skeletal material led to interpretations of mixtures of either Negroid and Malay or proto-Malay and Veddoid. The terminology has changed since that time. A few Chinese artifacts were found in early metal age sites.

Very little archaeological research was accomplished in eastern Indonesia. German Joseph Roder reported on rock paintings that he discovered in the Kei Islands and Seram. In 1937 he led an expedition in Mac Cluer Golf in western New Guinea. He was not able to complete the final report before the beginning of

World War II, but was finally able to publish it in 1959.

East Malaysia and Brunei

The early period of random finds in Sarawak, Brunei, and Sabah produced very little. "It did include, however, a time of world attention on Sarawak in the late 1870s when exploration of Sarawak caves and the Great Cave at Niah, in particular, was sponsored by Darwin, Huxley, and Wallace (Harrisson 1958, 550–560; 1970, 19) in an attempt to find the so-called 'missing link' in the evolution of man" (Solheim, et al. 1985, 12). "The reported results were that 'cave deposits of this part of Borneo are wholly without interest except to local naturalists'" (Solheim 1983, 35). This survey did, however, establish that there were cave and open sites with prehistoric and early historic remains, not only at Niah but also at the Bau Caves in southwestern Sarawak and at Santubong, at the mouth of the Kuching River (Harrisson 1954, 1958; Harrisson and O'Connor 1969, 3–6; Solheim 1961). No reports on these findings were published.

Banks, as an early curator of the Sarawak Museum, published a few descriptions of prehistoric artifacts he came across in Sarawak, and Ivor Evans, in what was then British North Borneo, did the same for North Borneo (1913, 154–158; 1922).

Philippines

There are several publications on the history of Philippine archaeology (Beyer 1947; Evangelista 1969; Solheim 1952a, 1953, 1968). This history refers primarily to the articles by Evangelista and Solheim (1968).

The one true archaeological survey during the nineteenth century was done by Frenchman Alfred Marche. In 1881 he made a systematic survey, primarily of cave sites, on two of the central Visayan Islands, the more important being of Marinduque. He published a travel account of this in French (1887), which has been translated into English (1970). Most of his collections are now in the Musée de l'Homme in Paris, while a few artifacts are in the Museum of Madrid. A brief article was published on a few of the wood carvings in the Musée de l'Homme

that he had recovered (Solheim and Gaynor 1978).

"Caves and open sites were casually explored in several localities in the Philippines by Feodor Jagor in 1860, J. Montano and Paul Rey from 1878–1881, and by Jose Rizal, Filipino national hero, and his party, in 1894. However, nothing significant resulted from these investigations" (Evangelista 1969, 99). Following Rizal's activities in Mindanao, until 1921 there was no further known archaeological activity. In 1921 HENRY OTLEY BEYER started gathering data on possible prehistoric finds. Up until this time it was believed that no "stone age" had existed in the Philippines.

From 1922 to 1924 Carl Guthe led an archaeological survey program, primarily in the Visayan Islands, on behalf of the University of Michigan. He had a boat to work from and as the result of about 15,000 miles of travel by sea and land about thirty-one tons of artifacts from 542 sites had been collected. He had been instructed to make only surface collections, but he was unable to follow these instructions at all times and, as a trained archaeologist, he made small test excavations at a few prehistoric sites. The expedition was focused on locating sites with Chinese and Southeast Asian porcelains and stonewares. Guthe published only three short reports on the expedition (1927, 1934, 1937; Solheim 1964a, 3).

Beyer, the father of Philippine anthropology and archaeology, first came to the Philippines in 1905 as a government ethnographer. He had no training in archaeology when he became interested in the prehistory of the Philippines. He did no fieldwork in archaeology before 1926. In late 1925 he was preparing to return to the United States to join the Department of Anthropology at Harvard when he fell and broke his leg. While he was recuperating, work on the dam and reservoir at Novaliches, to provide water for Manila, began and archaeological sites were discovered. When he was able he went to visit the sites and thereupon decided to forgo Harvard and organize excavation at Novaliches (Solheim 1969b).

Beyer was not a trained archaeologist and his methods were self taught, based on common sense and a very organized mind. His methods would not be considered "good" archaeology today, and criticism in the Philippines has tossed out most of his conclusions. However the generalizations he made, without presenting the data on which he based them, were on the whole quite accurate. His reconstructions of "waves of migration" have been shown to be most unlikely, but the dating for these waves and the areas from which he said they came match very well the times and areas with which contact has been hypothesized. His 1947 publication presents a very detailed history of archaeological finds in the Philippines.

In 1940 Olov R. T. Janse came to the Philippines from Vietnam to see if there were Dongson connections between the two areas. Thinking that Beyer was an amateur collector he did not work through him, and as a result found nothing of interest (Janse 1941, 1944, 1946). During World War II Beyer was not interned until the final six months of the war due to the intercession of Tadao Kano, a Japanese archaeologist in charge of museums in the Philippines. While he was unable to do any fieldwork during this time, he did much research and writing.

Taiwan

Probably the best history of Taiwan archaeology was one by Takeo Kanaseki and Naoichi Kokubu (1950). Written in Japanese, it was translated into Chinese. A brief history of Taiwan archaeology by Wu (1969) is the primary source for this article.

Archaeological research in Taiwan has not followed the trajectory that it did in the other Southeast Asian countries because the traditions that developed in Taiwan were the result of Japanese colonialism rather than western colonialism. Archaeology developed in close relationship with ethnology and the early Japanese focus in archaeological research was to relate the ethnic groups that were being studied at the time with prehistoric cultures. There are few if any reports suggesting any archaeological activities in Taiwan before the Japanese occupation began there in 1895.

There was very little communication between Japanese and western archaeologists until after the end of World War II. All publications on the archaeology of Taiwan were in Japanese or Chinese, resulting in an almost complete ignorance in the western world of what went on in Taiwan prehistoric research until well after the end of World War II. The first effective contact between Taiwan archaeology specialists and western archaeologists was in 1953 at the Eighth Pacific Science Congress and the Fourth Far-Eastern Prehistory Congresses Combined, held in Manila, where both Chinese and Japanese archaeologists from Taiwan took part.

Reports on archaeological subjects started appearing immediately in 1895 in the form of field notes that appeared in the Japanese archaeological journal *Zenruiqaku Zasshi*. "Three kinds of work may be distinguished among the sources: (1) Simple field notes, which include travel reports, site reports, and the description of artifacts; (2) Reports on excavations; and (3) Interpretations, which include theoretical analyses of data, discussions on the relationship between artifacts and the peoples, and discussions on the connections between Taiwan and other areas" (Wu 1969, 106).

In early 1897 Moshinori Ino and others discovered the Yuan-shan shell mound, one of the most important sites in Taiwan. Ino was an ethnographer and was the first to report impressed geometric decoration on pottery of the Ping-pu ethnic group, a kind of pottery latter found in archaeological sites. "He was the first person to carry out excavations in Peng-hu Island, and found that prehistoric communication existed between Taiwan and the Ryukyus and between Taiwan and Micronesia" (Ino 1907a, 1907b; Wu 1969, 106).

Ryuzo Torii presented the idea that the Yuan-shan culture might be related to a non-Taiwan culture (1897a). He was the first person to report the existence of the site of Pei-nan on the southeast coast of Taiwan (1897b), now the location of the largest excavation yet made in Taiwan. He also pointed out that there were prehistoric sites in the mountainous interior of Taiwan (1900). Torii authored one of the most important excavation reports of this early period (1911), and in his last paper (1926) he presented the first report on the megalithic culture in Taiwan.

It is not known under what authority or what source of funding this archaeological research took place. Wu has stated, however, that "a new trend, conducting organized excavations, had developed for the study of Formosan prehistory after the establishment of the Lecture Room of Folklore and Ethnology, Taihoku Imperial University" (1969, 107). Apparently, from about 1929 both authority and funding came through the Imperial University. New professional archaeologists became prominent in the field from this time. The most important of these were A. Matsumura, Takeo Kanaseki, Naoichi Kokubu, and Tadao Kano.

In about 1927 Matsumura discovered the Ken-ting site at the southern tip of Taiwan. Excavations were undertaken there in 1930, but other than brief preliminary papers, no final reports were published. In 1929 Kano listed 151 prehistoric sites that had been discovered and reported previous to that time. Many more were discovered in following years but little was published by other than those mentioned. The information on these sites comes from the Kanaseki and Kokubu report (1950). Kano was the most active, continuing fieldwork and publication until 1943, at which time he was moved by the Japanese military government to the Philippines to be in charge of the museums there. He worked closely with Beyer and informed him of Taiwan prehistory so that in later publications Beyer was the only English-writing archaeologist to be able to include data on Taiwan prehistory.

Adjustment Years, 1942–1959

Taiwan was the only country in Island Southeast Asia where fieldwork continued during World War II. In all the other countries fieldwork came to a virtual standstill with the beginning of the Japanese invasions. Unlike the abrupt beginning of this period at the end of the war, the ending varied for each country and was gradual in most cases. The year 1959 is an approximate average.

Indonesia

R. Soekmono, the director of the National Archaeological Institute of Indonesia in 1968, had this to say about the Dutch Archaeological Service after the end of World War II:

> When the Dutch came back to Indonesia after World War II and found that the Archaeological Service had become an institution of the Republic of Indonesia, they established another archaeological service that was staffed with the expert personnel of the prewar period, but it lacked the needed resources. It was not until 1950 that the Archaeological Service became united again with its branches at Prambanan and Bali. Since then it has functioned normally under the direction of Professor Bernet Kempers. (Soekmono 1969, 96)

Prehistoric research continued during the Japanese occupation, but at a much reduced pace. W. Rothpletz made a survey of the Bandung hill region in West Java, his report on which was published after the war (1951), as was the report by Bandi (1951) on the Bandung obsidian artifacts.

H. R. van Heekeren was the only prehistorian working with the Archaeological Service after the war. During the war he was a Japanese prisoner of war working on the Thai-Burma railroad, where he made archaeological discoveries. He returned to work in Indonesia in 1946, doing fieldwork in Central and South Sulawesi until the early 1950s on Paleolithic sites (1949a), Toala sites (1949b), and at Kalumpang (1950). D. A. Hooijer, the paleontologist, examined animal remains recovered by van Heekeren (1949). Van Heekeren continued working for the Archaeological Service until 1956, when he returned to the NETHERLANDS. He excavated in caves on Flores (1958b), on Patjitan sites in Java (1955a), in sites with stone sarcophagi in Bali (1955b), and urn burial sites in Java (1956b) and East Sumba (1956a).

East Malaysia (Sarawak and British North Borneo) and Brunei

The three generalized periods of archaeological activity in this region vary a bit for Sarawak because of one man, Tom Harrisson. Although he had visited Sarawak in the 1930s, his archaeological work there started after World War II, in 1947, and continued until his retirement in

1967. His research on Sarawak archaeology continued from a distance until 1975 and was published, after his death, in early 1976 (Solheim and Jensen 1977). His primary activities, as the Director of the Sarawak Museum in Kuching, were at Santubong, near Kuching, and at the Niah Caves, far to the northeast.

Harrisson's first indicated interest in Sarawak archaeology started in 1946 or 1947 when he was still with the British military (Solheim 1977a, 4). He was involved in the mapping of iron deposits at Santubong using military mine detectors and trained military personnel. When he visited the Niah Caves in 1947 to check on birds-nest collecting he noted possible prehistoric material there. Actual excavation started in the Bao Caves in 1949, not so much for the data to be obtained but as part of the training of future Sarawak Museum staff and of Harrisson himself. Harrisson, with no archaeological training himself, brought in Michael Tweedie, the Director of the Raffles Museum in Singapore, to provide the archaeological background (Harrisson and Tweedie 1951).

Excavations at six main sites in Santubong were the main training in archaeology for both Harrisson and the Sarawak Museum staff. Santubong had been known since the nineteenth century for stray finds of gold ornaments, stone and glass beads and bracelets, porcelains and stone wares, and a large quantity of iron slag. Common Chinese coins dated between A.D. 976 and 984. "The first Santubong digging was in 1949 and the first excavation in 1952. The Santubong archaeology through 1956 could be considered the completion of the training period of Sarawak archaeology" (Solheim 1983, 36–37). Harrisson published on a wide variety of archaeological subjects, based primarily on library research, during this period (Solheim and Jensen 1977).

The primary site in Brunei to date is Kota Batu (two miles from Brunei town), the location of the first Brunei Sultanate capital, with beginnings well before Islam came to the area. Tom Harrisson started looking over the area in 1951, did some testing in 1952, and, with Barbara Harrisson, made a preliminary excavation in 1953 (Harrisson and Harrisson 1956).

Philippines

Much of Beyer's valuable archaeological and ethnological library in his two houses in Ermita was destroyed during the battle of Manila. While he was able to save most of the ethnographic collections of the National Museum during the battle, the section of the museum where the archaeological collections were stored was gutted, the shelves and cabinets burned, and the artifacts deposited in a midden up to two meters deep on the basement floor. Beyer's office in a building near the palace was not hurt, so a portion of his library and collections were saved (Solheim 1969b, 12). Following the hostilities he completed the writing of his two major archaeological reports on the Philippines, published in 1948. Most of his collaborators were gone and he had lost contact with most of his collectors in the provinces so there was no field activity until 1950. In 1953 the Philippines hosted the Eighth Pacific Science Congress and Beyer organized the Fourth Congress of Far Eastern Prehistorians, held jointly. This was a major event in Southeast Asian and Pacific archaeology (see Indo-Pacific Prehistory Association).

Solheim came to the Philippines in late 1949 and spent a month in the field in 1950 excavating in a jar burial site on the Bondok Peninsula in southern Tayabas, southeast of Manila (Solheim 1951). In 1951 and 1953 Solheim was again in the field with several Filipino archaeology students, surveying and excavating on Masbate (Solheim 1954, 1968). In 1951 the first survey and excavation was of Batungan Mountain in Masbate, one of the small Visayan Islands. Several cave and rock shelter sites were tested and pottery similar to the earliest pottery in Micronesia was recovered from two sites. From other sites, pottery was discovered that was similar to the pottery from the Kalanay Cave Site. From one of these sites the first C-14 dating in the Philippines was done, giving a date of $2,710 \pm 100$ years ago (L274) (Solheim 1968). The excavation of the Kalanay Cave site on Masbate, in combination with the study of the earthenware pottery recovered by Guthe in the 1920s, led to the presentation of the Kalanay Pottery Complex in the Philippines (Solheim

1957c, 1964c), and later to the Sa-huynh-Kalanay Pottery Tradition, found widely in Island Southeast Asia and Vietnam (1959a, 1967c). In addition, proposed in the 1964 publication was the Bau-Malay Pottery Tradition, also found widely in Island and Mainland Southeast Asia (1959b, 1967d). In 1952 Solheim surveyed on Fuga Island, one of the Babuyan Islands just north of Luzon, and found several burial jar sites. In 1953 he made a small excavation of a burial jar on Batan Island, in the Batanes Islands north of the Babuyan Islands. The Fuga and Batan burial jars led to a summary article on burial jars in Island Southeast Asia (Solheim 1960).

Robert Fox completed his Ph.D. in cultural anthropology at the University of Chicago, but when he returned to the Philippines he became involved in archaeology. The three primary areas of exploration, excavation, and publication undertaken by Fox were at Calatagan, Batangas, the Tabon Caves in Palawan, and the Cagayan Valley of northern Luzon. As the chairman of the Department of Anthropology of the National Museum for many years Fox was involved in much more than those areas. In 1956 Fox and Evangelista surveyed and made small excavations in two jar burial sites in Sorsogon and Albay Provinces on the Bicol Peninsula (Fox and Evangelista 1957a, 1957b).

The Calatagan peninsula is at the very southwestern tip of Batangas Province, about 100 kilometers south of Manila. It was known that fourteenth- and fifteenth-century porcelains had been found there in the 1930s and some small excavations had been made by Janse in 1940 and Solheim in 1952 through 1953. Major excavations of several extensive burial sites were started by Fox in 1958 and a report was published in 1959. A description of the Calatagan earthenware pottery was published in 1982 (Main and Fox 1982). More details can be found in the Philippine section of *Asian Perspectives* Volumes 1 through 3 (1957–1959).

Taiwan

The transition period saw a change in the archaeologists in Taiwan from Japanese to Chinese. No fieldwork of note happened after the end of World War II until 1949 when Professor LI CHI founded the Department of Archaeology and Anthropology. While the department was active in research on the prehistory of the mainland, the group of eminent Chinese archaeologists that had moved from the mainland and were either with the university department or with Academia Sinica were not greatly interested in Taiwan's archaeology.

The first change appears to have developed as a result of the number of Chinese and Japanese archaeologists and cultural anthropologists who took part in the Eighth Pacific Science Congress and Fourth Far-Eastern Prehistory Congress held in Manila in 1953. As noted by Beyer (1956, 271–272) in the proceedings of the Congress, the five papers presented on Formosan archaeology were all by Japanese archaeologists. Shortly after the Congress Beyer received two letters from Li Chi telling him of two newly started excavations undertaken by the Department of Archaeology and Anthropology in Taiwan.

The first general knowledge of Taiwan prehistory among non–Chinese reading archaeologists came with a short article by KWANG-CHI CHANG (1956). Chang edited a much more ambitious review of the archaeology of Taiwan in 1963, which presented a foundation for the real beginning of Taiwan archaeological research by Chinese in Taiwan. This review included a site report on Tap'enk'eng by Pin-hsiung Liu of excavations made in 1962. The review provided the launching platform for a rejuvenated and reoriented program of Taiwan archaeology.

Local Archaeologists Take Over

In the 1960s local archaeologists gradually took over archaeological research in most of the countries of Southeast Asia. The training of local archaeologists was a major problem for all countries and the solution varied from country to country. None of the countries had a sufficient number of archaeologists to even approach extensive coverage for the total area of their country. Publication was and is another major problem, with the tradition of publishing final reports on excavated sites not yet established in Southeast Asia. Those reports that are published are usually preliminary reports, with very little detail.

Andaman Islands

The first archaeological work to be done in the Andaman Islands was by P. C. Dutta (1962) in 1959–1960. In 1985 Zarine Cooper located thirty-nine SHELL MIDDENS and excavated in some of these. Her first report was primarily concerned with the sites and the second (Cooper and Raghavan 1989) with the pottery recovered.

Indonesia

Peter Bellwood has published two different books that review the prehistory of Island Southeast Asia. The first of these (1978, 203–232) is a brief summary while the second (1985) is a detailed and lengthy account; however, both of these were the first coverage of Island Southeast Asian prehistory as a whole.

Bellwood and I. M. Sutayasa started a program of research in northern Sulawesi and the Talaud Islands, a string of islands running between eastern Mindanao in the Philippines and Sulawesi. The sites they discovered and reported (Bellwood 1976, 1980) date from 6000 B.C. to the present. The late-prehistoric to early-historic pottery reported showed a close relationship to pottery in the Philippines.

The first program of archaeological research in eastern Indonesia started in Irian Jaya in 1975, when Solheim began a one-year program of survey and excavation in coastal Irian Jaya, primarily on islands in Cenderawasih Bay, Waigeo, off the western tip of the Vogelkop, and east and west from Kaimana on the south coast. This program continued in 1990 with the testing of a site near Sorong on the north coast of the Vogelkop and a survey on Ternate and northwestern Halmahara in the Moluccas. In 1990 Bellwood started a program on Morotai, the most northerly of the Moluccas Islands. In 1992 the University of Hawaii, jointly with Universitas Pattimura on Ambon and the National Research Center of Archaeology, started a long-term program in the Moluccas. The program includes archaeological survey and excavation on the islands of Buru, Seram, and Ambon, under the direction of Bion Griffin of the Department of Anthropology, University of Hawaii.

In 1993 Irian Jaya Studies, a priority program of the Netherlands Organization for Scientific Research, started a long-term program of research of the Vogelkop (Birdshead) of Irian Jaya. Included in that multidisciplinary project is an archaeological survey and excavation under the direction of Gert-Jan Bartstra.

Much of the archaeological publication during the Dutch governance of Indonesia was in Dutch. As the Lembaga Purbakala dan Peninggalan Nasional and now the Pusat Penelitian Arkeologi Nasional (National Research Center of Archaeology) took over responsibility for archaeological research, most of their reports were published in Indonesian with only general surveys published in English. To keep up with Indonesian archaeology it is necessary to read Indonesian, which I do not do. Very kindly John Miksic has summarized the recent history of archaeology of Indonesia for me. Miksic taught archaeology for several years at Gaja Mada University in Yogyakarta and is now with the Department of History, Singapore National University. I present his paper in its original form, with thanks.

Indonesian Archaeology, 1957–1994

Archaeological research in Indonesia was practically dormant during the late 1950s and 1960s, as Indonesia experienced political turbulence. The most important research conducted in the 1960s was that of R. P. Soejono at Gilimanuk in western Bali, a large site containing many late prehistoric burials. Excavations were undertaken in 1963, 1964, 1973, and 1977. In 1977 Soejono obtained his Ph.D. in archaeology with a dissertation on late prehistoric burial sites in Bali. Gilimanuk occupied a major portion of this study, along with the sites of stone sarcophagi.

The tempo of archaeological research picked up in the 1970s, particularly after 1975, when administrative restructuring transformed the old system inherited from the Dutch of a single institution in charge of both research and conservation. Research became the sole responsibility of the newly formed National Research

Centre for Archaeology, while conservation of sites and monuments was entrusted to the Directorate for the Preservation and Protection of the National Heritage.

Prehistoric research since 1957 has been largely focused on the Lesser Sunda islands just east of Java, with secondary centers of research in Java and Sulawesi. Liang Bua, Flores, first examined by Dr. Th. Voerhoeven in 1950, has been the subject of several excavations in 1976, 1978, 1980, 1981, and 1982. Preliminary publications indicate that this site is extremely important, with a long series of occupations in several meters of deposit, displaying a sequence of development covering thousands of years.

Ian Glover's research in East Timor took place when that region was still under Portuguese colonial rule, but since 1975 it has belonged to Indonesia. His surveys and excavations there succeeded in establishing a general framework for prehistoric development stretching back to 13,500 B.P. (Glover 1986).

In south Sulawesi Glover excavated a number of cave sites. Leang Burung 2, the most significant, yielded flake tools dating to sometime between 17,000 and 29,000 B.P. Bellwood, in north Sulawesi examined the Paso midden, recovering much faunal material and tools dating to about 8500 B.P.

The Toalian stone tool technocomplex of south Sulawesi, appearing around 8000 B.P., already the subject of study before World War II, is now better known due to the efforts of Mulvaney and Soejono (1970) at Leang Burung 1, south Sulawesi, and Glover (1976, 1979) at Ulu Leang.

The Gunung Piring site on Lombok is another late prehistoric burial site with significant parallels to the Melolo burials on Sumba, excavated in the pre–World War II period. Excavations were conducted at Gunung Piring in the 1970s.

In Java, for the Pre-Metal Period, the most interesting information gathered over the past 20 years stems from Neolithic 17 workshop sites at Ponjen, Purbalingga, central Java, where excavations were conducted in 1983, 1984, and 1986, and Limbasari, excavated in 1981 and 1983.

The majority of Javanese sites excavated in the past two decades date from the late prehistoric period. Several are burial sites. These include Anyar, west Java, where jar burials were studied by van Heekeren in 1955; research resumed there in 1976. An other jar burial site at Terjan, Plawangan, north-central Java, was listed in Dutch inventories, but first excavated in 1977 and 1978.

For the late prehistoric and early historic period, much attention has been devoted to sites with megalithic remains. Haris Sukendar and co-workers have conducted wide-ranging surveys and excavations at such sites in Java, Sulawesi, and Sumatra. Teguh Asmar has revealed several painted slab graves on the Pasemah plateau, south Sumatra, similar to those recorded by van der Hoop in the 1930s. I Wayan Ardika discovered Romano-Indian rouletted ware on the north coast of Bali, the best-documented evidence for contact with the Indian subcontinent in the late prehistoric era. Edwards McKinnon has noted the discovery of the first Heger type I bronze kettledrums on the island of Borneo (from the Sambas region, at the northwestern tip of the island).

Some of the most exciting discoveries have been made at the oldest sites of Indonesian archaeology: the excavations of fossil man. Teams under Soejono, Jacob, H. Truman Simanjuntak, F. and A. Semah, and Djubiantono working at Sangiran and other sites in the Solo valley have obtained new fossils with dates as early as 1.2 million years B.P., and for the first time have documented human fossils and tools in direct association.

Research on the origins of agriculture and human impact on the prehistoric environment are progressing, but slowly. Palynological studies in Sumatra and Java have succeeded in providing some data, but we still lack evidence for the beginning of a lifestyle based on agriculture on these major islands. Other important gaps for future research to fill include the huge and undoubtedly important islands of Sumatra and Indonesian Borneo, where prehistoric research is still in its infancy.

During the period before 1975, the principal efforts of historical archaeologists in Indonesia were focused on research concerning monuments. The foremost project was the restoration of Borobudur, which was eventually completed in 1983. Other significant long-term projects were conducted in Trowulan, East Java, between 1976 and 1990 (fifteen years), and Banten Lama, West Java (1976–1985).

In the research strategy adopted for Trowulan, the center carried out a surface survey of an area 10 kilometers by 10 kilometers. The center's historical archaeologists then conducted excavations in several sectors: the Pendopo Agung ("Great Pavilion"), Pandan Sili, Klinterejo, Sentonorejo, Nglinguk, Sumurupas, Kejagan, Kedaton, Batok Palung, Wringin Lawang, and Blendren. Large quantities of artifacts were recovered, along with data on architecture, including nonreligious buildings. This site, the probable capital of the kingdom of Majapahit (thirteenth to sixteenth centuries) has been identified as the largest precolonial urban site in Indonesia.

Research has also been conducted sporadically in Sumatra. A branch office of the center has finally been established in Palembang, south Sumatra, and data are gradually accumulating on the kingdom of Srivijaya that was based there during the seventh to eleventh centuries (Manguin 1992), as well as later periods during which the site continued to be occupied. Other sites, including a trading post of the eleventh to thirteenth centuries at Kota Cina, north Sumatra, and a large complex of monuments at Muara Jambi of approximately the same period have also been investigated.

Research at the site of Banten Lama in West Java began in 1976 and continued for ten years. Banten continues the urban history of Indonesia from Trowulan, late classic period, into the early Islamic era. Excavation and survey here has succeeded in identifying units of activity within the site, including residential and occupational zones.

At all these sites, the work of analysis continues long after the excavations have been completed. Urban archaeology in Indonesia has made a promising beginning. Systematic surveys using standard sampling techniques are now employed, and there is reason to expect that the history of early complex society in Indonesia may soon become clearer.

Epigraphy, one of Indonesian archaeology's oldest subdisciplines, has contributed some important new information despite the small number of specialists in the field. Boechari, before his untimely death, contributed important new readings of Sumatran and Javanese inscriptions, as has Sukarto Kartoatmojo. J. G. de Casparis continues to add to his astounding output of valuable translations in a multitude of languages and scripts, facilitated by his incomparable experience in both South and Southeast Asia. In addition to new information provided by reading inscriptions discovered before 1957, new inscriptions continue to be found. One of the most important is the Wanua Tengah III inscription of A.D. 908. Discovered in November 1983 in Temanggung, Central Java, the find consists of two copper plates issued by King Balitung. The plates give a king list, the second of whom is said to have taken the throne in A.D. 746.

In the realm of spectacular discoveries, the Wonoboyo Hoard must assume a prominent place. In 1991 in this village near the site of the great Hindu complex of Prambanan, central Java, local residents discovered an enormous deposit of gold items, including coins and various other objects including jewelry and ritual accessories. The weight of gold recovered exceeds 30 kilograms. Although much gold of the Classic period is held in private and museum collections, this is by far the largest and best documented discovery. The fact that the gold was properly reported and delivered safely to the National Museum is an excellent indication of the level of awareness of modern Indonesians regarding the importance of archaeological studies and the pride that most Indonesians feel for their heritage.

John Miksic

Eastern Malaysia and Brunei
Tom Harrisson continued as director of the Sarawak archaeology program for another ten years, having developed a much more ambitious program and a number of well-trained staff. The major program under way was the exploration and excavation of the Niah Caves (Harrisson, T. 1957, 1958, 1959). While he published many

Gold plaque from Indonesia representing Vishnu (Gamma)

tery from Santubong and Niah (Solheim 1959, 1965; Solheim et al. 1959 and 1961). The most recent major report on the Great Cave at Niah is a Ph.D. dissertation by Zuraina Majid (1982).

Three of Harrisson's major publications were on Santubong, with Stanley O'Connor (1967, 1969, 1970) while the Harrissons were at Cornell University in the United States. Besides reporting on the Tantric shrine that they found there, one of the conclusions they arrived at concerning the iron industry they recovered was that the iron working was based on a technique from India and that a common stoneware ceramic artifact found was a crucible. These conclusions were later refuted, after Harrisson's death (O'Connor 1977; Christie 1990).

Some of Harrisson's more important published reports were on artifacts. With Lord Medway (1962) he did a study of the bone tools from Niah. He authored two reports on double spouted earthenware vessels (1971a, 1971b). He published a number of articles on prehistoric megaliths and the continuing megalithic traditions lasting until the recent past. Probably his two most important archaeological reports were his summaries of Borneo prehistory (1970, 1972).

Tom Harrisson was of such major importance to Sarawak, Borneo, and Southeast Asian archaeology that three different journals published special issues in his memory after his death in 1975. Solheim did an article in each of these on some phase of Harrisson's contribution to archaeology (1977a, 1977b; Solheim and Jensen 1977). Each of these special issues had several other articles on Harrisson's contributions. A more detailed review of the Niah program is found in Solheim 1977b.

Following the departure of Tom and Barbara Harrisson there were no archaeological staff with the Sarawak Museum who were trained to plan and direct major archaeological projects. As a result little archaeological research was done, other than needed salvage excavations, while the search went on to find a person who could be sent away for advance training. Several sites, near the coast and inland, were the subject of salvage operations and some twenty of these produced unexpected results. Tom Harrisson

papers, very few of these were site reports, and the two that could be so considered were done with Barbara Harrisson (Harrisson and Harrisson 1957; Harrisson, T., 1968). For Niah, Barbara Harrisson(1958, 1965, 1967, 1977a) published more substantive reports than Tom Harrisson.

Tom Harrisson brought in outside specialists to do special studies on both Niah and Santubong. Lord Medway, later the earl of Cranbrook, produced a large number of important papers on the animal bone recovered at Niah and other sites (*see* Index to Sarawak Museum Journal by Loh 1980, 171–172, 136). Tom Harrisson also brought in Sheilagh Brooks, a physical anthropologist, to join Barbara Harrisson in reporting on the cemetery burials (Brooks and Brooks 1968; Sheilagh, Brooks, et al. 1977; Harrisson, B. 1967), and the deep skull was reviewed by Brothwell (1960). Harrison brought in Solheim to work with the earthenware pot-

had been very interested in Chinese porcelains and stonewares. During his surveying no sites in Sarawak had been found with Ming ceramics in any quantity so he had hypothesized a "Ming gap" for Sarawak. Two sites found inland in the First Division had Ming and Sawankhalok wares of the fourteenth and fifteenth centuries in some quantity, illustrating that the "Ming gap" did not exist. A third inland site excavated was the first open site found from which a large number of stone tools and earthenware pottery were recovered in association (Chin and Nyandoh 1975; Chin 1977). The best illustrations of artifacts recovered by the Sarawak Museum programs were published by Chin (1980).

A Seameo Regional Centre for Archaeology and Fine Arts (SPAFA) ceramic workshop held in Kuching in 1981 included Chinese ceramic specialists. Further examination of the ceramics from Santubong proved that rather than most of the porcelain and stoneware dating from the tenth to the twelfth centuries as reported by Harrison (Harrisson and Harrisson 1957), it dated from the thirteenth to the fourteenth centuries with only a few shards of twelfth-century dating (Chin 1981). Solheim reported on the earthenware from this site (1965a) and later did a second report on this same pottery from other sites in Sarawak and Southeast Asia (1981).

Ipoi Datan was selected for advanced training in archaeology and for his master's thesis he reported on excavations at Gua Sireh, in the First Division of Sarawak. Solheim had made an excavation here in 1959 but because of an agreement with Tom Harrisson to publish the final report together, no final report was written before Harrisson died. From this site came a secure calibrated date for rice of 2,334 B.C. (Bellwood et al. 1992, 167) and a date for the earliest level of 21,630±80 (ANU 7048) (Datan and Bellwood 1991, 391).

Sabah archaeological research was started by the Harrissons. Tom Harrisson apparently first started exploring in Sabah in 1952 (Harrisson, B., and Ungap 1964, 664, Note 2). Tom revisited Sabah in 1964 and selected the Tapadong Cave area, on the Segama River, for survey under Barbara's supervision the same year. A number of rock shelters were discovered, many of

them containing carved wooden coffins with associated porcelains suggesting use over the last 700 years. (For a map showing locations of the Sabah caves and rock shelters, see Harrisson and Harrisson 1971, 37.) In several of these shelters were remnants of wooden platforms on which the coffins had been placed. A few of these had notched or perforated boards associated with them, which may have been a form of writing boards (Barbara Harrisson 1966). Numerous other caves and rock shelters were later found and tested, both in interior and in eastern Sabah. Some of these had much earlier deposits beneath the late burials in wooden coffins (Harrisson, T. 1966a, 1966b; 1967a, 90–91; 1967b, 145–147). Much more detail on the sites and their contents is found in Tom and Barbara Harrisson's book (1971). Tom remarked several times that the Sabah finds are quite different from the Niah materials and suggest close contact with neighboring Sulawesi.

Peter Bellwood started fieldwork in eastern Sabah in late 1979 with several major excavations, in cooperation with the Sabah Museum, in the same general area as the previous survey and testing done by the Harrissons. Three reports (1984, 1989, 1990) and a monograph (1988) edited by Bellwood present virtually a totally new understanding of eastern Sabah prehistory.

Bellwood's first research (1984) was in two nearby areas and included the Lake Tingkayu sites and the Madai sites. Lake Tingkayu was a no-longer-existent lake that had been formed when a lava flow had dammed a river. The lava flow is dated to about 28,000 years ago and the dam was broken through about 17,000 years ago, which drained the lake. Several open sites were located on the shore of this old lake. Surprisingly the stone tools included a number of bifacially flaked, very well-made, small and large tools, unlike anything found later in Southeast Asia. A later site formed after the lake had drained and dated between 17,000 and 12,000 years ago had much more typical Southeast Asian style unretouched stone tools.

Some of the Madai caves had occupations dating between 11,000 and 7,000 years ago with stone flaking similar to the post-lake site, but lacking the blade-like flakes of the earlier site. From about 4,000 to about 2,500 years ago the occupants of these caves made simple but good pottery and were probably Austronesian-speaking ancestors of some of the present day peoples of Borneo. The culture that followed, found in many more sites and dated between A.D. 1 and 1000, shows relationships to sites on the shores of the Sulu and Celebes Seas and wider areas, including similarities to the Niah Cave sites, but not a close resemblance. Finally, in the top levels, were remains like those reported by the Harrissons.

The report given at a conference in 1986 (1990) gave a more detailed account of the unusual flaked stone tools of the Tingkayu Industry. The book edited by Bellwood (1988) starts with the only detailed account of the expeditions from late 1979 to early 1987. This could be considered an almost final report of the fieldwork and research done during this period and involved a number of specialists presenting chapters on their work. A short postscript (1988, 276) concerns the content of probably the latest report (1989).

The final fieldwork in 1987 was in a series of rock shelters at Bukit Tengkorak. The new surprise from these sites, dated between 2,935 and 2,049 years ago, was that much of the obsidian used to make the common flake tools at the sites came from the Talasea obsidian sites in New Britain in Western Melanesia (Bellwood 1988, 149–151). This site was an important source for obsidian traded by people of the Lapita Culture in Melanesia. Obsidian from this source has been found as far south and east as Fiji and the Isle de Pines south of New Caledonia, where it existed during the same time period as at the Bukit Tengkorak sites.

Archaeological research in Brunei, again, was started by Tom Harrisson. On a visit in 1951 Tom selected three areas for tests to be made in the general area of the tomb of an early sultan of Brunei. What were thought to be southern Sung, Ming blue and white, and Sawankhalok stoneware from Thailand were recovered. In 1952 a small trench was dug and in 1953 an excavation was made. The report on this work (Tom and Barbara Harrisson 1956) was the first archaeological report for Brunei.

The recovered materials supported the legend that this was the area of the capital of the Sultans of Brunei and strongly supported that this had been a flourishing trading center for several hundred years before Islam came to Brunei.

Two programs needed to be completed in Brunei before Brunei archaeology could truly get under way. First, there needed to be a local person trained to be in charge, and second, there needed to be a physical base from which this work could be done. It was decided that Pengiran Shariffuddin should be trained for this work, that a national museum would be built for the base at the edge of the Kota Batu site, and that Shariffuddin would be the first curator of this museum. Shariffuddin first spent several years working with the staff of the Sarawak Museum and then studied in England, where he earned both parts of the Museum's Association Diploma (Tom Harrisson 1967a, 91; 1967b, 147). In 1967 a temporary museum building became available and Shariffuddin took over as director.

In 1968 an excavation at Sungai Lumut, forty-five kilometers north of Brunei town, was undertaken by the museum. The site was totally disturbed by farming, but produced a considerable quantity of South Chinese, Vietnamese, and Thai shards of porcelain and stoneware of primarily fourteenth- and fifteenth-century origin. One surprising result was that very little local earthenware was recovered in proportion to the high fired ceramics (Harrisson, B., and Shariffuddin 1969).

No excavation other than the 1956 testing had been done at Kota Batu by 1970. In 1968, however, a 122-meter drainage ditch was dug and 6,230 ceramic shards were recovered, without stratigraphic information. A detailed report was made by Barbara Harrisson in 1970 on this collection for comparative purposes with sites in Sarawak and the Philippines.

As of 1971 Brunei was the only country in Southeast Asia from which no Stone-age or Early Metal Age finds had been found. Tom Harrisson (1971c) remarked on this in an appeal to the public to help in locating early stone artifacts.

Dating of the Kota Batu site was enriched by a series of C-14 dates (Tom Harrisson 1971d).

While one questionable date of 95 B.C. was reported, the body of the dates was between A.D. 600 and 1300. Tom Harrisson was one of the pioneers in Southeast Asia in the study of beads. He summarized a number of these papers in a report (1973) comparing the beads recovered in Brunei to those that had been recovered in Sarawak.

Because of peaty soil and a high water table, much organic material, including wood, has been preserved in the Kota Batu site, the only such archaeological site known in Southeast Asia. Tom Harrisson (1974) reported on the wood remains excavated the first season at Kota Batu. He divided his subject into five parts: tree wood—1,577 pieces, coconut shell—399, other "nuts"—42, dammar (resin)—1,103, and charcoal—2,232. The tree wood included whole or partial: trays, bowls, and covers—16; dishes or wheels—6; kitchen utensils—11; tools for splitting or securing wood—8; spinning and weaving apparatus—17; fishing gear and boat parts—6; and toys—3 (8–10) The richness of this material from the small test excavation points to the wealth of the material that can be recovered when extensive excavations are made.

A site on the Tanjong Batu beach, the northeastern tip of Brunei, sixteen miles from Bandar Seri Begawan, the capital of Brunei, was discovered in 1974. A total of 199 primarily basal shards of small bowls were recovered, suggesting the possibility of a nearby shipwreck (Omar 1975). The shards were all considered to be Sung period (A.D. 917–1279), making them earlier than the great majority of the ceramics at Kota Batu and Sungai Lumut. Museum staff continued inspecting the site regularly and late in 1975 they discovered a polished stone adze, the first to be found in Brunei. Within days after this first discovery three more stone tools were turned over to the museum. All three of these were from the same area and had been found at about the same time as the first one (Omar and Shariffuddin 1976).

A new site, Kupang, was excavated by Omar and resulted in his M.A. thesis (1978). Unfortunately it has not been published; it appears to have been an important report for its treatment of the locally made earthenware. A brief report on the earthenware is included in an article on trade patterns between Brunei and neighboring areas from A.D. 700 to 1500 (Bellwood and Omar 1980). The site was first occupied around A.D. 750 according to C-14 dating. The earthenware is very similar to that reported by Solheim (1965a) from Tanjong Kubor in Sarawak. Bellwood and Omar name this pottery complex Tanjong Kubor (TK) ware. While they agree with Solheim that the TK ware is similar to pottery excavated in Cebu City in the Philippines, at Johore Lama in southern Malaysia near Singapore, and reported from Hong Kong, they do not go along with Solheim's calling this Bau-Malay and saying that it is found widely from about A.D. 700 up to the recent past in Island Southeast Asia, including the central and southern Philippines.

Philippines

Robert Fox continued as the primary archaeologist in the Philippines until he had a stroke in 1978. As chairman of the Department of Anthropology at the National Museum for many years, Fox helped to develop a number of well-trained Filipino archaeologists on the staff. He and his staff cooperated with the Department of Anthropology of the University of the Philippines in training a number of young archaeologists.

A great deal of archaeological fieldwork has been done by the National Museum, but unfortunately the museum does not have a regular publication. Many of the publications are short reports, put out on glossy paper for sale at the museum, and these do not receive wide circulation. A look at Fox's bibliography, which is considerable, shows that many of his works were short pieces issued with special museum exhibits, newspaper articles, articles in trade journals, and articles in other sorts of publications that did not receive circulation outside the Philippines. Looking at references to papers by the staff of the museum presented at international conferences you see that many references are to required reports to the museum on completed fieldwork. One Philippine journal that has carried a number of archaeological reports is the Philippine Quarterly of Culture and Society, published by San Carlos University in Cebu

City. Two reports that present more detail on developments in Philippine archaeology are by Ronquillo (1985) and Solheim (1974).

This article takes as the starting point of this final period the discovery of the TABON CAVES on the west coast of Palawan. Up to this time most of the archaeological work done by the museum staff was on late sites with quantities of trade porcelains from China and Mainland Southeast Asia.

The most important group of sites in the Philippines, the Tabon Caves, were discovered on the west coast of Palawan by Fox in 1962. By the end of the first season's survey forty caves and rock shelters had been found containing archaeological materials and many more were expected to be found in future seasons. The Tabon Caves and other sites in limestone outcrops along the west coast of Palawan were the main subjects of research from 1962 through 1966. Six periods of Pleistocene occupation were recovered with relatively unchanging flake tool assemblages, and C-14 dating from about 30,000 years ago to 9,250±250 years ago. A human skull cap was recovered, unfortunately from a disturbed location; at first it was thought to be between 22,000 to 24,000 years old, it is now thought to be around 15,000 years old. Above this was a jar burial assemblage with the pottery related to the Sa-huynh-Kalanay Pottery Tradition and dating roughly from 1,500 B.C., continuing into what Fox called the Metal Age with a few bronze and iron artifacts, now thought to date from about 400 B.C. to around A.D. 600. While no final reports have appeared, Fox (1970) made an important summary of many of the sites.

In a 1963–1964 ethnographic research program on the Kulaman Plateau in Mindanao, Marcelino Maceda of the University of San Carlos discovered a cave with limestone burial jars. Further nearby cave sites with limestone and earthenware burial jars were found in 1966 and followed up by excavations by Edward B. Kurjack and Craig T. Sheldon (Kurjack, Sheldon, and Keller 1971), all from Silliman University. One C-14 date on collagen for about the middle of the use of the cave is A.D. 585 (Kurjack et al. 1971, 147). While collagen dates are often

suspect, this date is at least reasonable. The pottery forms and uncommon decoration suggest relationships with both the Bao-Malay Pottery Tradition and the Sa-huynh-Kalanay Pottery Tradition.

A symposium was held in 1965 in honor of Beyer on his eighty-second birthday. The large volume of proceedings volume published (Zamora 1967) contains many important articles on Philippine archaeology and anthropology. Beyer died on 31 December 1966.

In 1966 a site was discovered within a Catholic church compound in the city limits of Manila. It was a cemetery with seventy-one burials and rich associated porcelain tradewares dating from the eleventh to the fourteenth centuries. After excavation it was developed into a site museum, open to the public daily (Fox and Legaspi 1977). An impressive book presented much of the porcelain recovered (Locsin 1967).

Fieldwork by Alexander Spoehr of the University of Pittsburgh in both archaeology and ethnology, starting in 1966 and completed in 1969, focuses on the Sulu archipelago and Zamboanga, Mindanao. This was to be a study of ethnic diversity and how different ethnic groups interacted through time. Excavations were made in sites ranging from early historic back to the early site of Balobok Rock Shelter on Sanga Sanga Island in the Sulu archipelago with C-14 dates of 6,650±180 years ago and 7,945±190 years ago. Most of the sites excavated were late historic. Spoehr only tested the rock shelter but reported that "the surface of the site and the excavations yielded a small collection of shards and shell and stone artifacts" (Spoehr 1973, 273). The shards included some red slipped pottery, one such shard with two horizontal rows of impressed circles, inlaid with lime (ibid., Fig. 117). This is similar to the earliest reported pottery in Micronesia and to that of two sites at Batungan Mountain on Masbate with a C-14 date of 2,710±100 years ago (Solheim 1968, 26, Figs. 5, 60). Spoehr's later date appears to be associated with the red slipped pottery. As Spoehr's dates were from shell, and so out of line with other dates from Island Southeast Asia, they came to be disregarded.

In 1992 the site was reinvestigated by a team for the National Museum and from Okinawa.

They found exactly the same artifacts, that is, shell tools, including shell adzes, stone tools and slipped potsherds, some with impressed decoration inlaid with lime, and very similar C-14 dates, made again on shell (Ronquillo 1993). This appears to be an extremely important site.

In 1968 Karl Hutterer (1969) started a field program in southwestern Samar along the Basey River and its tributaries. He located ten caves and/or rock shelters. Surface collections included Paleolithic style core and flake tools. From excavations he recovered some blade tools made from prepared cores, the first such tools recovered in the Philippines. Three polished stone adzes were recovered, as was earthenware pottery with forms and decoration similar to the Kalanay Complex pottery. Other sites had large quantities of Chinese and Southeast Asian porcelain and stoneware ceramics, indicating international trade. This research was the subject of Hutterer's Ph.D. dissertation at the University of Hawaii, which, unfortunately, has not been published.

Hutterer's work in Samar led to a survey of Buad and Daram Islands, small islands off the coast of southwestern Samar, where a large number of blades and prepared cores were recovered from the surface (Scheans et al. 1970; Cherry 1978). Many of the blades with silica gloss along the cutting edge indicated use in cutting some varieties of grass. Hutterer's Samar research also led to a field school in Samar for the Department of Anthropology, University of Hawaii, directed by David Tuggle. A preliminary research report on this project, edited by Tuggle and Hutterer (1972), was undertaken by the students from Hawaii. No final report has appeared.

A major problem for the study of Philippine prehistory is the popularity of ceramic collecting as the hobby of many wealthy Filipinos. Valuable ceramics and other artifacts were customarily buried with the dead in Southeast Asia and grave robbers were at their worst in the Philippines, locating cemeteries and looting them for their artifacts. The National Museum often found out about important sites after they had been systematically looted. One area with a high population in late prehistoric times and many cemeteries was the area surrounding Laguna de Bay. Leandro and Cecil Locsin were different sorts of collectors; realizing the damage done by looting, they had supported the excavation of the Santa Ana churchyard site. In 1967–1968 the Locsins supported a major excavation of three sites in Laguna and also supported the publication of a well-illustrated report on this work, which has yet to be published. The excavators were brought in from San Carlos University in Cebu. The two primary cultural horizons recovered, defined by the trade pottery of those periods, were of the Lower Sung and the Upper Sung/Yuan Dynasties of the twelfth to the fourteenth centuries. Below the Lower Sung three burials of what has been called "the Iron Age in the Philippines" were recovered. Earthenware pottery and no foreign trade porcelains were associated with these burials, and for the first time in the Philippines cremation burials and a crematorium were found.

Warren Peterson started archaeological survey and excavation in the Cagayan Valley of northern Luzon in 1968 as his Ph.D. dissertation research at the University of Hawaii. In the southern end of the valley he excavated the Pintu Rock Shelter where he found a core and flake tool industry, with flakes the more common. It was the first time flakes of this type had been found in the Philippines. Associated with these flakes from the middle level and upward was coiled or ring-built pottery. The earliest pottery from this site has a C-14 date of about 1,500 B.C., while the date for the bottom level is about 2,000 B.C. He later moved to the east coast of Luzon where he located an open site with clear evidence of houses built directly on the ground, the first such reported in the Philippines. "Flake and blade stone tools were also found, as well as a polished trapezoidal adze. Pottery in both layers was coiled or ring-built; red slipping was common. Three C-14 dates from samples of the floor of the house, in the deeper layer, varied from about 1,500 to 3,300 B.C." (Solheim 1974, 26–27).

Peterson continued working in the Philippines off and on and in 1978, while directing a field training program, he discovered the Payatas site within the city limits of Manila. From this site a number of small flakes were recovered with ground working edges and points. A number of postholes were found suggesting houses on probable prepared platforms. This site and its ground edge stone tools were also unique for the Philippines (Peterson 1979).

In 1971 the Ford Foundation approved a proposal by the National Museum of the Philippines and Solheim for the University of Hawaii to survey and test discovered sites in southeastern Mindanao. This was to be a part of a larger, long-term program of the United Nations Educational, Scientific, and Cultural Organization (UNESCO)–sponsored Malay Culture Project, which was to "explore and test archaeologically the broad triangular area from southeastern Mindanao on the north, northern Sulawesi on the southwest, and the western end of Irian Jaya on the southeast, including the Moluccas on the southern base line . . . an area which should prove to be central to the understanding of the movement of the Austronesian speaking peoples into Melanesia and the Pacific and which would be equally important in understanding the cultural and racial relationships between Indonesia and the Philippines" (Solheim et al. 1979, 1).

Work in the field started in June 1972 and continued into November. The two most important sites discovered were Asin Cave, on the east coast close to the southeastern tip of Mindanao, and Talikod Rock Shelter, on Talikod Island near Davao City. Asin Cave had been disturbed by an earthquake but had much restorable earthenware pottery from burial jars and associated smaller vessels. No porcelains, stonewares, or metal were present in the site. The earthenware included incised and painted pottery of the Kalanay Pottery Complex and several small pots with incised decoration over cord-marking (Solheim et al. 1979, 43–80, 117–121). Talikod Rock Shelter was only studied with two small test pits as it was close to the end of the fieldwork and the team could not stay over night on the island for security reasons. Stone flakes and worked shell, worked in a similar way as the stone flakes, were recovered in quantity. No polished stone tools were found. Two C-14 dates from one shell from this site were 3,950±90 years ago and 4,170±90 years ago (SUA-258). Two dates on partly fossilized worked shell were 7,320±100 years ago (SUA-256) and 7,620±100 years ago (SUA-257), but with the beginning of fossilization the dates are suspect (Solheim et al. 1979, 111, 116–117). Shell tools have been found at several sites on Palawan (Fox 1970, 60–64) and at Sanga Sanga with about the same dating.

A regional seminar on Southeast Asian Archaeology was held in Manila and Palawan from 26 June to 4 July 1972, with the financial assistance of the Ford Foundation. This was the first such seminar to bring together a number of the new and young native Southeast Asian archaeologists (Tantoco 1974). This sort of seminar became common with the development of SPAFA, much improving communication among the archaeologists of Southeast Asia. In connection with this seminar *A Selected Bibliography for the Study of Philippine Prehistory* was presented to all participants.

The primary emphasis of the National Museum's archaeology program moved from Palawan to the Cagayan Valley in northern Luzon in 1971. Three different areas of sites were developed over the next five years: on the western side of the Cagayan River, between the Cagayan and Chico rivers, near the mouth of the Cagayan River in the north, and to the east of the Cagayan River near Penablanca. The western sites were Pleistocene with a fossil fauna including Elephas, Stegodon, Rhinoceros, crocodile, giant tortoise, pig, and deer, possibly associated with flake and core tools. This was in the same area examined by von Koenigswald in 1953. The geological stratigraphy here is very complex and sites that were first thought to be Middle and Late Pleistocene may well be Late Pleistocene and Early Holocene.

In 1970 a shell mound was excavated at Lallo, in the north. Barbara Theil made a second excavation at this and other nearby sites in 1977. The most common artifact was pottery, some with an incised or impressed decoration of punctate straight or zigzag lines and rarely small impressed circles. This distinctive decoration is similar to rare decoration on a few shards from a Yuan-shan site in northern Taiwan; to pottery from the Batungan Cave sites in Masbate; to the earliest pottery on Saipan, Tinian, and Rota in the Marianas; and to pottery from the Kamassi site in central-western Sulawesi. There were also a few fired clay ornaments, either pendants or earrings (Theil 1986–1987a). Theil also excavated in two cave sites near Penablanca. Arcu Cave (Theil 1986–1987b) was a burial cave with C-14 dates from about 6,000 to 2,000 years ago. Six types of secondary burial included jar burial. Some of the bones were covered with red ochre. Associated with burials were flake tools, ornaments, shell bracelets, spindle whorls, and a stone barkcloth beater. Musang Cave had been used both for burials and as a habitation site; a lower level had dates between 11,500 and 9,000 years ago while the upper level had dates between 5,200 and 4,000 years ago. Ronquillo (1981) made a report on the stone tool technology of a third Pleistocene habitation cave in the same area.

By the mid-1970s, red-slipped and plain earthenware pottery had been dated back to 1,500 B.C. and earlier at a number of sites in the Cagayan Valley and on the adjacent east coast of Luzon. In 1978 Shutler made excavations at Andarayan and Fuga Moro Island in northern Cagayan Province. From these excavations considerable earthenware was recovered and a very successful attempt was made to work out a method to differentiate the plain and red-slipped wares of northern Luzon. By very detailed analysis of stages of manufacture and of the clay used, Snow and Shutler (1985) were able to define three pottery traditions, two of them starting around 800 years ago and continuing into specific ethnic groups today, and a third that appeared as early as 5,000 years ago and may be ancestral to the other two (147–148).

Karl Hutterer of the Department of Anthropology, University of Michigan, started, in cooperation with Silliman University, a long-range, interdisciplinary program in southeastern Negros called the Bais Anthropological Project. The researchers "gathered archaeological, ethnographic, biological and geological data to provide an overall understanding of prehistoric societies in Negros, and of 'how and why they evolved into the contemporary configurations

and cultural groupings of the island'" (Ronquillo 1985, 81; Hutterer and Macdonald 1979, 1982).

Robert F. Maher first made test excavations in Ifugao, northern Philippines, in 1961, but was unable to return again until 1973. His first purpose in working there was to find out the age of the Ifugao rice terraces: whether they were about 3,000 years old, as proposed by Beyer, or whether they were built by lowland farmers escaping to the mountains to get away from Spanish control, as proposed by Keesing and others. Maher excavated in three areas that he felt would represent a late location, a middle location that would be neither early nor late, and a site in the assumed earliest area of Ifugao occupation. The dates were 205≈/−100 years ago for the late location (Maher 1973, 52), 695±110 and 735≈/−105 years ago (Maher 1973, 55) from a midden at the medium location, and 2,950±250 years ago (Maher 1973, 56) from the oldest location on a house platform. While these did not date rice terraces they did show that the area with house platforms was occupied well before arrival of the Spanish. Maher did fieldwork in Ifugao in two more seasons, the final one in 1978. The report was published after his untimely death in 1987.

There has been a considerable amount of ethnoarchaeology done in the Philippines. In the 1950s Solheim published several papers on pottery manufacture. In the 1960s Daniel Scheans did a major work on pottery manufacture for ethnic groups all over the Philippines (1966). In 1969 Lionel Chiong, with Silliman University in Dumaguete, Negros Oriental, made a study of pottery manufacture in one barrio near Dumaguete (1975). Starting in 1974 Bion Griffin and Agnes Estioko-Griffin (Griffin and Griffin 1978) started a long-term program with the hunting and collecting Agta of northeastern Luzon. In Kalinga, starting in 1975 in the mountains of northern Luzon, William Longacre made a detailed ethnoarchaeological study of a pottery-making village (1981).

Rosa Tenazas (1974) excavated in a unique burial jar site in Barrio Magsuhot in southeastern Negros in 1974. The site had been discovered by farmers in 1972 and came to the attention of anthropologists at Silliman University. The first excavation by the university was conducted by Lionel Chiong but no reports were published. Some of the burials, either in large earthenware jars or in earthenware coffins, had over one hundred associated earthenware vessels. Several of the jars had human figures on their lids in deep relief, and hollow heads and relatively complete female figures were recovered. One unusual type of vessel was hollow with no bottom. No records were found of the excavations done by Chiong, but there was a collection of 141 pieces kept by the Silliman Anthropology Museum. A detailed study was made of this pottery (Mascunana 1986).

The Victoria Archaeological Survey (VAS) in Australia, under the leadership of Peter Coutts, made an agreement with the National Museum for an annual program of archaeological and ethnoarchaeological research on Panay. This program started in the field in 1976 with survey and testing. The decoration on pottery that was recovered is typical of what Beyer called Iron Age pottery (Coutts and Wesson 1978, 1979).

A final report on the Panay research was published in 1983 (Coutts). This goes into detail on the sites worked in 1980 but has little on the sites worked in earlier years, which were covered in the smaller, yearly reports. The one major excavation of the five years was of Lapuz Lapuz, a cave site in the interior (Coutts 1983, 22–103), and this is reported in great detail and well illustrated. The survey concentrated on cave and rock shelters and therefore does not give a full picture of Panay archaeology. Most, if not all, of the sites found were used by hunters and collectors who were in contact with probable farming people, as small quantities of simple earthenware were found in at least the upper levels of most sites. Virtually no porcelain or stoneware was found, even though the dating of the sites suggested that most of them were contemporary with open sites whose cemeteries had quantities of trade porcelains. In the early 1980s grave robbers discovered a site with possible pre-Sung Chinese ceramics near Butuan. The National Museum was told about this after much damage had been done and started exca-

vations finding Chinese Yueh-type pottery, the first time such pottery had been found in the Philippines. Of much interest were the remains of several wooden boats in the swamp, still in fair condition (Peralta 1980; Scott 1981). Research continued there into the 1990s. Most of the few published reports have been on zooarchaeology (Bautista 1991).

In 1981 the National Museum started a long-term exploration of the island of Bohol in the central Philippines. Led by Santiago, the expedition located over 130 caves and rock shelters, most of which contained archaeological sites.

Laura Junker, who as a graduate student had taken part in the Bais Anthropological Project, returned to Negros and made further excavations in Tanjay. This was part of a long-term study of international trade and its effects on the social and economic organization of prehistoric Negros (Junker 1993).

Archaeologists, ethnologists, and linguists from the University of Kumamoto in Japan made studies, surveys, and excavations in the Batanes Islands and the Cagayan Valley of northern Luzon in 1981 and 1982. A detailed preliminary report was published (Shirakihara 1983).

An exhibit of Philippine archaeological artifacts and art from collections of the National Museum, other museums in the Philippines and the United States, and private collections was shown in Hawaii, Los Angeles, Oakland, and Chicago in the United States. An impressive catalog was published to go with the exhibit and included a long article on Philippine prehistory (Solheim 1981).

With the beginning of underwater archaeology in Southeast Asia the National Museum has been involved in a number of underwater projects to salvage discovered shipwrecks. From these wrecks they recover data on international trade from the ninth to the eighteenth centuries as well as information on the ships and their equipment. The National Museum does not have the funds or staff to undertake these projects by itself so they are done as joint ventures. Shipwreck sites worked on include: a merchant boat located in 1982 southwest of Marinduque Island; a local boat found in 1983 at Puerto Galera, Mindoro; a sixteenth-century wreck located at the Royal Captain Shoal, a coral reef west of Palawan, in 1985; the *Griffin,* an East India Company boat found in 1985 northwest of Basilan, south of Zamboanga, Mindanao; and the galleon *San Jose,* found in 1986 near Lubang Island, Mindoro Province. In 1991 a two-season underwater project was started on the Spanish warship *San Diego,* which sank near Fortune Island on 14 December 1600. Over 34,000 artifacts were recovered from this ship, including porcelains and stonewares, earthenware vessels, a navigational compass and a maritime astrolabe, and organic materials.

The National Museum is conducting survey and limited excavation, led by Dizon and Santago, of stone remains not unlike the castles found on Okinawa, on the Batanes Islands, the most northerly of the Philippines Islands. These sites are located on hilltops and have been dated to the twelfth century. The most recent article summarizing Philippine prehistory was published in Hawaii in 1992.

Taiwan

The first major interdisciplinary program on Taiwan prehistory was organized by K.-C. Chang and carried out from July 1964 to July 1965 by the Department of Anthropology, Yale University, and the Department of Archaeology and Anthropology, National Taiwan University. The team was made up of five archaeologists, a palynologist, and a geologist. The primary sites excavated were Pa-li (the name shifted later to Tapenkeng), near Taipei, and Fengpitou, in southwestern Taiwan (Chang et al. 1969).

Chang organized an even more interdisciplinary team for a second major project in 1972 through 1974, sponsored by the same two institutions plus Academia Sinica in Taiwan. The team included experts in botany and palynology, archaeology, cultural anthropology, geography, geology, geomorphology, soil sciences, and zoology. Concerning this breadth Chang said: "Its breadth is not only intradisciplinary (for example, the study of the archaeology, the ethnohistory, and the ethnography of the modern inhabitants) but also interdisciplinary. Ours is a 'saturation' approach; we investigate many natural and humanistic scientific aspects of a small region—two river valleys—and seek to examine their interaction through a study of the ecosystems throughout their recent history" (Chang et al. 1974, 40–41). The two river valleys fall midway between the two major sites of the earlier program so the project also aimed to discover the relationships between the different cultures found at those sites. One of the archaeologists from Yale in this program produced two reports that present much of the archaeological results of this project (Dewar 1977, 1978).

Wen-hsun Sung made a small excavation at O-luan-pi, at the very southern tip of Taiwan, in 1966 (Sung et al. 1967) and reported extended burials in stone cist coffins with many associated artifacts but no metal. Later than the cist burials came a culture, which may have had metal associated, with flexed burials not in coffins. Another site at O-luan-pi, called O-luan-pi site II, was excavated in part by Li (1983) in 1982. He found four distinct cultural layers: OLP Prehistoric Cultural Phase I, without pottery, dated at about 5,000 years ago; OLP Prehistoric Cultural Phase II, with the same culture reported by Sung et al. (1967), dated about 4,000 years ago; OLP Phase III, with painted pottery, dated to about 3,000 years ago; and OLP Prehistoric Cultural Phase IV, with plain pottery, dated to about 2,500 years ago (Li 1983, 79–81). This report has 169 full-page color plates.

Li, in 1977, excavated at a site that has been called K'en-ting, about eight kilometers northwest of O-luan-pi, which had been discovered in 1930. The final report was his Ph.D. dissertation at SUNY-Binghamton University and unfortunately has not been published. However, he did publish an article, "Problems Raised by the K'en-ting Excavation of 1977" (1983). In this article he raised questions about Chang's considering the fine red ware phase as an invasion of a Lungshanoid culture from the China mainland. He presented reasonable arguments that the fine red ware evolved out of the earlier Corded Ware culture. This suggestion has come to be generally accepted. One of the important finds at K'en-ting was the impression of rice husks on several fine red ware shards. This gives the earliest date for rice in Taiwan. This date has been reported as ca. 3000 B.C. by Bellwood

(1985, 214) based on the thesis, but in an article Li states: "The beginning of rice cultivation in Taiwan is still in question, but its date has been push [sic] back to some 4,000 years ago by the K'en-ting excavation of 1977" (Li 1983b). A date for rice that is about as early comes from the site of Chih-shan-yen near Taipei. The author of this report (Wang 1983, 81) suggests a date of about 3,500 for the beginning of this site, but does not state in the brief English summary whether the rice was recovered from the very bottom of the site. Besides the rice there was much organic material in the lower layer.

Painan, Taitung, in southeastern Taiwan, is the largest site ever excavated in Taiwan and one of the most important. It was first reported in 1914 because of the several very large megaliths that were on its surface. It was investigated by Kano in 1928 and 1929 and trial excavations were made by Kanaseki and Kokubu in 1945. Excavations were undertaken by Sung from 1980 to 1982, when an area of 7,550 square meters was excavated and 1,025 stone cists recovered. Sung feels that the site was occupied by people of the same culture from about 3000 to 500 B.C. Besides the cist graves there were houses made from large stone slabs. A further report was published by Lien in 1989, but this was in Chinese.

The first human fossil remains in Taiwan were found in the Tsai-liao River, in Tso-chen Hsiang, Taiwan. These were seven skull fragments, some from the same skull, and two teeth, all identified as *Homo sapiens*. Three further skull fragments and two teeth from the same general location were reported by Lien. No artifacts were associated.

An International Conference on Anthropological Studies of the Taiwan Area: Accomplishments and Prospects was held in Taipei in late December 1985. Kwang-chou Li was the Executive Secretary of the Organizing Committee and on the editorial committee. Unfortunately he died during the editing of the proceedings. There were seven papers having to do with different applications of Taiwan archaeology in this book (Chang 1990).

In 1991 a bibliography of prehistoric archaeology was published. It is primarily of value to those who can read Chinese. The listing is divided into several parts, apparently by subject matter. The first part gives authors and articles that were published in English. At the end there is an index of authors, the authors writing in English listed first, in English. The authors writing in Chinese are listed in Chinese, in some cases with their names also in English. In the body of Chinese articles, many titles are listed as well in English, but many are not and the publications in which the articles were published are listed only in Chinese. The same authors, plus a host of others, compiled another very valuable book, this one only in Chinese except for a title page in English. Here are listed all the known prehistoric sites in northern and eastern Taiwan. Each site has one full page with a small map showing its location and for each group of sites in an area a foldout map showing the locations in a considerably larger area. There are 144 full-page color plates showing site locations and artifacts, with captions in Chinese.

Cheng-hwa Tsang did his Ph.D. dissertation research on the P'eng-hu Islands off the southwest coast of Taiwan. These are better known in the west as the Pescadores. His revised thesis (1995) is a final report of his research from 1983 to 1985 on those islands. The islands are closely related to the neighboring Taiwan coast but there are also strong indications of direct contact with the south coast of mainland China. One problem in the prehistory of the mainland of Taiwan is that there are very few sites with Corded Ware culture and these sites have very few artifacts other than some pottery. The Corded Ware site on P'eng-hu was a much richer site that those known from the mainland. For some reason these islands appear to have been uninhabited from about 4,000 years ago until the first historic occupation began in the early ninth century A.D. The ninety full-page color plates are impressive.

The Institute of History and Philology of Academia Sinica hosted an International Symposium on Austronesian Studies Relating to Taiwan in December 1995. A bound offset printing of most of the papers was presented to the participants at the conference and the proceedings are in press. Papers were presented by linguists, ethnographers, physical anthropologists, and archaeologists.

There has long been a debate between Peter Bellwood and Wilhelm Solheim II over the route of the movement of the speakers of Austronesian languages. Bellwood places this movement from south China to Taiwan and then south through the Philippines into eastern Indonesia and east into Melanesia. Solheim places the movement and expansion of his Nusantao Maritime Trading and Communication Network bringing the Malayo-Polynesian languages (the first branch from Austronesia) from south China south along the coast of Vietnam and one route from there extending to the west coast of Borneo, south around Borneo, east through the lesser Sundas, north along the coast of New Guinea and then out into Melanesia. Tsang, in a paper he presented (1995) said, "Based on the current archaeological evidence . . . I do not agree with Bellwood that 'Taiwan is a potentially vital area for the transmission of cultural innovations from the Asian mainland into the islands' . . . if he chooses to 'emphasize the importance of the Corded Ware–Yuan-chan cultural tradition.' Since the homeland of this tradition was most likely on the coast of the mainland between Fukien and Vietnam, as I mentioned previously, I would postulate that the Austronesian languages and cultures were probably transmitted into insular southeast Asian mainland rather than through the island of Taiwan."

Wilhelm G. Solheim II

Acknowledgments
My thanks to Wilfredo Ronquillo, director of the Archaeology Division of the National Museum, for bringing me up to date on recent archaeological activities in the Philippines.

References

Bamard, N. 1972. *Early Chinese Art and its Possible Influence in the Pacific Basin.* New York: Intercultural Arts Press.

Bandi, J. G. 1951. "Die Obsidianindustarie der Umgebung von Bandung in West Java." *Südsee-Studien:* 127–161. Basel: Museum for Völkerkunde.

Bautista, Angel. 1991. "A Zooarchaeological Perspective on the Ambangan Site, a Prehistoric Settlement in Butuan, Agusan del None, Southern Philippines." *Indo-Pacific Prehistory 17, vol. 1, Bulletin of the Indo-Pacific Prehistory Association* 10: 161–170.

Bellwood, Peter. 1976. "Archaeological Research in Minahasa and the Talaud Islands, Northeastern Indonesia." *Asian Perspectives* 19, no. 2: 240–288.

———. 1978. *Man's Conquest of the Pacific: The Prehistory of Southeast Asia and Oceania.* New York: Oxford University Press.

———. 1980. "The Buidane Culture of the Talaud Islands, North-eastern Indonesia." *Bulletin of the Indo-Pacific Prehistory Association* 2: 69–127.

———. 1984. "Archaeological Research in the Madai-Baturong Region, Sabah." *Bulletin of the Indo-Pacific Prehistory Association* 2: 69–127.

———. 1984–1985. "A Hypothesis for Austronesian Origins." *Asian Perspectives* 26: 107–117.

———. 1985. *Prehistory of the Indo-Malaysian Archipelago.* Orlando, FL: Academic Press.

———. 1988. *Archaeological Research in South-Eastern Sabah.* Monographs of the Sabah Museum. Kota Kinabalu.

———. 1989. "Archaeological Investigations at Bukit Tengkorak and Segarong, Southeastern Sabah." *Bulletin of the Indo-Pacific Prehistory Association* 9: 122–162.

———. 1990. "From Late Pleistocene to Early Holocene in Sundaland." In *The World at 18,000 BP,* 2: 255–263. Ed. C. Gamble and O. Softer. London: Unwin Hyman.

———. 1997. *Prehistory of the Indo-Malaysian Archipelago Revised Edition.* Honolulu: University of Hawaii Press.

Bellwood, Peter, and Matussin, Omar. 1980. "Trade Patterns and Political Developments in Brunei and Adjacent Areas, A.D. 700–1500." *Brunei Museum Journal* 4, no. 4: 155–179.

Bellwood, P. R., Gillespie, G. B. Thompson, J. S. Vogel, I. W. Ardika, and Ipoi Datan X. 1992. "New Sites for Prehistoric Asian Rice." *Asian Perspectives* 31, no. 2: 161–170.

Beyer, H. Otley. 1921. "The Philippines before Magellan." *Asia Magazine* 21: 861–866, 890, 892.

———. 1926. "Recent Discoveries in Philippine Archaeology." *Proceedings of the Third Pan-Pacific Science Congress* 2: 2469–2491. Tokyo.

———. 1947. "Outline Review of Philippine Archaeology by Islands and Provinces." *Philippine Journal of Science* 77, no. 3–4: 205–347.

———. 1948. "Philippine and East Asian Archaeology and Its Relation to the Origin of the

Pacific Islands Population." *National Research Council of the Philippine Bulletin no. 29*: 1–78.

———. 1951. "A Tribute to Van Stein Callenfels." *Journal of East Asiatic Studies* 1, no. 1: 77–81.

———. 1952. "Notes on the Archaeological Work of H. R. van Heekeren in Celebes and Elsewhere (1917–1950)." *Journal of East Asiatic Studies* 1, no. 3: 15–31.

———. 1956. *Proceedings of the Eighth Pacific Science Congress and the Fourth Far-Eastern Prehistory Congress: Proceedings of the Fourth Far-Eastern Prehistory and the Anthropology division of the Eighth Pacific Science Congresses combined. Part 1: Prehistory, Archaeology and Physical Anthropology.* Diliman, Quezon City: National Research Council of the Philippines.

Beyer, H. Otley, and Jaime C. de Veyra. 1947. *Philippine Saga—A Pictorial History of the Archipelago Since Time Began.* Manila: Evening News.

Brooks, Richard H., and Sheilagh T. Brooks. 1968. "Arm Position as Correlated with Sex Determination in the Niah Cave Extended Burial Series, Sarawak, Malaysia." *Sarawak Museum Journal* 16, no. 32–33 (n.s.): 67–74.

Brooks, Sheilagh T., Rodger Heglar, and Richard H. Brook. 1977. "Radiocarbon Dating and Palaeoserology of a Selected Burial Series from the Great Cave at Niah, Sarawak, Malaysia." *Asian Perspectives* 20, no. 1: 21–31.

Brothwell, D. R. 1960. "Upper Pleistocene Human Skull from Niah Caves, Sarawak." *Sarawak Museum Journal* 9, no. 15–16 (n.s.): 323–349.

Callenfels, P. V. van Stein. 1951. "Prehistoric Sites on the Karama River." *Journal of East Asiatic Studies* 1: 82–93.

Chang, Kwang-chi. 1956. "A Brief Survey of the Archaeology of Formosa." *Southwestern Journal of Anthropology* 12: 3711–386.

———. 1990. "Taiwan Archaeology in Pacific Perspective." In *Anthropological Studies of the Taiwan Area: Accomplishments and Prospects,* 87–98. Ed. K. C. Chang et al. Taipei: Department of Anthropology, National Taiwan University.

Chang, Kwang-chi, et al. 1969. *Fengpitou, Tapenkeng, and the Prehistory of Taiwan.* Yale University Publications in Anthropology no. 73. New Haven: Yale University Press.

———. 1974. "Man in Choshui and Tatu River Valleys in Central Taiwan: Preliminary Report of an Interdisciplinary Project, 1972–73 Season." *Asian Perspectives* 17, no. 1: 36–55.

Chang, Kwang-chih, ed. 1963. Special Taiwan Section of *Asian Perspectives* 7, no. 2: 195–275.

Cherry, Roger. 1978. "An Analysis of the Lithic Industry of Buad Island, Samar." *Philippine Quarterly of Culture and Society* 6: 3–80.

Chin, Lucas. 1977. "Trade Pottery Discovered in Sarawak from 1948–1976." *Sarawak Museum Journal* 20, no. 46: 1–7.

———. 1980. *Cultural Heritage of Sarawak.* Kuching: Sarawak Museum.

———. 1981. "Some Results on SPAFA Regional Seminar-cum-workshop on Ceramics of East and Southeast Asia and a Tentative Review on the Dating of Trade Ceramics Discovered in Sarawak." *Sarawak Museum Journal* 29, no. 50: 1–2.

Chin, Lucas, and R. Nyandoh. 1975. "Archaeological Work in Sarawak." *Sarawak Museum Journal* 23, no. 44: 1–7.

Chiong, Lionel T. 1975. "An Ethno-archaeology Study of the Pottery Manufactured in Daro, Dumaguete City, Negros Oriental, Philippines." M. A. thesis, Silliman University, Dumaguete City.

Christie, J. W. 1990. "Trade and the Santubopng Iron Industry." In *Southeast Asian Archaeology,* 231–240. Ed. I. Glover. BAR International Series.

Cooper, Z., and H. Raghavan. 1989. "Petrographic Features of Andamese Pottery." *Bulletin of the Indo-Pacific Prehistory Association* 9: 22–32.

Coutts, P. J. F. 1983. *An Archaeological Perspective of Panay Island, Philippines.* Cebu City, Philippines: University of San Carlos.

Coutts, P. J. F., and J. P. Wesson. 1978. "Field Reconnaissance of Eastern Panay Island, Philippines." *Philippine Quarterly of Culture & Society* 6, no. 1–2: 82–105.

Coutts, P. J. F., J. P. Wesson, S. Galuago, and D. Dinopol. 1981. "A Summary Report of the Fifth Australian Archaeological Expedition to the Philippines." *Philippine Quarterly of Culture and Society* 9: 77–110.

Datan, Ipoh, and Peter Bellwood. 1991. "Recent Research at Guan Sirih (Serian) and Lubang Angin (Gunung Mulu National Park)." *Indo-Pacific Prehistory 1990. Bulletin of the Indo-Pacific Prehistory Association* 10: 386–405.

———. 1993. "Recent Research at Guan Sirih (Serian) and Lubang Angin (Gunung Mulu National Park). Sarawak." *Sarawak Museum Journal* 64, no. 65 (n.s.): 93–111.

Dewar, Robert E., Jr. 1977. "Niu-ma-t'on, Ting-chieh, and Chiu-she: A Report of the Archaeology of Three Sites in the Tam River Valley." In

T'ai-wan Sheng Cho-shui hsi yu Ta-tü his Liu-yü K'ao-lcu Tiao-ch'a Po-kao, 65–161. Ed. K. C. Chang. Monograph Series of the Institute of History and Philology, Academia Sinica, no. 79.

———. 1978. "Ecological Context and the Prehistory of the West Central Taiwan Coast." *Asian Perspectives* 21, no. 2: 207–241.

Dutta, Pratap Chandra. 1962. "*A Trial Excavation of a Kitchen-midden at South Andaman.*" Vienna: Wiener Volkerkundliche Mitteilungen. X Jahre (N.F.), 5: 17–29.

Evangelista, Alfredo E. 1969. "The Philippines: Archaeology in the Philippines to 1950." *Asian Perspectives* 12: 97–104.

Evans, Ivor H. N. 1913. "On a Collection of Stone Implements from the Tempassuk District, British North Borneo." *Man* 13: 154–158.

———. 1922. *Among Primitive Peoples in Borneo.* London: Seeley, Service.

Fox, Robert B. 1970. *The Tabon Caves.* Monograph of the National Museum no. 1. Manila. National Museum.

Fox, Robert B., and Alfredo Evangelista. 1957a. "The Bato Caves, Sorsogon Province, Philippines." *Journal of East Asiatic Studies* 6: 49–55.

———. 1957b. "The Cave Archaeology of of Cagraray Island, Albay Province, Philippines." *Journal of East Asiatic Studies* 6: 57–68.

Fox, R., and A. Legaspi. 1977. *Excavations at Santa Ana.* Manila: National Museum.

Glover, Ian. 1976. "Ulu Leang Cave, Maros: A Preliminary Sequence of Post-Pleistocene Cultural Development in South Sulawesi." *Archipel* 113–154.

———. 1979. "The Late Prehistoric Period in Indonesia" In *Early South East Asia,* 167–184. Ed. R. B. Smith and W. Watson. London: Oxford University Press.

———. 1983. *Archaeology in Eastern Timor, 1966–67.* Terra Australis II. Canberra: Department of Prehistory, Research School of Pacific Studies.

———. 1986. *Archaeology in Eastern Timor.* Terra Australis 11. Canberra: Department of Prehistory, Research School of Pacific Studies.

Griffin, P. Bion, and Agnes Estioko-Griffin. 1978. "Ethnoarchaeology of Agta Hunter-Gatherers." *Archaeology* 31, no. 6: 34–43.

Guthe, C. 1927. "The University of Michigan Philippine Expedition." *American Anthropologist* 29, no. 1: 69–76.

———. 1928. "Distribution of Sites Visited by the University of Michigan Philippine Expedition 1922–1925." *Papers of the Michigan Academy of Science, Arts and Letters* 10: 79–89.

———. 1934. "Gold Decorated Teeth from the Philippine Islands." *Papers of the Michigan Academy of Science, Arts and Letters* 20: 7–2.

———. 1937. "A Burial Site on the Island of Samar, Philippine Islands." *Papers of the Michigan Academy of Science, Arts and Letters* 23: 29–35.

Harrisson, Barbara. 1958. "Niah's Lobang Tulang, Cave of Bones." *Sarawak Museum Journal* 8, no. 12 (n.s.): 596–619.

———. 1964. "Malaysian Borneo (Regional Report)." *Asian Perspectives* 8, no. 1: 92–97.

———. 1965. "Upiusing, a Late Burial Cave at Niah." *Sarawak Museum Journal* 12, no. 25–26; 83–116.

———. 1966. "Marker Devices in East Sabah Burial Caves." *Sarawak Museum Journal* 13, no. 27 (n.s.): 323–334.

———. 1967. "A Classification of Stone Age Burials from Niah Great Cave, Sarawak." *Sarawak Museum Journal* 15, no. 30–31 (n.s.): 126–200.

———. 1976. "Tom Harrisson. Living and Working in Borneo." *Borneo Research Bulletin* 8, no. 1: 25–30.

———. 1977a. "Tom Harrisson's Unpublished Legacy on Niah." *Journal of the Malaysian Branch Royal Asiatic Society* 50, no. 1: 41–51.

———. 1977b. "Tom Harrisson and the Uplands: A Summary of His Unpublished Ethnographic Papers." *Asian Perspectives* 20, no. 1: 1–7.

Harrisson, Barbara, and Tom Harrisson. 1968. "Magala—A Series of Neolithic and Metal Age Burial Grottos at Sekaloh, Niah, Sarawak." *Journal of the Malaysian Branch Royal Asiatic Society* 41, no. 2: 48–75.

Harrisson, Barbara, and P. M. Shariffuddin. 1969. "Sungei Lumut: A 15th Century Burial Ground." *Brunei Museum Journal* 1, no. 1: 24–56.

Harrisson, Barbara, and G. T. Bambin bin Ungap. 1964. "Tapadong—700 Years of Cave History in Sabah." *Sarawak Museum Journal* 11, no. 23–24 (n.s.): 655–665.

Harrisson, Tom. 1954. "Borneo Archaeology to 1954." *Sarawak Museum Journal* 6, no. 4 (n.s.): 188–192.

———. 1957. "The Great Cave of Niah: A Preliminary Report." *Man* 59: 161–166.

———. 1958. "The Caves of Niah: A History of Prehistory." *Sarawak Museum Journal* 8, no. 2 (n.s.): 549–595.

———. 1959. "New Archaeological and Ethnological Results from Niah Cave, Sarawak." *Man* 59: 1–8.

———. 1961a. "Niah Excavations, 1957–1961." *Asian Perspectives.*

———. 1961b. "The Borneo Finds." *Asian Perspectives* 5, no. 2: 253–255.

———. 1963. "100,000 Years of Stone Age Culture in Borneo." *Journal of the Royal Society of Arts* 112: 74–91.

———. 1964. "A Stone and Bronze Tool Cave in Sabah." *Asian Perspectives* 8, no. 1: 171–180.

———. 1966a. "'Turtle-Ware' from Borneo Caves." *Asian Perspectives* 9: 134–139.

———. 1966b. "Recent Archaeological Discoveriesn Malaysia, 1965; East Malaysia (and Brunei)." *Journal of the Malaysian Branch Royal Asiatic Society* 39, no. 1: 191–197.

———. 1967a. "East Malaysia and Bmnei (Regional Report)." *Asian Perspectives* 10: 85–92.

———. 1967b. "Recent Archaeological Discoveries in East Malaysia and Brunei." *Journal of the Malaysian Branch Royal Asiatic Society* 40, no. 1: 140–148.

———. 1968a. "New Analysis of Excavated Prehistoric Glass from Borneo." *Asian Perspectives* 1: 125–133.

———. 1968b. "A Rare Ceramic Bangle from Borneo." *Asian Perspectives* 11: 135–136.

———. 1968c. "Borneo's Prehistoric "Turtle Ware" and "Phallic-Top" Lidded Pots." *Asian Perspectives* 11: 119–123.

———. 1970. "The Prehistory of Borneo." *Asian Perspectives* 13: 17–46.

———. 1971a. "Niah Cave Double-Spouted Vessels." *Sarawak Museum Journal* 19, no. 38–39 (n.s.): 367–373.

———. 1971b. "Prehistoric Double Spouted-Vessels Excavated at Niah Caves, Borneo." *Journal of the Malaysian Branch Royal Asiatic Society* 44, no. 2: 35–78.

———. 1971c. "The Missing Brunei Stone Age." *Brunei Museum Journal* 2, no. 3: 81–88.

———. 1971d. "Deep Level Carbon Dates from Kota Batu, Brunei (95 B.C. to 1300 A.D.)." *Brunei Museum Journal* 2, no. 3: 96–107.

———. 1972. "The Borneo Stone Age—in the Light of Recent Research." *Sarawak Museum Journal* 20, no. 40–41 (n.s.): 385–412.

———. 1973a. "Ancient Glass Beads from Brunei and Sarawak Excavations (compared)." *Brunei Museum Journal* 3, no. 1: 118–126.

———. 1973b. "Carbon–14 Dates from Kota Batu, Brunei (Borneo)." *Asian Perspectives* 16, no. 2: 197–199.

———. 1974a. *Prehistoric Wood from Brunei, Borneo, Especially as Excavated at Kota Batu.* Monograph of the *Brunei Museum Journal* 2: 1–174.

———. 1974b. "The Megalithic in East Malaysia—II: Stone Urns from the Kelabit Highlands, Sarawak." *Journal of the Malaysian Branch Royal Asiatic Society* 47, no. 1: 105–109.

———. 1974c. "Double-Spouted Vessels, II: In West Malaysia and Singapore (From Prehistory to the Present Day)." *Journal of the Malaysian Branch Royal Asiatic Society* 47, no. 2: 139–147.

———. 1975. "Early Dates for 'Seated' Burial Matting at Niah Caves, Sarawak (Borneo)." *Asian Perspectives* 18, no. 2: 161–165.

Harrisson, Tom, and Barbara Harrisson. 1956. "Kota Batu in Brunei." *Sarawak Museum Journal* 7, no. 8 (n.s.): 283–319.

———. 1957. "The Pre-Historic Cemetery of Tanjong Kubor." *Sarawak Museum Journal* 8, no. 10 (n.s.): 18–50.

———. 1971. "The Prehistory of Sabah." *Sabah Society Journal* 4.

Harrisson, Tom, and Lord Medway. 1962. "A First Classification of Prehistoric Bone and Tooth Artifacts." *Sarawak Museum Journal* 10, no. 19–20 (n.s.): 335–362; a shortened version in *Asian Perspectives* 6: 219–229.

Harrisson, Tom, and Stanley J. O'Connor. 1967. "The 'Tantric Shrine' Excavated at Santubong." *Sarawak Museum Journal* 15, no. 30–31 (n.s.): 201–222.

———. 1969. *Excavations of the Prehistoric Iron Industry in West Borneo,* 2 vols. Southeast Asia Data Paper no. 72. Ithaca, NY: Cornell University.

———. 1970. *Gold and Megalithic Activity in Prehistoric and Recent West Borneo.* Southeast Asia Data Paper no. 77. Ithaca, NY: Cornell University.

Harrisson, Tom, and M. W. F. Tweedie. 1951. "Excavation of Gua Bungho in Southwest Sarawak." *Journal of the Polynesian Society* 60: 164–186.

Heekeren, H. R. van. 1945. "The Urn Cemetery at Melolo, East Sumba (Indonesia)." *Bulletin of the Archaeological Service* (Republic of Indonesia) 3: 1–24.

———. 1949a. "Preliminary Note on Palaeolithic Finds on the Island of Celebes." *Chronica Naturae* 105, no. 5: 145–146.

———. 1949b. "Rapport over de ontgraving van de Bola Bat nabij Badjo (Bone, Zuid Celebes)," *Oudheidkundig Verslag van de Oudheidkundige Dienst in Nederlandsch-Indie* 1941–1947: 89–108.

———. 1950. "Rapport over de ontgraving te Kamasi, Kalumpang, West Centraal Celebes." *Oudheidkundig Verslag van de Oudheidkundige Dienst in Nederlandsch-Indie* 1949: 26–48.

———. 1951. "The Urn Cemetery at Melolo, East Sumba (Indonesia)." *Berita Dinas Purbakala* 3: 1–24.

———. 1955a. "New Investigations on the Lower Palaeolithic Patjitan Culture in Java." *Berita Dinas Purbakala* 1: 1–12.

———. 1955b. "Proto-historic Sarcophagi on Bali." *Berita Dinas Purbakala* 2: 1–15.

———. 1956a. "The Urn Cemetery at Melolo, East Sumba." *Bulletin of the Archaeological Service of the. Republic of Indonesia* 3: 1–24.

———. 1956b. "Notes on a Proto-Historic Urn-Burial Site at Anjar, Java." *Anthropos* 51: 1194–1201.

———. 1957. *The Stone Age of Indonesia.* Verhandelingen van het Koninklijk Instituut voor Taal, Land- en Volkenkunde 21. The Hague: Martinus Mijhoff.

———. 1958a. *The Bronze-Iron Age of Indonesia.* Verhandellingen van het Koninklijk Instituut voor Taal-, Land- en Volkenkunde 22. The Hague: Martinus Nijhoff.

———. 1958b. "Prehistoric Research in Indonesia." *Annual Bibliography of Indian Archaeology* (1948–1953): lxxv–lxxxvii.

———. 1972. *The Stone Age of Indonesia.* 2d ed. The Hague: Martinus Nijhoff.

———. 1975. "Chronology of the Indonesian Prehistory." *Modern Quaternary Research in Southeast Asia* 1: 47–51.

Heine-Geldern, Robert. 1936. "Prehistoric Research in Indonesia." *Annual Bibliography of Indian Archaeology* 9: 26–38.

———. 1945. "Prehistoric Research in the Netherlands Indies." In *Science and Scientists in the Netherlands Indies,* 129–167. Ed. Pieter Honig and Frans Verdoom. New York: Board for the Netherlands Indies, Surinam and Curacao.

Hooijer, D. A. 1949. "The Pleistocene Vertebrates of Southern Celebes." *Chronica Naturae* 105, no. 5: 148–150.

Hoop, A. N. J. th. a Th. van der. 1940. "A Prehistoric Site Near Lake Kerinchi, Sumatra." In *Proceedings of the Third Congress of Prehistorians of the Far East,* 200–204. Ed. F. N. Chasen and M. W. F. Tweedie. Singapore: Government Printing Office.

Hutterer, Karl L. P. 1969. "Preliminary Report on Archaeological Fieldwork in Southwestern Samar." *Leyte-Samar Studies* 3: 37–56.

Hutterer, Karl L., and William K. Macdonald. 1979. "The Bais Anthropological Survey: A First Preliminary Report." *Philippine Quarterly of Culture & Society* 7, no. 3: 115–140.

Hutterer, Karl L., and William K. Macdonald, eds. 1982. *Houses Built on Scattered Poles: Prehistory and Ecology in Negros Oriental.* Cebu City: University of San Carlos Press.

Ino, Yoshinori. 1907a. "Legendary Stone Tools Among the Aborigines in Taiwan." *Zenruigaku Zashi* 22: 240–245 (in Japanese).

———. 1907b. "Stone Tools Found in Peng-Hu Island." *Zenruigaku Zashi* 23: 13–16 (in Japanese).

Janse, Olov R. T. 1941. "An Archaeological Expedition to Indo-China and the Philippines (Preliminary report)." *Harvard Journal of Asiatic Studies* 6, no. 2: 247–267.

———. 1944. "Notes on Chinese Influences in the Philippines in Pre-Spanish Times." *Harvard Journal of Asian Studies* 8: 34–62.

———. 1946. "Archaeology of the Philippine Islands." *Annual Report of the Board of Regents of the Smithsonian Institute,* 345–360. Washington, DC: Smithsonian Institution.

Junker, Laura Lee. 1993. "Archaeological Excavations at the 12–16 Century Settlement of Tanj Ay, Negros Oriental: the Burial Evidence for Social Stares-Symbolism, Head-Taking and Inter-Polity Raiding." *Philippine Quarterly of Culture and Society* 21, no. 1: 39–82.

Kanaseki, Takeo, and Naoichi Kokubu. 1950. "Outline of Prehistorical Researches in Taiwan." *Taiwan Wenhua* 6, no. 1: 9–15 (in Chinese).

Kurjack, E., C. T. Sheldon, and M. E. Keller B. 1971. "The Urn Burial Caves of Southern Cotabato, Mindanao, Philippines." *Silliman Journal* 18, no. 2: 127–153.

Li, Kyang-chou. 1983. "Problems Raised by the K'eng-Ting Excavation of 1977." *Bulletin of the Department of Anthropology* no. 43: 876–116.

Li, K-C., K-C. Chang, Y-K. Huang, C-W. Tsang, and C-Y. Tseng eds. 1995. *Austronesian Studies Relating to Taiwan.* Taipei: Academia Sinica, Institute of History and Philology, Symposium Series 3.

Lien, Chao-mei. 1990. "The Interrelationship of Taiwan's Prehistoric Archaeology and Ethnology." In *Anthropological Studies of the Taiwan Area: Accomplishments and Prospects,* 173–192. Ed. K. C. Chang et al. Taipei: Department of Anthropology, National Taiwan University.

Locsin, Leandro, and Cecilia Locsin P. 1967. *Oriental Ceramics Discovered in the Philippines.* Tokyo: Charles E. Turtle.

Loh, Chee Yin. 1980. "An Index to All Issues Published from 1911 to 1979." *Sarawak Museum Journal* 28, no. 49 (n.s.): 1–198.

Longacre, William A. 1981. "Kalinga Pottery: An Ethnoarchaeological Study." In *Pattern of the Past,* 49–66. Ed. Ian Hodder et al. Cambridge: Cambridge University Press.

Maher, R. F. 1973. "Archaeological Investigations in Central Ifugao." *Asian Perspectives* 16, no. 1: 39–70.

———. 1981. "Archaeological Investigations in the Burnay District of Southeastern Ifugao, Philippines." *Asian Perspectives* 24, no. 2: 223–236.

Main, Dorothy, and Robert B. Fox. 1982. *The Calatagan Earthenwares.* Monograph of the National Museum, 5. Manila.

Majiid, Zuraina. 1982. "West Mouth, Niah in the Prehistory of Southeast Asia." *Sarawak Museum Journal* (Special Monograph 3) 32, no. 52: 1–200.

Manguin, Pierre-Yves. 1992. *Excavations in South Sumatra, 1988–1990: New Evidence for Sriwijayan sites,* 62–73. Ed. Ian Glover. Hull, UK: Centre for South-East Asian Studies, University of Hull.

Marche, Alfred. 1887. *Lucon et Palaouan: Six Anées de Voyages aux Philippines.* Paris: librairie Hachette.

———. 1970. *Luzon and Palawan.* Translated by Carmen Ojeda and Jovita Castro. *Publications by the Filipinana Book Guild XVII.* Manila: the Filipiniana Book Guild.

Mascuñana, Rolando V. 1986. "The Bacong Artifacts in the Silliman Anthropology Museum Collection: A Morphological Analysis of Displayed Material Culture." In *Artifacts from the Visayan Communities: A Study of Extinct and Extant Culture,* 1–200. Dumaguete City, Philippines: Silliman University.

Miksic, John. 1977. "Archaeology and Paleogeography in the Straits of Malacca." In *Economic Exchange and Social Interaction in Southeast Asia,* 155–175. Ed. Karl L. Hutterer. Michigan Papers in South and Southeast Asia no. 13. Ann Arbor: Center for South and Southeast Asian Studies.

Mulvaney, D. J., and R. P. Soejono, 1970a. "Archaeology in Sulawesi, Indonesia." *Antiquity* 45: 26–33.

———. 1970b. "The Australian-Indonesian Archaeological Expedition to Sulawesi." *Asian Perspectives* 13: 163–177.

O'Connor, S. J. 1977. "Tom Harrisson and the Ancient Iron Industry of the Sarawak River Delta." *Journal of the Malaysian Branch Royal Asiatic Society* 50, no. 1: 4–7.

Omar, Matussin. 1975. "A Preliminary Account of Surface Finds from Fanjang Baty Beach, Muara." *Brunei Museum Journal* 3, no. 3: 158–174.

———. 1981. *Archaeological Excavations in Protohistoric Brunei.* Brunei Museum Special Issue no. 15.

Omar, Matussin, and P. M. Shariffuddin. 1976. "The Stone Age in Brunei." *Brunei Museum Journal* 3, no. 4: 127–141.

Peralta, Jesus T. 1979. "Robert Bradford Fox: Anthropologist." *Archipelago* 6: 8–12.

———. 1980. "Ancient Mariners of the Philippines." *Archaeology* Sept.-Oct.: 44–48.

Peterson, Warren. 1973. "Summary Report of Two Archaeological Sites from Northeastern Luzon." *Archaeology and Physical Anthropology in Oceania* 9, no. 1: 26–35.

Peterson, Warren, and the University of the Philippines Field School. 1979. "Archaeological Research in the Novaliches Watershed, Philippines." *Asian Perspectives* 22, no. 2: 120–139.

Ronquillo, W. 1981. "The Technological and Functional Analyses of the Lithic Flake Tools from Rabel Cave, Northern Luzon, Philippines." *Anthropological Paper no. 13.* Manila: National Museum.

———. 1985. "Archaeological Research in the Philippines: 1951–1983. *Bulletin of the Indo-Pacific Prehistory Association* 6: 74–88.

———. 1987. "The Butuan Archaeological Finds: Profound Implications for Philippine and Southeast Asian Prehistory." *Man and Culture in Oceania* 3 (Special Issue): 71–78.

Ronquillo, Wilfredo P., Rey S. Santiago, Shijun Asato, and Kazuhiko Tanaka. 1993. "The 1992 Archaeological Reexcavation of the Balobok Rockshelter, Sanga Sanga, Tawi Tawi Province, Philippines: A Preliminary Report." *Journal of Historiographical Institute,* Okinawa Prefectural Library, 18.

Rothpletz, W. 1951. "Alte Siedlungsplätze bei Bangung (Java) und die Entdeckung bronzezeitlicher Gussformen." *Südsee-Studien:* 77–126. Basel: Museum für Völkerkunde.

Rumphius, G. E. 1705. *'D'Amboinsche Rariteitkamer.* Amsterdam.

Scleans, Daniel J. 1966. "A New View of Philippines Pottery Manufacture." *Southwestern Journal of Anthropology* 22, no. 2: 206–219.

———. 1977. *Filipino Market Potteries.* Monographs of the National Museum, 3. Manila.

Scheans, D. J., K. L. Hutterer, and R. L. Cherry. 1970. "A Newly Discovered Blade Tool Industry from the Central Philippines." *Asian Perspectives* 13: 179–181.

Scott, William Henry. 1968. *Prehispanic Source Materials for the Study of Philippine History.* Manila: University of Santo Tomas Press.

———. 1977. "Maragtas and Kalantiaw: Controversial Prehispanic Law Codes." *Filipino Heritage* 3: 777–778.

———. 1981. "Boat-building and Seamanship in Classic Philippine Society." Anthropology Papers of the National Museum no. 9. Manila.

Shirakihara, Kasumi, ed. 1983. *Batan Island and Northern Luzon Archaeological, Ethnographical and Linguistic Survey.* Kumamoto, Japan: Faculty of Letters, University of Kumamoto.

Smith, Alfred. 1959. "Review of the *Bronze-Iron Age of Indonesia,* by H. R. van Heekeren." *American Anthropologist* 61, no. 2: 335–336.

Smith, R. B., and William Watson, eds. 1979. *Early South East Asia.* London: Oxford University Press.

Snow, G. E., and R. Shutler Onr. 1985. *The Archaeology of Fuga Moro Island, Cebu City, Philippines.* Cebu City: Carlos Publications, University of San Carlos.

Soejono, R. P. 1962. "Indonesia (Regional Report)." *Asian Perspectives* 6: 34–43.

———. 1969. "The History of Prehistoric Research in Indonesia to 1950." *Asian Perspectives* 12: 69–91.

———. 1970. "The Study of Prehistory in Indonesia: Retrospect and Prospect." *Asian Perspectives* 13: 11–15.

Soekmono, R. 1969. "Archaeological Research in Indonesia. A Historical Survey." *Asian Perspectives* 12: 93–96.

Solheim, Wilhelm G. II. 1951. "Preliminary Report on Archaeological Fieldwork in San Narciso, Tayabas, P.I." *Journal of East Asiatic Studies* 1, no. 1: 70–76.

———. 1952a. "Archaeology in the Philippines." *Journal of East Asiatic Studies* 1, no. 3: 63–64.

———. 1952b. "Paddle Decoration of Pottery." *Journal of East Asiatic Studies* 2, no. 1: 35–46.

———. 1953. "Philippine Archaeology." *Archaeology* 5, no. 3: 154–158.

———. 1954. "The Makabog Burial-jar Site." *Philippine Journal of Science* 83: 57–68.

———. 1957a. "Borneo. (Regional Report)." *Asian Perspectives* 1: 93–100.

———. 1957b. "Philippine Islands (Regional Report)." *Asian Perspectives.* 1: 101–107

———. 1957c. "The Kulanay Pottery Complex in the Philippines." *Artibus Asiae* 20, no. 4: 279–288.

———. 1958a. "Borneo. (Regional Report)." *Asian Perspectives* 2, no. 1: 59–61.

———. 1958b. "Philippines. (Regional Report)." *Asian Perspectives* 2, no. 1: 62–68.

———. 1958c. "The Present Status of the 'Palaeolithic' in Borneo." *Asian Perspectives* 2, no. 2: 83–90.

———. 1959. "Philippines (Regional Report)." *Asian Perspectives* 3, no. 1: 47–50.

———. 1959a. "Sa-huynh Related Pottery in Southeast Asia (ed.)." *Asian Perspectives,* 3, no. 2: 177–188.

———. 1959b. "Two Major Problems in Bornean (and Asian) Ethnology and Archaeology." *Sarawak Museum Journal* 9, no. 13–14 (n.s.): 1–5.

———. 1959c. "Further Notes on the Kalanay Pottery Complex in the P.I." *Asian Perspectives* 3, no. 2: 157–166.

———. 1960. "Jar Burial in the Babuyan and Batanes Islands and in Central Philippines, and Its Relationship to Jar Burial Elsewhere in the Far East." *Philippine Journal of Science* 89, no. 1: 115–148.

———. 1961. *Indonesia (2): COWA Surveys and Bibliographies. Area 20.* Cambridge, MA: Council for Old World Archaeology.

———. 1963. "Philippine Notes." *Asian Perspectives* 7, no. 1: 138–142.

———. 1964a. *The Archaeology of Central Philippines: A Study Chiefly of the Iron Age and Its Relationships.* Monographs of the National Institute of Science and Technology, 10. Manila: Bureau of Printing.

———. 1964b. "Pottery and the Malayo-Polynesians." *Current Anthropology* 5, no. 5: 360, 376–384, 400–403.

———. 1964c. "Further Relationships of the Sa-Huynh-Kalanay Pottery Tradition." *Asian Perspectives* 8, no. 1: 196–210.

———. 1965a. "The Prehistoric Earthenware Pottery of Tanjong Kubor, Santubong." *Sarawak Museum Journal* 12, no. 25–26 (n.s.): 1–62.

———. 1965b. "The Function of Pottery in Southeast Asia—from the Present to the Past." In *Ceramics and Man,* 254–273. Ed. Frederick R. Matson. Viking Fund Publication in Anthropology 41. Chicago: Aldine Press.

———. 1967a. "International Congresses and Symposia." *Asian Perspectives* 10: 1–8.

———. 1967b. "Southeast Asia and the West." *Science* 157: 896–902.

———. 1967c. "Two Pottery Traditions of Late Prehistoric Times in Southeast Asia." In *Historical Archaeological and Linguistic Studies in Southern China, S-E Asia and the Hong Kong Region,* 15–22. Ed. F. S. Drake. Hong Kong: Hong Kong University Press.

———. 1967d. "The Sa-huynh-Kalanay Pottery Tradition: Past and Future Research." In *Studies in Philippine Anthropology,* 151–174. Ed. Mario D. Zamora. Quezon City: Alemar Phoenix.

———. 1968. "The Batungan Cave Sites, Masbate, Philippines." In *Anthropology at the Eighth Pacific Science Congress,* 20–62. Ed. Wilhelm G. Solheim II. Asian and Pacific Archaeology Series no. 2. Honolulu: Social Science Research Institute, University of Hawaii.

———. 1969a. *Indonesia. Area 20. IV. 1969. COWA Surveys and Bibliographies.* Cambridge, MA: Council for Old World Archaeology.

———. 1969b. "H. Otley Beyer." *Asian Perspectives* 12: 1–18.

———. 1970. "Prehistoric Archaeology in Eastern Mainland Southeast Asia and the Philippines." *Asian Perspectives* 13: 47–58.

———. 1971. *Southeast Asia. Area 19, IV. 1970. COWA Surveys and Bibliographies* (with Jean Kennedy). Cambridge, MA: Council for Old World Archaeology.

———. 1974. "Potsherds and Potholes: Philippine Archaeology in 1973." Paper presented in Philippine panel, annual meeting Association for Asian Studies, Chicago, 30 March 1973, in *Philippine Studies: Geography, Archaeology, Psychology and Literature,* 15–43. Ed. Frederick L. Wernstedt, Wilhelm G. Solheim II, Lee Sechrest and George H. Guthrie, Leonard Casper. Northern Illinois University Center for SEA Studies, Special Report no. 10. DeKalb.

———. 1975a. "Review Article: *the Stone Age of Indonesia* by H. R. van Heekeren." *Asian Perspectives* 18, no. 2: 114–127.

———. 1975b. "Reflections on the New Data of Southeast Asian Prehistory: Austronesian Origin and Consequence." *Asian Perspectives* 18, no. 2: 146–160.

———. 1975c. "Jungere Steinzeit Sud-und Ostasiens." In *Handbuch der Urgeschichte, II: Jungere Steinzeit undSteinkupferzeit,* 425–450. Ed. Karl Narr. Bern and Munich: Francke Vefiag.

———. 1976. "Coastal Irian Jaya and the Origin of the Nusantao (Austronesian Speaking People)." In proceedings of *Colloquium 18 Le Premier Peuplement do l'Archipel Nippon et des Iles du Pacifique: Chronologie, Paleogeographie, Industries,* 32–42. Ed. Chosuke Serizawa. Paper presented at IXth International Congress of Prehistoric and Protohistoric Sciences, Nice, France.

———. 1977a. "Tom Harrisson and Borneo Archaeology." *Borneo Research Bulletin* 9, no. 1: 3–7.

———. 1977b. "The Niah Research Program." *Journal of the Malaysian Branch Royal Asiatic Society* 59, no. 1: 28–40.

———. 1981. "Philippine prehistory." In *The People and Arts of the Philippines,* 16–83. Ed. Father Gabriel Casal & Regalado Trota Jose, Jr., Eric S. Casino, George R. Ellis, and Wilhelm G. Solheim II. Los Angeles: Museum of Culture History, University of California–Los Angeles.

———. 1983. "Archaeological Research in Sarawak, Past and Future." *Sarawak Museum Journal* 32, no. 53 (n.s.): 35–58.

Solheim, Wilhelm G. II, and Nan Gaynor. 1978. "The Marche Cache." In *Filipino Heritage. The Making of a Nation,* 7: 1,752–1,754. Ed. Alfredo R. Rotes. Sydney: Hamlyn House.

Solheim, Wilhelm G. II, Barbara Harrisson, and Lindsey Wall. 1959. "Niah 'Three Colour Ware' and Related Prehistoric Pottery from Borneo." *Asian Perspectives* 3, no. 2: 167–176.

———. 1961. "Niah 'Three Colour Ware' And Related Prehistoric Pottery from Borneo." *Sarawak Museum Journal* 10, no. 17–18 (n.s.): 227–237.

Solheim, Wilhelm G. II, and Barbara Jensen. 1977. "Tom Harrisson—Bibliography of Publications Concerning Southeast Asian Prehistory." *Asian Perspectives* 20, no. 1: 13 –20.

Solheim, Wilhelm G. II, Avelino Legaspi, and Jaime S. Neff, S. J. 1979. *Archaeological Survey in Southeastern Mindanao.* Monograph of the National Museum, 8. Manila.

Solhelm, Wilhelm G. II, Floyd Wheeler, and Jane Allen-Wheeler. 1985. "Archaeology in Malaysia, Bmnei and Singapore." In *Malaysian Studies: Archaeology, Historiography, Geography, and Bibliography,* 1–83. Ed. John A. Lent and Kent Mulliner. DeKalb: Center for Southeast Asian Studies, Northern Illinois University.

Spencer, J. E., and G. A. Hall. 1961. "The Origin, Nature and Distribution of Agricultural Terracing." *Pacific Viewpoint* 2: 1–40.

Spoehr, Alexander. 1973. *Zamboanga and Sulu: An Archaeological Approach to Ethnic Diversity.* Ethnology Monographs of the Department of Anthropology, University of Pittsburgh, 1. Pittsburgh, PA.

Sung, Wen-hsün, Huang Shih-ch'iang, Lien Chao-mei, and Li Kuang-chou. 1967. "O-luan-pi: Tai-wan nan-tuan te shih-ch'ien [A prehistoric site at the southern tip of Formosa]." *Chung-kuo Tung-ya Hsiieh-shu Wei-yuan-hui Nien-pao* [Annual Bulletin of the China Council for East Asian Studies] 6: 1–43.

Tantoco, Rosario B., ed. 1974. *Proceedings of the First Regional Seminar on Southeast Asian Prehistory and Archaeology.* Manila: National Museum.

Tenazas, Rosa C. P. 1970. "Cremation Burial in the Philippines." *Philippine Historical Review* 3: 34–38.

———. 1974. "A Progress Report on the Magsuhot Excavations in Bacong, Negros Oriental, Summer 1974." *Philippine Quarterly of Culture and Society* 2: 133–155.

Thiel, Barbara. 1980. "Excavations in the Piñacanauan Valley, Northern Luzon." *Bulletin of the Indo-Pacific Prehistory Association* 2: 40–48.

———. 1986–1987a. "Excavations at the Lal-Lo Shell Middens, Northeast Luzon, Philippines." *Asian Perspectives* 27, no. 1: 71–94.

———. 1986–1987b. "Excavations at Arku Cave, Northeast Luzon, Philippines." *Asian Perspectives* 27, no. 2: 229–264.

———. 1988–1989. "Excavations at Musang Cave, Northeast Luzon, Philippines." *Asian Perspectives* 28, no. 1: 67–81.

Torii, Ryuzo. 1897a. "Pottery Techniques of the Ami Tribe, Eastern Taiwan." *Zenruigaku Zashi* 12: 360–373 (in Japanese).

———. 1897b "Distribution of the Aborigines in Eastern Taiwan." *Zenrugaku Zashi* 12: 378–413 (in Japanese).

———. 1900. "Past and Present Inhabitants at New-High Mountain." *Zenruigaku Zashi* 15: 303–308 (in Japanese).

———. 1911. "Maruyam Shell Mound, Taipei, Taiwan." *Zenruigaku Zashi* 27: 56 (in Japanese).

———. 1926. "Ancient Stone Artifacts in Taiwan." *Minzoku* 1: 3 (in Japanese).

Tsang Cheng-hwa. 1965. "New Archaeological Data from Both Sides of the Taiwan Straits and Their Implications for the Controversy about Austronesian Origins and Expansion." In *Austronesian Studies,* 185–226.

———. 1991. *Archaeology of the P 'eng-Hu Islands.* Taipei: Institute of History and Philology, Academia Sinica.

Tuggle, H. David, and Karl Hutterer. 1972. "Archaeology of the Sohoton Area, Southwestern Samar, Philippines." *Leyte-Samar Studies* 6: 1–104.

Wang Gungwu. 1958. "The Nanhai Trade." *Journal of the Malayan Branch of the Royal Asiatic Society* 31, no. 2.

Wang, T. S. 1983. *The Neolithic Site of Chih-shan-yen.* Taipei: Taipei Municipal Cultural Heritage Commission, Taiwan.

Wu, David Yen-ho. 1969. "A Short History of Archaeological Studies in Taiwan from 1895 to 1949: With a Bibliography." *Asian Perspectives* 12: 105–112.

Zamora, Mario D. 1967. *Studies in Philippine Anthropology (In Honor of H. Otley Beyer).* Quezon City: Alimar-Phoenix.

Israel

Archaeological fieldwork and research in Israel began long before the founding of the modern state in 1948. This article treats the history of archaeology in the region in nineteenth- and twentieth-century western Palestine in brief and then deals with developments in Israel after 1948 in greater detail.

The Formative Period in the Nineteenth Century

Archaeology in "the Holy Land," as Palestine under Ottoman Turkish rule was often called, began as part of the general rediscovery of the long-lost ancient Near East in the early to mid-nineteenth century. Discoveries of major monuments in Egypt and MESOPOTAMIA, as well as the recovery and decipherment of the earliest known written documents, beginning in the 1840s, soon galvanized interest in Palestine—especially as some of the most spectacular finds seemed to "prove the Bible."

Palestinian archaeology is generally said to have had its beginnings in the journeys of the Americans Edward Robinson and Eli Smith in 1838, pioneer mapmakers who first correctly identified more than 200 biblical and other ancient sites. The first actual clearance of ruins, however, was undertaken in 1850 by a French consular official, Felicien de Saulcy, who brought to light the so-called tombs of the kings in Jerusalem. The real archaeological turning point came with the great Survey of Western Palestine, which was sponsored between 1872 and 1878 by the British Palestine Exploration Society (PEF) and produced the first modern, reasonably accurate surveys and maps of western Palestine. The PEF also sponsored the first systematic below-ground explorations in Palestine, the soundings of C. W. Wilson and C. Warren near the Temple Mount in Jerusalem. The PEF's journal, the *Palestine Exploration Quarterly,* began publication in 1867 and is still published today. Other foreign archaeological societies for exploration and fieldwork in Palestine were founded at this time by the Americans (1870), Germans (1878), and French (1892).

The first real excavations, however, were those of the legendary SIR WILLIAM MATTHEW FLINDERS PETRIE at Tell el-Hesi in southern Palestine in 1890 (followed by the American F. J. Bliss in 1893). It was Petrie, long experienced in archaeology in Egypt, who intuitively laid the two foundations for all subsequent fieldwork: (1) stratigraphic excavation of multilayered tells or mounds and (2) comparative ceramic typology and chronology.

Twentieth-Century Palestinian Archaeology until World War I

The early twentieth century saw a flurry of large-scale archaeological projects in Palestine under several auspices. Excavations included those of Britain at Gezer (1902–1909); the United States at Samaria (1908–1910); and Germany at Ta'anach (1902–1904), Megiddo (1903–1905), Jericho (1907–1909), and Galilean synagogues (1905). Most of these excavations were amateurish when judged by more modern standards. Furthermore, results were often compromised by the typical combination of the excavators' colonialism, nationalism, adventurism, and above all by the "biblicism" that has been irresistible in this branch of archaeology. Only GEORGE REISNER's work at

Samaria in 1908–1910 rose above these limitations, but he was primarily an Egyptian archaeologist and the delay in the publication of his final report volumes until 1924 blunted his impact on the field. A final limitation on the development of Palestinian archaeology was the inefficient and even corrupt administration of antiquities and sites under Ottoman rule.

Archaeology from 1918 until 1948

The years between the two world wars constituted a "golden age" for Palestinian archaeology. The British Mandate government of 1918 established a modern Department of Antiquities and new antiquities laws. The department's journal, the *Quarterly of the Department of Antiquities in Palestine,* was published until 1950. The British themselves, often under the auspices of the PEF and the British School of Archaeology in Jerusalem, sponsored significant work at Ashkelon (1920–1922), Jerash in Transjordan (1923–1928), and the Carmel prehistoric caves (1925–1934) as well as work by Petrie at sites in the Gaza area (1926–1934), Jericho (1930–1936), Samaria (1930–1935), Lachish (1932–1938), Kh. el-Mefar (1935–1938), and other sites. In 1938, the Department of Antiquities, along with its collections and library, moved to a magnificent new facility, the Palestine Archaeological Museum, built in Jerusalem with funds from the Rockefeller family in the United States.

U.S. archaeology also flourished, largely under the aegis of the AMERICAN SCHOOL OF ORIENTAL RESEARCH, founded in 1900 and directed from 1920 to 1929 and 1933 to 1936 by WILLIAM FOXWELL ALBRIGHT, the leading U.S. archaeologist of his era and considered by many the father of "biblical archaeology." Among the U.S. excavations were those by Albright himself at Tell el-Fûl (1922), Bethel (1934), and especially Tell Beit Mirsim (1926–1934); by others at Tell en-Nasbeh (1926–1935) and Beth-shemesh (1928–1933); and Nelson Glueck's explorations in Transjordan (1932–1947). Parallel to "the Albright school" and its biblical orientation were large projects undertaken by secular U.S. institutions such as the University of Pennsylvania at Beth-Shan (1921–1933), the ORIENTAL INSTITUTE OF THE UNIVERSITY OF CHICAGO at

Megiddo (1925–1939), and Yale University at Jerash (1928–1934).

The Beginnings of a National School

It was during the period between the two world wars that Jewish scholars began to do firsthand work on the historical topography and archaeology of Palestine, then undergoing several waves of Jewish settlement from abroad. The Jewish Palestine Exploration Society had been founded in 1914 and was succeeded by the Israel Exploration Society after 1948.

The former society conducted the first Jewish excavations at the Hammath Tiberias Synagogue in 1921–1922, but the real pioneer of Jewish archaeology in Palestine was Eliezer Lipa Sukenik, who founded the Department (now the Institute) of Archaeology at the Hebrew University of Jerusalem shortly after its opening in 1925. Sukenik excavated the synagogue at Beth Alfa (1929) as well as many Jewish burials in Jerusalem and at Tel Gerisa (Tell el-Jerisheh, 1927). He also participated in the joint expedition to Samaria led by J. W. Crowfoot (1930–1935) alongside another pioneer of Jewish archaeology, Nahman Avigad. Another distinguished Jewish archaeologist and historian of the formative era was Benjamin Mazar (Maisler), who together with Avigad carried out extensive excavations in the Jewish necropolis at Beth Shearim (1936–1960). After joining the faculty of the Hebrew University, Mazar became the doyen of Jewish and later Israeli archaeology, training most of the next generation.

Other pioneer Jewish archaeologists of the British Mandate period were the prehistorian Moshe Stekelis; the classical archaeologist and art historian Michael Avi-Yonah; Ludwig A. Mayer, in Islamic art and archaeology; Immanuel Ben-Tor, Ruth Amiran, later chief archaeologist of the Israel Museum; and Shmuel Yeivin, later first director of the Israel Department of Antiquities. Other Jewish scholars in related fields of ancient Near Eastern, classical, and biblical studies were also active at this time, both at the Hebrew University and in the British-directed Department of Antiquities.

Although many publications appeared and interest in popular circles, especially among Jewish settlers in Palestine, grew enormously, no distinctive "Jewish school" emerged. Thus, foreign archaeologists continued to dominate the field under the colonialist regime in Palestine, as elsewhere in Transjordan, Syria, and Iraq. Nevertheless, by the eve of World War II, when all fieldwork came temporarily to an end, Jewish archaeologists were poised to come into their own. This pioneer generation—"the fathers of Israeli archaeology"—were deeply imbued with a love and firsthand knowledge of "the land of Israel" (Eretz-Israel), steeped in the classical academic tradition of European universities, influenced by the best of foreign scholarship and research (especially that of the Albright school), and experienced in field excavation.

Archaeology in the State of Israel

Almost immediately after the foundation of the state of Israel in 1948, Israeli archaeologists began work on their own even though they were now restricted to parts of western Palestine and even excluded from the Old City of Jerusalem. Israelis were also isolated from most foreign archaeologists, both archaeologists in Syria and Jordan and archaeologists from the United States, Great Britain, FRANCE, Germany, and other countries, as nearly all of them now chose to work in the West Bank or Transjordan. All the foreign institutes of archaeology, as well as the Rockefeller Museum and its facilities and publications, and even the Hebrew University of Israel were beset by enormous difficulties, including the war of independence, the absorption of a massive influx of immigrants, and severe economic and social difficulties. Archaeology was accorded a low priority.

Despite overwhelming odds, Israel quickly established a Department of Antiquities, on the old British model, and continued the tradition of the quarterly publication of the Department of Antiquities in Palestine with the launching of the *Israel Exploration Journal* in 1950. Limited salvage and excavation projects began, including Yeivin's work on many salvage projects, Mazar's excavations at Tel Qasile near Tel Aviv (1949–1950), and soon after the discovery and acquisition of some of the DEAD SEA SCROLLS, pioneer work in the publication of those manuscripts. Sukenik, and later his illustrious son Yigael Yadin, were instrumental in establishing a characteristic Israeli emphasis for the archaeology of the Second Temple period.

The development of a more self-conscious "national school" (although recognized as such only later) was owing largely to Yigael Yadin, who joined the faculty of the Hebrew University in 1954 after a term as chief of staff of the Israeli Defence Forces. He promptly launched large-scale and well-funded excavations by the Rothschild Foundation at the great site of Hazor in northern Israel (1955–1958 and 1968). There, alongside pioneers like Amiran and more recent archaeologists like Trude and Moshe Dothan, Claire Epstein, and Yohanan Aharoni, the first generation of native-born Israeli archaeologists was trained. These Hazor staff members, inspired by Yadin's charismatic personality, international standing, and sometimes mesmerizing vision, would become the architects of "the Israeli school" in the 1960s to the 1980s. Second only to Yadin's influence was that of the engineer and architect Immanuel ("Munya") Dunayevsky, whose primarily architectural approach remained a prominent feature of Israeli archaeology for a generation.

Other earlier Israeli fieldwork was prompted by the Dead Sea Scrolls research. The continued looting of caves, together with more systematic excavations of Qumran and the vicinity by foreign archaeologists working across the border in Jordan, necessitated a response by Israeli archaeologists. Pioneering expeditions were carried out in the Judean desert by Aharoni, followed by further survey and excavations led by Aharoni, P. Bar-Adon, and Yadin in 1961–1962. Spectacular finds were made from the Chalcolithic period (fourth millennium B.C.), and there were significant discoveries of manuscripts and other artifacts from the second Jewish revolt (under Bar-Kochba in A.D. 132–135). This work was followed immediately by Yadin's epochal project at Massada (1963–1964), which drew volunteers from all over the world, galvanized Israeli and Jewish interest in archaeology, and launched Yadin as an international celebrity. For many Israelis, Massada, the desert cliff-top fortress where Jewish insurgents made a last stand against the Roman legions, became a symbol of the identity of past and present in the restored state of Israel. Thereafter, archaeology would become a popular pastime, almost a secular religion for many Israelis, and a way of putting down roots in the Holy Land.

Other less spectacular excavations were carried out in the late 1950s and 1960s. Prehistoric caves in the Nahal Oren near the Carmel Ridge were excavated, sites of the Chalcolithic period in the Judean desert and the Beersheba basin were extensively investigated, and large Bronze- and Iron-Age mounds became the focus of long-running expeditions, such as those led by Aharoni and Amiran at Arad (1962–1984), Dothan at Tel Mor and Ashdod (1962–1972), and Biran at Tel Dan (1967). Nabatean-Byzantine sites in the Negev desert, such as Avdat and Mamshit/Kurnub, were excavated by A. Negev from 1959 to 1972, and the Roman port of Caesarea was explored by Negev and Avi-Yonah from 1956 to 1964. Synagogues and Jewish burials were also cleared at several locations.

During this period, the Institute of Archaeology at the Hebrew University, led principally by Mazar and Yadin, was the driving force behind Israeli archaeology. In 1962, however, a second Department of Archaeology was founded (now the Sonia and Marco Nadler Institute of Archaeology) at the newly opened Tel Aviv University. Largely as a result of Aharoni's initiative, this department's program was characterized specifically by his emphasis on regional archaeology, especially in the Negev desert. The institute's quarterly, *Tel Aviv,* began publication in 1974. Later, institutes of archaeology were established at Ben-Gurion University in the Negev and Haifa University. In 1965, the Israel Museum opened, and it included offices for the Department of Antiquities and a large wing for archaeological exhibits, collections, and work areas. This museum, in effect, finally replaced the old national center in the Rockefeller Museum in the Old City. By the 1980s, there were dozens of regional museums, including the large Museum Haaretz in Tel Aviv. Finally, the Hebrew University's new campus near the Israel Museum and the Knesset, replacing the one lost on Mt. Scopus in 1948, included facilities for the

Ruins of Massada in Israel (Corel)

continuation of the Institute of Archaeology, which flourished during the 1950s and 1960s. Its series of report volumes, *Qedem,* began appearing in 1975.

The 1967 war changed Israeli archaeology considerably as it opened the West Bank (the heartland of ancient Israel), the Golan Heights, and the Sinai to Israeli excavators. The latter two were largely *terra incognita,* and very extensive surveys soon began. Also, the Old City of Jerusalem now came into Israeli hands, and the first large-scale excavations ever undertaken there soon began, first under Mazar near the Temple Mount (1968–1978), then under Avigad in the Jewish Quarter (1969–1983). This work was followed by numerous other smaller projects that began in the 1970s and still continue. Indeed, the archaeology of Jerusalem has now become almost a separate specialization of Israeli archaeology, supplementing and often correcting more than a century of previous work. Finally, the new and expanding campus of the Hebrew University, again on Mt. Scopus overlooking the Old City, included the refurbishment and expansion of the old Institute and Department of Archaeology (now named the Philip and Muriel Berman Institute of Archaeology).

Israeli archaeology is divided by its practitioners into (1) prehistory; (2) Bronze/Iron Age archaeology, often termed *biblical archaeology* (although secular, without the theological overtones that the term carries in Europe and America); and (3) classical archaeology, including the Second Temple period. "Biblical archaeology" flourished particularly in the 1960s– 1980s, with excavations at Bronze- and Iron-Age sites, or Canaanite-Israelite sites, that could be identified in the Hebrew Bible (or Old Testament). These projects were too numerous to describe in detail, but among the most significant sites excavated were (from north to south) Dan (A. Biran), Acco (M. Dothan), Yoqneam (A. Ben-Tor), Dor (E. Stern), Tel Michal (Z. Herzog et al.), Tell Qasile (A. Mazar), Aphek (M. Kochavi and P. Beck), Shiloh (I. Finkelstein), Tel Batash/Timna (A. Mazar), Tel Miqneh/Ekron (T. Dothan and S. Gitin), Lachish (D. Ussishkin), Ashdod (M. Dothan), Tel Sera and Tel Haror (E. Oren), Deir al-Balah (T. Dothan), Tel Beersheva (Y. Aharoni), Tel Ira (Y. Beit-Arieh and V. Fritz).

The above were all tell sites or mounds, usually with long histories. Many smaller, one-period sites and cemeteries were also dug in the

1960s–1980s, however, ranging from Pale-olithic to Islamic, from north to south, and in-cluding the Israeli-occupied territories as well. In addition, the first systematic surveys were carried out in the latter regions, especially by younger archaeologists of the third generation, many of them from the Tel Aviv Institute of Ar-chaeology carrying out the emphasis of their mentor, Aharoni, concerning regional archaeol-ogy. Particularly noteworthy were the intensive surveys of the Galilee (Z. Gal and Y. Frankel), of the Samaria region (A. Zertal and I. Finkel-stein), the Judean highlands (A. Ofer), and the Sinai (E. Oren, Y. Beit-Arieh, and others). In Is-rael proper, surveys along the Mediterranean coast continued (R. Gophna and others), and there were very extensive surveys in the Negev (R. Cohen, M. Heimann, Y. Dagan, and others).

Classical archaeology was not neglected in the 1960s–1980s as there was a revival of inter-est in synagogues and Jewish settlements, with excavations by both local and foreign archaeol-ogists. Other classical and later period sites in-cluded sites in the Golan Heights, Caesarea, Herodian, Jericho, and the Herodium, and sev-eral Byzantine sites in the Negev as well as early Christian monasteries and churches. Underwa-ter and coastal archaeology also began in earnest, especially under the aegis of the Center for Maritime Studies of Haifa University. Fi-nally, prehistoric sites were not overlooked; in-deed research burgeoned.

In the 1990s, the Israeli school matured and several newer or intensified emphases developed:

1. In 1989, the old Department of Antiquities of the Ministry of Education and Culture was transformed into an independent body, the Israel Antiquities Authority, which has some 200 employees, and greatly expanded re-sources and responsibilities. It continues to publish the serial *Antigot* in both Hebrew and other languages as well as *Excavations and Sur-veys in Israel* and other materials.

2. More modern stratigraphic methods, hotly debated in the 1970s and even into the 1980s, were now taken for granted by a younger generation of archaeologists.

3. Some of the underlying socioanthropological theory and the emphasis on quantitative

methods, advocated by "the new archaeol-ogy" of the 1970s–1980s in America, was fi-nally adopted in Israel, although very selec-tively.

4. New large-scale projects were undertaken, often with subsidies from the Antiquities Au-thority designed to restore and develop key sites for tourism. The largest such project was the massive clearance and restoration of Roman-Byzantine Beth-shan, which even surpasses another Decapolis city, Jerash in Jordan. Other sites that underwent large-scale restoration were Dan, Hazor, Caesarea, Lachish, Beersheba, and Arad.

5. Both the Antiquities Authority and the sev-eral institutes of archaeology placed more emphasis on prompt publication, and the younger generation set a higher mark than their predecessors, both in preliminary and final reports.

6. It may be said that "the third generation" of Israeli archaeologists had finally "come of age" with the creation of a self-conscious, highly professional national school, one that was well organized and well supported. This school easily dominated the scene, in com-parison with the few remaining foreign-sponsored projects; few other than American projects persisted, and these were often joint Israeli-American enterprises.

Conclusion

Despite its rapid growth in just under fifty years and its complex character, Israeli archaeology throughout has had a certain consistent, distinc-tive character. First, it has been deeply grounded in traditional ancient Near Eastern scholarship. Second, it has taken the Bible (i.e., the Hebrew Bible or Old Testament) seriously, yet unlike American (and some European) "biblical archae-ology," it has maintained a professional, special-ized, and thoroughly secular character, utilizing the Bible, not as confessional literature, but largely as the foundation of national history and culture. Third, it has remained largely prag-matic, grounded in the realia, and has been pre-occupied more with description and classifica-tion than with explanation and little concerned with anything but the most basic theory.

Fourth, Israeli architecture emphasized large-scale architectural exposure rather than detailed stratigraphy and microphasing, and special emphasis has been laid on the clearance of living surfaces and exhaustive attempts to restore pottery assemblages. Fifth, Israeli archaeology (excluding prehistory) has been allied almost exclusively with the disciplines of history, philology, and comparative literature with anthropology playing a minor role, if any—in contrast to New World archaeology. Its adoption of aspects of the new archaeology has been slow, sporadic, and limited to such obvious practical strategies as ecological studies, regional surveys, and applied science in the analysis of certain materials. Deliberate, explicit research design is rare, and nomothetic approaches are almost unheard of. As Israelis argue, their connection with the land and its history is "direct and emotional," not theoretical; in any case, the urgency of salvage work and the necessities and hardships of so many excavations leave little time for reflection or comparisons with archaeology in other parts of the world. Thus, if archaeology in Israel is understandably somewhat parochial, it is also probably more intense, both professionally and popularly, than archaeology anywhere else.

A word should be added about foreign archaeology in Israel. Excavations sponsored by other nations have continued since the formation of the state of Israel, although on a relatively smaller and still-decreasing scale because of the dominance of the Israeli national school. The first postwar large-scale U.S. excavations were at Gezer (1964–1974, 1984, 1990); directed by G. E. Wright, W. G. Dever, and J. D. Seger, these excavations had a far-reaching significance in introducing methods of the new archaeology.

That tradition has continued largely with Gezer-trained excavators at Tell el-Hesi, a series of Galilean synagogue sites (E. M. and C. Meyers, J. F. Strange), at Lahav (J. D. Seger), at Tel Miqne/Ekron (S. Gitin, with T. Dothan), at Ashkelon (L. E. Stager), and other sites, both in Israel and Jordan. The old American School of Oriental Research, renamed the W. F. Albright Institute of Archaeological Research in 1968, continued its operations as a permanent in-country research institute. The British, French, and German institutes also continue to operate,

although all transferred most of their fieldwork to JORDAN after 1948. Alongside the *Israel Exploration Journal,* the journals of the foreign schools disseminate important information about archaeology in Israel, namely, the *Bulletin of the American Schools of Oriental Research, Levant* and the *Palestine Exploration Journal, Revue Biblique,* and the *Zeitschrift des Deutschen Palastina-Vereins.*

Bill Dever

See also Syro-Palestinian and Biblical Archaeology
References
Bar-Yosef, O., and A. Mazar. 1982. "Israeli Archaeology." *World Archaeology* 13: 310–325.
Ben-Tor, A., ed. 1992. The *Archaeology of Ancient Israel.* New Haven: Yale University.
Dever, W. G. 1985. "Syro-Palestinian and Biblical Archaeology." In *the Hebrew Bible and Its Modern Interpreters.* Ed. D. A. Knight and G. M. Tucker. Chico, CA: Scholars Press.
———. 1989. "Archaeology in Israel Today: A Summation and Critique." In *Recent Excavations in Israel: Studies in Iron Age Archaeology.* Ed. S. Gitin and W. G. Dever. Winona Lake, IN: For American Schools of Oriental Research.
Kempinski, A., and R. Reich, eds. 1992. The *Architecture of Ancient Israel.* Jerusalem: Israel Exploration Society.
Mazar, A. 1988. "Israeli Archaeologists." In *Benchmarks in Time and Culture: An Introduction to Palestinian Archaeology.* Ed. J. F. Drinkard, G. L. Mattingly, and J. M. Miller. Atlanta: Scholars Press.
———. 1990. *The Archaeology of the Land of the Bible ca. 10,000–586 B.C.E.* New York: Doubleday.
Moorey, P. R. S. 1991. *A Century of Biblical Archaeology.* Cambridge, UK: Lutterworth Press.
Silberman, N. A. 1982. *Digging for God and Country: Exploration. Archaeology and the Secret Struggle for the Holy Land, 1799–1917.* New York: Alfred A. Knopf.
Stern, E., ed. 1993. The *New Encyclopedia of Archaeological Excavations in the Holy Land.* 4 vols. New York: Scribners.

Italy

The history of Italian archaeology is dominated by the city of Rome, the grand imperial capital that was transformed into the seat of ecclesiastical power. Many Roman imperial buildings remained above ground and in use, and the description and exploration of these structures

Archaeological Sites in Italy

played a fundamental role in the development of archaeology in Italy. The earliest descriptions were probably offered with pilgrims to the Holy City in mind: the so-called Einsiedeln Itinerary (ca. A.D. 800) included descriptions of ancient monuments among those of the churches of Rome. A number of these monuments had ap-

parently disappeared by the time of the influential *Mirabilia Urbis Romae* (*Marvels of the City of Rome*; ca. 1140). The sack of Rome in A.D. 1082 had damaged a substantial part of the city. Just as serious was the mining of the city's ancient structures for building materials; the ninth century saw the start of this practice on a large scale, and it would continue for many hundreds of years.

Guides to the monuments of Rome appeared regularly from the thirteenth century onward. A notable description was written by the poet Petrarch (Francesco Petrarca, 1304–1374), who first visited Rome in 1337 and who collected, studied, and wrote about ancient inscriptions and coins. Such interests were, of course, normal for the educated classes in the early Renaissance, and collections of antiquities were commonplace among the great families, who often had their seats in imperial monuments. In Rome, for example, the Orsini family occupied the Mausoleum of Hadrian (Castel Sant'Angelo, later a papal fort), the Colonna family had the Baths of Constantine, and the Frangipani family fortified the Colosseum and the Arch of Titus.

The greatest of these noble families, the Medici, had their base in Florence. Cosimo the Elder (1389–1464) began the family's collection of antiquities, which was greatly expanded by Lorenzo "the Magnificent" (1448–1492). Competition between the aristocratic families and the papacy for ancient works of art became intense from this period on. Already there was concern for the fate of ancient monuments, particularly in Rome, as expressed by a papal bull issued by Pius II (r. 1458–1464) that threatened excommunication for those taking marble from Roman ruins. Stone from Roman monuments was disappearing at an astounding rate in the fifteenth century; under one of Pius's immediate predecessors, Nicholas V, over 2,500 cartloads of travertine were removed from the Colosseum by one contractor in one year. The ban, however, was honored more in the breach than the observance, and Pius's own ledgers record how he rebuilt the steps of Saint Peter's Cathedral with stone from the Colosseum. He was, though, a remarkable pope, who seems to have organized the first "systematic" excavation—an attempt to recover two large Roman ships submerged in Lake Nemi. The work was undertaken by the artist-architect Leon Battista Alberti (1404–1472), adviser to a number of popes between the 1430s and 1470s and author of a newly professional topographical work on ancient Rome, the *Descriptio Urbis Romae* (ca. 1440). The excavation of the Nemi ships was only partially successful. Their full excavation was undertaken by the Fascist government in the 1920s, and the level of the lake was lowered to reveal two enormous pleasure barges belonging to the emperor Caligula. (These were later burned by retreating troops in 1944.)

A number of important works of ancient art had never been buried—particularly coins and gemstones but also some large-scale sculptures, such as the equestrian statue of Marcus Aurelius on the Capitoline, the Capitoline She-Wolf, and *Lo Spinario*, all in bronze. These three statues were among those in the papal collection given by Pope Sixtus IV (r. 1471–1484) to the city of Rome in 1471. They were housed in the Palazzo dei Conservatori on the Capitoline Hill, which became the world's first public museum (the Musei Capitolini). Sixtus IV also forbade the unauthorized excavation of antiquities, which were beginning to flood out of Rome and sites such as Hadrian's Villa at Tivoli. This edict also had little effect; in the late fifteenth and early sixteenth centuries, excavations proliferated. Among the most notable was the discovery of the Domus Aurea (the Golden House of Nero) in central Rome. Part of this palace was discovered on the Oppian Hill, covered by the foundations of the later Baths of Titus; systematic visits to the underground chambers began around 1480. The style of wall painting seen there was immediately influential on contemporary wall painting (and the fantastic figures borrowed from these artificial grottoes, known as *grottesche*, are at the root of our word *grotesque*).

Many Roman monuments were ransacked during the sixteenth century, and perhaps more ancient sculpture was discovered in this century than in any other. Works such as the *Laocoon*, discovered in the Baths of Trajan in 1506 and seen immediately by Michelangelo, had a profound effect on contemporary artists. Typical of the period was the excavation of the enormous Baths of Caracalla, particularly under Paul III (r. 1534–1549), where teams worked in search of building material and ancient sculptures. A number of well-preserved works were discovered, such as the so-called Farnese Hercules and

The Canopus, Hadrian's Villa at Tivoli (from G. Piranesi, Le antichità romane *[Rome, 1756])*

the Farnese Bull. Paul III came from the powerful Farnese family, and many of the ancient sculptures discovered during the sixteenth century have retained the names of the aristocratic collections into which they passed. Many sculptures went into the VATICAN Collections (Musei Vaticani), established by Pope Julius II (r. 1503–1513); Paul III established the office of the Papal Commissioner of Antiquities (Commissario delle Antichità), which existed from 1534 until the formation of the modern archaeological bureaucracy in 1870 with the unification of Italy.

Paradoxically, although the sixteenth century witnessed a great deal of destruction of classical monuments, it was also a time when interest in such monuments peaked. Clearances in Rome produced much new information, and antiquarians and topographers as well as some of the greatest artists and architects of the day (such as Palladio and Raphael), were drawn into their

study. Excavations outside Rome began to grow in importance, not only in the environs of the city (such as at Hadrian's Villa at Tivoli) but also and particularly in Etruria. To this period can be dated the start of the patriotic Tuscan movement centered on the ETRUSCANS, with Cosimo I "the Great" de' Medici (1519–1574) crowned Magnus Dux Etruria (Grand Duke of Etruria). Etruscan tombs were opened at Chiusi, Volterra, Tarquinia, and elsewhere, and the images found in them had a demonstrable effect on the work of a number of Renaissance artists, such as Filippo Brunelleschi, Leonardo Da Vinci, and Michelangelo.

The pace of the discovery of ancient works of art slowed somewhat during the seventeenth century, although many new sculptures appeared, along with wall paintings that caused a sensation. One such painting was the so-called *Aldobrandini Wedding,* excavated on the Esquiline Hill in Rome in 1604 and much admired by visiting painters. During this century foreign visitors poured into Italy (with the more adventurous of them now also seeking to travel to GREECE). Among archaeologists (broadly defined) the Scotsman Thomas Dempster should be mentioned for his pioneering work on the Etruscans. His *De Etruria Regali Libri Septem* (Seven Books Concerning Etruria of the Kings) was produced by about 1620 under Medici patronage. Another prominent British visitor was the second duke of Arundel, who arrived in Italy with Inigo Jones in 1613 and excavated several houses in Rome. The ancient statues he took back to his galleries in the Strand in London appear to have started a craze for collection in Britain that grew considerably by midcentury. The artist Peter Paul Rubens spent the years 1600 to 1608 in Rome and was renowned both for his knowledge of antiquity and for his personal collection. The French classical painter Nicholas Poussin spent much of his life in Rome (from 1624 until his death in 1665); he introduced the artist Charles Le Brun to Rome in 1642. From this period dates the start of the great fascination with Rome on the part of the French kings, who saw themselves as successors to the Roman emperors. Le Brun was influential in the introduction of classical style to the court of a man who consciously associated himself with the emperor Augustus—Louis XIV (r. 1643–1715). Under Le Brun's guidance the French Academy in Rome was created in 1666. Many French artists studied at the academy, and a large collection of casts of ancient sculptures was assembled; ancient originals flowed back to France in such quantities that a papal edict sought to ban the export of antiquities.

Europe's oldest academy had been founded in Rome some sixty years before. The Accademia Nazionale dei Lincei (*lincei* from *lynxes,* meaning the sharp-eyed ones) was born in 1603 and soon counted Galileo Galilei among its members. Though this institution has gone through periods of inactivity and suppression, it has survived to the present day, and it still issues important archaeological publications, first among which is the *Notizie degli Scavi* (Excavation News). Antiquarian and topographical studies continued to appear in large numbers. A notable project from

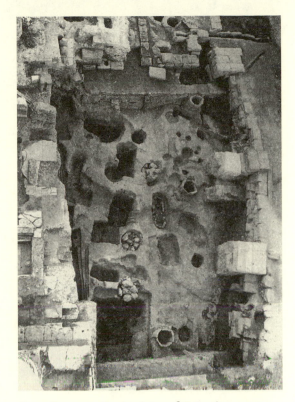

Forum Romanum: Overhead view of G. Boni's excavation of the proto-historical cemetery, ca. 1902 (Soprintendenza Archeologica di Roma)

the 1620s was the Museo Cartoceto (Paper Museum) of Cassiano dal Pozzo (d. 1657), who moved in the intellectual circle of the early Lincei. Dal Pozzo acquired and commissioned thousands of drawings of classical antiquities, although these had to coexist with representatives of his other interests, particularly in the natural sciences. Leonardo Agostini (1593–1669) became the antiquarian to the Barberini family on Dal Pozzo's recommendation and went on to become, in 1655, the pope's commissioner of antiquities, excavating in the Forum of Trajan and the Forum Romanum. He is best noted for his catalogs of ancient gemstones, *Le Gemme antiche figurate* (Ancient Figured Gems; 1657, 1669). At the same time, the huge topographical study of Famiano Nardini (d. 1661) appeared; his *Roma antica* (Ancient Rome) contained much new information and dealt with the city according to its fourteen ancient regions.

The eighteenth century opened with the astonishing discoveries at the buried city of Herculaneum from 1709 onward. The unearthed Roman cities of HERCULANEUM and POMPEII, discovered in 1748, became essential stopping points for aristocrats (especially British) wishing to round out their education. The golden age of the "grand tour" is often reckoned to be between 1713 and 1793, bounded by political developments that encouraged and then restricted travel. Early tourists included Thomas Coke, later the first earl of Leicester (from 1712), and Lord Burlington (from 1715), and the Society of Dilettanti was formed in London in 1733 for tour veterans. The Greek Revival style in buildings and gardens took hold in this period, and many large collections of antiquities were formed.

It would be some time before archaeologists and travelers ventured farther south into the Kingdom of the Two Sicilies, ruled by the Bourbon kings of Naples, but to the north archaeological inquiry was expanding. Work continued in and around Rome, especially on the Palatine (from the 1720s), in the burial monuments along the Via Appia, and in the villas at Tivoli. Farther north fascination with the Etruscans increased dramatically from the start of the eighteenth century. Interest in this culture, especially in Tuscany but more widely in Italy and Europe as well, was so fervent that a term has been used ever since to describe the passion: *Etruscheria*. The Accademia Etrusca was founded in Cortona in 1727, and many important excavations followed. The Lucretian motto of the academy—*obscura de re lucida pango* (I Reveal Clear Things about an Obscure Matter)—took some time to be fully realized. Tuscan patriotism and the politico-cultural ambitions of the grand dukes of Tuscany saw just about every advance in ancient arts and sciences attributed to the Etruscans, who were promoted as the "first" Italians. Such misapprehensions explain why Josiah Wedgwood's Staffordshire pottery, first produced in 1769, was named Etruria: his early models, painted vases from Etruscan tombs, were at the time thought to have been made in Etruria (whereas most had actually been imported from Athens). An important early Etruscologist was Antonio Gori, whose publications on Etruscan antiquities appeared between 1727 and 1762; he founded the Accademia Colum-baria in 1735 in Florence, which rivaled Cortona's Accademia Etrusca. Many of the worst excesses of the early Etruscologists were corrected later in the century—especially by Luigi Lanzi (1732–1810), who demonstrated (in 1789) that the Etruscan language was not derived from Hebrew and that most of the vases found in Etruscan tombs were in fact Greek.

Back in Rome the young Giovanni Piranesi arrived in the same year as the reigns of a series of enlightened popes began. Benedict XIV (r. 1740–1758) founded the Pontificia Accademia Romana di Archeologia (Pontifical Roman Academy of Archaeology), and Piranesi quickly graduated from being an engraver of archaeological vistas for grand tourists to being a full-scale topographer and archaeological draftsman. His forty-volume *Le Antichità romane (Roman Antiquities;* 1756) gained him great renown and was followed by many publications on Roman, Etruscan, and south Italian buildings and antiquities.

Perhaps the most notable arrival in the city of Rome was that of the German antiquarian JOHANN JOACHIM WINCKELMANN (1717–1768). Made papal commissioner of antiquities, he produced his highly influential *Geschichte der Kunst des Alterthums* (*History of Ancient Art*) in 1764. In it he proposed a chronological development for ancient sculpture, with a four-stage scheme in which Roman art belonged in the final phase of imitative works (Greek sculpture populated the "best" periods). Winckelmann was the first to attempt to understand ancient cultures on the basis of their art alone. From this time onward, ancient Greece would increasingly occupy the minds of European intellectuals. Winckelmann was part of the wider intellectual trend known as the Counter-Enlightenment, which reacted against the accumulated knowledge and reason of contemporary intellectual practice. This new romanticism sought truth and beauty in spontaneous, natural creation; the age of ancient Greece was seen explicitly, for the first time, as the childhood of Europe, and Greek culture was considered the foundation of all European culture, especially among German, Protestant intellectuals. There were political and religious dimensions to these ideologies. The Catholic

French kings identified strongly with the ancient Romans and saw their own realm as the New Rome; Protestant Germany looked increasingly to Greece in opposition, with a notable element to be found in Martin Luther's desire to understand the Bible purely from the Greek text alone, that is, unencumbered by translation into and commentary in Latin. It is therefore remarkable that in this climate, Winckelmann was the only non-Italian, non-Catholic scholar appointed as the pope's commissioner of antiquities (he converted to Catholicism to take up the post but is said to have been overheard singing Lutheran hymns at night in his rooms in the Vatican).

If ancient Greece, from this time on, became the focus of romantic, liberal, and bourgeois causes, Roman (and, more generally, Italian) antiquity suffered little for its continuing association with kings, popes, and aristocrats. Two particularly active popes, Clement XIV (r. 1769–1774) and Pius VI (r. 1775–1799), collected many new antiquities, reorganizing the Vatican galleries and creating the museum thereafter known as the Museo Pio-Clementino in their honor. Both employed Giovanni Battista Visconti, the energetic commissioner of antiquities, who made excavations both in Rome and at Tivoli, mainly in search of ancient statues. Visconti persuaded both popes to tighten conditions related to the issuance of export licenses for ancient works of art, which continued to flow out of the country. If not for these licenses, even more of the objects discovered by foreigners such as Gavin Hamilton (Scottish painter and dealer, d. 1798) would have made their way to northern Europe; Hamilton excavated at a large number of sites, including Tivoli, Rome, Gabii, and Ostia.

Focus on Pompeii and Herculaneum remained intense, especially in the second half of the century when the pace of excavation greatly increased. An interested onlooker and participant was the Englishman SIR WILLIAM HAMILTON, appointed extraordinary envoy to the court of Naples in 1764. His first collection of antiquities was published in lavishly illustrated volumes produced by the Comte d'Hancarville, a Frenchman. A number of spurious associations were used to argue for the high artistic and monetary value accorded painted pottery in antiquity. This sales pitch was certainly effective, as the British Museum bought the entire Hamilton collection (including over 700 painted vases) in 1772 for a large sum. Hamilton and d'Hancarville would perhaps be surprised to know that the ramifications of their arguments about artistic value are still ongoing in the study of Greek pottery. Taste in northern Europe was profoundly affected by the publication of these antiquities, with the influence heaviest in the decorative arts (e.g., Wedgwood's Etruria pottery in 1769) and interiors (e.g., the first suites decorated in neoclassical style in Spencer House, London, 1759).

South Italy and Sicily were slowly opening up to topographers, excavators, and travelers. Johann Wolfgang von Goethe, who was much influenced by the ideas of Winckelmann, toured Italy from 1786 to 1788 and visited Paestum (south of Naples) and a number of sites in Sicily that had, by the end of the century, been incorporated into the grand tour.

The years around 1800 brought considerable upheaval and activity to Italian archaeology. Napoleon's declaration of war on the Papal States saw 100 significant antiquities taken to Paris as a result of the settlement of 1797, among which were the *Laocoon* and the *Belvedere Apollo* (most were back in Rome by 1815, following Napoleon's fall). The short-lived republic under French occupation was overthrown in 1799, and the year 1800 saw the installation of a new pope and a new papal commissioner of antiquities, Carlo Fea, who was very active in the excavation and protection of antiquities until his death in 1836. Fea worked extensively with the French, who reoccupied Rome between 1808 and 1814 and who, in those short years, undertook an astonishingly large program of clearance, excavation, and repair. Major work was carried out in the Colosseum, Forum of Trajan, Basilica of Maxentius, Domus Aurea, and Pantheon, to name just a few. French work in the Forum Romanum, under Giuseppe Valadier and Carlo Fea, was the first systematic excavation undertaken in a zone ransacked for centuries; a new era of Roman archaeology had begun, in which Carlo Fea and Antonio Nibby were particularly prominent during the early years.

The Pontifical Roman Academy of Archaeology was refounded in 1810 and began the first of its numerous series of publications in 1821. Foreigners began to become more prominent in Italian archaeology, with the first formal foreign group established in 1823 by four scholars from northern Europe. The Roman Hyperboreans (*Hyperboreisch-römische Gesellschaft*) counted among their number the German Eduard Gerhard, who produced many reports of excavations and monuments in Rome and Etruria and is probably best remembered for his magisterial catalog of Etruscan engraved mirrors, *Etruskische Spiegel* (1840–1867). Gerhard oversaw the 1829 transformation of the Hyperboreans into the larger Istituto di Corrispondenza Archeologica, whose role was principally to publish new archaeological finds. One of Gerhard's first reports was an account of the excavations near the Etruscan city of Vulci (known at the time as Canino). Napoleon Bonaparte's estranged brother, Lucien, had been made prince of Canino by Pope Pius VII, and the chance discovery of an enormous necropolis in 1828 led to a large-scale program of excavation that saw many painted vases depart for the great museums of Europe (particularly in Germany). Pottery without figured decoration was ordered to be crushed underfoot as *poca roba* (small stuff), to prevent it from disrupting the market. Excavations were conducted throughout Etruria, with sensational results. The great early Etruscan "princely" tomb from Cerveteri, known as the Tomba Regolini-Galassi, was discovered in 1836; most of the finds are now in the Villa Giulia, a papal villa built in the mid-sixteenth century and converted into a museum for antiquities from the "Regione of Lazio" in 1889. The Frenchman Alessandro François's discovery of the François Tomb at Vulci crowned a career of excavation lasting over thirty years, and his description of the bodies and fabrics crumbling on contact with the outside air probably inspired the famous scene in Federico Fellini's film *Roma,* in which engineers digging a tunnel for the Metro suffer a similar phenomenon in the Roman chamber they discover. The important paintings in the François Tomb, apparently representing historical conflicts between Romans and Etruscans, were immediately recorded by the artist Carlo Ruspi, who had accurately reproduced a number of the painted decorations from Etruscan tombs being excavated in the necropolis of Tarquinia. These records preserve decorations that have mostly disappeared in since 1850. The British concentrated more on topography and the recording of extant monuments in Etruria than on excavation; several studies appeared in the 1830s and 1840s, before the publication of George Dennis's magnificent *Cities and Cemeteries of Etruria* (1848).

Slightly to the north, interest in the prehistory of Italy was sparked by Gozzadini's discovery of an Iron Age necropolis near his native Bologna in 1853. The people in the necropolis were cremated in biconical ash-urns in the European style; they were predecessors of the Etruscans, and their culture is known today as Villanovan, after the estate belonging to Gozzadini on which the necropolis was discovered. The principles associated with SIR CHARLES LYELL's new geology were being brought into Italy by naturalists and geologists and had an immediate effect on the study of prehistory, often known in Italy as *paletnologia*. The ideas of Thomas Henry Huxley, Charles Darwin, and others were fairly rapidly diffused in Italy, and the effect of the developing discipline of prehistory in SWITZERLAND on the many Italian political exiles who fled there was also significant. These factors were influential in the debates about the Bronze Age remains being excavated in the Po Valley, where the sodden soil allowed the preservation of wooden structures. The Bronze Age dwellings of the so-called Terramara culture could be compared with Swiss lake-dwellings and Scandinavian structures; links with northern Europe led to a widespread view that the people who built them were transalpine Indo-European migrants. For a time the Po Valley was regarded as the cradle of Italian civilization, since elements of the Terramara culture were argued to have moved south over time.

Fundamental for the development of Italian archaeology was the unification of Italy, begun in 1859. Giuseppe Garibaldi completed the process in 1870 by breaching the Aurelian Walls, which had served as the principal fortification of Rome since the third century A.D. The task of reorganizing archaeology was daunting for the new national government. Unified state structures had to be created throughout the country: museums, universities, an administration for carrying out archaeology, legislation. The process happened rather slowly because there was so much to be done for this new state and because money was always short. But it was achieved, even if strong regional peculiarities developed along the way. This was hardly surprising because in the series of small states that existed before 1859, archaeology was developed to widely differing degrees (the Papal States and the Kingdom of Sardinia representing the two ends of the spectrum).

Foreign archaeologists flooded into the country after reunification. The DEUTSCHES ARCHÄOLOGISCHES INSTITUT (German Archaeological Institute) was created out of the Istituto di Corrispondenza Archeologica in 1871, followed by the French School in 1873, the AMERICAN ACADEMY in 1894, and the British School in 1899. The Italians particularly admired the German education system, and contacts were encouraged by political factors, for Italy entered an alliance with Germany (and AUSTRIA) as the French attempted to intervene on behalf of the Papal States in the 1860s and 1870s. For archaeology the model was the new *Altertumswissenschaft,* or the science of antiquity, formed in the German and particularly the Prussian universities. "Science of antiquity" is perhaps a misleading translation, since in this system ancient texts had primacy, with great works of art next in line, and a strong streak of idealism ran through the research in which ideals and standards from antiquity were sought for application to modern times. But the scholarship was far more rigorous than the antiquarianism of the recent past, and the Italians struggled to emulate it; they had little to compare with the highly developed German system of gymnasium schools that produced hoards of students ready for university, already very well prepared in terms of the knowledge of ancient Greek and Latin. Important academic positions went to

northerners: Julius Beloch held the chair of ancient history in Rome from 1879 to 1929, and the country's most important chair of archaeology, in Rome, was awarded to Emanuel Löwy in preference to local candidates in 1889.

The textual/art-historical approach to archaeology was not all-consuming, however. One interesting exception was Giuseppe Fiorelli, made professor of archaeology in Naples in 1860. He was the first person at Pompeii to attempt controlled excavations, after the clearances conducted over the previous 100 years under the Bourbon kings of Naples. His field school (Scuola Archeologica di Pompei) was established in 1866 to train archaeologists in excavation methods, and Fiorelli was generally more interested in studying objects of all types in context rather than exploring the ideals encapsulated in works of high art. If Fiorelli's excavations cannot be described as truly stratigraphic, they at least proceeded down from above, rather than tunneling into Pompeian houses from the side, as had been the normal practice. The first classical archaeologist to dig with a properly stratigraphical method was Giacomo Boni, director of the excavations in the Forum Romanum from 1898 forward. Boni was trained as an architect, and his excavation techniques were thoroughly professional and were thrown into greater relief by barely supervised excavations conducted on public land as the city of Rome was rapidly redeveloped (to say nothing of the clearances on private land, which were not supervised at all). Boni was a friend of the great Italian prehistorian Luigi Pigorini, who dominated the field for half a century until 1925 (and who often visited the Forum excavations), and his methods were doubtless influenced by contemporary *paletnologia*. Boni is most famous for the discovery of the prehistoric cemetery in the Forum Romanum and the Lapis Niger nearby. This latter monument was a pavement of black stone in the Comitium, mentioned in Latin sources, and it was associated with a stone marker bearing an inscription in very archaic Latin (ca. 560 B.C.) that alludes to early kings. Both finds shed important new light on the early history of Rome and partly confirmed some of the ancient Roman traditions.

The Temple of Castor and Pollux, The Forum, Rome (Image Select)

Another important figure in Rome at the time was Rodolfo Lanciani, who was a professor of Roman topography from 1888 and dominant in that field until his death in 1929. Lanciani surveyed and published information on many monuments and significantly increased our knowledge of the ancient city of Rome at a crucial time, when so much evidence was being discovered and destroyed as the city was redeveloped. His accounts of current excavations in Rome and his history of excavations in the city from the Middle Ages, *Storia degli scavi di Roma* (*History of the Excavations of Rome;* 1902), brought him great renown, and many Victorian sitting rooms contained copies of his books, translated into English. Foreign topographers also worked in Rome; the German Karl Hülsen produced important books on the Forum Romanum (1904) and the overall topography of Rome (1907). The American Samuel Platner produced his topography of Rome in 1904; the

next year Thomas Ashby became director of the British School and produced a series of topographical works on Rome and the surrounding countryside over the succeeding quarter century. These two scholars collaborated on the *Topographical Dictionary of Ancient Rome* (1929), which is still widely used. In the same period the Istituto di Topografia Antica was founded by Giuseppe Lugli, a pupil of Lanciani's, and topography has remained a separate branch of archaeology to this day, with consequences both positive and negative.

South Italy and Sicily began to open up to serious archaeological inquiry with the end of the Kingdom of the Two Sicilies in 1860. The dominant personality in this regard was Paolo Orsi (1859–1935), one of the most significant figures in the history of Italian archaeology. After the disappointment of losing the chair of archaeology in Rome to Löwy in 1989, the young Orsi concentrated on the exploration of Sicily from his base at Syracuse, where he was inspector of antiquities. He initiated an incredible campaign of excavations at almost all of the type sites for Sicilian pre- and proto-history, turning from art to pursue stratigraphic excavations, typologies, and chronologies based on them, looking both at settlements and at the enormous cemeteries of Sicily. Orsi established the basic phases of Sicilian archaeology, which survive with little alteration to this day, and he did the first significant research on the interaction between Greek colonists and the indigenous populations. He worked mainly in Calabria during the first quarter of the twentieth century.

In southeastern Italy, the early excavations by the Duc de Luynes in the Temple of Apollo at Metaponto in 1828 represented an isolated phenomenon. Little systematic work was done before the beginning of the twentieth century. The growing importance of Taranto (site of the Spartan colony of Taras) as a naval base and industrial port stimulated development there, although a great deal was destroyed in the process. The fundamentally important late–Bronze Age site on the Scoglio del Tonno was completely erased by harbor works, although the superintendent, Q. Quagliati, was able to carry out a rescue excavation for four months. Only since 1990 have the enormous storerooms of the Taranto Museum been thoroughly researched, with the objects from the early excavations appearing in a series of well-illustrated volumes.

As the confident new Italian state emerged, overseas expeditions could be contemplated. Federico Halbherr began working at Gortyn in Crete in 1884, and with the foundation of the Italian mission to Crete in 1899 and then the Italian School of Archaeology in Athens in 1909, a number of other sites were explored. Italian work in Greece has concentrated on Crete and the Aegean Islands; Rhodes and Cos, occupied by Italy from 1912 on, were particular focuses of activity. Further work was carried out in Turkey and in Libya, particularly after the occupation of that country by Italian forces in 1914. The outbreak of World War I saw the exit of many of the German and Austrian professors from Italian universities, and since then foreigners have played less prominent roles in the history of Italian archaeology. In the 1920s Nationalism started to become an important force in Italian archaeology, particularly in excavations in the new national capital (*Roma Capitale*) and also in the new colonial possessions in North Africa and in what one might call the "cult of Romanness" (*Romanità*), exploited with flair by the Fascist administration (1922–1944). The Second Roman Empire set considerable sums of money aside for archaeological excavation and research. The Imperial Fora were thoroughly explored, and Augustus's famous Altar of Peace (Ara Pacis) was reconstructed, although in the wrong place and on the wrong axis. It has subsequently been demonstrated how this monument was a focal point of a symbolic landscape dominated by a huge sundial, the pointer of which was an Egyptian obelisk whose shadow penetrated the altar on the autumn equinox, Augustus's birthday. The wishes of the Fascist political masters often led to destructive haste in excavation. Huge areas of Ostia, the ancient port of Rome, were cleared by G. Calza between 1938 and 1942 for an international exhibition in Rome; although the city had been exceptionally well preserved by silt from the Tiber, most of the potentially useful information was lost in the rush. Given the concentration on Rome, the

study of Greek art and archaeology in these years could be an anti-Fascist statement, and the south Italian Società Magna Grecia, founded in 1920 and mainly interested in the Greek colonies of south Italy, became a focus of anti-Fascist activity. Its journal was closed down by the regime in 1932, and one of its leading members, Umberto Zanotti Bianco (doctor, sociologist, and southern statesman, as well as archaeologist) was confined by police to Paestum. This did, however, allow him to find and explore the great Sanctuary of Hera on the banks of the Sele River, together with Paola Zancani Montuoro. The methodologically rigorous excavation stood well apart from most of its Fascist-era contemporaries for its professionalism.

Classical archaeology had set down some solid positivist roots before the end of the nineteenth century, with figures such as Fiorelli, Boni, and Orsi prominent, but it moved instead in the direction of idealist, art-historical studies in the first half of the twentieth century. The importance in this trend to be attributed to the German Altertumswissenschaft, on the one hand, and the idealist thought of the philosopher Benedetto Croce, on the other, is still a matter of debate. Whatever the explanation, Italian classical archaeology and prehistory moved well apart in these years, and they have largely stayed apart since. The postwar years were dominated by the figure of Ranuccio Bianchi Bandinelli, who must have been a reluctant guide for Adolf Hitler in Rome on his official visit in 1938 (Hitler was reported to have been hugely impressed). Bianchi Bandinelli joined the Communist Party immediately after the war, and although he remained principally interested in art history, many of his students, still major figures today (e.g., Andrea Carandini, Filippo Coarelli, Mario Torelli), pursued more archaeological topics, often with an explicitly Marxist focus on social and economic history. This group had as its mouthpiece the Dialoghi di Archeologia (Archaeological Dialogues), founded in 1967, and efforts were made to bridge the gap with pre- and particularly proto-history, in which the leading figures were S. M. Puglisi and Renato Peroni.

The number of Italian archaeologists whose

Paolo Zancani Montuoro and Umberto Zanotti Bianco recover votive offerings from a sacred well in the Sanctuary of Hera at the mouth of the Sele River (6 kilometers north of Paestum), 1936. (Archivi Electa Milan)

work has been guided by political ideology has perhaps been overstated and in any case has declined in recent years. Anglophone theoretical archaeology cannot yet be said to have made a decisive impact. Some rather turgid theoretical works on Italian archaeology have appeared in English, at times accompanied by a disregard for the facts, which allows the doubters to feel their prejudices confirmed. However, foreign field methods have made quite an impact, their introduction into Italy sped by a number of foreign projects. In this context mention should be made of a series of surveys undertaken since the 1960s: by the British in the Tiber Valley (Ward-Perkins, Potter, and others) and the Marche (Barker), the Americans in Calabria (Ammerman) and Basilicata (Carter), and the Dutch in Puglia (Yntema and Burgers). Openness and generosity toward foreign teams has always characterized Italian archaeology, with notable benefits for all parties. A number of Italian universities have enthusiastically adopted information technology applications in archaeology, often backed by substantial grants from the European Union. Indeed, the economic and social benefits of a well-managed cultural heritage have become widely recognized recently in Europe in general and Italy in particular. A number of universities now offer programs in *Beni Culturali* (Cultural Heritage), with many students graduating to commercial cooperatives (often subsidized by the state in their early stages) that conduct excavations, organize museum displays, and develop cultural tourism. With a swelling corps of professionally trained archaeologists, able to apply their talents in universities, superintendencies, and private commercial enterprises, the future of Italian archaeology appears very bright.

Ted Robinson

See also Britain, Classical Archaeology; German Classical Archaeology; French Archaeology in the Classical World

References

Barbanera, M. 1998. *L'archeologia dei Italiani: Storia, metodo e orientamenti dell'archeologia classica in Italia.* Rome: Editori riuniti.

D'Agostino, B. 1991. "The Italian Perspective on Theoretical Archaeology." In *Archaeological Theory in Europe: the Last Three Decades,* 52–64. Ed. I. Hodder. London: Routledge.

de Grummond, N. T., ed. 1996. *An Encyclopedia of the History of Classical Archaeology.* Westport, CT: Greenwood Press.

Haskell, F., and N. Penny. 1982. *Taste and the Antique: the Lure of Classical Sculpture, 1500–1900.* New Haven: Yale University Press.

J. C. Harrington Medal in Historical Archaeology

In 1981, the SOCIETY FOR HISTORICAL ARCHAEOL-OGY (SHA) created the J. C. Harrington Medal, the highest award offered in the discipline. Medalists are selected for a lifetime of contributions to the field centered on scholarship. The first copy of the medal was struck in silver and was presented in January 1982 in a surprise ceremony to JEAN CARL (PINKY) HARRINGTON at the annual SHA conference in Philadelphia. All other copies are in antique bronze.

The list of recipients below reflects in a very general way the historical evolution of the discipline. To date, all medalists have been from North America (United States and CANADA), the region where the field has the deepest history going back to the 1930s, although the award is worldwide in scope. The names also in a vague fashion show the history of the discipline. The list includes researchers who were based in governmental agencies, museums, or similar institutions (COTTER, FONTANA, Harrington, HUME, KIDD, Quimby, South, and Woodward), transitional figures who started in such settings but spent much of their career in the academic world (Fairbanks, Jelks, and Smith), people who were always academics (Bass, DEETZ, Gilmore, Salwen, and Sprague), and, finally, Roberta S. Greenwood, the first archaeologist whose major contributions to scholarship were grounded in what has become

The J. C. Harrington Medal. The face bears the quotation "...beyond the strictly historical...," from one of Harrington's famous articles; the obverse shows the ground plans of three of the most famous sites Harrington and his wife, Virginia, excavated: Raleigh's 1585 Fort, Washington's 1754 Fort Necessity, and the nineteenth-century Mormon temple at Nauvoo. (Courtesy of the University of Pennsylvania Museum of Archaeology and Anthropology)

the primary support for the field since 1980, cultural resource management.

J. C. Harrington Medalists

Robert L. Schuyler

J. Paul Getty Museum
See Getty Museum

Jamestown, Virginia

Jamestown was the first North American community of European settlers to be the subject of a comprehensive, planned, and funded archaeological investigation. It was the first permanent English settlement in 1607, on Jamestown Island, Virginia, and is now part of Colonial National Historical Park. The archaeological work was begun in 1934 and was conducted in three campaigns, the last one continuing to 1997.

In 1934, work began with the objective of providing structure foundation plans for the newly established National Survey of Historic Sites and Buildings. This effort led to intractable differences between architects Henry Chandlee Forman and John Zaharov and archaeologists William John Winter, H. Summerfield Day, and Alonzo Pond. In 1936, order and firm direction were instituted by JEAN C. HARRINGTON, who was trained in both architecture and archaeology and had a grounding in data gathering. The project advanced under Harrington's effective direction with Civilian Conservation Corps labor until all work ended after the onset of World War II, which put an end to relief-supported archaeology in 1942. By then, Harrington's able staff of archaeologists, researchers, curators, and conservators had imposed orderly recording, data analysis, and conservation in the laboratory and had left a complete and extensive record of operations.

Investigations of Jamestown recommenced in 1954, with budgeted national park funds, under the direction of JOHN L. COTTER and with the assistance of Edward Jelks, Joel Shiner, Bruce Powell, Louis Caywood, and the curator, Paul Hudson. The deadline of 1957 was set, the 350th anniversary of the founding of Jamestown, for Cotter to compile all data into a single volume, *Archaeological Excavations at Jamestown, Virginia,* to be published in 1958 by the National Park Service.

In 1992, a five-year archaeological survey was established to extend archaeological sensing and testing over the entire island and to conduct an intensive search for archival data. This survey, conducted by a consortium of researchers from the College of William and Mary and Colonial WILLIAMSBURG, Inc., and funded by the National Park Service, was to bring Jamestown research up-to-date for the 400th anniversary in 2007.

John L. Cotter

See also Historical Archaeology

Japan

Each year from 1989 to 1999 more than 25,000 archaeological investigations took place in Japan, and the cost in the fiscal year of 1997 was over 132 billion yen (Center for Archaeological Operations 1999). The reasons for such scope and intensity of archaeological activities are the Japanese antiquarian tradition and the large number of amateur archaeologists, which creates a broadly based interest in archaeology; the assumed continuity of occupation of the archipelago and a strong affinity with those who left the archaeological remains; and the need to define the identity of Japanese people and their culture in today's global world. Archaeology in Japan, as in many other countries in East Asia, is

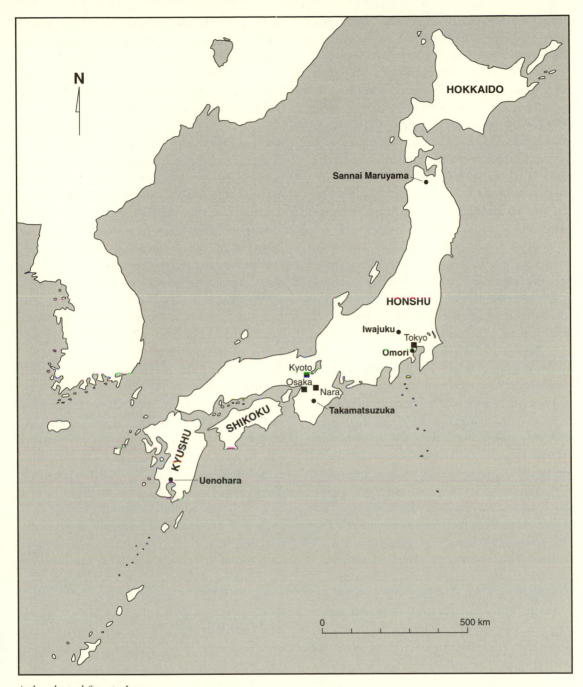

Archaeological Sites in Japan

national history that helps to define the present with reference to the past.

Premodern Interest in Archaeological Remains

Archaeological artifacts and features are mentioned in some of the earliest extant historical records (such as Kojiki 712, Fudoki 713, and Nihongi 720) that date to the early eighth century A.D. As elsewhere, these objects were attributed to supernatural origins, for example, stone arrowheads that often appeared after rainstorms were regarded as alarming signals from heaven that called for special rituals (Saito 1974, 1–12; Teshigawara 1988, 23, 26–28).

A rational approach to these remains began

during the Tokugawa period (A.D. 1603–1868) when peace prevailed and arts and scholarship flourished. One of the intellectual traditions out of which the "almost archaeology" of the Tokugawa period (Bleed 1986) grew was neo-Confucianism, which provided the ideological support for the hierarchical regime. For example, Arai Hakuseki (1656–1725), who served as an adviser to the Shogun government, came to believe that stone arrowheads were not the weapons of a heavenly army that had fallen from the sky but had been manufactured by human beings in ancient times.

Another tradition on which the "almost archaeology" of the Tokugawa period was based was the *kokugaku* ("national learning") school, which rejected the secular rationalism of Confucianism and turned instead to studies of such ancient texts as the *Kojiki*. It has been suggested (e.g., Yazawa 1985) that the concept of the ethnic homogeneity of the Japanese nation, which would be advocated by the national government in later years and which forms the theme of popular archaeology books today, originated with this group of scholars. The reverence for ancient emperors that the *kokugaku* promoted led to field studies of burial mounds *(kofun)*, with a view to their conservation and repair. Based on textual descriptions, but without firm evidence, many *kofun* were identified as imperial tombs. Although the identification had the positive effect of protecting the tombs from pot hunters, it also resulted in the current restriction on archaeologists' access to these remains.

Finally, there were a number of antiquarian groups active in Japan. One of these was the Rosekisha (Rock Fondlers' Club), of which the central figure was Seikitei Kiuchi (1728–1808), a wealthy official who lived near Kyoto. This group had several hundred members from various levels of society, including aristocrats, samurai, and Buddhist priests, who collected stones of unusual appearance, both natural and artifactual; held meetings to show their collections and compare notes; and published their findings with detailed descriptions and illustrations. These collectors represented the beginning of a broadly based amateur interest in archaeology, fostering the idea that archaeological inquiry was both fun and respectable. The club provided the necessary pool of human resources when, in response to threats to archaeological sites posed by the rapid economic development of the post–World War II years, a national system of salvage archaeology had to be put into place quickly.

Archaeology in the New Nation State

The political process that overthrew the Tokugawa Shogun government in 1868, reestablishing direct imperial rule (in theory at least), is referred to as the Meiji Restoration. The new Meiji government was committed to bringing Japan out of its isolation and to make it a modern nation state, and the introduction of archaeology as practiced in nineteenth-century Europe and America was a by-product of the arrival in Japan of scientists and technical experts whose special knowledge and skills were deemed useful by the new government. These experts included John Milne (1850–1913), an English seismologist who in 1876 became professor of geology at Tokyo University, where he remained until 1894; William Gowland (1843–1922), an English chemist who served as a consultant to the Mint from 1872 to 1888; and Edward Sylvester Morse (1838–1925), whose research trip to Japan in 1877 to study mollusks turned into a two-year appointment as professor of zoology at Tokyo University and who is generally credited, through his excavation of the Omori shellmound in Tokyo (Morse 1879a), as being the father of modern archaeology in Japan.

These scholars wrote books and articles about Japanese archaeology, most of which were published abroad in foreign languages and were read by very few Japanese. Nor did these men leave students who would become archaeologists. Being avocational archaeologists themselves, their impact on early Meiji Japan seems to have been through interaction with their Japanese counterparts, about whom it has been remarked "that there were more people interested in archaeology in Japan than anywhere else in the world" (Morse 1879b). Some examples of the interaction, where benefits seemed to have flowed in both directions, are summarized in English by Peter Bleed (1986) and Fumiko Ikawa-Smith (1982).

Although the introduction of the methods and concepts of western archaeology was accidental, the Meiji government took some deliberate measures to preserve the nation's archaeological heritage. It issued a series of edicts in 1871, 1874, and 1881 to help preserve ancient objects and to restrict the excavation of ancient tombs. It introduced the Law for the Preservation of Ancient Temples and Shrines in 1899, which was to become the basis for the 1950 Law for the Protection of Cultural Properties. The government also initiated, as early as 1871, the process that resulted in the establishment of the imperial museum (today's Tokyo National Museum) as the depository of the nation's heritage.

Archaeology as Science and Archaeology as History

The first generation of Japanese professional archaeologists was led by Shogoro Tsuboi (1863–1913), and he, along with several other science students of the time, formed the Anthropological Society of Tokyo (the precursor of the Anthropological Society of Nippon) in 1884. Having been sent to England to study anthropology (1889–1892), Tsuboi was appointed professor of anthropology within the College of Science at the University of Tokyo in 1893. Tsuboi is said to have emphasized the fact that he had not studied anthropology under Morse and made disparaging remarks about him (Goto 1977; Kudo 1977). Yet Tsuboi believed that anthropology should be considered part of zoology, and his position in what was to be called the *Jinshu ronso* ("race controversy") was the same as that of Morse.

The controversy was over whether the cord-marked *(jomon)* pottery from shellmounds was made by the ancestors of the aboriginal Ainu people who lived in northern Japan or by pre-Ainu inhabitants mentioned in Ainu legend. Morse, like Tsuboi, believed that the pottery makers were the pre-Ainu people while Heinrich von Siebold, John Milne, and Yoshikiyo Koganei (1859–1944) maintained that the pottery had been made by the Ainu. Koganei was a professor of anatomy at the University of Tokyo who had studied in Germany for five years (1880–1885). He based his arguments on an-thropometric data while Tsuboi, dismissing such data as useless, promoted the use of archaeological remains and ethnographic analogies. This preoccupation with the ethnic identity of the prehistoric pottery makers was to continue until Tsuboi's death.

This group of archaeologists was referred to as "the race archaeology school" or "the university school," in contrast to another group of archaeologists based at the Imperial Museum. Since the museum at that time employed scholars who continued the Tokugawa antiquarian tradition, the latter group was nicknamed "the museum school" or "the antiquarian school" (Terada 1980). Government policy at the time was to deposit the remains from prehistoric shellmounds in the Tokyo University Anthropology Department and those pertaining to the proto-historic and historic periods in the museum. The Anthropology Department of Tokyo University continued to be the major center for prehistoric research with a natural science orientation while more historically oriented work was conducted at the museum.

An additional major center for the latter kind of archaeology was created in 1913 when specialization in archaeology was formally recognized within the History Department of Kyoto University. Kosaku Hamada (1881–1938) was appointed professor of archaeology at Kyoto on his return from Europe in 1916. Most of his time in Europe (1913–1916) had been spent in England, where he studied with SIR WILLIAM MATTHEW FLINDERS PETRIE. Hamada's *Tsuron Kokogaku* (1922) is considered to be the first systematic statement in Japanese on the methods and theory of archaeology.

Stratigraphy, Typology, and Chronology

Hamada put archaeological methodology into practice at a series of excavations and in site reports, emphasizing the importance of stratigraphy and the need to define artifact types explicitly (e.g., Hamada 1918, 1919). At about the same time, Hikoshichiro Matsumoto (1919) used the stratigraphic principles of paleontology to argue that variations in ceramics were the result of chronological, rather than tribal, differences. From the 1920s until the end of World

War II in 1945, the separate disciplines of archaeology and anthropology were increasingly professionalized. In both cases, empirical evidence, based on stratigraphy, measurements, and typological classification and comparisons, were emphasized, with the ultimate goal of establishing a sound chronology.

It has been pointed out by many authors that the sociopolitical climate in the 1930s and 1940s favored such devotion to details rather than debate of any larger or more political issues. By this time, two kinds of prehistoric pottery, representing two separate cultures, were known. "Jomon," the Japanese translation of "cord marking" was used by Morse as a descriptive term for the Omori shellmound pottery, and it became established as the name for pottery found in similar shellmounds and, by extension, the name for the culture and the Stone-Age people who made it. A different kind of pottery, first recovered in Tokyo in 1884, was understood to belong to the bronze-using rice growers of the Yayoi period, a period that lasted a few centuries before and after the beginning of the Christian era. The occupation of the archipelago by these groups could not be easily reconciled with the official version of national history based on the eighth-century history texts of *Kojiki* and *Nihongi,* which attributed the founding of the imperial state to the descendant of the Sun Goddess in 660 B.C. Scholars who persisted in using archaeological data to interpret prehistory and proto-history ran the risk of losing their jobs, or even being imprisoned. Given those circumstances, the excessive empiricism of chronology building, with no apparent reference to "national history," was the prudent approach.

Early Post–World War II Years: Freedom of Inquiry

The end of World War II in 1945 meant the lifting of restrictions on historical inquiries, which made it possible to rewrite the history of Japan based entirely on archaeological evidence. The excavation of a Yayoi settlement site at Toro, near Shizuoka, between 1947 and 1950 dramatically underscored the new role that archaeology was to play in construction of national history in postwar Japan. Beginning shortly after the war, with severe shortages of such basic necessities such as shovels and food for the excavation crew, the Yayoi excavation was of a scale that had never occurred before in Japan, in terms of both expenditure and the number of participants. The investigation was both interdisciplinary and multi-institutional, with a large number of professionals and students and numerous local volunteers participating in unearthing the first rice paddies from an archaeological site as well as many artifacts, including wooden agricultural tools and building materials used for residential and storage structures. The excavation results were widely reported in the media, which raised the awareness of archaeology among the general public (Fawcett 1995). As W. Edwards (1991) notes, the image of the ancient, peaceful rice-growing village, recreated through archaeological investigation, supplied the new metaphor of continuity for the Japanese cultural and national identity, replacing the old mythological one made unacceptable by the war and defeat.

Another significant excavation took place in 1949, following the 1947 discovery of stone artifacts from an exposed Pleistocene formation by Aizawa Tadahiro (1926–1989), an amateur archaeologist, at Iwajuku about ninety kilometers north of Tokyo. The excavation by a team from the Meiji University provided the first convincing evidence for the existence of a Paleolithic period in Japan (Sugihara 1956). Within a few years of the excavation, the evidence for Paleolithic occupation had been confirmed at a number of other sites (Serizawa 1954; Serizawa and Ikawa 1960). The Iwajuku excavation not only added great temporal depth to the nation's history, it also gave the evidence a firm scientific basis: human occupation of the archipelago began in the geological past during the Ice Age, not in the mythical "age of gods."

The "scientific" approach during the early postwar years also involved making generalizations about the nature of past societies with reference to the theoretical framework of historical materialism. Seiichi Wajima (1909–1971) used the data and insights he had accumulated during the 1930s and 1940s to present an interpretative statement about prehistoric and proto-historic settlement systems, inferring social transformations that would have led to an early state with class differentiation (Wajima 1948). Similarly, Yukio Kobayashi (1911–1988) attributed class differentiation and state formation during the Kofun period (A.D. 300–600) to a rise in agricultural productivity that resulted from the widespread use of iron tools (Y. Kobayashi 1952). Such attempts at generalizations, however, were exceptional. For the majority of archaeologists, the particularist approach, with its emphasis on stratigraphic and typological evidence, which had been strongly entrenched in the 1930s, continued—and, in fact, continues to this day.

It was during this early postwar environment of freedom of speech, at a symposium in 1948, that Namio Egami first presented his thesis that the Japanese imperial family's ancestors had arrived relatively late in Japan and were the riders of horses from the continent (Egami 1962, 1964). Although this idea continues to be very popular with the reading public in Japan, and gained support of some foreign scholars (e.g., Hong 1988; Ledyard 1975), most Japanese archaeologists have dismissed it as being speculative and not worthy of serious rebuttal. It was only recently that one scholar decided to remedy the situation by presenting a counterargument (Sahara 1993).

International Contacts

Many Japanese archaeologists had studied abroad before World War II, and even during the early phase of the war, and a number of them had been engaged in archaeological investigations in the newly occupied areas of Manchuria, CHINA, Indochina, and the Pacific islands. As the war progressed they became increasingly isolated, and this isolation continued in the early postwar decades when foreign travel and the importation of foreign books were severely limited by economic conditions. Isolation ended gradually when a small number of young archaeologists were given the opportunity to study abroad and a few senior scholars were able to attend international meetings. International interaction has increased rapidly since the

A pottery jar from the Nagano-Ken jomon culture (3000–2000 B.C.), probably used for storing food (The Art Archive)

1970s, and Japanese archaeologists are once again engaged in overseas expeditions in places such as PERU, Alaska, and the Middle East.

Newly developed archaeological methods and techniques were introduced. Soon after radiocarbon DATING was developed, it was applied to samples from several Jomon sites, with occupation forces personnel and visiting U.S. archaeologists acting as intermediaries (Crane 1956; Crane and Griffin 1962; Libby 1951). These and subsequent determinations produced internally consistent, and surprisingly early dates, suggesting that Japanese pottery making was the earliest in the world.

A curious debate over the legitimacy of using radiocarbon dates in archaeological interpretation began. As noted elsewhere (Ikawa-Smith 1975, 15–17), the debate had little to do with the reliability of the method itself but instead concerned the integrity of archaeology as a historical discipline whose expertise resided in its ability to construct a chronology based on the study of artifacts rather than on technology. The resistance to the use of radiocarbon dating, however, was an exception. Other methods of dating were more readily accepted, as were various methods and techniques for identifying the sources of stones and clay, for enhancing artifact conservation, or for extracting more information about the use of plant and animal resources.

The periodical *Kokogaku to Shizen-kagaku* (Archaeology and Natural Science) was inaugurated in 1968, and the Association for Natural Science Approaches to Cultural Properties *(Bunkazai Kagakukai)* was formed in 1982. Its membership in 1998 was 830 and was evenly distributed between the natural sciences and humanities disciplines. A relatively large proportion of the work in this category is published in English (e.g., Akazawa 1980; Akazawa and Watanabe 1968; Koike 1979, 1986a, 1986b; Koike and Ohtaishi 1985; Matsui 1995, 1996; Minagawa and Akazawa 1992; Sato 1999; Yamamoto 1990).

In contrast to specific methods and techniques for analysis and conservation, theoretical and methodological concerns, particularly those of "the new archaeology" of the 1960s and 1970s, were not popular in Japan. This lack of interest was owing to North American archaeologists' concerns that archaeology should contribute to understanding the regularity of human behavior (Binford 1962; Longacre 1964; Taylor 1948)—a concern not shared by Japanese archaeologists. Archaeology in Japan had its roots in the Anglo-Saxon tradition of general anthropology in the 1880s, but early in the twentieth century it became a branch of history while *anthropology* came to mean biological anthropology alone.

One topical area in which the theoretical interests of both Japanese and Anglo-Saxon archaeologists overlapped was in the study of settlement systems. In the case of Japanese archaeology, however, this was the continuation of an interest that dated back to the 1930s (e.g., Akamatsu 1937; also see Sasaki 1999) rather than a new direction. North American settlement archaeology was presented in summary translations (Keally 1971) and its historical background explained (T. Kobayashi 1971). The large-scale excavations in Japan that began in the late 1960s provided an opportunity to put this methodology into practice. In the settlement pattern studies that developed as a result (T. Kobayashi 1980; T. Kobayashi, Oda, Hatori, and Suzuki 1971; Oda and Keally 1973), however, the emphasis was on the construction of settlement typology, in the empirical tradition of Japanese archaeology.

Economic Expansion and the Restructuring of Archaeological Operations

As the Japanese economy recovered through the 1950s and 1960s, large development projects threatened a number of archaeological sites. There was a popular movement to protect the nation's cultural heritage, which led to the revision of the 1950 Law for the Protection of Cultural Properties in 1959, making it mandatory to investigate sites, at the developer's expense, if the development project could not be modified to avoid site destruction. In the same year (1959), 345 notices of excavation were filed, of which 227 were purely academic in purpose and 118 were to investigate sites to be destroyed. The ratio of the academic to salvage excavations became reversed in 1963, when the former numbered 209 as opposed to 227 salvage operations. This reversal marked the beginning of a radical change in the nature and scope of archaeological operations in Japan.

Ten years later, in 1973, the figures were 203 academic versus 1,863 emergency excavation notices, for a total of 2,066. In 1983, academic excavations went down to 137 while emergency excavation notices shot up to 14,403. The figure for the fiscal year of 1997 was 409 academic excavations and 34,957 emergency operations, for a total of 35,366 notices (down from 41,555 in 1996, presumably the result of the economic situation). The total expenditure for emergency excavations in 1997–1998 was 132 billion yen (Center for Archaeological Operations 1975, 1989, 1999). The expenditure for the academic excavations is not known, but it would be miniscule by comparison.

Japan now has a very elaborate system of salvage archaeology involving three levels of government (national, prefectural, and municipal) and affiliated nonprofit corporations

(Barnes 1990; Fawcett 1990, 1995; Habu and Fawcett 1999; T. Kobayashi 1986; Pearson 1992; Tanaka 1984; Tsuboi 1986; and Tsude 1995). According to the Center for Archaeological Operations (1999), the total number of people employed at the prefectural and municipal levels as administrative archaeologists in 1997–1998 was 6,872. There must have been an additional hundred or so working at the national level with the Agency for Cultural Affairs and its institutes in Tokyo, Nara, and elsewhere.

Hiroshi Tsude (1995), using figures from a few years earlier, estimates the total number of archaeologists in Japan at 5,700, of which 300 are in academic departments, 700 in museums, and the remaining 4,700 (or 82 percent) engaged in the administration of cultural resources management. In spite of their large numbers, cultural resources management archaeologists are always pressed for time, starting one operation after the other, conducting excavations, and preparing mandatory excavation reports, which are technically excellent but purely descriptive. They have little time to fully digest their findings and formulate any syntheses. Nor could the very small number of "academic" archaeologists keep up with the rapidly accumulating data and come up with syntheses and theoretical formulations. Japanese archaeologists are drowning in a flood of data.

The Archaeology of National Origins

The allocation of such huge resources to archaeological activities is feasible in Japan because of the high level of interest in the discipline by the tax-paying public. Spectacular results of excavations are widely reported on television and in newspapers and attract a large number of visitors to the sites. The Sannai Maruyama site, a very large Jomon period site at the northern end of Honshu, dating to about 3500–2000 B.C., featuring six enormous wooden structures and about 700 pit-house remains, received over 1 million visitors between 1994 and 1997 (Habu and Fawcett 1999). At the opposite end of the archipelago, some 160,000 visitors went to the Uenohara site to see evidence of settled village life as early as 9,500 years ago when the site was opened to

the public over the summer holidays in 1997 (*Weekly Asahigraph* 1997, 17). These on-site interpretation events are some of the measures Japanese archaeologists have taken to keep the public informed of the significance of their activities, but they are, in fact, responding to the public's demand for information about the nation's past.

Public interest in archaeology in Japan is the legacy of long-term antiquarianism, but the level of the interest has risen in recent years, partly because of a series of spectacular finds, starting with the 1972 discovery of a painted tomb of Takamatsuzuka. There is also an increasing and perceived need for the Japanese people to define their distinctiveness as Japan takes its place the among the nations of the world. The interest in archaeology grew hand in hand with the growth of the discourse called *Nihonjinron* ("theory about the Japanese") and *Nihonbunkaron* ("theory about Japanese culture"), both of which purported to explain what was distinctly Japanese. Archaeological finds became relevant within this context because archaeological remains, even those of the 9,500-year-old Jomon villagers, are perceived as the remains of Japanese ancestors. A large number of archaeology books are published, some with beautiful photographic illustrations and others in convenient pocketbook format, bearing titles and subtitles like "The Origins of the Japanese," "Japan's Cultural Roots," and "Where Did the Japanese Come From?"

Archaeology thrives in Japan because it is perceived not as an abstract academic exercise but as a means to elucidate the nation's past, as a substantial contribution to increasing the Japanese peoples' understanding of who they are. In Japan, archaeology is national history, helping to define the present with reference to the past.

Fumiko Ikawa-Smith

References

Akamatsu, Keisuke. 1937. "Kodai shuraku no seisei to hatten" [Process of Formation and Development of Prehistoric and Early Historic Settlements]. *Keizai Hyoron* 4, no. 2. Reprinted in *Kodai Shuraku no Keisei to Hatten Katei,* 141–207. Tokyo: Akashi Shoten, 1990.

Akazawa, Takeru. 1980. "Fishing Adaptation of Prehistoric Hunter-Gatherers at the Nittano Site, Japan." *Journal of Archaeological Science* 7: 325–344.

Akazawa, Takeru, and Hitoshi Watanabe. 1968. "Restoration of Body Zize of Jomon Shell-mound Fish (Preliminary Report)." In *Proceedings of the VIIIth International Congress of Anthropological and Ethnological Science, Tokyo-Kyoto,* 3:193–197.

Barnes, Gina L. 1990. "The Origins of Bureaucratic Archaeology in Japan." *Journal of the Hong Kong Archaeological Society* 12: 183–196.

Binford, Lewis R. 1962. "Archaeology as Anthropology." *American Antiquity* 28: 217–225.

Bleed, Peter. 1986. "Almost Archaeology: Early Archaeological Interest in Japan." In *Windows on the Japanese Past: Studies in Archaeology and Prehistory,* 57–67. Ed. R. Pearson, G. L. Barnes, and K. L. Hutterer. Ann Arbor: Center for Japanese Studies, University of Michigan.

Center for Archaeological Operations. 1975. *Maizo Bunkazai Nyusu* [CAO News] no. 2. Nara National Institute for Cultural Properties Research.

———. 1989. *Maizo Bunkazai Nyusu* [CAO News] no. 66. Nara National Institute for Cultural Properties Research.

———. 1999. *Maizo Bunkazai Nyusu* [CAO News] no. 89. Nara National Institute for Cultural Properties Research.

Crane, H. R. 1956. "University of Michigan Radiocarbon Dates I." *Science* 124: 671.

Crane, H. R., and J. B. Griffin 1962. "University of Michigan Radiocarbon Dates III." *Radiocarbon* 4: 45.

Edwards, W. 1991. "Buried Discourse: The Toro Archaeological Site and Japanese National Identity in the Early Postwar Period." *Journal of Japanese Studies* 17: 1–23.

Egami, Namio. 1962. "Light on Japanese Culture Origins from Historical and Archaeology and Legend." In *Japanese Culture,* 11–16. Ed. R. J. Smith and R. K. Beardsley. New York: Wenner-Gren Foundation for Anthropological Research.

———. 1964. "The Formation of the People and the Origins of the State in Japan." *Memoirs of the Toyo Bunko* 23: 35–70.

Fawcett, Clare P. 1990. "A Study of the Socio-Political Context of Japanese Archaeology." Ph.D. dissertation, McGill University, Montreal.

———. 1995. "Nationalism and Postwar Japanese Archaeology. In *Nationalism, Politics, and the Practice of Archaeology,* 232–246. Ed. P. L. Kohl and C. Fawcett. Cambridge: Cambridge University Press.

Goto, Kazutami. 1977. "Morse to kaizuka kenkyu" [Morse and Shellmound Research]. *Kokogaku Kenkyusu* 24, nos. 3–4: 114–121.

Habu, Junko, and Clare Fawcett. 1999. "Jomon Archaeology and the Representation of Japanese Origins." *Antiquity* 73: 587–593.

Hamada, Kosaku. 1918. "Kawachi Kou sekkijidai iseki hakkutsu hokoku" [Report of the Excavation of the Stone Age Site at Kou, Province of Kawachi]. *Kyoto Teikoku Daigaku Bunka Daigaku Kokogaku Kenkyushitsu Hokoku,* no. 2.

———. 1919. "Yayoi-shiki doki keishiki bunrui zuroku" [Catalog of the Classification of Yayoi Pottery]. *Kyoto Teikoku Daigaku Bunka Daigaku Kokogaku Kenkyushitsu Hokoku,* no. 3.

———. 1922. *Tsuron Kokogaku.* Tokyo: Daitokaku.

Hong, Wontack. 1988. *Relationship between Korea and Japan in Early Period: Paekche and Yamato Wa.* Seoul: Pan Korea Book Corporation.

Ikawa-Smith, Fumiko. 1975. "Japanese Ancestors and Palaeolithic Archaeology." *Asian Perspectives* 18.

———. 1982. "Co-traditions in Japanese Archaeology." *World Archaeology* 13: 296–309.

Keally, Charles T. 1971. "Setorumento arkeoroji" [Settlement Archaeology]. *Shinano* 23, no. 2: 200–209.

Kobayashi, Tatsuo. 1971. "Amerika kokogaku ni okeru 'setorumento akeroji' seiritsu no haikei" [Background of the Formation of "Settlement Archaeology" in American Archaeology]. *Shinano* 23, no. 2: 195–200.

———. 1980. "Jomon jidai no shuraku" [Settlements during the Jomon Period]. *Kokushigaku* 110–111: 1–17.

———. 1986. "Trends in Administrative Salvage Archaeology." In *Windows on the Japanese Past: Studies in Archaeology and Prehistory,* 491–496. Ed. R. J. Pearson, G. L. Barnes, and K. L. Hutterer. Ann Arbor: Center for Japanese Studies, University of Michigan.

Kobayashi, Tatsuo, Shizuo Oda, Kenzo Hatori, and Masao Suzuki. 1971. "Nogawa sendoki jidai iseki no kenkyu" [Study of the Preceramic Site, Nogawa]. *Kaiyonki Kenkyu* 10, no. 4: 231–252.

Kobayashi, Yukio. 1952. "Kofun jidai bunka no seiin ni tsuite" [Formation of the Kofun-Period Culture]. In *Nippon Minzoku* [Japanese People]. Tokyo: Iwanami shoten.

Koike, Hiroko. 1979. "Seasonal Dating and Valve-paring Technique in Shell Midden Analysis." *Journal of Archaeological Science* 6, no. 1: 63–74.

———. 1986a. "Jomon Shell Mounds and Growth-line Analysis of Molluscan Shells." In *Windows on the Japanese Past: Studies in Archaeology and Prehistory,* 267–278. Ed. R. J. Pearson, G. L. Barnes, and K. L. Hutterer. Ann Arbor: Center for Japanese Studies, University of Michigan.

———. 1986b. "Prehistoric Hunting Pressure and Paleobiomass: An Environmental Reconstruction and Archaeozoological Analysis of a Jomon Shellmound Area." In *Prehistoric Hunter-Gatherers in Japan,* 27–53. Ed. T. Akazawa and C. M. Aikens. Tokyo: University of Tokyo Press.

Koike, Hiroko, and N. Ohtaishi. 1985. "Prehistoric Hunting Pressure Estimated by the Age Composition of Excavated Sika Deer *(Cervus nippon)* Using the Annual Layer of Tooth Cement." *Journal of Archaeological Science* 12: 443–456.

Kudo, Masaki. 1977. "Tsuboi Shogoro to sono shuhen" [Tsuboi Shogoro and His Contemporaries]. *Kokogaku Kenkyu* 24, nos. 3–4: 190–208.

Ledyard, G. 1975. "Galloping along with the Horseriders: Looking for the Founders of Japan." *Journal of Japanese Studies* 1: 217–254.

Libby, W. F. 1951. "Chicago Radiocarbon Dates II." *Science* 114: 295.

Longacre, William A. 1964. "Archaeology as Anthropology: A Case Study." *Science* 144: 1454–1455.

Matsui, Akira. 1995. "Postglacial Hunter-Gatherers in the Japanese Archipelago: Marine Adaptations." In *Man and Sea in the Mesolithic,* 327–334. Ed. Anders Fischer. Oxford: Oxbow Books. Monograph 53.

———. 1996. "Archaeological Investigations of Anadromous Salmonids Fishing in Japan." *World Archaeology* 27, no. 3: 444–460.

Matsumoto, Hikoshichiro. 1919. "Miyatojima Satohama oyobi Kesen-gun Osozawa kaizuka no doki" [Pottery from the Satohama on Miyatojima and from Osozawa Shellmound in Kesen County]. *Gendai no Kagaku* 7, nos. 5–6. Reprinted in *Ronshu Nippon Bunka no Kigen,* 1:117–216. Ed. Yukio Kobayashi. 1970.

Minagawa, Masao, and Takeru Akazawa. 1992. "Dietary Patterns of Japanese Jomon Hunter-Gatherers: Stable Nitrogen and Carbon Isotope Analyses of Human Bones." In *Pacific Northeast Asia in Prehistory: Hunter-Fisher-Gatherers, Farmers,* and *Sociopolitical Elites,* 59–67. Ed. Aikens, C. Melvin, and Song Nai Rhee. Pullman: Washington State University Press.

Morse, Edward S. 1879a. "Shell Mounds of Omori." *Memoirs of the Science Department, University of Tokio, Japan.* Vol. 1, pt. 1.

———. 1879b. "Traces of an Early Race in Japan." *Popular Science Monthly* 14: 257–266. Reproduced in part in Japanese translation in *Ronshu Nippon Bunka no Kigen 5: Nippon Jinshuron, Gengogaku,* 54–60. Ed. Jiro Ikeda and Susumu Ono. Tokyo: Heibonsha, 1973.

Oda, Shizuo, and Charles T. Keally. 1973. *Musashino Koen Site.* Tokyo: Nogawa Excavation Project, Tokyo Metropolitan Government.

Pearson, Richard. 1992. "The Nature of Japanese Archaeology." *Asian Perspectives* 31, no. 2: 115–127.

Sahara, Makoto. 1993. *Kibaminzoku wa Konakatta* [Horseriders Did Not Come]. Tokyo: NHK Books.

Saito, Tadashi. 1974. *Nippon Kokogakushi* [The History of Japanese Archaeology]. Tokyo: Yoshikawa Kobunkan.

Sasaki, Ken'ichi. 1999. "A History of Settlement Archaeology in Japan." *Journal of East Asian Archaeology* 1: 324–352.

Sato Yoichiro. 1999. "Origin and Dissemination of Cultivated Rice in Asia." In *Interdisciplinary Perspectives on the Origins of the Japanese,* 143–153. Ed. Keiichi Omoto. Kyoto: International Research Center for Japanese Studies.

Serizawa, Chosuke. 1954. "Kanto oyobi Chubu chiho ni okeru Mudoki bunka no shumatsu to Jomon bunka no hassei ni kansuru yosatsu" [Preliminary Observation on the End of the Nonceramic Culture and the Beginning of Jomon Culture in Kanto and Chubu Districts]. *Sundai Shigaku* 4: 65–106.

Serizawa, Chosuke, and Fumiko Ikawa. 1960. "The Oldest Archaeological Materials from Japan." *Asian Perspectives* 2, no. 2: 1–39.

Sugihara, Sosuke. 1956. *Gumma-ken Iwajuku hakken no sekki bunka* [Stone Age Remains Found at Iwajuku, Gumma Prefecture]. Reports of the Research by Faculty of Literature, Archaeology I. Meiji University.

Tanaka, Migaku. 1984. "Japan." In *Approaches to the Archaeological Heritage,* 82–88. Ed. H. Cleere. Cambridge: Cambridge University Press.

Taylor, Walter W. 1948. *A Study of Archaeology.* Memoir of the American Anthropological Association, no. 69.

Terada, Kazuo. 1980. *Nippon no Jinruigaku* [Anthropology in Japan]. Tokyo: Shisakusha.

Teshigawara, Akira. 1988. *Nippon Kokogakushi* [The History of Japanese Archaeology]. Tokyo: University Tokyo Press.

Tsuboi, Kiyotari. 1986. "Problems Concerning the Preservation of Archaeological Sites in Japan." In *Windows on the Japanese Past: Studies in Archaeology and Prehistory*, 481–490. Ed. R. J. Pearson, G. L. Barnes, and K. L. Hutterer. Ann Arbor: Center for Japanese Studies, University of Michigan.

Tsude, Hiroshi. 1995. "Archaeological Theory in Japan." In *Theory in Archaeology, a World Perspective*, 298–311. Ed. Peter J. Uko. London and New York: Routledge.

Wajima, Seiichi. 1948. "Genshi shuraku no kosei" [Organization of Prehistoric Settlements]. In *Nihon Rekishigaku Koza* [Lectures in Japanese History], 1–32. Ed. Tokyo Daigaku Rekishigaku Kenkyukai. Tokyo.

Weekly Asahigraph. 1997. No. 3950 (26 December). Tokyo: Asahi Shimbunsha.

Yamamoto, Kaoru. 1990. "Space-Time Analysis of Raw Material Utilization for Stone Implements of the Jomon Culture in Japan." *Antiquity* 64, no. 245: 867–888.

Yazawa, Kosuke. 1985. "Taminzoku shakai to shiteno Nippon" [Japan as a Multiethnic Society]. *Koza Nippon no Rekishi* 13: 25–47.

Jarmo

Most famous as the focus of ROBERT BRAIDWOOD's research into the history of the DOMESTICATION OF PLANTS AND ANIMALS, Jarmo is a Neolithic village site in the Zagros Mountains of Iraqi Kurdistan. The site was occupied for several centuries between 9000 and 8000 B.P., and the careful excavation of the site by Braidwood and his multidisciplinary team between 1948 and 1954 made it possible for archaeologists to examine evidence of plant and animal remains as well as more traditional information, such as artifacts and architecture.

Tim Murray

See also Mesopotamia

Jefferson, Thomas (1743–1826)

Statesman, president of the United States of America, diplomat, scientist, revolutionary, and architect, Thomas Jefferson was born on the frontier in Virginia, the son of a surveyor/explorer who had married into one of the best families in the district. He had a classical education and from 1760 to 1762 studied mathematics, science, and philosophy at the College of William and Mary. Jefferson began to study law and was admitted to the bar in 1767, working as a successful lawyer until the beginning of the War of Independence in 1776, when he began a full-time career in politics.

Jefferson had been left substantial property by his father, on which he began to design and build the mansion of Monticello. In 1770 he was appointed county lieutenant and in 1773 surveyor of the county, and he soon became involved in local politics, being elected as a member of the county government and contributing to the framing of local legislation. He was elected by the Virginia convention to serve in Congress and was then elected along with others to draw up the Declaration of Independence. At the age of 33 Jefferson helped to found a new nation.

After some time as governor, congressman, and American diplomat in Paris, Jefferson became the first secretary of state under the constitution from 1790 until he retired briefly to Monticello in 1793, vice-president in 1795, and president from 1800 until 1809, with ALBERT GALLATIN as his secretary of the treasury. The high point of his administration was the Louisiana Purchase, which added impetus to the proposed Lewis and Clark expedition. Jefferson was passionately interested in and supportive of this expedition, and wrote the biography of the explorer Meriwether Lewis, who had been his private secretary.

Jefferson was also involved in the intellectual life of the new nation. The American Philosophical Society (APS), based on the model of the Royal Society of London, had been founded in 1743 by a small group of eminent Americans. Under the presidency of Thomas Jefferson (1797–1815) the society became an intellectual influence on post-Revolutionary and newly na-

Thomas Jefferson (Ann Ronan Picture Library)

tionalist America, a de facto scientific adviser to the government. The society wrote the charter for the government's great western exploratory expedition led by Lewis and Clark, and later contributed to the Lond Expedition of 1819 and the Wilkes Expeditions of 1838 and 1842, both of which were anthropological in objective. Under Jefferson's presidency the APS took an interest in archaeology, linguistics, and anthropology.

Jefferson was a pioneer in the study of archaeology, paleontology, ethnology, geography, and botany in America and he amassed a collection of Indian vocabularies that were unfortunately lost. Through the APS Jefferson became associated with the important scientific societies of Europe and America. He was elected in 1801 to the Institute of France in recognition of his reputation in FRANCE as an intellectual—and not as a politician. He corresponded with a great many scientists across the world and across America and wanted the best of foreign knowledge to be available to Americans. After his final retirement from politics he helped to found the University of Virginia and he established a school of builders in Virginia and tried to establish formal instruction in architecture.

He kept up with his voluminous correspondence and he continued to advise his political colleagues. To reduce his debts Jefferson sold his collection of some 10,000 books to the new Library of Congress.

Tim Murray

Jenné and Jenné-jeno

Jenné and Jenné-jeno (ancient Jenné) are successive tell settlements in the upper inland Niger Delta of Mali, and together, they span over two millennia of continuous occupation on the floodplain. Both have been designated World Heritage Sites by the United Nations Educational, Scientific, and Cultural Organization. The forty-five-hectare tell of Jenné is inhabited today by a population of about 10,000.

Historical sources, such as the account of the French explorer Réné Caillié (1830) and local *tarikhs* (histories written in Arabic), detail the central role that Jenné has played in the commercial activities of the western Sudan during the last 500 years. In the famous "golden trade of the Moors," gold from mines far to the south was transported overland to Jenné, then transshipped on broad-bottom canoes (pirogues) to Timbuktu, and then sent by camel to markets in North Africa and Europe (Bovill 1968; Levtzion 1973). Leo Africanus (1896) reported in 1512 that the extensive boat trade on the middle Niger involved massive amounts of cereals and dried fish shipped from Jenné to provision arid Timbuktu. Today, the stunning mud architecture of Jenné in distinctive Sudanic style is a legacy of the settlement's early trade ties with North Africa.

Systematic archaeological research at Jenné began in 1994 with a coring project (McIntosh et al. 1996) and continued with excavations in 1998 on the proposed site of the new Jenné museum. Cultural deposits descended over six meters and began with material dating to the early second millennium A.D.

Three kilometers to the southeast, the thirty-three-hectare mound of Jenné-jeno attracted little attention during the colonial period despite its thick surface carpet of broken pottery and numerous mud brick wall foundations. Scientific excavations in the 1970s and

1980s revealed that Jenné-jeno was founded ca. 250 B.C. by iron-using peoples who cultivated rice, millet, and sorghum; herded stock; and engaged in fishing and hunting (S. K. McIntosh 1995; S. K. McIntosh and R. McIntosh 1980). The deposits dating to this early period are almost six meters down from the highest part of the mound.

Careful evaluation of deposits from numerous other excavation units at Jenné-jeno and two other nearby sites provided evidence for the rapid growth of the mounds throughout the first millennium A.D. Jenné-jeno itself reached its maximum extent of over seventy-five acres by A.D. 850. Intensive surface survey of the mounds located within a four-kilometer radius of Jenné (sixty-nine in all) indicated that the majority were occupied by at least A.D. 800–1000, creating a remarkable concentration of population (10,000–27,000 people) within the integrated multisite system known as the Jenné-jeno urban complex.

Those discoveries marked the end of assumptions that urban settlements and long-distance trade in West Africa were secondary to the development of the trans-Saharan trade by North African Arabs after the ninth century. Settlement at Jenné-jeno declined after A.D. 1200, and the settlement was completely abandoned by A.D. 1400. Most of the nearby mounds followed the same pattern. Their demise was concomitant with the period of early settlement documented at Jenné, but the reasons for this shift in settlement location are not yet understood.

Susan McIntosh

See also Africa, Sahara; Africa, Sudanic Kingdoms
References
Africanus, Leo. 1896. *The History and Description of Africa.* Ed. R. Brown; trans. J. Pory. 3 vols. London.
Bovill, E. W. 1968. *The Golden Trade of the Moors.* 2d ed. Oxford: Oxford University Press.
Caillié, R. 1830. *Travels through Central Africa to Timbuktu and across the Great Desert to Morocco: Performed in the Years 1824–1828.* 2 vols. London.
Levtzion, N. 1973. *Ancient Ghana and Mali.* London: Methuen.
McIntosh, R., P. Sinclair, T. Togola, M. Petrén, S. K. McIntosh. 1996. "Exploratory Archaeology at Jenné and Jenné-jeno, Mali." *Sahara* 8: 19–28.
McIntosh, S. K., ed. 1995. *Excavations at Jenné-jeno, Hambarketolo, and Kaniana: The 1981 Season.* University of California Monographs in Anthropology no. 20. Berkeley: University of California Press.
McIntosh, S. K., and R. J. McIntosh. 1980. *Prehistoric Investigations in the Region of Jenné, Mali.* Cambridge Monographs in African Archaeology no. 2. 2 vols. Oxford: B.A.R.

Jericho
See Israel; Jordan; Kenyon, Kathleen Mary; Syro-Palestinian and Biblical Archaeology

Jerusalem
See Israel; Kenyon, Kathleen Mary; Syro-Palestinian and Biblical Archaeology

Johnny Ward's Ranch
In late 1959 and early 1960, volunteer members of the Arizona Archaeological and Historical Society carried out excavations on eleven Sundays in a period site in southern Arizona designated Ariz. EE: 5:6 in the Arizona State Museum survey system. The efforts were directed by archaeologists BERNARD L. FONTANA and J. Cameron Greenleaf, but of the fifty-eight people who volunteered their efforts, only four or five had had previous archaeological experience.

Fontana had chosen the site because he mistakenly believed it represented the adobe ruins of San Ignacio de Sonoitac, a mid-eighteenth-century mission visiting station built and administered by Jesuit missionaries before their expulsion from New Spain in 1767. Excavations and subsequent documentary research indicated the site was instead one that had been occupied between 1859 and 1903 and had served variously as a ranch for the family of Johnny Ward and other English-speaking settlers, headquarters for a mining and milling company, a house and store, and a dwelling for Chinese gardeners. Not wanting to disappoint the volunteers

Johnny Ward's Ranch (January 16, 1961), Patagonia, Arizona. Excavation of this late nineteenth-century site by Bernard L. Fontana, J. Cameron Greenleaf, and members of the Arizona Archaeological and Historical Society helped to initiate an expansion in the type and age of historic sites worked on in the American West. (Bernard Fontana)

who had worked so diligently on the excavation, Fontana and Greenleaf analyzed the artifacts, nearly all of them mass produced and machine-made, as carefully as if they had been hand-crafted objects of the pre-Industrial Revolution. The results of their analyses were published as "Johnny Ward's Ranch: A Study in Historic Archaeology" in the society's journal, *The Kiva* (28, no. 12, October-December 1962).

The study was the first in the annals of U.S. archaeology to take seriously the products resulting from the ideas of interchangeable parts and mass production by machines. Pioneering descriptive and historical studies of square-cut nails, wire nails, tin cans, metallic cartridges, ironstone ceramics, machine-blown bottles, and similar artifacts were presented. The report became the first to give credence and respectability to what came to be labeled "tin can archaeology," and as such it became a landmark in the history of archaeology in the United States.

Bernard L. Fontana

See also United States of America, Prehistoric Archaeology

Jordan

The area known today as Jordan (Transjordan) lies between Palestine (Cisjordan or modern ISRAEL and the Palestinian Territories) and MESOPOTAMIA and is intimately connected to these surrounding regions of the Near East, in both geography and history (see map). This brief survey of the development of archaeology in Jordan will outline the major phases of exploration and the relationship of work in this region to the broader development of archaeology in the Middle East.

The Earliest Phase of Exploration, 1805–1918

"Who that has ever traveled in Palestine has not longed to cross the Jordan valley to those mysterious hills that close ever eastward view with their long horizontal outline, their overshadowing height, their deep purple shade?"

With these words from his 1856 travel log, Arthur Stanley, the dean of Westminster in London, summed up the relationship between Palestine and Transjordan for the earliest ex-

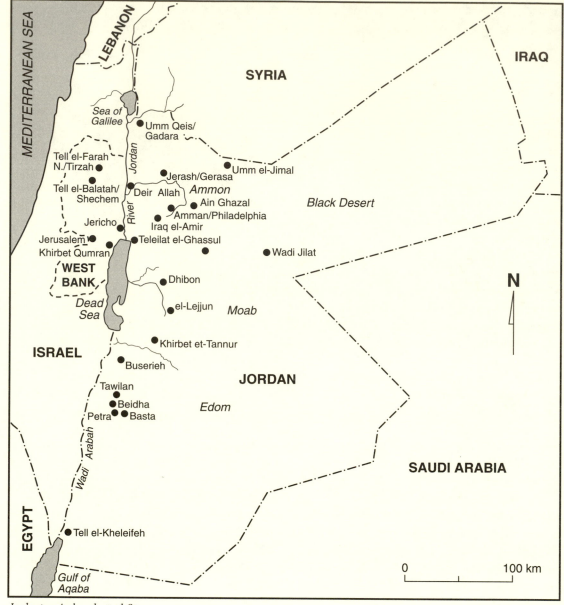

Jordanian Archaeological Sites

plorers of the Levant. At the time of his visit Transjordan was a place less traveled, largely unknown, and poorly explored, yet it was of great interest primarily due to the connections between the two regions in historical and biblical accounts. Interest in the ancient Near East was growing, and discoveries in both Palestine and MESOPOTAMIA were prompting scholars to explore the history of the region in the contexts of the biblical and classical references.

Exploration began somewhat later in Transjordan than in Cisjordan or Palestine, however,

and the country received only occasional attention from scholars and travelers during the earliest part of the nineteenth century. The first explorations in Transjordan were undertaken largely by antiquarians and biblical scholars intent upon recording sites of historical or biblical significance. Explorers such as the German Ulrich Jasper Seetzen, who visited between 1805 and 1807, and the Swiss Johann Ludwig Burckhardt, who visited between 1810 and 1812, were among the first to record some of the great sites of classical antiquity, including Jerash/Gerasa and Amman/Philadelphia (Seetzen) and Petra (Burckhardt). Others followed, including the Americans Edward Robinson and Eli Smith, who, though their visits were brief, are considered to be the fathers of historical geography in the region. Unfortunately, their extensive work in Palestine (1837–1838, 1851–1852) was not duplicated east of the Jordan River.

One of the reasons why comparatively little exploration was undertaken through the 1800s was the political instability of the region. The population was a combination of settlers living in villages and Bedouin tribes, although under Ottoman Turkish rule, there was little protection or rule outside the more densely populated regions. The activities of the Bedouin, who were occasionally aggressive toward the villages and travelers, made exploration difficult and often dangerous. Foreigners' visits to Transjordan were therefore sporadic and usually directed to specific known sites, since their primary focus was on the "Holy Land" (Cisjordan or Palestine) and its historical geography.

By the mid-nineteenth century Ottoman dominance of the region began to increase, and Ottoman governors were eventually appointed at Irbid to oversee the district of Ajlun (1851) and at Salt to oversee the central district of Belqa (1868). One of the main reasons for this growing political dominance of Transjordan was the need to control the Haj route for Islamic pilgrims to make their way to Mecca between Damascus and the Hejaz. And one of its outcomes was an increase in the exploration of the region by westerners.

The Development of Jordanian Archaeology during the British Mandate, 1918–1946

After World War I came to a close, the Sykes-Picot agreement established a British mandate in Palestine and Transjordan in 1918, and the area came under the control of the British Empire. Appropriately, the authorities established a department of antiquities in Palestine in 1920, led by the English archaeologist JOHN GARSTANG, and three years later a department of antiquities was set up in Amman to oversee the region of Transjordan.

With the advent of British rule, archaeologists found the territory more accessible and safer to explore, and during the mandate period they laid some of the major groundwork for our understanding of the archaeology and history of these regions. Research was not, however, restricted to British interests: several international schools, including some from FRANCE, Germany, and the United States, carried out significant projects in the southern Levant in these years.

A great deal of the work was concentrated in Palestine, but some was also conducted at various major sites of classical antiquity in Transjordan, including Amman, Jerash/Gerasa, and Petra. At Petra the earliest systematic excavations were undertaken in 1929 by George Horsfield, the first director of the Transjordan Department of Antiquities. Horsfield, a student of Garstang, worked on several of the major tombs of Petra, including the Palace Tomb, al-Kazneh, the Urn Tomb, and the Tomb of the Roman Soldier. In 1924 he also initiated the first work at Gerasa/Jerash, where he devoted considerable energy to clearing and reconstructing several of the site's major monuments, including the south and north theaters, the Propylaeum of the Temple of Artemis, and the Nymphaeum. Four years later he was joined by an Anglo-American expedition from the British School of Archaeology in Jerusalem and Yale University, led by John Crowfoot; in 1930 a team from the AMERICAN SCHOOLS OF ORIENTAL RESEARCH (ASOR), under the direction of Clarence Fisher and later Nelson Glueck (in 1933 and 1934), also began to work with Horsfield. At Amman work on the citadel was carried out by the Italian Archaeological Mission beginning in 1927 and concluding in the 1930s, and from 1936 on other parts of the city were studied by the director of the Transjordan Department of Antiquities, G. Lankester Harding. Overall, these excavations revealed the exceptional state of preservation of many of the sites of classical antiquity. Efforts were begun to preserve them from the destruction that would ensue from development and expanding populations in the region.

Other notable projects in the British mandate period included the discovery of Teleilat el-

View from the colonnaded street of the rock-cut palace and Corinthian Tombs at Petra (©Roger Wood/CORBIS)

Ghassul, one of the key sites of the Chalcolithic period in the southern Levant, near the shores of the Dead Sea. Work at this site by Alexis Mallon and Robert Koeppel of the Pontifical Biblical Institute (PBI) in Jerusalem between 1929 and 1938 revealed, perhaps for the first time, the extent of the richness of Jordan's prehistoric archaeology.

The work of Nelson Glueck during his terms as director of the American Schools of Oriental Research Institute in Jerusalem (1932–1933, 1936–1940, and 1942–1947) had a lasting impact upon Transjordan. Glueck, a student of the great U.S. archaeologist WILLIAM F. ALBRIGHT, was one of the pioneers of archaeological survey in Transjordan. Between 1932 and 1947 he surveyed more than a thousand sites, including many that were previously unknown. As a student of biblical history, Glueck particularly focused upon the biblical kingdoms of Ammon, Moab, and Edom. His extensive survey work included mapping, photography, and site collections, and it set the precedent for all subsequent archaeological surveys in the region. His four-volume report entitled *Explorations in Eastern Palestine* (1934–1951) is still consulted extensively by those working in Jordan, and although it contained some errors, it was, in general, remarkably accurate. His two popularizations of the archaeology of the region, *The Other Side of Jordan* (1940) and *Deities and Dolphins: The Story of the Nabataeans* (1966), brought the antiquities of Jordan to a wider readership. Glueck also undertook two excavations in Transjordan, first (1937–1938) at Khirbet et-Tannur, a Nabataean temple site in the Wadi al-Hasa, and later (1938–1940) at the site of Tell el-Kheleifeh, which he believed to be Solomon's seaport Ezion Geber. These two periods of the Iron Age and the Nabateans were to be the main focus of Glueck's career, which was inspirational to the generation of archaeologists that followed.

Archaeology in the Hashemite Kingdom of Jordan, 1946–1967

After 1946, when Transjordan became an independent kingdom under the rule of the Hashemites, the area underwent a period of steady growth in terms of the development of a national archaeology. The retreat of British sovereignty in the region did not mean an immediate withdrawal of British interests or support, and G. L. Harding continued as director of what was now the Department of Antiquities of Jordan until 1956. Harding served as director of this department for twenty years (1936–1956) and was instrumental in the formation of archaeological policies that helped to establish the national school of archaeology in Jordan. In 1951 he founded the *Annual of the Department of Antiquities of Jordan,* which reported on the yearly archaeological work in the country, and later he wrote the first major popularization of the archaeology of Jordan, *The Antiquities of Jordan* (1959).

During the Hashemite period and following the partition of Palestine and the formation of the state of Israel (in 1948), the Department of Antiquities of Jordan was also responsible for the archaeology of the portion of Palestine that came to be known as the West Bank. This region included many of the major biblical sites, among them Jerusalem. Many of the international schools preferred to continue to work in this region, and major excavations in the former Transjordan were less frequent than might otherwise have been expected.

Some of the best-known projects include those by English archaeologist KATHLEEN KENYON, who carried out a series of excavations at Jericho from 1952 to 1958, when she was director of the British School of Archaeology in Jerusalem (BSAJ); later, from 1961 to 1968, Kenyon excavated in Jerusalem itself at the "City of David" (Ophel), working with a multinational team under the auspices of the Palestine Exploration Fund. The 1956–1968 fieldwork directed by G. E. Wright at Tell el-Balatah (Shechem), which was sponsored by Drew University and McCormick Theological Seminary (and later Harvard University) and affiliated with ASOR, was the principal U.S. excavation during this period. The École Biblique et Archéologique Française excavated the site of Tell el-Farah, associated with biblical Tirzah, under the direction of R. De Vaux from 1946 to 1960 and later conducted studies at Qumran (as will be discussed).

Outside of the West Bank and in Jordan proper, excavations began at the site of ancient Dhiban/Dibon under F. Winnett, W. Reed, and D. Tushingham (1950–1956) and at Deir 'Alla under H. J. Franken and a Dutch team from Leiden University (1960–1967). The German Evangelical Institute also began work at Umm Qeis, the Decapolis city of Gadara, in 1966. Other notable work included that by British archaeologist Peter Parr and U.S. archaeologist Philip Hammond, who led teams at Petra between 1954 and 1968, as well as renewed work at Teleilat Ghassul by R. North and the PBI (1960) and later Basil Hennessey under the auspices of the BSAJ (1967). U.S. work conducted with ASOR affiliation was also undertaken at 'Iraq el-Amir (1961–1962) and at Bab edh-Dhra (1965–1967) under Paul Lapp, then director of the American School in Jerusalem.

Perhaps the most spectacular archaeological achievement of this period was the discovery of the DEAD SEA SCROLLS. Local Bedouin found these biblical and extrabiblical texts dating to the first and second centuries A.D. in caves along the northwestern shore of the Dead Sea. This discovery led to a series of concentrated excavations at the various caves and later at Khirbet Qumran under the Jordanian Department of Antiquities, the Palestine Archaeological Museum, and the École Biblique et Archéologique Français under the direction of De Vaux (1951, 1953–1956). The finds from both the caves and the nearby site at Qumran (thought to be the complex associated with the writers of many of the scrolls, the Essenes) have significantly influenced modern research on the Bible, enabling insights into the early biblical communities in the region.

This period of archaeological research both in the West Bank and in Jordan itself established a pattern of archaeological fieldwork being conducted by schools from most of the major western powers; it also represented the longest phase of uninterrupted research in the region. The effects of this work are still being felt, with many of the principal researchers in the field of Levantine archaeology having "cut their teeth" during this time and on many of these projects; these individuals (who are only now retiring) have in turn been instrumental in establishing the study of Levantine archaeology in many countries. The 1946–1967 period also established the practice of having the Jordanian Department of Antiquities partner with of the international schools in the documentation, publication, and preservation of the rich archaeological heritage of Jordan.

Archaeology in Jordan, 1967 to the Present

Following Jordan's loss of the West Bank during the Six-Day War in 1967, Jordanian archaeology once again focused on land east of the Jordan River. Many of the international schools (British, U.S., German) set up "temporary" offices in Jordan (Amman) at this time, in order to continue archaeological research but avoid excavation in the Israeli occupied territories, which would have breached UN rules. The American Schools of Oriental Research in Jerusalem was the first institution to set up a "branch office" in support of research in Jordan in 1968, and British researchers soon followed suit. Within a few years, in 1971, the American Center for Oriental Research (ACOR) was founded, and somewhat later, in 1978, British archaeologists formalized their shift from Jerusalem to Amman via the establishment of the British Institute at Amman for Archaeology and History (now the Council for British Research in the Levant), under the direction of Crystal Bennett.

The founding of headquarters in Amman for many of the international schools at this time marked a transition or a break in the direction of archaeological research in Jordan and in Israel and the West Bank. From this point forward archaeological work in Israel and Jordan developed along independent lines, with increasingly little contact between the scholars of both countries. This situation was equally true for the indigenous archaeologists (Israeli and Jordanian) and for the archaeologists from the international schools. In particular, many of those formally working in Jordan were reluctant to jeopardize the situation by making contacts and pursuing active research west of the Jordan Rift. Consequently, archaeology in Israel developed on an independent trajectory and along specific national lines in a way that was distinctly different from the archaeology in Jordan.

The national school in Israel sought its roots in the archaeology of ancient Israel and Judah and in Jewish history in general, but archaeology in Jordan was less political. The populations in Jordan were largely Bedouin and were not particularly interested in developing a history of occupation for the region along the lines being pursued by Israeli biblical archaeologists: they claimed no distinctly historical links with either the Nabataeans or the Iron Age kingdoms of Ammon, Moab, and Edom. Given this move away from a focus upon a narrowly defined and specific culture-historical approach, archaeological work in Jordan was much more diverse, and a number of specific subfields of archaeology were free to develop.

Nonetheless, some Jordanian researchers were interested in biblical archaeology and the study of the Bronze and Iron Ages, as expressed in the excavations of Crystal Bennett in Edom at sites such as Tawilan and the ancient Edomite capital at Buserieh (1968–1974, 1980). There were, however, just as many scholars who focused upon the world of classical and late Antiquity, up to and including the Islamic periods. The wealth of extremely well preserved and important sites from these periods in Jordan (often due to the lack of continuous occupation at the site in modern times) no doubt contributed to this tendency. Sites such as Petra, Jerash, Gadara, and Amman were obvious attractions for researchers, but some smaller sites also had great appeal, among them Umm el-Jimal, a Roman-Byzantine city on the desert fringe (excavated since 1973 by Calvin College), and the Roman Legionary Fort at el-Lejjun (studied by S. Thomas Parker), a spectacularly preserved fortress of the Roman limes, or frontier. Both projects have contributed to our understanding of life on the fringes of the Roman and Byzantine Empires.

Perhaps the least expected direction of archaeological work in Jordan since 1967 came with the advances of the "New Archaeology" in the 1970s and 1980s, which saw the expansion of anthropological archaeology in the country and an increase in research on the earliest prehistory of the region, from the Paleolithic until the end of the Neolithic period. Up to that point Jordan was known largely for the richness of its numerous well-preserved sites of classical antiquity and the Bronze and Iron Ages. No one could have predicted that so many spectacular prehistoric sites, many in excellent condition, would also be found. The expansion of a scientific and specifically anthropological approach to prehistoric archaeology in Jordan has been one of the most significant advances since the 1980s. This research has been undertaken in the context of a distinctly environmental approach, which has focused on understanding the development of the region in the late Pleistocene and Holocene, the adaptation of early modern humans to the region and its environment, and the development of societies and the transition to settled life.

Projects that have contributed to this research are numerous, but a few of the key efforts are worthy of special mention. These include the pioneering work of English archaeologists Diana Kirkbride (at Beidha) and, more recently, Andrew Garrard. While assistant director and then director of the British Insti-

tute at Amman, Garrard oversaw work at sites in the Azraq Basin and at Wadi Jilat (1982–1989), which trained a generation of British prehistorians and environmental archaeologists. Also noteworthy is the work of Gary Rollefson and others at the now famous site at 'Ain Ghazal, perhaps one of the most spectacular (and largest) Neolithic settlements in the Levant; it has produced spectacular finds, including two groups of nearly life-size anthropomorphic figurines. Still other sites in the vicinity of Petra—such as Basta, excavated by Hans Nissan, Nans Georg Gebel, and Zeidan Kafafi—have shown the wealth and extent of the prehistoric occupation of Jordan in virtually every environmental and geographic zone, from the Mediterranean to the steppe and desert.

The increasing role of survey work in recent years has complemented the part played by excavation in revealing the archaeology of Jordan. Extensive surveys have covered many Jordanian regions, including the Black Desert (A. Betts), the Kerak Plateau (M. Miller), the Wadi al-Hasa and the Southern Ghor and Northeast Arabah (B. MacDonald), and a great many others (see Banning in MacDonald, Adams, and Bienkowski 2001). All of these surveys have been instrumental in helping to piece together the many thousands of archaeological sites in Jordan from all periods, which are in turn recorded in the Jordanian Antiquities Database and Information System (JADIS)—a computer database of all archaeological sites in Jordan. This tool for the management of cultural resources allows for the preservation and conservation of Jordan's rich cultural heritage.

Last but by no means least is the significant part played by Jordanians in both the Department of Antiquities and the various archaeology departments in the nation's universities. The hospitality and partnership of Jordanians in the ongoing development of archaeology and the cultural-resource management of archaeological sites in the kingdom has been one of the keys to the vast amount of work undertaken since 1946. In this regard the Department of Antiquities has been fortunate to have had directors of vision and energy who carried on the work of Horsfield and Harding, including (but not limited to) Adnan Hadidi, Ghazi Bisheh, Safwan Tell, and Fawaz al-Khrayshah.

The future of archaeology in Jordan is bright, with many Jordanians taking an active interest in the history and archaeology of their country, as evidenced by the thriving archaeology departments at the University of Jordan (Amman), Yarmuk University (Irbid), and Mutah University (Kerak). Many of the graduates in the field are employed in the Department of Antiquities and other aspects of Jordanian heritage. Often working in partnership with international research projects, they are now creating a distinctive Jordanian archaeology.

Russell B. Adams

See also Syro-Palestinian and Biblical Archaeology

References

Glueck, Nelson. 1934. *Explorations in Eastern Palestine* I. Annual of the American Schools of Oriental Research 14.

———. 1935. *Explorations in Eastern Palestine II.* Annual of the American Schools of Oriental Research 15.

———. 1937. *Explorations in Eastern Palestine III.* Annual of the American Schools of Oriental Research 18–19.

———. 1940. *The Other Side of Jordan.* New Haven. (Rev. ed., 1971, Cambridge, MA: American Schools of Oriental Research.)

———. 1951. *Explorations in Eastern Palestine IV.* Annual of the American Schools of Oriental Research 25–28.

———. 1966. *Deities and Dolphins: The Story of the Nabataeans.* London.

Harding, G. L. 1959. *The Antiquities of Jordan.* London: Lutterworth Press.

King, Philip J. 1983. *American Archaeology in the Mideast: A History of the American Schools of Oriental Research.* Winona Lake, IN: Eisenbrauns.

MacDonald, B., R. B. Adams, and P. Bienkowski, eds. 2001. *The Archaeology of Jordan.* Sheffield, UK: Sheffield Academic Press.

Sauer, J. 1997. "Archaeology in Jordan." In *The Oxford Encyclopedia of Archaeology in the Near East,* 3:51–56. Ed. E. M. Meyers. Oxford: Oxford University Press.

Stanley, A. P. 1856. *Sinai and Palestine in Connection with Their History.* London: John Murray.

Journal of Field Archaeology

The *Journal of Field Archaeology (JFA),* a quarterly periodical, was founded in 1974 by James R. Wiseman and has been substantially supported since that time by Boston University, whose trustees hold the copyright. Originally the journal was published at Boston University on behalf of the Association for Field Archaeology, but when that organization was dissolved in 1989, its remaining assets were transferred to *JFA.* Three years earlier, the general editorship had passed to Creighton Gabel, who continued in that capacity until 1994. In 1995, Ricardo J. Elia became editor. During most of the *JFA*'s history, the managing editor has been Al B. Wesolowsky, another professional archaeologist, while David Ford, as the long-term art director, has contributed greatly to the quality of the graphics.

The stated purpose of the journal was, in particular, to provide a forum for the publication of field reports in recognition of the fact that such venues were becoming increasingly limited even as the discipline grew. At the same time, the *JFA* has welcomed submission of specialized technical and methodological studies, ranging from materials science and field techniques to ethno-archaeology and experimental archaeology. On occasion, survey articles providing historical perspectives on, or summarizing recent research in, major world areas also have been published. No restrictions have ever been placed on the geographical or temporal focus of contributions.

In addition to full-length articles and briefer research reports, some special feature sections have appeared for a number of years. One was "The Archaeometric Clearinghouse" edited by Curt W. Beck (Vassar College) from 1974 to 1993; with a new title, "Archaeological Science Review," this special section subsequently came under the editorship of Julian Henderson of Sheffield University in England. Reflecting the growing concern about the illicit trafficking in antiquities, "The Antiquities Market" section likewise began to appear in the first year of publication, with Karen Vitelli (Indiana University) assuming direct responsibility for it in 1976, replaced by Ellen Herscher of Washington, D.C., in 1984 and by Timothy Kaiser (University of

Toronto) in 1990. "Public Archaeology Forum," devoted to recent and current developments in archaeological resource management, including legislation, came under the guidance of Hester Davis (Arkansas Archeological Survey) in 1986, having been published previously (from 1977) as "Rescue and Preservation" with Thomas King (U.S. National Park Service) as editor. Book reviews, initiated in 1989, were first edited by Norman Hammond (Boston University), who was succeeded in 1992 by Curtis Runnels, also of Boston University.

Now *JFA* occupies a niche that incorporates an emphasis on field reports and publication of other forms of basic archaeological research; an explicit recognition of the interdisciplinary aspects of the field, including scientific approaches as adjuncts to, or components of, archaeological investigations; and a deep interest in professional ethics and responsibility with respect to, among other things, the protection of the world's archaeological heritage.

Creighton Gabel

See also United States of America, Prehistoric Archaeology

K

Karageorghis, Vassos (1929–)

Vassos Karageorghis dominated Cypriot archaeology in the latter half of the twentieth century. He studied archaeology at the Institute of Archaeology at London University (Ph.D. awarded in 1957). Shortly after CYPRUS gained independence from Great Britain, he became director of the Department of Antiquities, and after retiring from that position, he established the Archaeological Research Unit of the newly founded University of Cyprus. He has been a visiting scholar at a variety of universities in Europe and the Americas and is currently director of the Leventis Foundation. His primary field of research has been on the Iron Age and the late Bronze Age of Cyprus, with major, large-scale excavations at Salamis, Kition, Maa-Palaekastro, and Pyla-Kokkinokremnos; the results of all have been efficiently and comprehensively published. He has written widely on specific Cypriot issues as well as on the relationship between Cyprus and surrounding regions. Among his major contributions is a series of monographs on Cypriot terracotta models. Through the Leventis Foundation he has provided funds to several major museums to develop new displays of their Cypriot material, and he has done much to establish the place of Cyprus internationally, in part by encouraging foreign excavators to work on the island. His activities in repatriating looted antiquities have also been of particular significance.

David Frankel

Karnak and Luxor

The temples of Karnak and Luxor are located on the east bank of the Nile at the modern city of Luxor (ancient Thebes) in southern Egypt. The two temples formed the religious heart of the city of Thebes. The urban remains of ancient Thebes cluster around Karnak extending southwards toward Luxor temple. Much of the standing remains of these great stone temples were exposed through unscientific excavation during the nineteenth century. However, modern archaeological excavation and epigraphic recording of scenes and texts, as well as the analysis and interpretation of these massive buildings, is likely to continue for the foreseeable future. Conservation and reconstruction of the Karnak and Luxor temples continues to be a major activity of the Egyptian Supreme Council of Antiquities and numerous foreign projects conducting work at Luxor.

The majority of the visible architecture of the Karnak and Luxor temples dates to the New Kingdom (Dynasties 18–20, ca. 1550–1070 B.C.) and later periods. Alterations and additions to Karnak and Luxor temples did not cease until the beginning of the Christian Period in the first century A.D. Karnak and Luxor temples are among the best-preserved temple sites in Egypt. Profusely decorated with scenes and texts, the temples provide an unparalleled glimpse into the religious life of ancient Egyptian society.

The main temple at Karnak (known in ancient Egyptian as *Ipet-Sut*) was dedicated to the god Amun(-Re), a deity who rose to prominence in the Middle Kingdom (ca. 2050–1750 B.C.) and who became the premier state god during the New Kingdom. Flanking the Karnak precinct of Amun-Re on its south and north side respectively are satellite precincts dedicated to

Ruins at Luxor, Egypt (Image Select)

Mut (the consort of Amun-Re) and Montu (a falcon god associated with warfare). Shrines and subsidiary temples dedicated to many additional gods (including Khonsu, Osiris, Maat, and others) are located within these three main precincts. The Luxor temple (which was known as *Ipet-Resyt*) is located two kilometers south of Karnak. The temple was dedicated to a form of the god Amun known as Amenope. In ancient times, the Luxor and Karnak temples were linked by a processional route that is still lined today with human-headed sphinxes added by the Late Period king Nectanebo I. An annual religious festival known as the Opet Festival was the most significant religious ceremony in the life of ancient Thebes. During this festival a statue of Amun was carried out of the Karnak temple to Luxor temple for the enactment of religious rites that celebrated the association between the pharaoh and Amun.

The visible ruins of Karnak (including the temple precincts of Amun, Mut, and Montu) cover an area of more than 50 hectares (50,000 square meters), making the agglomeration of ancient ruins one of the most extensive in the world and a bewildering spectacle to the modern visitor. The early history of the Karnak temple may perhaps be linked with Montu, who was the original god of ancient Thebes. The rise to prominence of Amun-Re during the Middle Kingdom (ca. 2050–1750 B.C.), however, served to realign any prior associations of Karnak. The oldest known architectural remains in Egypt date to the Middle Kingdom and indicate the presence of a state temple dedicated to Amun-Re that is now destroyed and buried beneath the extensive New Kingdom remains. The earliest still-standing part of the temple includes early 18th Dynasty structures erected by Amenhotep I, Thutmosis I, and the female pharaoh Hatshepsut. Behind these, extensive reconstruction undertaken by the mid-18th Dynasty king Thutmosis III (ca. 1479–1425 B.C.) has erased much of the earlier 18th Dynasty and pre–New Kingdom temple. Excavation has, however, revealed a number of early buildings that in ancient times had been dismantled and reused as construction fill. These include the nearly perfectly preserved shrines of Senwosret

I (Dynasty 12), Amenhotep I, and Hatshepsut (Dynasty 18). Adjacent to the temple's inner core is the Sacred Lake, a feature that symbolized the primeval waters of Nun that existed at the beginning of creation.

The history of the Amun temple at Karnak during the New Kingdom and later periods is one of expansion outward from this older temple core. A series of halls and pylons were added by successive kings. In total, ten different pylons with associated courtyards and other features extend along the temple's central east-west axis and on a secondary north-south axis that linked the Amun temple with the precinct of Mut. Fronting the 18th Dynasty section of the temple is the famous Great Hypostyle Hall, which was initiated by Seti I and completed by his son Ramses II during the 19th Dynasty. The present entrance to the temple is through the incomplete First Pylon, which dates to the Late Period.

Much of Karnak is decorated with extensive scenes and texts that illustrate the religious associations between the pharaoh and the divine realm of the gods. Some sections are decorated with historical texts commemorating the military achievements of the New Kingdom rulers. One such text, the "Annals of Thutmosis III," provides considerable detail on the military activities and organization of Egypt's empire during the 18th Dynasty. While the massive stone remains of Karnak and Luxor temples provide evidence on the religious life of ancient Egypt, surrounding the temples were extensive concentrations of storerooms, workshops, and houses. At the height of its power during the New Kingdom the temple establishment of Amun involved more then 80,000 people, both at Thebes and elsewhere in Egypt. Ongoing archaeological work promises to further our understanding of the intertwined religious, economic, and political roles of the temples of Karnak and Luxor.

Josef Wegner

See also Egypt, Dynastic

References
Afrère, S., et al. 1991 *L'Égypte Restituée vol. 1: Sites et temples de Haute Égypte.* Paris: Editions Errance.

Baines, John, and Jaromír Malek. 1980. *Atlas of Ancient Egypt*. New York: Facts on File.

Kemp, Barry. 1989. *Ancient Egypt: Anatomy of a Civilization*. New York: Routledge.

Murnane, William. 1983 *The Guide to Ancient Egypt*. New York: Facts on File.

Shafer, Byron E., ed. 1997. *Temples of Ancient Egypt*. Ithaca, NY: Cornell University Press.

Strudwick, Nigel. 1999. *Thebes in Egypt: A Guide to the Tombs and Temples of Ancient Luxor*, Ithaca, NY: Cornell University Press.

Kastelic, Jožef (1913–)

The Slovenian archaeologist, ancient historian, and poet Jožef Kastelic graduated in classical philology and ancient history from the University of Ljubljana in 1939 and completed his Ph.D. at the same university in 1943. Between 1942 and 1968, Kastelic worked at the National Museum in Ljubljana and became its director in 1945. He was also professor of classical archaeology, Roman provincial archaeology, and ancient history at the University of Ljubljana between 1968 and 1983 and professor of ancient history at the University of Maribor (Slovenia) between 1985 and 1989. Kastelic is a member of German Archaeological Society, the Institute of Etruscan and Italic Studies in Florence, and the Italian Institute of Pre- and Protohistory.

One of the most influential archaeologists in SLOVENIA, Kastelic is credited along with colleague JOSIP KOROŠEC for the revival of archaeological work in Slovenia and Yugoslavia after World War II. He continued the National Museum's long tradition as the central and national archaeological institution and established some of the important series and journals: *Arheoloski katalogi, Situla,* and *Argo*. Kastelic organized many influential exhibitions, such as *Umetnost alpskih Ilirov in Venetov* (Situla Art between Po and Danube) in Ljubljana in 1962. He was one of the founders of early Slavic archaeology in Slovenia after 1945. Between 1948 and 1949, he excavated at large early Slavic cemetery in Bled (see *Slovanska nekropola na Bledu* [Ljubljana 1950] and *Slovanska nekropola na Bledu* [Ljubljana 1960]). Kastelic excavated a large barrow in STIČNA between 1946 and 1953 and participated in many joint Yugoslav research projects, among

them research in Yugoslav Macedonia at the sites of Demir Kapija and Trebeniste. As the head of the Department of Archaeology at the University of Ljubljana, he decisively molded and defined its new and articulated structure in the 1960s and 1970s.

Bojan Djuric

References

"Opuscula Iosepho Kastelic sexagenario dicata." 1974. *Situla* (Ljubljana) 14–15. Contains bibliography.

Keller, Ferdinand (1800–1881)

Ferdinand Keller was the founder of the lake-dwellings theory, a member of the old bourgeoisie of Zurich, and an English teacher at the Technicum there, and he was the most prominent archaeologist in SWITZERLAND in the nineteenth century.

After studying theology and then natural science in Paris, Keller went to England where he was a private tutor, and where he met SIR RICHARD COLT HOARE in Wiltshire. Colt Hoare was the owner of a rich collection of prehistoric relics, and although Keller was primarily fascinated by Celtic antiquities, he was strongly influenced by a visit to the Salisbury burial mounds and Stonehenge.

He returned to Zurich and discovered the Burgholzli mounds, which led him to found the Antiquarian Society of Zurich in 1832, the first organization of its kind in Switzerland. His interests went beyond prehistory to include all vestiges of the past, from Roman colonies to religious architecture, not forgetting medieval paleography. Thanks to his eclecticism, his mastery of languages, and his easy social nature, he was constantly in contact with a very large network of archaeologists and antiquarians both in Switzerland and abroad. His correspondence remains an extraordinary source of original information, and much of it is yet unpublished.

Despite the variety and quantity of his research, it was the discovery of the lake dwellings themselves that gave him exceptional fame. During the winter of 1853–1854, a record lowering of the water level in Lake Zurich led to the discovery, in Obermeilen, of pile fields accompanied by potsherds and tools of stone, antler, and wood. Informed of the discovery by a schoolteacher, Keller immediately recognized the significance of the find and interpreted the remains as dwellings on pile-supported platforms above the water. Thus, even though pile stumps had been observed a few years before on the shores of Lake Bienne, it was only when Keller got interested in them that research on the Swiss lake dwellings began to get real attention in Europe.

It is with regard to the lake dwellings that Keller's contribution to archaeological research in Switzerland can best be evaluated. Although his work was always serious and well documented, it was not intrinsically innovative; neither was he a master of archaeological excavation. Even if Keller did observe a three-age division in the remains, he did not attach much importance to it. In fact, he gathered all remains from the Neolithic to the Iron Age together and attributed them to a homogeneous Celtic population.

Keller's genius lay in his ability to extrapolate material from data on lake dwellings and other sites to provide coherent and global interpretations. The force of Keller's dynamism swept along numbers of specialist naturalists, geologists, botanists, and zoologists. He also managed to interest the public and to keep its interest without entering into or using ethnic customs and religion as explanations. Keller controlled and dominated Swiss archaeology, and his interpretations, however erroneous, remained almost irrefutable and encouraged research instead of blocking it. He can be seen as more of a learned nineteenth-century antiquarian, because of his background in the natural sciences, than as an archaeologist.

Marc-Antoine Kaeser

References

Keller, F. 1837. "Die keltischen Grabhugel im Burgholzli und die Graber auf der Forch." *Mitteilungen der Antiquarischen Gesellschaft in Zurich* 1: no pagination.

———. 1854. "Die keltischen Pfahlbauten in den Schweizerseen." *Mitteilungen der Antiquarischen Gesellschaft in Zurich* 9: no pagination.

———. 1858–1879. "Pfahlbauberichte 2, 3, 4, 5, 6, 8. [Lake Dwelling Reports, 2–6, 8.]." *Mitteilungen der Antiquarischen Gesellschaft in Zurich* 12, 13, 14, 15, 20: no pagination.

Martin-Kilcher, S. 1979. "Ferdinand Keller und die Entdeckung der Pfahlbauten." *Archaologie der Schweiz* 2: 3–11.

Meyer von Knonau, G. 1882. "I. Lebensabriss des Stifters der Gesellschaft Dr. Ferdinand Keller." In *Denkschrift zur funfzigjahrigen Stiftungsfeier der Antiquarischen Gesellschaft in Zurich,* 1–48. Ed. G. Meyer von Knonau and G. Finsler. Zurich: Burkli.

Schneider, B. 1991. "Ferdinand Keller und die Antiquarische Gesellschaft Zurich." *Archaologie der Schweiz* 14: 14–18.

Kendrick, Sir Thomas Downing (1895–1979)

Kendrick was born in Birmingham, England, and won a scholarship to Oriel College, Oxford, in 1913. He joined the army and survived the fighting in France, although he was severely wounded. He returned to Oriel in 1919 and read anthropology and later studied and published on the prehistoric archaeology of the Channel Islands.

In 1922 he began working at the BRITISH MUSEUM in the department of British and medieval antiquities. He became assistant keeper in 1928, keeper in 1938, and director and principal librarian from 1950 until his retirement in 1959. Kendrick's primary interest was in Anglo-Saxon art and he was responsible for the display of the great SUTTON HOO treasure to the public after the war. He also made the his area of expertise accessible, publishing *The Axe Age* (1925), *The Druids* (1927), *A History of the Vikings* (1930), *Anglo-Saxon Art to AD 900* (1938) and *Late Saxon and Viking Art* (1949). He ensured that the museum was as significant to scholars as it was popular.

Kendrick maintained his interest in archaeology, publishing *Archaeology in England and Wales 1914–1931* with CHRISTOPHER HAWKES in 1932 and editing several volumes of *The County Archaeologies*. His greatest contribution to the history of archaeology was his magnificent *British Antiquity* (1950), which remains essential reading in this field. He was made a fellow of the British Academy in 1941 and was a fellow of the

Society of Antiquaries, of which he was secretary from 1940–1950.

Tim Murray

See also Britain, Prehistoric Archaeology

Kent's Cavern

Kent's Cavern, a limestone cave on the Devonshire coast near Torbay, England, was first excavated in a systematic and serious way by John MacEnery, a local Catholic priest, in 1825, 1826, and 1829. MacEnery found what he considered to be clear evidence of the bones of extinct animals and ancient stone tools in the same strata. Geologist WILLIAM BUCKLAND persuaded MacEnery that this could not be the case, and the publication of his memoir on the site had to wait until 1859, eighteen years after his death.

The site was excavated twice before 1859, in 1841 by R. A. C. Austen and in 1846 by WILLIAM PENGELLY, who was later to gain fame as the excavator of BRIXHAM CAVE. Both excavators were persuaded of the association that Buckland had so strongly opposed. After the recognition of high (greater or longer) human antiquity, the British Association for the Advancement of Science funded Pengelly's return to Kent's Cavern between 1865 and 1878.

Tim Murray

References

Van Riper, A. Bowdoin. 1993. *Men among Mammoths: Victorian Science and the Discovery of Human Prehistory.* Chicago: University of Chicago Press.

Kenyon, Kathleen Mary (1906–1978)

Kathleen Mary Kenyon, the eldest daughter of Sir Frederic Kenyon, was born on 5 January 1906 in England and died at the age of seventy-two on 24 August 1978 at her place of retirement in South Wales. Her father was keeper of manuscripts at the BRITISH MUSEUM. She attended St. Paul's Girls' School in London and her studies were so successful there that she became "head girl." She then studied at Somerville College, Oxford University, and received her degree in history in 1929. As she had already decided to make archaeology her career, she seized the op-

Kathleen Kenyon (Image Select)

portunity she was offered upon graduation from college to become a photographer and excavator with GERTRUDE CATON-THOMPSON on a British Association expedition to GREAT ZIMBABWE in southern Rhodesia (modern Zimbabwe).

Between 1930 and 1935, Kenyon continued her training and fieldwork with the legendary SIR MORTIMER WHEELER at the Roman town of Verulamium near St. Albans, England. Her important contribution was the uncovering of the Roman theater there, the only public monument of its kind in the British Isles.

Kenyon spent the summer months from 1931 to 1934 on her first Near Eastern archaeological project. She worked on the Palestine Exploration Fund's Crowfoot expedition to Samaria. She applied and refined her Romano-British field-training techniques to her excavations at Samaria, which made her a pioneer along with SIR WILLIAM MATTHEW FLINDERS PETRIE, GEORGE A. REISNER, and Clarence Fisher in the introduction of methods of stratigraphical digging to archaeological excavations, with drawn sections, at ancient Near Eastern sites.

In 1935, Kenyon helped Wheeler establish the Institute of Archaeology at London Univer-

Jordanian archaeological workers excavating a tower near the Dead Sea believed to date to 7000 B.C. (© Bettmann/ CORBIS)

sity. She was the first honorary secretary of that institute, was its acting director from 1942 to 1946, and from 1948 to 1962 held the lectureship in Near Eastern Archaeology there. She then served as principal of St. Hugh's College, Oxford, until her retirement in 1973.

Apart from her extensive work on Romano-British sites and in Zimbabwe and Samaria during the 1930s and 1940s, Kenyon conducted major archaeological expeditions at the Roman town of Sabratha in Tripolitania (Libya in north Africa) and at two famous biblical sites in Palestine, Jericho (1952–1958) and Jerusalem (1961– 1967). It was her pioneering work in uncovering the earliest known stages in the history of mankind at Jericho that made Kenyon world famous as both a personality and an archaeologist. Her last fieldwork on Mt. Ophel in the 1970s, the biblical site of Jerusalem, was conducted as a rescue operation because of ur-

ban development in East Jerusalem. The work served as the basis for Kenyon's being able to correct and clarify much of the nonstratigraphical work carried out in Jerusalem during the nineteenth century.

Kenyon received many honors during her long and distinguished career, which culminated in her being created a Dame Commander of the Order of the British Empire in 1973. She wrote many archaeological articles and excavation reports, the most widely read being *Archaeology in the Holy Land* (1st ed., 1960; 4th ed., 1979), which has been translated into a number of foreign languages.

Thomas A. Holland

References

For references, see *Encyclopedia of Archaeology: The Great Archaeologists, Vol. 2,* ed. Tim Murray (Santa Barbara, CA: ABC-CLIO, 1999), pp. 491–493.

Khirokitia-Vouni

The world heritage site Khirokitia-Vouni is the most extensively excavated aceramic Neolithic settlement on CYPRUS. It was initially excavated by PORPHYRIOS DIKAIOS between 1936 and 1946. Limited work was later carried out by Nicholas Stanley Price and Demos Christou, and since 1977 Alain Le Brun has continued excavations at the site. It is the type site for the Cypriot aceramic Neolithic period (early Neolithic or Khirokitia culture).

A very extensive area of the site has been cleared, revealing a closely packed array of circular houses of varied size. Most have very substantial stone foundations, with mud brick superstructure and flat roofs. In the larger examples, interior space may have been increased by platforms or mezzanine floors. A substantial stone "wall" running up the slope the full length of the excavated area has been variously interpreted, most recently as a formal boundary of the settlement marking off the safe interior from a hostile exterior. As the settlement grew, new houses were erected outside the wall, and a new wall, with a complex entry, was built. Intramural burials are a feature of the site. The economy of Khirokitia was based on an array of plants, many or which were imported to Cyprus at the beginning of the Neolithic period, and by a range of imported animals, primarily sheep, goat, pig, and deer.

David Frankel

References

Dikaios, P. 1953. *Khirokitia.* Oxford.

Le Brun, A. 1981. *Fouilles recentes a Khirokitia (Chypre) 1977–1981.* Paris.

———. 1989. *Fouilles recentes a Khirokitia (Chypre) 1983–1986.* Paris.

Kidd, Kenneth E. (1906–1994)

Kenneth E. Kidd was the pioneer founder of Canadian HISTORICAL ARCHAEOLOGY. His initial training and fieldwork were in ethnology (his M.A. thesis at the University of Toronto was on Blackfoot ethnography) and prehistoric archaeology. In 1935, he joined the Department of Ethnology at the Royal Ontario Museum where he was assigned in 1941 to excavate one of the most famous sites in CANADA, the Jesuit Mission of Sainte-Marie (1639–1649) established in Huron Territory (Ontario). His two-year project at this site basically created Canadian historical archaeology and his book, *The Excavation of Ste. Marie I,* is very likely the first professional site report for any historic site in North America published as a separate book (Kidd 1941).

Unlike a number of his contemporaries in the United States, including J. C. HARRINGTON and JOHN L. COTTER, Kidd did not abandon prehistoric studies for Euro-American sites. His primary interest in the contact period kept him firmly committed to both types of archaeology. In 1948 he authored a significant report, "The Excavation of a Huron Ossuary," and that article was followed by a popular synthesis, *Canadians of Long Ago: The Story of the Canadian Indian,* published in 1951 (Kidd 1948, 1951). His career-long focus on contact situations drew him into a lifelong study of European trade goods, especially glass beads, and in 1970, he and his wife, Martha Ann Kidd, summarized years of museum and archival research in "A Classification System for Glass Beads for the Use of Field Archaeologists" (Kidd and Kidd 1970). This system, although weakened by his choice of an impressionistic color-coding typology, was the first important guide to an artifact category found in historic sites on every continent.

In 1964, Kidd left the museum world to become the first holder of chair of the new Department of Anthropology at Trent University in Peterborough, Ontario, where he taught until his retirement in 1973. At Trent he made historical archaeology central to the curriculum and also established one of the first Indian-Eskimo studies programs in Canada.

Kidd was one of the few members of his pioneering generation who had a keen interest in the history of archaeology. He synthesized and surveyed Ontario archaeology in several articles across the decades and his article "Historical Site Archaeology in Canada" (Kidd 1969) is the only national history for that field in Canada.

In 1985, the Society for Historical Archaeology honored Kidd with its highest award, the J. C. HARRINGTON MEDAL, and in 1993, he was presented with the Commonwealth Medal for the

125th Anniversary of the Confederation of Canada.

Robert L. Schuyler

References

Kidd, Kenneth E. 1948. "The Excavation of a Huron Ossuary." *Bulletin of the Society for American Archaeology no. 1.*

———. 1949. *The Excavation of Ste. Marie I.* Toronto: University of Toronto Press.

———. 1951. *Canadians of Long Ago: The Story of the Canadian Indian.* Toronto, New York: Longmans, Green.

———. 1969. "Historical Site Archaeology in Canada." *National Museum of Canada Anthropological Papers no. 22.*

Kidd, Kenneth E., and Martha Ann Kidd. 1970. "A Classification System for Glass Beads for the Use of Field Archaeologists." *Canadian Historic Sites: Occasional Papers in Archaeology and History, no. 1.*

Kidder, Alfred Vincent (1885–1963)

Kidder grew up in Cambridge, Massachusetts, and as a young man befriended many of Harvard's great scientists, such as geologists RAPHAEL PUMPELLY and Alexander Agassiz and anthropologists LEWIS HENRY MORGAN and FREDERIC WARD PUTNAM from the PEABODY MUSEUM, through his family connections. Kidder began studying medicine at Harvard in 1904, but changed to archaeology after participating in EDGAR LEE HEWETT's field school and meeting Alfred Marsten Tozzer, professor of archaeology.

In 1909 Kidder entered graduate school at Harvard to begin work on his doctorate in anthropology under the supervision of Egyptologist GEORGE REISNER, art historian George Chase, and anthropologist Franz Boas. Kidder continued to excavate during the summer, in 1910 in Newfoundland, and in 1912 at historic Pueblo ruins in the Gobernador and Largo canyons in New Mexico. In 1914 Kidder received his Ph.D. on the style and decorative motifs of Pueblo pottery, suggesting that ceramic materials could be used as a gauge of cultural development in the American Southwest, similarly to what was being done by archaeologists at Old World sites in Europe, Africa, and Asia.

Kidder is best remembered for his pioneering approach to the study of Pecos Pueblo (1915–1924) in New Mexico, which had been occupied in both prehistoric and historic times. The connection between potsherds and stratigraphic excavation would be the hallmark of Kidder's work at Pecos Pueblo, conducted on a massive scale. His use of stratigraphy not only introduced this method of relative dating to archaeology but also brought a sense of the spatial distribution of territory under the control of a specific prehistoric culture. Moreover, Kidder established the value of stratigraphy to Americanist archaeology. While waiting to be inducted into the army in 1917 Kidder spent two months living at the First Mesa in Hopi Indian country and traveling around Hopi territory. Using ethnographic data from cultural anthropology and melding it with excavation data into a workable whole, Kidder's data from this period raised the science of archaeology to a new interpretive level. In 1920 Kidder was able to return to Pecos Pueblo, where he employed a multidisciplinary approach to resolve its archaeological problems—physical anthropologists, pottery analysts, ethnographers, engineers, and agronomists were some of the members of the team that studied the Pecos Pueblo material—the first long-term and multi-disciplinary project in North American archaeology.

In 1929 Kidder began the second half of his archaeological career by becoming the director of the Carnegie Institute's Division of Historical Research in Washington, D.C. Kidder now turned his attention for the most part to the MAYA of Central America, and introduced his "pan-scientific"/multi-disciplinary approach to resolving Mayan archaeological problems. While this approach was never fully realized, it did succeed in collecting data about the Mayan habitat, agricultural base, technology, and living descendants. Kidder and Charles A. Lindbergh worked jointly on the aerial discovery of Mayan sites throughout the Yucatán and in other locations and began to use the airplane as a tool to trace possible trade routes between Mayan cities. Kidder employed longtime friend and colleague SYLVANUS G. MORLEY to continue his groundbreaking work deciphering Mayan hieroglyphics. Kidder himself excavated the Kaminaljuyu mounds in GUATEMALA, and encouraged the careers of two Mayan archaeologists: Anna O. Shepard and TATIANA PROSKOURIAKOFF. During this time Kidder was also concerned with the importance of the environment and its influence on human culture. He included a concentration on environmental factors in his program of Mayan archaeology, a far-sighted move in 1953, since today's archaeology considers this type of research as routine for most field/site analysis.

After World War II the Carnegie Institution began to allocate more of its resources to the "hard sciences" and less to the human and social ones, eventually closing down the Division of Historical Research, but not before Kidder proposed that the institution underwrite the use of radiocarbon DATING for archaeology. Kidder retired in 1950, but until his death he continued to act as mentor for many archaeology students and colleagues and he taught a graduate course in archaeology at the University of California at Berkeley. As a reflection of the esteem in which he was and is still held, the Alfred Vincent Kidder medal was created by the SOCIETY FOR AMERICAN ARCHAEOLOGY, and is awarded every three years to an outstanding Americanist.

Douglas R. Givens

References

For references, see *Encyclopedia of Archaeology: The Great Archaeologists, Vol. 2*, ed. Tim Murray (Santa Barbara, CA: ABC-CLIO, 1999), pp. 357–367.

Kings Bay Plantations

Because of construction of the Kings Bay Naval Submarine Base, researchers from the University of Florida investigated six plantations on the southernmost part of the Georgia coast from 1977 to 1985—Cherry Point, Kings Bay, Harmony Hall, Marianna, Point Peter, and New Canaan. These plantations were small, middle, and large according to land- and slave-holdings categories developed by historians. Charles H. Fairbanks and Robin Smith conducted the testing from 1977 to 1980, while William H. Adams directed the testing and data recovery phases from 1981 to 1985. Thomas H. Eubanks directed the excavation of the McIntosh Sugar-

house in 1981 and 1985, and in 1981, this project was the first to make field use of microcomputers linked as smart terminals to the mainframe. In 1985, the project also made the first use of video camera/computer interfacing to produce artifact illustrations successfully.

The Kings Bay project was unique because it investigated all the plantations located between Crooked River and St. Marys River, a distance of over eight miles, and these were historically linked into a single community. Previous plantation archaeology had generally focused on big plantations, but at Kings Bay small and middle-sized ones were also investigated.

Because these plantations were geographically close, the environmental differences were largely nil, an especially important point for the zooarchaeological study. The faunal analysis done by William Richard Adams at Indiana University was by far the most detailed for historical sites on the coast—27,353 bone fragments from planter sites and 10,552 fragments from slave sites. Using calculations of meat weight, it was found that planters ate considerably more wild food than slaves did and utilized a wider variety of wild species.

Ceramic analysis, coupled with analogous historical documentation, suggests that slaves on task-system plantations like these had the ability and capital to engage in the market economy to support themselves. This greater economic freedom and market participation by slaves provided them with a means to control much more of their own lives than on the more-paternalistic gang-system plantations.

William H. Adams

See also Flowerdew Hundred Plantation

Kitchenmidden Committee

The Danish zoologist JAPHETUS STEENSTRUP began researching the shell banks of northern DENMARK in the 1820s in order to understand sea- and land-level changes. Initially, he believed that the enormous mounds of shells were the result of geological change—that they had been washed up by the sea. However, in the course of his excavations he found artifacts, bones, and hearths that he dated to the Stone Age period.

In 1848, the Danish Academy of Sciences established a multidisciplinary committee to study SHELL MIDDENS, or kitchen middens, and geological and sea-level changes. Steenstrup, the geologist Forchammer, and the archaeologist JENS JACOB WORSAAE reexamined the shell banks. In 1850, they discovered the enormous shell bank at Melgaard and recovered numerous implements and bones from it. Although it was Worsaae who suggested that the enormous piles of shell represented the remains of meals eaten by Stone Age people over a long period, Steenstrup coined the name *kitchen middens*.

All three men studied and recorded over fifty shell banks habitation sites in Jutland and Zealand in Denmark and in Scania in SWEDEN. In the early 1850s, they published six volumes of reports on these kitchen middens, demonstrating that they were of human origin and mapping patterns in accumulation. They also proved that the middens were occupied seasonally, and this fact, along with the distributions of hearths and artifacts, provided evidence of human behavior and activities.

Steenstrup disagreed with Worsaae about the age of the middens, believing that they were Neolithic or Stone Age but that they were contemporaneous with the builders and occupants of the Megalithic tombs. Worsaae rightly believed them to be earlier. In lectures in 1857, Worsaae argued for a chronological division of the Stone Age into two periods; the shell bank kitchen middens were from the earlier period, and the Megalithic tomb period was later.

Steenstrup's successful collaboration with Forchammer and Worsaae was the first of many successful collaborations between archaeologists, geologists, and biologists in Scandinavia and elsewhere. Steenstrup proved the importance of understanding the paleoenvironment to the study of archaeology, and his pioneering study of post-glacial flora was among the first of many significant contributions by biologists to archaeological chronology—with palynology, dendochronology, and carbon−14 DATING reaching their apogee in the twentieth century.

Tim Murray

See also Archaeometry

Klemenc, Josip (1898–1967)

The Slovenian archaeologist and ancient historian Josip Klemenc graduated in archaeology in 1920 and in history and geography in 1921 from the University of Zagreb, Croatia. He received his Ph.D. in archaeology from the same university in 1929 for his thesis on the dislocation of the Roman Army in Pannonia in the first century A.D. Between 1922 and 1942, he worked in the Archaeological Museum in Zagreb, where he became a curator. In 1946, Klemenc was appointed professor of classical archaeology and ancient history in the newly established Department of Archaeology at the University of Ljubljana, SLOVENIA, which produced the first generation of Slovenian archaeologists after World War II.

Klemenc's professional interests focused principally on the ancient topography, epigraphy, and numismatics of the Roman provinces of Noricum and Pannonia. In pre–World War II Yugoslavia, he initiated the study of archaeological topography, and between 1936 and 1939, he published three volumes of *Archaeologische Karte von Jugoslawien: Blatt Ptuj* (1936), *Blatt Zagreb* (1938), and *Blatt Rogatec* (1939), the first and the third with B. Saria. However his most influential work is associated with his discovery of Roman funerary art in Slovenia. In the Roman cemetery in Sempeter near Celje, the Roman colony of CELEIA, he discovered and studied sculptural remains that today represent the best examples of high-quality provincial art in Noricum.

Bojan Djuric

References
Klemenc, J. 1972. *Anticne grobnice v Sempetru* [Ancient Aediculae in Sempeter]. Ljubljana.

Knossos

Although the German archaeologist HEINRICH SCHLIEMANN had sought permission from the Turkish authorities to excavate at Knossos in the 1880s, the site is inextricably linked with the career of SIR ARTHUR EVANS. Knossos lies in the north part of central Crete, quite close to the present coastline. Although settlement is thought to have begun around 6000 B.C., it is clear that the large palace structure that lies at the core of

Palace in ancient Knossos with reconstructed balustrade and fresco (Image Select)

the site existed by about 1900 B.C. Evans's excavation of Knossos began in 1900, and the task was to tax his excavation and conservation skills until 1929. Although there has been considerable discussion of the conservation strategies followed by Evans and his associates, and about his emphasis on the "Minoan" civilization as being of Indo-European origin, there is no doubting the magnificent achievement of his major publication of the site, *The Palace of Minos at Knossos* (four volumes between 1921 and 1935). At Knossos, Evans had "found" the Minoan civilization, and, following Schliemann, he had further enhanced the links between myth and history.

Tim Murray

References

Evely, D., Hupres-Broch, H., and Momigliano, N. 1994. *Knossos, a Labryinth of History: Papers Presented in Honor of Sinclair Hood.* Athens: British School of Athens.

Kondakov, Nikodim Pavlovich (1844–1925)

The son of a freed serf and steward of princely estates, Kondakov went to school in Moscow, and in 1861 was sent to study at the University of Moscow with Slavic historian, philologist, and folklorist Ivonvich Buslayev. In deference to his teacher's dislike of Darwinism and prehistoric archaeology, Kondakov studied Classical and Byzantine art, graduating in 1866 and becoming a teacher at his old school.

In 1871, after traveling abroad to study classical monuments, Kondakov was appointed to the professorial chair of the theory and history of art at Novorossiysk University in Odessa. Scholars at this university were actively studying the local classical monuments of the Northern Black Sea coast and Kondakov participated in the excavation of the necropolis of the ancient Nimphaeum in Kerch, in the Crimea, where members of both the Greek and Scythian aristocracy were buried—the best excavated, researched, and recorded necropolis in the ancient world. Between 1873 and 1884 Kondakov traveled to major centers in Europe and the Near East, visiting libraries and museums and writing a monumental synthesis on the history of Byzantine art, his doctoral thesis *The History of Byzantine Art and the Iconography of the Miniatures of Greek Manuscripts.* This won the Gold Medal of the Russian Archaeological Society and resulted in his appointment to the influential Emperor's Archaeological Commission, whose three members were in charge of all archaeological activity in RUSSIA.

In 1888 Kondakov became professor of art history at Petersburg University and principal curator of medieval antiquities at the Imperial Hermitage Museum. In 1889 he became an academician (member of an imperial academy of eminent academics). He published six volumes of *Russian Antiquities in Monuments of Art* and a work on Russian archaeology, *Russian Hoards,* in 1898. In the latter Kondakov researched burial mounds, hoards, and other finds "in all aspects of their style, typical form of subjects, (and) its historical changes," using the iconographic typology developed in his thesis and transforming it into an archaeological typology. Kondakov continued to travel extensively and to publish his research on Byzantine art, which he described as the result of three different cultural and aesthetic traditions and influences—Hellenism, Greek–Egyptian–Near Eastern Orientalism, and the nomads from the steppes of the Black and Caspian Seas, Central Asia, and Southern Siberia.

At the end of the nineteenth century Russian prehistoric archaeology came of age. In 1899 ALEKSANDER VASILIY SPITSYN's *The Settling of Ancient Russian Tribes According to Archaeological Data* and GORODCOV's "Russian Prehistoric Ceramics" were published, the latter becoming the basis of all typological work by Russian archaeologists. Kondakov returned to the analysis of Byzantine art, writing *Iconography of Our Lady, Connections of Greek and Russian Icon-Painting with Italian Painting of the Early Renaissance* in 1911 and the two-volume *Iconography of Our Lady* in 1914–1915.

Kondakov's work, which redefined Russia and Russian culture as an expression of the Orthodox East as distinct from the cultural traditions of the West, also argued for Byzantium as the prototype for the contemporary Tzarist Russian empire. Both had unified Europe and Asia, and both justified Orthodoxy and autocracy. However this meant that liberal intellectuals and revolutionaries identified Byzantine influence with the maintenance of the monarchy and the social and political order. Kondakov was socially and politically conservative despite his background; closely connected with the church, he was readily admitted to the palace of Tsar Nicholas II as the court's expert on icon-painting.

Kondakov was 73 when the Russian Revolution began. During the Civil War (1918–1920) he lived in Odessa in territory occupied mainly by anticommunist White Russians and by supporting troops of the European powers. When they lost he went into exile in Istanbul, Sofia, and finally in Prague in Czechoslovakia in 1921, where his pupils organized what became the Kondakov Institute after his death in 1925. The institute became important for the study of CZECH Byzantine art and Slav philology and history, moving to Belgrade, Yugoslavia, after the German invasion, where it was destroyed in 1944 during a German air raid. Kondakov's numerous pupils have occupied leading positions within Soviet academe. He is now recognized as the founder of Russian archaeology.

Leo Klejn

References
For references, see *Encyclopedia of Archaeology: The Great Archaeologists, Vol. 2,* ed. Tim Murray (Santa Barbara, CA: ABC-CLIO, 1999), pp. 165–174.

Korea

Archaeological research on Korean Peninsula has about 100 years of history, which can be roughly divided into two halves. During the first half, Japanese scholars had exclusive access to, and control of, archaeological research and interpretation in the few years before the Japanese annexation of Korea in 1910 and during their colonial rule of the peninsula from 1910 to 1945. The second half started with the defeat of JAPAN at the end of World War II and the division of the Korean Peninsula into North and South Korea in 1945. Archaeological developments in the divided Korea have taken place with very little interaction between the two Koreas.

Archaeological Research before 1945

Before the modern discipline of archaeology was introduced to Korea, a number of Korean writers provided their own interpretations of archaeological sites and artifacts such as dolmens, stone daggers, and arrowheads. Their views were similar to those of their European counterparts prior to the development of archaeology in that they regarded stone tools as thunderbolts or elf arrows. One of the first scholars to consider prehistoric artifacts as human tools and weapons, i.e., as valuable historical data, was Kim Jeong-hui (1786–1856), a well-known writer, calligrapher, and painter. His survey of the Silla royal tombs in Kyongju resulted in an article that discussed the location of King Jinheung's tomb from a historical and geographical approach (Yi 1988). His identification of inscribed roof tiles from the Pyongyang area as those of the western Han dynasty of China on the basis of calligraphic style is the first example of archaeological research in Korea. However, his activities were isolated incidents and had no effect on the development of archaeology in Korea.

Modern archaeological activity in Korea began during the decline of the Joseon dynasty and the subsequent growth of Japanese influence during the late nineteenth and early twentieth centuries. Even before the Japanese annexation of Korea in 1910, Japanese scholars such as Sekino Tadashi, Torii Ryuzo, and Imanishi Ryu surveyed various archaeological sites on Korean Peninsula and in northeast CHINA. The earliest known archaeological excavations in Korea were all conducted by Japanese archaeologists in 1909 at the Baekje royal tombs in Buyeo and at a Silla royal tomb in Kyongju by Sekino Tadashi. The brick chamber tombs of the Chinese Lelang commandery in Pyongyang were excavated by Sekino Tadashi and Imanish Ryu. It is clear that the Japanese scholars were mainly interested in the royal tombs of Korea for their well-furnished burial goods, and it is also evident that they wanted to use them to highlight the foreign rule of Korea—in an attempt to legitimize Japan's rule of Korea, beginning with the Protectorate Treaty of 1905 and culminating in official annexation in 1910.

After annexation, the Korean Governor General's Office played an important role in establishing archaeological institutions, regulating and managing cultural properties, and deciding major policies concerning archaeological research in Korea. The office established the Museum of the Governor General's Office in 1915 to accommodate its own collection of Korean artifacts, and it organized the Committee for the Investigation of Korea Antiquities (Chosen koseki chosa iinkai), which would not only serve as the main consulting body for archaeological activities initiated by the colonial government but also conduct surveys, excavations, reconstruction, and preservation works throughout Korea. Scholars who participated on this committee included Sekino, Imanishi, Kuroita Katsumi, Hamada Kosaku, Harada Yoshito, Ikeuchi Hiroshi, and Umehara Sueji.

The office also laid the legal foundations for the preservation of archaeological remains by promulgating the first laws regulating cultural properties in 1916 (Pai 2000). For the first thirty years of the twentieth century, all archaeological research and excavation in Korea was organized, sponsored, and supervised by the Governor General's Office. After 1935, a semi-official Society for the Study of Korean Antiquities (Chosen koseki kenkyukai) replaced the Governor General's Office as the major sponsor of archaeological research in Korea.

During Japan's colonial rule of Korea, Japanese archaeologists identified and excavated thousands of archaeological sites, the majority of which were burials, such as the graves of the Lelang commandery in Pyongyang and the royal tombs of Silla in Kyongju; Baekje in Seoul, Gongju, and Buyeo; and Goguryo in Pyongyang and Ji'an in northeastern China, which was also under the rule of Japan at the time. Ancient buildings, monuments, and remains in several capitals of Korean dynasties and kingdoms, such as Seoul (Joseon dynasty), Gaeseong (Goryeo dynasty), Pyongyang, Gongju, Buyeo, and Kyongju, were thoroughly surveyed, photographed, recorded, and classified. Other kinds of archaeological sites, such as historic fortresses, Buddhist temples, prehistoric graves, and shell middens, were also surveyed, and a number of important ones were excavated.

As a result, Japanese researchers prior to 1945 produced a huge amount of archaeological data that could be used to understand the prehistory and history of Korea. A framework

Bas relief on the wall of a Buddhist temple in Sokkuram, Korea (Image Select)

for prehistoric and early historic Korea was composed, the study of which had been handicapped by the existence of few contemporary written records. The institutional and legal system for archaeological research established by the Japanese colonial government became the foundation for archaeological research in independent North and South Korea after World War II.

However, Japanese archaeological research in Korea had a number of shortcomings, biases, and unfavorable side effects. Archaeological activities were strictly limited to Japanese scholars, and research institutions and museums never hired or trained Koreans. At the end of World War II, there was not a single Korean who had received any training at the innumerable excavations conducted by the Japanese. Archaeological reports and museum catalogs were printed in both Japanese and English, and occasionally in classical Chinese, but never in Korean.

The archaeological past of the Korean Peninsula apparently belonged only to the Japanese and not to the Koreans. Archaeological information was used to legitimize Japan's colonial rule of Korea by highlighting alleged evidence of Japan's past conquests of the peninsula and the presumed lack of indigenous developments in premodern Korea. The results of Japanese archaeological research were selectively used to highlight the common ancestral origins of the Korean and Japanese races, the assertion that Japanese emperors ruled Korea between the fourth and seventh centuries, the overwhelming influence of Chinese civilization on Korea and the consequent lack of unique Korean origins, and the backwardness and stagnation of Korean civilization (Hatada 1981). Archaeological knowledge was not used to illustrate the distinctive nature and original development of Korean prehistoric or historic culture.

After conducting thousands of surveys and excavations in Korea, the Japanese left behind only a few excavation reports, monographs, catalogs, and articles. Many of the excavations were simply treasure-hunting expeditions conducted without any scientific record-keeping. It is unfortunate that precious archaeological information was lost forever as a consequence. There is no primary archaeological data from the sites the Japanese considered to be the most important and worthy of their excavation.

South Korean Archaeology after 1945

After the defeat of Japan in 1945, the Korean Peninsula was divided into southern and northern halves by the Allied forces. In South Korea, which was controlled by the U.S. forces, the newly founded National Museum in Seoul started archaeological activities in 1946 with the excavation of a Silla tomb in Kyongju. Kim Jae-won was appointed as the first director of the museum. He had received his postgraduate education in archaeology in Europe during the colonial era, but he had no experience of excavation in Korea. Excavations of tombs of the historical period continued, but the museum's work was soon halted by the outbreak of the Korean War (1950–1953).

In the 1950s, the National Museum and a few university museums excavated prehistoric and historical sites of various kinds. The people who participated in the excavations include some of the first generation of Korean archaeologists, such as Jin Hong-seop, Yun Mu-byeong, Kim Won-yong, and Kim Jeok-hak, most of whom had no formal training in archaeology. However, the organization of an exhibition of Korean art that toured major museums in the United States and Europe between 1958 and 1960 resulted in limited archaeological excavation because of the limited number of museum staff members who were available for fieldwork.

In 1961, the Department of Archaeology and Anthropology was established at Seoul National University, and Kim Won-yong, who had recently received his Ph.D. from New York University, became the senior member of the faculty, marking a new era of formal education in Korean archaeology. A doyen of Korean archaeology, Kim Won-yong played the most significant role in training young archaeologists and establishing the basics of Korean prehistory and art history. Graduates from this department have become the major players in Korean archaeology and art history as professors in universities, curators in national and private museums, and bureaucrats in government offices in charge of managing cultural properties.

During the 1960s and 1970s, most archaeological fieldwork was conducted by university museums, the National Museum, and the newly established Institute of Cultural Properties. Excavations of two royal tombs of Silla, the Tomb of Heavenly Horse and the Great Tomb of Hwangnam, in Kyongju and the discovery of the Tomb of King Muryeong, the only intact royal tomb of a great king of Baekje, in Gongju, were of great significance during this period. In addition, the first examples of Acheulean hand-axes in East Asia were discovered in Jeongokni. A Neolithic SHELL MIDDEN site at Yeoncheon in Busan, and a number of Bronze-Age settlement and burial sites were excavated, all of which filled significant gaps in Korea's prehistory.

One of the major accomplishments of Korean archaeology during this period was to overcome the colonial legacy of Japanese archaeologists. In both North and South Korea, archaeologists discovered a number of Paleolithic sites that confirmed a long sequence of cultural development on Korean Peninsula. They also proved that the Japanese interpretation of the so-called Chalcolithic age was wrong by confirming the existence of Neolithic and Bronze Ages in successive chronological order. As archaeological data accumulated, it became apparent that the Korean Peninsula was neither a backward nor a stagnant area of prehistoric cultural development, as the Japanese scholars had tried to portray it. On the contrary, newly discovered archaeological data in both Korea and Japan suggested that the major sources of stimulus for new cultural development in the Yayoi and Kofun periods of Japan were often the ancient societies of the Korean Peninsula.

Since the 1980s, enormous economic development has caused the destruction of numerous archaeological sites, and in order to protect the cultural heritage, legal codes were revised to require mandatory archaeological fieldwork before public and private construction projects could begin. In an attempt to meet the increasing demand for archaeological fieldwork, a number of new archaeological institutions for cultural resource management (CRM) were launched. These institutions took much of the CRM burden from the university museums, which had conducted most of the archaeological excavations until the 1980s. In order to cope with the changing environment of archaeological research, a number of new scholarly associations were organized in the late 1980s around research areas and topics. These included the Yeongnam Archaeological Society, the Honam Archaeological Society, the Hoseo Archaeological Society, and the Society for the Study of Korean Neolithic Age. These associations continue to help develop more-detailed studies of each area and thematic topics, but they could lead to an overspecialization and minimal scholarly communication across regional or thematic boundaries.

In recent years, an enormous amount of new archaeological data has been produced each year from hundreds of excavations by CRM projects. As a result of this explosion in archaeological fieldwork, a new picture of Korean prehistory and early history is slowly emerging. Chronological and geographical blanks in the archaeological data are being rapidly filled in, and new archaeological information has forced scholars to reexamine the traditional views of Korean pre- and proto-history.

North Korean Archaeology after 1945

In North Korea, the archaeological and historical interpretation of the past has always been closely intertwined with the political and ideological currents of the North Korean regime. After the Soviet forces took control of the northern half of Korean Peninsula at the end of World War II in 1945, the socialist authorities paid immediate attention to archaeological and historical heritage. In 1946, the Provisional People's Committee of North Korea promulgated laws and regulations for the preservation of national treasures, ancient sites, scenic spots, and natural monuments. The authorities also established historical museums and organized the Committee for the Preservation of Ancient Sites in Pyongyang and in each province. In the same year, a Neolithic shell midden in Songpyeongdong, Unggi, was excavated by North Korean archaeologists, the first recorded case of an excavation by Koreans. The excavation of a number of prehistoric sites continued until the outbreak of the Korean War.

After that war, archaeological fieldwork was actively carried out in conjunction with national reconstruction and industrialization projects. The leader of the archaeological team was Do Yu-ho, who had studied prehistory at the University of Vienna in Austria during the colonial period. He trained a number of other scholars, including Kim Yong-gan, Hwang Gi-deok, and Kim Yong-nam. Archaeological surveys and excavations in the 1950s accumulated new archaeological data and made it possible for North Korean archaeologists to establish a basic chronology for Korean archaeology, confirming the existence of Paleolithic and Bronze-Age cultures in Korea and overcoming the colonial legacy of Japanese archaeologists.

With this new body of accumulated archaeological data, North Korean scholars began to develop their own interpretations of early Korean history in the 1960s. Their attention focused on the issue of Gojoseon (Old Joseon, or Korea) and its location, territory, cultural sphere, time of formation, and nature of its social organization. The location of Gojoseon on the Liaodong Peninsula in northeastern China was accepted in the 1960s. This period was a golden age for North Korean archaeology, and it was much more advanced than that of South Korea. The most important cultural and historical archaeological theories were Marxism, historical materialism, and unilinear cultural evolutionism.

In the early 1970s, a new state doctrine of *juche,* or self-reliance, was established as the pillar of political ideology and propaganda in an attempt to idolize the North Korean leader Kim Il-sung. As a result, archaeological interpretation was under the direct influence of the ideology of the state and the ruling Workers' Party, and consequently, archaeology and historiography in North Korea became stagnant. In the 1980s and 1990s, archaeological research in North Korea was not as active as it had been in the 1960s, primarily because of the poor economic conditions of the country. The number of archaeological sites that were discovered and excavated decreased. Archaeological research in North Korea became dormant, with few archaeological discoveries reported and few original archaeological studies published.

In the early 1990s, a new framework for Korean prehistory was developed by North Korean archaeologists after the alleged discovery of the so-called tomb of Dangun in the Pyongyang area. This was scientific evidence of the existence of the mythical first Korean ancestor, born as the result of a union between a she-bear and the son of heaven according to various written sources of the twelfth century A.D. In order to emphasize the importance of the cultural accomplishments of Dangun and his successors, the earlier chronological framework of the 1960s was abandoned and a totally new picture of prehistoric Korea presented, but without any objective evidence. Archaeology in North Korea has now become a tool of state doctrine, part of the political propaganda of a chauvinist nationalism, and it can no longer be regarded as an independent scientific discipline.

Korean Archaeology in the New Millennium

Korean archaeologists will face many daunting challenges in the early decades of the new millennium. There is so much new archaeological data reported each year in South Korea that it has almost become impossible for even a Korean archaeology specialist to digest and make sense of it all. It is becoming more difficult to synthesize data and provide consistent and comprehensive interpretations of Korean prehistory and early history. This task will only be possible if there is cooperative work among specialists from different periods and themes.

Korean archaeology will need an independent framework of interpretation for both prehistoric and historical archaeology. Archaeological interpretation in Korea remains superficial, with most research being focused on typological studies and the periodization of artifacts and sites, with rudimentary explanations based on diffusion and migration. Historical archaeology does not provide alternative explanations. Historical records are considered to be of primary importance, and this attitude limits and dictates the interpretation of archaeological data. Korean archaeology must become more independent in its theory and methodology so it will be no longer considered a subdiscipline of historiography.

In both North and South Korea, archaeological research was almost exclusively practiced by Koreans in the last half of the twentieth century. Foreigners are still not allowed to excavate an archaeological site in South Korea, and in North Korea, there is no known case of foreign archaeological research. Except for only a few Japanese scholars and still fewer western scholars, Korean archaeology is still very much isolated from the outside world. In order to internationalize Korean archaeology, reports and papers must be published with English abstracts, cooperative fieldwork with foreign institutions should take place, and Koreans should be trained in foreign archaeology. There is still only a single monograph on Korean archaeology in English, and that by a western scholar (Nelson 1993).

The last, but hardly the least, challenge to be faced by Korean archaeologists may be the possible reunification of the two Koreas. Between North and South Korea there are huge differences in theory, methodology, empirical data, and the very practice of archaeology. Even before unification there should be some kind of constructive engagement among archaeologists from the two Koreas, which should include joint field surveys and excavations as well as the exchange of personnel and archaeological collections.

Yangjin Pak

References

Choi, Mong-lyong, et al. 1992. *Hanguk Seonsa Gogohaksa* [History of Korean Prehistoric Archaeology]. Seoul: Kkachi.

Hatada, Takashi. 1981. *Shin Chosenshi nyumon* [New Introduction to Korean History]. Tokyo: Ryukei shosha.

Nelson, Sarah M. 1993. *The Archaeology of Korea.* Cambridge: Cambridge University Press.

Pai, Hyung Il. 2000. *Constructing "Korean" Origins: A Critical Review of Archaeology, Historiography, and Racial Myth in Korean State-Formation Theories.* Cambridge, MA: Harvard University Asia Center.

Yi, Seon-bok. 1988. *Gogohak Gaeron* [Introduction to Archaeology]. Seoul: Iron gwa silcheon.

Korošec, Josip (1909–1966)

The Slovenian archaeologist Josip Korošec was involved with Neolithic, Eneolithic, and early Slavonic archaeology in SLOVENIA in the first decades after World War II. He graduated in classical philology in Belgrade in 1936 and specialized at Karl's University in Prague (receiving his Ph.D. in 1939). Between 1939 and 1945, he was curator of archaeology in the Provincial Museum in Sarajevo, between 1945 and 1947, he was curator in the City Museum at Ptuj, and beginning in 1947, he was at Ljubljana University where he founded the Department of Archaeology and was professor of prehistoric and early Slavonic archaeology.

In 1948, Korošec was one of the initiators of the Institute of Archaeology at the Slovenian Academy of Arts and Sciences. He founded the central national archaeological journal *Arheoloshi vestnik* in 1950, and in 1964, he founded the journal for Paleolithic, Neolithic, and Eneolithic archaeology, *Porocilo o raziskovanju paleolita, neolita in eneolita v Sloveniji*. He was also a correspondent member of the Yugoslav Academy of Arts and Sciences in Zagreb, the DEUTSCHES ARCHÄOLOGISCHES INSTITUT (German Archaeological Institute) in Berlin, and the Institute for Pre- and Protohistory in Florence.

Besides academic and organizational work, his contribution to field archaeology was significant. Korošec conducted several excavations, of which the most important were the prehistoric and early Slavonic site of Ptuj, the Ljubljana marshes, and the Neolithic site of Drulovka, all in Slovenia. In the other republics of the former Yugoslavia, Korošec excavated Danilo near Sibenik and Bribir near Zadar (both in Croatia) as well as Amzabegovo in Macedonia. He collaborated on fieldwork and analyses with his colleague and wife, Paola Korošec.

Korošec introduced VERE GORDON CHILDE's concept of culture into Slovene archaeology. According to Korošec, culture could be divided into the material and spiritual. The cultural group was determined culturally, geographically, chronologically, and ethnically, providing an entity with a certain degree of common economic and social organization. In 1947, Korošec published his first large synthesis on the history of Slavs in Slovenia, *Staroslovenska grobisca v severni Sloveniji*. This work was opposed to Nazi archaeology, which had also sought support for German ethnogenesis in sites in Slovenia in or-der to justify German geopolitical appetites. Paradoxically, the conceptual framework of GUSTAV KOSSINNA's *Siedlungsarchaeologie* (settlement archaeology), the basis of German expansionist theses, was nevertheless applied to Korošec research on early Slavonic sites. However, Korošec 's work on the theoretical considerations and definitions of archaeology, and its relationships with other social and humanist sciences and history, set the pattern for the future development of archaeology in Slovenia. He published numerous works—13 books, 116 discussions, 106 book reviews, 20 surveys—and his synthesis *An Introduction to the Material Culture of the Slavs in Early Medieval Period* (1952) is still one of the cornerstones of Slovenian national archaeology.

Irena Mirnik Prezelj

References
Grafenauer, B. 1967. "J. Korošec." *Zgodovinski casopis* (Ljubljana) 21: 238–246. Includes bibliography.
Klemenc, J. 1966. "In memoriam, J. Korošec." *Arheoloski vestnik* (Ljubljana) 17: 3–7.

Kossinna, Gustaf (1858–1931)

Born in East Prussia, the son of a secondary school teacher, Kossinna absorbed the German nationalist ethic prevalent in the education system of the time—the direct result of contemporary politics when Prussia was leading German unification. He attended the Universities of Gottingen, Leipzig, Berlin and Strasbourg. In Berlin Kossinna studied German philology, history and geography, but it was lectures on German and Indo-European linguistics that particularly interested him, and the problem of the location of the original Indo-German homeland (Urheimat) was to preoccupy him for his entire life. In 1881 he received a doctorate for his thesis on the linguistic subject "Ancient Upper-Frankian Written Monuments." In 1892 he started to work as a librarian at the University of Berlin.

Kossinna's interests in the original German homeland, and the roots of the German language and its ancient vocabulary sparked his interest in the material culture of ancient Germans. During the 1880s he began to read archaeological literature and to attend meetings of the Berlin Anthropological Society, founded by RUDOLF VIRCHOW and Adolf Bastan in 1869. Virchow was the head of German prehistoric archaeology for over thirty years and argued that the laws of culture might mirror those of biology. Kossinna developed the idea of identifying ancient peoples such as Slavs and Germans from their contemporary descendants, transferring ideas of biological transmission into ideas about the transmission of cultural traditions, succession, and continuity. In 1895 Kossinna gave the paper "The Prehistoric Spreading of Germans in Germany" at the annual meeting of the Anthropological Society, arguing that material culture (burials and artifacts) was a more precise indicator of the boundaries of early Germany than literary sources, and that prehistoric German territory could be determined by excavating prehistoric cultures.

Virchow died in 1904 and Kossinna succeeded him to the chair of prehistory at Berlin University. In 1905 he published "Ornamental Iron Spear-Heads as an Indication of Eastern Germans," in which he asserted the identification of cultures by one category of artifact and one identifying attribute—seeing national particularities in every detailed manifestation of national culture. Kossinna resented any criticism of his simplistic ideas, and surrounded himself with acolytes, whom he sought to place in key positions within German archaeology. In 1911 Kossinna's methodological work *The Origins of the Germans and the Method of "Residence Archaeology"* not only took his critics to task but also spelled out his "ethnographic prehistory" or "archaeology of spreading," an autochthonistic thesis that supported the primacy of continuity, of an age-long habitation of the same territory of Germans by Germans.

These arguments were further developed in the book *German Prehistory, An Extraordinarily National Science,* published that same year. Kossinna insisted that despite the opinions of classical writers, early 'Germans and their ancestors (Fore-Indo-Germans) were not barbarians but were in fact far more cultured than anyone else—they were the first to domesticate horses and invent the alphabet and bronze. Other cultures such as the French, CELTS, and Dacians and Slavs were belittled. For Kossinna the purpose of archaeology lay in connecting the German past to the German present and the German future, which was why archaeology was of vital importance for the nation. He acclaimed the outbreak of World War I as the fulfillment of the original "destiny" of the German people.

Kossinna took the German defeat of 1918 very hard but he continued to develop his claim that territorial rights were determined and measured by the duration of a people's residence on that territory, and that the descendants of former possessors, even of those from very ancient times, had the right to drive present inhabitants away. Kossinna saw archaeology as a means of proving territorial claims—as a weapon of interstate geopolitics and a potential rationale for extended international and national conflicts. His book *The Origin and Expansion of Germans in Prehistoric and Early Historic Times,* published in two parts in 1927 and 1928, completed links between his "residence archaeology" and his racial theories.

When Hitler came to power the "extraordinarily national" archaeology of Kossinna was mobilized in the service of Nazism and its territorial claims. Kossinna's pupil Hans Reinert was placed at the head of the State Union of German Prehistory and Kossinna's books were reissued many times. While Kossinna did see and express some of the really vital questions about the possibilities, uses, and developments of archaeology, such as the ethnic determination of cultures, the possibility of genetic connections with cultures, culturogenesis (the origin of a certain culture), and the connection of culturogenesis with the origin of peoples and their languages, his conclusions were dangerously simplistic, uncritical, untestable, imbalanced, and wrong. His work is all but ignored.

Leo Klejn

See also German Prehistoric Archaeology
References
For references, see *Encyclopedia of Archaeology: The Great Archaeologists, Vol. 2,* ed. Tim Murray (Santa Barbara, CA: ABC-CLIO, 1999), pp. 233–246.

Kostenki

First excavated in 1879 by Russian archaeologists A. Polyakov and A. SPITSYN, Kostenki was the focus of long-term excavation for much of the twentieth century. Extending about 10 kilometers on the banks of the River Don to the south of Voronezh, Kostenki is in fact a complex of twenty-five surface and stratified open sites, which in some instances extend up to 2 kilometers away from the river.

The excavation of these sites has produced a large assemblage of items of material culture for the period 35,000 B.P.–11,000 B.P., including stone and bone tools, ivory Venus figurines, animal figurines carved from bone and stone, and features that have been interpreted as rectangular long houses. Although that interpretation is now being questioned on the basis that what was thought to be contemporary evidence now seems more likely to be the result of multiple occupations. The other "dwellings"—small houses made of mammoth bone—continue to be accepted as evidence of single occupations.

Tim Murray

See also Russia

Kostrzewski, Józef (1885–1969)

Józef Kostrzewski was an outstanding Polish prehistorian. He initially studied medicine at the University of Wroclaw, but in 1909–1910 he took two semesters of archaeology under Wlodzimierz Demetrykiewicz at the Jagiellonian University in Cracow. He continued prehistoric studies in Berlin under GUSTAF KOSSINNA and received his Ph.D. in 1914. The first year of his studies was spent in London, engaged in self-education at the BRITISH MUSEUM. In 1912, the first year of his independent research, Kostrzewski excavated a site in Siedlemin, near Jarocin (Wielkopolska) in POLAND. In 1914, his first book, *Wielkopolska w czasach przedhistorycznych* (Wielkopolska in the Prehistoric Period), was published. A second edition was published in 1923, the same year he became an assistant in the prehistory section of the Museum of the Society of Friends of Sciences in Poznan. He defended his postdoctoral disserta-

Józef Kostrzewski (Arkadiusz Marciniak)

tion on prehistory, written under the supervision of the anthropologist Jan Czekanowski, the classical archaeologist Edmund Bulanda, and the geologist Jozef Siemiradzkion, at Jan Kazimierz University in Lvov in 1919.

Kostrzewski was one of the founders of the Poznan University, in 1919, and he became head of the Department of Archaeology there. In 1920, he was one of the coorganizers of the Polish Prehistoric Society, whose aim was to support studies in prehistory and to encourage archaeology. It was composed of fans of archaeology from all over Poland and its journal, *Przeglad Archeologiczny* (Archaeological Review), has been published ever since.

In 1924, Kostrzewski successfully combined the collections of the two Poznan museums: the Polish one, or Mielzynskis's Museum, and the German one, or Wielkopolskie Museum. A prehistoric section located in the Wielkopolskie Museum was established with Kostrzewski as its head, and it came to contain one of the most valuable archaeological collections in Poland. Kostrzewski began to develop his autochthonic theory of the origin of Slavs, and in 1926, he began editing the popular journal *Z Otchlani Wiekow* (From the Abyss of Ages), which became not only a great success but also an excellent instrument for the propagating of archaeology among the general public. His work at the museum and his research and publications ensured that the department in Poznan became a strong archaeological center in both the interwar and the postwar period. Thanks to the efforts of Kostrzewski, the Poznan Prehistoric School was established, and by the end of 1926, he was the dominant figure in archaeology in Poland, as the head or the founder of most Poznan archaeological institutions.

In 1934, Kostrzewski initiated and led the excavation of a Lusatian culture fortified settlement, BISKUPIN, in Poland. Biskupin became an example of modern archaeological research and the use of new preservation methods, as well as a training site for new staff. A wide information and promotional campaign launched by Kostrzewski generated considerable interest in the excavations from within Poland and from abroad. In 1936, he began excavating the strongholds of the early Piasts in Gniezno, Poznan, and Klecko.

During World War II, Kostrzewski changed his name to avoid detention. This was a period of intense work, and his *Kultura prapolska* (Pre-Polish Culture), published in 1947, was one of his greatest achievements. Two years after the Polish edition, a French translation appeared *(Les origines da la civilisation polonaise, préhistoire-protohistoire),* which was an outstanding synthesis of the whole problem of Polish tribal and early Piast culture while, at the same time, being an original introduction to the celebration of the millennium of the Polish state. The work was characterized by a broad and comprehensive approach to the problems it raised as well as by an innovative application of the achievements of other branches of science, such as ethnography and history.

After the war, in March 1945, Kostrzewski again became the head of the prehistoric section in the Wielkopolskie Museum and assumed a teaching position at the university. At the suggestion of the Institute for the Research on Slavic Antiquities, the excavations in Biskupin were resumed in 1946. His postwar academic career was marked by his anti-German attitude, and Kostrzewski struggled to prove the Polish origins of the so-called regained territories (the northern and western parts of today's Poland).

In 1950, because he was a scholar who did not want to comply with the indoctrination and ideologization of public and academic life resulting from communist rule in Poland, he lost his position as head of the university department and retired. In 1956, during the period of considerable political freedom after Stalin's death, he again became the head of the Archaeology Department. He retired finally in 1960, and because he had educated a large group of active archaeologists, he can be considered the proper founder of the Poznan school of prehistory.

Over his long professional career Kostrzewski showed interest in all periods of Polish prehistory. By studying all of its history, he developed the most accurate typological and chronological descriptions of successively identified cultures and leading groups of monuments. His research involved classifying and describing source materials, and he intentionally did not try to include a discussion of economic and settlement relations or relationships with the natural environment. Neither did he directly refer to the discoveries of the natural scientists. For him, the basic unit of study was an archaeological culture and a local group. Each culture, after sublimation, became a real and independent unit that was capable of unrestricted migration, making its own relations, transferring its own features, or mixing with other cultures.

Kostrzewski's main works were typically idiographic in character, and he himself was a typical empiricist, rarely explaining the theoretical and methodological assumptions he referred to. He was also interested in the problem of the continuity of settlement patterns in a given territory. In his work, he took a positivist approach and adopted intuitive antinaturalism. For Kostrzewski, induction was the fundamental procedure used in obtaining valid knowledge.

He supported the theory of autochthonism of the Slavs, based on the premise that from the time of the Lusatian culture (late Bronze Age to the early Iron Age) until the early Middle Ages there is an observable continuity in settlement patterns and in cultural development. He also emphasized the cultural unity of the region and attributed it to Slavic forefathers. His main concern was to formulate an approach that would synthesize particular fragments of the prehistory of Polish territories.

The second edition of his *Wielkopolska w czasach prehistorvcznych* (Wielkopolska in the Prehistoric Period), published in 1923, was considered the fundamental model for all approaches to the synthesis of the prehistory of the territories of Poland. Kostrzewski was particularly interested in synthesizing long periods in the prehistory of Poland, for example, from the Neolithic Age to the great migration period, considered in *Prehistoria ziem polskich* (1948; Prehistory of the Polish Lands) and *Pradzieje Polski* (1965; Prehistory of Poland). He was also the author of regional syntheses: the one already mentioned about Wielkopolska as well as others about Pomerania and Silesia.

Arkadiusz Marciniak

Koumbi Saleh

The forty-four-hectare tell of Koumbi Saleh is one of the great urban sites of Africa. In the eastern Hodh, several miles from Mauritania's border with Mali, the site comprises over sixty mounds, delimited by large streets, of debris from collapsed buildings constructed with plaques of locally available schist. A main attraction of the site since its discovery in 1914 by Bonnel de Mezières, a French civil servant, has been its putative identification as the capital of the Empire of Ghana as described by the Arab chronicler al B'akri in 1068. Virtually all pre-1970s archaeological work at the site, by Bonnel de Mezières, Raymond Mauny, and others, was undertaken primarily to evaluate this identification.

The archaeological material encountered in the course of these early, quite extensive excavations was given only summary treatment, and no full excavation reports were ever published. Beginning in 1975, French archaeologist Sophie Berthier's excavations, by contrast, considered the site in archaeological rather than historical terms and focused on the study of architectural evolution at the site and the characterization of material culture through time. Berthier's work was undertaken as part of more extensive excavations at and around the Koumbi Saleh mosque that were directed by Serge Robert. To date,

Berthier's work is the only publication to have emerged from that extensive project.

Berthier conducted excavations during four field seasons on a single building in the north central part of the site not far from the Grande Place, a large public area. She concluded that of the thick deposits encountered, half belonged to a period of "grand urbanization," dated by twelve radiocarbon determinations on charcoal to the eleventh–fourteenth centuries. Architecture at that time was very distinctive and commonly included rectangular and triangular wall niches, the use of paving stones on floor, step, and terrace surfaces, and the use of painted schist wall plaques. By the late fourteenth century, the buildings had been abandoned.

Strongly focused on architectural evolution, Berthier's work is thin with regard to analyses and interpretations that illuminate the changing nature of subsistence and trade at the apparent capital of the empire. The extensive areas of Koumbi Saleh that lack stone ruins still remain to be investigated, and among these may be the remains of the indigenous town in which the pagan king (ghana) lived, described by al-Bakri as separate from the stone-built town inhabited by Muslims and northern traders.

Susan McIntosh

See also Africa, Francophone
References
Berthier, S. 1997. *Recherches archéologiques sur la capitale de l'Empire de Ghana.* International Series no. 680. Oxford: British Archaeological Reports.
Bonnel de Mezières, A. 1920. "Recherche sur l'emplacement de Ghana (fouille à Koumbi Saleh et Settah)." *Comptes Rendus de l'Académie des Inscriptions et Belles Lettres* 12: 227–273.
Mauny, R., and P. Thomassey. 1951. "Campagne de fouilles à Koumbi Saleh (Ghana?)." *Bulletin de l'Institut Français de l'Afrique Noire* B, no. 13: 438–462.
———. 1956. "Campagne de fouilles de 1950 à Koumbi Saleh (Ghana?)." *Bulletin de l'Institut Français de l'Afrique Noire* B, no. 18: 117–140.
Robert, D., and S. Robert. 1972. "Douze années de recherches archéologiques en République islamique de Mauritanie." *Annales de la Faculté des Lettres, Dakar* 2: 195–233 (pp. 221–226 concern Koumbi Saleh).

Kourion

Kourion (Curium), an Iron Age and Roman site on the south coast of CYPRUS, has been the target of numerous projects. Some of the best-known finds by LUIGI PALMA DI CESNOLA (including much gold jewelry now in the Metropolitan Museum in New York) came from his work on Iron Age royal tombs in 1873. Additional recent work by Demos Christou (Department of Antiquities, Cyprus) has clarified details of those tombs and of Cesnola's activities.

There have been numerous and extensive excavations of the classical city by a series of archaeologists. Between 1933 and 1954, George McFadden and others excavated on behalf of the Pennsylvania University Museum. The Department of Antiquities has been conducting excavations on the Acropolis since 1964, and A. H. S. Megaw worked on the early Christian basilica for Dumbarton Oaks in Washington, D.C. Between 1980 and 1983, Diana Buitron and David Soren excavated at the Sanctuary of Apollo. The site has well-preserved Roman buildings, including a theater, many of which are decorated with mosaics. The theater and many other structures have been substantially restored.

David Frankel

References

A Guide to Kourion. 1987. Nicosia: Bank of Cyprus Cultural Foundation.

Soren, D., and J. James. 1988. *Kourion: The Search for a Lost Roman City.* New York: Doubleday.

Kozłowski, Leon (1892–1944)

Leon Kozłowski was one of the most important Polish archaeologists of the first half of the twentieth century, and he represented a generation of archaeologists who, for the first time, had professional careers in archaeology. He was a student of Erazm Majewski, studied archaeology under Wlodzimierz Demetrykiewicz at the Jagiellonian University in Cracow in 1912–1913, and continued under the supervision of R. Schmidt at the University of Tübingen in Germany. In 1921–1939, he was professor of archaeology at the Jan Kazimierz University in Lvov.

Kozłowski was the author of very modern syntheses about the Paleolithic, Neolithic, and

Leon Kozłowski (Arkadiusz Marciniak)

Bronze Ages in POLAND. These are *Starsza epoka kamienna* (1922; Palaeolithic or Early Stone Age), *Mlodsza epoka kamienna* (1924; Neolithic or Late Stone Age), and *Wczesna, starsza i srodkowa epoka bronzu w Polsce w swietle subborealnego optimum klimatcznego i jego wplyw na ruchy etniczne i zaludnienie Polski* (1928; Early and Middle Bronze Ages in Poland in the Light of Subboreal Climatic Optimum and Its Influence on the Ethnic Movements and Population of Poland). In his work on the Neolithic period, he distinguished many archaeological cultures that have remained correct until the present, and he presented a very clear chronological division for the period.

Kozłowski's works are characterized by methodological correctness. He would define the notions present in archaeological discourse, for example, that of archaeological culture, and his work contained geological backgrounds, hydrographic conditions, climate and soil characteristics, and an assessment of their impact on prehistoric settlement systems. While analyzing flint assemblages he focused his attention on raw materials, the technology used, and tool functions. His works were richly illustrated with detailed tables. His other important works are *Wenedowie w zrodlach historycznych i w swietle kartografii przedhistorycznej* (1937; Weneds in Historical Sources and in the Light of Prehistoric Cartography) and *Zarys pradziejow Polski poludniowo-wschodniej* (1939; Prehistory of South-East Poland, an Outline).

Kozłowski's scientific activities are characterized by the collection of different kinds of data and by the formulation of generalizations regarding particular periods, areas, and problems. These two characteristics were important features of Polish archaeology during the first half of the twentieth century and his work is still stimulating for later generations of Polish archaeologists. He introduced the results of European archaeological research on relative chronology into the milieu of Polish archaeology, and he regarded a typological-comparative method as fundamental for archaeology. Kozłowski emphasized the necessity of withdrawing from simple nineteenth-century evolutionism, with its linear perception of the development of cultural phenomena. He noticed the importance of environmental factors and diffusion in shaping the development of prehistoric communities, mainly their migration. He carried out many large-scale excavations and numerous field surveys, and his excavations, modern for their time, were characterized by methodical correctness and complexity.

Kozłowski was active politically. In the 1930s he was minister for agriculture and agricultural reforms, undersecretary in the Ministry of Finance, and prime minister of the Polish government from 1933 to 1934.

Arkadiusz Marciniak

Kromdraai

Kromdraai is a South African site containing evidence of early hominids. In 1938, R. Broom recovered a hominid from the site and named it *Paranthropus Robustus*—it is now thought to be an australopithecine. The site was reexcavated by C. K. Brain between 1955 and 1956 and by Elizabeth Vrba between 1977 and 1985. A total of thirteen hominid fossils have been recovered.

Tim Murray

See also Africa, South, Prehistory

Krukowski, Stefan (1890–1982)

Stefan Krukowski was an influential Polish archaeologist and a great personality. His only teacher of prehistory was Erazm Majewski, and he never completed any formal studies in archaeology, being completely self-taught. He was commissioned to conduct his first fieldwork by Majewski in 1908. In 1911, he published his first paper, on studies carried out in the Kielce district. In 1914, he started working in the anthropology workshop of the Warsaw Scientific Society, and this event marked the beginning of his almost total devotion to the Stone Age. At the same time, he also began important studies of the caves in the Cracow-Wielun range, such as Okiennik Cave. During World War I, he continued his research in Russia, in the Caucasus, on the Paleolithic site of KOSTENKI.

Krukowski's professional career and research were especially intense between 1919 and 1939. From 1918 to 1925, he worked in the prehistory section of the Institute of Anthropological Studies of the Warsaw Scientific Society. At the same time, he was keeper of archaeological monuments for the southern Warsaw district until 1928, and in that year he became a curator in the newly founded State Archaeological Museum in Warsaw. His research focused on the development of proper scientific methods applicable both in fieldwork and in interpretation, and his work was closely associated with the natural sciences, primarily geology.

Of great importance was his collaborations with the outstanding geologist Jan Samsonowicz. Their work led to the discovery of a unique mine of striped flint in KRZEMIONKI OPATOWSKIE in 1922, shallow mines of chocolate-colored flint near Lysogory, and grey-white spotted flint in Swieciechow near Annopol. In 1928, he took up the study and protection of the mine in Krzemionki Opatowskie, and in 1939, he published *Krzemionki Opatowskie,* a research questionnaire in which the author described the standard features of the mine such as the mining field, shafts, underground headings, dumps, and mining tools. He also discussed the organization of the work, the spatial relations between mines and the settlements they were connected to, and the social aspects of the distribution of flint axes.

Stefan Krukowski (Arkadiusz Marciniak)

ritory of Poland, drew differences among them, and illustrated their influence on the morphological diversity of flint inventories. He examined the possibility and mechanics of studying raw materials distribution and the possible ways that prehistoric societies obtained them. His work matched the highest standards of the day.

He was also the author of an overview of the Paleolithic age of Poland, published in 1948 as the synthesis *Prehistoria ziem polskich* (Prehistory of the Polish Lands), written jointly with JOZEF KOSTRZEWSKI and Roman Jakimowicz. In 1976, Krukowski published another synthesis of the Polish Paleolithic and Mesolithic ages entitled *Skam 71,* in which he presented his theory of genetic prehistory. It was an original study, but because of its complicated terminology and hermetic language, its reception was limited. He also created a dictionary of concepts to be used in archaeology.

Genetic prehistory, Krukowski's original contribution, was an attempt to provide new directions in Stone Age archaeology, and developed toward the end of the 1960s, it was hoped it would provide an alternative to traditional Paleolithic prehistory. Krukowski pointed out the necessity of studying all flint assemblages, such as raw material, blanks, and waste, not just tools. The objective of genetic history was to determine the origin, formation, and purpose of stone tool industries. A crucial aspect in its determination was the study of flint blanks, which enabled him to recognize the unintended effects of the producers on the basis of a detailed analysis of all artifacts making up a given inventory. Genetic prehistory and the flint blank method permitted the separation of industries in mixed inventories.

Arkadiusz Marciniak

Krukowski was a researcher of Paleolithic cave camps such as Ciemna and Okiennik, of loess and sand sites, and of mines. He examined the locations of the sites in POLAND of Piekary, Gora Pulawska, Grzybowa Gora, Swidry Wielkie, Wieliszew, and Oronsko. He also organized and led a research campaign to Rydno, in which he focused on the systematic identification of a settlement complex in connection with the oldest mine, hematite processing and distribution, and a chocolate-colored rock bed.

After World War II, he had trouble finding a permanent position. In 1956, he received the title of professor extraordinarius.

The first part of his first work, synthetic in character, *Pierwociny krzemieniarskie gornictwa transportu i handlu w holocenie polskim* (Beginnings of Flint Mining, Transportation, and Trade in Holocene of Poland) was published in 1920, and the second part was published in 1922. In this work, Krukowski was concerned with the origins of material used for flint tools. He described his search for siliceous rocks in the ter-

Krzemionki Opatowskie

The site of Krzemionki Opatowskie is located about ten kilometers southeast of Ostrowiec Swietokrzyski, Tarnobrzeg voivodeship, in POLAND. It is the best known as "the black and white striped flint mine," within an agglomeration of some excellent and characteristic flint mines in the northern and northeastern parts of

Flint mine at Krzemionki Opatowskie, showing rock pillars (Arkadiusz Marciniak)

cient system of ventilation. Loopholes were punctured near the bottom and near the top of the neighboring underground headings, making possible the circulation of air between the main shafts and the systems of corridors surrounding them. Workers in the mine used a set of mining tools made from flint and stone (chocks, axes, and flint picks), from antlers (chocks, axes), and probably from wood. The quarry or open-cast mine was used to exploit the relatively scarce good-quality material found on the weathered external layer. Across the area of the whole mine, and particularly surrounding earlier shaft funnels, there are banks of waste limestone debris. Around the main field area there are remains of flint-making workshops, which produced semimanufactured tools, mainly axes and chisels.

The flint mine in Krzemionki Opatowskie was established by people of the Neolithic "Funnel Beaker Culture." It was exploited later by people of the "Globular Amphorae Culture," and it remained in use until the beginning of the Bronze Age. Specialized miners, living in neighboring settlements, worked the mine. In some of the bigger settlements around the mine (such as "Gawroniec" in Cmielow) there is evidence of the mass production of semimanufactured axes and chisels. A very elaborate and specialized mining and production group emerged in this area.

The flint tools (mainly axes and chisels) made from the raw material exploited in Krzemionki Opatowskie were distributed over very large areas, sometimes for more than five hundred kilometers from the mine. They can be found from the Sambia peninsula in the north, Rugen Island and Elbe river-basin in the west, and in southern Bohemia, Moravia, and Slovakia in the south. Large numbers of striped flint tools can be found in the territories of the southeastern group of Funnel Beaker Culture. Total production of the flint mine from Krzemionki Opatowskie has been estimated at around eight million semimanufactured artifacts.

The flint mine at Krzemionki Opatowskie was found by Polish geologist Jan Samsonowicz in 1922, and the first systematic excavations were undertaken by Jozef Zurowski in the years

the Swietokrzyskie Mountains. This was a big flint basin in a small region, and it was developed during the Paleolithic. Krzemionki Opatowskie is the unique site of this type in Europe.

The flint mine was exploited via a system of shafts and underground headings, and also, to a lesser degree, in a quarry (opencast) system. The mine consisted of more than one thousand shafts, a few meters in width and four to ten meters in depth. Slightly above the bottom of the shaft, there was a system of corridors alongside a siliceous rock, about sixty centimeters in height. These were sometimes enlarged in the form of bigger stalls (up to twelve by eighteen meters). The shape of the system of corridors was the result of the siliceous rock distribution, and the siliceous concretion was approximately ten to fifteen centimeters thick. For the sake of security in the mine, numerous rock pillars were left in place as mining progressed, along with other consolidations, such as limestone dumps or intentional filling by debris from mining. There was a relatively effi-

between 1924 and 1927. STEFAN KRUKOWSKI and Zygmunt Szmit started their researches in Krzemionki Opatowskie in 1928. In the same year Krukowski became the curator of the mine. The mine has been protected by law since 1928. Krzemionki Opatowskie is an open archaeological museum at present, and it is still a center of archaeological interest, mainly from the State Archaeological Museum in Warsaw.

Arkadiusz Marciniak

Kuwait

See Arabian Peninsula

L

La Madeleine

La Madeleine is the type site of the Magdalenian industry of the Upper Paleolithic period in Europe, about 16,000–10,000 B.C. The rock shelter lies on the outskirts of Les Eyzies in the Perigord region of southwestern FRANCE and was excavated in the mid-nineteenth century by ÉDOUARD LARTET and HENRY CHRISTY. The site yielded stone and bone tools of distinctive form, but it is most notable for producing evidence of mobiliary (portable or parietal) art in the form of carved and incised bone, antler, stone, and ivory. The people who made these are referred to as Magdalenian and they hunted deer or ibex.

Tim Murray

See also Breuil, Henri; Lithic Analysis
References
Gamble, C. 1986. *The Paleolithic Settlement of Europe.* Cambridge: Cambridge University Press.

La Tène

The eponymous site of the later phase of Iron Age civilization (500 B.C. until the Roman Conquest) of La Tène, SWITZERLAND, covers the whole of Celtic Europe. Discovered in 1857 by Hans Kopp, who "fished" for Friedrich Schwab, the archaeologist of Bienne, the site was first considered to be a lake dwelling based on examples of Stone and Bronze Age villages on the Swiss lakes. Such an interpretation had the advantage of extending the custom of lake dwelling, which was felt to be specifically Swiss, until the Roman occupation.

In no time, La Tène achieved international fame. In 1872, HANS HILDEBRAND suggested giving the name to a specific culture of the Iron Age, and the definition was ratified by an international congress held in Stockholm in 1874. Hildebrand, however, attributed the differences between the two cultures that he had defined, Hallstatt (early Iron Age) and La Tène (later Iron Age), to geographical variation. It was EDOUARD DESOR, an archaeologist and geologist from Neuchâtel, who deserves all the credit of having, as early as 1865 (and more explicitly in 1868), clearly established a chronological succession for the Iron Age. This feat was achieved by means of comparisons with Tiefenau (Bern), Alesia (France), and the Celtic site of Marzabotto (northern Italy) on the one hand and the burial mounds of the Swiss Neuchâtel area and the Austrian burial place of Hallstatt on the other.

The site of La Tène includes two bridges, named Vouga and Desor after the early excavators. The bridges crossed a lateral, little active (or maybe dead) arm of the river Thielle, which was totally filled in when discovered. The bridges are near the Thielle's egress from Lake Neuchâtel, which is linked by this river to Lake Bienne. The river separates the foothills of the Jura mountain chain from the Swiss plateau, and this archaeologically rich site has seen successive excavations. Unfortunately, some of the work has not been a credit to Swiss archaeology. During the fifty years following La Tène's discovery, looting of the site was more common than archaeological research, particularly during the first Jura Surface Waters Regulation Scheme (1869–1883), which lowered water levels by 2.70 meters and left the surface of the site exposed.

The difficulty of excavating the site, by dragging or fishing and then by excavating in the wa-

Reconstruction of a grave found in France, La Tène period (The Art Archive / Musée des Antiquités St. Germain en Laye / Dagli Orti)

ter, does not explain the lack of care taken while doing it. Many of the archaeologists who participated in the site's "exploitation" were much more conscientious elsewhere. These archaeologists probably tolerated the looting of the La Tène site by many collectors because they judged it too late to carry out any serious archaeological work there, owing to technical difficulties. It is certain that the relative typological homogeneity of the material tempered their scientific fervor by taking away a good part of what generally motivated stratigraphic observations.

They also recognized that important reshapings of the strand at the head of the lake, which is often marked by violent storms, had drastically changed the terrain so that artifact position would have seemed of little significance. And last but not least, the considerable extension of the site, together with the absence of practical landmarks, might have made attempts of planimetric documentation seem useless. In the accounts of the excavations, archaeologists, once their booty was listed, endeavored to justify

their scientific carelessness by the devastated condition of the site around the area of their findings. These important finds were dispersed into many private collections, and they can be found in museums all over the world. There is no complete inventory of the artifacts.

When professional excavations began at La Tène in 1907, the site was considered to be almost exhausted. Local authorities created the Societe d'Histoire et d'Archeologie de Neuchâtel and granted it financial support to undertake new excavations. The society gave the Commission des Fouilles de La Tène full responsibility for the work. Excavations, supervised by William Wavre and then Paul Vouga (famous for his work on lakeshore Neolithic), lasted until 1917. Vouga's systematic excavations, as well as his attempts to understand former work, resulted in the following picture.

The two bridges are set more than 100 meters apart, and a fence runs alongside the bank, probably to strengthen it. To the south, there were some buildings, whose plans are not clear, and the layout of these vestiges, found amid the beams and the pillars of the bridges and also up- and downstream, are not very well known. The finds extend to almost the whole range of what one can expect to find in an archaeological site: weapons, tools, ornaments, and implements made of iron, but also of bronze, wood, and bone; potsherds, baskets, fabrics, and leather articles. Zoological and anthropological remains were also various and numerous: bones of horses, oxen, pigs, sheep, goats, and dogs as well as several human skeletons.

Most of the archaeological material (nearly 90 percent) has been assigned to the middle La Tène period (approximately 270–150 B.C.) while the Vouga bridge, upstream, can be dated to 252 B.C. by dendrochronology. The rest of the finds provide isolated evidence of the occasional frequention of the shore during the final La Tène period and then during the two first centuries A.D.; the Desor bridge could well be Roman.

There have been many hypotheses about the function of the site, as well as about the circumstances of its abandonment. The site was set in a strategic place, straddling the Swiss plateau and the foothills of the Jura, and the quality, richness, and variety of vestiges were unique. The layout of the objects was also striking, with concentrations in several zones of different types of artifacts, such as swords, spears, or horse bits and rings.

Thus, the site has been regarded as an *oppidum* (fortified town), or a place of refuge; as a military post with an arsenal; and as a trading place with a port or a frontier post. The interpretation most favored by the majority of scientists was formulated by Klaus Raddatz in 1952: La Tène was a place of sacrifice, a hypothesis that could be easily combined with any one or more of the above-mentioned functions. It is based on the characteristics of the site's animal bones, which totally contradict the usual data for a settlement place. It is reinforced by the presence of "new" objects and of wrapped or "mutilated" human skeletons—one of which was found with a rope around its neck (E. Vouga 1885, 32).

Controversy about the nature of the La Tène site is still far from over. In a study of the Celtic bridge of Cornaux a few miles downstream, Hanni Schwab is convinced of the trade and craft functions of La Tène. According to her, the site would have been suddenly devastated, like the bridge of Cornaux, by a big rise in the lake's water level shortly before mid-first century B.C. This point of view has not been favorably received, but Schwab must be given credit for showing that evidence for a definitive interpretation of the site, whose last excavations date back more than three-quarters of a century and whose material has not yet been entirely studied, is too weak and incomplete for any final resolution.

Marc-Antoine Kaeser

See also Celts

References

Desor, E. 1864. "Les constructions lacustres du Lac de Neuchâtel: III—Age du Fer." *Musée Neuchâtelois* 1: 63–69.

———. 1865. *Les palafittes ou constructions lacustres du Lac de Neuchatel.* Paris: Reinwald.

———. 1868. "Le tumulus des Favargettes." *Musee Neuchatelois* 5: 229–242.

Dunning, C. 1990. "La Tène." In *The Celts: Exhibition Catalogue,* 366–368. Milan: Bompiani.

Egloff, M. 1989. "Des premiers chasseurs au début du christianisme." In *Histoire du Pays de Neuchatel,* 1:13–171. Hauterive: Attinger.

———. 1991. "L'artisanat celtique d'après les trouvailles de La Tène?" In *The Celts: Exhibition Catalogue,* 369–371. Milan: Bompiani.

Hildebrand, H. 1872–1880. "Studier i jamforande fornforskning I: Bidrag till spannets historia." *Antiqvarisk Tidskrift for Sverige* 4: 1–263.

Jacob-Friesen, G. 1980. "Ein Jahrhundert Chronologie der vorromischen Eisenzeit in Mittel und Nordeuropa." *Bonner Jahrbucher* 180: 1–30.

Kaenel, G. 1991. "La Tène (canton de Neuchatel), un site mythique qui n'a pas livre tous ses secrets." In *Les Celtes dans le Jura: L'age du fer dans le massif jurassien (800–15 av J.-C.),* 117–118. Ed. P. Curdy, G. Kaenel, and M.-J. Rouliere-Lambert. Yverdon, Switz.: Cornaz.

Muller, F. 1990. *Der Massenfund von der Tiefenau bei Bern: Zur Deutung latenezeitlicher Sammelfunde mit Waffen.* Antiqua no. 20. Basel: Schweizerische Gesellschaft fur Ur- und Fruhgeschichte.

Navarro, J.-M. de. 1972. *The Finds from the Site of La Tène. 1: Scabbards and the Swords Found in Them.* London: Oxford University Press.

Raddatz, K. 1952. "Zur Deutung der Funde von La Tène." *Offa. Berichte und Mitteilungen aus dem Schleswig-Holsteinischen Landesmuseum fur Vor- und Fruhgeschichte in Schleswig und dem Institut far Ur- und Fruhgeschichte an der Universitat Kiel* 11: 24–28.

Schwab, H. 1989. *Archéologie de la 2e correction des eaux du Jura,* Vol. 1, *Les Celtes sur la Broye et la Thielle.* Archeologie fribourgeoise no. 5. Fribourg: Editions Universitaires Fribourg.

Vouga, E. 1885. *Les Helvetes à La Tène.* Neuchâtel: Attinger.

Vouga, P. 1923. *La Tène: Monographie de la station.* Leipzig: Hiersemann.

La Venta

A major Olmec site in Tabasco, MEXICO, near the southern coast of the Gulf of Mexico, La Venta is located on top of a salt dome and is surrounded by swampy terrain. The site was discovered in 1925, when large earth structures and massive stone monuments were found. It was once thought to be a "vacant" ceremonial center, with little cultivable land in the immediate environs and the surrounding rural populace using the uninhabited site for public rituals. Recent excavations, however, have revealed that this view was in error. We now know that by 2000 B.C. there were already farmers in the region, subsisting on its maize and rich estuarine and marine resources. The prized land for farming was along river levees, annually renewed with rich silt.

The farming hamlets gradually grew into larger villages, and signs indicate a developing social stratification. By 1150 B.C. construction had begun on the large earth mounds that formed the ritual heart of the site. After the downfall of the nearby OLMEC site of San Lorenzo, about 900 B.C., La Venta became the most important site in the region. The ceremonial center of La Venta includes dozens of earth mounds and platforms. Its largest pyramid, over 30 meters high, has been argued by some to have the form of an effigy volcano. Another earth platform, possibly the royal palace compound, is over 320 meters long, 260 meters wide, and up to 7 meters high.

Excavations in La Venta in the 1940s revealed

Jade Olmec carved head (Image Select)

additional huge stone monuments that are among the hallmarks of Olmec civilization. Some eighty monuments have been found to date, weighing up to 35 tons. They include colossal heads (probably the portraits of rulers), thrones, and a wide variety of other sculptures. Later in La Venta's history, probably after 800 B.C., a more narrative art was executed. Monuments called "stelae" portray scenes of several interacting figures, carved in low relief.

Among the most dramatic discoveries at La Venta are the appropriately called "massive offerings." One of these offerings involved the digging of a huge pit, which was then filled with twenty-eight layers of roughly shaped serpentine blocks, weighing 1,000 tons in total. The offering was covered with a mosaic mask, also made of serpentine blocks, and different-colored clays.

La Venta's heyday was between 900 and 400 B.C. The site displays many of the hallmarks of later Mesoamerican civilization: an extensive ceremonial heart for the enacting of public rituals, rich dedicatory offerings, carved stone monuments, elaborate burials, writing, objects carved in jade, and so on.

Stone Olmec carved head (Gamma)

Some time around 400 B.C. the site was destroyed. Many of its stone monuments were smashed or defaced, and the ceremonial center was abandoned. Offerings made after the site's abandonment indicate that it may have remained a place of pilgrimage for centuries; even a Spanish colonial olive jar has been found at the site, apparently buried as an offering.

Peter Mathews

See also Mesoamerica

Laetoli

Lying on the edge of the African Serengeti to the south of OLDUVAI GORGE in northern Tanzania, the site of Laetoli was discovered by LOUIS LEAKEY and MARY LEAKEY in 1935. The area was subsequently worked on by Ludwig Kohl-Larsen (1938–1939), and its status as a fossil locality was confirmed. Mary Leakey returned to the area (particularly the nearby Garusi River valley) in 1974 and recovered hominid fossils that have been classified as *Australopithecus afarensis* or *africanus*. These are the remains of

small, lightly built human ancestors. *Afarensis* is dated 3.75–3 million years ago, while *Africanus* lived about 3–2 million years ago. More exciting was the 1978 discovery by Paul Abell of trails of hominid footprints left in the volcanic ash, which made it clear that these hominids walked upright.

Tim Murray

See also Africa, East, Prehistory; Africa, South, Prehistory

References

Hay, R. L., and Leakey, M. D. 1982. "The Fossil Footprints of Laetoli." *Scientific American,* 246: 50–57.

Language and Archaeology
Introduction

The criteria for integrating linguistic and archaeological evidence vary according to the nature of the problem and the questions posed. The use of linguistic evidence in archaeological analysis also varies in type and degree depending upon the theoretical approach of the researcher. Generally, linguistic reconstructions help archaeologists to test hypotheses regarding social and political change and regional interactions, to explain the distribution of intrusive archaeological assemblages and changes in settlement patterns, and to identify the linguistic structure and identity of ancient texts.

Archaeology and historical linguistics also intersect when written texts survive for or about the culture under study. Although written texts may provide a rich source of information, historical references can be vague, inaccurate, or culturally biased. Oftentimes hypotheses tested without them can be equally productive.

Historical Linguistics

Nineteenth-century European linguists working at the University of Leipzig, referred to as Neogrammarians by their elders, developed principles and a method of comparison that successfully accounted for linguistic change over time. They demonstrated that the linguistic processes that produced change in prehistoric languages are observable and operative in transforming living languages. They showed how most of the modern linguistic groups in Europe and some others in the Near East and India developed from a common ancestral language, Indo-European. Neogrammarians were able to reconstruct a basic vocabulary and associated cultural traits for a proto-language they called Proto-Indo-European and to propose a geographic homeland for the Indo-European people (Labov 1994).

Research in the past twenty-five years has demonstrated that the degree of regularity and the mechanical principles of the Neogrammarians are essentially correct. Refinements in typological classifications and linguistic geography and advances in sociolinguistic methods of data collection and quantitative analysis have all helped to illuminate some features of the past that previously remained unexplored and beyond explanation (ibid.).

Combining Archaeology and Language

European scholarship conceived the seminal theoretical and methodological models for archaeological, historical, and linguistic investigations that continue to be reworked, discarded,

and rediscovered today. Europe has also provided the proving ground for interdisciplinary debates (Trigger 1989). In the early twentieth century, European archaeologists combined the reconstructions of historical linguists with their own empirical evidence to propose locations for an Indo-European homeland and to reconstruct the lifeway of Indo-Europeans (Mallory 1991).

As the number of excavated sites increased and the stratigraphic and geographic distributions of artifacts became clearer, disputes arose among archaeologists over the origins of specific European cultures. Fueled by nationalist and regional fervor of the early twentieth century, archaeologists like GUSTAF KOSSINNA insisted upon a local origin for the succession of artifact types while Carl Schuchhart identified materials from different areas with separate ethnic groups whose migrations could be identified by their material remains (Mallory 1991). VERE GORDON CHILDE favored continuous diffusion of cultural traditions from outside Europe (Renfrew 1987). The active role that interdisciplinary scholarship played in these debates lessened considerably after World War II as a result of the misuse of combined archaeological and linguistic findings by Nazi Germany to substantiate Nazi racial beliefs and to justify German territorial expansion (Mallory 1991).

The debate over independent local innovation versus cultural diffusion (see Childe's theory above) has been ongoing in archaeology since the turn of the century, and similar debates have also set the course of research in linguistics. By the 1960s the importance of internal factors as the cause for change took precedence in some research over external factors (Trigger 1989). Those scholars whose results were partly based upon diffusion, migration, and interdisciplinary data found it necessary to argue their case on several fronts. Such a defense was necessary in 1987 after the publication of Collin Renfrew's book, *Archaeology and Language: The Puzzle of Indo-European Origins*. Scholarly response to Renfrew's proposal linking the spread of agriculture into Europe with the arrival of Indo-Europeans raised both strong objections and support from other scholars and his use of linguistic data has made a strong case for the need for interdisciplinary research. The challenges to Renfrew's hypotheses have also led to a resurgence of research linking archaeological data and linguistic reconstructions (Anthony 1995, Mallory 1991).

Research combining historical linguistics and archaeology has developed to varying degrees in other parts of the world (Blench and Spriggs 1999). In the Americas combinatory research on prehistory has remained intermittent and marginal compared to its seminal position in Europe. The lack of written records for most of American prehistory and incomplete synchronic data for many of the language families in the Americas have produced a different approach to interdisciplinary research (Hymes and Fought 1975). The interests of nineteenth- and early-twentieth-century Americanists differed significantly from their European counterparts, with the primary focus of archaeologists being restricted to the American prehistoric period represented by visible remains (Wauchope 1962). The search for evidence of prehistoric European connections also minimized interest in ancient American languages and culture (ibid.). Even after the focus of archaeological inquiry shifted to the prehistory of indigenous non-European peoples, linguists and anthropologists, spearheaded by Franz Boas, concentrated on salvaging the language and culture of modern populations before they disappeared (Hymes and Fought 1975). The data they collected was needed for historical and comparative work, and the collection of linguistic data from modern indigenous languages and culture continues to be a focal point of linguistics and anthropology.

With rigorous linguistic reconstructions for American proto-languages running behind other prehistoric inquiry, archaeologists and historical linguists in the Americas in the early twentieth century did not pursue combinatory research. The period after World War I produced discoveries that were documented and described by the researchers, leaving explanation and testable hypotheses to the next generation of archaeologists (Sabloff 1990). The close working relationships between the archaeologists and anthropologists studying the ancient Maya of MEXICO, GUATEMALA, and Honduras (e.g., J. E. THOMPSON with Wisdom and SYLVANUS MORLEY with Villa Rojas) suggests that they may have shared their undocumented inferences with each other and that the unpublished theories of archaeologists were the impetus for the conclusions of anthropologists (Becker 1979). From the first publications of the art and writing of the Maya of MESOAMERICA, decipherment and interpretation of inscriptions was left to epigraphers (scholars who study writing systems) from various fields including art history, social anthropology, engineering, architecture, and archaeology (Coe 1992). Mayan historical linguists have maintained a marginal position in the decipherment process, instead concentrating on reconstructing vocabulary for proto-languages and identifying linguistic homelands and cross linguistic areal traits (Campbell et al. 1986, Campbell and Kaufman 1976, Kaufman 1976).

Shared motivation to understand the social reality of prehistoric populations throughout the world makes future collaborations between archaeologists and linguists likely. Controversial linguistic dating methods such as glottochronology and mass comparison are also being tested (Greenberg et al. 1986, Marcus 1983a). Dynamic models and theories to predict social responses to ecological, social, and political change continue to be developed by archaeologists and linguists (Trigger 1989, Labov 1994). Both disciplines use geographic models for determining the rate of differentiation and expansion of linguistic populations, the spread of technology, and the migratory trajectory of prehistoric groups (Nichols 1993). Settlement pattern studies continue to be used to compare aspects of spatial organization of ancient societies with expressions of space and worldview in linguistic reconstructions (Trigger 1989).

Judith Storniolo

See also German Prehistoric Archaeology; Linear A/Linear B; Maya Epigraphy

References
Anthony, David W. 1999. "Horse, Wagon and Chariot: Indo-European Languages and Archaeology." *Antiquity* 69, no. 264: 554–565.
Becker, Marshall. 1979. "Priests, Peasants and

Ceremonial Centers: The Intellectual History of a Model." Pp. 3–20 in *Maya Archaeology and Ethnohistory*. Ed. Norman Hammond and Gordon R. Willey. Austin: University of Texas Press.

Blench, Roger, and Matthew Spriggs, eds. 1999. *Archaeology and Language IV: Language and Cultural Transformation*. London: Routledge.

Campbell, Lyle, Terrence Kaufman, and Thomas C. Smith-Stark. 1986. "Meso-America as a Linguistic Area." *Language* 62, no. 3: 530–570.

Campbell, Lyle, and Terrence Kaufman. 1976. "A Linguistic Look at Olmecs." *American Antiquity* 41: 80–89.

Coe, Michael D. 1992. *Breaking the Maya Code*. New York: Thames and Hudson.

Greenberg, Joseph H., C. H. Turner, and S. Zegura. 1986. "The Settlement of the Americas." *Current Anthropology* 27: 477–488.

Hymes, Dell, and John Fought. 1975. *American Structuralism*. The Hague: Mouton Publishers.

Kaufman, Terrence. 1976. "Archaeological and Linguistic Correlations in Mayaland and Associated Areas in Meso-america" *World Archaeology* 8: 101–118.

Labov, William. 1994. *Principles of Linguistic Change: Internal Factors*. New York: Blackwell Publishers.

Mallory, James. 1975. *In Search of the Indo-Europeans*. London: Thames and Hudson.

Marcus, Joyce. 1983a. "The Genetic Model and the Linguistic Divergence of the Otomangueans." Pp. 4–12 in *The Cloud People: Divergent Evolution of the Zapotec and Mixtec Civilizations*. Edited by Kent V. Flannery and Joyce Marcus. New York: Academic Press.

Nichols, Johanna. 1992. *Linguistic Diversity in Space and Time*. Chicago: University of Chicago Press.

Renfrew, Colin. 1987. *Archaeology and Language: The Puzzle of Indo-European Origin*. New York: Cambridge University Press.

Sabloff, Jeremy. 1990. *The New Archaeology and the Ancient Maya*. New York: Scientific American Library.

Trigger, Bruce G. 1987. *A History of Archaeological Thought*. Cambridge: Cambridge University Press.

Wauchope, Robert. 1962. *Lost Tribes and Sunken Continents*. Chicago: University of Chicago Press.

Lapita Complex

See Polynesia; Papua New Guinea and Melanesia

Lartet, Édouard (1801–1871)

Lartet studied law in Toulouse before going to Paris in 1821 as a young lawyer, where he became interested in archaeology and paleontology. He returned to work as a lawyer in southwestern FRANCE and was paid by his clients with fossil bones and prehistoric tools, which they knew were his passion. He began to study the local Tertiary deposits, and in 1834 discovered the rich fossil site of Sansan.

Further encouraged by famous scientists at Paris's National Museum of Natural History, Etienne Saint Hillaire and, later, Adrien Jussieu, Lartet continued to search the fossil deposits of France. In 1837 he found the remains of a fossil ape called Pliopithecus, and in 1856 remains of another fossil ape—Dryopithecus. In 1853 he returned to Paris to undertake full-time paleontological research, where he met JACQUES BOUCHER DE PERTHES. Lartet began to believe that animals and humans had evolved over a much longer period of time than was thought, and that Boucher des Perthes's discoveries in the Somme gravels were proof of this. Lartet also presented his finds from the Aurignac rock shelter in the French Pyrenees as evidence of humans being contemporary with extinct animal species, and, like the work of Boucher des Perthes, it was rejected by the Academies des Sciences in Paris.

In 1861 Lartet proposed a chronology for human skeletal and cultural remains based on fossil animal bones found with them in cave sites. While his chronology eventually proved to be limited, it established him as one of the founders of human paleontology. Sponsored by English prehistorian and banker HENRY CHRISTY, he began to explore cave sites in the Perigord and Dordogne regions of France, where he discovered the famous Paleolithic sites of LA MADELEINE, Les Eyzies and LE MOUSTIER, providing further evidence of phases of human development based on archaeological stratigraphy. Lartet also published on the development of the human brain in fossil mammal species.

In 1865 he became a member of the Société d'Anthropologie de Paris, and in 1869 its president and professor of paleontology at the National Museum of Natural History. Ill health caused his early retirement from both these positions.

Tim Murray

See also Lithic Analysis
References
Wangernez, J. 1986. Édouard Lartet, 1801–1871: "Le Gersois Fondateur de la Paléontologie Humaine." *Le Mois Scientifique Bordelais* 66: 1–3.

Lascaux

Lascaux, a cave occupied during the Magdalenian period in the Dordogne region of FRANCE, was discovered by four boys in 1940, and it remains among the most spectacular collection of Paleolithic wall art yet found. It is best known for its 600 magnificent paintings of aurochs (wild cattle), horses, deer, and signs of various kinds, but it also contains almost 1,500 engravings dominated by horses. The best-known feature is the great Hall of the Bulls, which contains several great auroch figures, some of them five meters in length, the largest figures known in Ice Age art. The hall also contains an enigmatic figure, called "the unicorn." A shaft features a painted scene of what seems to be a bird-headed man with a wounded bison and a rhinoceros, and the scene has often been interpreted in shamanistic terms, though with little justification.

Stone tools for engraving were found in the cave as well as many lamps, 158 fragments of pigment, and color-grinding equipment. Scaffolding was clearly used in some galleries to reach the upper walls and ceiling. Much of the cave floor was lost when the site was adapted for tourism, but it was probably never a habitation—it is more likely it was visited only briefly for artistic activity or ritual. Charcoal fragments from the cave floor have provided radiocarbon dates around 17,000 years ago and in the ninth millennium B.P.

The cave was closed to tourists in 1963 because of pollution that resulted in a "green sickness," consisting of a proliferation of algae, and

Archaeologist exploring Lascaux Caves (Gamma)

a "white sickness" of crystal growth. It was possible to reverse the effects of the green sickness and arrest the development of the white, but to ensure the survival of the cave's art, the number of visitors had been drastically reduced. As compensation, a facsimile cave, a complete copy of the original cave and its details, Lascaux 2, is now open nearby.

Paul Bahn

See also Rock Art

Latvia
The Main Periods in the History of the Archaeology of Latvia

For a long time after World War II the traditional subdivision of time concerning the investigation of the history of archaeology in the main publications and surveys (Moora 1952; Graudonis 1967; Šnore 1974) was into four periods. This division is based on the political situation in the Baltic states during the eighteenth through the twentieth centuries. The *first period* of archaeological study, from the middle of the

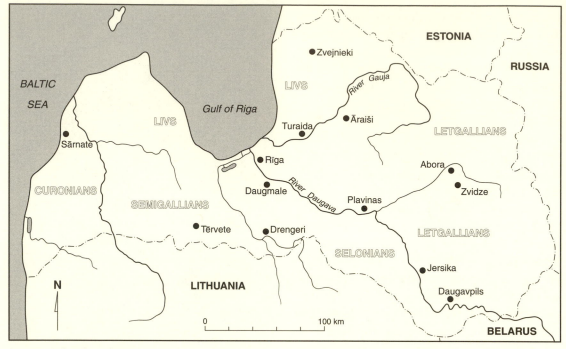

Latvian Archaeological Sites

nineteenth century to the founding of the independent republic of Latvia in 1918, belongs to the Baltic Germans. The *second period* was an important short-term period that included the foundation of the national school of archaeologists and the appearance of the works of the first generation of Latvian archaeologists in independent Latvia (1918–1940). The *third period* was that of a new political regime—the Soviet occupation—when a new generation of archaeologists appeared who continued the traditions and skills of the first generation of Latvian archaeologists (1940–1941; 1945–1990). The *fourth period* was the time of an independent development of Latvian archaeology at an international level (1990–present).

The first period of the history of archaeology in Latvia—the Baltic German period—can be divided into three phases. Well-known amateur archaeologists of the first phase during the nineteenth century were Friedrich Kruse, who published *Necrolvonica oder Alterthumer Liv-, Esth- und Curland* in Dorpat (Tartu 1842) and K. K. Bahr, who described the graves of Livs in *Die Graber der Liven* (Dresden 1850). Local antiquarian Carl Sievers (1814–1879) carried out the first amateur excavations of the Stone Age settlements in

Zvejnieki and Rinnukalns between 1874 and 1875. The first systematic classification of Stone Age artifacts was elaborated by professor C. Grewingk (1819–1887) in Dorpat, Tartu province (1865, 1874, 1887). The further subdivision of the first period of the history of archaeology in Latvia was determined by the fact that Russian archaeologists joined the investigation of the Baltic provinces, along with the Baltic German amateurs and specialists, before preparing for the Tenth All-Russian Archaeological Congress in Rīga in 1896. During the second short phase Baltic German archaeologists and Russian archaeologists organized excavations. The most significant excavations were carried out by Russian specialist J. Romanov in the Lettgallian cemetery of the tenth through twelfth centuries at Odukalns and cremations of the Curonians of the eleventh through the fourteenth centuries in Western Latvia at Pasilciems. These scientific investigations matched the scale of those in the 1890s. N. Haruzin published a report about the archaeology inside the Baltic provinces of Russia, including Estland, Livland, and Curland, which contained many criticisms about the methodology of investigations by Baltic German amateurs (Haruzin 1894). The introduction to the catalog of the Tenth All-Russian Archaeological Congress was written by a German archaeologist in Dorpat, Tartu province, Professor Richard Hausmann (1842–1918)—the 1890s' foremost specialist in the early Iron Age archaeology of the eastern Baltic region.

The *third phase* of the first period of archaeological investigations in Latvia, at the beginning of the twentieth century, was marked by great activities of German specialists. R. Hausman's publication, *Prahistorische Archaologie von Estland, Livland, Kurland* (Dorpat 1910) was the first elaborate chronology of prehistory that met European standards for archaeological science at the beginning of the twentieth century. A. Bielenstein, the famous ethnographer and ethnologist, at the end of the nineteenth century (1899) described the Latvian hillforts. A bibliography of the archaeology of Livland, Estland, and Curland until 1913 was published by A. Buchholtz and A. Sprekelsen (Rīga 1914). The first scientific typological and chronological survey of the prehistory of the eastern Baltic area, including Latvia, *Die baltischen Provinzen Kurland, Livland, Estland,* was published by Max Ebert (1913).

The *second period* in the history of archaeological investigations in Latvia refers to the years of the independent Republic of Latvia (1918–1940). Max Ebert, who worked at Albertus University in Koenigsberg, and Francis Balodis, who was on the staff of the Saratow University in Russia, became the first professors and heads of the Department of Archaeology in the faculty of Philology and Philosophy during the first years of the independent Latvia. Francis Balodis became the head of the department in 1924, after his return from Saratow. These two famous, academically educated specialists were the founders of the National School of Latvian archaeologists. In later archaeological investigations the best specialists were students Voldemārs Ģinters, Eduards Šturms, F. Jākobsons, Elvīra Šnore, Rauls Šnore, Ādolfs Karnups, and Pēteris Stepiņš. The large-scale excavations at the Lettgallian, Semigallian, and Liv hillforts of the tenth through the thirteenth centuries were organized by these archaeologists. Excavations of barrows and cemeteries of the Iron Age

and early Middle Ages increased artifact collections. New specialists focused interest on the new discoveries from the late Iron Age via investigations of hillforts, cemeteries, the material culture of native peoples, and their social life and ideology. Investigations of Stone- and Bronze Age monuments began with the excavations of the Sārnate peat bog settlement and the Neolithic sanctuary on the littoral of the Baltic Sea, the Ģipka lagoon. Excavations of the Stone Age monuments in the inner regions of the Lake Lubāna Wetland were carried out (Iča). The first publications of the new investigations appeared in the popular periodical *Senatne un Māksla* (*Antiquity and Art*), which was edited by Francis Balodis between 1936 and 1940. The investigators were full of good ideas for carrying on the work of the first generation of Latvian archaeologists, but they were interrupted by the first Soviet occupation in 1940. Because it was feared that archaeology would encourage nationalist tendencies (and therefore lead to revolt against occupation), the KGB persecuted many archaeologists during World War II and the period following the war. The Russians sought to crush local identity, as Stalin was doing throughout the USSR. Francis Balodis emigrated. V. Urtāns—who was to become one of the best archaeologists of the second generation of Latvian archaeologists—was arrested and sent to the Siberian gold mines. Ernests Brastiņš, the famous topographer and investigator of Latvian hillforts, was deported from Latvia and was later sentenced to death.

The beginning of the third period in the history of archaeology in Latvia was dramatic as it included changes in the political situation in Latvia during two different occupation regimes: Soviet and German Nazi. For several years the departments of the History of Latvia at the University in Rīga were closed. Latvian archaeologists of the second generation graduated from the university at the end of the German Nazi occupation or at the beginning of the Soviet occupation. At the end of the war senior archaeologists F. Balodis, Voldemārs Ģinters, and Eduards Šturms emigrated to Sweden and Germany. After the war, in 1946, two other specialist archaeologists—R. Šnore and Ā. Karnups—were deported. The peaceful development of archaeological investigations was reinstated very slowly. Two academically educated specialists—E. Šnore and L. Vankina—were the first to begin new archaeological investigations. Then new enthusiasts entered the field of Latvian archaeology—among them J. Graudonis, Ē. Mugurēvičs, and Ā. Stubavs.

The three phases of Soviet, or postwar, Latvian archaeology were outlined by Ē. Mugurēvics (1999). New excavation projects were realized by archaeologists during the *first phase*. The archaeologists of the Institute of History of Latvia were very active during the 1950s and 1960s. Extensive excavation works were carried out under the guidance of Latvian archaeologists of the first generation E. Šnore and E. Brīvkalne at the Letgallian hillfort Asote and the Semigallian hillfort of Tērvete. The Lettgallian cemetery of the tenth through the thirteenth centuries Pildas Nukši was excavated. During this phase archaeological materials—the results of excavations and typological studies, as well as reports of more serious investigations—were published in the new periodical of Latvian Archaeology: *Arheoloģija un Etnogrāfija* (*Archaeology and Ethnography*) between 1959 and 1998.

The *second phase* of the third period (1960–1974) was marked by long-term, large-scale excavations in the flooded zones at hydro-power stations at Plaviņas and Rīga and along the middle and upper flow of the river Daugava. Attention was directed to publishing the results of excavations at the hillfort Asote (1961), the medieval economic contacts of the Lettgallians and the Slavs (1965), the late Bronze Age in Latvia (1967), and the Cloth of the Lettgallians (1970). Intensive work at the Lake Āraiši fortress discovered much of the inhabited area with well-preserved remains of timber dwellings and a large number of wooden artifacts. Excavations of complexes at Stone Age monuments in the Lake Lubāna Wetland and at Zvejnieki on the bank of Lake Burtnieki uncovered the need for further investigation of the Mesolithic, Neolithic, and early-Bronze Age periods of Latvia. Interdisciplinary studies (paleocarpology, palinology, radiocarbon dating, etc.) were used. A monograph of the Sarnate peat

bog settlement was published (1970). It was the first research work about the Neolithic period in the littoral of the Litorina sea. The results of these and other archaeological discoveries were published in the *Archaeology of Latvia* (1974), written by eleven authors, the first popular publication about archaeological investigations in Latvia. The work detailed the elaborate typology and chronology of artifacts and monuments, reconstructions of buildings and hillforts, economy, ideology, and ethnogenesis of native people.

During the *third phase* of the postwar investigations (1975–1989) work concentrated in the flooded zone of the Daugavpils hydro-station along the upper part of the Daugava River (1982–1987). Long-term protective excavations were carried out in the Naujiena stone castle and town (Dunaburg) of the fourteenth and fifteenth centuries, the Slutiški late-medieval cemetery of the fifteenth through the seventeenth centuries, and twenty other monuments. The conservation work on the Stone Age settlements in large areas of the Lake Lubāna Wetland was duplicated in the Zvidze, Kvāpāni, Sūḷagals, and Iča settlements. New evidence of the transformation from a hunter-gatherer society to one of farming and stock breeding were found. An intensification in the publication of monographs was marked during this term. Two monographs about the Lake Lubāna Wetland settlements (Loze 1979; 1988) and one about the Stone Age burial field in Zvejnieki (Zagorskis 1987) were published. Three monographs about the Bronze Age by Graudonis and Vasks and several on the Middle Ages (Mugurevics; Šnore; and Zariņa), as well as a book on early medieval coins (Berga) added to the number of publications.

The *fourth period* of archaeological investigation began during yet another new political situation after the restoration of the Republic of Latvia. The independent development of archaeological investigations prompted wider interest in the publication and interpretation of basic materials, which were in the Funds of Museums in Latvia for a long time. The catalog *The Stone Age Lake Lubāna Collection* (1999) contained more than 3,000 drawings of bone and antler artifacts. Surveys of Old Town Rīga (1998) and the castles of the Archbishop of Rīga during the Livonian period and later (1999) were detailed and included architectural studies across the territories of present-day Latvia. Publication of the compiled works of the talented Latvian archaeologist Fēliks Jākobsons (1896–1930) is the best example of the strong interest in Latvian cultural heritage (1999). A connoisseur of Eastern Prussian archaeological materials, Jākobsons, who graduated from the Albertus University in Koenigsberg, described and illustrated the archaeological material lost during World War II in Eastern Prussia (now the Kaliningrad district of Russia).

The organization of international conferences in Latvia—especially for discussing themes concerning the Baltic Sea during the Stone and Bronze Ages (1995) and in the Middle Ages (1992)—helped to make contacts between archaeologists from opposite sides of the Baltic. Such important changes mark new approaches in the development of the archaeology of Latvia. New projects, such as the excavation of a Neolithic ritual place of the inhabitants of Litorina littoral of 5000 B.C. and a study of the influence of Stone Age people on the environment in the Lake Lubāna Wetland, began. Another prospective project is in the area of the Dubna River system (a tributary of the Daugava), which includes the excavation of the hillfort Jersika, inhabited during the Iron Age and early Middle Ages. Two stone and brick castles of the Livonian period—Turaida and Cēsis (1974–1999)have been excavated. The archaeological excavations in Old Town Rīga continue. Special attention is being paid to the "Blackheads building"—the only secular building that has survived since the fourteenth century. A special work about the "Black-heads building" project is scheduled for publication.

Personalities

Archaeologist *Jānis Apals* (1930–) received his doctorate in history from the State University in Rīga. He is a senior researcher in the Department of Archaeology at the Institute of History of Latvia and pioneered investigations of underwater Viking age monuments in the lakes of Latvia, where remains of ten underwater fortresses were discovered. He was an organizer of the excavations at Lake Āraiši—the primary extensively excavated and reconstructed monument of the Viking age in the Baltic states.

Professor Dr. Francis Balodis (1882–1947) was the first academically educated Latvian archaeologist and the founder of the Latvian National School of Archaeology. Balodis studied in Dorpat (Tartu), Moscow, and Munich Universities and is a specialist in the archaeology of the Iron and Middle Ages, Egyptology, and the History of Art. Balodis was a professor at the universities of Moscow and Saratov (Russia) from 1918 to 1924, the chair of Archaeology and the dean of the faculty of Philosophy and Philology in Rīga (1924), the pro-rector of the State University in Rīga (1931–1933), head of the Monument Protection Board (1932–1940), and the editor of the periodical *Senatne un Māksla* (*Antiquity and Art*) from 1936 to 1940. Balodis excavated the Middle Age hillfort Jersika (Gersike) and the Raunas Tanisa hillfort. Beginning in 1940, he worked in Sweden as an Egyptologist.

Ernests Brastiņš (1892–1941) studied at the Art School in Saint Petersburg. During World War I he worked in the Russian Army as a topographer. Brastiņš was a pioneer in the field of, and the author of a topographic survey of, Latvian hillforts with the remains of wooden constructions, surveying in total 282 sites between 1922 and 1927. He was the director of the Museum of War in Rīga, where a Department of Latvian Hillforts was organized. He was arrested and deported by Soviet political bodies to Astrakhan (Lower Volga), where he was sentenced to death in 1941.

Voldemārs Ģinters (1899–1979), a Ph.D., studied at the state universities in Rīga and Koenigsberg. Ģinters was the director of the State Museum of History in Rīga from 1934 to 1945. He specialized in the archaeology of the Middle Ages and was one of the best methodologists of excavations. Ģinters organized investigations at hillforts in Daugmale and Mežotne (1938–1939; 1942). At the end of World War II Ģinters emigrated to Sweden, where he became a researcher at the State Museum of History in Stockholm.

Jānis Graudonis (1913–) is a member of the Academy of Sciences of Latvia. He studied at the State University in Rīga and was an assistant at the Institute of the History of Latvia from 1947 to 1948. When the Institute was repressed by Soviet political bodies, Graudonis returned to the Institute of History in 1958. Specializing in the Bronze and Early Iron Ages and the Late Middle Ages, Graudonis led large-scale excavations in the flooded zones of the Pļaviņas and Rīga hydro-stations along the middle flow of the Daugava River. He excavated at the Turaida brick castle, built and occupied between the thirteenth and seventeenth centuries, for nearly twenty-five years, from 1978 to 1999. Graudonis was chairman of the second conference of the Association of European Archaeologists in Rīga in 1996.

Ādolfs Karnups (1904–1973), an archaeologist and ethnologist, studied at the State University in Rīga, then was head of Department of Ethnography at the State Museum of the History of Latvia until 1946. Karnups specialized in the archaeology of the Middle Ages. He led large-scale excavations at the Talsi hillfort from 1936 to 1937. Arrested after World War II by Soviet repressive bodies, Karnups was at first sentenced to a death but afterwards was deported to Siberia, where he remained until 1955. He was the head of the Department of Prehistory at the Museum of History of Medicine in Rīga from 1955 to 1973. His specialty during the post-Siberian period was the history of the folk medicine of the early medieval period.

Ēvalds Mugurēvičs (1931–) studied at the State University in Rīga and was the head of the Department of Archaeology at the Institute of the History of Latvia from 1971 to 1995. Mugurēvičs's specialties are the archaeology of the Middle Ages of the Livonian period (the end of the twelfth century through the first half of the sixteenth century A.D.) and early written sources. Mugurēvičs led large-scale excavations in the flooded zone of the Pļaviņas hydro-station from 1958 to 1965 and was the administrator and coordinator of excavations in the flooded zones of the Rīga and Daugavpils hydro-stations (1966–1974; 1982–1987). He also led excavations in castles of the medieval period in Western

Latvia (Rēzekne, Saldus, Piltene, Dundaga, and Sabile). His specialty is the adoption of Christianity in Livonia. He has been a member of the board of the INTERNATIONAL UNION OF PREHISTORIC AND PROTOHISTORIC SCIENCES since 1994, and the president of the National Committee of Historical Sciences in Latvia since 1992.

Elvīra Šnore (1905–1996) studied at the State University in Rīga. Šnore was the founder of the study of scientific archaeology of the Middle Ages in Latvia with emphasis on earlier local inhabitants of the Iron Age (third to eighth centuries)—the Letgallians, Selonians, and Livs—and their material culture until the Middle Ages.

Šnore was the head of the Department of Archaeology of the State Museum of History from 1933 to 1944 and senior researcher at the Department of Archaeology of the Institute of History of Latvia from 1946 to 1984. She led archaeological excavations in the ninth-to-thirteenth-century hillfort of Asote from 1949 to 1954 and in the flooded zones of the Pļaviņas and Rīga hydro-stations, as well in the Lettgallian cemeteries of the Nukši and Kivti peoples of the thirteenth through the seventeenth centuries.

Rauls Šnore (1901–1962), archaeologist and numismatist, studied at the State University in Rīga. Specializing in Iron Age archaeology in Latvia, Šnore was the director of the Museum of History in Rīga from 1936 to 1941, the manager of the Central Museum of History in Cēsis, Valmiera, and Valka from 1942 to 1946, the scientific director of the Rīgas Duomo Museum, and an assistant professor at the State University in Rīga from 1945 to 1946. Arrested in 1946 and sentenced to ten years of exile in prison, Šnore was deported to the republic of Mordovia and returned to Rīga in 1955 as an invalid. He excavated some Neolithic sites on the bank of Lake Lielais Ludzas in the last years of his life.

Adolfs Stubavs (1913–1986) studied pedagogy and received his doctorate in history at the State University in Rīga. He was head of the Department of Archaeology at the Institute of History of Latvia from 1958 to 1971. Stubavs's specialty was the early and late Middle Ages. He led large-scale excavations at the Ķentes hillfort (fifth–ninth centuries A.D.), the Koknese hill-fort and castle (thirteenth–seventeenth centuries), and the Salaspils stone castle of the Livonian order (thirteenth–seventeenth centuries). Stubavs was the foremost specialist in the classification and elaboration of the main types of Latvian hillforts.

Professor Dr. *Eduards Šturms* (1895–1959) studied at the State University in Rīga and at Koenigsberg. Šturms was the pioneer of systematic investigations of Stone and Bronze Age monuments in Latvia (1927–1940, 1943), including the Sārnate peat bog settlement, Pūrciems dune dwellings on the littoral of the Litorina sea, an Iča settlement in the Lake Lubāna wetland, and Rēznas barrows of the Bronze Age. At the end of World War II Šturms emigrated to West Germany. He led the Latvian Department of the Institute of Investigations of Baltic States from 1953 to 1955 and was guest professor at the University of Bonn from 1955 to 1959 and a corresponding member of the DEUTSCHES ARCHÄOLOGISCHES INSTITUT (German Archaeological Institute) from 1954 to 1959.

Vladislavs Urtāns (1921–1989) received his doctorate in history at the State University in Rīga. Arrested and deported to Siberia by Soviet political bodies in 1941, Urtāns returned to Rīga in 1946, and graduated from the State University in 1949. Urtāns was a researcher in the Archaeology Department at the Museum of the History of Latvia from 1947 to 1950 and at the Museum of History and Art in Madona from 1951 to 1958 and senior researcher at the Museum of the History of Latvia from 1958 to 1976. Specializing in the archaeology of the Iron and Viking Ages, Urtāns was one of the best specialists of typology studies of the Iron Age of Latvia. He led large-scale excavations in the flooded zones of the Pļaviņas and Rīga hydro-stations, and at the Daugmale, Aizkraukle, and Madalāni hillforts of the tenth through the twelfth centuries (1966–1987).

Lūcija Vankina (1908–1989) received a doctorate in history at the State University in Rīga and then became head of the Department of Archaeology of the Museum of the History of Rīga from 1946 to 1986. Vankina specialized in the Stone Age Archaeology of Latvia and excavated at the Sārnate wetland settlement from 1949 to 1959.

Anna Zariņa (1921–) studied at the Latvian Academy of Agriculture. Zariņa is a pioneer and a primary specialist in the investigation and reconstruction of the archaeological textiles of the ancient Livs and Letgallians. She led large-scale excavations in the flooded zones of the Pļaviņas, Rīga, and Daugavpils hydro-stations from 1963 to 1986.

Archaeological Monuments

Latvian hillforts are fortifications on hills that had special wooden palisade defensive systems and a high rampart and ditches on one side. Dwellings and buildings for special crafts were located inside the plateau and the outer fort. Chronologically hillforts can be dated to a wide period, from the beginning of the first millennium B.C. until the tenth through thirteenth centuries A.D. A topographic survey of these forts was done by E. Brastiņš in the 1920s and the work was continued by specialists from the State Inspection of Monument Protection beginning in 1950 under the guidance of J. T. Urtāns.

Abora is the main permanent settlement of the Late Neolithic Corded Ware Culture (CWC) in the Lake Lubāna Wetland of Latvia, where remains of material culture from 4490 to 3770 B.P. were preserved in peat. The wooden dwelling constructions, fishing devices, and some burials of flexed individuals of the CWC were discovered between 1964 and 1965 and in 1970 and 1971. Abora is the main location where amber is processed in present-day Latvia. From there amber artifacts and ornaments were exchanged across Eastern Europe—in the basins of the Volga and Dnieper Rivers (4490–3770 B.P.). Abora is the main source of information on the subsistence strategies of CWC people in Latvia, who were hunter-gatherers, and there is evidence of farming and stock breeding.

Āraiši Lake Fortress is a Viking Age fortress on an island on the Āraiši Lake in eastern Latvia, discovered by Count C. G. Sieverss in 1876 and excavated by Latvian archaeologist Jānis Apals from 1965 to 1969 and from 1975 to 1979. The fortress was the subject of extensive discussions as to whether it was a pile dwelling in the lake

(Virchow 1877) or a pile dwelling on the island (Bielenstein 1970). Lowering the level of the lake in 1965 helped researchers to discover the structure of the fortress. The surface of the island was covered by a horizontally laid thick lattice of logs that covered an area about twenty-eight by thirty-five meters. Remains of 145 wooden constructions—dwellings and fortification systems of five phases of habitation—were discovered lying directly one over the other without any archaeological break. The dwellings of the first stage were built in A.D. 830 and the dwellings of the third stage in A.D. 890. These were timber log dwellings, of yoke-angle construction. The buildings of the first three stages were built in the center of the fortress, but during the fourth and fifth stages buildings were also located along the perimeter of the settlement. The unique reconstruction of the fortress Āraiši was elaborated on by Jānis Apals and architect Dzintars Driba (1987–1992). Reconstruction was finished in the 1980s. The Open Air Museum on island Āraiši was organized by the Inspection of Monument Protection at the Ministry of Culture of Latvia and the Foundation of the Āraiši Lake Fortress.

Daugmale, at 3,800 square meters, is one of the largest hillforts in Latvia. The town covered two hectares and included a port (ninth through twelfth centuries A.D.) in the lower flow of the Daugava River. Daugmale was inhabited by Semigallians in the ninth century and by Livs in the tenth through the twelfth centuries. It was an economic, political, cultural, and transit trading center, as well one of the largest craft centers (iron, bronze, bone, antler, amber, and pottery processing) of the Livs before the adoption of Christianity in the thirteenth century.

Drenģeri-Čunkāni, the largest investigated cemetery of the Semigallians of the seventh through the tenth centuries A.D., lies in the southeastern part of Semigallia. Excavations in 1982 through 1991 by Māris Atgāzis and Viktorija Bebre discovered 697 graves in lines without the secondary filling of the territory of cemetery with new deceased individuals. It is evidence of the peaceful development of Semigallian society in the period before the first

Catholic bishops came from Germany and fought for the adoption of Christianity among the pagan natives.

Jersika (Gersike) was the Lettgallian (*letti, letthigali*) economic, political, and cultural center in the tenth through the twelfth centuries A.D. It sits on the sixteen-meter-high bank of the middle flow of the Daugava River between two valleys. Jersika is one of the best-fortified hillforts, with a defensive system built up by an oak log rampart. Inside are camera-shaped buildings full of earth and stones. The area of the flattened plateau was 100 meters by 75 meters. Jersika was the residence of Wissewalduc, Rex de Gerceke (Heinrici Chronicon, XXIX.4), who displayed great resistance to the Catholic bishops, including Albert, during the adoption of Christianity. Jersika was burned twice between A.D. 1209 and 1215 by Crusaders. The Lettgallians lost their independence gradually. In A.D. 1239 Jersika was only a *locum castri* (local camp). Archaeological excavations carried out by Francis Balodis (1939) and Antonija Vilcāne (1995–1999) revealed that the hillfort had been burned down.

Lubāna Lake Wetland lies in the middle part of the East Latvian lowland. It is a region of concentration of Stone Age settlements (30 units), which were discovered in the 1960 and 1970s. The wetland was the main region of postwar excavations of Stone Age settlements, and boasts well-preserved organic materials. It is the best region for elaborating Stone Age chronology (70 radiocarbon data) and for reconstructing subsistence strategy and cultural development in Latvia during the period from 7110 to 3640 B.P. It was the main center for amber processing in the inland territories of the eastern Baltic during the Neolithic period.

The *Lubāna Lake Collection* contains more than 3,000 stray finds of late Paleolithic, Mesolithic, and Neolithic bone and antler artifacts. The collection was gathered from the bottom of Lake Lubāna by local people between 1937 and 1939 after the water level was lowered and includes harpoons, slotted points, spearheads, daggers, knives, arrowheads, fishhooks, and cult objects. The collection was subsequently passed into the hands of the Board of Antiquity in Rīga.

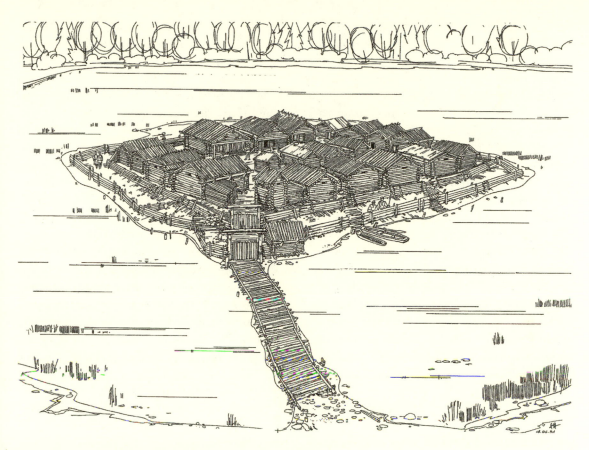

Drawing of the reconstruction of the ninth-century A.D. Lake Āraiši Fort (Archeological Society of Northern Germany)

Rīga Old Town is the oldest part of the capital of Latvia. The first systematic excavations of Rīga Old Town were carried out after World War II, when some remains of old town dwellings were discovered in the so-called Bishops Albert Square on the bank of the river Rīdzene, a tributary of the river Daugava. The excavations were done by archaeologists of the Museum of History of Rīga and Navigation and of the Institute of History of Latvia under the guidance of Andris Caune. Archaeologists discovered and reconstructed the first village of the local people—the Livs—and specified the border of their first cemetery, from the end of the twelfth century. Reconstructions of some dwellings were shown, based on the discovered remains of wooden and stone buildings of the twelfth through the fifteenth centuries. Clay and stone stoves, warm-air stoves, and tile stoves had been arranged inside the houses. Simpler timber houses and iron and bronze processing places, dated by C-14 to A.D. 1100–1210

were excavated. These buildings were built shortly before the Duomo was constructed in A.D. 1211. Four towers and a defense wall of Rīga Old Town were investigated, as well underground passages from the seventeenth and eighteenth centuries A.D. Special attention was paid to the river Rīdzene embankment, where remains of an old ship were found in the 1930s. During the 1970s and 1980s dwellings of Rīga Old Town were a special subject of Andris Caune's investigations. In the 1990s protection works—excavations in the area of the foundation and cellar of the House of Black-heads, the oldest public building remaining from the fourteenth century—were continued by archaeologists under the guidance of A. Caune. Now the building is entirely reconstructed. Another project—the excavation of the cemetery of monks in the Duomo garden (thirteenth–eighteenth centuries A.D.)—was led by Andris Celmiņš. More than 800 graves were discovered.

Rīga , measuring fifty square kilometers, was the second completely investigated region in Latvia. More than sixty archaeological sites were found in the lower flow of the river Daugava in the flooded zone of the Rīga hydro-station (built between 1966 and 1975). The most important discoveries were in the late Bronze Age fortified settlement and in the burial field, where finds included 247 wooden coffins and evidence of twenty-one cremations under the cultural layer of the Ķivutkalns settlement on Dole island (Graudonis). The first late Paleolithic site near the bank of the Baltic Ice Lake was found in Salaspils Laukskola by Zariņa, and during the excavations flint artifacts of Arensburg and Swiderian cultures were discovered (Zagorsaka). It is currently the only excavated late Paleolithic site in Latvia. The complexes of the Middle-Ages monuments of twelfth- and thirteenth-century stone castles, towns, churches, and cemeteries of the first Livonian bishops, as well as the villages and cemeteries of the local people—the Livs—were discovered in Ikšķile by Graudonis and in Mārtiņsala by Mugurēvičs.

Pļaviņas is a region of concentration of archaeological monuments in the flooded zone of the hydro-station (built between 1958 and 1965) in the middle flow of the river Daugava. Important excavations were carried out at the late Bronze Age fortified settlement in Mūkukalns by Graudonis and at the Letgallian hillfort Oliņkalns of the tenth through the twelfth centuries by Mugurēvičs. Protective investigations of the stone and brick castles of the Rīgas Archbishop and the Livonian order included Koknese (thirteenth through seventeenth centuries A.D.) by Stubavs, and Sēlpils (fourteenth through eighteenth centuries) by Šnore and Zariņa. During the excavations discoveries were made in the towns of the owners of castles as well as in the villages of the local people—the Lettgallians and the Selonians. For the first time in the eastern Baltic, wooden plates and shields with polychrome paintings (white, red, and black) were found in the three graves of Selonian barrows at Lejas-Dopeles (tenth–eleventh centuries).

Sārnate, the first discovered wetland settlement of the Neolithic Sārnate culture, is in the territory of the ancient lagoon of the Litorina Sea. The settlement now lies near the Latvian western coast of the Baltic Sea. The first five wooden dwellings in the peat were discovered by Šturms between 1938 and 1940, and twenty items were discovered by L. Vankina between 1949 and 1959. The dwellings contained a rich complex of wooden hunting, gathering, farming, and domestic utensils. The pottery style represented a special coastal variant of middle Neolithic ceramics and is genetically linked with the pottery of the Ertebolle-Ellerbeck cultures in the west Baltic area (4630–4510 B.P.).

Tērvete was the main political center of the northwestern Semigallians under the guidance of Dux Semigallorum Viesthardus at the beginning of the thirteenth century and Rex Semigalliae Nameisis in the second half of the thirteenth century. The first excavations of the Tērvete hillfort in 1866 and 1892 were by Bielenstein and Hausman. Large-scale investigations were organized in 1930 through 1960 by Emīlija Brīvkalne and a wooden defensive system and previously inhabited plateau inside the hillfort were discovered. Tērvete had the best fortifications of the Semigallian forts at the end of the twelfth century and into the thirteenth century, when the political situation changed and the peaceful development of the Semigallians, as well as the Letgallians, Curonians, and Livs, was interrupted by the crusaders of the Teutonic or Sword Brethren Order. Two defensive systems with two rows of palisades surrounded the hillfort Tērvete and an eight-meter-high rampart was built on the east side of the hillfort. The area of the hillfort was 1,000 square meters and the defensive system included a high log wall along the edge of the hillfort. A double log wall was built in the lower part of the palisade. The defensive system was supplemented by tower-shaped buildings. Special cameras (towers) full of earth and stones were built inside the log walls. In the battle near Saule in 1236 Semigallians conquered the Sword Brethrens Order. It was the end of this order, and some time afterward the new Livonian Order formed from its remains. According to the data from excavations at the Tērvete hillfort and written sources, the hillfort was burned down in 1272. Seven years later Rex Nameisis renewed the hillfort, but in 1280, because it was so difficult to fight against the very active invaders, the Semigallians burned down their own wooden castle and went to the southern part of northern Lithuania.

Turaida was the brick castle of the archbishop of Rīga in the thirteenth and fourteenth centuries. The remains of the Livs hillfort (eleventh–twelfth centuries) were discovered under the cultural layers of the remains of the castle. The Turaida castle of the Livonian period, situated on the high bank of the river Gauja in the eastern part of Latvia, was investigated fully and reconstructed partly between 1974 and 1999.

Zvejnieki, a Stone Age burial field in the northeastern part of Latvia, is the biggest in Northern Europe. It was excavated by Francis Zagorskis (1929–1986) during the period from 1965 to 1971. Single, double, and group burials of the late Mesolithic and early, middle, and late Neolithic periods (6775–5100 B.P.)—totaling 308 individuals—were discovered. Rich bone, flint, and slate implements represented the funerary inventory. Red or blue clay masks with amber disks and rings in the eye sockets were discovered in some graves of people of the Comb and pit ceramic cultures. Figurines of elk heads, birds, male faces, and female figures were ritual objects.

Zvidze, in the Lake Lubāna Wetland, is a Neolithic settlement of the first farmers in the eastern Baltic region that is situated on the border of moraine plain and the ground of the old Lake Lubāna basin. Zvidze was excavated from 1973 to 1975 and from 1981 to 1984. The archaeological evidence of farming—wooden tools; spades; mattocks; cereal and grain processing tools; spinning and weaving implements; and tools for processing hemp, nettles, and flax—were discovered inside the remains of the wooden dwellings, which were of standing pole construction with ridged roofs. It was suggested that these people adopted agriculture as a result of diffusion between 5000 and 4700 B.P.

Baltic Nationalities

Curonians—Western Baltic people (*kurši*) described in early written chronicles such as Heinrici Chronicon and Livlandische Reim-schronik as *curones,* who lived in the eighth through the thirteenth centuries A.D. in the territory of the western part of Latvia and the northwestern part of Lithuania.

Lettgalians—Eastern Baltic people (*latgaļi*), described in Heinrici Chronicon and Livlandische Reimchronik as *Letti* or *Letthigalli,* who lived in the eighth through the thirteenth centuries in the territory of the eastern part of present-day Latvia, east of the river Daugava.

Livs—Finno-Ugric people (*lībieši*), described in Livlandische Reimchronik as *Līven* or *Līwen,* who lived during the tenth through the thirteenth centuries in the lower flow of the rivers Gauja and Daugava, as well on the littoral of northwestern Latvia. The main excavated monuments are two villages and a cemetery dating to the tenth through the thirteenth centuries, Salaspils Laukskola in the lower part of the river Daugava. A rich inventory included bronze ornaments, tortoise-shaped fibulas, and remains of textiles including small bronze ornaments on the edges of the villaine, a special cape worn by women (Zariņa).

Selonians—Baltic people (*sēļi*), described in Heinrici Chronicon as *sēlen,* who lived in the ninth through the thirteenth centuries in the territory of the southeastern part of present-day Latvia, to the south of the river Daugava, and in the northern part of present-day Lithuania.

Semigallians—Baltic people (*zemgaļi*), described in Heinrici Chronicon and Livlandische Reimchronik as *Semigally,* who lived in the basin of river Lielupe and in the northern part of present-day Lithuania during the ninth through the thirteenth centuries. The main excavated archaeological monuments are the hillforts Mežotne (excavated by Voldemārs Ģinters) and Tērvete.

Institutions

Latvian Board of Antiquities (1923–1940)—A protection, registration, documentation, coordination, and administration center for archaeological monuments in Latvia. The Monument Protection law was accepted in the independent republic of Latvia in 1923 and supplemented in 1932, when professor Francis Balodis became the head of the board. More than 1,412 monuments and 148 reports of archaeological excavations, together with lists of 28,500 artifacts, were registered during the first fifteen years of the activities of the board.

Latvian University (founded 1919)—The only educational institution with archaeology as an academic discipline in the independent republic of Latvia. The Chair of Archaeology was founded by the Faculty of Philology and Philosophy in 1922. Professor Max Ebert (1879–1929) came to Rīga from the Albertus University of Koenigsberg. During the short term of his work at the university, archaeology became an academic discipline. The first three students, Voldemārs Ģinters, F. Jākabsons (1896–1930), and Eduards Šturms, continued their studies at the Albertus University of Koenigsberg. Max Ebert was displaced by professor Francis Balodis, the only academically educated Latvian archaeologist, who worked in Moscow and Saratow Universities and at the Institutes of Archaeology from 1912 to 1924. The first generation of Latvian archaeologists were trained during the 1920s. Elvīra Šnore, Rauls Šnore, Ādolfs Karnups, and Pēteris Stepiņš were the top students of professor Francis Balodis. In the first year of Soviet occupation, 1940, Balodis emigrated to Sweden. Šturms, now associate professor, continued to manage archaeological courses during the Soviet and German Nazi occupations. In 1944 Šturms emigrated to Germany. The first educational works at the university in the postwar period were organised by Rauls Šnore, but he was the subject of political repression. The Chair of Archaeology disappeared for a long time. Between 1950 and 1980 there were a few courses in protohistory from Professor Ēvalds Mugurēvičs, the foremost specialist in late Middle Ages archaeology in Latvia. In present-day Latvia there are only two archaeologists on the staff of the Department of Archaeology—Professor Andrejs Vasks, who specializes in the Bronze Age, and Associate Professor Armands Vijups, who specializes in the theory of archaeology. Only six people have completed master's theses.

Institute of History of Latvia—The scientific center of investigation of the prehistory and history of Latvia was founded in 1936. A Department of Archaeology was organized in the Institute of History and Material Culture of the Academy of Science after World War II (in 1947). In the new political situation some archaeologists began to investigate an urgent theme—the contacts between the people of the Iron Age of East Latvia and the Slavs during the tenth through the thirteenth centuries. The Chair of Archaeology at the university was not restored. Marxist methodology was used. Using Marxist methodology, Estonian academician Harri Moora (1952) published a special survey of the prehistory and early Middle Ages of Latvia. Excavations concentrated in the east and middle parts of Latvia. The Letgallian early medieval cemetery Pildas Nukši, which contained more than 250 graves, was investigated and the survey published in 1954. The Lettgallian hillfort Asote of the tenth through the twelfth centuries was excavated in 1949 through 1954 by Šnore, and the Semigallian hillfort Tērvete of the tenth through the twelfth centuries was investigated in 1951 through 1960. A unique clay tile painting of a piper was found inside a dwelling on the palisade of the Tērvete hillfort. Latvian archaeologists of the second generation—Emīlija Brīvkalne, Jolanta Daiga, Jānis Graudonis, Ēvalds Mugurēvičs, Ādolfs Stubavs, and Anna Zariņa—continued the excavation. The first published monograph, "Asote Hillfort" (Šnore) appeared in 1961; the second, about the contacts between the Lettgallians and the Slavs in the tenth through the thirteenth centuries, in 1965 (Mugurēvičs). Two other monographs were devoted to Lettgallian clothes (Zariņa) and to Late Bronze and Early Iron Age (Graudonis). The first excavations of the Stone Age monuments on the bank of Lake Lielais Ludzas were carried out at the end of the 1950s by Rauls Šnore and Francis Zagorskis. The second region of investigation was the Lake Lubāna Wetland in the 1960s. Discovery of twenty-five new settlements with well-preserved organic materials in the Lake Lubāna Wetland allowed the organization of large-scale protection excavations in the zones of building and melioration (Loze). Excavations were carried out by Zagorskis and Ilze Loze. Fieldwork was stimulated during the investigation of three building and flooded zones of hydro-stations at Pļaviņas, Rīga, and Daugavpils (1958–1974; 1982–1987). The excavations of Old Town Rīga were continued. The funds of the Department of Archaeology of the Latvian Institute of History (the second main archaeological repository in Latvia) contain more than 176,000 artifacts and altogether 1.8 million accounting units, including archival data (1995).

Museum of the History of Latvia—The main archaeological repository of Latvia, founded on the basis of collections from the Committee of Science of Latvian Society in 1869 and the German Duomo Museum in 1936. The first expeditions for gathering stray finds (1894, 1895) and the first exhibition during the Tenth Archaeological Congress in Rīga (1896) were organized by the Latvian Society. A Department of Archaeology at the museum appeared in 1924, in the first years of independent Latvia, with the Stone, Bronze, and Iron Age sections. The department contained more than 10,000 artifacts in 1936, 130,000 in 1981, and 180,000 in 1999. Since 1930 the museum has been managed by the Board of Monument Protection. The department has included archaeologists Elvīra Šnore and Voldemārs Ģinters. Large-scale excavations at Mežotne and Dignāja hillfort were carried out during the 1930s. After the German Army occupied Rīga, work in the museum was reduced. Before the Soviet Army came some collections were prepared for evacuation and sent to Germany. At the end of the war the director of the museum, Voldemārs Ģinters, left Latvia and the Latvian collections were returned from Germany. During the Soviet period Lūcija Vankina—another second generation Latvian archaeologist—was the head of the Department of Archaeology. The department took part in the works at the Sarnate peat bog settlement and in the flooded zones of the Pļaviņas and Rīga hydro-stations. Archaeological exhibitions were organized several times; the best one was in 1975, when Swedish archaeologists came to Rīga for three days.

Museum of the History of Rīga and Navigation— The oldest museum in Latvia contains one-third of the main repository of archaeological collections in Latvia (140,000 artifacts). It contains the first collection of natural and historical materials, as well as pieces of art gathered by doctor N. Himzel and donated to the city after his death. In accordance with the decision of the town council his collections were made part of the museum in 1773. The collections were supplemented with artifacts from the Society of History and Antiquity of the Baltic provinces of Russia from 1858 to 1890 and then moved into the Duomo Museum (1891), where they were exhibited together with the coin collections. The first excavations in Rīga Old Town were carried out in 1938 (after the reorganization of the museum in 1936). A Department of Archaeology was founded in 1949.

Ilze Loze

References

Apals, Jānis. 1994, 1995. "Reconstruction der befesting Inselsiedlung der 9 Th-s in Āraiši (Lettland)." *Experimentale Archaeologie:* 97–110.

Apals, Jānis, et al. 1974. *Latvijas PSR arheoloģija.* Rīga.

Balodis, Francis. 1938. *Latvian History: Latvian Prehistory and Protohistory.* (In Latvian.) Rīga.

———. 1939. "The Hillfort Jersika." *Senatne un Māksla* IY: 65–80.

Brastiņš, Ernests. 1923. *Latvian Hillforts: Kuršu zeme* [Curonian land]. Rīga.

———. 1926. *Zemgale un Augšzeme* [Semigallian and Selonian Land]. Rīga.

———. 1928. *Latgale* [Letgallian Land]. Rīga.

———. 1930. *Vidzeme* [Middle Land]. Rīga.

Caune, Andris. 1984. *Dwellings of Rīga in the Twelfth Thirteenth Centuries* (In Russian.) Rīga.

Caune, Andris, ed. 1998. *The Ancient Rīga—Investigations in Archaeology and History of Rīga.* Rīga.

"Das Jubilaum des Arch. Ēvalds Mugurēvičs." *Arh. un Etnogr.* 18 (1996): 7–20.

Die Wohninsel Āraiši. 1993. Cēsis.

"Dwellings of Āraiši Fortress [Yoke Angel Construction)." (In Latvian.) *Arheoloģija un Etnogrāfija* 11 (1974): 141–153.

Ģinters, Voldemārs. 1936a. "Excavations in Daugmale Hillfort in 1935–36." *Senatne un Māksla* 1: 87–105; 4: 15–44.

———. 1936b. *Prehistory of Latvian Folk Clothes* (In Latvian.) Rīga.

———. 1939. "Ancient Hillfort Mežotne." *Senatne un Māksla* 1: 63–96; 4: 15–45.

Graudonis, Jānis. 1967. *The Late Bronze Age and Early Iron Age in Latvia.* (In Russian.) Rīga.

———. 1994. *Dictionary of Archaeological Terminology—in Latvian—Russian—German—English.* Rīga.

———. 1999a. *Archaeological Excavations in the Turaida Brick Castle—Investigations of Rīga Archbishops' Castles.* Rīga.

———. 1999b. *Archaeological Investigations of the Brick Castle in Turaida—Compiled Issue: Investigations of the Castles of the Archbishop of Rīga.* Rīga.

Graudonis, Jānis, R. Denisova, and R. Grāvere. 1985. *Bronze Age Burials at Ķivutkalns.* (In Latvian.) Rīga.

Graudonis, Jānis, et al. 1974. *Latvijas PSR artheoloģija.* Rīga.

Indreko R. *In Memoriam: Šturms Eduards* In monograph, 405–411. Compiled by J. Ozols.

Karnups, Ādolfs. 1936. "Excavations at Talsi Hillfort Talsi." *Senatne un Māksla* 4: 67–86.

———. 1937. "Excavations at Talsi Hillfort Talsi" *Senatne un Māksla* 4: 74–93.

———. 1938. *Der Burger Talsi. Conventus primus historicum Balticorum—Rigae.*

Late Neolithic and Early Bronze Age of the Lubana Lowland. 1979. (In Russian.) Rīga.

Latvian Historians. Archaeologists Elvīra Šnore and Rauls Šnore. 1997. (In Latvian.) Rīga.

———. 1974. Riga, 211–213; fig. 173.

———. 1974b. Rīga, 2207–2209.

Loze, I. 1979. *Late Neolithic and Early Bronze Age in the Lake Lubāna Plain.* (In Russian.) Rīga.

———. 1988. *Stone Age Settlements of the Lubāna Lowland.* (In Russian) Rīga.

———. 1998. "The Adoption of Agriculture in the Area of Present-Day Latvia (The Lake Lubāna Basin)" In *Beyond Balkanization—Baltic-Pontic Studies,* 59–84. Vol. 5. Poznan.

Mugurēvičs, Ēvalds. 1965. *East Latvia and Neighbouring Countries during the Tenth–Thirteenth Centuries.* (In Russian.) Rīga.

———. 1977. *Castle Districts of Oliņkalns and Lokstene.* (In Latvian.) Rīga.

———. 1993. *Heinrici Chronicon.* Rīga: Zinātne.

———. 1998. *Livlandische Reimchronic.* Rīga: Zinātne.

———. 1999. "The Works of Archaeologists of the Latvian Institute of History in the Post War Years (1946–98)." *Inside Latvian Archaeology:* 141–152.

Mugurēvičs, Ēvalds, ed. *Artheoloģija un Etnogrāfija* (1971–2000).

Mugurēvičs, Ēvalds, et al. 1974. *Latvijas PSR artheoloģija.* Rīga.

"Neolithic Amber Ornaments in the Eastern Part of Latvia." *Przeglad Archaeologiczny* 23 (1975): 59–82.

The Newly Discovered Hillforts in the Eastern Part of Latvia. 1995. Rīga.

"Planning the Buildings in the First Stage of Habitation of the Āraiši Lake Fortress." 1987. (In Latvian.) In *Proceedings of Academy of Sciences of Latvia,* 81–97.

Šnore, Elvīra. 1961. *Hillfort Asote.* (In Latvian.) Rīga.

———. 1987. *Cemetery Kivti (Seventh–Twelfth Centuries).* (In Latvian.) Rīga.

———. 1993. *Barrows of the Early Iron Age in the Eastern Part of Latvia.* (In Latvian) Rīga.

Šnore, Elvīra, ed. 1974. *Latvijas PSR artheoloģija (Archaeology of Latvian SSR).* Rīga.

Šnore, Elvīra, and Anna Zariņa. 1980. *Ancient Sēpils.* (In Latvian.) Rīga.

Šnore, Rauls. 1938a. "Investigations in Prehistory of Latvia during the 20 Years of State." *Senatne un Māksla* 4: 39–96.

———. 1938b. *Zur Typologie der fruhen Silberbarren in Lettland—Conventus primus historicum Balticorum.* Rigae.

———. n.d. "History of Economy in Latvia during the Prehistory and Protohistory Period." Prepared manuscript. Latvian Department, Academic Library, Rīga.

Stubavs, Adolfs. 1974. "Classification and Typology of Latvian Hillforts." (In Latvian.) *Artheoloģija un etnogrāfija* 11: 74–88.

———. 1976. *The Hillfort and Settlement of Ķentes Hillfort.* (In Latvian.) Rīga.

Šturms, Eduards. 1970. "Die steinzeitlichen Kulturen der Balticums." S. 298, 58 Taf. *Antiquitas* 3, 40, Bd. 9. Bonn.

Urtāns, J. 1992. "Ernests Brastiņs—Investigator of Latvian Hillforts." *Journal of Institute of History of Latvia* 4: 195–200.

———. 1994a. *Arheologs Vladislavs Urtāns.* Rīga.

———. 1994b. *Latvian Hillforts: The Originality of the Archaeological Reality.* Amsterdam.

Urtāns, Vladislavs. 1961. "The Owl Fibula." *Arheoloģija un etnogrāfija* 3: 39–60.

———. 1977. *The Eldest Deposits in Latvia.* (In Latvian.) Rīga.

Vankina, Lūcija. 1970. *Wetland Settlement of Sārnate.* (In Russian.) Rīga.

———. 1999. *The Collection of Stone Age Bone and Antler Artefacts from Lake Lubāna.* Rīga.

Vilsone, M. 1973. *Archaeological Excavations in Rīga Old Town and Their Role in the Investigations of the*

History of Capital. Rīga: Museum of History of Rīga and Navigation. 1772–1973.

Zagorska, I. 1996. *The First Radiocarbon Data from the Stone Age Burial Field in Zvejnieki—The Application Methods in Archaeology.* Helsinki.

Zagorskis, F. 1987. *Stone Age Burial Field.* (In Latvian.) Rīga.

Zariņa, Anna. 1970. *Cloth of Ancient Letgallians (Seventh–Thirteenth Centuries)* (In Latvian.) Rīga.

———. 1988. *Cloth of Livs Tenth–Thirteenth Centuries.* (In Latvian.) Rīga, 1988, 107 pages.

———. 1999. *The Ancient Clothes of Latvians (Seventh–Seventeenth Centuries).* (In Latvian.) Rīga.

Zariņa, Anna, et al. 1974. *Latvijas PSR arheoloģija.* Rīga.

Zemītis, G. 1996. "The Rampart of Hillfort Daugmale." *Arheoloģija un Etnogrāfija* 18: 118–223.

———. 1999. *Department of Archaeology at the History Museum of Latvia—Inside Latvian Archaeology.* Gotteborg.

Austen Henry Layard (Ann Ronan Picture Library)

Laugerie Haute and Laugerie Basse

First dug in 1868 by ÉDOUARD LARTET as part of his Dordogne campaign with HENRY CHRISTY and subsequently explored by DENIS PEYRONY and FRANÇOIS BORDES, these two adjacent rock shelters in the vicinity of Les Eyzies in the Dordogne have, between them, yielded a complete sequence of Upper Paleolithic industries in southwestern FRANCE. The Laugerie sites are type sites for the Aurignacian, Gravettian, Solutrean, and Magdalenian periods, and there is a particularly fine representation of Magdalenian art objects in Laugerie Basse.

Tim Murray

See also Lithic Analysis

References

Gamble, C. 1986. *The Paleolithic Settlement of Europe.* Cambridge University Press.

Layard, Sir Austen Henry (1817–1894)

Born in Paris and raised in SWITZERLAND, Layard studied law and then practiced for six years, at the end of which he set out to ride overland to Ceylon. He got no further than IRAN, where he spent a year with a group of nomads. Arriving in Baghdad in 1842 he was sent back to Constantinople (later Istanbul) to brief the British Ambassador on his travels. On the way he visited what was thought to be the ancient city of NINEVEH, at Khorsabad, where French diplomat PAUL EMILE BOTTA was excavating.

After several years as a diplomatic agent in Turkey Layard persuaded the British Ambassador Sir Stratford Canning to sponsor his excavation of the mounds in northern MESOPOTAMIA—in competition with the French. In 1845 at the mound of NIMRUD Layard discovered several Assyrian royal palaces, one of which was that of Ashurnasirpal II, and bas-reliefs similar to those discovered by Botta at nearby Khorsabad. Both Layard and Botta were only interested in the most spectacular finds of statuary and portable architectural remains to be displayed in their national museums. Tunneling and trenching around these larger pieces destroyed much other archaeological information and smaller or fragile artifacts.

In 1847 Layard began shipping his finds back to London where reports of them had already caused a sensation. They were put on display in the BRITISH MUSEUM where they aroused not only great public interest but also further spon-

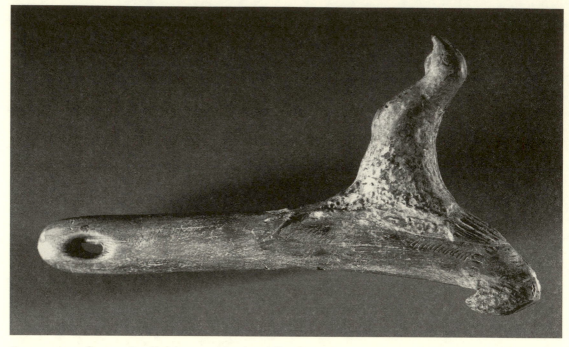

Reconstruction of a pierced staff with a carved heath cock found at Le Mas d'Azil (Gianni Dagli Orti / Corbis)

sorship of Layard's work by the English government. Returning to Mesopotamia in 1849 Layard excavated the mound of Kuyunjik opposite Mosul, which was in fact Nineveh (and not Khorsabad as Botta had claimed). He found Sennacherib's palace, and the royal library and archives, which contained thousands of clay tablets. Layard continued to dig the mounds around Mosul and then moved into southern Mesopotamia where he tested the sites of Babylon and Nippur. In 1851 he supervised the packing of another hundred or so cases of Assyrian artifacts and returned to England where he published *Discoveries in the Ruins of Nineveh and Babylon* and *the Monuments of Nineveh* (1853), both of which were bestsellers. The exhibition of these extraordinary finds generated an Assyrian fashion and style in contemporary jewelry, hair and beard styles, theatrical productions, decoration, painting, poetry, and architecture, and provoked much controversy among scholars about biblical credibility and progress.

Layard himself left archaeology and took up politics and diplomacy. He became a member of Parliament and English ambassador to Madrid and Constantinople. In the latter position he was to encounter and help HEINRICH SCHLIEMANN. The British excavation of Mesopotamia was continued by Hormuzd Rassam and William Kennett Loftus until 1855, and sponsored by the British Museum and a private Assyrian Excavation Fund. Scholars such as HENRY RAWLINSON began to decipher the cuneiform tablets that Layard had shipped home, although it was to take another thirty years to complete the task.

Tim Murray

See also French Archaeology in Egypt and the Middle East
References
Lloyd, S. 1984. *The Archaeology of Mesopotamia,* rev. ed. London: Thames and Hudson.

Le Mas D'Azil

Le Mas D'Azil, a cave system with occupation deposits, is the type site of the Azilian industry dated to the Mesolithic/Epipaleolithic period (about 11,500–9500 B.P.) in FRANCE. Located in the Ariège region in the French Pyrenees, this huge and complex site, first dug by French historian EDUOARD PIETTE in 1887, is also rich in Aurignacian and Magdalenian artifacts, particularly carved and incised antler and bone art works as well as painted pebbles.

Tim Murray

See also Lithic Analysis
References
Gamble, C. 1986. *The Paleolithic Settlement of Europe.* Cambridge: Cambridge University Press.

Le Moustier

Le Moustier is the type site of the Mousterian industry (from the Middle Paleolithic period, 180,000–30,000 years ago) found in Europe and northeastern Africa and into central Asia. The rockshelter site was first excavated by ÉDOUARD LARTET and HENRY CHRISTY as part of their work in southwestern FRANCE, which began in 1863. Although there is still debate about the nature of Mousterian assemblages, it is often assumed that there is an association between Neanderthal remains and the Mousterian. Difficult problems related to the explanation of variability within Mousterian assemblages remain and were at the center of celebrated exchanges between prehistorians FRANÇOIS BORDES and LEWIS BINFORD.

Tim Murray

See also Lithic Analysis
References
Gamble, C. 1986. *The Paleolithic Settlement of Europe.* Cambridge: Cambridge University Press.

Leakey, Louis Seymour (1903–1972)

Leakey was born in Kenya, East Africa, to missionary parents and grew up among the tribal Kikuyu. He went to secondary school in England and then to St John's College Cambridge in 1922 where he studied languages, archaeology, and anthropology. In 1926 he returned to East Africa and began to investigate the prehistory of the Rift Valley, which he published in *Stone Age Cultures of Kenya Colony* (1931). He married the artist and archaeological draftsperson Mary Douglas Nichol in 1936.

Between 1936 and 1962 many examples of Australopithecus (small-brained, bipedal ho-minid fossils, extant between five million and one million years ago) were found in South Africa (at the sites of Sterkfontein, KROMDRAAI, Makapansgat, and SWARTKRANS), firmly establishing the study of the earliest archaeological records in the world. Unlike many of his European contemporaries Louis Leakey believed that Africa, and not Central Asia, was where humanity had originated. During the 1940s Louis and MARY LEAKEY pioneered Paleolithic "living-floor" archaeology at OLORGESAILIE, investigating fossil pollens and paleo-environmental data in an attempt to more fully interpret the stone tools from the same levels. They also began looking for the makers of the Oldawan stone tools they had found in the ancient deposits of the OLDUVAI GORGE, an ancient lake basin in northern Tanzania in the East African Rift Valley. In 1959 the hominid cranium, called *Zinjanthropus* (East African man) *boisei* or OH 5 was found. "Zinj" was the first hominid to be dated by the potassium-argon (K/Ar) method, a new technique, and was found to be 1.7 million years old. *Zinjanthropus* was also the first hominid to be excavated on television, and event that not only captured public imagination but also grabbed the attention of the American National Geographic Society, who were to provide ongoing financial support for the Leakeys' work. "Zinj" also caused some scientific controversy.

Louis Leakey first concluded that OH 5 was *the* ancestor of modern humans and not another ancestral form of the South African Australopithecines—which in fact it subsequently became. Then the remains of another, more advanced hominid (i.e., with a larger brain capacity) were found close by, and in 1964 Leakey claimed that this find, *Homo habilis,* superceded OH 5 as *the* early human ancestor, directly connected to *Homo sapiens.* While Leakey's simplistic views on human evolution have now been generally rejected, his finds were a significant contribution to the knowledge of fossil human evolution. International funding for research in this area increased and archaeologists and Paleo-anthropologists from America and Europe began to work in Africa searching for the origins of the whole of humanity. Leakey's work had shifted interest from Europe and Asia

Louis and Mary Leakey excavating in Tanganyika, 1961 (Bettmann/Corbis)

to the southern hemisphere, and to the development of world archaeology and prehistory.

In addition to the Olduvai material, Louis Leakey's work on the Miocene fauna of western Kenya and the early hominid remains from Rusinga Island, Songhor, and Fort Ternan were great contributions to African prehistory. He spoke Kikuyu fluently and his 1937 to 1939 detailed study of the people and their culture was published in 1977 by his wife. Louis Leakey became curator of the Coryndon Museum in Nairobi in 1940, and he established the Centre for Prehistory and Paleontology in 1962, which became the International Louis Leakey Memorial Institute for African Prehistory after his death.

Tim Murray

See also Dart, Raymond Arthur; Africa, East, Prehistory; Africa, South, Prehistory; Laetoli

References

Isaac, G., and E. R. McCown, eds. 1976. *Human Origins: Louis Leakey and the East African Evidence.* Menlo Park, CA: Benjamin.

Leakey, Mary Douglas (1913–)

Mary Leakey is the daughter of the landscape painter Erskine E. Nichol and the great-great-great-granddaughter of JOHN FRERE, the antiquarian squire who argued for the antiquity and human origins of stone tools at the end of the eighteenth century. Mary Douglas Nichol had an informal education and was a talented artist with an interest in archaeology. She illustrated GERTRUDE CATON-THOMPSON's book *The Desert Fayum* (1934), and, impressed by her talents, LOUIS LEAKEY asked her to illustrate his popular book on prehistory, *Adam's Ancestors* (1934). They were married in 1936 and worked together in East Africa for more than thirty years.

Before 1972 it is almost impossible to separate Mary's contributions to East African archaeology from Louis's—they were an archaeological field team. Mary was there at Rusinga, OLDUVAI, and OLORGESAILIE, and she contributed to and wrote many of the scholarly publications on their work. She seems to have left the publicity, funding, and the big-picture debates to Louis and to have preferred to continue with and supervise the painstaking analysis required by every find at every excavation.

After Louis Leakey's death in 1972 Mary began to work at the Pliocene site of LAETOLI, southeast of Olduvai. From 1974 to 1981 she and her collaborators found numbers of new mammalian species, among which, dated to about 3.7 million years ago, were the hominid fossils of what was called *Australopithecus afarensis.* In 1976 a trail of fossil animal footprints were found, some of which were hominid, and in 1978 two long trails of fossil hominid footprints were uncovered and dated to about 3.5 million years ago. These footprints confirmed what had only been inferred from skeletal remains, that the small-brained *Australopithecus* hominids were bipedal.

Mary Leakey also contributed to the practice of field archaeology through her paleo-environmental "living floor" work and through her development of field museums, where finds were left in-situ. She also conducted a major study of rock art at Kondoa-rangi in Tanzania, published in her book *Africa's Vanishing Art: the Rock Paintings of Tanzania* (1951).

Tim Murray

See also Dart, Raymond Arthur; Africa, East, Prehistory; Africa, South, Prehistory

References
Morrell, V. 1995. *Ancestral Passions: The Leakey Family and the Quest for Humankind's Beginnings.* New York: Simon and Schuster.

Lepinski Vir

Excavated by Serbian archaeologist Dragoslav Srejovic' between 1967 and 1971, Lepinski Vir lies in the Djerdap Gorge of the Danube River in Serbia. Lepinski Vir has an interesting and long sequence of occupations from hunter-gathering/foraging/agricultural societies. Although there are disagreements about the dating of the site, it is generally believed that it was occupied around 7000 B.C. by people foraging in the forests for game and in the river for fish, and that by 5000 B.C., the occupants of the site were managing cattle, sheep, pigs, and goats. Lepinski Vir is also notable for the remains of houses found on the site and the presence of limestone sculptures found in the remains of the houses. There is some speculation that the site was in fact occupied by the local farming Starcero cultures.

Tim Murray

Lepsius, Karl Richard (1810–1884)

Lepsius was born in Germany and educated at the universities of Leipzig, Gottingen, and Berlin. After completing his doctorate in Classical archaeology in 1833 Lepsius went to Paris to further his studies. JEAN FRANÇOIS CHAMPOLLION's new ancient Egyptian grammar had just been published and Lepsius became interested in Egyptian hieroglyphics. He supported and defended Champollion's system of decipherment and he contributed to further understanding of ancient Egyptian through his recognition of syllabic signs and their similarities to Coptic.

Lepsius spent many years visiting the European collections of Egyptian antiquities before traveling to Egypt in 1842 with the Prussian Expedition (1842–1845). He was accompanied by a number of Prussian scholars and skilled draftsmen to survey and record monuments and collect antiquities. The expedition sent back more than 15,000 artifacts, papyri, and plaster casts, drawings, plans, and maps to Prussia. Between 1849 and 1859 Lepsius published *Monuments in Egypt and Ethiopia,* the results of the expedition, in twelve folio volumes. The Swiss Egyptologist EDOUARD NAVILLE completed another five volumes in the series after Lepsius's death.

In 1865 Lepsius became keeper of the Egyptian collections in the Berlin Museum. He returned to Egypt the following year to record the monuments of the eastern Delta and the Suez regions, during which he discovered Tanis, the capital of Egypt during the twenty-first dynasty. Here he excavated the Canopus Decree, a useful linguistic adjunct that helped to prove that the Rosetta Stone was translated correctly. Lepsius edited the principal German journal of Egyptology, which is still published today, for over twenty years and completed over 142 publications on ancient Egypt. His last visit to Egypt was for the opening of the Suez Canal in 1869.

Tim Murray

References
Ceram, C. W. 1967. *Gods, Graves and Scholars.* Harmondsworth, UK: Pelican.

Leroi-Gourhan, André (1911–1986)

André Georges Léandre Leroi-Gourhan was born in Paris on 25 August 1911. He acquired his education almost entirely outside any conventional context. Although he did attend the seminars given by the sociologist Marcel Mauss and the sinologist Paul Granet during the 1930s, Leroi-Gourhan remained proudest of the autodidactic and eclectic periods of his life, probably because they allowed him to stay outside an academic system that did not impress him.

After World War I, the Durkheimian school, under Marcel Mauss, opened up to oriental studies, to linguistics, and to a comparative approach. Leroi-Gourhan founded a school of prehistory in its own right, countering the existing culture-historical and typological vision of archaeology with the synthetic, anthropological, and semiological approach of "prehistoric ethnology."

During the 1930s, Leroi-Gourhan was in charge of reorganizing the Arctic section of the Trocadéro Museum (later the Musée de l'Homme) in Paris, and this daily involvement with artifacts and collections was to have a lasting effect on him. It was during this period that he became conscious that the comparative method could be substituted for the standard approach of the "hard" sciences, i.e., that he would be able to validate his interpretation of archaeology only when it could be based on an abundance of data and a range of varied regularities so that no other interpretation could account for all of them.

Leroi-Gourhan laid the foundations for the ethnology of stone toolmaking techniques, a very original approach that combines a systemic analysis of comparative syntheses with the development of methodological tools to be used for particular case studies. The publication of *Évolution et techniques* (Evolution and Techniques) in 1943 established the specific epistemology for this technological approach and announced the concept of *chaîne opératoire* (chain of operation). *Évolution et techniques* is in fact an *inventaire raisonné* (reasoned inventory) that allows us to appreciate the physical effectiveness and the relative complexity of a tool or a toolmaking technique as well as to identify possible substitutes for it. Moreover, this inventory allows us to discern the principles shared by the techniques used in a community and to understand their ethnicity.

Leroi-Gourhan presented his *inventaire raisonné* in the form of tree-like diagrams, or dendrograms. Those ubiquitous and recurrent instances of solutions that were physically functional were brought together under the term *tendance* ("tendency"), and he broke each technical process or artifact down into a group of attributes he included in the category he called *faits* ("instances of techniques"). Between the two extremes of *tendance* and *faits,* the dendrogram represents a hierarchical classification of artifacts and technical processes according to their *degrés de fait* ("degrees of specificity"). If we move from the trunk (the *tendance,* or the invariant aspect of technique) toward the branches, the technical characteristics retained in the diagram are further and further apart, i.e., they are increasingly culturally different from one another. But reading it the other way around, we gradually move from the different instances to what these different phenomena have in common.

In proposing the notion of "favorable environment," Leroi-Gourhan also indicated how the "continuity of the technical environment" plays a role in the adoption or rejection of a borrowed item or an innovation: the intellectual assessment of this novelty should be compatible with the mental representations that the group has of its techniques. The criteria distinguished by Leroi-Gourhan to establish technical classifications were those he thought would be able to elucidate the evolution of human technical behavior, and those that would allow him to understand the logic of transformations that accounted for the existence of forms of techniques judged to be increasingly effective.

He believed that the study of techniques had to be linked to the question of the technicity of living beings, "dealing simultaneously with" organic structures, neuro-motor equipment and manifestations of the mind. This fundamental notion of technicity incited him to articulate the philosophical, genetic, and epistemological investigations that he was to develop in such a prophetic fashion in *Le geste et la parole* (Word and Action; 1964–1965). In this work, Leroi-Gourhan developed his ideas about exteriorization and "ethnic becoming" (épiphylogenèse), which he saw as the progressive liberation of a memory that articulates three levels: individual, socioethnic, and specific. The idea that a kind of rationality plays its part in the course of history has, moreover, invited a comparison between Leroi-Gourhan's work and that of Karl Marx.

If his career was that of an academic (he was professor at the University of Lyon until 1956, at the Sorbonne until 1968, and finally at the Collège de France until 1982), he lived, above all else, as a philosopher, and he was an astonishing character. When most of his colleagues regarded excavation as being of secondary importance, he took his students into the field. In this context, the excavations at the sites of Arcy-sur-Cure, Les Mournouards, and PINCEVENT were of great importance. During three decades, several hundred students from many countries took courses in excavation at these centers, and they were deeply influenced by the experience. Here, Leroi-Gourhan laid the foundations of both spatial analysis and funerary archaeology *à la française*.

In the 1960s, Leroi-Gourhan's approach seemed on the point of imposing itself on the archaeological sphere, but this was not to be. Three factors contributed to this missed opportunity. First was Leroi-Gourhan's personality: he was a man who had accumulated degrees and honors; a man who could read Chinese, sing in Russian, and speak Japanese; a man who had reorganized museums and updated methods of excavation and the interpretation of prehistoric art; a man who predicted, in 1965, the advent of hypertexts and electronic libraries. At the same time, however, as an archaeologist he had made no spectacular discoveries. He was a thinker who found it hard to communicate, a keen do-it-yourself man who worked without funds, and a professor who did not leave a single distinguished student behind.

The second factor involved a change of direction in his intellectual development, which had lasting consequences. After the publication of *Le geste et la parole* and the discovery of the Magdalenian site at Pincevent in 1964, Leroi-Gourhan abruptly lost interest in the synthetic approach that he had developed until then; the often intuitive yet profoundly lucid, coherent, and penetrating predictions and interpretations he expressed in *Le geste et la parole* were for him an end in their own right. It was as if, after Pincevent, the structuring of prehistoric space became the locus of his activities. This bifurcation brought him the disapproval of English and American scholars who generally only knew of him from a few translated texts, essentially texts on Paleolithic art (*Le geste et la parole* did not appear in English until 1993). The third factor consisted of the institutional gap between ethnology and archaeology, a gap that thwarted all attempts by his followers who tried to maintain the unity of prehistory and ethnology that Leroi-Gourhan had believed in. Not one of his students was both an archaeologist and an ethnologist, all of them were either one or the other.

Leroi-Gourhan's experience resembles that of Lévi-Strauss in that the history of a discipline can be identified with the intellectual history of an exceptional personality. But unlike Lévi-Strauss, Leroi-Gourhan's paradoxical nature has contributed to the situation today, in which he is ignored by a large non-French part of the scientific community. But, as he had intended, the implications of his work go far beyond the archaeology and the ethnology of techniques. His general hypotheses concerning the process of hominization, which raise the question of Being, are today being placed into a wider philosophical perspective. His analysis of post-Neanderthal "epiphylogenesis" has been repositioned in the context of the cognitive sciences and is the origin of highly up-to-date investigations in other disciplines.

Anick Coudart

See also France; Lithic Analysis
References
For references, see *Encyclopedia of Archaeology: The Great Archaeologists, Vol. 2,* ed. Tim Murray (Santa Barbara, CA: ABC-CLIO, 1999), pp. 663–664.

Lhwyd, Edward (1660–1709)

Lhwyd was born into a well-established Welsh family and educated at Jesus College, Oxford, where he became a friend of Dr. Robert Plot, philosopher, antiquarian, and first keeper of the ASHMOLEAN MUSEUM. Lhwyd assisted with the development of the natural science collections of shells and botanic specimens and became interested in the study of fossils, or "formed stones." He was convinced they were the petrified remains of organisms that had died long ago, and like the eminent Oxford scientist Robert Hooke thought they might be evidence of huge changes to the earth. Lhwyd identified, classified, and published a large range of fossils in the Ashmolean's collection in 1691.

Lhwyd's interests broadened from fossils to include stone implements and British antiquity in general, and he became friends with the antiquarian JOHN AUBREY. He was recruited in 1693 to contribute to Edmund Gibson's revised edition of WILLIAM CAMDEN's *Britannia,* the first attempt at an update of this great work since it had been translated into English in 1610 and gone out of print in 1637. Lhwyd eventually became responsible for researching and writing about the whole of Wales, and he undertook an antiquarian tour in support of this task during the summer of 1693.

Lhwyd's additions to the Welsh sections of *Britannia* were outstanding. Indeed, his additions transformed the Welsh sections from a rather inadequate sketch of unfamiliar terrain to the most rewarding part of the new volume when it was published in 1695. In his contributions Lhwyd did more than any of his predecessors to enlarge the understanding of the societies that inhabited Britain before the Romans. He formed a picture from material remains supplemented by folklore and Classical reports, and drew attention to the high degree of social organization and technical prowess needed to erect the great stone complexes. He made it clear, too, that the Britons had considerable metalworking skills, noting the discovery of several caches of weapons, axe-heads, bolts, daggers, and swords.

Lhwyd's research for *Britannia* inspired him to undertake a work that would bring together his knowledge of Celtic languages and ancient British antiquities and his interest in natural history. In 1707 he published his *Glossography,* the first part of the projected larger *Archaeologia Britannica,* which confirmed Lhwyd's preeminence as a Celtic scholar. The *Glossography* was a substantial folio and a remarkable achievement of comparative philology. Lhwyd demonstrated the relationship between the Celtic languages surviving in western Europe, and he included Welsh and Irish dictionaries and a Cornish grammar. He was able to make some progress in reconstructing the ancient Gallic language spoken in Gaul in Roman times. Lhwyd's travels between 1697 and 1701 were an impressive testimony to the thoroughness of his research. He made the first antiquarian tour of the Scottish highlands and visited Scottish antiquaries. He collected Gaelic manuscripts and local customs and folklore. He recorded local dialects and details of towns, villages, and local place names. He sought information about barrows, burial chambers, standing stones, and inscribed stones. He looked at coins and brass utensils, flint arrowheads, and prehistoric implements and fossils.

Unfortunately much of the vast store of information Lhwyd accumulated was lost. After the *Glossography* his heath failed and he never completed the second part of the *Archaeologia Britannica,* the proposed great compendium of the Celtic culture of western Britain. He died in 1709 and his papers were dispersed, and many of them were later destroyed by fire. Because of the limited appeal of the *Glossography* and its incomplete status Lhwyd's reputation was not as great as it should have been. Yet his work is a lasting record of his exceptional powers as an interpreter of prehistoric remains and proves his worth as an incomparable topographer and local historian. His philological research effectively laid the foundations for all later study of the Celtic languages of the British Isles and Brittany.

Graham Parry

See also Britain, Prehistoric Archaeology

References

For references, see *Encyclopedia of Archaeology: The Great Archaeologists, Vol. 1,* ed. Tim Murray (Santa Barbara, CA: ABC-CLIO, 1999), p. 37.

Li Chi (1895–1979)

Li Chi was born in Hubei province in CHINA into a wealthy family. In 1918 he went to the United States to study psychology and sociology at Clark University in Massachusetts, and then to Harvard University, where he earned a Ph.D. in anthropology in 1923, after which he returned to China and taught at Nankai University.

Between 1925 and 1926 Li excavated a Neolithic Yangshao Culture site in southern Shanxi province, making him the first Chinese scholar to undertake modern archaeological fieldwork. In 1928 he became the first head of the department of archaeology at the Academia Sinica, established to excavate the three-thousand-year-old capital of the Shang culture at ANYANG. These excavations shaped modern archaeology in China through their recruitment and training of young Chinese archaeologists (including XIA NAI, later director of the Institute of Archaeology) and their use of modern field archaeology techniques in combination with traditional Chinese historiography and antiquarianism. The site also yielded oracle bone inscriptions that proved to be the first written documents in China, and the ceramic and bronze vessel nomenclature and typology used by Li at Anyang still dominates the archaeology of China. His book *The Formation of Chinese People: An Anthropological Inquiry* was published in 1928.

The Sino-Japanese War in 1937 and then World War II put an end to all archaeology in China. In 1949 Li went to Taiwan with the Nationalist government, and he did not work on mainland China again. He founded the Department of Archaeology and Anthropology at National Taiwan University, the first university program in China to train professional archaeologists, and published his synthesis of archaeological and historic material *The Beginnings of Chinese Civilization* in 1957. Li spent most of his time on the conservation and publication of the Anyang material, which was completed as *Anyang Excavations* in 1977.

Tim Murray

See also Island Southeast Asia

Libby, Willard Frank (1908–1980)

Born in Colorado and raised in California, Willard Libby was a farmer's son. He began studying mining engineering at the University of California, Berkeley, in 1927 and changed to chemistry, which interested him more. He received a Ph.D. in 1933 after studying low-energy radioactive nuclei. From 1933 to 1941 he taught chemistry at Berkeley.

In 1941 Libby joined the Manhattan Project (the development of a nuclear bomb) at Columbia University in New York City, where he worked on gas diffusion techniques for separating uranium isotopes into fissionable material. In 1945 he became professor of chemistry at the University of Chicago and began working at the Institute of Nuclear Studies. It was here that Libby proved that the amount of radiocarbon in all living plants and animals begins to decay at death at a known rate—so that it would be possible to measure the amount of time since the organism has died by measuring the amount of radiocarbon remaining in it. The accuracy of this technique was tested by comparison with proven other DATING techniques such as tree-ring dating, and the first actual C-14 dates appeared in 1949.

Radiocarbon dating revolutionized archaeology in the twentieth century. It began a new era—no longer did archaeologists have to spend so much time developing and testing chronologies for their material—they had an accurate method for dating any organic material from the last 70,000 years and they could now pursue other imperatives and new ideas and new directions in their discipline. In 1959 Libby became professor of chemistry at the University of California, Los Angeles, and in 1960 he received the Nobel Prize for chemistry for his work on radiocarbon dating.

Libby was one of the United States' major postwar nuclear scientists. In 1954 he was appointed by President Eisenhower to serve on the Atomic Energy Commission, the first chemist to do so. He was mainly interested in the effects of nuclear fallout and was also involved in international efforts for peaceful uses of nuclear power, serving as vice-chairman of the American delegation to the First International Conference on Peaceful Uses of Atomic Energy in Germany in 1955.

Tim Murray

See also Douglass, Andrew Ellicot

Lindenschmidt, Ludwig (1809–1893)

German prehistorian and scholar who helped to found the Romisch-Germanische Zentral Museum at Mainz, where he was director until his death.

During the first half of the nineteenth century Germany, like England, was full of enthusiastic antiquarians eagerly excavating and founding museums and equally eager to establish a significant and ancient German past. This latter obsession was the result of contemporary German political fragmentation, which would persist until the 1870s. Political fragmentation was reflected in the fragmentation of collections of archaeological material—of find contexts and artifacts and scholarship—unlike in Scandinavia, where CHRISTIAN J. THOMSEN, BROR HILDEBRAND, and HANS HILDEBRAND were beginning to organize and study large, national, and lengthy homogenous archaeological collections and consequently develop theories, such as the THREE AGE SYSTEM, about European prehistory.

In 1866 Lindenschmidt was one of the founding editors of the periodical *Archiv fur Anthropologie,* which became the forum for German anthropologists who lacked any formal and national organizations. In 1870, the same year as German political unification, the German Society for Anthropology, Ethnology and Prehistory was founded. The *Archiv* became its journal, and continued to be published until World War II. Lindenschmidt, like his fellow prehistorians, was interested in "archae-geography," the elucidation of ethnic questions via archaeological evidence, issues that occurred in the work of RUDOLF VIRCHOW and continued with GUSTAF KOSSINNA. This preoccupation explains their critical stance toward, and even rejection of, the Three-Age theory. Until the 1880s Lindenschmidt refused to accept the idea of separate Bronze and Iron Ages and continued to emphasize the importance of southern Europe and the Mediterranean for the development of prehistoric metallurgy in central Europe.

Tim Murray

See also German Prehistoric Archaeology
References
Sklenár, K. 1983. *Archaeology in Central Europe: The First 500 Years.* Leicester, UK: Leicester University Press.

Linear A / Linear B

The Linear B script was in used in Minoan Crete and Mycenaean GREECE in the period between 1450 and 1200 B.C. An earlier script, called Linear A, had been devised in Crete in the period between 1700 and 1450 B.C. Linear B has been translated, but Linear A still provides a challenge.

The story of the decipherment of Linear B really begins with English archaeologist SIR ARTHUR EVANS at KNOSSOS, the royal city of Crete, at the beginning of the twentieth century. During his excavations at that site, Evans discovered many small clay tablets covered with linear script. These were different from the hieroglyphs, which he had also observed carved into seals and small gems, found by himself (and others) on Crete and in Greece. Beginning in 1909 with the publication of *Scripta Minoa I,* Evans was able to publish only a small fraction of the tablets he had excavated by the time the fourth volume of the *Palace of Minos* was published in 1935. The point has often been made (not least by those most directly responsible for the translation of Linear B) that this slow rate of publication may have delayed the eventual decipherment of Linear B, but it is equally true that subsequent discoveries such as American archaeologist CARL BLEGEN's 1939 recovery of the Mycenaean archive at the Palace of Nestor at Pylos in Greece provided vital clues.

Building on work by A. E. Cowley, Alice Kober, and E. J. Bennett, Jr., a young English architect Michael Ventris (1922–1956)—at first working essentially alone but later with the Cambridge philologist John Chadwick—was able to overcome the problems posed by the shortage of published texts to produce the fundamentals of a decipherment of Linear B in

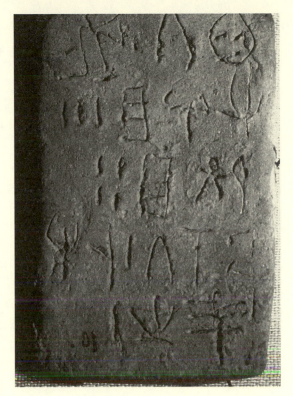

Early Minoan writing (AAA)

1952. The most significant element of his decipherment was the argument that Linear B was, in fact, an ancient form of Greek. Ventris and Chadwick went on to complete the task of decipherment in the years before the former's untimely death in a road accident.

It is not without some irony that the first major test of the Ventris-Chadwick decipherment was provided by none other than Carl Blegen, who had returned to Pylos in 1952 and discovered a further 300 tablets. The fact that these could be read, even though they (and other Linear B documents) are primarily invoices and the "paperwork" involved in the administration of palace business, at once brought history closer to the Minoan and Mycenaean world. The fact that the last kings of Crete were Greek speakers has led to a reevaluation of Evans's argument that the Minoans had conquered the Mycenaeans. It is now thought that the reverse is true and that around 1450 B.C. Knossos was conquered by the same people who ruled at Pylos and Mycenae.

Tim Murray

References

Doblhofer, Ernst. 1961. *Voices in Stone.* London: Picador.

Lithic Analysis

Stone artifacts are studied by archaeologists because they are durable and frequently found on archaeological sites of almost every age. Consequently, much has been written about their analysis and interpretation. This article considers the history of three approaches to the study of stone artifacts: (1) factors contributing to variation in the composition and characteristics of stone artifact assemblages, (2) functionalist interpretations of artifact assemblages, and (3) idealist interpretations of material remains.

Functionalist and idealist approaches reflect a fundamental debate in archaeology about whether humans are passive participants or active agents in their worlds. Functionalist approaches seek to explain the role of artifacts in the evolution and/or behavior of different groups. Idealist approaches seek to understand the knowledge and belief systems of the makers of artifact assemblages. Fundamental to both approaches is an understanding of why recurring artifact forms (i.e., types) exist, as well as the factors contributing to variation in the composition of artifact assemblages.

Dimensions of Artifact Variability

For much of the twentieth century, archaeologists attributed the similarities and differences between artifact assemblages to a single variable: the cultural idiosyncrasies, or traditions, of different groups of people. The best known work in this regard is FRANÇOIS BORDES's study of variation in Lower and Middle Paleolithic assemblages from southwest France (Bordes 1961). Bordes formulated a typology to describe the sixty-three different tool types (i.e., artifact forms) recognized as regular components of Lower and Middle Paleolithic assemblages. He then characterized the artifact assemblages recovered from the various layers of different rock-shelter deposits in terms of the relative proportion of each made up by those sixty-three tool types. Comparison revealed repeated patterns of assemblage composition, allowing the definition of six distinctive facies. Bordes could find no association between facies and environment or between facies and time, leading him to suggest that each distinctive suite of artifacts represented a different cultural tradition. The interdigitating of facies over a long period of time in a relatively small area led Bordes to describe these cultural traditions as tenacious.

In the 1950s Bordes's approach to assemblage analysis and interpretation was pioneering. Earlier studies, such as that of DENIS PEYRONY, had characterized assemblages in terms of the presence or absence of a few distinctive artifact types (the type fossil approach). In contrast, Bordes's approach involved the analysis of entire artifact assemblages and separated information about the way that tools were made (technology) from the types of tools that were produced (typology).

Since Bordes's studies, archaeologists have come to appreciate that a whole array of variables has contributed to the similarities and differences in the composition of the assemblages they study. However, four variables are considered fundamental to any attempt to understand assemblage composition: the flaking qualities and edge properties of the raw materials from which the artifacts were made, the techniques used to make the artifacts, the uses to which the artifacts were put, and culturally ordained rules about what an artifact of a particular function should look like (this variable is usually referred to as style). In the latter part of the twentieth century archaeologists strove to disentangle the impact that each of these variables had on the composition of artifact assemblages from different time periods.

Even as Bordes was discussing the impact of cultural traditions on artifact assemblages, other archaeologists, such as CHARLES MCBURNEY and J. D. CLARK, were investigating the possibility that recurring assemblage types might represent seasonal or functional differences in activities undertaken at different sites. These types of inquiries are often linked to the work of L. R. BINFORD, who, in the 1960s and early 1970s, published a series of papers exploring the possibility that variations in the composition of

Lower and Middle Paleolithic artifact assemblages might result from differences in function rather than from different traditions for making tools designed for particular tasks—that is, culture (see, e.g., Binford and Binford 1969). One stimulus for this idea came from studies of Lower Paleolithic assemblages and the observation that the geographic and temporal scale of variation in artifact assemblages was far greater than the spatial and temporal boundaries of cultural entities. However, the key stimulus came from studies of the material culture of contemporary hunting-and-gathering communities. The Binfords observed that these communities used different tool kits at different times and in different places, in response to seasonal and temporal variation in the availability of plant and animal resources. It was argued that the same organizing principles—the use of different items of material culture for different purposes in different contexts—would have influenced the behavior of prehistoric hunters and gatherers and, therefore, the composition of the archaeological assemblages they left behind.

Binford and Binford used multivariate statistics to explore the co-occurrence of artifact types. This technique revealed the existence of five recurring sets of artifact types, each of which was interpreted as a functionally distinct tool kit. The three sites investigated were found to contain different groups of tool kits, and each was consequently interpreted as a different type of site within a wider settlement system. Almost two decades later microscopic analyses of the wear traces preserved on the edges of Middle Paleolithic artifacts from the Middle East and France provided a direct test of the functions of the tool clusters identified by the Binfords. Perhaps the most important result of these use-wear studies was the observation that, during the Middle Paleolithic, there was no direct relationship between the form of a tool and the use to which it was put (Shea 1992). This undermined the specific functional interpretations that the Binfords had offered for each of the tool clusters they had described but not necessarily the underlying logic of their approach.

Subsequent studies (such as those of H. L. Dibble) of the impact of edge resharpening on the form of a tool have underscored the importance of establishing the reasons for the existence of recurring forms before offering explanations for assemblage variation. These studies have shown that many of the tool types described by Bordes actually represent different stages in a sequence of edge modification. Tools become blunted during use, and a resharpening of those blunted edges results in a change in the shape of the tool. Not all of the sixty-three tool types that Bordes had identified represented either culturally determined templates or tools fashioned for a particular task.

Similar changes in the interpretation of Acheulean hand-axes have also been made. In the first half of the twentieth century archaeologists often argued that hand-axes were better made and more refined in later, rather than earlier, time periods. Thus, measures of the degree of two-dimensional symmetry, extent and refinement of retouch, and/or overall shape were used to establish the relative chronology of otherwise undated assemblages from Africa, the Middle East, and Europe. Underlying these schemes was the assumption that the shape of a hand-axe was controlled primarily by the amount and refinement of retouch and thereby provided a measure of the technical sophistication of the toolmaker.

In the late 1970s Peter Jones undertook a series of knapping experiments designed to investigate the effects of the flaking properties and the form of particular raw materials on both the shape and the durability of the working edges of axes recovered from sites at OLDUVAI GORGE. He found that the classic teardrop shape of the hand-axe inevitably resulted when an attempt was made to maximize both the length of the cutting edge and the weight of the axe at the same time; in other words, the fundamental determining factor with respect to hand-axe shape was neither style nor the technological proficiency of the knapper. Instead, variations on the teardrop shape of experimental hand-axes were shown to be related to the properties of the raw material and the form of the tool blank from which the axe was fashioned, the quality of the working edge on the finished tool, and the amount of resharpening undertaken on the axe edges.

Studies such as those by Dibble and by Jones, which emphasized raw material properties and resharpening, do not deny the possibility of using stone to obtain information about cultural affiliation, but they do highlight the fact that many variables contribute to the final form of an artifact. Consequently, approaches such as the one developed by Bordes, which makes quite specific assumptions about the reasons why artifacts of different shape exist, have fallen out of favor. In response, many researchers have shifted their attention to other variables affecting artifact form and assemblage composition, especially techniques of artifact manufacture.

Initial studies of the ways in which tools were made were intended to characterize the stone-working techniques of a particular portion of the archaeological record (such as the Acheulean, Middle Paleolithic, or Upper Paleolithic). Most of these studies were based on the experimental replication of forms recovered from archaeological sites, and they provided a basis for outlining the development of stone technologies over time. However, it was soon realized that studies investigating different ways of reducing a waterworn cobble, an Acheulean hand-axe, or a Levallois core had the potential to provide more detailed information about the relationship between stone-working techniques and the composition of artifact assemblages. Investigations into the different techniques that can be used to reduce Middle Paleolithic Levallois cores are a good example (Dibble and Bar-Yosef 1995).

During the 1970s and 1980s studies of artifact resharpening, raw material variability, and manufacturing techniques showed that recurring artifact types result from a complex series of processes and should not be interpreted simply as culturally ordained tool types. As a consequence, discussions about the impact of cultural tradition on artifact assemblages have begun to involve a much more detailed consideration of the concept of style and culture. Some archaeologists have explored the behavioral significance of style in contemporary settings for particular types of artifacts; other researchers have examined the theoretical and methodological problems that arise from attempts to interpret particular features of artifacts as indicative of specific cultural traditions.

Different researchers hold quite varied views about the role played by style in human societies, about the types of information that style conveys, and, therefore, about how style can be identified. Some archaeologists, such as Wiessner, regard style as a form of nonverbal communication that conveys information about both individual and group identity. For cognitive archaeologists (such as Ian Hodder) style is a symbolic expression of social relations, and the aim of analysis is to investigate the meaning of the symbols that style embodies. However, there is no general agreement that style is always symbolic or that it is always intended to convey specific information. For example, J. R. Sackett (1982) distinguishes between style as symbol (iconological style) and style that simply reflects the choices that individual artisans made in producing functionally equivalent objects (isochrestic style). He also distinguishes between passive style (regularity in artifact form, arising from shared traditions) and active style (intended to convey specific information).

Attempts to refine the concept of style and make it more amenable to archaeological analysis and interpretation do not actually resolve the archaeologist's dilemma about whether stylistic causes and effects operate independently of functional causes and effects. The obvious solution is to hold one source of variation constant in order to identify the effects of another. However, this approach assumes that it is possible to identify functionally equivalent artifacts and/or that it is possible to identify the options from which the prehistoric knapper made his or her choices during artifact manufacture. This notion is not as straightforward as it might at first seem. Types or attributes that appear to be functionally redundant in one context may not be so in another. Furthermore, what is functionally redundant in any context is actually in the mind of the maker, and it is therefore impossible to assess interpretations of patterned variation as isochrestic style. Consequently, techniques for identifying the contribution of style to differences (and similarities) in the composition of artifact assemblages are not well developed, and

they rely on reductive analytical strategies, which presuppose the independence of the different dimensions of artifact variability.

In the final analysis current arguments about style are based on different ideas about the information contained in patterned archaeological data. On the one hand, the debate involves a return to the dispute between Bordes and Binford: whether artifact assemblages are cultural markers or markers of functionally distinct tool kits. On the other hand, much has been learned about the interdependence of different dimensions of artifact variability in different contexts. Reductive analytical techniques cannot incorporate all the potential contributors to stone artifact assemblage variability, but there can be no doubt that these have enhanced archaeologists' understanding of the factors contributing to the similarities and differences between artifact assemblages from different time periods. Archaeologists can now pursue a broader array of interpretative approaches, depending on the information they choose to generate from the artifact assemblages under investigation.

Functionalist Approaches

Functionalist approaches use ecological and evolutionary theory, together with paleoenvironmental information, to investigate the interrelationships between ecological and environmental variables and aspects of a society's economic, social, and political structures—in particular, the role these institutions played in the survival and success of different human societies. Debate about the causes of Middle Paleolithic artifact variability underscored how little was known about the relationship between stone artifact assemblage composition, site function, site layout, and seasonal variation in foraging activities. As a consequence, Binford, John Yellen, and others initiated ethno-archaeological research during the 1960s designed to identify in human behavior those regularities that can be assemblages.

Binford's study of the activities of the Nunamiut people of Alaska ultimately provided the theoretical underpinning for an approach to stone artifact analysis and interpretation that became known as technological organization (Nelson 1991). The investigation focused on the relationship between particular aspects of Nunamiut behavior and the material record these people were creating, rather than relying on descriptions they provided about the activities in which they were engaged. Binford found, for instance, that there were no simple relationships between assemblage composition and site function, even though the artifacts that accumulated at different sites exhibited patterns that archaeologists could detect. The form and design of artifacts, their functions, and the extent to which they were reused varied, depending on the way that resources in different parts of the landscape were employed. Thus, Binford showed that explanations for the similarities and differences in the composition of artifact assemblages were likely to involve a complex series of cause-and-effect statements integrating aspects of technology, the strategies used to acquire resources, and patterns of movement across the landscape.

More recently, archaeologists interested in the problem of technological organization have begun to draw on the theories and methods of evolutionary ecology. This approach involves an application of the ideas explored in recent decades by evolutionary biologists with the aim of understanding the extent to which evolution shapes behavior—in other words, to assess the role that specific behaviors play in the survival and reproductive success of individual members of a social group. Archaeologists employing the principles of evolutionary ecology have sought to establish a link between the way in which artifacts were made and used and the exploitation of specific items contributing to the diet. For example, the acquisition of raw materials, the fashioning of these into tools, and the use, maintenance, and discard of the tools have been analyzed and interpreted in the same way as other behaviors—it is assumed that natural selection will have played a role in shaping the stone technology employed by a particular group of people to gain access to particular resources.

As in studies of foraging behavior, attempts to adapt the theory of evolutionary ecology to stone technology involve a cost-benefit analysis based on the assumption that, all other things being equal, natural selection will have created the optimal solution to an adaptive problem. However, nothing is ever truly "equal," and the purpose of the cost-benefit analysis is not to identify the optimal technological solution with respect to a particular problem. Rather, the aim is to identify the optimal strategy identified on theoretical grounds, to compare it with the actual strategy employed, and to seek an explanation for the differences between the two. For this reason an optimization model provides archaeologists with a heuristic device rather than an analytical tool.

Given the difficulties of identifying the actual costs and benefits of different technological strategies employed in the past, archaeologists have tended to use qualitative methodologies to assess the relative costs and benefits of different types of technologies. A number of researchers (such as R. Torrence) have explored the concept of risk and the ways in which technology could be used to reduce the probability that the costs incurred in the capture of a specific item of prey would exceed the benefits associated with its capture. Risks are assessed in terms of the consequences of failing to access a specific resource, and inferences are made about the suitability of different artifacts for acquiring that resource. It is assumed that the artifacts used to acquire specific prey items have to be available and in good working order at the precise moment that the prey is captured. It is further assumed that the time and resources expended in developing technologies that would ensure the capture of a particular prey item are proportional to the consequences of failing to acquire it. The prey items associated with the greatest risk are those that are mobile and available only at one location and only for a short period of time. In such situations more time and effort would be expended in making the artifacts needed to exploit these types of food sources than in making artifacts used to capture sedentary food sources available throughout the year.

M. Nelson (1991) and others have built on these ideas to try to characterize different types of stone technologies and the types of foraging strategies for which they are most likely to have been employed. In these studies curated, expedient, and opportunistic technologies are distinguished from each other in terms of the amount of planning involved in their execution.

Curated technologies are those that involve anticipation of future needs, which may include the acquisition, transport, and stockpiling of raw materials and/or finished tools. Time is invested in preparing and transporting raw materials and in making, maintaining, and transporting tools. The reward for this is the immediate availability of usable tools when the need for them arises. Expedient technologies are those in which tools are made and repaired at the place of use. In contrast to curated technologies, expedient technologies involve an expenditure of minimal time and energy on the manufacture, reshaping, and resharpening of tools. Finally, opportunistic technologies are those that involve no forward planning at all. The acquisition of raw materials and the manufacture and maintenance of tools are flexible and reflect immediate responses to unanticipated conditions. Typically, artifacts are manufactured from whatever materials are at hand and are discarded immediately after use.

Attempts have been made to relate these different types of technologies to the forms of particular tools and to the composition of entire artifact assemblages through two interrelated concepts: tool design and site function. Archaeologists whose artifact assemblages contain tools that were used in food procurement (as opposed to those used to make other tools) have expended some effort in trying to develop ways of analyzing tool design. These researchers argue that tools used at the moment that a prey item is captured or harvested are subject to the greatest design constraints. As a consequence, most of the relevant studies have focused on various forms of weapons, such as spear points and other types of projectiles.

A number of researchers have used the concept of risk to analyze patterns of group mobility, insofar as mobility can be reconstructed on the basis of the distribution of artifacts made from raw materials of known origin. It is suggested that highly mobile groups tended to accumulate artifact assemblages containing a wide range of raw materials, collected from various raw material sources visited in the course of

other subsistence activities (i.e., the collection of raw materials was an embedded activity). This collecting strategy would have reduced the risk of being without a raw material when it was needed for tool manufacture. Assemblages associated with highly mobile groups also tend to contain only small numbers of artifacts: tools and tool blanks made from large blocks of durable and easily worked materials that could be readily fashioned into functionally specific tools (thus, the risk of being without a particular tool when it was needed was also minimized). Less-mobile groups tended to make more use of local material because distant sources of stone were visited only rarely. These groups also economized on the use of exotic stone by resharpening as much as possible tools made from the less accessible materials.

In sum, functional studies have continued to emphasize investigating the multiple causes that give rise to artifact form. Various approaches to modeling the reasons for variable artifact form and assemblage composition have been undertaken, integrating aspects of technology, tool design, resource acquisition, and mobility. The common theme of these studies is the desire to understand the role stone artifacts played in the evolution and/or behavior of different human groups.

Idealist Approaches to Artifact Analysis

Discussions about the art, religion, and beliefs of ancient peoples have been present throughout the history of the discipline of archaeology, but the development of formal analytical and interpretative frameworks for the study of these phenomena dates only to the early 1980s. Just as there are a variety of ways of investigating the functional (or evolutionary) significance of artifacts, there are also a variety of ways of investigating what artifacts can reveal about the cognitive abilities of our ancestors or about the conceptual frameworks of past human societies. Some researchers have applied concepts and methods developed in linguistics or psychology to the problem of interpreting artifact assemblages in cognitive terms, but the most influential of the current approaches to this problem of gaining insight into the prehistoric mind through the analysis of artifact assemblages is undoubtedly the *chaîne opératoire* (operational sequence). This is a concept borrowed from ethnologists to describe how a particular society acquires and uses materials, and it was introduced into archaeology by the French archaeologist-ethnologist ANDRÉ LEROI-GOURHAN.

Like the functionalists, idealists have come to appreciate that the causes underlying variation in stone artifact assemblages are multidimensional and that to understand this variation requires consideration not only of the types of tools in the assemblages under study but also of the ways in which raw materials were procured, the conceptual schemes that underlay the production of the tools, and the actual techniques employed in their manufacture and maintenance. Practitioners of the *chaîne opératoire* approach view technology as the process whereby natural materials are transformed into cultural objects, and since technology is both artificial and deliberate, they argue that it must have mental antecedents (see, e.g., Schlanger 1994). Thus, identification of the series of events that ends with the loss or discard of stone tools is seen to provide a key to the "mind in action." The ultimate goal is to use the chaîne opératoire to document differences in the stone-working skills exhibited by different members of a social group or to document the evolution of technical skills through the course of human history. This approach is often employed by researchers interested in the evolution of human intelligence.

Idealists do not conceive of the mind either as a "black box" or as a "mental template." Their concern is to determine what prehistoric knappers knew about stone working, how they acquired that knowledge, how they organized themselves on the basis of that knowledge, and how they used, maintained, transformed, transferred, and even forgot it (Schlanger 1994, 148). It is therefore the identification of the body of knowledge with which a prehistoric knapper worked—as embodied in the sequence of activities associated with stone tool production—that allows the archaeologist to see the mind in action.

Insights into this knowledge are obtained by investigating what it is that the knapper needs to know, for example, in order to produce a blade. Here a distinction is drawn between the more abstract, conceptual knowledge that a knapper must have to begin blade production and the practical knowledge or procedural know-how that is required to actually make a blade. In other words, there will be a difference between the conceptual sequence applied to the problem of blade manufacture in the abstract and the actual sequence of events of a particular knapping episode. This is because materials are neither standardized in shape nor homogeneous in composition. Contingency is accepted as part of the process of transforming raw materials into tools. Therefore, there is feedback between the material being worked and the knapper working that material.

The documentation of a chaîne opératoire relies heavily on information obtained through the experimental knapping and refitting analyses that are the primary sources of information about the conceptual knowledge and procedural know-how required for the manufacture of particular tools. The chaîne opératoire itself is a description of the sequence of behaviors, actions, and gestures involved in the making of a particular tool type—from the acquisition of raw materials to tool manufacture, use, and edge maintenance to, finally, the loss or abandonment of tools or the materials from which they were made (see, e.g., Schlanger 1994). At each stage in the analysis, consideration is given to the context within which behaviors, actions, or gestures take place and to the constraints that impinge on their execution. For example, understanding raw material acquisition requires information about the distribution of materials in time and space, the flaking properties and edge qualities of those materials, and their suitability for a specific task. Information is also needed about the settlement system and foraging activities with which the acquisition of the raw material had to be integrated.

Like the functionalists, idealists have advocated the integration of technological information with settlement pattern data. However, idealist analyses of these data are aimed at documenting the ways in which space was used, so as to establish a basis for inferring something about the value past societies placed on different activities. Such inferences can be made on the basis of an examination of the distribution of artifacts marking different stages in the production and use of tools.

Conclusion

The history of approaches to the study of stone artifacts charts the enrollment of an increasing number of variables to explain variation in artifact form and assemblage composition. The early- to mid-twentieth-century preoccupation with artifact form as a means of accessing information about past cultures has been replaced by a broader array of approaches that investigate both the reasons for the existence of different artifact types and the variations in their patterns of co-occurrence. These approaches investigate the impact of raw material properties, techniques of artifact manufacture, the uses to which artifacts were put, and the effects of resharpening on artifact form and assemblage composition, in addition to style. Both functionalist and idealist approaches recognize the importance of analyzing stone artifacts in relation to other artifacts and in relation to other categories of archaeological data, including their position on a landscape. Attempts are made to integrate information generated from the analysis of different categories of archaeological data in order to assess the behavioral information that can be gleaned from the stones themselves. The ubiquity and durability of stone artifacts means that they will always be an important source of information about past human behavior.

Nicola Stern and Simon Holdaway

References

Binford, L. R., and S. R. Binford. 1969. "Stone Tools and Human Behavior." *Scientific American* 220: 70–84.

Bordes, F. 1961. "Mousterian Cultures in France." *Science* 134: 803–810.

Dibble, H. L., and O. Bar-Yosef, eds. 1995. *The Definition and Interpretation of Levallois Technology.* Monographs in World Archaeology, no. 23, Madison, WI: Prehistory Press.

Gardin, J.-C., and C. S. Peebles, eds. 1992. *Representations in Archaeology.* Bloomington: Indiana University Press.

Isaac, G. Ll. 1986. "Foundation Stones: Early Artifacts as Indicators of Activities and Abilities." In *Stone Age Prehistory: Studies in Memory of Charles McBurney.* Ed. G. N. Bailey and P. Callow. Cambridge: Cambridge University Press.

Jones, P. R. 1994. "Results of Experimental Work in Relation to the Stone Industries of Olduvai Gorge." In *Olduvai Gorge,* vol. 5, *Excavations in Beds III, IV and the Masek Beds, 1968–1971.* Ed. M. D. Leakey and D. A. Roe. Cambridge: Cambridge University Press.

Nelson, M. 1991. "The Study of Technological Organization." *Method and Theory in Archaeology* 3: 57–100.

Sackett, J. R. 1982. "Approaches to Style in Lithic Archaeology." *Journal of Anthropological Archaeology* 1: 59–112.

Schlanger, N. 1994. "Mindful Technology: Unleashing the *Chaîne Opératoire* for an Archaeology of Mind." In *The Ancient Mind: Elements of Cognitive Archaeology,* 143–151. Ed. C. Renfrew and E. B. W. Zubrow. Cambridge: Cambridge University Press.

Shea, J. J. 1992. "Lithic Microwear Analysis in Archaeology." *Evolutionary Anthropology* 1:143–150.

Torrence, R. 1989. *Time, Energy and Stone Tools.* Cambridge: Cambridge University Press.

Lithuania

The history of archaeology in Lithuania mainly began in the nineteenth century. The first information about single archaeological objects was obtained during the sixteenth century, while Lithuania was a grand duchy, but during the period when Lithuania and POLAND formed a single state (1569–1795), there was little interest in the past, and only a few mentions about stray finds survive from that era.

Lithuania as Part of the Russian Empire (1795–1918)

It was while Lithuania was part of the Russian Empire that the study of archaeology began, with the main feature being the search for the oldest roots and evidence of states and nations. Archaeology in Lithuania started in a small local museum in Barzdžiai in western Lithuania in 1812. The museum was founded by the landowner

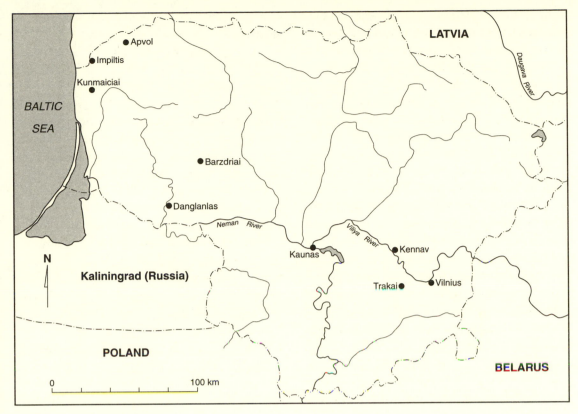

Lithuanian Archaeological Sites

Dionizy Paskiewicz (1765–1830), and it contained primarily accidental finds.

Francziszek Wilczynski (1796–1859) undertook the first large excavations of hill-forts and burial mounds in eastern Lithuania, and the first book on Lithuanian archaeology was published in 1842 (Tyszkiewicz 1842). The antiquities in this book were divided according to the types of objects and artifacts found. The author, Count Eustachy Tyszkiewicz (1814–1873), was the first scholar in Lithuania to understand the significance of archaeology as an organized social science. On his initiative, the Archaeological Commission and the Museum of Antiquities were established in 1855 in Vilnius. The commission started to systematize and generalize archaeological finds and to publish archaeological works, such as the catalog of the museum. Each month, the members of the commission met to listen to and discuss lectures on history and archaeology, and several of them began excavations.

Russian authorities discovered that the Archaeological Commission was attempting to elucidate and describe the culture of ancient Rzuczpospolita, a Baltic late Neolithic, shoreline living, maritime economic (seals and fish) culture who also domesticated livestock. Because they considered that attempt to be politically dangerous, they closed the commission down after an insurrection in 1863. The Museum of Antiquities was reorganized, and any developments in Lithuanian archaeology ceased for twenty years. During that period, only private individuals continued to excavate.

When the Lithuanian national liberation movement began in the nineteenth century, it alerted the interests of Russian scientists to this part of their empire. From 1888 to 1889, Eduar Wolter (1856–1941) and a local landowner, Wandalin Szukiewicz (1852–1919), excavated medieval grave fields in southern Lithuania, and Szukiewicz, on his own, excavated some Iron Age burial mounds. At the same time, in central Lithuania, Tadeusz Dowgird (1852–1919) excavated Iron Age grave fields and burial mounds and kept precise documentation of his work. In 1884, Fiodor Pokrovskij (1855–1903) was appointed director of the Museum of Antiquities in Vilnius. He revived the study of archaeology at the museum, excavated burial mounds in eastern Lithuania, and published reports of these excavations. He questioned and interviewed local people about archaeological sites and finds and collected and published all of this information in archaeological maps (Pokrovskij 1893, 1899). In 1893, the Ninth Congress of Russian Archaeology was held in Vilnius, and this meeting presented the achievements of archaeology to the local people and encouraged their further support of it.

At beginning of twentieth century, the Russian Imperial Archaeological Commission in Saint Petersburg began to take some interest in, and control of, archaeological excavations in Lithuania. It issued permits and demanded reports and information concerning finds. Large excavations were begun and photographed. The commission sent archaeologists to investigate burial mounds and hill-forts, and it supported the work of interested amateurs. One of these was Ludwik Krzywicki (1859–1941), who, during his summer vacations between 1900 and 1913, surveyed and excavated hill-forts and published information concerning their artifacts. From 1911 to 1914, the local archaeological commission in Vilnius registered artifacts from a medieval–new age town, and this information was published in Russian, Polish, and Lithuanian. At the end of nineteenth and during the early years of the twentieth century, private archaeological collections and amateur excavations to enrich them became popular. World War I terminated the work of non-Lithuanian archaeologists and was responsible for the destruction of the majority of extant archaeological collections.

First Lithuanian Republic (1918–1940)

The main feature of the history of archaeology during the period of the first republic was the creation of a national school of archaeology. In 1919, the State Archaeological Commission was established to protect sites of cultural significance, but the initial activities of the commission were not productive because of conflict over different methods of conservation and protection.

In fact, archaeology in Lithuania was primarily the work of individuals. In the 1920s, the Russian ALEKSANDER SPICYN (SPITSYN) (1858–1931) was invited to write the first general work about the antiquities of Lithuania using prewar data (Spicyn 1925), which had been already divided into different archaeological cultures. At the same time, Colonel Petras Tarasenka (1892–1962) collected information about different archaeological sites and finds, and between 1926 and 1928 he published three books about archaeological knowledge and the protection of archaeological heritage. His most important contribution in these books was the first comprehensive archaeological map of Lithuania (Tarasenka 1928). In 1930–1934, General Vladas Nagevičius (1881–1954) excavated the hill-forts of Apuolė and Impiltis in western Lithuania, and with the support of specialists from different sciences, he used aerial photography and film-making and completed many different analyses of the material found. The 1920s also saw the foundation of many regional museums in Lithuania to house collections of finds from destroyed archaeological sites.

In 1934, the State Archaeological Commission was reorganized, and the protection and registration of archaeological sites was improved, with guards placed at various sites to stop their destruction by plough. In 1936, the new museum of Vytautas Great was established in Kaunas. It strove to create separate laws of cultural values to protect and rescue sites from destruction by excavation. The head of prehistory department in this museum, Jonas Puzinas (1905–1978), became the first professional Lithuanian archaeologist. Having taken an archaeology degree in Germany, Puzinas divided all the archaeological material in the museum into the common Baltic periods and chronological order. In 1938, the museum opened a new archaeological exhibition, the study of which was published (Puzinas 1938) and became the first scientific manual of Lithuanian archaeology. Puzinas trained a new generation of Lithuanian archaeologists. In 1939, the capital of Lithuania, Vilnius, which had been occupied by the Polish since 1920, was returned, and the center of Lithuanian archaeology was transferred there.

Part of the U.S.S.R. (1940–1991)

World War II and the subsequent Soviet occupation of Lithuania interrupted any further archaeological work, and publications stopped. In 1940, the occupation government passed a law of cultural monuments protection, which had been prepared by an independent Lithuania and was really only a piece of political propaganda. Archaeology was centralized in order to achieve greater Soviet control. In 1941, the Academy of Sciences was created; in it, was an Institute of History and within that, a Department of Archaeology. During fighting in Lithuania, many parts of archaeological collections in local museums were destroyed. In 1944, to escape repression, Puzinas and his best student, Marija Gimbutienė (or Gimbutas, 1921–1994), went to western Europe. Gimbutienė completed her thesis in Germany in 1947, writing on Lithuanian grave-field data and separating it into cultural-chronological groups linked to some historic Baltic tribes. In Lithuania, the field archaeologist Pranas Baleniūnas (1900–1965) was arrested and imprisoned in northern Russia.

The main features of Lithuanian archaeology during the years the country was a Soviet socialist republic were the accumulation of archaeological sources and the investigation of the ethnic genesis of the Baltic tribes. In 1945, Lithuania had only four archaeologists left, and they had sole responsibility for re-creating and developing the discipline. The training of archaeologists never stopped, testimony to the work of Pranas Kulikauskas (b. 1913) and Regina Kulikauskienė (b. 1916). Marxism was compulsory, and its impact on Lithuanian archaeology directed research into areas of socioeconomic formation, productive forces, and relations to production. The Russian language was used, and the works of former investigators were ignored. The center for archaeology in Lithuania became the Institute of History, which issued the permits for excavations. Archaeology at Vilnius University consisted only of producing students.

Archaeological surveys and excavations of grave fields began in 1948, and before long, excavations became large and rapid—however, there were no journals in which to publish archaeological articles in the first postwar decade in Lithuania. In 1949, P. Kulikauskas finished his thesis on a grave field at Kurmaičiai in western Lithuania. At the beginning of Soviet rule, archaeologists copied prewar work but included the necessary Marxist changes. This work was narrow and purely historical in treatment, written according to preconceived social evolutionary schemes created by the Communist Party, and there was only one way to investigate and publish results. The highest achievement of this Stalinist style of Marxism in archaeology was the preliminary edition of the *History of Lithuanian SSSR* (*Lietuvos TSR istorija* 1953), which divided prehistory into the stages of development of primitive society.

After the death of Joseph Stalin in 1953, the Soviet states started to become more liberal, and so did archaeology. During this time, new humanitarian directions were created, and archaeological investigations were included in economic development projects. A new postwar generation of archaeologists started to work. Excavations took place at new building sites and large infrastructure building projects, such as the building of the Kaunas water reservoir in 1953–1957, excavations at Castle Trakai in 1951–1962, and work on the Vilnius lower castle in 1955–1961, which led to the adaptation of some of these buildings as museums. However, the law for the protection of cultural monuments was often ignored at the time, and many archaeological sites were destroyed. Still, new kinds of archaeological monuments, such as Stone Age settlements, were excavated. The liberalization of archaeology spread to the analysis of archaeological material using traditional chronological-typological methods, more choice in the direction of investigations, and the creation of larger archaeological generalizations, which could include the material of former investigators.

The first books on Lithuanian archaeology since World War II were published, including those dealing with archaeological finds, hillforts (Tarasenka 1956), and archaeological stones (Tarasenka 1958). Marxist interpretations of prehistory were consolidated in the *History of Lithuanian SSR* (*Lietuvos TSR istorija* 1957, 5–37), and the main achievement of this period in archaeology was a synthesis of Lithuanian prehistory (Kulikauskas, Kulikauskienė, and Tautavičius 1961). This book built on the prewar work of Puzinas and used new information from archaeological investigations and thirteenth-century materials and earlier. Written in Lithuanian, it consolidated the periodization of prehistory and the main typology and chronology of its artifacts.

After 1961, Lithuanian archaeology began a period of systematization of archaeological materials. In 1962, the leader of Lithuanian archaeology was Adolfas Tautavičius (b. 1925), a graduate of Soviet times. Archaeological conferences were held every two years, and since 1966, a scientific-information edition was published every two years (*Archeologiniai,* eighteen issues before 1999). A general work concerned with trade relations was published (*Lietuvos gyventoju prekybiniai rysiai* 1972), and the results of the period of systematization of archaeological materials in 1974–1978 were published in four volumes of collective work by ten people (*Lietuvos TSR archeologijos atlasas* 1974–1978), which describes Stone Age settlements, hill-forts, grave fields, burial mounds, and some artifacts.

There were many different innovations in archaeology, such as plastic facial reconstruction, the filming of excavations (from 1965 by Vytautas Urbanavičius), investigations of the Bronze Age (from 1967 by Algimantas Merkevicius), and investigations of iron smelting (from 1969 by Jonas Stankus). In 1965, radiocarbon analysis began, and human skeletal material has been collected and investigated since 1970. Large-scale excavations of medieval–new age grave fields began in the oldest Lithuanian towns. R. Kulikauskienė and Rimutė Rimantienė completed the first doctorate in archaeology (Rimantienė 1971; Volkait-Kulikauskienė 1970), and a list of state-protected archaeological sites (3,367 objects) was prepared and published (*Lietuvos TSR istorijos ik kultûros paminklu sarasas* 1973).

In 1979, Lithuanian archaeologists began to investigate ethnic genesis. There was a huge amount of accumulated archaeological material that required new qualitative research and synthesis, so interrepublic conferences concerning ethnic genesis and ethnic history were organized in 1979, 1981, and 1991. Investigations became complex and included historians, ethnologists, linguists, and anthropologists. Also in 1979, the first volume of nonperiodical archaeological information was published (*Lietuvos archeologija* 1979–1999), which opened up the market for larger publications about excavated materials and for separate investigations. The first synthetic studies for different prehistory periods were published—the Stone Age (Rimantien 1984) and the old Iron Age (Michelbertas 1986)—as well as a general work about Lithuanian ethnic genesis (*Lietuvių etnogeneze* 1987).

In 1988, a short but eventful period of perestroika, which took the shape of a national independence movement in Lithuania, began. This policy was manifest in archaeology by the creation of new organizational structures. For instance, a separate group of archaeologists was organized by the Society of Lithuanian archaeologists and founded within the Institute of History in 1989, the result of excavations in Vilnius lower castle, and a chair of archaeology was founded at Vilnius University in 1990. Also in 1990, the inspection of cultural heritage, a serious attempt at protecting archaeological heritage, was established. In 1989, the first archaeological museum in Kernavė opened. Existing archaeological organizations were enlarged, and new archaeologists were allowed to be independent. In science, censorship was abolished, and computers began to be used. Relations among the archaeologists in the various Soviet socialist republics were broken up, and the search for new contacts in archaeology from the West started—with Poland and Sweden.

Second Lithuanian Republic (1991–)
After the putsch of August 1991 in Moscow, Lithuania, which had proclaimed its independence in 1990, became a recognized independent state, and after liberation from Marxist fetters, archaeology returned to fundamentals. New di-

rections and themes were formulated, the archaeology of foreign countries was taught, relations with foreign archaeologists and at foreign archaeological sites began, and material, including archaeological data, that had never been published before appeared in print. Lithuanian archaeological material was now also being discussed by foreign researchers (*Archaeologia*, 1995–1998).

In 1994, the popular archaeological magazine *Baltų archaeologija* was first published, and in 1998, Eugenijus Jovaiša produced the first Lithuanian archaeological compact disc, which was concerned with a grave field from the first to the fourth centuries in Dauglaukis in western Lithuania (Jovaiša 1998). Beginning in 1993, Lithuania began to award its own doctoral other degrees in archaeology. The publishing of archaeological books by different organizations increased. With the weakening of state support for archaeology, fieldwork became smaller and more concentrated on the excavation of hillforts and barrow mounds, which had been destroyed by nature and human factors, and also on rescue excavations in the old towns, which were being enlarged. In 1995, underwater archaeological research started at Lake Vladas Žulkus. In Lithuania at present there are more than sixty trained archaeologists working, one professor (Mykolas Michelbertas), eight postdoctoral scholars, and nineteen Ph.D. students.

Gintautas Zabiela

References

Alseikaitė-Gimbutiėn, M. 1947. *Die Bestattung in Litauen in vorgeschichtlichen Zeit* [The Burial Customs in Lithuania in Prehistory Time]. Tübingen.

Archaeologia Baltica. 1995–1998. Ed. Vytautas Kazakevičius. 3 vols. Vilnius.

Archeologiniai tyrinėjimai Lietuvoje [Archaeological investigations in Lithuania]. 1966–1998. Vilnius.

Baltų archaeologija [Archaeology of Balts]. 1994–1998. Ed. Algirdas Girininkas. Vilnius. Nos. 1–12.

Jovaiša, E. 1998. *Žvilgsnis į "aukso amžiu"* [Look into the "gold age"]. Vilnius.

Kulikauskas P., R. Kulikauskiene, and A. Tautavičius. 1961. *Lietuvos archeologijos bruožai* [Sketches of Lithuanian Archaeology]. Vilnius.

Kulikauskas P., and G. Lietuvos Zabiela. 1999.

Archeologijos istorija (iki 1945 m.) [History of Lithuanian Archaeology until 1945]. Vilnius.

Lietuvių etnogeneze [Ethnogenesis of Lithuanians]. 1987. Ed. Regina Kulikauskiene. Vilnius.

Lietuviu liaudies menas [Folk Art of Lithuanians]. 1958. Vol. 1. Vilnius.

Lietuvos archeologija [Archaeology of Lithuania]. 1979–1999. 18 vols. Vilnius.

Lietuvos gyventoju prekybiniai ryšiai I-XIII a [Trade Relations in Lithuania in 1st–13th Centuries]. 1972. Vilnius.

Lietuvos TSR archeologijos atlasas [Atlas of Archaeology in Lithuanian SSR]. 1974–1978. 4 vols. Vilnius.

Lietuvos TSR istorija [History of Lithuanian SSR]. 1953. Ed. Juozas Žiugžda. Vilnius.

———. 1957. Ed. Juozas Žiugžda. Vol. 1. Vilnius.

Lietuvos TSR istorijos ik kultūos paminklų sąrašas [List of Historical and Cultural Monuments in Lithuanian SSR]. 1973. Vilnius.

Michelbertas, M. 1986. *Senasis geležies amžius Lietuvoje* [Old Iron Age in Lithuania]. Vilnius.

Pokrovskij, F. V. 1893. *Arkheologicheskaya karta Vilienskoi gubernii* [Archaeological Map of Vilnius Government]. Vilnius.

———. 1899. *Arkheologicheskaya karta Kovienskoi gubiernii* [Archaeological Map of Kaunas Government]. Vilnius.

Puzinas, J. 1935. *Vorgeschichtsforschung und National- bewusstsein in Litauen* [Investigations of Prehistory and National Consciousness in Lithuania]. Kaunas.

———. 1938. "Naujausių proistorinių tyrimų duomenys" [Data of New Prehistorical Investigations]. *Senovė* [Antiquity] (Kaunas) 56, no. 7: 175–304.

Rimantienė, R. 1971. *Paleolit i mezolit Litvy* [Palaeolithic and Mesolithic in Lithuania]. Vilnius.

———. 1984. *Akmens amžius Lietuvoje* [Stone Age in Lithuania]. Vilnius.

Spicyn, A. 1925. "A. Litovskije drievnosti" [Lithuanian Antiquities]. *Tauta ir žodis* [People and Word] (Kaunas), pp. 112–171.

Tarasenka, P. 1928. *Lietuvos archeologijos medžiaga* [Material of Lithuanian Archaeology]. Kaunas.

———. 1956. *Lietuvos piliakalniai* [Hill-forts in Lithurania]. Vilnius.

———. 1958. *Pėdos akmenyje* [Feet in Stone]. Vilnius.

Tyszkiewicz, E. 1842. *Rzut oka na žródla archeologii krajowej* [Look to the Sources of Land Archaeology]. Vilnius.

Volkaite-Kulikauskienė, R. 1970. *Lietuviai IX-XII a* [Lithuanians in the Ninth–Twelfth Centuries].

Zabiela, G. 1998a. "Application of Alternative Methods in Lithuanian Field Archaeology (up to 1996)." *Archaeologia Baltica* (Vilnius) 3: 143–158.

———. 1998b. "Arkheologiya v Litvie v 1991–1996 gg: dostizhenya i problemy" [Archaeology in Lithuania in 1991–1996: Achievements and Problems]. *Rosiiskaya arkheologiya* [Russian Archaeology] (Moscow) no. 3: 237–244.

Ljubljansko Barje

Ljubljansko Barje, known also as the Ljubljana Marsh or the Laibacher Moor, is a complex of prehistoric pile-dwelling sites in SLOVENIA. The term *Ljubljansko Barje* is frequently used as a synonym for Copper- and Bronze Age pile dwellings in the marshland south of Ljubljana in a Pleistocene tectonic depression of approximately 170 square kilometers. It is presumed that a shallow lake existed there before the formation of marshes in about 2000 B.C.

The first pile dwellings were discovered by DRAGOTIN (KARL) DEZMAN, curator of the Provincial Museum of Carniola, Ljubljana, in 1875 near the village of Ig, fifteen kilometers south of Ljubljana. Between 1875 and 1877, he conducted several excavation campaigns in which he researched an area of more than 10,000 square meters. Archaeological excavations revealed very rich, ornamented pottery; clay figurines; stone, wooden, and bone implements; and some of the earliest metal finds in Slovenia. These finds made the Ig pile dwellings one of the most various and attractive prehistoric sites of central Europe at the time. Nevertheless, Dezman succeeded in publishing only brief notices and some interim excavation reports.

Initially, the pile dwellings were attributed to the Stone Age, but later they were thought to be Bronze Age in origin. The first more-detailed cultural attribution of the dwellings was given by M. Hoernes in 1898, who placed the finds from Ig into the context of the Bandkeramik culture. European archaeologist VERE GORDON CHILDE, in *The Danube in Prehistory* (1929), associated the Ig pile dwellings with Slavonian cul-

ture and placed them in the Copper Age (Danubian IV phase). The Slovenian archaeologist RAJKO LOZAR attributed "the Ljubljana pottery" to the northern cultural circle, especially to the Globular Amphora culture of the late Neolithic period.

After World War II, from 1953 to 1981, the Department of Archaeology at the University of Ljubljana (consisting of JOSIP KOROŠEC, Tatjana Bregant, and Zorko Harej) organized several larger excavations on newly discovered sites in the Ljubljansko Barje. The results of these excavations demonstrated the existence of a long-lived settlement system extending from the late Neolithic to the early Bronze Age. The first catalog of finds from the Ig dwellings was published by the Slovenian archaeologists Josip Korošec and Paola Korošec in 1969. They classified the pottery from Ig into two cultural and chronological groups originating from the Slavonian (Vucedol) culture complex. The first Ig phase was placed in the early Copper Age, and the second, in the late Copper Age and transition to the Bronze Age.

The most complete chronological and cultural study of pottery from Ljubljansko Barje was published by Hermann Parzinger (Parzinger 1984). He defined seven phases (from the end of the Neolithic to the early Bronze Age) and placed the Ljubljansko Barje pile dwellings in the context of the middle Danubian cultural region (Lengyel, Baden, Vucedol cultures). However, he also demonstrated the presence of cultural elements associated with northern Italian cultures (Lagozza, Remedello, and Polada).

Tatjana Greif

References

Harej, Z. 1986. *Kultura kolisc na Ljubljanskem barju.* Ljubljana.

Korošec, P., and J. Korošec. 1969. *Najdbe s koliscarskih naselbin pri Igu na Ljubljanskem barju.* Ljubljana.

Parzinger, Hermann. 1984. "Die Stellung der Uferrandsiedlungen bei Ljubljana im aneolithischen und fruhbronzezeitlichen Kultursystem der mittleren Donaulander." *Arheoloski vestnik* 35: 13–75.

Louvre

Established in 1793, the Musée du Louvre in Paris, FRANCE, originally included the royal collections and artifacts seized from émigré royalists and the church after the revolution. The museum's collection (which included a large number of pieces derived from the Classical Roman and Greek cultures) was dramatically increased when art works looted from ITALY by the victorious French armies were sent back to Paris after 1794. Although many of these works were returned after Napoleon's fall in 1815, the nucleus of the great museum called the Louvre was firmly established. Although it is justly famous for its collection of paintings, the Louvre also houses major collections of antiquities, particularly those drawn from the classical world, Egypt, and ancient Assyria.

The classical collection had its roots in the royal collections of François I and Henri IV, and it was supplemented by purchases of materials originally looted by the French armies. After 1815, the collection was expanded by donations (such as *Venus de Milo* in 1821), by purchase, and by pieces retrieved from excavations. The Egyptian collection has a long history as well. Founded by JEAN-FRANCOIS CHAMPOLLION in 1827, the collection was greatly expanded through the efforts of French collectors and excavators in Egypt, the most notable being AUGUSTE MARIETTE working at Saqqara. Of almost equal importance is the Assyrian collection founded in 1847, which is based around the work of PAUL-EMILE BOTTA and Ernest Renan. Staff members of the Louvre continue to be active in archaeological research all over the world.

Tim Murray

References

Gould, C. H. M. 1965. *Trophy of Conquest: The Musée Napoleon and the Creation of the Louvre.* London: Faber.

Lozar, Rajko (1904–1985)

The Slovenian archaeologist, ethnographer, and art historian Rajko Lozar graduated in art history and classical archaeology from Ljubljana University in 1925 and received his Ph.D. in Roman provincial archaeology in Vienna in 1927. Between 1928 and 1940, he was curator of archaeology in the National Museum in Ljubljana, in 1940–1945, he was director of the Slovene Ethnographic Museum in Ljubljana, and in 1941–1942, he was a lecturer in prehistory at the University of Ljubljana. After 1945, he migrated first to Austria and then, in 1950, to the United States where he was director of the Rahr Civic Center and Public Museum in Manitowoc, Wisconsin, between 1956 and 1969.

Lozar was predominant in Slovenian archaeology in the period between the two world wars, mainly owing to the fact that he was the only professional archaeologist in SLOVENIA at the time. This research and museum work encompassed archaeology, art history, and ethnography as well as the protection of cultural monuments and university teaching. As a scholar with a background in Classical and humanist sciences, he was influenced by the culture-history approach in central European archaeology during the first decades of the twentieth century. He applied the specific approach that he had developed first as an art historian to his archaeological studies in prehistory, to the Roman and early medieval archaeology of Slovenia, and to the study of the evolution of style and key forms. He partly ignored typological studies based on discretely delimited units and contexts, considering form as the general expression and synthesis of individual and local cultural development, not as a manifestation of the spiritual culture only. His major works in this area are "Ornamenti noriskopanonske kamnoseske industrije" (1934a; Ornaments of the Norico-Pannonian Stonecutting Industry), "Predzgodovina Slovenije, posebej Kranjske, v luci zbirke Mecklenburg" (1934b; Prehistory of Slovenia, especially Carniola, in the Light of Mecklenburg Collection), and "Studija o ljubljanski keramiki" (1941b; Study of Pottery from the Late Copper Age Sites in Ljubljana Marsh).

He was also one of the pioneers of early Slavic archaeology in Slovenia. His study on Slavonic pottery, "Staroslovansko in srednjevesko loncarstvo v Sloveniji" (1938; Early Slavic and Medieval Potmaking in Slovenia), was the first attempt at a chronological and typological systematization of pottery from Slavic sites in Slovenia. At the end of his professional career in archaeology in Ljubljana, he published the first historical and critical synthesis of Slovenian archaeology: "Razvoj in problemi slovenske arheoloske vede" (1941a; Development and Problems of Slovenian Archaeological Discipline). As an ethnographer, Lozar edited and contributed important texts to the *Narodopisje Slovencev* (*Ethnography of the Slovenes*) published in 1944.

After 1945, Lozar left Slovenia for political reasons. He lived in Austria until 1950 when he moved to Manitowoc, Wisconsin, where he worked as the director of local city museum. After leaving Slovenia, he lost all professional contacts with contemporary Slovenian archaeologists.

Predrag Novakovic

References

Gabrovec S. 1987. "Rajko Lozar." *Arheoloski vestnik* (Ljubljana) 38: 435–441.

Lozar, R. 1934a. "Ornamenti noriskopanonske kamnoseske industrije." *Casopis za zgodovino in narodopisje* 29: 99–147.

———. 1934b. "Predzgodovina Slovenije, posebej Kranjske, v luci zbirke Mecklenburg." *Glasnik Muzejskega drustva za Slovenijo* 15: 5–19.

———. 1938. "Staroslovansko in srednjevesko loncarstvo v Sloveniji." *Glasnik Muzejskega drustva za Slovenijo* 20: 180–225.

———. 1941a. "Razvoj in problemi slovenske arheoloske vede." *Zbornik za umetnostno zgodovino* 17: 107–148.

———. 1941b. "Studija o ljubljanski keramiki." *Glasnik muzejskega drustva za Slovenijo* 22: 1–35.

Charles Lyell (Ann Ronan Picture Library)

Lyell, Sir Charles (1797–1875)

Born in Scotland, Lyell studied geology at Oxford University with WILLIAM BUCKLAND. In 1819 he moved to London to study law and was admitted to the bar, but never practiced. Instead he took up the study of geology and scientific writing, supporting himself financially through private means and from the sale of his enormously influential books. Lyell was professor of geology at King's College, London, between 1831 and 1833 and was knighted in 1848.

His three-volume *Principles of Geology* (1830–1833) described modern and uniform long-term geological changes and argued against the prevailing catastrophism of his time as unscientific and based on biblical chronology. Lyell also contributed to the development of paleontology and Tertiary studies and helped to establish the Eocene, Miocene, and Pliocene periods, based on animal extinctions.

While Lyell rejected Lamarck's evolutionism, he argued that extinction was the normal course of nature. He gradually accepted Charles Darwin's theories after the publication of *On the Origin of Species* (1859) but the question of human origins and human-ape connections remained a problem for him. In his book *Geological Evidence of the Antiquity of Man* (1863) he promoted arguments for the long antiquity of human history, convinced by evidence, provided by WILLIAM PENGELLY and HUGH FALCONER from BRIXHAM CAVE and other sites, of man-made tools being found with extinct fauna. In 1859 Lyell and the rest of the committee of the Geological Society of London followed JOSEPH PRESTWICH and JOHN EVANS to Abbeville in France to pass judgment on the validity of the fossil and tool finds in the

Somme gravels by JACQUES BOUCHER DE PERTHES. It was the English scholars' international recognition of Boucher de Perthes that further assisted in his work being finally accepted by the French Academie des Sciences—and the reality of high human antiquity was accepted by the scientific establishment.

Tim Murray

See also Britain, Prehistoric Archaeology

Machu Picchu

Located to the northwest of Cuzco in PERU, the site of Machu Picchu is spectacularly situated on a ridge high in the Andes. The settlement comprises temples, tombs, houses, and agricultural terracing made from local stone with the same high-quality techniques that were so common among the INCA. A place of considerable mystery, this "lost" city was brought to the attention of the outside world in 1911 by Hiram Bingham, an American explorer. He photographed the site and returned the next year to complete the job of mapping and undertaking limited ex-

cavations—in part funded by the NATIONAL GEOGRAPHIC SOCIETY. Subsequent research has dispelled much of the mystery surrounding the site. It is now quite generally accepted that the site was not unknown to the Spanish and that it was built during the reign of the Inca king Pachacuti (A.D. 1438–1471).

Tim Murray

References
Bingham, Hiram. 1977. *Lost City of the Incas: The Story of Machu Picchu* (reprint of 1948 ed.). New York: Atheneum.

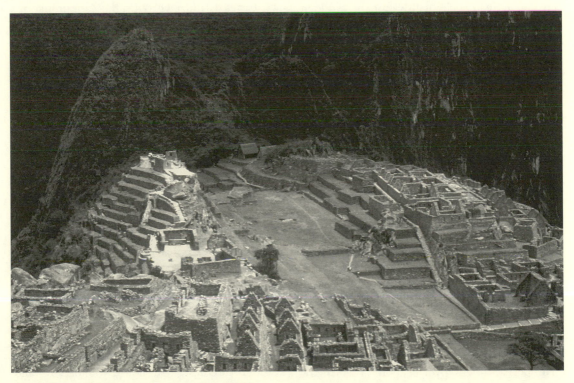

An aerial view of the ruins at Machu Picchu. (CFCL)

Madagascar

Madagascar, situated in the western Indian Ocean, is the fourth-largest island in the world. About 400 kilometers from Africa, which lies to the west, the island is itself a small continent with diversity in all aspects of the environment: physical, climatic, and biological. Archaeology is the main discipline that can help to reconstruct the past in Madagascar. Apart from an Arab script of perhaps the fourteenth century, written sources are available only from the nineteenth century, and oral traditions go back no further than the fifteenth century.

A brief review of the philosophical approaches to understanding Madagascar's past from an archaeological point of view is useful. Madagascar is about 1,580 kilometers north to south and 580 kilometers east to west and covers some 587,000 square kilometers. Human settlements, right from the beginning, seem to have adapted to its different physical environments. The arid southern and western part, the cool central highlands, and the humid eastern forests have developed societies with economies comprising, respectively, gathering and hunting, herding, irrigated rice cultivation or swidden (slash and burn) cultivation. Although Madagascar is not far from Africa, the language used throughout the island is of Southeast Asian origin, an Austronesian language close to the one spoken on Borneo. Nevertheless, some African vocabulary does exist, and this linguistic synthesis has defined the much-studied problem of the first human settlement of Madagascar, which has fascinated researchers, including archaeologists, for more than a century.

The origin and settlement of Madagascar have been key research problems since the beginning of the twentieth century. Based on evidence, settlement is believed to be less than 2,000 years old. Who were the first inhabitants and when did they arrive? Folktales record myths about first inhabitants and past environments. These myths, for example, refer to "the Lalomena," "the red beast," perhaps the pygmy hippopotamus, and "the Vorombe," "the big bird," perhaps the Aepyornis, both of which are indigenous to Madagascar.

Interest in the past is important for the Malagasy people themselves, and the Malagasy concept of the past and its periodization are consistent across the island. Six main periods, sometimes with subdivisions, characterize this concept of the past: faha-gola ("faha, in the Malagasy concept, states the period, and "gola" is used to point very old times, the unknown first settlement), faha-vazimba (the vazimba are said to have been the first inhabitants met on the island by new migrants around the fifteenth century), faha-gasy (the period when the ancestors of actual inhabitants settled on the island), faha-mpanjaka (the period when the kings reigned), faha-vazaha or faha-zanatany (the period of colonization), and faha-leovantena (the period of independence). This periodization also comes down from oral traditions.

Linguistic and historic studies provide some chronological points of reference that are useful in understanding the settlement of Madagascar. The seventh to the tenth centuries A.D. marked the coming of migrants from Southeast Asia via Africa. In the eleventh century, Shirazi migrants reached the Comoros and the northern part of Madagascar, and in the twelfth and thirteenth centuries, Islamized groups, the Zafiraminia, arrived in the southeastern part of the country. The thirteenth and fourteenth centuries saw the arrival of two other Islamized groups, the Zafikazimambo and the Anakara, in the same region. About 1500, the supremacy of the Arab traders in the Indian Ocean declined and the Europeans arrived.

The past has always fascinated all Malagasy people, and each family has traditions about its own history. Among the better known nineteenth-century scholars who began to record the history of Madagascar was Raombana, secretary to Queen Ranavalona I (1828–1857). When very young, Raombana and his twin brother Rahaniraka had been sent to England by King Radama I to be educated, and they stayed there for ten years. Because Raombana was descended from a former king and princes in the highlands and because of his English education, he developed an interest in the past of his country. He visited and described house foundations and other archaeological features at Ifanongoavana, noted in oral traditions as the first settlement of migrants from the eastern coast to the highlands. These migrants were said to be the ancestors of the kings of the central highlands who tried to unify Madagascar in the late eighteenth and nineteenth centuries. Raombana's observations were useful in guiding the recent excavations of David Rasamuel at Ifanongoavana (Rasamuel 1984).

European voyagers who went to Madagascar before the nineteenth century described ancient settlements. One of those voyagers, Flacourt, spent twenty years on the far southeastern coast and wrote a book about the region in the seventeenth century. Flacourt noted the site of Antranovato, literally "the house of stone," which was probably erected by the Portuguese in the sixteenth century. In the eighteenth century, Nicholas Mayeur noted the fourteenth- or fifteenth-century site of Vohemar in the northeastern part of the island and another, which he did not name, in the northwestern part, which he thought were connected to Vohemar. Many other people contributed to the historical and archaeological studies of Madagascar during the late nineteenth century. The most prolific and significant was Alfred Grandidier, who insisted that the Malagasy ancestors came largely from Southeast Asia and denied any significant African influence, in opposition to Gabriel Ferrand. In addition to his studies of history, ethnography, and environment, Grandidier also excavated the remains of extinct subfossils. Bones taken to the Musée d'Histoire Naturelle in Paris had traces of cutting by iron tools on them, and they have recently been confirmed and dated by accelerator techniques to the first century A.D.

Despite occasional mentions of stone tools, there is no evidence of Paleolithic flake stone industries like those in the nearby Africa. The oldest site dated by radiocarbon (728–764 A.D.) is a rock shelter in the far north of the island, the lowest level of which contains traces of human occupation. New methods of research, specifically paleoecological studies of lake sediments, indicate that the first extensive human impact on vegetation is found in sediments dated about 1,500–2,000 years ago.

There has been an evolution in the archaeological assessment of Madagascar's history. The French, during the colonial period, excavated the sites of early ports, the most significant being Vohemar on the northeastern coast, which was excavated by Elie Vernier and Gaudebout in the 1940s. The results of this excavation were used to justify contemporary French occupation because they indicated that Madagascar had been colonized before. The inhabitants' intellectual development was evident: their material culture was rich, and in their tombs, jewels and finely worked vessels of chlorite schist were found. Colonial administrators who wrote descriptions of the regions where they stayed proposed that the island's initial settlement was recent, but as a result of oral traditions, these assertions would be corrected by the results of later research.

The first to initiate truly scientific archaeological research in Madagascar was a Frenchman, Pierre Verin, who went to Madagascar in the 1950s as a trainee in the colonial administration. Fascinated by the country and its inhabitants, he began to learn the language and to understand the Malagasy, an experience that greatly influenced his attitude toward Madagascar. Moreover, his anthropological and archaeological education at Yale University had provided him with theoretical and methodological insights, and his subsequent research in Polynesia had motivated him to study Madagascar because of its connection to Austronesian voyagers who had settled in both regions in the past. Returning to the island in the early 1960s, Verin began and developed archaeological research at the University of Madagascar (now University of Antananarivo), and geographers helped him locate and study unknown and earlier sites on the island. In the first edition of the journal *Taloha* (literally, "before nowadays"), the results of research on the first human settlement of Talaky on the far southern coast, dated by radiocarbon to the eleventh century A.D., were published, and Verin began a survey to trace the human settlement of the island. In the 1970s, he studied Islamic sites along the northern coast, which he termed "echelles." One of these sites, Mahilaka, was reported in his doctoral thesis

(Verin 1975).

Besides surveys and fieldwork, other techniques were developed to record all fortified sites and to develop a comprehensive typology and historical interpretation of their growth. Adrien Mille (1970) has subsequently worked intensively with aerial photos of a limited area in the highlands around Antananarivo and has counted more than 16,000 fortified (ditched or walled) sites. The results were reported in his thesis (Mille 1971), which is a fundamental document for all who want to engage in archaeology in the highlands. This pioneer research was later continued by Raharijaona Victor (1988) in the southern part of the highlands.

During the 1970s, U.S. archaeologist Henry Wright created a ceramic chronology of the sites from finds, especially ceramics recovered from survey and excavation. The availability of transport to Antananarivo and interest in Merina state formation (seventeenth to eighteenth centuries A.D.) concentrated archaeological attention on the central highlands. This interest spread in the early 1980s to intensive surveys, using the same methods already developed in the highlands, of other regions, and these surveys provided much additional information about little-known regions. Thus, in the very southern part of the island (the Androy region), Jean-Pierre Emphoux and Chantal Radimilahy (from 1978 to 1981) then Georges Heurtebize (1986) undertook surveys and excavations of sites that enabled a correction of the old assertions about dates for the first occupation of the southern arid zone. The work helped to increase knowledge about the material culture, settlement, subsistence, and social organization from the beginning of the second millennium. At the same time, Malagasy archaeologists compiled information from oral traditions about recent periods and contributed to the archaeological map by showing the types of sites by period for each region surveyed, and in 1973 Jean-Aime Rakotoarisoa studied and mapped the nineteenth-century Merina state fortresses throughout the island.

During the 1980s, new areas of inquiry developed such as the development of iron metallurgy, the study of specific sites—especially royal ones in the highlands—and human impact on the environment. Excavations of large areas took place, test trenches being considered insufficient to offer an image of past life. Royal sites were explored in detail to illustrate this approach. Thus, David Rasamuel (1984) and Rafolo Andrianaivoarivony respectively studying the sites of Ifanongoavana and Lohavohitra, both from the fifteenth or sixteenth century (and until the eighteenth century for Lohavohitra), reported their results.

Most of the archaeological work since the 1960s had been intended to clarify national and regional identities in the way each archaeologist thought to be the best, and it has provided as many answers as it has questions. The answer to establishing how and when the island was inhabited remains open to interpretation with similar remains found in sites that are far from each other. How can they be related? One way is through written sources, which are available only after the seventeenth century. The testimony of travelers during their reconnaissance of the island during the colonial period of the nineteenth century provides a lot of information, and the continuum of the Malagasy culture has helped to clarify some questions. However, the gaps in the archaeological map still need to be filled in.

Chantal Radimilahy

References

Battistini, R., P. Verin, and R. Rason. 1963. "Le site archéologique de Talaky, cadre géographique et géologique, premiers travaux de fouille, notes éthnographiques sur le village actuel proche du site." In Annales de l'Universite de Madagascar 1:113–128.

Dewar, R. 1986. "Ecologie et extinction des subfossiles de Madagascar, traduit par Pierre Verin." Taloha 10. Civilisation de Madagascar, Revue du Musée d'Art et d'Archéologie, Université de Madagascar.

Gaudebout, P., and E. Vernier. 1941. "Notes sur une campagne de fouilles a Vohemar, Mission Rasikajy 1941." Bulletin de l'Academie Malgache, n.s., 24: 110–114.

Grandidier, G. 1899. "Fouilles dans les ruines arabes de Mahanara (côte nord-est)." In Journal Officiel (Tananarive), 29–31.

———. 1905. "Les animaux disparus de Madagascar, gisements, époques, et causes de leur disparition." La Revue de Madagascar (Paris) 8: 111–128.

Milee, A. 1970. "Contribution à l'étude des villages fortifiés de l'Imerina ancien (Madagascar). Thèse de IIIème cycle, Clermont-Ferrand.

Radimilahy, C. 1998. "Mahilaka." Studies in African Archaeology (Uppsala) 15.

Raharijoana, V. 1988. Étude du peuplement de l'espace d'une vallée des hautes terres centrales de Madagascar: Archéologie de las Manamona (Xve–XVIe siècles). Thèse de doctorat d'état. Paris, Sorbonne.

Rasamuel, D. 1984. "Alimentation et techniques anciennes dans le Sud de Madagascar, à travers une fosse à odures du XIme siècle." Études Ocean Indien 4: 81–109.

Verin, P. 1975. "Les chelles anciennes du commerce sur les côtes nords de Madagascar." Lille: Service de Reproduction des Thèses, Université de Lille III.

Magdalenska Gora

Magdalenska Gora is an early–Iron Age site in Dolenjska (lower Carniola) in SLOVENIA. It comprises a hill-fort settlement covering an area of about thirteen hectares. Some forty earthen burial barrows have been documented in its immediate vicinity, and twenty-two of them, containing at least 1,000 graves, were the subject of extensive excavations at the end of the nineteenth century and the beginning of the twentieth by the Narodni Muzej or National Museum; the Naturhistorisches Museum, Vienna; and the PEABODY MUSEUM, Harvard University. Burial was largely inhumation, although a considerable number of cremation graves in the barrows have been found as well. The number of graves in the barrows varies from 2 to more than 350, but the average number of graves per barrow is between 20 and 60.

The burials cover a period of approximately 500 years, from the eighth to the fourth century B.C., with the majority of graves belonging to fifth or fourth century. Numerous rich princely and warrior graves make Magdalenska Gora one of the important centers for the Dolenjska group of the Hallstatt (early Iron Age) culture. The graves are characterized by ornamented bronze vessels of the situla type, different types of helmets, horse-riding equipment, weapons (axes, spearheads, arrowheads), great quantities of personal ornament (fibulae, pendants, necklaces, bracelets), and elaborate ceramic vessels. The site was not completely abandoned after the fourth century B.C., as some LA TÈNE (later Iron Age) cremation graves were found in the cemetery as well.

Peter Turk

See also Austria; Celts

References
Hencken, H. 1978. "The Iron Age Cemetery of Magdalenska Gora in Slovenia." Bulletin of the American School of Prehistoric Research 32.

Maghreb

The study of prehistoric archaeology in the Maghreb (Morocco, Algeria, Tunisia) has been dominated by French archaeologists. The earliest were primarily avocational (Sheppard 1990), and they maintained close ties with archaeological and anthropological societies of metropolitan France and often published their findings in journals such as L'Anthropologie, although they also developed active local societies with a strong archaeological focus (e.g., La Société de Géographie et d'Archéologie de la Province d'Oran, La Société Archéologique de Constantine, and La Société de Préhistoire de Tébessa). In the late 1920s and 1930s and again in the 1970s, research by North Americans brought different perspectives to the interpretation of the later prehistory of the region (Sheppard 1990).

From its inception, the study of prehistoric archaeology in the Maghreb has concentrated on later prehistory (i.e., late Pleistocene and Holocene). This trend began with one of the earliest of the avocational archaeologists, Duprat, who first remarked in 1894 on the distinction in stone artifact size at various landsnail shell middens (called escargotières, see Gobert 1937). For the next forty or fifty years, archaeological research and debate in the Maghreb centered on these materials and those that either immediately preceded or succeeded them.

In 1910–1911, in a serial article, De Morgan, Capitan, and Boudy reported stratified assemblages of stone tools from sites in southern Tunisia, which they called Capsian. The stratigraphically lower assemblages contained large-backed blades, burins, and thick scrapers. The upper, or younger, assemblages were described as more refined, containing backed bladelets, small scrapers, fragments of engraved ostrich eggshell, and polished bone tools. Arguing that the Capsian took the place in North Africa of the European Upper Paleolithic, De Morgan proposed a subdivision: the more refined material was named Capsian superior, and the assemblage dominated by large tools was called Capsian inferior. This division, which essentially mirrors that of the modern Upper Capsian and typical Capsian persists today (Lubell, Sheppard and Jackes 1984).

Another early archaeologist was Paul Pallary, whose research in coastal caves and shelters resulted in the 1909 publication of *Instructions pour les recherches préhistoriques dans le Nord-Ouest de l'Afrique*. Pallary noted the similarity of the coastal North African lithics to Iberian materials that had been published earlier by Siret in *Les premiers âges du métal dans le Sud-Est de l'Espagne* (H. Siret and L. Siret 1887) and named the microlithic industry found in Maghreb coastal sites the Iberomaurusien. Based upon the "warm" fauna associated with this industry, Pallary thought that it must be later than the French Magdalenian, with its "cold" fauna, and that it therefore bridged the period between the Paleolithic and the Neolithic.

Attempts to correlate North African discoveries with those in Europe led to the formation of two schools. Members of the first, "the diffusionists," rejected the importance of independent development and saw similarity in archaeological industries as evidence of direct contact and/or diffusion of ideas. Members of the other school saw the development of local chronology and the definition and description of sequences as being the matters of primary concern. The diffusionist argument was championed by Capitan who, in the 1910–1911 serial article, argued counter to De Morgan, that the similarity between the Aurignacian and the Capsian was probably evidence of an exchange of ideas or people across a Mediterranean land

bridge (De Morgan, Capitan, and Boudy 1910–1911, 226). The great French archaeologist HENRI BREUIL (1912, 183) agreed, stating that the Capsian was middle Aurignacian and might have influenced the development of the French Aurignacian by way of Spain, thus further bolstering Pallary's ideas.

By correlating North African and French assemblages, the early Maghreb archaeologists hoped to develop a chronology for a regional sequence. Foremost among these archaeologists was Albert Debruge, a civil servant in the Algerian city of Constantine and an active member of the Constantine Archaeological Society, which charged him with responsibility for the excavation of Mechta El Arbi in eastern Algeria. From this site Debruge reported a lithic industry totally lacking in burins and geometric microliths and exhibiting what he thought were Mousterian affinities. He attributed the bone industry, which had no affinity with European materials, to intrusive Neolithic burials and made Mechta the type site for his "Aurignacien ancien" (Debruge 1923). Numerous human skeletons were studied by Bertholon, who concluded they were Neanderthaloid (Mercier and Debruge 1912). Considerable disagreement arose among the anthropologists, but all ultimately concurred that the skulls were not Neanderthal (Mercier 1915; Pond, et al. 1928).

Debruge found few geometric microliths in central Algerian sites, but further east, the numerous geometric microliths in the sites near Tebessa posed a problem for the Aurignacian school since they were not often found in the French Aurignacian period but rather in the post-Paleolithic Tardenoisian period (Coutil 1912). As a result, Debruge adopted a cautious stand on the Tebessa assemblages, a caution not exercised by Maurice Reygasse, principal administrator of the Commune Mixte of Tebessa and the most active archaeologist in that region. From 1917 on, Reygasse divided the Capsian of the Tebessa region into three Aurignacian civilizations (Reygasse 1920), the last being the *Tardenoisien le plus pur* ("the purest Tardenoisian"). For Reygasse, the abundance of geometrics that began in the middle Aurignacian period was evidence of the development of geometrics in

North Africa prior to the French Tardenoisian period, and he concluded that the richness of the Maghreb Aurignacian confirmed the African origin of the Aurignacian period in general (Reygasse 1922, 194–203). This position was difficult to refute without dating sites, but work along these lines was being undertaken as early as 1910 by Eugène G. Gobert in Tunisia.

Gobert, one of the foremost avocational archaeologists working in the Maghreb, was a medical doctor in Gafsa. He followed De Morgan's view that the Capsian bore no necessary relationship to the French Aurignacian (Gobert 1910, 595), and working within the geological paradigm of French archaeology, he began to systematically excavate sites and develop a regional chronology based on rock-shelter stratigraphy and interassemblage comparison. He observed that virtually all Capsian sites in southern Tunisia contained geometric microliths when the deposits were screened. Therefore, if geometrics were a fossil directeur, or marker fossil, Capsian assemblages should all be Holocene (i.e., Tardenoisian) in age. Gobert attributed the rarity of geometrics in the sites investigated by Debruge to poor excavation techniques, a view not entirely substantiated by later reinvestigations at Mechta el Arbi (Balout 1955, 380).

Gobert (1910, 595) also argued that Capsian sites contained a warm vertebrate fauna of zebra, ox, antelope, and ostrich, which, since it was little different from the fauna associated with Neolithic sites, indicated a similar age. This argument was countered by the diffusionists, who invoked a less severe climate for North Africa during the Upper Paleolithic, owing to its more southerly latitude. It was into this atmosphere of controversy that the U.S. Logan Museum at Beloit College in Wisconsin launched a North African program of research through contacts with members of the diffusionist school. In 1925, Alonzo Pond visited Reygasse in Tebessa and then joined a Franco-American expedition on its trip south to Tammanrasset in central Sahara.

With Dubruge's official guidance, Pond began excavating at Mechta El Arbi in 1926 and then worked on the Mediterranean coast in 1927 and in eastern Algeria in 1929; finally, with a contingent of fourteen American students, he conducted a three-month campaign of excavation on the southern edge of the Constantine plain near Canrobert (now Oum el Bouaghi) in the Aïn Beïda region in 1930. The research methods used during these expeditions were models for their time (Lubell 1992; Sheppard 1990, 1992) as they included systematic survey, surface collection, accurate measurement and plotting of sites on topographic maps (including an identifying number for each), excavation by arbitrary levels, and screening of all excavated deposit through a very fine mesh (Pond, Chapius, Romer, and Baker 1938). In addition to the quantitative study of all the stone tools recovered, the Logan Museum expeditions were also exceptional for the recovery and detailed identification of faunal and human remains, studies of modern snail populations, and sufficient conservation of charcoal samples that, fifty years later, they provided reasonable carbon–14 dates (Sheppard 1984). The standards of research and publication set by Pond were unequaled by North African archaeologists for another twenty years.

Using faunal data and the prevailing understanding of glacial climates, Pond's colleague Collie (1928) argued that North Africa provided a suitable environment for the early development of the Aurignacian culture during the Würm Glacial period prior to the diffusion of the Aurignacian to Europe. Differences between the lithic assemblages of Europe and North Africa were assumed by Collie to reflect either divergence after movement to Europe or the advanced features of the original culture in Africa (Collie 1928, 45). Although Collie described the Aurignacian tool types, he did not attempt any detailed numerical comparison of North African and French assemblages. It is apparent that regardless of poor chronology and limited data, Collie thought he had a rather compelling argument for the origin in North Africa of the French Upper Paleolithic culture.

If Collie was the grand theoretician, Pond was the methodical field-worker concerned with the practical problems of describing and comparing archaeological assemblages. Pond (et al, 1928, 58) noted that many forms of tools, and especially the bone tool industry, bore little or no resemblance to the known Aurignacian assemblages while Romer (1928) concluded that the crania from Mechta El Arbi were related to neither Neanderthal nor Cro-Magnon beings but were likely ancestors of modern North Africans.

Pond did not make many statements concerning European and African relationships. However, based on his study of museum collections in Italy, his reading of Raymond Vaufrey's (1928) study of the Italian Paleolithic, and the work of LOUIS LEAKEY, Pond did hypothesize that man originated in Africa and entered Europe via either the Nile Valley and the Near East or the Sahara and Spain. He argued that Collie's hypothesis of movement of the Aurignacian culture across a land bridge from Tunisia to Italy was not supported by stone tools found at Italian sites. It was the study of this material that subsequently lead Vaufrey to work in North Africa and refute the Aurignacian-Capsian connection.

Vaufrey was a student of the great French archaeologist MARCELLIN BOULE (see Roubet 1979), who had a strong interest in paleontological evidence for Pleistocene land bridges across the Mediterranean. Boule sent Vaufrey first to Italy and then, in 1927, to North Africa to search for animal and stone tool evidence for such connections. Vaufrey quickly demonstrated the lack of evidence for an Italian-Tunisian land bridge and went on to complete a comparative study of archaeological materials from southern Tunisia and eastern Algeria, often with the collaboration of Gobert. Between 1931 and 1933, Vaufrey tested a large number of sites throughout this region (Vaufrey 1955), often excavating in small units down to sterile soil or bedrock and screening all deposits (Roubet 1979, 29). The resulting collection was then selected with a bias in favor of formal retouched tools. In 1933, he published an article in *L'Anthropologie* that provided the standard interpretation of the Capsian for the next thirty years.

Vaufrey divided the Capsian into a chronological sequence from typical Capsian to Capsian superior to Neolithic in the Capsian tradition. The typical Capsian was characterized by numerous backed blades, lateral burins, endscrapers, backed bladelets, and varying amounts of geometric microliths and microburins. The major characteristic of Capsian superior was the marked decrease in the number of large tools and a great increase in the number and variety of microlithic tools, especially geometrics. Vaufrey created two facies, the "intergétulonéolithique" of Tunisia (elongated scalene triangles and truncations) and the "Capsien supérieur typique" in Algeria (triangles and equilateral trapezes). Both facies contained a more varied and abundant bone industry than that found in the typical Capsian. The Neolithic in the Capsian tradition was characterized by the complete disappearance of most typical Capsian elements, a reduction of the number of geometric forms, and the introduction of bifacial points. Vaufrey concluded that from a typological viewpoint, the Capsian had a Mesolithic, or at most a final Paleolithic, character and that it was not ancestral to the Aurignacian period.

In addition to defining the industries and providing a temporal framework, Vaufrey formalized knowledge concerning the geographical distribution of the Capsian. He noted that the typical Capsian was confined to the region south of Tebessa in Algeria and Tunisia while the Capsian superior spread throughout the Constantine plains and south to the northern edge of the Sahara. This is essentially the distribution known today (Camps 1974, 117). In 1955, Vaufrey published his synthesis, *Préhistoire de l'Afrique,* the first book of which is entitled *Le Maghreb.* In addition to a wealth of data and interpretations on all periods, Chapter 2 of this work presents an excellent summary of the history of archaeological research in the Maghreb up to the 1950s.

Vaufrey subsequently focused his interest on the portable and rock art of the Maghreb and attempted to develop a chronology for rock art and investigate the relationship between artifacts from the Capsian and those of neighboring regions, notably Egypt and Spain (Roubet 1979, 42–46). Noting a resemblance between the Neolithic in the Capsian tradition and many other industries throughout Africa, he postulated a spread of the former throughout Africa.

After World War II, the number of archaeologists working on the later prehistory of the Maghreb increased dramatically. Some (R. de Bayle des Hermens, G. Camps, H. Camps-Fabrer, H. J. Hugot, J. Tixier, G. Souville) were trained professionally by Lionel Balout, who replaced Maurice Reygasse in 1947 as the professor of prehistory at the University of Algiers and established the Centre de Recherches Anthropologiques, Préhistoriques et Ethnographiques (CRAPE) at the Bardo Museum in 1952 following the Second Pan-African Congress of Prehistory held in Algiers (Balout 1952; Roubet, Hugot, and Souville 1981).

Abbé Jean Roche, a student of Teilhard de Chardin and Breuil who also worked with CAMILLE ARAMBOURG, Henry Vallois, and Vaufrey, was one of the first to reintroduce fully modern methods of excavation and analysis. His work on the Moroccan Epipaleolithic period at Taforalt and other sites (Roche 1963) was exemplary and, despite continued research and cataloging of sites in Morocco (e.g., Souville 1973), has little competition for innovation and thoroughness.

Avocational archaeology also continued. Among the best practitioners was Jean Morel (1896–1981) who published eighty-eight papers on the prehistory of the Maghreb between 1946 and 1981 (others appeared posthumously), several of which were methodologically innovative and/or theoretically sophisticated and whose critiques of work by others was always thoughtful (e.g., Morel 1974, 1978a, 1978b, 1981).

In 1955, Balout published his magisterial *Préhistoire de l'Afrique du Nord, essai de chronologie,* which became, and to some extent remains, the standard reference work on the prehistory of Africa. Balout also established the journal *Libyca,* which became the preferred publication venue for reports on Maghreb prehistory (although publication since the mid-1980s has been problematic). Gabriel Camps, who succeeded Balout at the University of Algiers and CRAPE, encouraged a number of younger archaeologists (including Ginette Aumassip, Claude Brahimi, and Colette Roubet). Camps conducted a series of important excavations at

sites in Algeria and the Sahara (e.g., Camps 1968), often in collaboration with Henriette Camps-Fabrer (e.g., Camps and Camps-Fabrer 1964), who was responsible for two major reports, *Matière et art mobilier dans la préhistoire Nord-Africaine et Saharienne* (1966) and a monograph on Medjez II (1975). In 1974, Gabriel Camps published a sequel to Balout's 1955 treatise, *Les civilisations préhistoriques de l'Afrique du Nord et du Sahara,* which integrated what was then known from chronometric dating with the vast quantities of archaeological, paleoenvironmental, and paleontological data amassed since the 1950s (*see* Camps 1975).

Among the younger generation of French or French-trained archaeologists, several stand out: Ginette Aumassip, for a long series of investigations on the Saharan Neolithic (e.g., Aumassip 1973, 1980–1981); Claude Brahimi, for his brief but influential research on the Iberomaurusian (Brahimi 1970); Danilo Grébénart, for his reassessment of Relilai and other sites in the Tebessa and Ouled-Djellal regions (Grébénart 1976); Jacques Tixier, for his systematization of Maghreb lithics (Tixier 1963, 1967); and Colette Roubet, for her interdisciplinary work on the Neolithic of Capsian tradition (Roubet 1979). To these, we can add the research of a small number of archaeologists not trained in the Francophone tradition: Antonio Gilman (1975), David Lubell (Lubell 1984, 1992; Lubell et al. 1975, 1976, 1982–1983, 1984), and Peter Sheppard (1984, 1987). Algerian archaeologists more recently educated in France and Algeria have begun to publish in the journal *Libyca* (e.g., Ferhat 1984–1986; Hachi 1982–1983; Heddouche 1982–1983, 1984–1986) and elsewhere (Sahnouni 1987, 1991).

Although the emphasis in Maghreb prehistory, both in research and in publication, has been on the later Pleistocene and Holocene, earlier periods have not been entirely neglected. For the most part, investigations of these, beginning as early as the 1920s (e.g., Lecointre 1926), have been concentrated in Morocco, have been carried out by trained geologists and paleontologists, and have resulted in a series of important publications on the industries and environments of the Lower Paleolithic. These include Arambourg's monograph *Mammifères fossiles du Maroc* (1938), Bourcart's article "La géologie du quaternaire au Maroc" (1943), and especially a publication by Neuville and Ruhlmann, *La Place du Paléolithique Ancien dans le Quaternaire Marocain* (1941). An account of the history of research on earlier Maghreb prehistory is given by Pierre Biberson in two volumes published in 1961: *Le Cadre paléogéographique de la préhistoire du Maroc Atlantique* and *Le Paléolithique inférieur du Maroc Atlantique*. Biberson took over the research of Neuville and Ruhlmann at the Casablanca quarries following World War II, and there he was responsible for excavation of the Acheulean levels at Sidi-Abderrahman Extension.

Little systematic research other than Biberson's has been done on Lower Paleolithic materials in the Maghreb. The state of knowledge in the early 1970s is reviewed by Freeman (1975).

Other than the Moroccan sites, significant localities include Aïn Hanech (Arambourg 1947; Sahnouni 1987, 1991) and Ternifine (Arambourg 1963; Balout, Biberson, and Tixier 1967; Geraads, Hublin, Jaeger, Tong, Sen, and Toubeau 1986) in Algeria; Sidi Zin in Tunisia (Gobert 1950; Gragueb 1980); Erg Tihodaine in the Algerian Sahara, where Reygasse began work in the 1930s (Reygasse 1935), followed by Arambourg in the 1940s and 1950s (e.g., Arambourg and Balout 1955), and more recently by Thomas (1977). DESMOND CLARK (1992) provides a brief, more recent overview.

The Middle Paleolithic is even less well documented. The classic Maghreb industry of this period is the Aterian, first identified by Pallary in 1911 but named by Reygasse in 1922 and then defined by him in 1930 (Debénath 1994; Ferring 1975). Characterized by the use of the Levallois technique and the presence of stemmed (pedunculate) artifacts, Aterian assemblages date between 40,000 and 20,000 years ago and are found from the Atlantic coast of Morocco to the Nile Valley. Although a Mousterian origin is almost certain, Mousterian sites are rare. Wengler's doctoral thesis, "Cultures préhistoriques et formations quaternaires du Maroc Oriental: Relations entre comportements et paléoenvironnements du Paléolithique

Moyen" (1993), provides some clarification. It is now generally accepted that there are no known examples of *Homo sapiens neandertalensis* in the Maghreb (or elsewhere in North Africa). Even though the makers of the North African Mousterian are unknown, all fossils found in association with Aterian assemblages are accepted as anatomically modern *Homo sapiens* (Debénath 1994). Unresolved are questions of the affinity and origins of later (Iberomaurusian and Capsian) populations, a point discussed at length in Lubell, Sheppard, and Jackes (1984) and in a series of articles and monographs by Chamla (e.g., 1968, 1970, 1973, 1975, 1978; see also Briggs 1955).

David Lubell and Peter Sheppard

See also Africa, Francophone; Lithic Analysis; Rock Art

References

Arambourg, C. 1938. *Mammifères fossiles du Maroc.* Mémoires de la Société des Sciences Naturelles du Maroc, 46.

———. 1947. "Les vertébrés fossiles des formations continentales des plateaux constantinois (note préliminaire)." *Bulletin de la Société d'Histoire Naturelle de l'Afrique du Nord* 38: 45–48.

———. 1963. *Le gisement de Ternifine: L'Atlanthropus de Ternifine.* Archives de L'Institut de Paléontologie Humaine, 32.

Arambourg, C., and L. Balout. 1955. "L'ancien lac de Tihodaïne et ses gisements préhistoriques." In *Congrès Panafricain de Préhistoire. Actes de la IIe Session, Alger, 1952,* pp. 281–295. Ed. L. Balout.

Aumassip, G. 1973. *Néolithique sans poterie de la région de l'Oued Mya (Bas-Sahara).* Mémoires du CRAPE, 20. Algiers: SNED.

———. 1980–1981. "Ti-n-Hanakaten, Tassili-n-Ajer, Algérie. Bilan de 6 campagnes de fouilles." *Libyca* 28–29: 115–127.

Balout, L. 1952. *Actes du Congrès Panafricain de Préhistoire.* Paris: Arts et Métiers Graphiques.

———. 1955. *Préhistoire de l'Afrique du Nord, essai de chronologie.* Paris: Arts et Métiers Graphiques.

———. 1967. "Procédés d'analyse et questions de terminologie concernant l'études des ensembles industriels du Paléolithique inférieur en Afrique du Nord." In *Background to Evolution in Africa,* pp. 701–735. Ed. W. W. Bishop and J. D. Clark. Chicago: University of Chicago.

Balout, L., P. Biberson, and J. Tixier. 1967. "L'Acheuléen de Ternifine (Algérie), gisement de l'Atlanthrope." *L'Anthropologie* 71, 3–4: 217–238.

Biberson, P. 1961a. *Le Cadre paléogéographique de la préhistoire du Maroc Atlantique.* Service des Antiquités du Maroc, Fascicule 16.

———. 1961b. *Le Paléolithique inférieur du Maroc Atlantique.* Service des Antiquités du Maroc, Fascicule 17.

Bourcart, J. 1943. "La géologie du quaternaire au Maroc." *Revue Scientifique* 3, no. 224: 311–336.

Brahimi, Cl. 1970. *L'ibéromaurusien littoral de la région d'Alger.* Mémoires du CRAPE, 13. Paris: Arts et Métiers Graphiques.

Breitborde, L. B., ed. 1992. *Alonzo Pond and the Logan Museum Expedition to North Africa: The 1985 Beloit College Symposium.* Logan Museum Bulletin, new series, 1, 1.

Breuil, H. 1912. "Les subdivisons du Paléolithique supérieur et leur signification." In *Congrès Int. d'Anth. et d'Arch. Préhistoriques: Comptes rendu de la XIV ème Session, Geneva,* pp. 165–240.

———. 1937. *Les subdivisions de Paléolithique supérieur et leur signification.* 2d ed. Paris: Lagny.

Briggs, L. C. 1955. *The Stone Age Races of Northwest Africa.* Bulletin of the American School of Prehistoric Research, 18. Cambridge, MA: Peabody Museum, Harvard University.

Camps, G. 1968. *Amekni, néolithique ancien du Hoggar.* Mémoires du CRAPE, 10.

———. 1974. *Les civilisations préhistoriques de l'Afrique du Nord et du Sahara.* Paris: Doin.

———. 1975. "The Prehistoric Cultures of North Africa: Radiocarbon Chronology." In *Problems in Prehistory: North African and the Levant,* pp. 181–192. Ed. F. Wendorf and A. E. Marks. Dallas: Southern Methodist University Press.

Camps, G., and H. Camps-Fabrer. 1964. *Le nécropole mégalithique du Djebel Mazela à Bou Nouara.* Mémoires du CRAPE, 3.

Camps-Fabrer, H. 1966. *Matière et art mobilier dans la préhistoire Nord-Africaine et Saharienne.* Mémoires du CRAPE, 5.

———. 1975. *Un gisement capsien de faciès sétifien: Medjez II, El Eulma (Algérie).* Paris: CNRS.

Chamla, M. C. 1968. "L'évolution du type de Mechta-Afalou en Algérie occidentale." *C.R. Acad. Sci., Paris* 267: 1849–1851.

———. 1970. *Les hommes epipaléolithiques de Columnata (Algérie occidentale), etude anthropologique.* Mémoires du CRAPE, 15.

———. 1973. "Etude anthropologique de l'homme capsien de l'Aïn Dokkara (Algérie orientale)." *Libyca* 21: 9–53.

———. 1975. "La diversité des types humains dans les gisements capsiens." In H. Camps-Fabrer, *Un gisement capsien de faciès sétifien: Medjez II,* pp. 373–376. Paris: CNRS.

———. 1978. "Le peuplement de l'Afrique du Nord de l'Epipaléolithique à l'époque actuelle." *L'Anthropologie* 3: 385–430.

Clark, J. D. 1992. "The Earlier Stone Age / Lower Palaeolithic in North Africa and the Sahara." In *New Light on the Northeast African Past,* pp. 17–37. Ed. F. Klees and R. Kuper. Cologne: Heinrich-Barth-Institut.

Collie, G. L. 1928. *The Aurignacians and Their Culture.* Beloit College Bulletin, 26, 2. Beloit, WI.

Coutil, L. 1912. "Tardenoisien, capsien, gétulien, ibéro-maurusien, tellien, loubirien, généyenien, intergétulo-nolithique." *Congr. Int. d'Anth. et d'Arch. Préhistorique: C. R. XIVème Session, Geneva,* 1:310.

De Morgan, J., L. Capitan, and P. Boudy. 1910–1911. "Etude sur les stations préhistoriques du Sud-Tunisien." *Revue de l'Ecole d'Anthropologie* 20: 105–136, 206–221, 267–286, 336–347; 1911: 217–228.

Debénath, A. 1994. "L'atérien du nord de l'Afrique et du Sahara." *Sahara* 6: 21–30.

Debruge, A. 1923. "Essai de chronologie sur "les escargotières." *Recl. des Notes et Mém. de la Soc. Arch. de Constantine* 44: 61.

Ferhat, N. 1984–1986. "Le gisement acheuléen de la Zaouia Sidi El Hadj Belgacem, Timimoun (Sahara algérien)." *Libyca* 32–34: 81–95.

Ferring, R. 1975. "The Aterian in North African Prehistory." In *Problems in Prehistory: North African and the Levant,* pp. 113–126. Ed. F. Wendorf and A. E. Marks. Dallas: Southern Methodist University Press.

Freeman, L. G. 1975. "Acheulean Sites and Stratigraphy in Iberia and the Maghreb." In *After the Australopithecines,* pp. 661–743. Ed. K. W. Butzer and G. Ll. Isaac. The Hague: Mouton.

Geraads, D., J.-J. Hublin, J.-J. Jaeger, H. Tong, S. Sen, and P. Toubeau. 1986. "The Pleistocene Hominid Site of Ternifine, Algeria: New Results on the Environment, Age, and Human Industries." *Quaternary Research* 25: 380–386.

Gilman, A. 1975. *The Later Prehistory of Tangier, Morocco.* Bulletin of the American School of Prehistoric Research, no. 29.

Gobert, E. G. 1910. "Recherches sur le Capsien,

1re série." *Bulletin de la Société Préhistorique Française* 6: 595–604.

———. 1937. "Les escargotières: le mot et la chose." *Revue Africaine* 81: 639–645.

———. 1950. "Le gisement Paléolithique du Sidi Zin." *Kharthago* 1: 1–64.

Gragueb, A. 1980. "Un nouveau gisement Acheuléen dans la Vallée de l'Oued Mellegue (Nord-Ouest de la Tunisie)." *L'Anthropologie* 84: 359–379.

Grébénart, D. 1976. *Le capsien des régions de Tébessa et d'Ouled-Djellal (Algérie)*. Etudes Méditerranéennes, 1. Aix-en-Provence: Editions de l'Université de Provence.

Hachi, S. 1982–1983. "Les industries du Paléolithique inférieur des Ajjers. Point des connaissances." *Libyca* 30–31: 19–58.

Heddouche, A. 1982–1983. "Les galets aménagé de Bordj Tan Kena-Illizi (Algérie)." *Libyca* 30–31: 9–18.

———. 1984–1986. "Etude de l'industrie du gisement néolithique de Bordj Tan Kena-Illizi (Algérie)." *Libyca* 32–34: 139–157.

Lacorre, F. 1949. "Le gétulo-capsien: Abri 402 et Ain Metherchem." *Bulletin de la Société Préhistorique Française* 50: 258–273.

Lecointre, G. 1926. *Recherches geologiques dans la meseta marocaine.*" Mémoires de la Société des Sciences naturelles du Maroc, 14.

Lubell, D. 1984. "Paleoenvironments and Epi-Paleolithic Economies in the Maghreb (ca. 20,000 to 5000 B.P.)." In *From Hunters to Farmers: The Causes and Consequences of Food Production in Africa*, pp. 41–56. Ed. J. D. Clark and S. A. Brandt. Berkeley: University of California Press.

———. 1992. "Following Alonzo's Trail: Paleoeconomic Research in Algeria since 1930." In *Alonzo Pond and the Logan Museum Expedition to North Africa: The 1985 Beloit College Symposium*, pp. 49–57. Ed. L. B. Breitborde. Beloit, WI.

Lubell, D., J.-L. Ballais, A. Gautier, and F.A. Hassan. 1975. "Prehistoric Cultural Ecology of Capsian Escargotières I: Preliminary Results of an Interdisciplinary Investigation in the Chéria-Télidjène Region 1972–73." *Libyca* 23: 44–121.

Lubell, D., and A. Gautier. 1982–1983. "Prehistoric Cultural Ecology of Capsian Escargotières II: Report on Investigations Conducted during 1976 in the Bahiret Télidjène, Tébessa Wilaya, Algeria." *Libyca* 30–31: 59–142.

Lubell, D., F. A. Hassan, A. Gautier, and J.-L. Ballais. 1976. "The Capsian Escargotières." *Science* 191: 910–920.

Lubell, D., P. Sheppard, and M. Jackes. 1984. "Continuity in the Epipalaeolithic of North African with Special Emphasis on the Maghreb." In *Advances in World Archaeology*, 3:143–191. Ed. F. Wendorf and A. Close. New York: Academic Press.

Mercier, G. 1915. "L'Homme de Mechta-Chteaudun (Algérie)." *Bulletin de la Société Préhistorique Française* 12: 160–166.

Mercier, G., and A. Debruge. 1912. "La station préhistorique de Mechta Chteaudun." *Recl. des Notes et Mém. de la Soc. Arch. de Constantine* 46: 287–307.

Morel, J. 1974. "La faune de l'escargotière de Dra-Mta-El-Ma-El-Abiod (Sud-Algérien): Ce qu'elle nous apprend de l'alimentation et des conditions de vie des populations du Capsien supérieur." *L'Anthropologie* 78: 299–320.

———. 1978a. "L'Industrie lithique de l'escargotière de Dra-Mta-El-Ma-El-Abiod dans le sud-est Algérien: Sa composition et son évolution." *L'Anthropologie* 82: 335–372.

———. 1978b. "Les sources d'alimentation des épipaléolithiques de Tamar Hat et le problème des origines de la domestication en Afrique du Nord." *Bulletin du Musée d'anthropologie préhistorique de Monaco* 22: 72–78.

———. 1981. "Nouvelles réflexions sur l'alimentation et le mode de vie des Capsiens de Dra-Mta-el-Ma-el-Abiod dans la région de Tébessa (Est Algérien)." In *Préhistoire Africaine: Mélanges offerts au doyen Lionel Balout*, pp. 189–194. Ed. C. Roubet, H.-J. Hugot, and G. Souville. Recherche sur les Grands Civilization, Synthèse no. 6. Paris: Editions ADPF.

Mortillet, G. de. 1882. *La préhistorique: Antiquité de l'homme*. Paris: Reinwald.

Neuville, R., and A. Ruhlmann. 1941. *La Place du Paléolithique Ancien dans le Quaternaire Marocain*. Collection Hespéris, Institut des Hautes-Etudes Marocaines, 8.

Pallary, P. 1909. *Instructions pour les recherches préhistoriques dans le Nord-Ouest de l'Afrique*. Mémoires de la Société Historique Algérienne. 3.

Pond, A., L. Chapius, A. Romer, and F. Baker. 1938. *Prehistoric Habitation in the Sahara and North Africa*. Logan Museum Bulletin, 5. Beloit, WI.

Pond, A., A. Romer, and F. Cole. 1928. *A Contribution to the Study of Prehistoric Man in Algeria, North Africa*. Logan Museum Bulletin, 2. Beloit, WI.

Reygasse, M. 1920. "Etudes de paléthnologie

maghrébine (nouvelle série)." *Recl. des Not. et Mém. de la Soc. Arch. de Constantine* 52: 513–570.

———. 1922. "Etudes de paléthnologie maghrébine—2ème série." *Recl. des Not. et Mém. de la Soc. Arch. de Constantine* 53: 159–204.

———. 1935. "Decouverte d'ateliers de technique acheuleene dans les Tassili des Ajjers (Erg Tihodaine)." *Bulletin de la Société Préhistorique Française* 6: 358–362.

Roche, Abbé Jean. 1963. *L'Epipaléolithique Marocain.* 2 vols. Lisbon: Livraria Bertrand.

Roubet, C. 1979. *Economie pastorale préagricole en Algérie Orientale: Le Néolithique de tradition capsienne, exemple: l'Aurès.* Etudes Antiquités Africaines. Paris: CNRS.

Roubet, C., H. Hugot, and G. Souville. 1981. *Préhistoire africaine: Mélanges offerts au Doyen L. Balout.* Synthèse 6. Paris: Rech. Civilisations.

Sahnouni, M. 1987. *L'industrie sur galets du gisement villafranchien supérieur de Aïn Hanech.* Office des Publications Universitaires, Algiers.

———. 1991. "Étude comparative des galets taillés polyhédriques, subsphériques, et sphériques des gisements d'Aïn Hanech (Algérie orientale) et d'Olduvai (Tanzanie)." *L'Anthropologie* 97, no. 1: 51–68.

Saxon, E., Λ. E. Close, C. Cluzel, V. Morse, and N. J. Shackleton. 1975. "Results of Recent Investigations at Tamar Hat." *Libyca* 22: 49–91.

Sheppard, P. 1984. "A Study of Technological and Stylistic Variability in Capsian Stone Tool Assemblages." Ph.D. dissertation, University of Toronto, Canada.

———. 1987. *The Capsian of North Africa: Stylistic Variability in Capsian Stone Tool Assemblages.* BAR International Series, no. 353. Oxford: British Archaeological Reports.

———. 1990. "Soldiers and Bureaucrats: The Early History of Prehistoric Archaeology in the Maghreb." In *A History of African Archaeology,* pp. 173–188. Ed. P. Robertshaw. Portsmouth, NH: Heinemann.

———. 1992. "Snail Shells and Paradigms: The Role of the Logan Museum Expedition in North African Prehistory." In *Alonzo Pond and the Logan Museum Expedition to North Africa: The 1985 Beloit College Symposium,* pp. 33–44. Ed. L. B. Breitborde.

Siret, H., and L. Siret. 1887. *Les premiers âges du métal dans le Sud-Est de l'Espagne.* Louvain: Anvers.

Siret, L. 1924. "La taille de trapèzes tardenoisien." *Revue Anthropologique* 34: 115–134.

Souville, G. 1973. *Atlas préhistorique du Maroc, 1: Le Maroc Atlantique.* Paris: CNRS.

Thomas, H. 1977. *Géologie et paléontologie du gisement Acheuléen de l'Erg Tihodaine, Ahaggar—Saharien Algérien.* Mémoires du CRAPE, 27. Algiers: SNED.

Tixier, J. 1963. *Typologie de l'épipaléolithique du Maghreb.* Mémoires de CRAPE, no. 2. Paris: Arts et Métiers Graphiques.

———. 1967. "Procédés d'analyse et questions de terminologie concernant l'études des ensembles industriels du Paléolithique récent et de l'Epipaléolithique dans l'Afrique du Nord-Ouest." In *Background to Evolution in Africa,* pp. 771–820. Ed. W. W. Bishop and J. D. Clark. Chicago: University of Chicago.

Vaufrey, R. 1928. *Le Paléolithique Italien.* Mémoire 3. Paris: Archives de l'Institut de Paléontologie Humaine.

———. 1933a. "Notes sur le Capsien." *L'Anthropologie* 43: 457–483.

———. 1933b. "Stratigraphie et répartition des faciès capsiens." *L'Anthropologie* 43: 648–649.

———. 1955. *Préhistoire de l'Afrique.* Vol. 1, *Le Maghreb.* Paris: Marron.

Wengler, L. 1993. "Cultures préhistoriques et formations quaternaires du Maroc Oriental: Relations entre comportements et paléoenvironnements du Paléolithique Moyen." Doctoral thesis, University of Bordeaux 1.

Mallowan, Sir Max (1904–1978)

Born in London and educated at New College, Oxford, Max Mallowan claimed to have first excavated Victorian china shards when he was four years old in Bedford Gardens, Kensington. In 1925, after finishing university and hoping to avoid a career in the Indian Civil Service, he was taken on as a field assistant at the Iraqi site of Ur of the Chaldees by English archaeologist SIR LEONARD WOOLLEY. It was there that Mallowan met the novelist (Dame) Agatha Christie, whom he married in 1930.

Mallowan worked in MESOPOTAMIA with Woolley for five years and became field director for joint excavations by the BRITISH MUSEUM and the British School of Archaeology in Iraq, which had been founded by a legacy from GERTRUDE BELL. He excavated at the Quyunjik mound at NINEVEH, at the village site of Arpachiyah, and

Max Mallowan and his wife, Agatha Christie, leave their home in London at the start of their journey to northern Iraq for archaeological research. (Bettmann/Corbis)

then in Syria at Chagar Bazaar and Tell Brak, where he discovered third-millenium shrines and the Palace of Naram-Sin.

Between 1940 and 1945, he served as a liaison officer with the Allied forces in North Africa. In 1947, Mallowan took up the chair of western Asiatic archaeology at London University and returned to Iraq as director of the British School, where he began to excavate SIR AUSTEN HENRY LAYARD's great site of NIMRUD. Over the next twelve years the site provided a wealth of architectural remains, artifacts, and texts, which were published in the monumental two-volume work *Nimrud and Its Remains* (1966). In 1962, he returned to Oxford as a fellow of All Souls College, was vice-president of the British Academy in 1961–1962, and trustee of the British Museum from 1973 to 1978. He was editor of *Iraq* (1948–1971) and an advisory editor of *ANTIQUITY*. He became a commander of the Order of the British Empire in 1960 and was knighted in 1968.

Tim Murray

References
Mallowan, Max. 1977. *Mallowan's Memoirs.* London: Collins.

Malmer, Mats P. (1921–)
Malmer was born in Scania, SWEDEN, and studied prehistory at Lund University, receiving his Ph.D. in 1962. Malmer moved to Stockholm to become head of the Stone and Bronze Age Department at the Museum of National Antiquities in 1959, where he began to publish on archaeological methodology and theory while continuing extensive excavations. In 1970 he became professor of archaeology at Lund University, and in 1973 he was appointed to the chair of archaeology at the University of Stockholm.

Malmer is a key figure in discussions within Scandinavian archaeology on quantitative and taxonomic methods and the interpretation of archaeological data. His most significant influence has been to introduce and argue for the rational replacement of the predominant induc-

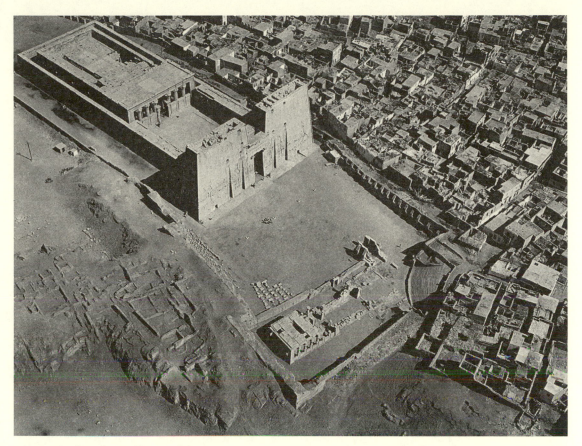

The Temple of Horus at Edfu, one of the most complete extant temples in Egypt and one of the many sites excavated by Auguste Mariette (Marilyn Bridges / CORBIS)

tive approach with a rational use of hypothesis and verification, a method in line with the hypothetico-deductive methods of logical positivism.

Malmer has also published in the area of rock carvings and museum studies, and his excavations of sites, and papers and reports on these, range from the Mesolithic to the medieval.

Marie Louise Stig Sørensen

References

For references, see *Encyclopedia of Archaeology: The Great Archaeologists, Vol. 1,* ed. Tim Murray (Santa Barbara, CA: ABC-CLIO, 1999), pp. 207–209.

Mariette, Auguste (1821–1881)

Auguste Mariette was born in Boulogne, France, and briefly lived and taught drawing and French in England. He developed an interest in Egyptology through the illustrations and notes of his cousin Nestor L'Hote, who had been a draftsman on JEAN-FRANÇOIS CHAMPOLLION's expedition to Egypt between 1828 and 1829. Mariette taught himself hieroglyphics from Champollion's grammar and dictionary, studied Coptic, and began working at the LOUVRE Museum, where he completed an inventory of all of the Egyptian inscriptions in the collection.

In 1850 the Louvre sent him to Egypt to collect papyri but instead he began excavating the Saqqara Serapeum, the huge subterranean gallery containing the sacred Apis bulls. He also located the Fifth Dynasty tomb of Ti at SAQQARA. In 1855 the Louvre appointed him Assistant Conservator and he returned to Egypt to excavate at Giza, Thebes, ABYDOS, and Elephantine.

In 1858 Mariette was appointed the first director of the new Egyptian Antiquities Service by the joint ruling Pashas of Egypt. The National Museum in Cairo was founded in that same year, the first museum of its kind in the Near East. As director of the service Mariette was in charge of all the excavations in Egypt, preventing the wholesale pillaging and plundering of sites, and ensuring that the museum began collecting, conserving, and preserving antiquities.

Mariette himself excavated more than thirty-five sites in Egypt over the next thirty years, which included 300 tombs at Saqqara and the clearance of the temples of Luxor, Medinet Habu, Dendera, and Edfu. Despite later criticism by WILLIAM MATTHEW FLINDERS PETRIE and GEORGE REISNER for his unscientific excavation techniques, Mariette's contributions to Egyptian archaeology were enormous. He published five volumes on *Dendera* (1875), and a catalogue of finds from *Abydos* (1880). He helped with the libretto for Verdi's great Egyptian opera *Aida,* which celebrated the opening of the Suez Canal. He was succeeded by Gaston Maspero.

Tim Murray

See also Egypt, Dynastic; French Archaeology in Egypt and the Middle East

References

France P. 1991. *The Rape of Egypt: How the Europeans Stripped Egypt of Its Heritage.* London: Barrie and Jenkins.

Marr, Nikolay
See Russia

Marshall, John Hubert (1876–1951)

John Hubert Marshall became director-general of the Archaeological Survey of India in 1902 and relinquished the position in 1928, although he continued to work for the survey in nonadministrative positions until 1934. When the English viceroy of India, Lord Curzon, arrived in India in 1900, he felt it necessary to formulate an integrated archaeological policy on the part of the government of India rather than depending on a few "surveyors" in the provinces for archaeological investigations and the Public Works Department for monument conservation. Curzon chose Marshall as the director-general for the formulation and execution of this policy.

Conservation policy was laid down in an of-ficial resolution in 1903 and subsequently incorporated in a manual (Marshall 1923), which still remains the bible of conservators in India. The main emphasis was on the preservation of the originality of the monument. The Ancient Monuments Preservation Act of 1904 empowered the government to acquire nonliving monuments (i.e., monuments not being used for current religious worship) for conservation, to prohibit traffic in antiquities both to and from British India, to provide for keeping antiquities in situ or in site museums, and, finally, to prohibit the excavation of ancient sites by irresponsible persons.

In 1906, the Archaeological Survey of India became a permanent central government department with an elaborate and well-controlled hierarchy of officials, various administrative circles, and a "branch" of epigraphy. What has happened since then is an increase in the number of "circles" and "branches" with consequent changes in territorial jurisdictions and responsibilities. However, the basic pattern laid down by Marshall has remained intact. The work of excavation and exploration was divided among circles, and reports appeared in the survey's Annual Reports, the publication of which—for the year 1902–1903—began in 1904. There was a well-defined policy regarding the basic research based on the exigencies of Indian conditions and best expressed by Marshall himself:

From the time of its reorganization in 1902 it has been the design of the Department to take in hand the excavation of the great buried cities of antiquity; but, before this design could be carried out, it was deemed advisable to re-examine some of the Buddhist sites which had already been partially uncovered, in order to coordinate the results obtained by earlier excavators and to check the often unreliable conclusions which they had drawn. For all practical purposes this part of the program was completed in 1910, by which time much solid work had been done at Charsada, Rajgir, Saheth-Maheth, Kasia, Sarnath, and other spots, and secure foundations laid for operations in another and more difficult field. Then followed the exploration of the town of Bhita, a small and well-defined site near Allahabad. Here, for the first time in India, well-preserved remains of houses, shops and streets, dating as far back as the Mauryan epoch, were laid bare, and numerous minor antiquities recovered, which help us materially to visualize the everyday life of the towns-people in those early days. These discoveries gave a promise of a still richer spoil awaiting the spade at the more important centers of ancient civilization; and this promise has since been amply fulfilled. At Taxila the results obtained have been epoch-making.

The site of Pataliputra, the capital of the great Mauryan empire, which was singled out for excavation simultaneously with that of Taxila, offers to the digger a far less favourable field than the latter; for it has been inundated for centuries past by the waters of the Ganges, and its monuments, if they have not altogether perished, are buried at a depth of 20 feet or more below the surface. (Marshall 1916, 24–27)

After 1924, the focus of archaeological effort shifted to INDUS VALLEY CIVILIZATION sites and to the excavations at Taxila, where Marshall himself excavated until the early 1930s. The method of excavation adopted by him and his officers may simply be described as excavating stratum by stratum, the component of each stratum being structures. Several publications by Marshall will always be regarded as being among the great volumes of Indian archaeology: the report of his detailed work at the Buddhist monument site of Sanchi (Marshall and Foucher 1983), the report of his work at Taxila (Marshall 1951), his analysis of Indus civilization (Marshall, ed. 1931), and last, but not least, his *Conservation Manual* (Marshall 1923).

Marshall also wrote two guidebooks on Sanchi, which contains Buddhist stupas from the third century B.C. onward, and a third guidebook on Taxila, which contains the ruins of Indian cities from pre-third-century-B.C. levels to early centuries A.D. The modern Archaeological Survey of India, and to some extent its counterparts elsewhere in SOUTH ASIA, have continued this tradition of producing definitive guidebooks on various monuments and sites under their care. The main emphasis of Marshall's interpretation of the Indus civilization was on its indigenousness and its intimate blending with the later Indian historic tradition.

The impact of John Marshall on the Indian archaeological scene will be clear from the tribute paid to him by a nationalist Indian archaeologist more than fifty years after his departure from the Indian archaeological scene:

The large exposed and conserved sites we see, the gardens around the monuments which we appreciate, the museums we enter and the objects we admire, the objects on which much of our own perception of our past is based—these are all intimately linked with the period which we here have called "the John Marshall period" in the history of Indian archaeology. It was an orderly and secure archaeological universe which, despite threats of retrenchment and financial stringency, went about its own way, building up the archaeological image of and ancient India in its manifold colours and nuances. (Chakrabarti 1988, 169–170)

Dilip Chakrabarti

References

Chakrabarti, D. K. 1988. *A History of Indian Archaeology from the Beginning to 1947*. Delhi. Munshiram Manoharlal Publishers.

Marshall, J. 1916. *Indian Archaeological Policy*. Calcutta.

———. 1923. *Conservation Manual*. Calcutta.

———. 1951 *Taxila*. Cambridge: Cambridge University Press.

Marshall, J., ed. 1931. *Mohenjodaro and the Indus Civilization*. London.

Marshall, J., and A. Foucher. 1983. *The Monuments of Sanchi*. Delhi.

Mason, Otis Tufton (1838–1908)

Mason was educated at Columbian College (now George Washington University), from which he graduated in 1861. Mason worked as the principal of a primary school and then in 1872 was appointed to the Department of Ethnology in the SMITHSONIAN INSTITUTION. He became one of the founders and leaders of American museum science and in 1902 was appointed head curator of anthropology.

Mason was especially interested in the technological aspects of human culture, and his papers on Native American basketry, textiles, and weapons were invaluable contributions to ethnology and are still important sources of information. He was also the author of two popular science books: *Woman's Share in Primitive Culture* (1894) and *The Origin of Inventions* (1895). In 1879 he was one of the founders of the Anthropological Society of Washington and he made many contributions to its journal *American Anthropologist*.

Tim Murray

See also United States of America, Prehistoric Archaeology

Masson, V. M.
See Russia

Maya Civilization

One of the great cultures of MESOAMERICA, Maya civilization extended throughout southern MEXICO and northern Central America. The Maya territory included what are now the southernmost Mexican states of Yucatán, Campeche, Quintana Roo, Tabasco, and Chiapas, as well as all of BELIZE and GUATEMALA and the westernmost parts of Honduras and EL SALVADOR.

In terms of geography the Maya area is often divided into three regions. The northern two regions (called the northern and southern lowlands, respectively) are formed by the low, limestone shelf that is the Yucatán Peninsula. Here the natural vegetation is tropical forest, featuring true high-canopy "jungle" in the south but becoming increasingly low and thorny as one moves to the northwest of the peninsula. Because of the porous limestone bedrock, there are few rivers in these regions. Particularly in the northern lowlands, access to water has traditionally been from *cenotes,* or natural sinkholes, in the limestone formations. The third region, the southern highlands, is much more mountainous, formed in large part by a string of volcanoes that lie along the Pacific coast.

The florescence of Maya civilization was the classic period, from A.D. 250 to 900, and it was centered in the Maya lowlands. Before this time, however, there was a long period of cultural development, both in the lowlands and in the southern highlands.

The history of human occupation in the Maya area stretches back at least 12,000 years, as shown by the scattered remains of hunting camps. A subsistence based on hunting and gathering lasted for millennia, but evidence suggests that by about 2000 B.C. there were farming villages in some parts of the Maya area and that by 1000 B.C. most of the Maya area was inhabited by village agriculturalists.

Until very recently, it was thought that the earliest development of more complex cultures in the Maya area began in the south—along the rich terrain of the Pacific piedmont and in the adjacent highlands of Guatemala and Chiapas—with temple-pyramids and carved stone monuments, as well as settlement and burial evidence indicating an increasingly stratified society. Although there certainly was impressive development in the southern highlands, it is now clear that there was also very early cultural development in the southern lowlands. In northern Guatemala, excavations at sites such as Nakbe and El Mirador have uncovered the remains of huge temple-pyramids built in the late centuries B.C. and possibly extending back as far as 600 B.C. By the late centuries B.C. there were numerous cities with massive public architecture in the southern Maya lowlands, and by the early centuries A.D. society was becoming increasingly stratified under hereditary rulers who probably gained most of their power initially through their reputations as spiritual leaders and their ability to mediate with the supernatural world on behalf of their people. Huge mask panels modeled in stucco adorned the front facades of many pyramids: these incorporated symbols of kingship on heads that were surrounded by cosmological symbolism. The stage was set for the greatest florescence of Maya civilization—the classic period.

The classic period was initially defined by the span of time during which carved stone monuments incorporating hieroglyphic dates were erected at a host of Maya cities. Conventionally, the period ranges from A.D. 250 to 900. During this time dozens of cities grew up, each with its own hereditary kings and each controlling a territory usually not more than about 50 kilometers in diameter. These city-states, as they have been called by some scholars, were organized into wide-ranging alliance networks.

Not all of the earlier great cities survived into classic times: El Mirador and Nakbe, for example, collapsed in late-preclassic times. Two cities that apparently capitalized on the collapse of the others (if they were not directly responsible for it) were TIKAL and Kalak'mul (Calakmul); in classic times they grew to dominate the Maya world, and they were deadly enemies. Hieroglyphic records show how most other sites were organized into either the Tikal or Kalak'mul spheres, and battles were continually taking place between sites on either side of the divide in a kind of "proxy" war. Occasionally there were major wars that could even wreak havoc on Tikal and Kalak'mul themselves. In A.D. 562 the city of Caracol, under the aegis of Kalak'mul, attacked Tikal, and its city was sacked. Tikal was again attacked in A.D. 679, but not too long afterward, in A.D. 695, Tikal reasserted its power by capturing and sacrificing the king of Kalak'mul.

Until the 1970s most scholars assumed that Maya subsistence was based solely on the "slash-and-burn" system of agriculture that is widespread in the Yucatán Peninsula today. It is now clear, however, that the Maya had a wide range of agricultural techniques, including more intensive "raised-field" agriculture, agricultural terracing, and extensive backyard gardens. The Maya had few domesticated animals (with dogs, an important food source, and turkeys chief among them), but they augmented their diet through hunting and fishing. It may seem strange that water was a problem in such a wet environment, but in many sites it was, due to the porous limestone bedrock and the general lack of groundwater. The Maya solved the problem by constructing reservoirs—lining the "borrow pits" they used for quarrying their construction stone and underground cisterns with lime plaster.

Modern tourists are attracted to the sites of ancient Maya cities because of the distinct character each possesses. Although they all have many features in common, individual site layout and architecture vary widely. Cities have an open plan, with temple-pyramids and palaces arranged around plazas. Further out from the center, elite and commoner residential compounds also incorporate buildings arranged around courtyards, and these are scattered across the landscape (usually on higher, well-drained terrain) with open spaces between them that would have been used for household gardens.

The formal public architecture and art of classic Maya centers is prodigious. From great temple-pyramids such as those at Tikal to more intimate buildings such as those of the royal palace at PALENQUE, there is almost an infinite variety of styles. Maya art, too, had many different forms and styles, from huge public monuments (stelae) erected in plazas to recount the exploits of the kings to smaller, beautifully carved jades worn by individuals in life and buried with them after death.

One of the greatest features of Maya civilization is its hieroglyphic writing system. Inscriptions were carved on stone and wood, modeled in stucco, and painted on murals and ceramics; several thousand inscriptions survive, most of them from the classic period spanning from about A.D. 200 to 900. Increasingly over the past few decades, Maya glyphs, as they are called, have been translated by epigraphers—to the point that over 90 percent of most texts can now be read. Mayan hieroglyphic inscriptions address a variety of subjects. Most of the stone monument texts are framed in the political history of the various city-states, detailing the exploits of the kings and momentous events in the history of the state. Other inscriptions describe various rituals and ceremonies conducted, in most cases, by the king. Still others are more personal, such as the "name tagging" of ceramic vessels and other objects.

One of the most debated aspects of Maya archaeology is the collapse of classic Maya civilization. The facts are clear. During the ninth century A.D., city after city in the southern Maya lowlands collapsed. Monuments ceased to be carved, building construction was stopped (sometimes in the middle of a project), and there is evidence of a massive population drop (as much as 90 percent over a century) in some cities. In effect, the lights went out all over the

Mayan codex section from the Mayan-Troano-Codex (Image Select)

peninsula in cities that had flourished for hundreds of years.

Over the decades many causes have been proposed to explain this societal and demographic collapse, from earthquakes, hurricanes, floods, or droughts to peasant revolt or civil war. Recent research has revealed that the collapse was probably the result of a combination of factors that snowballed to the point at which they overwhelmed classic Maya society. Ecological problems and warfare seem to have been foremost among these factors.

Evidence shows there were massive ecological problems in the Maya lowlands during the eighth and ninth centuries A.D., when deforestation appears to have caused sheet erosion in some regions; no doubt, changes to rainfall patterns occurred as well. Skeletal evidence indicates that dietary deficiency (reflecting both a growing population and an inadequate supply of food resources to support that growth) was an increasing problem by the beginning of the eighth century. The situation was critical by the ninth century.

There is now evidence that warfare was endemic in the Maya lowlands, especially during the second half of the classic period. In large part this was due to the fierce rivalry between polities, but it also seems that an increasing factor in the violence was competition over resources, including food. Evidence even suggests there were fortified maize fields by late in the classic period.

Some scholars have argued that the word *collapse* is, in fact, inappropriate for describing the momentous events of the ninth century in the Maya lowlands. It is clear that the century saw the demise of the ruling elites who had dominated Maya society for the previous 700 years or longer: stone monuments documenting royal histories were no longer carved, and some palaces were sacked. In certain sites, such as Tikal, there is also evidence of massive population loss, but whether this was due to warfare and such factors as endemic disease or to outmigration is not clear. What is clear, however, is that in many parts of the Maya lowlands, life continued. In Belize the effects of the "collapse" do not seem to have been so severe, but it is

northern Yucatán where most of the dramatic postclassic developments took place.

In late-classic times there were many large cities in northern Yucatán. One of them, CHICHÉN ITZÁ, would come to dominate most of the northern part of the peninsula for the terminal classic period, and some scholars extend this site's dominance as far as A.D. 1200. After the decline of Chichén Itzá, politics in the northern peninsula were again factionalized until a new city arose to dominate the area. This was the city of Mayapan, which flourished between about A.D. 1280 and 1450. Following the collapse of Mayapan, which documentary sources of the sixteenth century ascribe to internal revolt, the peninsula again reverted to petty competing kingdoms. This was the situation that the Spaniards encountered when they arrived on the scene in the early 1500s. It was also a factor in the Spaniards' conquest of Yucatán. It took the Spaniards over twenty years to gain a secure foothold in northern Yucatán, and one kingdom in the central part of the peninsula remained independent, practicing traditional Maya ceremonies (including human sacrifice) until 1697.

The heritage of classic Maya civilization is still very much alive. Approximately seven million Maya people still live in their ancient homeland, and two dozen Mayan languages continue to be spoken today. In some cases Maya people continue to practice traditional rituals, such as house dedication ceremonies, that are almost identical with those described in ancient hieroglyphic texts.

Peter Mathews

See also French Archaeology in the Americas; Maya Epigraphy

References

Schele, L., and P. Mathews. 1998. *The Code of Kings: The Language of Seven Sacred Maya Temples and Tombs.* New York: Scribners.

Maya Epigraphy

Among the many achievements of MAYA CIVILIZATION was the development of a writing system. Maya writing, which was probably stimulated by the slightly earlier OLMEC script, was the most complete expression of a writing system devised by any of the civilizations of MESOAMERICA. The decipherment process, to which numerous scholars have contributed over many decades, has been a gradual one, but the language is now largely deciphered and understood.

The history of research into Maya epigraphy started with a Spanish priest named Diego de Landa, who wrote a treatise on the Maya of northern Yucatán in the mid-sixteenth century. He included a brief but garbled account of Maya writing—the closest thing we have to a Rosetta stone for the Maya script. Although Landa completely misunderstood the nature of the script (he assumed it was an alphabetic system, when in fact it is composed of syllable signs and word signs), he did elicit from an informant some forty signs and their (approximate) phonetic value.

Little more was done with the script until the mid-eighteenth century. At that time explorers were beginning to penetrate the thick tropical forest of the Yucatán Peninsula, where they would discover ruined cities of classic Maya civilization. One of these explorers, JOHN LLOYD STEPHENS, produced some best-selling "travel books" that were beautifully illustrated by his artist companion, FREDERICK CATHERWOOD. These books stimulated other explorers to follow in their footsteps, and by the end of the nineteenth century most of the great classic Maya cities had been discovered. Meanwhile, discoveries of another sort were being made in Europe: three painted books or codices (at least one of which was probably included in treasure sent by Hernán Cortés to the king of Spain) were rediscovered, and it was recognized that they were written in Maya script. By 1900 several Maya sites had been explored quite scientifically, and their stone monuments and inscriptions were faithfully recorded in photographs and drawings. The stage was set for the decipherment process to begin.

The earliest attempts at decipherment took two directions. One involved an intensive analysis of the chronological component of Maya texts. Most Maya inscriptions have a calendrical framework in which dates are recorded at the beginning of sentences. Many of the details of the calendar were known from writers such as Landa and also from the remnants of the calendar that have survived to the present day. Although the Maya calendar is quite complex, with several intermeshing cyclical counts, it was almost completely deciphered by 1900.

The other direction of research involved non-calendrical glyphs. The focus (especially at first) was on the codices, and there was much discussion concerning the nature of the script. Early on it was determined that the script was not alphabetic. But was it syllabic or logographic in nature? Between 1890 and 1914, as intense discussion on this issue continued, much of the general content of the codices was worked out, and signs were read correctly in some cases.

By the beginning of the twentieth century the recently deciphered calendrical component of Maya writing dovetailed nicely with the new phase of Maya research: large-scale excavations of classic Maya sites by prominent research institutions, especially ones based in the United States. Chronology, of course, was a major component of this work, and since the carved Maya monuments usually contained dates that were assumed to be contemporary with their carving, the race was on to find more and more monuments. Hundreds of new inscriptions were discovered during the first half of the twentieth century, and they provided the chronological framework for the new excavations (even though the correlation between the Maya and Christian calendars was not completely agreed upon during these decades).

Gradually, the dates recorded on the carved monuments became all-consuming to scholars, many of whom came to believe that dates were all that the inscriptions contained. Depicting the Maya as a society of rural peasant farmers watched over by small groups of ascetic calendar priests, these scholars contended that it would have been sacrilegious to record anything other than the calendar (personal histories, for example) in Maya texts.

This view was to change dramatically at the end of the 1950s, largely through the work of two researchers. In 1958 the Mexican scholar Heinrich Berlin published two articles in which he identified glyphs that referred in some way to individual Maya cities. The following year he

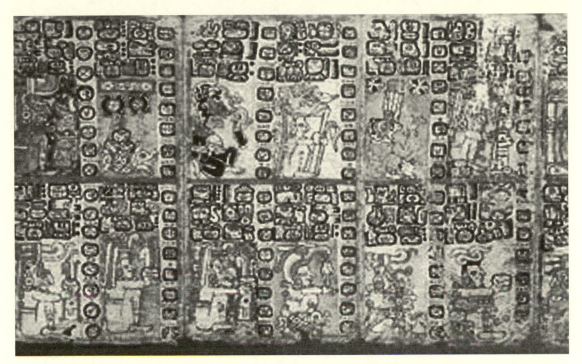

Mayan lintel listing the nine generations of rulers at Yaxchilan ca. A.D. 450–550 (Image Select)

isolated personal-name glyphs carved in a royal tomb at PALENQUE. It was beginning to appear that history was indeed recorded in the Maya hieroglyphs. In 1960 the issue was put beyond doubt with the publication of a brilliant paper by the U.S. scholar TATIANA PROSKOURIAKOFF. This paper dealt principally with the inscriptions from the site of Piedras Negras: Proskouriakoff showed that the carved stone monuments were grouped into "sets," each of which addressed the reign of an individual king. She identified birth and coronation glyphs and also showed that the same pattern seemed to occur in other classic Maya sites. Much of the work in the decades following the publication of Proskouriakoff's paper has focused on deciphering the exploits of the various Maya kings and their relationships—both peaceful and bellicose—with one another.

Meanwhile, advances were being made on another front. By the early 1950s a thorny issue concerning Maya writing was being revisited—whether the script was purely logographic (made up of word signs) or whether it contained syllabic signs. On two previous occasions, in the 1890s and 1930s, proponents of

"phoneticism"—who believed that syllabic signs were a component of Maya script—had lost the debate. Now a young Russian scholar, Yuri Knorosov, was renewing the battle. He had an advantage over earlier researchers in that he had studied other writing systems and thus knew the kinds of features and structures to expect in ancient scripts. He argued that Maya script contained both logograms and syllabic signs and (acknowledging earlier work) that Landa's "alphabet" was in fact primarily a list of syllabic signs corresponding to the pronunciation of the Spanish letters Landa had elicited. In this way—and by using examples drawn mostly from the codices—Knorosov proposed correct readings of many Maya syllabic signs; he also gave the first plausible account of the structure of Maya writing. Although his work was heavily criticized by several scholars (led by Sir Eric Thompson), his arguments gradually gained favor, and today they form the basis on which the very successful phonetic decipherment of Maya writing has been made.

In many ways research since the 1960s has been a refinement and extension of the foundations laid by Proskouriakoff, Berlin, and

Knorosov, but even since the 1960s tremendous advances have been made. Syllabic readings of some 150 signs have been deciphered, and the majority of logograms can also be read, in large part because they are often accompanied by "phonetic complements" that give partial phonetic clues to their reading. Most of the Maya inscriptions in stone, wood, and other media can be almost completely read in ancient Mayan and translated. Although many contain erudite references to long-lost rituals and esoteric ceremonies, they are increasingly understood with the aid of archaeological findings, ethnohistorical and ethnographical parallels, and, in some cases, knowledge of the practices of contemporary Maya.

The Maya hieroglyphs were written over almost 2,000 years. The script contains about 800 different signs, some 400 of which were in use at any one time. Of these, between one-quarter and one-third were syllabic signs, the rest being logograms. Inscriptions were generally arranged in a system of double columns, in which the material would be read from left to right and top to bottom within two columns of text, before proceeding to the next two columns on the right. The script is written predominantly in one language (called Eastern Cholan), which is most closely related to a subgroup of Mayan languages still spoken across the base of the Yucatán Peninsula. The script was later adopted and used for inscriptions in at least one other language (Yucatec Mayan, still spoken in the northern half of the peninsula).

Most of the surviving Maya inscriptions are historical in general content, although they also contain a wealth of information on sociopolitical and geopolitical structure as well as details of ceremonies and rituals. Four Maya bark-paper books survive; they deal principally with astronomical and astrological matters. Various sixteenth-century commentators said the script was used to record information on history, genealogy, prophecy, maps, trade and tribute, astronomy, astrology, ritual and religious ceremonies, mythology, songs and poetry, and disease and medicine. Most of these topics are at least touched upon in the corpus of Maya hieroglyphic inscriptions that survives as testimony to the wonderful achievements of this ancient American civilization.

Peter Mathews

References

Coe, M. 1992. *Breaking the Maya Code*. London: Thames and Hudson.

McBurney, Charles (1914–1979)

Charles McBurney was a distinguished Paleolithic archaeologist who spent his entire professional career at Cambridge University, apart from his war service in North Africa—an experience that led him to return to Libya, where he did much of his fieldwork.

McBurney was born in the United States and lived in Stockbridge, Massachusetts. He was privately educated in Europe before going to Cambridge in 1933, where he studied under DOROTHY GARROD, Miles Burkitt, and GRAHAME CLARK. After graduating he began a doctoral dissertation on the Lower Paleolithic of Europe, embracing the major geographic study of the distribution of the Acheulean or hand-axe industries. The principal conclusions of this work were published in 1950.

World War II shaped much of McBurney's career. After its conclusion he returned to Cyrenaica, in Libya, to work with the geologist Richard Hey, and he discovered numbers of Mousterian, Aterian, and Upper Paleolithic sites. Henceforth, his interests were firmly fixed on this period, covering the last 150,000 years, although he remained highly conversant with problems of the Lower Paleolithic. In Cyrenaica McBurney first excavated the open site of Hajj Creiem and the cave of Hagfet et Dabba, where he found a new industry that he named the Dabban. Then, in 1948, he found the great cave that most attracted his attention: the HAUA FTEAH near the coast in northern Cyrenaica. This vast sinkhole, 60 meters in diameter, was large enough to contain the whole camp. Excavations proceeded to a depth of 13 meters. The Haua Fteah became one of two very major pieces of fieldwork in McBurney's career, and it presented a classic archaeological sequence through the last glaciation. Its publication in monograph form in 1967 was a signal achievement. The site included hominid remains but is mainly known for its Middle and Upper Paleolithic sequences. McBurney related it to the eastern Mediterranean and the cave sequence of Israel. He regarded the enigmatic pre-Aurignacian blade industry as a precursor of the Upper Paleolithic but also noted significant differences.

The Upper Paleolithic proper began with the Dabban and extended through great depths of Oranian (Iberomaurusian) deposits. McBurney was able to show that the coastal sequence was clearly different from those of the inland. He was thus one of the first archaeologists to document clearly and come to terms with contemporary rather than evolutionary variation in a Paleolithic region and to provide a possible cultural explanation for it.

These insights show that McBurney, who was sometimes described as a traditionalist with regard to Paleolithic interpretation, was greatly ahead of his time in many ways. His cultural ideas were more consonant with the "New Archaeology" than with any typecast view. Rather than having a supposed traditionalist's notion of constant, gradual change, McBurney was particularly concerned with measuring rates of change. He therefore invested heavily in radiocarbon dates for calibrating the Haua Fteah sequence. The technique was new but well applied by H. de Vries at Groningen University.

McBurney was among the first Paleolithic archaeologists to favor quantitative techniques for the description of stone industries. Although his enthusiasm for statistical analysis was not shared by all his contemporaries, his suspicion of typologies, which he felt were not objectively applied, was farsighted. His skepticism about applications of the Bordes typology has been borne out by more recent work in Europe. His statistical approach is best exemplified by his analyses of the stone industries and faunal remains from the cave of Ali Tappeh in Iran near the Black Sea.

McBurney's other fieldwork was wide-ranging, including, for example, that on the Lower Paleolithic at Hoxne, Suffolk. He carried out a reconnaissance of British Upper Paleolithic sites but was more preoccupied with the origins of the Upper Paleolithic. These he felt lay even far-ther east than the great sequences investigated by Garrod and others in Palestine. He led expeditions to Iran and Afghanistan on this search, but difficulties of time, logistics, and politics prevented him from excavating early deposits. Modern research has shown the earliest Upper Paleolithic emerging as technical change arising in the Negev and Lebanon.

His last great piece of fieldwork, parallel to that at Haua Fteah, was in the cave of La Cotte de Saint Brelade on the island of Jersey in the English Channel. This was carried out as a training excavation for the Cambridge Department of Archaeology over many successive Easter vacations and published posthumously under the editorship of P. Callow and K. Scott.

McBurney's enthusiasm for the Paleolithic was tremendous and on a par with that of J. DESMOND CLARK for African prehistory. He had great influence, although relatively few people completed Ph.D.'s under his supervision. His firm and even uncompromising views distanced him from some potential followers of Paleolithic archaeology at a time when there was a great attraction to the economic prehistory championed by ERIC HIGGS at Cambridge as a rival calling. Yet McBurney's intellectual rigor, which his students sometimes found restrictive, stimulated free thinking and scientific honesty. His former students speak fondly of him and carry forward many of his principles but have not been disciples in any strict sense.

He had no love of theory for its own sake. McBurney's distinction is that he is remembered not for a typology but for two great excavations and a set of principles—a scientific code of practice for handling lithic material and cultural problems. He saw no connection between archaeology and social anthropology as practiced at Cambridge but was a supporter of ethnographic studies and ethno-archaeology. He had a great respect for the Soviet archaeologist SEGEI SEMENOV and worked hard to introduce microwear studies to Britain. These started to reach fruition through the work of his own students, such as Derek Roe and GLYN ISAAC. This observation provides some indication of McBurney's long-term influence. His was approximately the third generation of Paleolithic archaeologists since the beginnings laid by JACQUES BOUCHER DE PERTHES and ÉDOUARD LARTET; his greatest achievement is not so much to have taught a fourth generation but to have sewn ideas and strongly inspired a successor generation that is broadly scattered around the world.

John Gowlett

See also Africa, Francophone; Africa, Sahara; Africa, Sudanic Kingdoms; Britain: Prehistoric Archaeology

References

For references, see *Encyclopedia of Archaeology: The Great Archaeologists, Vol. 2*, ed. Tim Murray (Santa Barbara, CA: ABC-CLIO, 1999), p. 726.

McCarthy, Fred D. (1905–1997)

Although Fred McCarthy spent the bulk of his career at the Australian Museum in Sydney, his interests extended beyond museum work to include foundational studies in Australian prehistoric archaeology, comparative archaeological research in INDONESIA, ethnographic fieldwork in Arnhem Land and Cape York (both in Australia), and the key administrative role of first principal of the Australian Institute of Aboriginal Studies. McCarthy is most famous as the excavator of the Lapstone Creek rock shelter in the Blue Mountains outside of Sydney (1935–1936), where the reality of cultural change in prehistoric Australia was demonstrated, and as a stone tool typologist with the publication (with Elsie Bramell and H. V. V. Noone) of *The Stone Implements of Australia* (1946). McCarthy was awarded an Honorary Doctor of Science by the Australian National University in 1980.

Tim Murray

References

Specht, J. 1993. *F. D. McCarthy, Commemorative Papers (Archaeology, Anthropology, Rock Art).* Sydney: Australian Museum.

Meadowcroft Rock Shelter

Meadowcroft is a rock shelter in southwestern Pennsylvania (United States) with a long series of stratified, multicomponent deposits spanning a period from 14000 B.C. to ca. A.D. 18. Fortu-nately, Meadowcroft is not subject to weathering degradation due to freezing and thawing, which can either preserve or destroy the archaeological record, as limestone rock shelters often are. Meadowcroft is oriented east-west with a southern exposure about 15 meters above Cross Creek, a tributary of the Ohio River. The overhang is 13 meters above the present floor. Local springs are abundant and the prevailing wind across the shelter opening ventilates smoke and insects.

The environment surrounding Meadowcroft was favorable to both occupation and preservation 16,000 years ago. The site was occupied intermittently by groups representing all major cultural stages in North America and has some of the earliest reliable evidence of people in North America. The climate indicated by pollen studies suggests an open spruce/pine forest with some open tundra and little hardwoods for occupation at around 16,000 years ago. Elsewhere in similar environments caribou and mastodon would be subsistence mainstays, but there are no extinct Pleistocene fauna at Meadowcroft. This raises the question of whether the age of the site dates to the Holocene or whether it was used during a warmer climate that supported different species.

Meadowcroft is the oldest documented site for Paleo-Indian occupation. The site contains lithic blades dating to 14,000 years ago, following migration over the Bering Strait. Excavation begun in 1973 by Adovasio et al. began with mapping and trenching; all artifacts were processed and labeled on site. The most common cultural features found were firepits, ash and charcoal lenses, firefloors, and refuse or storage pits. A total of seventy samples were prepared for radiocarbon DATING from the excavation at that time, and some forty more have been obtained since. The radiocarbon dating confirms an early (pre-Clovis) occupation of 14,000 years ago. Other artifacts recovered include lithic, bone, wood, shell, basketry, cordage, and ceramic materials. The lithic collection is not only the earliest securely dated collection of tools in eastern North America, but also among the earliest reliably dated assemblages recovered in the Western Hemisphere. Lithic production at the site shows evidence of highly skilled craftsmen in the manufacture of flaked stone implements. In addition to lithics, faunal remains include animal bone (deer, elk, bear, raccoon, and the nocturnal flying squirrel), mollusk shells, feathers, claws, insect carapaces, egg shells, and fish scales—up to 117 species in all.

All of the data recovered from Meadowcroft suggest its use as a station for hunting, collecting, and food processing. The significance of the rock shelter in North American archaeology has necessitated close scrutiny of the available data, particularly the concern of contamination of radiocarbon samples. Consensus calls for ongoing clarification of dating the rock shelter, yet the general antiquity of the site is not in question. While numerous studies compare Meadowcroft to related assemblages across North America, a final report has yet to be published.

Danielle Greene

See also Lithic Analysis; United States of America, Prehistoric Archaeology

References

Bonnichsen, Robson, and Karen L. Turnmire. 1999. *Ice Age People of North America: Environments, Origins, and Adaptations.* Corvallis: Oregon State University Press for the Center for the Study of the First Americans.

Dillehay, Tom D., and David J. Meltzer. 1991. *The First Americans: Search and Research.* Boca Raton, FL: CRC Press.

Ericson, Jonathon E., R. E. Taylor, and Rainer Berger, eds. 1982. *Peopling of the New World.* Los Altos, CA: Ballena Press.

Thomas, David Hurst. 1989. *Archaeology.* Fort Worth: Holt, Rinehart and Winston.

Medieval Archaeology in Europe
Introduction

Medieval archaeology as a subject with its own identity is a relatively recent phenomenon, but the study of the material culture of the Middle Ages has a much longer history, set in the context of a series of cognate disciplines. This fact is important for understanding the development of the subject as many of the areas of concern and types of research questions have derived from these other disciplines. Moreover, just as

Roman archaeology was often undertaken by people who had a background and interest in classical sources, with the inevitable biases in the evidence collected and researched, the same is the case with medieval archaeology. Medieval archaeology as a distinct academic discipline taught through defined modules and courses in universities is an even more recent phenomenon, as yet present in only some European countries, with the result that much of medieval archaeology is practiced by people trained in other branches of archaeology or in cognate disciplines. This situation continues to affect the research questions and priorities in the subject, although medieval archaeology has matured considerably over the last half century.

Many of the major structures and sites of importance in medieval archaeology have never been abandoned or forgotten and continue in use, albeit often in a very different context. These range from churches and cathedrals to castles and palaces and more mundane structures such as water mills, bridges, and field systems. Moreover, many portable artifacts, which tend to have belonged to the elite, have never entered the archaeological record but have continued to serve a function to the present day. These include religious items such as illuminated manuscripts, reliquaries, and church plate and secular objects such as royal regalia, armor, and weaponry. A great deal of the study of the material culture of the Middle Ages has been undertaken by architectural historians, art historians, historical geographers, and historians of particular activities such as naval or military historians, and numismatists. To varying degrees these scholars have incorporated the primary study of material evidence into their research and even have carried out excavations to reveal such remains.

Medieval archaeology has two separate traditions, early and late. The first is associated with the early Middle Ages, also often called the migration period, which ran from the end of the Roman period in those areas affected by the Roman Empire until the eleventh to thirteenth centuries A.D. depending on the region. The second is concerned with the late Middle Ages when the power of the international church and the developing structures of feudalism created a different set of social and economic dynamics and a very different range of archaeological evidence. In all areas, the early and later traditions of medieval archaeology have been treated separately, and in many regions the early medieval phase has been more closely linked with later prehistory. There are three main reasons for this division, which are worth exploring. All three play a part in all regions and countries, but in different situations their relative importance has varied. In many countries there has been discussion of these issues, and debates about the value or impediment that such a set of attitudes and structures creates, and it is in the context of these debates that the subject area of medieval archaeology was formed.

The first reason for the division between early and late medieval derives from the remote past and relates to broad cultural influences across the European continent. There was not the same Roman period break in cultural chronologies north of the Rhine and the Danube that occurred to the south, where the Roman Empire held greater sway. Where there was no significant Roman horizon (that is, artifacts that denote behavioral and cultural changes), apart from imported prestige goods, cultural groups whose burials often contained grave goods and settlements consisting of defended hilltops and lowland settlements with only timber structures (which leave little obvious surface remains) continued right up to the arrival of Christianity and developed feudalism in the second millennium A.D. Even where there was Roman political and cultural control, this control broke down and was replaced with a far less complex socioeconomic system, which left evidence far more similar in its characteristics to that of the late Iron Age cultures that were spread across Europe before the Roman Empire.

Indeed, the dating and identification of the post-Roman phases became clear to antiquarians across Europe only in the mid-nineteenth century. This period can be linked with movements of populations across Europe, the collapse of the complex Roman Empire, and in the succeeding centuries the development of smaller and then ever-larger kingdoms, which were the genesis of the modern European states. The early medieval evidence is much more similar in the types of settlement, cemetery, and artifactual evidence to that from late prehistory than to the evidence from the Roman or later Middle Ages.

The second reason for the division of the subject into early and late medieval units relates to nineteenth-century attitudes toward the past. This reason is directly linked to the remains, particularly the difference between the pagan, unsophisticated early medieval remains and the cultured, Christian remains of the later Middle Ages. Interestingly, in areas such as Ireland where Roman influence was irrelevant, the early medieval period was essentially Christian and the archaeology is linked to the later medieval rather than to the prehistoric. This division between pagan/barbarian and Christian/civilized Europe has implications that have been, and continue to be, played out through history in legislation, state administrative structures, museum responsibilities, and academic teaching and research.

The third reason relates to documentation and attitudes of both nonmedieval archaeologists and scholars from other disciplines such as history. Archaeology of any note has often been seen as being credible only within a prehistoric or proto-historic period. When documents become more numerous, it has often been thought that archaeology no longer had a role, except, perhaps, to provide illustrative material or to fill in a few gaps in the written documentation. This attitude pervades much of European scholarship to this day and until recently was even more widespread. Medieval archaeologists have had to fight this definition of archaeology, and this fight has occurred mainly in the context of later medieval archaeology. Still, postmedieval and historical archaeologists have also had this mission.

Given the paucity of texts for the early medieval period, archaeology has often been recognized as having a role there, although in relatively well-documented areas such as Ireland some historians completely ignore or denigrate the contribution that any study of material culture can make. Documentary sources are more plentiful for the later Middle Ages (though very often they are limited in their range of subject matter), which means that much prejudice still remains concerning the archaeology of this period. For example, in Belgian-Dutch bibliographical reviews, archaeology is included only up to the ninth century A.D. In many countries, medieval archaeology refers only to the later Middle Ages, though gradually the term *medieval* is being applied to both early and late periods.

The development of early and later medieval archaeology needs to be distinguished given the diverse attitudes to each held in the past. Different traditions developed in each country, often related to the relative visibility of remains and the associations of structures and artifacts with the development of nation states and national identities, although sometimes traditions have been shaped by the influence of particular individuals and their concerns. Nevertheless, each subject area can be followed through a series of phases that, with roughly the same chronologies, can be traced across much of Europe.

Early Descriptions and Investigations

Medieval archaeology in one sense began in the Middle Ages when excavations were made to recover the physical remains and associated belongings of saints, although both the methods and motivations would be alien to archaeologists today. Most early antiquarian records deal with prehistoric and Roman antiquities, but some early medieval material was noted. In England, the works of John Leland, WILLIAM CAMDEN, and WILLIAM STUKELEY all included a small amount of medieval ecclesiastical material. Scandinavian scholars, including Henrik Rantzau, JOHAN BURE, and OLE WORM, recorded runestones and burial monuments.

One of the most notable discoveries was that of the Frankish King Childeric's grave, found in 1653 in Tournai, Belgium, at the church of St. Brice. A range of artifacts, including the king's seal ring, were recovered and published by Jean-Jacob Chifflet in 1655. Unfortunately, much of the material was stolen in 1831 and has never been recovered. It was in the eighteenth and the first part of the nineteenth century that medieval archaeological remains became of increasing interest, although the period of the En-

lightenment in the eighteenth century encouraged an emphasis on classical ruins at the expense of those from the Middle Ages.

In early medieval archaeology, the focus was on the recovery of grave goods, largely from chance discoveries of unmarked cemeteries on the Continent, and recovery was sometimes followed by more systematic digging. Barrows attracted the attention of antiquarians, and while many had prehistoric origins, some were early medieval in date and others had been reused at that time and contained early medieval burials. Some of the earliest excavations conducted with some scientific rigor were those by the antiquarian and scholar Professor Olaf Rudbeck at Old Uppsala, SWEDEN, in the late-seventeenth century. In England during the early eighteenth century Saxon barrows were unearthed in Kent; at the time they were considered casualties of Caesar's invasion. Later in the century the antiquarians Bryan Faussett and James Douglass were active in excavating barrows and tumuli; they also kept excellent records, and their archives and some finds are now in British museums. Work in Wiltshire was subsequently carried out in style by WILLIAM CUNNINGTON and RICHARD COLT HOARE.

With the rise of the Romantic movement during the early nineteenth century, medieval ruins attracted much more attention than ever before, although this attention did not often lead to greater study. Rather, the neglected structures were to create an impact and stir the emotions, and some were modified by additions or selective demolition to heighten their effect, although some clearance of rubble did take place, as with the Cistercian abbeys of Tintern in Wales and Fountains in England. This increased awareness did lead to more serious research in some cases, such as the discovery of architectural fragments and grave slabs, and made such sites well known to subsequent generations. More obviously, archaeological interest relating to later medieval evidence at this time was also engaged with regard to remains, either ruins or buildings, still in use. In DENMARK, churches were recorded by N. L. Høyen, and in Sweden, P. Härnquist made a study of a Franciscan convent before a new building was constructed on top of it, but such work was exceptional for the time. In England, Britton and Rickman identified the major styles of architecture and placed them in chronological sequence.

An Antiquarian Structure

Two important parallel developments in the nineteenth century affected the development of the various strands of medieval archaeology. One was the establishment of national and local societies with an interest in archaeology, and the other was the development of legislation to protect monuments and (of special importance for later medieval archaeology) buildings such as abbeys and castles. Universities did not develop a great interest in medieval archaeology at this stage, although a chair in the archaeology and history of medieval art was established at the University of Cracow (in Poland) in 1866.

More national societies developed to enlarge the small number, such as the SOCIETY OF ANTIQUARIES OF LONDON, that had been founded in the later eighteenth century, and many of them included early and later medieval archaeology within their interests. Examples include the British Archaeological Association for the Encouragement and Prosecution of Researches into the Arts and Monuments of the Early Middle Ages, founded in 1843, which soon had 1,200 members. The following year, the Society for the Preservation of Norwegian Antiquities was established, marking the change in that country to a more organized attitude to medieval archaeology. The joint German historical and antiquarian societies agreed in 1852 to found two museums, an act that institutionalized the divide between early and late medieval archaeology. Early medieval archaeology was within the purview of the Central Roman and Germanic Museum in Mainz, which also dealt with prehistoric and Roman material, and late medieval evidence was the responsibility of the Germanic National Museum established in Nuremberg for Christian German material with an emphasis on high art linked to architecture.

By the middle of the nineteenth century, many regions across Europe had or were establishing local museums and antiquarian societies. Members of the landed gentry and minor aris-tocracy, professional classes, and the more intellectual of the merchant and industrial classes were able to share their interest in the past, of which the medieval was a part and often a very visible one. Much of the archaeology had direct links with the present ecclesiastical structures and the estates and castles of the elite; other elements related to earlier medieval evidence associated with ethnic groups that had migrated and established the precursors of the developing nation states. In Germany, local societies began to emerge in the 1820s, and the Christian Middle Ages became a popular subject of interest in antiquarian circles, following on from developing interests in classical and prehistoric archaeology. Local societies in Italy began to form in the later nineteenth century, though medieval material was of only marginal interest in that country.

Merovingian cemeteries were excavated across FRANCE, often because of accidental discoveries caused by building work, and the finds were recorded by local antiquarian societies and sometimes partially published in their proceedings. Despite the seventeenth-century Childeric find, there was much doubt as to the dates and cultural attributions of the graves until the middle of the century. Major row-grave cemeteries were excavated at Nordendorf and Oberflacht in Germany in the 1840s, and the dating of such graves was ascertained through associated coin finds at Selzen, near Mainz, published in 1848. In eastern Europe, most attention was also given to early medieval material, particularly from cemeteries.

Barrow digging continued as an antiquarian pursuit throughout the nineteenth century. In RUSSIA, barrow cemeteries of the ninth to thirteenth centuries A.D. were investigated, most notably at Gnezdovo near Smolensk. Bateman, Atkinson, and Mortimer worked extensively in northern England, and by this time Anglo-Saxon burials were being clearly distinguished from prehistoric ones. Finds in all countries were often reported at local and national meetings; some finds were put in local museums at this time while others remained in private hands either to be lost, sold on the antiquities market, or later deposited in an institution. Some burials were recorded with fine line drawings or watercolors, but generally recording was minimal or of very low quality throughout Europe.

Some early medieval settlements were located and excavated in Germany, notably those defended with earthworks. These were linked with historical campaigns and conflicts, especially those between the Romans and Germans and between the Saxons and Franks. Excavation led to typological classification of the fortifications by German archaeologist Carl Schuchhardt from the 1880s.

National legislation and administrative structures for the protection of monuments, such as the Service des Monuments Historiques in France (founded in 1830), began during the nineteenth century, and the conservation of individual buildings, with reference to the medieval period, was usually the primary concern of such organizations. An unusual development was that of Carcassonne in southern France, where attempts were made to protect a whole quarter of the town, although doing so involved extensive construction in a style considered appropriate by the supervisor of the restoration Viollet-le-Duc. Elsewhere, medieval properties came under state care by one means or another. Many ruined churches had been passed to the board of works in Dublin when the Church in Ireland was disestablished in 1869, and in England, legislation to protect monuments was first enacted in 1882, although some castles and palaces were already under state care.

In Ireland, much survey was undertaken, helped by the high quality of the first edition of the Ordnance Survey maps of the country published from the 1840s. Many significant regional surveys of early medieval earthen ring forts, stone cashels, and promontory forts were published, in which other later medieval earthwork sites such as mottes (mounds) and moats were also noted. In England, Scotland, and Wales, the Ordnance Survey subsequently carried out detailed mapping, again noting many earthwork sites and the presence of ruins, often of medieval date.

Later medieval churches and monasteries were popular subjects of investigation. More frequent observations were made in Scandinavia, including some for Lund Cathedral in Sweden, which were recorded during restoration work from the 1830s onward. Likewise in Norway, Trondheim Cathedral and the wooden stave churches were recognized as being in need of preservation and restoration. In Sweden the Munkeliv monastery in Bergen and ecclesiastical structures in Oslo were examined, as were ecclesiastical structures in Trondheim and Bergen in Norway. In Finland, the Franciscan church at Kåkar was excavated by K. A. Bomansson, and the Birgittine convent of Nödendal was studied by R. Hausen. In Germany, a national monuments commission founded in 1835 led to the publication of inventories of monuments of artistic and architectural merit. The construction of architectural typologies, dated where it was considered appropriate by links to documentary sources, was undertaken across Germany and Austria.

Although walls could be stripped of plaster, excavation was not a research tool. In Great Britain, many monasteries were investigated by trenching to reveal wall lines and to allow the reconstruction on paper of the monastic plans, and cathedrals and churches were also often excavated, frequently in association with building works. Here, the Gothic revival led to the extensive restoration of a large numbers of parish churches and cathedrals and a few castles. Such work caused a reaction to excessive interference with standing fabric, and the Society for the Protection of Ancient Buildings was founded in 1877 by the pre-Raphaelite artist and conservation leader William Morris.

Castles often attracted attention, largely as architectural subjects although occasionally as sites for the excavation of finds and site clearance. German excavations began in the early nineteenth century, and important publications had begun to appear by the middle of the century. The results of work on Castle Tannenberg were published in 1850 by J. V. Hefner and J. W. Wolf, and C. A. von Cohausen used excavation evidence to ascertain details about the Ingelheim Palace published in 1852–1853. Detailed architectural study of the building was begun by Clemen in 1888, and an overview of German castles was produced by Piper in 1896. In

Poland, work began at Kobiernice in the 1880s as well as on the castle hill of Halich (now in Russia).

Urban archaeology received some attention at this time, but it was patchy. The institutional buildings of Göteborg, Sweden, were studied by Berg, but when he extensively excavated at the town of Kunghälla, he did not note structural evidence from the town itself, despite the many finds, but he did report on a monastery and castle adjacent to the settlement. An unusual example of continuous research on an urban center from the later nineteenth century can be seen at Lund, Sweden, where Karlin collected finds and recorded structures and stratigraphy while sewers were being dug. He later carried out excavations in various parts of the city. During the construction of railway works in Oslo, Norway, the architects recorded finds and deposits revealed by that construction.

Intermittent Interest

In the early twentieth century, there was a shift in activity associated with later medieval archaeology, and the clearance of ruins and their display for the public became common at this time. In England, the Office of Works carried out many programs. For instance, the visible ruins of the late medieval town of Old Sarum near Salisbury were excavated and consolidated before World War I, and after the war there was a program to work on abbeys such as Fountains, Byland, and Whitby. Even poor-quality excavation recovered significant amounts of early medieval material, though its context remains difficult to interpret.

In SPAIN, the study of medieval archaeology was largely architectural, such as Asturian, Visigothic, and Mozarabic buildings of various kinds. Later medieval studies of castles and churches were also carried out. In Bohemia, the Benedictine abbey on Ostrov Island in Prague was excavated by Davle. A study of castles was carried out by the architect G. Fischer for Norway, and work began on the Prague castle, which has been continuously investigated since 1925. British official interest in recording archaeological and architectural heritage was reflected in the establishment of royal commissions for England, Wales, and Scotland, and county volumes appeared steadily after 1908.

The discovery of timber buildings through the identification of postholes by Carl Schuchhardt in the first decade of the twentieth century would lead in due course to tremendous changes in research interests and interpretation, but at the time, such discovery was not widely appreciated. The first large-scale excavation of a medieval settlement was in the 1930s when P. Grimm excavated Hohenrode, in Germany, which was occupied from the tenth to the fourteenth centuries A.D. The resulting wide-ranging report indicated the potential of such studies, but the excavation was not emulated. Rescue excavations on Frankish settlements included Gladbach and an Alemannic settlement at Merdingen, in Germany. One of the great discoveries of the period was that of the Viking Oseberg ship and its contents in Norway in 1904.

There was some important academic consolidation, and some important museum studies were undertaken on the collections assembled during the nineteenth century. Notable examples of such work for early medieval material include the typological classification of Germanic art styles by B. Salin, typologies of Anglo-Saxon brooches by. E. T. Leeds, and corpora of Viking material across Europe by Shetelig. Work on classification was stimulated and continued, with coin-dated Austrasian material published by Werner. Cemetery evidence was dominant, and it was often used to indicate settlement patterns, with variables of time, space, and ethnicity. Examples include K. Schuhmacher for the Rhineland and Leeds for England. The possibility of understanding Slavic material culture was appreciated by L. Niederle, who published a series of volumes on such evidence over a period of fifteen years. Later medieval artifact studies developed in some areas at this time, such as on Bohemian ceramics and on a range of finds in London, which were cataloged and published extensively for the first time.

Urban archaeology continued at Lund, Sweden, but the efforts in this city were not emulated elsewhere. Instead, evidence was collected by amateurs, often local government officials, clergymen, or architects. Such piecemeal recording was widespread in Scandinavia, examples being the work of O. A. Digre, who examined many development sites in Trondheim, Norway, and P. Fardelin, who did the same on the island of Gotland, Sweden. Research excavations by H. Jankuhn began at Hedeby, in southern Denmark, in the 1930s and was continued after World War II.

A range of specialities developed during this period. These are most obvious in early medieval archaeology, where subdivisions based on regional and chronological units, often linked to ethnic groups, were established. These still continue to this day, and since World War II have been supported by specialist societies or conferences, which may also incorporate multidisciplinary work by literary, toponymic, historical, and art history scholars.

Post–World War II Expansion

The massive urban destruction in many parts of Europe during World War II resulted in an unrivaled opportunity to examine urban evidence for medieval towns, though the possibility was not always seized with great enthusiasm. Great progress was made in northern Europe and to a certain extent in Britain, but in other countries, such as France, rebuilding took place without excavation. It was in this period that the full potential of urban archaeology began to be realized, although often the organizational structure and methods of funding were adequate in only a few regions. Elsewhere much evidence was lost, but at least the loss was noted, and in subsequent decades better facilities could be established for urban excavation.

In eastern Europe, state archaeological services were founded that accepted the importance of medieval archaeology. Each country established an academy of sciences, and within such a framework research programs were established and linked to nationalist and political themes. These included examination of the great Moravian state in Czechoslovakia and the Old Russ in Russia. In Poland, a center for the study of the Polish state was established in 1948, and about a third of all excavations in that country up to the mid-1960s were on medieval sites. The massive destruction of Warsaw and many trading cities on the Baltic coast gave opportunities for excavation before reconstruction or redevelopment.

In Britain, a pressure group called Rescue lobbied for excavation on many threatened medieval sites, and the importance of urban archaeology was highlighted by Carolyn Heighway. Excavations of the city of Winchester by Martin Biddle of the University of Pennsylvania were influential in Britain and some areas of Europe for indicating the potential for large open-area excavation in towns and for the examination within one town of various elements that, together, allowed for overall urban development to be understood within a historic framework. Methodological developments such as the design of recording forms and the elaboration of the Harris matrix for the elucidation and display of stratigraphic sequences also had widespread repercussions for medieval archaeology and beyond.

In France, the University of Caen has been the leading academic center for medieval archaeology, particularly through its Medieval Research Center, established in 1951 by Michel de Bouard. It has stimulated a number of initiatives, including biennial Chateau Gaillard conferences on castles, studies of pottery production, and urban archaeology. It was through the center that the journal *Archéologie Medievale* was first published in 1971.

Castle excavations have continued, and in Germany information concerning significant assemblages of pottery and other finds began to be published in the 1960s; previously only architectural details and sequences of structures had received much attention. In England, the origin of earthen castles was the focus of a concerted research campaign in the 1960s, and a similar study was undertaken in Northern Ireland. Castles of native princes have more recently been subjected to excavation in Wales to complement the already extensive studies of those built by the English. The changing interests and priorities of castle archaeology can be appreciated on a European level through *Château Gaillard,* the proceedings of the conference held every two years since the 1960s.

It was not until the beginning of the 1950s that rural medieval archaeology developed in any significant way, and this interest was inspired by the development of open-area settlement excavation in Denmark by Hatt and Steensberg. In England, the fieldwork identifying medieval villages as earthworks by Maurice Beresford was a vital step, and it was consolidated by a long-term research project at Wharram Percy by Beresford and John Hurst. Partly because of this work, the Medieval Village Research Group was established, and it was followed by the Moated Sites Research Group. The recognition of other forms of medieval settlement in the countryside led to the eventual merger of the two groups to form the Medieval Settlement Group.

From a British origin, such special interest groups have taken on a wider European dimension, and their annual reports have included frequent short reports and some longer papers on Continental material. One of the landmarks of medieval archaeology was the establishment of the Society for Medieval Archaeology in England in 1956 and the publication of the first volume of its journal, *Medieval Archaeology,* the following year. The European scale of medieval archaeology was indicated by a conference held at Rotterdam in the Netherlands in 1966, and a review of urban archaeology was later distilled at an Oxford, England, conference in 1975; the proceedings of both conferences were subsequently published and had considerable impact.

Early medieval studies continued have an ethnic basis, but social questions began to be considered and grave goods were used to establish patterns of ranking. The use of documentary sources to provide a social structure expected in the burial finds was widespread. An early example was W. Veeck in the 1930s, but most studies were undertaken in the 1960s and 1970s by R. Christlein and H. Steuer in Germany and J. Shepherd and C. Arnold in England. In eastern Europe, the role of the Slavs was a major early medieval theme, one that combined both burial and settlement archaeology. The International Union of Slavonic Archaeology was established in 1965 at Warsaw, and subsequent conferences have been held every five years in other cities in eastern Europe.

Typological studies continued for the early

medieval material, with examples including the K. Böhner refining chronologies for the Trier region in Germany and SIR JOHN MYRES's extensive studies of Anglo-Saxon cremation urns. Early medieval cemetery studies have also developed with greater care and consideration being given to skeletal remains, other evidence from the graves and their fills, and structural features around the graves. Cremation cemeteries have also been studied with regard to cremation pyres and the cremated remains within the vessels. Several major rich burial sites were excavated during the twentieth century under high-quality archaeological conditions. Two Frankish graves were recovered from under Cologne Cathedral in Germany and one from Saint-Denis in France, all in 1959. The boat burial and impressive assemblage of artifacts from Mound 1 at SUTTON HOO were recovered in 1939, and there were further archaeologically significant but less spectacular findings at the site in the 1980s and 1990s.

Recent Developments
Medieval archaeology has continued to expand across Europe, although the amount of rescue excavation has often declined as planning procedures have reduced the amount of destruction. Moreover, a reduction of state funding, replaced by developer funding, has meant that mitigating strategies are often favored by developers. A trend for conservation that started in Britain has now spread to Scandinavia and is becoming increasingly favored in other areas. In contrast, the study of standing remains in a fully archaeological sense has become far more important.

The application of scientific methods in medieval archaeology has been rapid in recent decades. For some early medieval archaeological sites radiocarbon DATING offers some potential, although in most situations its precision is too crude to improve on artifactual dating. More success has been obtained with archaeomagnetic dating, and dendrochronology has been of particular importance. The latter has been applied to structural timbers in standing buildings and in waterlogged situations such as wrecks and waterfronts, and the method has provided dates similar in precision to those in documented sources across much of northern and western Europe. In ceramics, the use of thin sections has been effective in identifying clay sources and trade patterns, and x-ray florescence and other analytical techniques have also been applied.

In some regions and countries, medieval archaeology has only developed as an activity with a separate identity in recent decades. A good example of this is Italy, where apart from nineteenth-century interests associated with major ruins, the Roman past was the dominant concern. The full development of medieval archaeology there has come about through a few significant academics and opportunities for rescue archaeology, and the publication of the national periodical *Archeologia Medievale* since 1974 has provided a vehicle for much innovative and important work. An even later start can be identified in Spain. Although some aspects were developed in the early part of the century, it was the foundation of the Spanish Association of Medieval Archaeology in 1980 that defined the subject, with *Acta Medievalia* being published from that year. Since 1985, a biennial conference has been held in Spain, and *Boletin de Arqueologia Medieval* has appeared since 1987.

The increasing European identity of medieval archaeology, confidence in its intellectual integrity, and the development of wide-ranging research themes have been manifested by several relatively recent developments. One initiative was the establishment of the European Symposium for Teachers of Medieval Archaeology, first held in Lund, Sweden, in 1990 and held regularly since. Another was the innovative international conference Medieval Europe held in YORK, England, in 1992. With a series of seven parallel thematic sessions, each headed by keynote papers, case studies and overviews were offered from all over Europe. A subsequent medieval Europe conference was held in Bruges, Belgium, again with major thematic strands, and it demonstrated the expanding and increasingly sophisticated nature of medieval archaeology.

As yet there is no substantial Europe-wide synthesis of early or late medieval archaeology, and even national syntheses have only recently

appeared in a few countries. Medieval archaeology is a young aspect of archaeology in its present form, and a great deal was achieved in the last half on the twentieth century, but it is in the twenty-first century that it will mature into a coherent and fully confident section of the discipline.

Harold Mytum

See also Novgorod

References

Andersson, H., and J. Wienberg, eds. 1993. *The Study of Medieval Archaeology: European Symposium for Teachers of Medieval Archaeology, Lund, 11–15 June 1990.* Stockholm: Almqvist and Wiksell International.

Barley, M. W., ed. 1977. *European Towns: Their Archaeology and Early History.* London: Academic Press.

Fehring, G. 1991. *The Archaeology of Medieval Germany, an Introduction.* London: Routledge.

Klindt-Jensen, O. 1975. *A History of Scandinavian Archaeology.* London: Thames and Hudson.

Renaud, J. G. N., ed. *Rotterdam Papers: A Contribution to Medieval Archaeology.* Rotterdam: ROB.

Melanesia

See Papua New Guinea and Melanesia

Mercati, Michele (1541–1593)

Although Greek and Roman writers had been aware that some people had made and used stone tools, this knowledge was lost during the Dark Ages after the fall of Rome. It was rediscovered during the Renaissance as scholars began to have access to ancient documents and to question medieval oral and written knowledge.

Michele Mercati was superintendent of the Vatican Botanical Gardens in Rome and physician to Pope Clement VII. He also created one of the first mineralogical collections in Europe, which distinguished between minerals and metals in its display. A contemporary of the antiquarians WILLIAM CAMDEN, JOHAN BURE, and OLE WORM, Mercati was interested in new interpretations of evidence rather than the acceptance of traditional explanations of it. And like them, too, he was interested in chorology and geography.

In 1570, Mercati wrote *Metallotheca Vaticana, opus posthumum,* in which he argued that before the use of iron, stone tools might have been made out of flint to be used "in the madness of war." Mercati believed that fossils were organic in origin and that many of the flints called *ceraunia,* or "thunderstones," had been fashioned by hand and not by natural forces such as lightning. He cited biblical and classical sources, such as Lucretius, for the use of stone tools. In making these arguments he would have been familiar with the ethnographic specimens from the New World sent as presents to the VATICAN.

Mercati's ideas were not accepted by the learned world, and his book was not published until over 100 years after his death. Its appearance prompted the French scholar Antoine de Jussieu to write a paper to the Académie des Sciences on the possible human origins of stone tools and ethnographic comparisons in 1723. Mercati's ideas were echoed by English aniquarians WILLIAM DUGDALE in the seventeenth century and JOHN FRERE in the late eighteenth century.

Tim Murray

References

Ceram, C. 1967. *Gods, Graves and Scholars.* Harmondsworth, UK: Pelican.

Mesoamerica

Coined in 1943 by the scholar Paul Kirchoff, the name *Mesoamerica* is used to describe the culture area of the ancient civilizations of central and southern MEXICO and northern Central America. The name was partly based on analogy with the term MESOPOTAMIA, since the geographic region involved lies between the great landmasses of North and South America.

More than a geographic entity, however, Mesoamerica was a cultural entity. The peoples inhabiting the area shared a great many cultural traits that very clearly separated them from the peoples to their north and south. These traits included subsistence based on agriculture (the Mesoamerican cultigens maize, beans, and squash being the most important crops); cities with ceremonial precincts containing temple-pyramids; a fatalistic religion with a largely shared cosmology and pantheon of gods; the practice of human sacrifice; a ritual calendar of 260 days; and a ballgame played with a solid rubber ball.

Although Mesoamerican cultures shared many cultural traits, there were also differences among them. First and foremost of these differences was language: dozens of different languages were spoken by the various peoples of Mesoamerica, including Nahuatl (the language

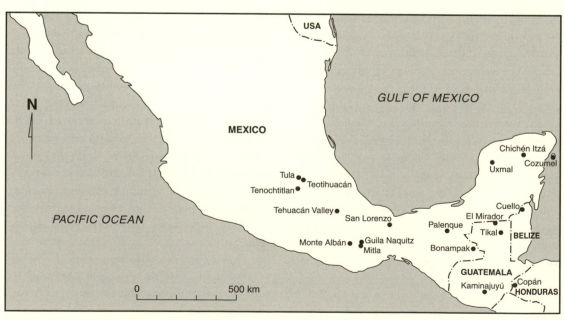

Mesoamerican Archaeological Sites

of the AZTECS), about thirty different Mayan languages, the Zapotec and Mixtec languages of Oaxaca, and the Tarascan or Purépecha spoken in western Mexico.

The OLMECS, who flourished between about 1200 and 400 B.C., are considered to have had the first complex society in the area, and it appears that they developed many of the cultural patterns that later became the hallmarks of Mesoamerican civilization. Other Mesoamerican groups adopted these patterns, adding their own distinctive characteristics.

Peter Mathews

See also Belize; Guatemala; Maya Civilization

Mesolithic Europe
See Europe, Mesolithic

Mesopotamia
History of Excavation

The origins of Mesopotamian archaeology lie in nineteenth-century adventurism, tempered by the practical intelligence and broad learning that was the Victorians' defining hallmark. A handful of intrepid travelers (notably Pietro della Valle, L'Abbé de Beauchamp, and Karsten Niebuhr) had ventured through Mesopotamia in earlier centuries, stopping at NINEVEH, Babylon, and other sites whose identification survived in local folklore. Some brought back occasional inscriptions and other artifacts but, despite legends of buried treasure, none attempted any significant excavations.

A major turning point came in the first decades of the nineteenth century when Babylon, Nineveh, and a number of other Mesopotamian sites were systematically inspected and surveyed by Claudius Rich, a talented linguist who was the East India Company's resident in Baghdad (in what is now Iraq). Rich's accounts of his discoveries (1813, 1818, 1836, and 1839), and the collection of his finds bought by the BRITISH MUSEUM in 1825, inspired the first generation of Mesopotamian explorers. First in the field were the French, under PAUL-ÉMILE BOTTA, who after brief soundings at Nineveh in December 1842 spent two seasons (1843–1844) excavating the

Palace of Sargon II at Khorsabad (ancient Dur Sharrukin), the third of four Assyrian capitals (the others being Ashur, Kalhu [NIMRUD], and Nineveh). Botta was relatively well financed by the LOUVRE Museum and approached his task with the discipline of a trained surgeon and naturalist, although not yet with any understanding of the principles of stratigraphy. Botta was succeeded by Victor Place, who led from 1852 to 1854.

The first British excavations were made by AUSTEN HENRY LAYARD, who had set out overland from England in 1839 intending to reach Ceylon, but having been captivated by the Assyrian sites resolved to stay and dig. Eventually gaining the financial support of the British ambassador in Istanbul, Sir Stratford Canning, Layard, aged only 28, began excavating at Nimrud (ancient Kalhu, which he believed to be Nineveh) in November 1845. There he immediately came upon the palace of the ninth-century B.C. Assyrian King Ashurnasirpal II. During the next eight years Layard and his assistant Hormuzd Rassam uncovered no less than eight royal palaces, as well as temples and other imposing structures, whose sculpted bas-reliefs, ivory carvings, and cuneiform tablets (written in the then-still-undeciphered Assyrian language) were a revelation to Victorian Britain, whither the major finds were shipped.

Layard's priorities, as prescribed by the British Museum, were "to obtain the largest possible number of well-preserved objects at the least possible outlay of time and money." His method was equally direct: he dug trenches along the sides of the palace rooms to expose the whole of the carved stone slabs without removing the earth from the center. Consequently few of the chambers were fully explored and many small objects and other evidence were left or lost. There was no recognition in this method of the stratigraphic principles—rudimentary as they still were—now beginning to be observed in the excavation of European prehistoric sites. It did however provide enough trophies of art (including some three kilometers of sculpted wall reliefs), architecture, and inscriptions to sustain the British Museum's grudging and inadequate support.

The initial phase of Assyrian excavation by

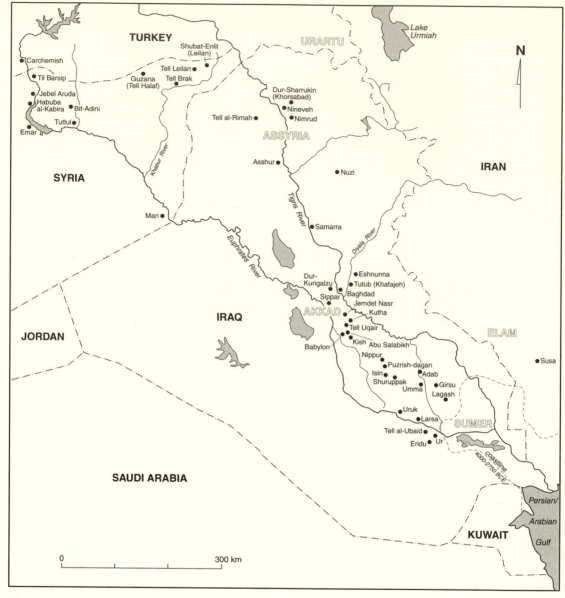

Mesopotamian Archaeological Sites

both the French and the British ended in 1853. Their success inspired a number of exploratory soundings at Babylonian sites in the 1850s but with limited results, due largely to the excavators' unfamiliarity with mud-brick architecture. Hormuzd Rassam returned to the field in 1878 and worked through 1882 at widely scattered sites in Assyria and Babylonia, but his careless methods rendered even the more important finds less useful than they should have been. An additional setback was the loss of nearly all of Victor Place's finds from Khorsabad, and some of the British finds from Nineveh, in a disastrous sinking of the cargo rafts at Qurnah in 1855.

While Botta and Layard had been digging, scholars in Europe were working to decipher the cuneiform script of the Mesopotamian monuments. The key to their understanding lay in a trilingual inscription, in Old Persian, Babylonian, and Elamite, of Darius at Behistun in western IRAN. The Indo-Iranian Old Persian text provided the basis for deciphering the Semitic Babylonian, and in 1857 a blind test of the four leading ex-

The arrival of a colossal Assyrian statue of a winged bull at the British Museum in 1852 (Illustrated London News, *28 February 1852*)

perts on an inscription from Assyria confirmed that the code had indeed been cracked.

The Assyrians were known from the Bible and from Greek authors before their archaeological discovery, and fitted into an existing (if still unreliable) historical framework. The next major phase of discovery, on the other hand, revealed a culture for which there was no comparable background: that of the Sumerians. From 1877 to 1881 and from 1888 to 1900 a French team under Ernest de Sarzec excavated at Telloh, the site of ancient Girsu in the city-state of Lagash, bringing to light the first substantial evidence of the Sumerian culture that had flourished in the third millennium B.C. French work continued here under other directors until 1933. As well as sophisticated works of art (notably the "Stele of the Vultures" and statues of Gudea), thousands of clay tablets with Sumerian writing were discovered. These were mostly economic accounts from the temple administrations and formed the basis for reconstructing early Sumerian economy and society.

These finds established Sumer as home to the earliest literary culture in Mesopotamia. Still earlier stages of this development were traced from 1912 by a German team at Uruk (Biblical Erech, modern Warka), where a sequence of two monumental temple complexes was uncovered, along with examples of linear pictographic writing, an ancestor of the Sumerian cuneiform script, on stone and clay tablets. This remains the first evidence of writing yet recovered from anywhere in the world (Late Uruk period, ca. 3400 B.C.).

The meticulous excavations at Uruk were themselves based on the exemplary standards set by other German teams under Robert Koldewey at Babylon (1899–1913) and at Borsippa and Fara (1901–1903), and under Walter Andrae at the first Assyrian capital, Ashur (1903–1914). These excavations made great advances in the recovery of mud-brick architecture, which earlier excavators had not recognized or had ignored. At Ashur, Andrae also cut a deep sounding (a trench or hole) in the Ishtar Temple, establishing the first significant stratigraphical history of a Mesopotamian site. The expedition to Babylon uncovered the spectacular remains of the city of Nebuchadnessar, another name resonant with biblical associations. Unfortunately, virtually nothing has been recovered of Babylon's earlier grandeur, when it was the capital of the dynasty of Hammurabi in the eighteenth and seventeenth centuries B.C.

After an exploratory season in 1884, the first major American excavations began under H. V. Hilprecht, J. P. Peters, and J. H. Haynes at the Sumerian cult center of Nippur in 1887 and continued intermittently up until the 1980s. The thousands of texts from this site, mostly school exercises in Sumerian, form the backbone of our knowledge of Sumerian literature. Four Sumerian and Akkadian sites of the third and second millennia B.C. were excavated in the Diyala region in the 1930s by a Chicago expedition under HENRI FRANKFORT, whose close analysis of the ceramic typology and glyptic and sculptural art found formed the basis of the first systematic periodisation of third-millennium Mesopotamia (1929, 1931).

A hiatus in excavation during World War I was followed by the creation of the nation of Iraq and the establishment of a department of antiquities under GERTRUDE BELL. Expeditions returned to earlier Assyrian (Khorsabad, Nineveh) and Sumerian (Tello, Kish, Jemdet Nasr, Fara) excavations, and started at many new sites. The most important of these was the joint U.S.-British expedition (1922–1934) under C. LEONARD WOOLLEY to the Sumerian city of Ur. This was the first British expedition to emulate the care and precision of the Germans, to which Woolley added his own talent for inspired improvisation (as in his use of plaster to recover the forms of perished wooden objects). Woolley recovered important remains of Neo-Babylonian and Isin-Larsa period housing, and established a deep stratigraphical sequence for early Sumer, but the most celebrated finds then and since were the richly furnished "Royal" Tombs of ca. 2600 B.C. (in fact probably priestly burials). This was the first and only time Mesopotamia has yielded "treasure" that ranks in the popular conception with the finds of Bronze-Age Greece and Egypt. Woolley's excavations at nearby al-Ubaid (1923–1924) recovered evidence of the earliest (fifth millennium B.C.) settled presence in the alluvium, known since as the Ubaid culture.

The period up to World War II also saw an expansion of activity in the hilly uplands surrounding the Tigris-Euphrates valleys at sites like Tepe Gawra, Tell Brak, Arpachiyeh, HASSUNA, Samarra, and Tell Halaf, where rain-fed agriculture had supported pre-Ubaid village communities. Continuing discoveries in this "fertile crescent" (extending beyond Mesopotamia from Palestine through Syria and Turkey and down western Iran), especially by American archaeologist ROBERT BRAIDWOOD in the 1950s at JARMO, have documented this region's crucial role in the early DOMESTICATION OF PLANTS AND ANIMALS, and, at some Samarran sites, early irrigation. Evidence of Paleolithic activity in the Kurdish mountains was found in the 1920s by English archaeologist DOROTHY GARROD.

The broad chronological and cultural outlines of Mesopotamian archaeology having now been defined, the period after World War II saw a proliferation of excavation at sites of nearly all periods and regions, some continuing long-established expeditions (Uruk, Nippur), others recommencing at earlier excavations (Tell Brak, Nimrud, Sippar, Babylon), and others starting on new sites. In the 1970s and 1980s a large number of rescue excavations were undertaken in areas designated for flooding by the Hamrin, Haditha, and Eski Mosul dams in Iraq (and for dams in Syria and Turkey), some with startling results. The German and Dutch excavations at Habbuba Kabbira and Jebel Aruda in Syria uncovered hitherto-unsuspected outposts of early Sumerian culture ("colonies") along the Upper Euphrates. Survey and limited excavation along the Arabian side of the Gulf from the 1950s on has indicated an Ubaid-period Mesopotamian presence (fifth millennium B.C.) along this littoral, a prelude to the well-documented Gulf trade with Meluhha (Indus Valley) of the third through the second millennia B.C. A number of area surveys of Babylonia by American archaeologist ROBERT MCCORMICK ADAMS in the 1960s and 1970s illuminated demographic patterns that have had a significant impact on models of early state development.

Intellectual History

The great popular and scholarly interest in Mesopotamian archaeology in the nineteenth century was sustained both by the historical-scientific empiricism of the age and, at the other extreme, by its connection to the Bible. For generations of people steeped as much in biblical history as they were in pagan art (the Elgin marbles had arrived a generation earlier), the Assyrian reliefs showing Sennacherib's siege of Lachish and King Jehu prostrating himself before Shalmanesser III brought the Bible vividly to life as no previous discoveries had done, and each new shipment of finds was assured a sensational reception as they arrived at the British Museum. Layard's account of his excavations, *Nineveh and its Remains* (1849; popular edition 1851), became a railway-stand bestseller. Its 8,000 sales in 1849, he boasts in one letter, "will place it side by side with *Mrs Rundell's Cookery*." Bible fever reached its climax with George Smith's discovery at the British Museum in 1872 of the "flood tablet" from the library of Ashurbanipal at Nineveh, bearing an account of the "Babylonian Noah," Utnapishtim. Smith had little trouble securing support from the *Daily Telegraph* for an expedition to Nineveh to find the missing portion of the tablet.

The biblical origin of the flood story was only one of a series of such firsts that established Mesopotamia in the scholarly consciousness as the original source of civilization: the first writing, a complex society, the presence of cities, bureaucracy, a primitive democracy, monumental art, and much else. On its periphery lay the fertile crescent, the source of the first agriculture and animal husbandry, or so it was long believed. *Ex Oriente Lux* (OSCAR MONTELIUS; VERE GORDON CHILDE)—from this heartland of invention many of the key developments in technological, social, and political evolution were thought to have radiated out, illuminating Europe and other areas of the old world with the benefits of civilized life. Although many of these ideas have been much modified and their naïve diffusionism tempered, Mesopotamia's status as a source of "origins" remains. Text books on world archaeology inevitably (and rightly) cite Sumer's role as a precociously early complex society, which had a significant impact on its neighbors and arguably on the early course of old world history as far afield as China.

The most successful integration of Mesopotamian evidence into a continental and global perspective has been in prehistory, for which the exclusively archaeological data is directly accessible to researchers from other regions and cultures. With the historical periods, on the other hand, an enormous weight of historical and textual evidence, requiring a familiarity with a number of ancient and modern languages, has tended to insulate Mesopotamia from cross-disciplinary analysis; where it has been attempted, such analysis has tended to yield superficial and unreliable results. The continuing divide between text-based Assyriologists and artifact-based archaeologists represents a further barrier to synthetic interpretation. Unlike classical archaeologists and Egyptologists, few Mesopotamian archaeologists can claim more than a working grasp of the textual evidence—and few Mesopotamian philologists and linguists can claim a strong grasp on the archaeological evidence. Some scholars have attempted to integrate the material and textual data, but very few have made significant original contributions in both fields. Moreover, within Assyriology itself the discipline is increasingly split into temporal and cultural specialisms corresponding to the main textual corpuses: Archaic, E.D.-Ur III Sumerian, Akkadian, Old Babylonian, Old Assyrian, Middle Babylonian/Assyrian, Neo-Assyrian, Neo-Babylonian, Achaemenid, and Seleucid-Parthian. Accessibility to this increasingly fragmented world is still hampered by a scarcity of textbooks and general surveys that are taken for granted in the archaeology of other cultures.

As is clear from the historical outline above, the major landmarks in Mesopotamian archaeology are either discoveries or technical advances in methods of retrieval and documentation. There is little here that might count as intellectual history in the sense of a theoretical interpretive (and predictive) framework for understanding the archaeological record in social, historical, or anthropological terms. Progress has thus tended to be measured in empirical terms—the recovery of more and better evidence—rather than theoretical ones. Surveys of archaeological theory tend to make little reference to Mesopotamia, reflecting the difficulty in divining any distinctive evolving body of analytical and interpretive principles. This contrasts particularly with the history of European prehistory, in which such theory-building has played a leading role.

The primary reason for the dearth of theory has been the abundance of direct nonarchaeological evidence for the nature of Mesopotamian society, religion, history, literature, science, and much else in the tens of thousands of cuneiform documents recovered from Mesopotamian sites. Much of what a theoretical framework might hope to deliver in more general terms is here delineated in precise and vivid detail. There remains of course the challenge of synthesizing this highly particularistic evidence into general patterns of social, historical, and cultural behavior, for which methodological principles must be brought into play. But the resulting construction remains nonetheless far richer and more verifiable than would be possible from the archaeological material alone. In these circumstances the general neglect of theory is understandable, if not always beneficial.

In the first half of the twentieth century, two individuals stand out for their more profound theoretical contributions to Mesopotamian archaeology: Vere Gordon Childe and HENRI FRANKFORT. Childe looked to the East for the source of key technological innovations—in particular bronze-working and agriculture—that, through their diffusion to Europe, determined the course and nature of Bronze Age culture in that area (Childe's primary area of expertise). Childe approached such developments within a Marxist framework, one predicated upon assumptions of historical determinism and cultural materialism. Indeed it is the application of these supposed universal principles of social and economic evolution to the understanding of archaeological remains that has underpinned Childe's continuing interest in archaeological theory; otherwise works such as *The Most Ancient East* (1928), which ends with a chapter on "Proofs of Diffusion," and *Man Makes Himself* (1936), with its Durkheimian characterisation of a depersonalised Oriental despotism, would long ago have been consigned to the realm of historical curiosities.

Childe's work on the Near East, which largely synthesised existing data, was more influential among Europeanists than Near Easterners, and this remains true today. Henri Frankfort, on the other hand, had a significant impact on his own and subsequent generations of Near-Eastern scholars both as an excavator and as a synthesiser of archaeological and textual evidence. Beyond his work on the iconography of cylinder seals and sculpture, and the periodization of the Early Dynastic period, all of which remain fundamental today, Frankfort wrote in a more speculative vein on what he called the *mythopoeic* (myth-making) culture of Mesopotamia. As the name implies, this approach took its point of departure from the cuneiform literary tradition, in particular the myths, which Frankfort saw as "a carefully chosen cloak for abstract thought" (1948), supplemented by anthropological insights into the conceptual frameworks of other nonwestern societies.

The mythopoeic approach was applied most fruitfully in Frankfort's analysis of the origins of civilization in Mesopotamia and Egypt around 3000 B.C., where it provided a basis for understanding the many cultural dissimilarities that cut across these two cultures' parallel technological trajectories. On the other hand, Frankfort's work on the "intellectual adventure" of the ancient Near East had little direct impact on his more typological and art historical discussions of the archaeological record, which tended to be influenced instead by his readings in German art theory, especially as transplanted to the Warburg Institute in London, of which Frankfort became director in 1949. Here archaeology provided illustration of ideas inspired by textual sources rather than vice versa. His last book on *The Art and Architecture of the Ancient Orient* (1954) is largely traditional in approach, with no conspicuous dependence on a supposed Mesopotamian *Weltanschauung*. Indeed, while Frankfort saw himself primarily as an archaeologist, his most significant legacy may turn out to be in the empathetic conceptualization of ancient cultural experience (an aspect of his thought much influenced by R. G. Collingwood's 1946 book *The Idea of History*)—a conceptualization that proceeded primarily from literary sources. It remains true nonetheless that Frankfort, more than any of his peers or successors, attempted to break down the barriers between different classes of evidence so as to recreate Mesopotamian culture in the round. He is not alone in having failed entirely to bring all of these aspects together in one seamless narrative.

The intellectual history of Mesopotamian archaeology since World War II has been sporadic and largely reactive to challenges from other arenas, notably the New Archaeology, processual and postprocessual archaeology, and the *annales* school of historiography. By and large, the vigorous debates that have taken place in archaeological theory over the past forty years have received little direct input from Mesopotamian (or other Near Eastern) research, and figures like Childe and Frankfort, who engaged actively with the major intellectual currents of their time, do not come easily to mind. As in Syro-Palestinian archaeology (but unlike in Egyptology) the bifurcation of Mesopotamian archaeology from the text-based study of history and culture continues to play a significant role in defining the lines of current research. Interest in the broader social and historical dynamics of Mesopotamia still looks more to textual than to archaeological data for its primary validation, thereby defusing the motivation for the higher level theory that animates prehistoric studies elsewhere. Advances in archaeological theory and practice have tended to be correspondingly more methodological and technical. It remains a matter of disagreement among archaeologists to what extent this lack of theory is an intellectual failing or a welcome reflection of Mesopotamia's greater variety and abundance of direct evidence of cultural motivation and behavior.

The influence of processual theory has been most apparent in the emphasis, from the 1970s, on defining sociopolitical processes, notably the rise of social complexity and early state development in the Uruk period. This work was greatly facilitated by the extensive surveys of settlement patterns in the Mesopotamian alluvium by Robert McCormick Adams and others in the 1960s and 1970s. The dynamics of core/periphery relations—especially relevant to resource-poor Mesopotamia—have become much more nuanced, especially between the cities of southern and northern Mesopotamia. As everywhere, diffusionism is strongly out of favor, with northern Mesopotamia emerging as a primary center of independent innovation. More sophisticated, model-oriented discussions of the nature of trade and other forms of economic and non-economic exchange have drawn from a variety of theoretical positions, including Marxism and processual theory. Also owing something to these trends has been the greater appreciation of the technological and social functionality of many classes of artifact (seals and sealings, pottery, figurines, elite status markers, and texts qua objects), all generating a greater interest in domestic archaeological contexts. Within both newer and older theoretical positions may be seen the expanding utilization of scientific analytical tools, especially in the retrieval and interpretation of biological remains, in dating, and in the reconstruction of technologies of metallurgy, ceramics, glass-making, etc. In cuneiform studies the use and abuse of "historical" sources has been much discussed in the past twenty years, turning the focus onto the contextual understanding of texts as instruments of contemporary ideology and propaganda. Here archaeology has been ahead of the trend in its longstanding appreciation of the propagandistic nature of public art.

Anthropology has featured intermittently in Mesopotamian archaeology as a basis for comparative interpretation, especially in reconstructions of a (semi-) nomadic lifstyle among communities of the Zagros frontier and in work on prehistoric sites. In investigations of historical periods its application has been scarcer, restricted largely to categories like pottery that bridge the prehistoric/historic divide.

The art-historical analysis of Mesopotamian culture is less developed than in the classical world or Egyptology for reasons both internal and external to the subject. Among external factors is the fact that relatively few Mesopotamian archaeologists have a strong background in the principles and methodology of art history. Exceptions (notably H. Frankfort, P. Amiet and E. Porada) have had a dispro-

Gold helmet, Mesopotamia, ca. 2500 B.C. (Image Select)

But it is considerably coarser-grained and often more speculative than art history in the sense that this discipline is generally understood.

Timothy Potts

See also Bell, Gertrude

References

Curtis, J. E. 1982. *Fifty Years of Mesopotamian Discovery, The Work of the British School of Archaeology in Iraq, 1932–1982.* London: British School of Archaeology in Iraq.

Groenewegen-Frankfort, H. A. 1951. *Arrest and Movement: An Essay on Space and Time in the Representational Art of the Near East.* London: Faber and Faber.

Harper, P. O., et al., eds. 1995. *Assyrian Origins, Discoveries at Ashur on the Tigris.* New York: Metropolitan Museum of Art.

Hilprecht, H. V. 1903. *Explorations in Bible Lands during the 19th Century.* Philadelphia: A. J. Holman.

Kuklick, B. 1996. *Puritans in Babylon: The Ancient Near East and American Intellectual Life, 1880–1930.* Princeton, NJ: Princeton University Press.

Larsen, M. T. 1996. *The Conquest of Assyria, Excavations in an Antique Land 1840–1860.* London and New York: Routledge.

Lloyd, S. 1963. *Mounds of the Near East.* Edinburgh: Edinburgh University Press.

———. 1980. *Foundations in the Dust, The Story of Mesopotamian Discovery.* Rev. ed. London: Thames and Hudson.

Wengrow, D. 1999. "The Intellectual Adventure of Henri Frankfort: A Missing Chapter in the History of Archaeological Thought." *American Journal of Archaeology* 103, no. 4: 597–613.

portionate impact on the field. More inhibiting have been a variety of internal factors, in particular ignorance of key aspects of how art was conceived and made in Mesopotamia: the lack of virtually any basis for attributing works to individual hands or names, which has forced the reconstruction of broader styles, schools, and traditions; ignorance of the functional priorities of the artist (ritual, propagandistic, apotropaic, etc.) vis-à-vis any artistic/aesthetic ambitions; ignorance of the degree of artistic latitude allowed to artists (minimal?); ignorance of the aesthetic and other categories in which they conceived the success or failure of a work of art (an area now being profitably investigated by I. Winter); and, perhaps most compromising of all, an inability in most contexts to define criteria for distinguishing conscious difference of style from unintentional difference of quality (or conception or execution). This leads to arbitrary and subjective value judgments, as in the common postulate of "crude" or "schematic" styles, when it is not clear that style is involved at all, but rather competence.

Most of what goes under the name of art history in Mesopotamian studies has been in the nature of iconographical and typological analysis, often with a view to defining period, cultural, ethnic, or regional styles, and thence to tracing patterns of influence and diffusion. Under the circumstances this is often all that can be done, and it has yielded many significant results.

Mexico

Archaeological research in Mexico has a long, complex history covering over 150 years and the careers of hundreds of archaeologists. Part of this history has been summarized in fairly recent surveys (Bernal 1979; García Mora et al. 1987–1989; Willey and Sabloff 1980), but much of it remains to be written. This article examines some of the central developments in Mexican archaeology with an emphasis on the work since 1940 when the quantity and types of investigations increased at an accelerated pace.

The evolution of Mexican archaeology as a scientific discipline generally has been closely connected with the development of archaeology and anthropology in the rest of the world and with specific processes in the historical, political, and social configuration of Mexico. During the twentieth century, archaeology related directly to the political and ideological needs of the Mexican national state. Starting with the dictatorship of Porfirio Díaz, which was ended by a revolution in 1911, and continued by subsequent postrevolutionary movements, the monuments of the pre-Hispanic peoples have been utilized as an ideological base for an ethnic and cultural identity to fortify the growing nationalist sentiments needed by the new groups in power. Since the nineteenth century, Mexican nationalist governments have promoted a series of laws and regulations to conserve and protect historical and archaeological patrimony, and these laws and regulations were truly advanced for the time. The first of these, a law prohibiting the export of antiquities, dates to 1827, shortly after Mexico's independence from Spain.

Nationalist movements have largely determined and defined one of the major traditions of archaeological research in Mexico: archaeology centered on the exploration, restoration, and reconstruction of ancient buildings and monumental sites or "zones." This tradition started at the end of the nineteenth century, and although there have been changes in key concepts, techniques, and goals, it is still the major type of archaeology today, stimulated and maintained by the state because of the political and ideological functions of archaeological monuments.

The Beginnings of Archaeology in Mexico

The beginning of archaeology in Mexico can be divided into two periods: the first starting around 1840 and ending in 1880; the second extending between 1880 and 1910, during which time there was a notable increase in the number of scholars interested in the pre-Hispanic cultures of Mexico.

The most influential scholarly work that mentioned ancient Mexico and was published before the first initial period were the studies of the naturalist and philosopher Alexander von Humboldt (1814). Other important contributions were the books recording visits to MAYA ruins written by JOHN L. STEPHENS (1841) and illustrated by FREDERICK CATHERWOOD. These do not indulge in speculations typical of the time proposing migrations of peoples from the Old World to explain the origins of American civilizations. Both Stephens and Catherwood attributed the ruins of Yucatán, Chiapas, and Central America to the ancestors of the contemporary Maya, and this conclusion helped change the interpretations of many scholars in the Americas and Europe concerning the cultures of pre-Hispanic Mexico.

Between 1840 and 1870, the French priest Abbé Brasseur de Bourbourg established himself as the first general Mesoamericanist. His contributions were mainly in linguistics and ethnohistory, but he also advanced archaeological knowledge considerably through his effort to establish ties between contemporary indigenous peoples and pre-Hispanic cultures using Spanish colonial documents and native histories from the sixteenth century. He learned several Maya languages, made some of the first attempts to translate Maya hieroglyphs, and edited the first published edition of the *Popol Vuh* (the most important surviving Maya epic cycle). He also discovered and edited an encyclopedic sixteenth-century account by Bishop Landa of Maya culture in Yucatán at the time of the Spanish conquest. The Landa manuscript contains descriptions of some of the hieroglyphs that eventually made possible the first successful phonetic translations of ancient Maya writing.

During the same period, early syntheses of ancient highland Mexican history were made by Garcia Icazbalceta and Orozco y Berra. Their work is especially important because, in some cases, it is based on native codices and other original manuscripts that have since disappeared. In 1858, the geographer García Cubas published a geographical and statistical atlas of Mexico that included a number of archaeological sites, and in the 1870s, he produced important descriptions of TEOTIHUACÁN and Tula.

The French archaeologist-explorer Désiré Charnay arrived in Mexico in 1858 and continued his investigations there until the 1880s. His contributions include the introduction of photography to record monuments in the Maya area and the use of plaster molds to produce accurate copies of monuments (Graham 1971). In Tula, Hidalgo, the site of the ancient TOLTEC capital Tollan, Charnay made some of the first extensive excavations of ancient residential architecture in MESOAMERICA. He was also the first to notice and publish similarities between the art and buildings of Tula and CHICHÉN ITZÁ in Yucatán (Charnay 1885).

The thirty years from 1880 to 1910 saw a great increase in the number of scholars studying pre-Hispanic Mexican cultures. Three important Mexican investigators of this period were Del Paso y Troncoso, A. Peñafiel, and Leopoldo Batres. Although the first two were principally historians, Del Paso y Troncoso was also director of the national archaeological museum and published studies of ancient ceramics and monuments. Subsequently, he spent years editing colonial texts from archives in Spain and elsewhere in Europe, and these are invaluable sources of cultural information for both historians and archaeologists. Peñafiel made some of the first systematic studies of ancient Mexican ruins, which were published in Spanish in Berlin (Peñafiel 1890). He also produced analyses of toponyms and other linguistic topics useful to archaeologists.

Batres's work is still controversial because of his role as the "official" archaeologist for the Porfirio Díaz dictatorship. He excavated key sites including MONTE ALBÁN, Mitla, Xochicalco, and TENOCHTITLÁN and is best known for the massive restorations at Teotihuacán that were made in preparation for the 1910 celebration of the centenary of Mexico's independence from Spain. Batres's archaeological work in general was not as bad as many of his critics have maintained, and his programs have historical importance because they marked the beginning of the tradition of direct intervention by the Mexican state in the exploration and restoration of ancient monumental sites.

The end of the nineteenth century and the first years of the twentieth witnessed basic contributions to Maya studies, especially in epigraphy. The first corpus of inscriptions from major Maya centers, many only recently discovered, was published by Maudslay and Maler, and their reports also contain photographs of monuments that since have disappeared or have been damaged. The quality of Maudslay's photographs and his drawings of inscriptions set the standard for decades and is superior to that of American SYLVANUS MORLEY's (1938) publications. The first decipherments of dates in Maya texts were proposed by Forstemann, Goodman, and Bowditch, and their chronology for the Maya area served as the basis for correlating relative chronological sequences in other regions of Mesoamerica.

During the 1890s, the American Edward Thompson did fieldwork in northern Yucatán, including a regional study around Labna and excavations at Chichén Itzá. His removal of subaquatic items from the cenote or "sacred well" of Chichén caused serious problems between the Mexican government and Harvard University because Thompson clandestinely sent many of the items to the PEABODY MUSEUM where they remained for several decades before being returned to Mexico.

WILLIAM H. HOLMES of the SMITHSONIAN INSTITUTION made basic contributions in several fields of archaeology, and his famous 1886 study concerning the origins of ceramics in the Americas included data from Mexico, and some aspects of it are still valid. Shortly afterward, Holmes made a pioneer study of architectural planning in Teotihuacán and several other ancient Mexican cities. He promoted the systematic analysis of lithic, shell, and other archaeological materials and was the first to excavate pre-Hispanic obsidian mines in Mesoamerica, producing an outstanding report on the quarries of the Sierra de Pachuca, Hidalgo, in 1900. Another pioneer investigator was the Czech ALES HRDLICKA. His main contributions were to physical anthropology, but he also did archaeological work on the northern periphery of Mesoamerica at La Quemada, Zacatecas, and a series of centers that would later be used to define the Chalchihuites culture.

Without doubt, the most important Mesoamericanist during the decades before 1910 was the German scholar Eduard Seler, and his vast works are still necessary reading in many fields. He made the first systematic studies of ancient Mexican and Maya iconography, and his analyses of codices, religions, and calendars are classics (Coe 1993). Seler made numerous field trips to Mexico and Central America and published descriptions of sites and monuments in regions as diverse as GUATEMALA, Chiapas, Oaxaca, Los Tuxtlas (Veracruz), and Zacatecas, among others. His study of the areas influenced by the major city of Teotihuacán, based mainly on the analysis of museum collections, was the direct precursor for the concepts of cultural unity that would be used to define Mesoamerica (Bernal 1979, 142). Seler knew several of the major pre-Hispanic languages and also made key contributions in ethnology and ethnohistory.

The Expansion of Mexican Archaeology
In 1911, at the beginning of the armed conflicts of the Mexican Revolution, the Escuela Internacional de Arqueología y Etnografía Americana (International School of American Archaeology and Ethnography) was founded in Mexico City. On the basis of agreements between the Mexican government and universities and museums in Germany, France, and the United States, the school functioned as a research institute. Even though it existed formally only until 1920, the institute's activities were of such importance that its foundation clearly marked a new period in the development of Mexican archaeology. Directors included some of the greatest anthropologists in the Americas—Eduard Seler, Franz Boas, Alfred Tozzer, and MANUEL GAMIO—and the programs were truly anthropological, with important studies in ethnology and linguistics in various regions of Mexico, despite the violence of the revolution (Rivermar 1987). Heroic linguistic investigation was done by Boas (1917) in studying speakers of archaic Nahuatl (the language spoken by the Aztecs) in the remote Oaxaca coastal town of Pochutla, but such work may have been routine for a man who was studying the Eskimos of central Greenland in the 1880s.

The school's central contribution to archaeology was the introduction of stratigraphic excavations in Mexico. In 1912, Gamio conducted a series of stratigraphic excavations at San Miguel Amantla (Azcapotzalco), which provided the basis for the first ancient culture sequence in the basin of Mexico. Boas and Gamio also extensively studied the collections of the national museum from sites in the basin of Mexico and published a catalog based on this work. Tozzer excavated Teotihuacán-period residences at Santiago Ahuizotla in the west-central basin near Azcapotzalco and identified a new ceramic complex called Coyotlatelco. It was eventually shown that this complex was part of a cultural tradition that appeared between the collapse of the Teotihuacán state and the rise of the Tula.

The sequence for the basin of Mexico proposed by the members of the International School consisted of three different cultures: archaic (which is now called formative), Toltec (related to the culture of Teotihuacán), and AZTEC. This chronological framework was partially modified by Alfred Kroeber in 1925, and in 1938, George Vaillant, on the basis of numerous stratigraphic excavations, published a more detailed chronology. The cultural sequence for the basin that is currently used was formulated by Pedro Armillas in 1950 on the basis of excavations at Teotihuacán along with the investigations of Vaillant and Sigvald Linne and the work of Acosta at Tula. Despite these modifications, it is fair to state that the investigations of the International School correctly identified the principal cultures of the basin of Mexico in the proper chronological order.

The outstanding figure in Mexican archaeology during the revolution and the decade of the 1920s was Manuel Gamio (González Gamio 1987), who had been one of Boas's students at Columbia University in 1910–1911. Gamio was the last director of the International School, and between 1917 and 1922, supported by funds from the Mexican government, he planned and directed the first multidisciplinary anthropological project in the Americas on the population of the Teotihuacán Valley. The program comprised archaeology, ethnography, demography, geology, and environmental and agricultural studies and investigated the people of the Teotihuacán Valley from pre-Hispanic times to the twentieth century. The project's findings were published in five volumes, and it was one of the most successful large-scale anthropological projects ever attempted, with a very advanced level of research for its time. The project's most important archaeological work was Gamio's excavations of the Ciudadela complex in the center of Teotihuacán where he uncovered key information concerning the origins of the ancient city.

During the same period, Gamio organized several other archaeological projects including excavations of the main plaza of Tenochtitlán and important studies of the early sedentary, or archaic, cultures in the basin of Mexico. Gamio collaborated with B. Cummings in excavations of the early urban site of San Cuicuilco, which had been nearly covered by ancient lava flows. After the 1920s, Gamio devoted most of his efforts to social anthropology and to setting up government programs to improve the living conditions of Mexico's indigenous peoples. He founded the National Institute of Indigenous Groups and directed it and other institutes for many years. He is one of the key figures of Mexican anthropology during the twentieth century, and his thinking strongly influenced government policy concerning the pre-Hispanic past and the problems of contemporary indigenous people.

In 1915, Herbert Spinden published an influential synthesis of early cultures in the Americas that was partly inspired by the studies of Gamio and others of Mexico's archaic cultures. Spinden's work contained hypotheses about the origins of agriculture and sedentary populations and caused a controversy among archaeologists that lasted for several decades (Willey and Sabloff 1980). Spinden's other fundamental contribution was his doctoral thesis (Spinden 1913), which was one of the key early analyses of Maya civilization and provided a corpus of monuments in chronological order determined by dated inscriptions and styles using his own Maya calendar correlation. In this work, Spinden proposed that the basic content of the inscriptions is historical and that the major Maya sites were true cities, not just ceremonial centers. These ideas were criticized by distinguished Mayanists like Morley and J. E. S. THOMPSON, and nearly fifty years passed before most investigators realized that Spinden was correct (Marcus 1983).

In 1914, Morley obtained long-term support from the Carnegie Institution for an ambitious program of multidisciplinary studies of the Maya. The Carnegie program, which lasted for over forty years, was directed successively by Morley, ALFRED V. KIDDER, and H. E. D. Pollock and organized important archaeological projects in Mexico, Guatemala, and Honduras. Its staff included many notable archaeologists: J. E. S. Thompson, TATIANA PROSKOURIAKOFF, Ricketson, Ruppert, Morris, Wauchope, A. L. Smith, R. E. Smith, the great linguist Ralph Roys, and others. For nearly thirty years, Morley explored the Maya lowlands and recorded hundreds of inscriptions, which were published in five volumes (Morley 1938).

The principal Carnegie project in Mexico during the 1920s involved the excavation and restoration of buildings at Chichén Itzá (Morris, Charlot, and Morris 1931; Rubbert 1952), and during the same decade, the number of archaeological projects in the central Mexican highlands increased. Initially these were led by Gamio, as "director of anthropology" for the federal government, and later they continued through the efforts of Ignacio Marquina, head of the national Department of Pre-Hispanic Monuments founded in 1925. In 1923, Marquina, trained as both an architect and an archaeologist, began a project at the Aztec center of Tenayuca and achieved a thorough analysis of the construction phases and ceramic sequences of the main pyramid and associated structures (Marquina et al. 1935). Marquina's program at Tenayuca produced one of the best architectural restorations in Mesoamerica.

Eduardo Noguera was responsible for ceramic analyses in Tenayuca. During the 1920s he excavated at Teotihuacán and surveyed a series of archaic (formative) sites in the basin of Mexico including Zacatenco, Ticoman, and El Arbolillo, which were subsequently excavated by George Vaillant. Noguera successfully used seriation techniques on surface collections at early sites and published a book on the archaic cultures of the basin in 1925. Also during the 1920s, Tulane University organized an archaeological and ethnographic survey of Tabasco, Chiapas, and southern Veracruz directed by Blom and La Farge. The first detailed descriptions of gulf coast OLMEC centers, especially LA VENTA, Tabasco, were published, and thus the debate concerning the possible roles of the Olmec in the origins of Mesoamerican civilization began. Blom and La Farge did not use the term *Olmec;* it was Hermann Beyer who named this newly discovered culture in a review of their report.

Beyer investigated Mesoamerican iconography and writing systems during the 1920s and 1930s and was the liaison between Mexican and German anthropologists. In 1919, he founded the important *Journal El Mexico Antiguo,* and between 1919 and 1924, he taught archaeology at Mexico's National Museum.

Beyer's outstanding student, the young lawyer Alfonso Caso, soon became a central influence on Mexican archaeologists in terms of both his investigations and his work as director of government institutes and programs (Bernal 1979). From his first fieldwork at Tizatlan, Tlaxcala, in 1927, Caso had an intense interest in many fields of archaeology and anthropology. He produced a major study of Zapotec stelae in 1928, and in 1930, he started his project at Monte Albán and other sites in Oaxaca, work that lasted eighteen field seasons with the collaboration of JORGE ACOSTA, IGNACIO BERNAL GARCIA, Eulalia Guzman, Anna Shepard, and others. The work at Monte Albán became one of the most important government projects of this period, and Caso was soon famous for his discovery of a Mixtec treasure in Tomb 7 at Monte Albán. The project included the exploration and restoration of many of the principal buildings on Monte Albán's main plaza along with surveys and excavations of other centers in the valley of Oaxaca. By the late 1930s, this research had produced one of the first detailed regional chronologies and ceramic sequences in Mesoamerica, although the final publication of these results came only years later (Caso and Bernal 1952; Caso, Bernal, and Acosta 1967).

During the 1920s and 1930s, Caso began his significant studies of ancient writing and codices in Oaxaca and related investigations of religion and calendar systems. Like Gamio, the numerous contributions of Caso to anthropology go beyond archaeological investigation. He was the founder and first director of the National Institute of Anthropology and History (1939), director of the National Institute of Indigenous Groups, president of the National University,

and a federal government cabinet minister (España Caballero 1987). Despite these bureaucratic duties, his academic production was vast, and several books on Mixtec codices have been published based on manuscripts Caso completed before his death in 1970.

The use of stratigraphic excavations to establish ceramic sequences and basic chronologies for Mexico's major regions was the major concern of archaeologists during the 1930s. For central Mexico, the most important cultural sequences were proposed by Vaillant and Noguera. Vaillant's work is still very influential although his premature death prevented him from publishing reports of all his excavations. Many of the ceramic type and cultural phase names he presented in syntheses (Vaillant 1938, 1941) are still in use, and his publications concerning central Mexican formative sites are of very high quality. He was perhaps the first archaeologist to identify Olmec traits in some highland formative cultures.

Noguera worked in numerous areas, especially Puebla, the basin of Mexico, and western Mexico, and produced publications about ceramics and chronology. He eventually wrote the only general summary of ceramic sequences for Mesoamerica (Noguera 1967). Another important synthesis of cultural chronologies for the central highlands was published in 1975 by Krickeberg using both ethnohistorical and archaeological data.

Sigvald Linne of the Ethnographical Museum of Stockholm directed an important program during the 1930s to define the principal area of influence of the Teotihuacán state by excavating at Teotihuacán, Calpulalpan, and other highland centers. His work marked a considerable advance over the previous studies of this problem by Seler and others. Linne did some detailed excavations of very large Teotihuacán residences in two sectors of the ancient city called Xolalpan and Tlamimilolpa.

The Mexican government sponsored excavation and restoration projects at the Aztec period centers of Malinalco and Calixtlahuaca in the state of México (García Payón 1936, 1939) and at Tzintzuntzan, Michoacán, the capital of the Tarascan people (Rubin de la Borbolla 1941). It is important to note that even through there had been little research in Mesoamerica concerning preceramic/presedentary cultural horizons, the Mexican scholar Pablo Martínez del Río published an important study on the origins of man in the Americas in 1936.

One of the best summaries of Mexican archaeology during this period was published by J. E. S. Thompson in 1933. Thompson did some of his most important Maya fieldwork during the 1930s, mainly in Belize but also in Quintana Roo, Campeche, and Yucatán, and he made a key contribution (Thompson 1935) in correcting the correlation between the Maya and European calendars, a correlation that is still used today.

Mexican government projects in the Maya lowlands included the architectural and iconographic studies of Miguel Angel Fernandez at Chichén Itzá in 1935, at Tulum in 1938, and at PALENQUE and Acanceh, also in 1938. The report on Acanceh is especially significant because of the discovery of Teotihuacán-style architecture in northern Yucatán. Wilfredo Du Solier (1938), also of the Department of Pre-Hispanic Monuments, produced an excellent ceramic sequence for the Totonac center of El Tajin in north-central Veracruz and subsequently excavated a series of cities of the Huasteca people on the northeastern frontier of Mesoamerica. Joaquin Meade was another investigator active in the Huasteca during the 1930s and 1940s.

In 1937, a project started in the Tuxtlas mountains of southern Veracruz under the direction of Juan Valenzuela and Karl Rubbert, whose investigations revealed evidence of long-distance commercial systems during the early classic period (A.D. 300–600) linked with the expansion of the Teotihuacán state. At the site of Matacapan, investigators identified several Teotihuacán-style buildings that may have been used by merchants from that great highland city.

During the final part of the 1930s, a number of important programs began on the west coast of Mexico, such as the work of Isabel Kelly (1938) and G. F. Ekholm (1942) in Sinaloa. The basic goal of both archaeologists was to establish regional chronologies based on ceramic sequences.

Some historical surveys (Bernal 1979; Willey and Sabloff 1974) have observed that Mexican

archaeology before 1940 was largely centered on the definition of ceramic sequences and relative chronologies for specific sites and regions. Most research concentrated on three areas: the central Mexican highlands (especially the basin of Mexico), the Maya lowlands, and Oaxaca. In general, the largest unit of investigation was a specific ruin or "site," and although stratigraphic excavations were common, they were mainly confined to relatively small test pits or trenches. Throughout most of the Americas during this period, many archaeological reports were essentially what GORDON WILLEY and Jeremy Sabloff (1974) call "potsherd chronicles." These were cultural reconstructions limited chiefly to descriptions of artifact types and the definition of supposedly related typologies, and there was not much effort to obtain a global vision concerning other aspects of ancient cultures.

Despite this generalized pattern in archaeology before 1940, there were some notable exceptions, such as Gamio's project in the Teotihuacán Valley, the investigations of Seler throughout Mesoamerica, and those of Linne in the central highlands. Although the pre-1940 concentration on chronologies and the definition of cultural sequences seem to contemporary archaeologists to constitute very limited goals, these objectives were fundamental during this period because without the chronological ordering of different cultures, no more anthropological archaeology would have been possible in subsequent periods. The pre-1940 investigations constituted an essential initial stage for obtaining preliminary knowledge concerning the archaeology of Mexico's numerous regions, many of which had a pre-Hispanic past that was previously almost unknown.

Another important activity during this period involved the Mexican "institutional archaeology" tradition of excavating and reconstructing large monumental centers. Some of the best monumental reconstructions ever done date to this period: Gamio's work at the Ciudadela plaza in Teotihuacán, Marquina's project at Tenayuca, and the Carnegie Institution program at Chichén Itzá.

Work in MAYA EPIGRAPHY was very successful during this period. The decipherment of Maya dates established the first absolute chronology in Mesoamerica, and the projects of Maudslay, Maler, Morley, and others who discovered and recorded a preliminary corpus of Maya inscriptions made possible the subsequent breakthroughs in the deciphering of this writing system.

Consolidation

In some ways, the 1940s constituted a period of consolidation and critical reviews of previous investigations in Mexico. During the second half of the decade, however, a series of projects began that had new kinds of objectives and new fields of study.

In 1940, the social anthropologist Clyde Kluckhohn published a severe criticism of archaeological investigation in Mexico and Central America. He was especially critical of the tendency of archaeologists to study pre-Hispanic cultures in terms of isolated elements such as architecture, ceramics, and inscriptions, and he argued that there was little commitment to produce syntheses concerning the totality of a culture similar to the analyses that ethnologists were making of living peoples. These criticisms were expanded and essentially codified by his archaeologist student WALTER TAYLOR (1948), whose work was a forerunner of some of the concepts "the new archaeology" of the 1960s. Pedro Armillas similarly criticized traditional Mesoamerican archaeology in Mexico during the same period.

The 1940s began with debates among archaeologists concerning two poorly understood cultures: the Toltecs and the Olmec. The Toltecs were mentioned in many pre-Hispanic chronicles as the ancestors of the Aztecs and some other peoples. Their empire, which was said to have reached its apogee during the tenth or eleventh century A.D., had its capital city called Tula, or Tollan, somewhere in the central highlands. Charnay (1885) and others had proposed that the center called Tula in the state of Hidalgo was the legendary Tollan, but many early-twentieth-century archaeologists, including Gamio and Vaillant, thought that Teotihuacán was the Toltec capital.

In 1941, the distinguished ethnohistorian Jiménez Moreno had analyzed the place-names and geographical regions mentioned in the chronicles concerning the location of ancient Tollan and had showed that most of the places were clearly identified with the area of Tula, Hidalgo. In 1940, with the support of the newly founded National Institute of Anthropology and History, Jorge R. Acosta began the first of nearly twenty archaeological field seasons at Tula, and the first roundtable conference of the Mexican Society of Anthropology was organized the next year with Tula and the Toltecs as its theme. Over thirty archaeologists discussed the significance of the findings of Jiménez Moreno and Acosta and concluded that Tula, Hidalgo, was the Tollan described in the chronicles of central Mexico.

The Olmec were the subject of the second roundtable conference of the Mexican Society of Anthropology, held in 1942 with Caso, M. Stirling, M. Covarrubias, and Jiménez Moreno as key participants. Discussions centered on Stirling's recent investigations of Olmec centers in Veracruz and Tabasco, especially his discovery of Stela C at Tres Zapotes, Veracruz, which had an inscribed date corresponding to 32 B.C. The iconographic studies of Caso and Covarrubias, and the ethnohistorical syntheses of Jiménez Moreno, all presented cases for the great antiquity of the Olmec. On the basis of these investigations, the majority of the roundtable participants concluded that, as Caso had proposed, the Olmec were "the mother culture" of Mesoamerican civilizations such as the classic Maya, Teotihuacán, and Zapotecs of Monte Alban. The chronological placement of the Olmec was debated until the 1950s when radiocarbon dating showed that this culture existed at least as early as 1000 B.C., during the formative period.

During the 1940s, many Mayanists, including Morley and Thompson, did not accept that the Olmec were older than the Maya of the classic period (A.D. 300–900). In 1941, Thompson published a complex analysis that tried to demonstrate that the Olmec were a postclassic culture of the fourteenth or fifteenth century A.D. Stirling continued excavating Olmec sites during the 1940s at La Venta, Tres Zapotes, and San Lorenzo, and Covarrubias (1943, 1946a, 1946, 1949) excavated Tlatilco in the basin of Mexico where he found evidence for the early expansion of Olmec culture beyond the Gulf coast of Veracruz and Tabasco.

In *Mexico South* (1946b), Covarrubias published the first detailed summary of the Olmec civilization, including a brilliant analysis of iconography. One of the finest books ever written about Mexico, the work includes chapters on the archaeology, ethnography, folklore, and history of the peoples of the Isthmus of Tehuantepec in Southern Mexico.

The 1940s ended with a transformation of the fields of study and theoretical goals of Mexican archaeology. Investigations were made based on the theories of cultural evolution and Marxism, often with an emphasis on the development of social stratification and the interrelationships between human populations and their natural environments. Paul Kirchhoff, Pedro Armillas, and Othón de Mendizábal were pioneers in these new research orientations. Mendizábal, principally a social anthropologist, used archaeological and ethnological data and published a series of analyses concerning the economic systems of specific native groups and the cultural evolution of major regions in the central highlands (Mendizábal 1946).

Paul Kirchhoff, a German social anthropologist who went to Mexico during the 1930s, made fundamental contributions to archaeology. In 1943 he produced the first coherent definition of Mesoamerica (it was Kirchhoff who proposed the term) as a cultural area, mainly using ethnohistoric and ethnographic traits to define the cultural elements. He also published studies of the ecological variations in Mesoamerica and neighboring areas, attempting to correlate them with different social structures, subsistence systems, and patterns of resource exploitation among pre-Hispanic peoples. He wrote ethnohistorical analyses of ancient chronicles, concentrating especially on histories of the Toltecs and the migrations of different ethnic groups in central Mexico. His classes on Marxism, social organization, ethnology, and other subjects in the National School of Anthropology and History profoundly influenced several generations of Mexican anthropologists and archaeologists.

The investigations and classes of Pedro Armillas during the 1940s and 1950s also had

A carved statue found in the ancient Toltec city of Tula (Gamma)

profound effects on the development of Mexican archaeology. He was the original exponent of cultural ecology in Mesoamerican studies, and his many students have generated projects and investigations inspired by his ideas. Armillas was instrumental in disseminating the writings and concepts of VERE GORDON CHILDE in Mexico, writings concerning cultural evolution, urbanism, and other fundamental processes.

Armillas did fieldwork in many regions. His excavations in Teotihuacán formed the basis for his (1950) chronology of the basin of Mexico, which is essentially still valid. Using data from surveys of various regions in the state of Guerrero, he proposed a model for the major systems of agriculture in Mesoamerica (1947). He studied fortified centers in the central highlands (1948) and conducted surveys in the Valley of Puebla-Tlaxcala in an attempt to correlate specific centers with ethnic groups mentioned in pre-Hispanic chronicles. In 1949 he published a famous essay proposing a framework for cultural evolution in Mesoamerica, emphasizing technology and socioeconomic processes. In field exercises for classes at the National School of Anthropology, he organized a project at Xochicalco on the gulf, including one of the first settlement pattern studies in Mesoamerica (Sanders 1956).

The theoretical propositions of Armillas caused long-standing debates concerning the criteria for defining the concepts of state and civilization. Armillas proposed that urbanism is the key factor and that the great highland cities, especially Teotihuacán, constituted the principal centers of culture evolution in Mesoamerica. Other archaeologists, especially Caso and Bernal, contended that cultures outside the highlands, such as the Olmec and the Maya, played even more important roles in the evolution of Mesoamerican civilization than did the Teotihuacán (Sanders and Price 1968).

In contrast to earlier periods, various 1940s projects consisted of regional studies with objectives that went beyond merely establishing local cultural chronologies. At the beginning of the decade, Alberto Ruz Lhullier did a survey of the Campeche coast that in some ways was a precursor of later settlement pattern investigations. During the late 1940s, Ruz began a program at Palenque that produced important findings, including the 1952 discovery of the royal tomb in the Temple of the Inscriptions.

In 1943, the Carnegie Institution published an excellent report by Rubbert and Denisson of surveys in the jungles of Campeche, Quintana Roo, and the Petén of Guatemala, discovering important centers including El Mirador. During the same period, Pollock did an encyclopedic survey of Maya architecture in central Yucatán, especially in the Puuc area (Pollock 1980).

Other areas of Mexico began to be studied systematically: Rubin de la Borbolla, Moedano, Porter, and Estrada Balmori conducted a series of surveys and excavations in Guanajuato and Michoacán, especially in the regions of Chupicuaro, Tzintzuntzan, and Zinapécuaro, in which they investigated sites of many different periods. Corona Núñez (1942, 1946) studied Tarascan sites at this time, and Isabel Kelly studied numerous regions in western Mexico, especially in Michoacán, Jalisco, Sinaloa, and Colima (Kelly 1945–1949, 1980).

In 1944, Ekholm presented a detailed study of cultural sequences in the Huasteca of the northern Gulf coast, and his work is the source for the chronological framework that is still being used for this region. During the 1940s and 1950s, José García Payón directed key investigations in north-central Veracruz and eastern Puebla surveying major regions and excavating many sites, including El Tajín, Misantla, Zempoala, Castillo de Teayo, and Xiutetelco.

An important interdisciplinary project was organized by Espejo, Barlow, Griffin, and Franco at Tlatelolco in the basin of Mexico in which they attempted to correlate ethnohistorical reconstructions and events with archaeological data. Griffin and Espejo (1947, 1950) defined four general complexes of Aztec ceramics that became fundamental components of most late pre-Hispanic chronologies for central Mexico. At San Cristóbal Ecatepec in the northern basin, Du Solier (1947–1948) made thorough excavations of a long series of occupations from the late formative period (500 B.C.) until the Spanish conquest in the sixteenth century.

Also during the 1940s, several investigations of Pleistocene early hunters began. The discovery of an apparently very early human burial at Tepexpán (near Teotihuacán) by De Terra (1946) was followed by Aveleyra's (1952) more reliable find of stone tools associated with a mammoth kill at Santa Isabel Ixtapan. Several other early sites were investigated, and by 1950, there was sufficient information for Aveleyra to write a book on the prehistory of Mexico. In 1952, the Department of Prehistory of the National Institute of Anthropology was founded with Pablo Martinez del Rio as its first director.

The National School of Anthropology, the key institution for archaeological teaching and investigation, was founded in 1937. During the 1940s and 1950s this school was one of the best places to study anthropology. The students came from many countries in the Americas and Europe, and the distinguished faculty included Wigberto Jiménez Moreno, Paul Kirchhoff, Pedro Armillas, Pedro Bosch Gimpera, Juan Comas, Miguel Covarrubias, Calixtla Guittierrez Holmes, Barbro Dahlgren, Roberto Weitlaner, Javier Romero, and Pablo Martínez del Rio.

Some of the students' theses became Mesoamerican classics: Pedro Carrasco (1950) on the Otomi, Arturo Monzón (1949) on the Aztec *calpulli* (units of social organization), Anne Chapman (1957) on Mesoamerican ports of trade, and Acosta Saignes (1945) on Aztec merchants. Central concepts for the influential Mesoamerican studies of Angel Palerm, Eric Wolf, and William Sanders also originated when they were students at the National School of Anthropology.

During the 1950s, an increasing number of projects studied the relationships between pre-Hispanic peoples and their geographical setting and natural environment. Many of these investigations were based on settlement pattern analyses that were introduced in Mesoamerican archaeology by Gordon Willey in his 1953 Belize Valley project. Gordon Childe, JULIAN STEWARD, and Karl Wittfogel were the sources of many of the theoretical frameworks of archaeological investigations during this period, and in varying degrees, these theorists had materialist perspectives influenced by Marxism.

Childe had a profound effect on archaeology throughout the world, and in Mexico, his thinking on social evolution and his concepts of "Neolithic revolution" and "urban revolution" were commonly used. Steward's theories concerning "multilineal evolution" and his studies of culture change in relation to human adaptations to the natural environment formed an essential theoretical basis for settlement pattern studies, which have been a central part of Mexican archaeology for several decades.

Childe's and Steward's ideas were often combined with the more controversial theories of Wittfogel about "hydraulic societies" and the roles of irrigation in the development of civilization. In the 1950s, key works included studies by Palerm (1957) concerning ecological potential and cultural development, Sanders's (1956, 1957) analyses of irrigation systems and settlement patterns in the central highlands, interdisciplinary programs by Lorenzo and others (Lorenzo, Mooser, and White 1956) concerning the paleoenvironments of the basin of Mexico, and Rene Millon's early investigations of the roles of irrigation at Teotihuacán.

In the 1950s, there were also some major findings in several fields of Maya archaeology. Ruz continued his extensive excavation and restoration program at Palenque, and at Dzibilchaltun in northern Yucatán, E. W. Andrews IV started a multifaceted project that eventually produced important publications. Subsequent investigations continued for three decades. The Carnegie Institution's last project, centered at Mayapan, involved some essentially new field methodologies for Maya studies, including the excavation of numerous habitational structures and the production of a detailed map of the entire settlement (Pollock, Roys, Proskouriakoff, and Smith 1962). During the same period, the Mormon Church began a long-term program in Chiapas directed by the New World Archaeological Foundation (Lowe 1959), and it produced dozens of important site reports.

Some crucial contributions were also made in Maya epigraphy. The Russian Yuri Knorosov published preliminary phonetic translations of hieroglyphic texts and thus supplied the methodology for the revolution in Maya decipherments that was to take place during the 1970s and 1980s. Unfortunately, Knorosov's work was vigorously attacked by Thompson, and few Mayanists during the 1950s, with the exception of David Kelley, attempted phonetic translations of hieroglyphs. Despite the mistaken refutations of phoneticism, Thompson produced fundamental analyses in his *Maya Hieroglyphic Writing: An Introduction* (1950) and *A Catalogue of Maya Hieroglyphs* (1962).

In 1958, H. Berlin identified what he called "emblem glyphs" on monuments that appeared to be the names of cities or symbols of royal dynasties. In 1959, Proskouriakoff published the first of several key studies proposing that the principal subjects of texts on Maya monuments concerned historical events, especially details of the lives of the kings and nobles who ruled specific centers or regions. The work of Proskouriakoff and Berlin soon caused a reorientation of Maya epigraphic studies because the two men rejected the interpretations of the previous generation of Mayanists headed by Morley and Thompson, who thought the inscriptions were principally religious and calendric in nature without much historical content. The importance of Knorosov's phonetic analyses was not fully accepted until nearly twenty years later.

Major projects along the Gulf coast of Veracruz and Tabasco included García Payón's excavations at El Tajín and Zempoala and his surveys in various regions (1954, 1955). Medellín Zenil established ceramic sequences in the Totonicapán and other areas of south-central Veracruz (1953, 1960), and in extensive excavation at La Venta, Tabasco, by Drucker, Heizer, and Squier 1959) many offering and monuments were uncovered. This work obtained the first radiocarbon dates for the Olmec culture, placing it tentatively between 1000–400 B.C., thus confirming the Olmec chronology proposed by Caso and Covarrubias.

In the Valley of Oaxaca, Bernal and Paddock excavated various centers as part of the investigation program for the newly founded Universidad de las Americas, and in the basin of Mexico, Piña Chan excavated formative sites while investigating some of the problems relating to early cultures there that had previously been defined by Vaillant, Noguera, and Covarrubias. In surveying the northern basin, Tolstoy (1958) refined ceramic typologies for some phases of the classic and postclassic periods, and Sejourné (1959) made controversial nonstratigraphic excavations in Teotihuacán that uncovered many murals and provided information concerning the planning and internal structure of residential buildings.

Richard MacNeish's (1958) project in Tamaulipas in northeastern Mexico was significant because it attempted to investigate the early domestication processes for basic food plants such as maize and beans, a problem MacNeish would study more thoroughly later in his multidisciplinary project in the Tehuacán Valley.

The 1950s produced some ambitious general syntheses of Mesoamerican archaeology. In Marquina's (1951) encyclopedic study of pre-Hispanic architecture, still an indispensable work in Mesoamerican studies, he cited and analyzed numerous unpublished reports from the archives of the Department of Pre-Hispanic Monuments in enriching his coverage of poorly known cultures and regions. Two book-length essays on cultural definitions of Mesoamerica were published by Olivé (1958) and Piña Chan (1960).

Contemporary Mexican Archaeology

Most of the concepts and theories currently in use by Mesoamerican archaeologists emerged, close to their present form, during the 1960s and 1970s. In some cases, the theoretical and methodological goals of new projects are so ambitious that there are lapses of as much as ten to twenty years between the beginning of fieldwork and the publication of the detailed "final reports."

Mexican archaeology experienced some radical changes during the 1960s with numerous debates concerning the validity of the theory, methods, and objectives of traditional archaeology. Some of the debates were influenced by the development of "the new archaeology" in the United States, especially by the ideas and theories of LEWIS BINFORD. Among younger Mexican archaeologists there was an even stronger interest in Marxism and the use of historical materialism to study social process and attempt to discover general "laws" of social development. This shift toward Marxism was part of a much larger intellectual and political process that eventually resulted in the student movement of 1968 that changed key aspects of the contemporary Mexican political system. So far, the best Marxist analyses have been produced by social anthropologists such as Bonfil and Olivera, and although numerous archaeological projects have used Marxist interpretive frameworks, no rigorous materialist syntheses have appeared similar to the ones that Childe produced for ancient peoples in the Old World. Some of the best materialist studies using archaeological and ethnohistorical data concern the development of social stratification and state-level societies (Batra 1969; Carrasco, ed., 1976; Carrasco and Broda 1978).

Starting in the 1960s, the National Institute of Anthropology and History steadily grew and diversified, and there was a considerable increase in the number of archaeologists on its staff. Laboratories for geological, biological, and ecological analyses were set up in the Department of Prehistory, and the Departments of Salvage Archaeology and Subaquatic Archaeology were founded. The Archaeology Department in the new (1964) National Museum of Anthropology was expanded, and during the 1970s and 1980s, the National Institute of Anthropology and History founded regional centers staffed by archaeologists in principal Mexican states. The National Autonomous University of Mexico developed specific institutions for anthropological and archaeological research, including the Center for Maya Studies and the Institute for Anthropological Investigations. Some state governments and state universities founded or expanded archaeology programs, the largest of which was organized by Veracruz University in Jalapa.

Since the beginning of the 1960s, the number of both national and foreign archaeological projects in Mexico has greatly increased, and they focus on studying regions and cultural processes that previously received little or no attention. The most representative programs include three long-term projects that began in 1960 in the central highlands: William Sanders's Teotihuacán Valley project, Rene Millon's study of urbanism at Teotihuacán, and Richard MacNeish's multidisciplinary program investigating the origins of agriculture in the Tehuacán Valley in the state of Puebla. Partially based on previous theoretical frameworks, these projects now involved much more ambitious research designs that meant many seasons of fieldwork done by large staffs of archaeologists and students.

Sanders's work consisted of the first systematic settlement pattern survey of a large region in Mexico. His field methodology was based principally on Willey's pioneer study in the VIRÚ VALLEY of PERU, and his initial theoretical goals centered on Steward's and Armillas's conceptions of cultural ecology. Sanders soon expanded the project to include the entire basin of Mexico—with the collaboration of Jeffrey Parsons, Richard Blanton, and others—and during nearly fifteen years of investigations, his project recovered crucially important information concerning hundreds of settlements and 3,000 years of human occupation. The surveys are especially significant because they recorded many sites that since have been destroyed by the growth of modern Mexico City and its suburbs.

Sanders, Parsons, and Santley published a general summary of the project in 1969, and Parsons's volumes (1971) on the settlement systems for specific areas of the basin provide a further wealth of data.

Millon's (1973, 1981) Teotihuacán project produced the first detailed study of urbanism in Mesoamerica. His staff mapped the entire pre-Hispanic city, which covered nearly twenty square kilometers, and the published map in book form is a model of rigorous archaeological reporting. Fieldwork combined excavations and surface surveys helped to define different periods of growth in the ancient city and to identify specific neighborhoods and craft areas. The initial mapping program produced many subsequent investigations by project members such as George Cowgill's statistical analyses of social organization, Rattray's fine ceramic chronology, and Spence's studies of obsidian tool production.

MacNeish's archaeobotanic project in the Tehuacán Valley was primarily dedicated to analyzing domestication processes for maize and other key Mesoamerican cultivated plants. Fieldwork concentrated on the excavation of deep deposits in dry caves and regional settlement pattern studies covering several thousand years of occupations from early preceramic horizons until the sixteenth-century A.D. Spanish conquest (Byers and MacNeish 1967–1976). This work obtained valuable information concerning the origins of agriculture and settled life, the development of irrigation systems, and the evolution of complex societies. The Tehuacán project was a truly multidisciplinary program as it integrated the archaeologists' research with that of biologists, botanists, geologists, and other specialists who studied materials in the archaeological record that commonly had been ignored in previous Mesoamerican studies: plant remains, animal bones, pollen, human coprolites, fiber textiles, etc.

The three long-term projects made fundamental contributions to the development of archaeology in Mexico. Their central significance goes beyond their extensive findings concerning specific peoples and cultural processes and lies chiefly in their theoretical and methodological frameworks. These provided new perspectives in archaeological investigation such as the study of pre-Hispanic cities in their totality as complex integrated cultural systems instead of limiting investigation to the monumental ceremonial centers or other sectors of a city, as if they were isolated from the rest of settlement. Another contribution was the perspective of settlement pattern studies that transcended the concept of isolated sites and organized archaeological investigation in terms of regional settlement systems or other groups of sites forming larger analysis units. New investigations inspired by these projects modified and expanded the kinds of problems and information being studied, recovered more data about many specific cultural processes, and provided a more integrated vision of pre-Hispanic societies.

During the following decades, settlement-pattern studies became common in Mexico, and some of the first projects of this type were salvage archaeology programs undertaken by the National Institute of Anthropology and History. Fieldwork and excavation were coordinated with the construction of hydroelectric dams and modern irrigation systems, such as (during the 1960s and 1970s) the projects of Infiernillo, Palos Altos, and La Villita in Guerrero; La Angostura, Mal Paso, Chicoasen, and Itzantun in Chiapas; Chicayan in Veracruz; and Pujalcoy in San Luis Potosí. More recently, a number of salvage settlement pattern and excavation programs have been carried out in conjunction with the construction of natural gas lines. The quantity of salvage investigation has increased greatly since 1970, and it now forms an integral part of Mexican government archaeology. One of the most extensive accumulations of salvage data came from nearly twenty-five years of excavation during the installation of Mexico City's subway system.

Some of the major nonsalvage regional studies include projects in the Puebla-Tlaxcala, the Valley of Oaxaca, the Komchen (Yucatán), the Coba (Quintana Roo), the Rio Bec and the Tula area. There were also French and Mexican surveys in the Huasteca (Ochoa 1979).

Two key regional projects investigating the origins of Mesoamerican civilization among the Gulf coast Olmec were centered at San Lorenzo Tenochtitlán in Veracruz (Coe and Diehl 1980) and La Venta in the state of Tabasco (González Lauck 1988). The San Lorenzo project included ecological and agricultural studies that provided crucial data concerning Olmec subsistence, and the La Venta project made settlement pattern studies of sites that were over 3,500 years old.

In the field of what Latin Americans call "prehistoric archaeology," the study of very early human occupations of the late Pleistocene and later preceramic times, there have been important changes. Multidisciplinary projects investigating long sequences of occupations for specific regions, in conjunction with detailed reconstructions of paleoclimates and paleoenvironments, are now the norm. In the southern basin of Mexico, a major program at the site of Tlapacoya by the Department of Prehistory (Lorenzo and Mirambell 1986; Niederberger 1976) uncovered one of the earliest sites in the Americas, over 20,000 years of human occupations. A probable long occupation by early hunters was investigated by Irwin-Williams (1978) at Valsequillo in Puebla. A multidisciplinary project concerning the origins of agriculture and settled life was directed by Kent Flannery (1986) in the Valley of Oaxaca.

As part of the growing interest in studying social and economic processes, new techniques and theoretical goals have been developed for the analysis of archaeological materials, especially ceramics and lithics. Ceramics are no longer studied exclusively to establish chronologies and occupation sequences but also to identify artifact functions, activity areas, and technological processes. Numerous programs investigate ceramic production (workshop) and trade systems with the aid of petrographic and trace element analyses (Rice 1986).

Lithic artifacts and tools were only briefly described in Mesoamerican reports before the 1960s, but LITHIC ANALYSIS has improved greatly and now the technological production sequences and specific functions of tools are investigated. Use/wear functional studies are common, and there is considerable research concerning lithic workshops, mining, and trade systems (Gaxiola and Clark 1989).

Historical archaeology, investigating cultures

Mayan ruins at Uxmal (Danny Lehman / CORBIS)

dating after the Spanish conquest, is a relatively new field in Mexico, but since the 1960s, there have been several large projects and many smaller ones that have excavated structures and settlements from the sixteenth to the nineteenth centuries (Charlton 1972; Juárez Cossío 1984; Lee and Markman 1977; Vega Sosa 1979). These programs usually benefit from parallel investigations of historical archives in Mexico and Spain.

Maya epigraphy has provided one of the greatest breakthroughs in Mesoamerican archaeology in recent years. Based on the previous studies of Knorosov, Proskouriakoff, Thompson, Berlin, Kelley, and others, the decipherment of texts has advanced to the point that there are now partial translations of many inscriptions. Recent work by Floyd Lounsbury, LINDA SCHELE, Peter Mathews, Stuart, and others have identified royal dynasties and many historical events for some of the principal classic Maya centers, and these scholars also have verified the phonetic structure of much of Maya writing (Coe 1993). There is literally a flood of publications containing translations of inscriptions and new historical summaries largely

based on epigraphic studies (Schele 1982; Schele and Freidel 1990).

Large government projects dedicated mainly to the excavation of main plazas or "monumental zones" of ancient centers are still common, but they vary greatly with regard to theoretical frameworks, field techniques, and objectives. Some of the most significant of these programs include the Teotihuacán project directed by Bernal during the 1960s, which principally concentrated on the exploration and reconstruction of buildings on the Street of the Dead. The more recent Teotihuacán projects directed by Rubén Cabrera have extensively excavated the area of the Ciudadela, especially the Temple of Quetzalcoatl (Cabrera, Rodriguez, and Morelos 1982; Cabrera et al. 1989), and have produced important data on the functioning of the Teotihuacán state.

The Cholula project directed by Marquina at the end of the 1960s excavated and reconstructed architectural complexes near the Great Pyramid and produced some excessively restored buildings. This program also included ethnohistorical and ethnological investigations (Marquina 1970). The recent excavation of the Templo Mayor and other structures on Tenochtitlán's main plaza (López Luján 1993; Matos Moctezuma 1982) received a large amount of financial support from the government and generated great interest among the Mexican public. This program has resulted in a major new museum and research center for Aztec studies and an important series of publications.

There are many other projects investigating monumental centers such as Teotenango, Xochicalco, Uxmal, Yaxchilan, Palenque, BONAMPAK', Pomona, Tonina, Chichén Itzá, El Tajin, Cacaxtla, Monte Albán, and La Quemada. Some of these projects are limited to the excavation and conservation of monumental architecture while others combine those activities with more extensive investigations that delimit the total settlement and study specific areas outside the monumental zone.

More than 100 archaeological zones in Mexico are open to the public, and tens of thousands of other sites have been identified in surveys or other investigations. There is growing debate among archaeologists concerning priorities for the investigation and conservation of this ancient cultural patrimony. With the growth of modern Mexico, and especially with the expansion of numerous towns and cities and the common use of mechanized agriculture, many archaeological sites are in danger of being destroyed. Nearly all future archaeology in Mexico will in some sense be salvage archaeology.

In recent decades a number of major syntheses and new journals dedicated partially or entirely to Mesoamerican archaeology have been published. Some of the most influential of these include *Handbook of Middle American Indians* (Bricker and Sabloff 1981; Wauchope 1964–1971); *Mexico: Panorama histórico y cultural* (1974–1976) and *La antropología en Mexico: Panorama histórico* (García Mora et al. 1987–1989), both published by the National Institute of Anthropology and History; and the journals *Latin American Antiquity, Ancient Mesoamerica, Arqueologia* (INAH), and *Arqueologia Mexicana*.

Robert H. Cobean and
Alba Guadalupe Mastache Flores

References

Acosta Saignes, M. 1945. "Los pochteca: Ubicación de los mercaderes en la estructura social tenochca." *Acta Antropologica* 1, no. 1.

Andrews, E. W. 1980. *Excavations at Dzibilchaltun, Yucatán, Mexico.* New Orleans: Tulane University.

Armillas, P. 1947. "Notas sobre sistemas de cultivo en Mesoamerica." *Anales del INAH* 3: 85–114

———. 1948. "Fortalezas mexicanas." *Cuadernos Americanos* 7: 143–163.

———. 1949. "Tecnologia, formaciones socioeconómicas, y religión en Mesoamerica." In *Twenty-ninth International Congress of Americanists,* 19–30. Mexico City.

———. 1950. "Teotihuacan, Tula, y los toltecas: Las culturas post-arcaicas y pre-aztecas del Centro de Mexico, excavaciones y estudios 1922–1955." *Runa* 3: 37–70.

Aveleyra, L. 1952. "Asociación de artefactos con un mamut en el Pleistoceno superior de la Cuenca de México." *Revista Mexicana de Estudios Antropologicos* 13: 3–30.

Bartra, R., ed. 1969. *El modo de produccion asiatico.* Mexico: Ediciones ERA.

Berlin, H. 1958. "El glifo emblema en las inscripciones maya." *Journal de la Société des Americanistes* 52: 91–99.

Bernal, I. 1979. *Historia de la arqueología en Mexico.* Porrua.

Boas, F. 1917. "El dialecto mexicano de Pochutla." *International Journal of American Linguistics* 1: 9–44.

Bricker, V. R., and J. A. Sabloff, eds. 1981. *Supplement to the Handbook of Middle American Indians I.* Austin: University of Texas Press.

Byers, D. S., and R. MacNeish, eds. 1967–1976. *The Prehistory of the Tehuacan Valley.* Austin: University of Texas Press.

Cabrera, R., I. Rodriguez, and N. Morelos, eds. 1982. *Memoria del proyecto arqueologico Teotihuacan.* Mexico City: SEP, Instituto Nacional de Antropología e Historia.

Cabrera, Rubén, et al. 1982. *Teotihuacan 80–82: Primeros resultados.* México : SEP, Instituto Nacional de Antropología e Historia.

Cabrera Castro, R, G. L. Cowgill, S. Sugiyama, and C. Serrano. 1989. "El proyecto templo de Quetzalcóatl." *Arqueologfa* 5: 51–79. Mexico City: INAH.

Carrasco, P. 1950. *Los otomfes: Cultura e historia prehispanica de los pueblos Mesoamericanos de Habla Otomiana.* Mexico City: UNAM.

———. 1976. *Estratificacion social en la Mesoamerica prehispanica.* Mexico City: SEP-INAH.

Carrasco, P., and J. Broda, eds. 1978. *Economfa polftica e ideologfa en el Mexico prehispanico.* Mexico City: Editorial Nueva Imagen.

Caso, A., and I. Bernal. 1952. *Urnas de Oaxaca.* Mexico City: INAH.

Caso, A., I. Bernal, and J. Acosta. 1967. *La ceramica de Monte Albán.* Mexico City: INAH.

Chapman, A. C. 1957. "Port of Trade Enclaves in Aztec and Maya Civilization." In *Trade and Market in Early Empires.* Ed. K. Polanyi, C. M. Arensberg, and H. W. Pearson. Glencoe, IL: Free Press.

Charlton, T. 1972. "Populations Trends in the Teotihuacan Valley, A.D. 1400–1969." *World Archaeology* 4: 106–123.

Charnay, D. 1885. *Les anciennes villes du Nouveau Monde.* Paris: Hachette.

Coe, M. D. 1993. *Breaking the Maya Code.* New York: Thames and Hudson.

Coe, M. D., and R. A. Diehl. 1980. *In the Land of the Olmec: The Archaeology of San Lorenzo Tenochtitlan.* Austin: University of Texas Press.

Corona Núñez, J. 1942. "Origen probable de los habitantes primitivos de Michoacan." *Universidad Michoacana* 4, no. 18: 82–113.

———. 1946. "Cuitzeo, estudio antropo-geografico." *Acta Antropológica* 2, no. 1: 1–70.

Covarrubias, M. 1943. "Tlatilco: Archaic Mexican Art and Culture *DYN* 4–5: 40–46.

———. 1946a. "El arte olmeca o de la Venta." *Cuadernos Americanos* 4: 153–179.

———. 1946b. *Mexico South: The Isthmus of Tehuantepec.* New York: Alfred Knopf.

———. 1949. "Tlatilco: El arte y la cultura preclásica del Valle de Mexico." *Cuadernos Americanos* 9: 149–162.

Drucker, P., R. F. Heizer, and R. J. Squier. 1959. *Excavations at La Venta, Tabasco, 1955.* Washington, DC: Smithsonian Institution.

Du Solier, W. 1938. "La ceramica arqueológica del Tajin." *Anales del Museo Nacional de Mexico* 3: 147–192.

———. 1947–1948. "Ceramica arqueológica de San Cristobal Ecatepec." *Anales del INAH* 3: 27–57.

Ekholm, G. F. 1942. *Excavations at Guasave, Sinaloa, Mexico.* New York: American Museum of Natural History.

España Caballero, A. 1987. "La practica social y el populismo nacionalista." In *La antropologza en Mexico: Panorama histórico,* 2: 223–288. Ed. Carlos García Mora. Mexico City: INAH.

Flannery, K. V. 1986. *Guila Naguitz: Archaic Foraging and Early Agriculture in Oaxaca.* New York: Academic Press.

Freidel, D. A., and J. A. Sabloff. 1984. *Cozumel: Late Maya Settlement Patterns.* New York: Academic Press.

García Mora, C., et al., eds. 1987–1989. *La antropología en Mexico: Panorama historíco.* 15 vols. Mexico City: INAH.

García Payón, J. 1936. *Zona arqueologica de Tecaxic Calixtlahuaca.* México: Talleres gráficos de la nación.

———. 1939. "El edificio monolitico de Malinalco es de cultura Azteca." *Cuadernos Americanos* 27: 22–228.

———. 1953–1954. "Exploraciones en El Tajin, Temporadas. 1953–1954." *Direccion de Monumentos Prehispanicos* 2. Mexico City: INAH.

———. 1955. "La ofrenda del Altar de la Gran Piramide, Zempoala, Ver." *El Mexico Antiguo* 8: 57–65.

Gaxiola, M., and J. E. Clark, eds. 1989. *La obsidiana en Mesoamerica.* Mexico City: Instituto Nacional de Antropología e Historia.

González Gamio, A. 1987. *Manuel Gamio: Una lucha sin final.* Mexico City: UNAM.

González Lauck, R. 1988. "Proyecto arqueológico La Venta." *Arqueologia* 4. Mexico City: INAH.

Griffin, J. B., and A. Espejo. 1947. "La alfareria correspondiente al ultimo periodo de ocupación nahua del Valle de Mexico." *Tlatelolco a traves de los tiempos* 9: 10–26.

———. 1950. "La alfareria correspondiente al ultimo periodo de ocupación nahua del Valle de Mexico." *Tlatelolco a traves de los tiempos* 11: 15–66.

Grove, D. C., ed. 1987. *Ancient Chalcatzingo.* Austin: University of Texas Press.

Humboldt, A. von. 1814. *Researches concerning the Institutions and Monuments of the Ancient Inhabitants of America.* London.

Irwin-Williams, C. 1978. "Summary of Archaeological Evidence from the Valsequillo Region, Puebla, Mexico." In *Cultural Continuity in Mesoamerica,* 7–22. Ed. David Browman. The Hague: Mouton.

Juárez Cossío, D. 1984. *San Jeronimo: Un ejemplo de argueologta historica.* Thesis, Escuela Nacional de Antropología e Historia. Mexico City: Instituto Nacional de Antropología e Historia.

Kelly, I. T. 1938. *Excavations at Chametla, Sinaloa.* Iberoamerica 14. Berkeley: University of California.

———. 1945. *Excavations at Culiacan, Sinaloa.* Iberoamerica 25. Berkeley: University of California.

———. 1945–1949. *The Archaeology of the Autlan-Tuxcacuesco Area of Jalisco: I The Autlan Zone, II The Tuxcacuesco Zapotitlan Zone.* Iberoamerica 26–27. Berkeley: University of California.

———. 1980. *Ceramic Secuence in Colima: Capacha, an Early Phase.* Anthropological Papers 37. Tucson: University of Arizona.

Kirchhoff, P. 1943. "Mesoamerica, sus limites geograficos, composición etnica y caracteres culturales." *Acta Americana* 1: 92–107.

Krickeberg, W. 1975. *Las antiguas culturas americanas.* FCE. Mexico City.

Kroeber, A. L. 1925. "Archaic Culture Horizons in the Valley of Mexico." *University of California Publications in American Archaeology and Ethnology* 17–70, 373–408.

Lee, T., and S. D. Markman. 1977. "The Coxoh Colonial Project and Coneta, Chiapas, Mexico: A Provincial Maya Village under the Spanish Conquest." *Historical Archaeology* 11: 56–66.

Lopez Luján, L. 1993. *Las ofrendas del Templo Mayor de Tenochhtlan.* México City: Instituto Nacional de Antropología e Historia.

Lorenzo, J. L., and L. Mirambell. 1986. *Tlapacoya: 35,000 anos de historia del Lago de Chalco.* Mexico City: INAH.

Lorenzo, J. L., F. Mooser, and S. E. White. 1956. *La Cuenca de Mexico: Consideraciones geologicas y arqueologicas.* Mexico City.

Lowe, G. W. 1959. *The Chiapas Project, 1955–1958.* New World Archaeological Foundation Papers 1, 3. Provo, UT.

MacNeish, R. S. 1958. *Preliminary Archaeological Investigations in the Sierra de Tamaulipas, Mexico.* American Philosophical Society 48: Pt 6.

Maler, T. 1901. *Researches in the Central Portion of the Usumacinta Valley.* Memoirs 2, 1. Cambridge MA: Peabody Museum.

Marcus, J. 1983. "Lowland Maya Archaeology at the Crossroads." *American Antiquity* 48: 454–488.

Marquina, I. 1951. *Arquitectura prehispanica.* Mexico City: INAH.

———. 1970. *Proyecto Cholula.* Investigaciones 20. Mexico City: INAH.

Martínez del Río, P. 1936. *Los ortgenes americanos.* Mexico City.

Matos Moctezuma, E. 1982. *El Templo Mayor de Tenochtitlan.* Mexico City: INAH. Meade, J. 1939. "Exploraciones en la Huasteca potosina."

XXVII Congreso Internacional de Americanistas 2: 12–24.

Medellín Zenil, A. 1953. "Secuencia cronológico cultural en el centro de Veracruz." *Revista Mexicana de Estudios Antropologicos* 13: 371–378.

———. 1960. *Ceramicas del Totonacapan: Exploraciones en el centro de Veracruz.* Jalapa, Mex: Universidad Veracruzana.

Mendizábal, M. O. de. 1946. *Obras completas.* 6 vols. Mexico City.

Millon, R. F. 1954. "Irrigation at Teotihuacan." *American Antiquity* 20: 177–180.

———. 1973. *Urbanization at Teotihuacan, Mexico.* Vol. 1, *The Teotihuacan Map.* Austin: University of Texas Press.

———. 1981. "Teotihuacan: City, State, and Civilization." In *Supplement to the Handbook of Middle American Indians,* 198–243. Ed. V. R. Bricker and J. A. Sabloff. Austin: University of Texas Press.

Monzón, A. 1949. *El calpulli en la organizacion social de los Tenochca.* Mexico City.

Morley, S. G. 1938. *The Inscriptions of Peten.* 5 vols. Washington, DC: Carnegie Institution.

Morris, E. H., J. Charlot, and A. A. Morris. 1931. *The Temple of the Warriors at Chichén-Itza, Yucatán.* Publication 406. Washington, DC: Carnegie Institution.

Niederberger, C. 1976. *Zohapilco: Cinco milenios de ocupacion humana en la cuenca de Mexico.* Mexico City: INAH.

Noguera, E. 1967. *La ceramica arqueológica de Mesoamerica.* Mexico City: UNAM.

Olivé, J. C. 1958. "Estructura y dinamica de Mesoamerica: Un ensayo sobre sus problemas conceptuales." *Acta Antropologica* 2da. epoca, 3. Mexico City.

Palerm, A. 1957. "Ecological Potential and Cultural Development." *Social Science Monographs* (Pan-American Union) 3: 1–38.

Parsons, J. R. 1971. *Prehistoric Settlement Patterns in the Texcoco Region.* Memoirs of the Museum of Anthropology. Ann Arbor: University of Michigan.

Piña Chan, R. 1958. *Tlatilco, INAH, investigaciones 1 y 2.* Mexico City.

———. 1960. *Mesoamerica.* Memorias 6. Mexico City: INAH.

Pollock, H. E. D. 1980. *The Puuc: An Architectural Survey of the Hill Country of Yucatán and North Campeche, Mexico.* Memoirs 19. Cambridge, MA: Peabody Museum of Archaeology and Ethnology.

Pollock, H. E. D., R. L. Roys, T. Proskouriakoff, and A. L. Smith. 1962. *Mayapan, Yucatán, Mexico.* Publication 619. Washington, DC: Carnegie Institution.

Rice, P. M. 1986. *Pottery Anaylsis: A Sourcebook.* Chicago: University of Chicago Press.

Rivermar Pérez, L. 1987. "En el marasmo de una rebelión cataclismica." In *La antropología en Mexico: Panorama histórico,* 2:91–131. Ed. Carlos García Mora. Mexico City: INAH.

Rubbert, K. 1952. *Chichén Itza: Architectural Notes and Plans.* Publication 595. Washington, DC: Carnegie Institution.

Rubbert, K., and J. H. Denisson. 1943. *Archaeological Reconnaissance in Campeche, Quintana Roo, and Peten.* Publication 543. Washington, DC: Carnegie Institution.

Rubin de la Borbolla, D. F. 1941. "Exploraciones arqueológicas en Michoacan, Tzintzuntzan, temporada III." *Revista Mexicana de Estudios Antropologicos* 5: 5–20.

Ruz Lhullier, A. 1954. "Exploraciones en Palenque, 1952." *Anales del INAH* 6: 79–110.

———. 1969. *La Costa de campeche en los tiempos prehispanicos.* Serie Investigaciones 18. Mexico City: INAH.

Sanders, W. T. 1956. *The Central Mexican Symbiotic Region: A Study in Prehistoric Settlement Patterns in the New World.* 23: 115–127. Viking Foundation Publications in Anthropology.

———. 1957. "Tierra y agua." Ph D. dissertation, Harvard University.

Sanders, W. T., J. R. Parsons, and R. S. Santley. 1969. *The Basin of Mexico: Ecological Processes in the Evolution of Civilization.* New York: Academic Press.

Sanders, W. T., and B. Price. 1968. *Mesoamerica: The Evolution of a Civilization.* New York: Random House.

Schele, L. 1982. *Maya Glyphs: The Verbs.* Austin: University of Texas Press.

Schele, L., and D. Freidel. 1990. *A Forest of Kings.* New York: William Morrow.

Sejourné, L. 1959. *Un palacio en la ciudad de los Dioses: Teotihuacan.* Mexico City: Instituto Nacional de Antropología e Historia.

Spinden, H. J. 1913. *A Study of Maya Art: Its Subject Matter and Historical Development.* Memoirs 6. Cambridge, MA: Peabody Museum of Archaeology and Ethnology.

Stephens, J. L., and F. Catherwood. 1841. *Incidents of Travel in Central America, Chiapas, and Yucatán.* 2 vols. London.

Taylor, W. W. 1948. *A Study of Archaeology.* Memoir 69. American Anthropological Association.

Terra, H. de. 1946. "New Evidence for the Antiquity of Early Man in Mexico." *Revista Mexicana de Estudios Antropologicos* 8: 69–88.

Thompson, J. E. 1933. *Mexico before Cortes.* New York, London: C. Scribner's Sons.

———. 1935. *Maya Chronology: The Correlation Question: Contributions to American Archaeology.* Publication 456. Washington, DC: Carnegie Institution.

———. 1950. *Maya Hieroglyphic Writing: An Introduction.* Publication 589. Washington, DC: Carnegie Institution.

———. 1962. *A Catalogue of Maya Hieroglyphs.* Norman: University of Oklahoma Press.

Tolstoy, P. 1958. *Surface Survey of the Northern Valley of Mexico: The Classic and Post-Classic Periods.* Transactions of the American Philosophical Society 48, 5. Philadelphia: American Philosophical Society.

Vaillant, G. C. 1938. "A Correlation of Archaeological and Historical Sequences in the Valley of Mexico." *American Anthropologist* 40: 535–573.

———. 1941. *Aztecs of Mexico.* Garden City, NY: Doubleday, Doran.

Valenzuela, J. 1938. "Las exploraciones efectuadas en Los Tuxtlas, Veracruz." *Anales del Museo Nacional de Mexico,* 3:83–108. Mexico City.

Vega Sosa, C. 1979. *El recinto sagrado de Mexico.* Tenochtitlan, Mex: INAH.

Wauchope, R., ed. 1964–1971. *Handbook of Middle American Indians.* Austin: University of Texas Press.

Willey, G. R., and J. Sabloff. 1974. *A History of American Archaeology.* London: Thames and Hudson.

———. 1980. *A History of American Archaeology.* 2d ed. London: Thames and Hudson.

Minoan Civilation

See Evans, Sir Arthur; Knossos; Linear A / Linear B

Moche

Moche is the name of the dominant culture on the north coast of PERU from the first to the seventh centuries A.D., known as the early intermediate period. The culture was first identified in the Moche Valley and was centered on the

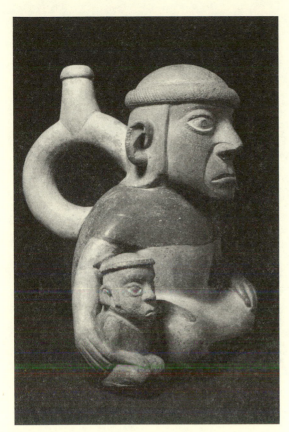

A typical Mochica pottery effigy jar picturing a mother and child (Burstein Collection/Corbis)

large pyramid sites of HUACA DEL SOL and Huaca de la Luna. During the course of Moche history, a distinctive pottery style developed, one that emphasized accurate observation of everyday life. Moche culture was also rich in other areas of the decorative arts.

Uncertainty still surrounds the political organization of the Moche culture, which appears to have been based around social stratification. The erection of large pyramids, first at Huaca del Sol and later at Galindo and Pampa Grande, indicates that although the core territory of the Moche culture may have retreated from the coast in the early seventh century A.D., some continuity in forms of political organization may have continued. The cause of the downfall of the Moche is also widely debated. It has been argued that adverse weather patterns generated by the El Niño current attacked the fundamentals of the Moche economy; other people have suggested that Moche was adversely affected by

the rise of the Huari state. Whatever the reason or reasons, it is clear that the Moche culture had been influenced by the earlier Chavín cultural forms and that it in turn influenced the Chimú and other cultures that followed it.

Tim Murray

See also Sipan
References
Donnan C. B. 1976. *Moche Art and Iconography.* Los Angeles: Latin American Center, University of California–Los Angeles.

Mohenjo Daro
See Indus Civilization; South Asia

Monte Albán

A major site and center of Zapotec civilization in southern MEXICO, Monte Albán is a huge hilltop site adjacent to the modern city of Oaxaca. Monte Albán is located in the center of the three major arms of the Valley of Oaxaca and is surrounded by rugged mountains. The Zapotecs are members of an ethnic group that is still widespread in Oaxaca today, and there is no doubt that their ancestors built Monte Albán.

Prior to 500 B.C., the Valley of Oaxaca had seen a long period of cultural development that had given rise to a number of chiefdoms, each containing a central town with several hundred inhabitants and public ceremonial buildings surrounded by smaller agricultural villages. The settlement and demography of the valley changed radically in 500 B.C., however. Monte Albán was founded on top of a 400-meter-high hill on what had previously been bare land. The hill was leveled, and settlement began in three discrete localities on the hilltop. From this fact some scholars have argued that Monte Albán represents the coming together in a central place by the people of the three arms of the valley, and certainly, the valley and its preexisting towns and villages saw a temporary reduction in population after the founding of Monte Albán.

Over the following centuries, Monte Albán grew enormously in population and power, and it came to dominate the entire Valley of Oaxaca as well as lands beyond. There are some indica-

The ruins of Monte Albán in Mexico (Gamma)

tions that this domination was not necessarily entirely peaceful—several hundred famous "danzante" (the term derived from the view of nineteenth-century explorers that the figures were dancers) sculptures dating to 500–200 B.C., probably illustrate captured individuals and perhaps represent communities brought under the sway of Monte Albán.

The height of Monte Albán's power was between the third and early-eighth centuries A.D., and its culture at this time is often referred to as classic Zapotec civilization. This was the time when the huge central Mexican city of TEOTI-HUACÁN dominated the political map of ancient Mexico. Monte Albán was in contact with Teotihuacán, and indications are that the relationship was a smooth one, for some carved stones at Monte Albán show what appear to be peaceful emissaries arriving from Teotihuacán and being greeted by the Zapotec rulers of Monte Albán.

By A.D. 500, Monte Albán had a population of more than 20,000, with the vast majority of people living on artificial terraces on the hillside surrounding the ceremonial heart of the city. Higher up the hill, adjacent to the center, nobles lived in palace compounds, many of which included family tombs built underneath a central patio. The central, ceremonial part of Monte Albán is extremely impressive. Originally, an area measuring some 250 by 700 meters was cleared on the very summit of the 400-meter-high hill. Then a series of temples and other public structures was built in three parallel north-south rows, and at the northern end of these a huge palace complex was constructed. These buildings featured a type of architectural facade, widespread in MESOAMERICA at the time, called talud-tablero—a sloping base to each platform surmounted by vertical panels. The talud-tablero at Monte Albán is in a distinctive local style of architecture appropriately called "the classic Zapotec" style.

Sometime during the mid-eighth century Monte Albán went into decline, which has generally been linked with the decline of Teotihuacán shortly before. At the time, trade routes throughout Mesoamerica were disrupted, and perhaps there was no longer the need for a strong, centralized Monte Albán to act as a buffer to Teotihuacán's might. Whatever the reason, by A.D. 900 Monte Albán was declining into ruin. Perhaps as many as 4,000 people were still living on the flanks of the hill, but the great palaces and temples were in disrepair. When Mixtec peoples invaded the Valley of Oaxaca during the fourteenth century, they settled at the base of the hill. They did find and use some of the earlier Zapotec tombs, scooping the old Zapotec inhabitants to one side and burying their own elite members there. One such tomb, with the prosaic designation Tomb 7, was particularly rich. The burial was that of a fourteenth-century Mixtec prince, and he was accompanied by several sacrificed servants as well as magnificent works of art in gold, silver, and precious stones.

Peter Mathews

See also Maya Civilization
References
Blanton, R. 1978. *Monte Albán: Settlement Patterns at the Ancient Zapotec Capital.* New York: Academic Press.

Montelius, Gustaf Oscar Augustin (1843–1921)

Born in Stockholm, SWEDEN, and educated at Uppsala University, Montelius finished his Ph.D. in 1869. From 1863 to 1880 he worked at the Museum of National Antiquities in Stockholm in various capacities, and finally as senior executive officer. From 1907 to 1913 he was state antiquarian, head of the Central Board of Antiquities and the Museum of National Antiquities. Montelius was a fellow of the Swedish Academy and a member of its Nobel Prize Committee.

When Montelius started as a prehistorian in the mid-1860s knowledge of chronological details in European archaeology was almost nonexistent. In spite of a long research tradition, Scandinavian archaeology had not yet advanced beyond a division of the Stone Age into an earlier (Mesolithic) and a later (Neolithic) phase. There was a similar division of the Bronze Age into two stages, and a division of the Iron Age into three periods. In most other parts of Europe, prehistoric research had not even reached that level of chronological understanding. Consequently archaeologists were limited in their ability to interpret prehistoric life and society in any depth. Montelius clearly recognized this problem and throughout his career as an archaeologist he was engaged in creating reliable time scales for prehistoric Europe. No other single researcher did so much to develop traditional archaeological DATING methods as Montelius. Largely because of his efforts and methodological examples, prehistoric archaeology in northern Europe by the end of the century had access to a fairly detailed and reliable chronology, both in relative and absolute terms. In fact, Montelius's work left its mark on the development of prehistoric chronology in other parts of Europe as well as in the Near East.

As a prehistorian, Montelius did not have much interest in theory. He was primarily an empiricist and his strength lay in his supreme ability to collect information; to systematize, digest, and generalize great quantities of archaeological data; and to present his results in a clear and convincing way. Given his systematic nature, energy, and curiosity, it is remarkable that Montelius did not become a prominent excavator.

Aside from chronologies, Montelius was also interested in issues of prehistoric culture. He was an energetic popularizer. Many of his scientific works were edited for the general public, with less emphasis on chronological problems and more discussion of general cultural and social perspectives. He became a central figure in European archaeology. Many of his works were published in major European languages, and his extensive international network of contacts was facilitated by his proficiency in German, French, Italian, and English.

Bo Gräslund

See also Classification
References
For references, see *Encyclopedia of Archaeology: The Great Archaeologists,* Vol. 1, ed. Tim Murray (Santa Barbara, CA: ABC-CLIO, 1999), pp. 162–163.

Montfaucon, Bernard de (1655–1741)

De Montfaucon was a French Benedictine monk, paleographer, philologist, and antiquary, who published several histories and translations from Greek. In 1685 de Montfaucon published an account of the excavation of a megalithic stone tomb at Cocherel that contained polished stone axes. He ascribed the tombs to a people who had no knowledge of iron, and in passing referred to the possibility of a three-age sequence—stone, copper, and iron—of human development. In reaching this conclusion he was undoubtedly influenced by contemporary archaeological research in England and Scandinavia.

From 1698–1701 de Montfaucon worked in the Vatican Library in Rome, publishing his travels and experiences in *Diarium Italicum*. For the next twenty years he prepared his monumental fifteen-volume *L'antiquité expliquée et representée en figures* (1722–1724), comprising an enormous amount of source material and iconographical data from the ancient world. His aim was to illustrate and describe the monuments of antiquity in order to explain them and attempt to reconstruct the past. It was both a scientific and an educational work—and de Montfaucon suggested that a serious student could take up to two years to do it justice. His work was to have an enormous impact on subsequent antiquarian studies and the beginnings of an archaeology based on illustration and interpretation.

Tim Murray

References
Schnapp, A. 1996. *The Discovery of the Past*. London: British Museum Press.

Morgan, Lewis Henry (1818–1881)

Born in New York State, Lewis Henry Morgan studied law at Union College in Schenectady and moved to Rochester in 1844. He became wealthy through investments in railways and iron smelting and was thus able to devote all of his time to his scholarly interests after 1860. Morgan took part in the literary and scientific societies of his day, joining the American Association for the Advancement of Science in 1856, presiding over the newly created anthropology section in 1873, and becoming the association's president in 1879. He was made a member of the National Academy of Sciences in 1875.

Morgan's passion was for Native American Indian ethnology, and his first book, *League of the Iroquois* (1851), is still the best ethnography on the subject. He undertook fieldwork among the Ojibwa in Michigan, out of which grew modern kinship studies such as those outlined in *Systems of Consanguinity and Affinity* (1871). In *Ancient Society, or Researches in the Line of Human Progress from Savagery through Barbarism to Civilization* (1877), the influence of the evidence of human antiquity recently discovered in Europe moved Morgan in the direction of evolutionism.

The impact of his work was enormous—Karl Marx, Frederick Engels, John Lubbock, and Charles Darwin all read and considered it, and in the next generation, Lorimer Fison, the Australasianist; Adolph Bandelier, Mesoamerican and southwestern archaeologist and historian; and JOHN WESLEY POWELL, head of the Bureau of American Ethnology and leading classifier of Native American languages in his day, were all Morgan's students and successors. He was also a major influence on the outstanding anthropologists W. H. R. Rivers, A. R. Radcliffe-Brown, and Claude Lévi-Strauss.

Tim Murray

See also United States of America, Prehistoric Archaeology

References
Morgan, L. H. 1964 *Ancient Society*. Ed. Leslie A. White. Cambridge, MA: Belknap Press.

Morley, Sylvanus Griswold (1883–1948)

The son of a former military academician and mine owner, Sylvanus Morley corresponded with FREDERIC WARD PUTNAM of Harvard University's PEABODY MUSEUM from the age of fifteen. To please his father, Morley first studied to be a civil engineer but then began studying anthropology at Harvard. His earlier fascination with Egypt gave way, under Putnam and Alfred Tozzer's encouragement, to an abiding interest in the Maya of Central America.

After his graduation from Harvard Morley was sent by the ARCHAEOLOGICAL INSTITUTE OF AMERICA to the Yucatán in MEXICO to study linguistics. There he met Mesoamerican archaeologist Edward Thompson at the site of CHICHÉN

Itzá. Other travels through the Yucatán convinced Morley to abandon linguistics for a career in archaeology. Back at Harvard in 1905 he studied anthropology under Tozzer and read Daniel Brinton's *Primer of Maya Hieroglyphics*—his first exposure to a subject that would become his lifelong forte.

In 1907 Morley participated in EDGAR LEE HEWETT's field-methods school in archaeology in the Southwest, along with ALFRED V. KIDDER. His engineering training in areal survey proved to be invaluable, and he continued to work for Hewett until 1915, when he was hired by the Carnegie Institution's new Department of Central American Archaeology. His first book, *Introduction to the Study of the Maya Hieroglyphs,* a synthesis of what was then known about MAYA EPIGRAPHY, was published in the same year. In the *Supplementary Series in the Maya Inscriptions* (1916) Morley brought together drawings of all lunar glyphs, thereby allowing John Edward Teeple to solve the riddle of the lunar count.

Over the next decade Morley searched and surveyed some of the most inaccessible parts of Mayan territory. Traveling by mule and camping with few creature comforts, surrounded by jungle, suffering from malaria, and surviving Mexican bandits, Morley visited Copan, Tulum, and Uaxactun. The artist WILLIAM HENRY HOLMES and archaeologist Samuel Lothrop were part of his field team. From 1917 to 1919 he worked for U.S. naval intelligence in Washington, D.C., before returning to the field in 1919. Until 1922 Morley spent most of his time in the Petén looking for Mayan date inscriptions, and he visited COSTA RICA and GUATEMALA to study Mayan influences there. In 1920 he completed the *Inscriptions of Copán,* the first book to discuss in detail all the texts of a single site.

Morley's available time for deciphering glyphs was seriously eroded by the constraints of field trips and lecture tours for the Carnegie Institution. He still managed to provide a number of the meanings for glyphs and demonstrated that almost every Mayan monument was erected to "mark the close of a katun (a period of time in the Mayan calendar) or one of its quarters." Perhaps as important to Mayan archaeology as his scholarly work was his insistence that the public become aware of the achievements of the Maya. He delivered lectures throughout the United States and wrote popular articles on the MAYA CIVILIZATION.

Morley's plan of making a thorough study of the Maya at Chichén Itzá, which was why the Carnegie Institution had employed him, was never realized, for it was overtaken by his desire to find and decipher Mayan glyphs. As early as 1925 the institution began to consider a leadership change and a reorganization. Kidder was appointed as director of the new Division of Historical Research in an attempt to introduce a multidisciplinary strategy to the Mayan project. Morley continued his pioneering work on Mayan glyphs until 1947, when he became director of the Museum of New Mexico in Santa Fe.

Douglas R. Givens

References

For references, see *Encyclopedia of Archaeology: The Great Archaeologists,* Vol. 1, ed. Tim Murray (Santa Barbara, CA: ABC-CLIO, 1999), pp. 323–324.

Morocco

See Maghreb

Mortillet, Gabriel de (1821–1898)

Gabriel de Mortillet studied to be a priest in Grenoble and then went to Paris to study engineering. His fascination with geology and conchology (the study of shells) soon eclipsed his interest in engineering, and his radical socialist political beliefs led to his exile to Savoy, ITALY, in 1848. Four years later Mortillet cataloged the geological collections at the museum in Geneva, and in 1854 he moved back to Savoy to look after the museum in Annecy, until the province was annexed by FRANCE in 1857. From 1858 until 1863 Mortillet worked in Italy for the Lombard-Venetian Railway Company and began his research into prehistory, prompted by his interest in the discovery of Neolithic settlements in the lakes of SWITZERLAND.

In 1864 Mortillet returned to Paris and founded the prehistory review *Les Materiaux pour l'Histoire Positive et Philosophique de l'Homme,* becoming a conservator at the Musée des Antiquités Nationales at Saint-Germain-en-Laye in 1868. There, he drew up the classification of stone-tool technology whose denominations have remained standard until the present day; this work represents his major contribution to the science of prehistory in the nineteenth century. Mortillet argued against ÉDOUARD LARTET's classification of Paleolithic material based on faunal assemblages and argued for classification based on stone-tool types.

From 1880 onward Mortillet was one of the prime movers of a group of scientists, mostly anthropologists, who called themselves "scientific materialists," and between 1884 and 1887 he founded and ran the review *L'Homme,* in which their arguments and positions were promulgated. Mortillet became anticlerical and denounced the Catholic Church for its interpretations of scientific data, arguing for the separation of science and religion that became a political struggle for the separation of church and state. After 1870 and the defeat of France by the Prussians, his arguments took on a nationalist tone.

Mortillet also participated in the debate over the existence of an intelligent human ancestor in the Tertiary period, provoked by the discovery of incised bones and apparently worked flints in Tertiary soils. Some prehistorians, such as JEAN LOUIS ARMAND DE QUATREFAGES, argued for an intelligent human being created by God in the beginning. Mortillet, faithful to his concept of evolution, deduced from the flints the existence of a transitional creature between man and ape—the missing link, which he called *anthropopithecus* and to whom he devoted many pages in his book *Le préhistorique* (1883). His creation was replaced by EUGENE DUBOIS's *Pithecanthropus erectus,* discovered in Java in 1894, which destroyed the concept of evolution promulagated by Mortillet, suggesting that the transformation of species was neither as linear nor as simple as the French prehistorian had thought.

Mortillet's philosophical beliefs also had a strong impact on the debate about prehistoric art and religion. He was certain that Paleolithic peoples were primitive and, as savages, on a lower rung of the ladder of biological and cultural development, far removed from modern people. However, discoveries of art objects, funeral practices, and cave-art galleries inevitably raised a few problems for a priori ideas about primitive beings. Mortillet refused to see any symbolic value in Paleolithic art and denied the existence of anything abstract. Eventually, as the evidence accumulated, Paleolithic art was recognized by other prehistorians such as EMILE CARTAILHAC, breaking down the equation of the primitive with the barbarian.

In key academic positions for half a century, Mortillet was both a great theoretician and the leader of a school. A controlling influence, he helped to train, through his writing and teaching, a large proportion of the French prehistorians of the second generation and significantly assisted in establishing the discipline of prehistory in France.

Nathalie Richard; translated by Judith Braid

References

For references, see *Encyclopedia of Archaeology: The Great Archaeologists,* Vol. 1, ed. Tim Murray (Santa Barbara, CA: ABC-CLIO, 1999), pp. 106–107.

Most na Soči

Most na Soči, also known as Sveta Lucija or Santa Lucia, is an early–Iron Age site in the subalpine area of western SLOVENIA at the confluence of the rivers Soča (Isonzo), Idrijca, and Baca. The cemetery was extensively excavated between 1884 and 1902 by Carlo Marchesetti, the curator of the Trieste City Museum, and by Joseph Szombathy, the curator of the Naturhistorisches Museum in Vienna.

More than 6,400 graves were discovered during the excavations, making Most na Soči one of the largest prehistoric cemeteries in this part of Europe. The burial rite was almost exclusively cremation in a flat grave; only 10 percent of the cremation graves were deposited in urns. Grave goods comprised personal ornaments (fibulae, pins, bracelets, pendants, necklaces, etc.).

The cemetery is divided chronologically into six phases between the eighth and fourth centuries B.C. Weapons (spearheads and axes) were absent throughout most of this period, only appearing in the last phase, i.e., in the fourth century. Culturally, the community living in Most na Soči had strong ties with Paleovenetic groups in northeastern ITALY (especially with the Este group) and with the Dolenjska (lower Carniola) group in Slovenia.

The settlement was partially excavated between 1971 and 1982 by Drago Svoljsak, the curator of the Regional Museum in Nova Gorica. These excavations revealed thirty early–Iron Age houses as well as some later structures. In the early Iron Age, Most na Soči was an open settlement—which means that no defensive structures were recorded—divided into dwelling and craft sections (the latter including metallurgical activities).

Peter Turk

References

Gabrovec, S., and D. Svoljsak. 1983. *Most na Soci* I. Ljubljana: Narodni Museum.

Marchesetti, C. 1893. "Scavi nella necropoli di S. Lucia presso Tolmino." *Bolletino della Societa adriatica di scienze naturali in Trieste* 15: 3–336.

Terzan B., F. Lo Schiavo, and N. Trampuz-Orel. 1984–1985. *Most na Soci II*. Ljubljana: Narodni Museum.

Moulin Quignon

Second only to the PILTDOWN FORGERY, Moulin Quignon is one of the most celebrated frauds of prehistoric archaeology. By the end of 1859, the argument about whether human beings had a high antiquity (certainly extending back to the time of extinct animals) had been won by JACQUES BOUCHER DE PERTHES, HUGH FALCONER, and others through the patient excavation of sites such as BRIXHAM CAVE and the reexamination of the English sites of KENT'S CAVERN and Hoxne and the Somme River gravels in FRANCE. However, at none of those sites had the excavators been able to locate the bones of the oldest humans, and they based their arguments on the presence of artifacts in very old deposits.

Boucher de Perthes sought to solve this problem by offering his workmen the sum of 200 francs or the first human bones to be retrieved from his sites. On 23 March 1863, one of his workmen recovered a human tooth (in association with two axes). A week later, Boucher de Perthes's joy knew no bounds when another tooth and the right half of a human lower jaw were retrieved from the same deposit.

Many of the scientists most directly concerned with the debate about high human antiquity flocked to the site, in particular ARMAND DE QUATREFAGES, Falconer, JOHN EVANS, and JOSEPH PRESTWICH. Early conviction that Boucher de Perthes had made a significant discovery was (on the English side at least) replaced by skepticism when Prestwich and Evans announced that some of the stone artifacts recovered from the site were fakes.

Falconer reexamined the tooth and the jaw and pronounced them modern, a conclusion that sparked a storm of controversy. In an attempt to resolve the dispute, ÉDOUARD LARTET proposed a committee of inquiry that would provide each side with the opportunity to state its case in open discussion. This event took place on 9 May 1863 and was attended by most of the disputants (with the exception of Boucher de Perthes). Argument raged about whether the stone tools were fakes (resolved in the negative after the committee visited the site on the 13 May and observed the excavation of more artifacts that Prestwich thought were genuine) and about whether the jaw was modern and had been introduced to the deposit (the argument favored by Falconer but not endorsed by the committee).

The matter did not end there. Returning to England, Falconer urged Prestwich and Evans to return to the site and excavate under controlled conditions. Evans arranged for Henry Keeping (the excavator of Brixham Cave) to visit the site (between 3 June and 6 June), and his assessment, reported by Evans and supported by Evans's continued analysis of the previously excavated tools, was highly negative. Evans closed the circle by making a strong case that the jaw had been taken from the nearby site of Mesnières, which had been visited by one of the workmen from Moulin Quignon.

There was never any admission (certainly not by Boucher de Perthes) that there had been any fraud. Nonetheless, the evidence mounted by Falconer, Evans, and Prestwich about the jaw and the associated artifacts effectively consigned the remains to obscurity in the store of the

The Great Mound at Moundville in Alabama (Hulton Getty)

Musée de l'Homme in Paris. Interesting questions continue to be unanswered. Who was to have profited from the fraud? Was it the workmen to get their 200 francs, Boucher de Perthes to obtain a crowning achievement and recognition, or Quatrefages (an opponent of Darwin), who could now demonstrate that from the time of earliest human occupation of the earth the physical form of human beings had hardly changed? Perhaps it was simply that both Boucher de Perthes and de Quatrefages seized an opportunity provided by the quarry workers, nothing more.

Tim Murray

References

Van Riper, A. Bowdoin. 1993. *Men among the Mammoths: Victorian Science and the Discovery of Human Prehistory.* Chicago: University of Chicago Press.

Moundville

Moundville, a site comprising twenty large mounds distributed around a central plaza, is located in Alabama. Considered by many people to be among the largest of such sites in the Mississippian culture, Moundville has been explored by antiquarians and archaeologists since the late 1860s. The first extensive excavations, undertaken by U.S. archaeologist Clarence B. Moore, occurred in 1905 and 1906.

The site has proved to be exceptionally rich in material culture and in food remains, and these have, in conjunction with evidence of house plans and site layout, allowed archaeologists to construct a viable site history. Moundville was first occupied around A.D. 1050 and gradually grew in size, complexity, and importance over the next 350 to 400 years. The site is thought to have been abandoned around A.D. 1550, and it is now interpreted as being the most important residential, religious, and political center of the surrounding region.

Tim Murray

See also Atwater, Caleb; United States of America, Prehistoric Archaeology

References

Knight, Vernon J., Jr., and Vincas Steponaitis. 1998 *Archaeology of the Moundville Chiefdom*. Washington, DC: Smithsonian Institution Press.

Müller, Sophus Otto (1846–1934)

Sophus Müller was born in Copenhagen, DENMARK, the son of a numismatist and museum director. Enrolling at Copenhagen University in 1864 to study classics, he attended JENS JACOB WORSAAE's lectures on archaeology and read the work of English geologist CHARLES LYELL. After graduating in 1871 Müller worked as a teacher, but he gradually became associated with the collections in Copenhagen and with Worsaae, the curator of the Royal Museum of Nordic Antiquities (after 1892 the National Museum).

Müller begun to publish articles on the Danish Iron and Bronze Ages and traveled to the major museums and collections in central, western, and northern Europe. In 1878 he was employed as a scientific assistant to his father in the Department of Numismatics at the museum. He kept in contact with Worsaae and his group and participated in the activities of the museum. He also began publishing the *Nordic Journal* in Stockholm. In 1880 he received a Danish doctoral degree for his dissertation on animal ornamentation in Scandinavia.

In 1885 he became a curator at the Royal Museum and seven years later was named codirector of the new National Museum, with responsibility for prehistoric, ethnographic, and classical collections. During his tenure the National Museum assumed all the main tasks arising from archaeology's emergence as a discipline: publications, the preparation of finds for exhibition or storage, excavations, inspections, conservation, and the training of the next generation of archaeologists. The teaching of archaeology disappeared from the university and was taken over the by National Museum. Remaining at the museum until his retirement in 1921, he effectively dictated and controlled Danish archaeology during this period.

Müller also had extensive excavation experience, and the context of the finds he worked on always played a paramount role in his analysis and interpretations. He was at times a publicist, and he was also well traveled. He was therefore familiar with much of the prehistoric material then known and housed in the main European museums and collections. From 1881 on he was secretary of the Royal Nordic Antiquaries Society and editor of its journal, *Yearbook for Nordic Archaeology*.

Müller is one of the key figures in the nineteenth-century development of the methods and theories of archaeology. His dispute with OSCAR MONTELIUS about typology has been characterized as the first methodological debate on such issues—an illustration opposing an essentially objective and subjective methodology and how each methodology could affect the discipline. Müller also defined several significant cultural sequences in Danish prehistory and laid a solid foundation for future studies. His works include various illustrated manuals, such as *The Arrangement of Denmark's Prehistoric Objects* (1888–1895). Much of this work still constitutes the backbone of the discipline in Denmark, and researchers actively draw upon it today. Müller can be credited with establishing the fundamental themes of Danish archaeology—wide-ranging research, penetrating analysis, and a profound respect for source material.

Marie Louise Stig Sørensen

References

For references, see *Encyclopedia of Archaeology: The Great Archaeologists*, Vol. 1, ed. Tim Murray (Santa Barbara, CA: ABC-CLIO, 1999), pp. 207–209.

Mulvaney, John (1925–)

John Mulvaney is an Australian archaeologist who trained at Cambridge University after completing a history degree at the University of Melbourne. On his return to Australia Mulvaney followed the pioneering work of NORMAN TINDALE and FRED MCCARTHY at Fromm's Landing and Kenniff Cave (among other sites). He noted that there was clear evidence for cultural change in prehistoric Australia, and his work at Kenniff Cave revealed conclusive evidence (through radiocarbon DATING) of the Pleistocene occupation of Australia.

Apart from this demonstration of high human antiquity in Australia, Mulvaney forged much of the agenda of Australian prehistoric archaeology in the 1970s with the publication of his *Prehistory of Australia* in 1969 (now in its third edition). Specifically interested in Australian prehistory as a central element in the story of Aboriginal Australia, Mulvaney championed the notion of archaeology and anthropology working together to enlighten non-Aboriginal Australians about the richness and variety of pre- (and post-) European life in Australia. Of equal importance was Mulvaney's service to his profession through his membership in key government committees and investigations, his advocacy of the cause of preserving the human heritage of Australia, and his defense of the principles of liberal inquiry.

Tim Murray

References

Bonyhady, T., and T. Griffith, eds. 1996. *Prehistory to Politics: John Mulvaney, the Humanities and the Public Intellectual*. Carlton: Melbourne University Press.

Mycenae

See Greece

Myres, Sir John Linton (1869–1954)

John L. Myres attended Winchester School and then New College, Oxford. After completing his undergraduate degree he became a fellow of Magdalen College, Oxford, and visited the Mediterranean in 1892, where he worked with SIR JOHN EVANS on Crete. By comparing Cretan vases with vase fragments found by SIR WILLIAM MATTHEW FLINDERS PETRIE in Egypt, Myres was able to argue for trade links between the ancient civilizations of Crete and Egypt. He joined the British School's excavation of Palakastro and Petsofa on Crete and published his finds.

In 1894 Myres began excavating on CYPRUS at Kition, and with a German colleague, he wrote the catalog of the Cyprus Museum. In 1907 he became a professor of Greek and a lecturer in ancient geography at Liverpool University, but three years later he returned to Oxford as the new Wykeham Professor of Ancient History, a position he held until 1939. He wrote the popular study *The Dawn of History* in 1911 and contributed several chapters to the Cambridge Ancient History. During World War I his detailed knowledge of the geography and people of the eastern Mediterranean was put to use when he led raiding operations from a former royal yacht onto the coast of TURKEY. He was made a commander of the Royal Navy and was awarded the Order of the British Empire and the Greek Order of George I.

In 1927 on the death of SIR ARTHUR EVANS, Myres took on the task of completing the editing and publishing of the Linear B tablets from KNOSSOS, and he was pleased that when Michael Ventris deciphered it in 1952, Linear B proved to be Greek. In 1930 Myres's best-known work—*Who Were the Greeks?*—was published, followed by *Herodotus, Father of History* and *Geographical History in Greek Lands* in 1953. In all these works he used not only the classics but also a multidisciplinary approach, combining ancient history, archaeology, geography, and anthropology. He was knighted in 1943 and won the Victoria Medal of the Royal Geographic Society in 1953. During World War II, once again using his great geographic knowledge of the eastern Mediterranean, he edited handbooks for naval intelligence. He was president of the Royal Anthroplogical Institute from 1928 to 1931, president of the Hellenic Society from 1935 to 1938, and chairman of the British School at Athens from 1934 to 1947.

Tim Murray

See also Childe, Vere Gordon; Greece: Linear A/ Linear B

References

Myres, John Linton. 1943. *Mediterranean Culture*. Cambridge: Cambridge University Press.